SIXTEENTH CANADIAN EDITION

RAGAN

MACROECONOMICS

CHRISTOPHER T.S. RAGAN
McGILL UNIVERSITY

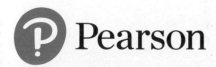

Pearson Canada Inc., 26 Prince Andrew Place, North York, Ontario M3C 2H4.

978-0-13-483582-2

1   20

Library and Archives Canada Cataloguing in Publication

Ragan, Christopher T. S., author
   Macroeconomics / Christopher T.S. Ragan, McGill University. —
Sixteenth Canadian edition.

Includes index.
Issued in print and electronic formats.
ISBN 978-0-13-483582-2 (hardcover).—ISBN 978-0-13-522072-6 (looseleaf).—
ISBN 978-0-13-523344-3 (HTML)

   1. Macroeconomics—Textbooks. 2. Macroeconomics—Canada—
Textbooks. 3. Textbooks. I. Title. II. Title: Ragan macroeconomics.

HB172.5.R35 2019   339   C2018-905868-4
                                               C2018-905869-2

Brief Contents

PART 1   **What Is Economics?**   **1**

Chapter 1   Economic Issues and Concepts   1
Chapter 2   Economic Theories, Data, and Graphs   26

PART 2   **An Introduction to Demand and Supply**   **49**

Chapter 3   Demand, Supply, and Price   49

PART 7   **An Introduction to Macroeconomics**   **461**

Chapter 19   What Macroeconomics Is All About   461
Chapter 20   The Measurement of National Income   485

PART 8   **The Economy in the Short Run**   **507**

Chapter 21   The Simplest Short-Run Macro Model   507
Chapter 22   Adding Government and Trade to the Simple Macro Model   535
Chapter 23   Real GDP and the Price Level in the Short Run   558

PART 9   **The Economy in the Long Run**   **579**

Chapter 24   From the Short Run to the Long Run: The Adjustment of Factor Prices   579
Chapter 25   Long-Run Economic Growth   608

PART 10   **Money, Banking, and Monetary Policy**   **641**

Chapter 26   Money and Banking   641
Chapter 27   Money, Interest Rates, and Economic Activity   669
Chapter 28   Monetary Policy in Canada   698

PART 11   **Macroeconomic Problems and Policies**   **729**

Chapter 29   Inflation and Disinflation   729
Chapter 30   Unemployment Fluctuations and the NAIRU   752
Chapter 31   Government Debt and Deficits   779

PART 12   **Canada in the Global Economy**   **803**

Chapter 32   The Gains from International Trade   803
Chapter 33   Trade Policy   828
Chapter 34   Exchange Rates and the Balance of Payments   852

Mathematical Notes   M-1
Timeline of Great Economists   T-1
Index   I-1

Contents

List of Boxes ix
To the Instructor x
To the Student xv
Acknowledgements xvi
About the Author xvii

PART 1
What Is Economics? 1

Chapter 1	Economic Issues and Concepts	1
1.1	What Is Economics?	3
	Resources	4
	Scarcity and Choice	4
	Four Key Economic Problems	8
	Microeconomics and Macroeconomics	9
	Economics and Government Policy	9
1.2	The Complexity of Modern Economies	10
	The Nature of Market Economies	11
	The Decision Makers and Their Choices	13
	Production and Trade	15
1.3	Is There an Alternative to the Market Economy?	17
	Types of Economic Systems	17
	The Great Debate	19
	Government in the Modern Mixed Economy	20

Summary 21
Key Concepts 22
Study Exercises 22

Chapter 2	Economic Theories, Data, and Graphs	26
2.1	Positive and Normative Statements	27
	Disagreements Among Economists	28
2.2	Building and Testing Economic Theories	30
	What Are Theories?	30
	Testing Theories	31
2.3	Economic Data	34
	Index Numbers	34
	Graphing Economic Data	37
2.4	Graphing Economic Theories	38
	Functions	38
	Graphing Functions	39
	A Final Word	44

Summary 44
Key Concepts 45
Study Exercises 45

PART 2
An Introduction to Demand and Supply 49

Chapter 3	Demand, Supply, and Price	49
3.1	Demand	50
	Quantity Demanded	50
	Quantity Demanded and Price	51
	Demand Schedules and Demand Curves	52
3.2	Supply	57
	Quantity Supplied	57
	Quantity Supplied and Price	58
	Supply Schedules and Supply Curves	58
3.3	The Determination of Price	62
	The Concept of a Market	62
	Market Equilibrium	63
	Changes in Market Equilibrium	65
	A Numerical Example	67
	Relative Prices	68

Summary 69
Key Concepts 70
Study Exercises 70

PART 7
An Introduction to Macroeconomics 461

Chapter 19	What Macroeconomics Is All About	461
19.1	Key Macroeconomic Variables	462
	National Product and National Income	462
	Employment, Unemployment, and the Labour Force	467
	Productivity	469
	Inflation and the Price Level	471
	Interest Rates	474
	Exchange Rates and Trade Flows	476
19.2	Growth Versus Fluctuations	479
	Long-Term Economic Growth	479
	Short-Term Fluctuations	480
	What Lies Ahead?	481

Summary 481
Key Concepts 482
Study Exercises 482

WL 02.11.2019 1014

**Chapter 20 The Measurement of National
              Income   485**
20.1 National Output and Value Added   486
20.2 National Income Accounting:
        The Basics   488
      GDP from the Expenditure Side   490
      GDP from the Income Side   493
20.3 National Income Accounting:
        Some Further Issues   496
      Real and Nominal GDP   496
      Omissions from GDP   499
      GDP and Living Standards   502
Summary   503
Key Terms   504
Study Exercises   504

PART 8
The Economy in the Short Run   507

**Chapter 21 The Simplest Short-Run Macro
              Model   507**
21.1 Desired Aggregate Expenditure   508
      Desired Consumption Expenditure   509
      Desired Investment Expenditure   516
      The Aggregate Expenditure Function   520
21.2 Equilibrium National Income   522
      A "Demand-Determined"
        Equilibrium   522
      Equilibrium: Desired AE = Actual Y 523
21.3 Changes in Equilibrium National
        Income   524
      Shifts of the AE Function   524
      The Multiplier   526
      Economic Fluctuations as
        Self-Fulfilling Prophecies   529
Summary   531
Key Concepts   532
Study Exercises   532

**Chapter 22 Adding Government and Trade to the
              Simple Macro Model   535**
22.1 Introducing Government   536
      Government Purchases   536
      Net Tax Revenues   536
      The Budget Balance   537
      Provincial and Municipal
        Governments   537
      Summary   537
22.2 Introducing Foreign Trade   538
      Net Exports   538
      Shifts in the Net Export Function   539
      Summary   541

22.3 Equilibrium National Income   541
      Adding Taxes to the Consumption
        Function   542
      The AE Function   542
      Equilibrium National Income   544
22.4 Changes in Equilibrium National
        Income   544
      The Multiplier with Taxes
        and Imports   545
      Net Exports   546
      Fiscal Policy: Government
        Spending and Taxation   547
22.5 Demand-Determined Output   549
Summary   551
Key Concepts   552
Study Exercises   552

Appendix to Chapter 22   556
An Algebraic Exposition of the Simple
  Macro Model   556

**Chapter 23 Real GDP and the Price Level
              in the Short Run   558**
23.1 The Demand Side of the Economy   559
      Exogenous Changes in the Price
        Level   559
      Changes in Equilibrium GDP   560
      The Aggregate Demand Curve   561
23.2 The Supply Side of the
        Economy   564
      The Aggregate Supply Curve   565
      Shifts in the AS Curve   566
23.3 Macroeconomic Equilibrium   567
      Changes in the Macroeconomic
        Equilibrium   568
      Aggregate Demand Shocks   569
      Aggregate Supply Shocks   572
      A Word of Warning   573
Summary   575
Key Concepts   575
Study Exercises   576

PART 9
The Economy in the Long Run   579

**Chapter 24 From the Short Run to the Long Run:
              The Adjustment of Factor Prices   579**
24.1 Three Macroeconomic States   580
      The Short Run   580
      The Adjustment of Factor Prices   580
      The Long Run   581
      Summary   581

24.2	**The Adjustment Process**	582
	Potential Output and the Output Gap	582
	Factor Prices and the Output Gap	582
	Potential Output as an "Anchor"	585
24.3	**Aggregate Demand and Supply Shocks**	585
	Positive *AD* Shocks	586
	Negative *AD* Shocks	588
	Aggregate Supply Shocks	590
	Long-Run Equilibrium	591
	The Canadian Wage-Adjustment Process: Empirical Evidence	592
24.4	**Fiscal Stabilization Policy**	594
	The Basic Theory of Fiscal Stabilization	594
	Automatic Fiscal Stabilizers	598
	Limitations of Discretionary Fiscal Policy	600
	Fiscal Policy and Growth	602
Summary		603
Key Concepts		604
Study Exercises		604

Chapter 25	**Long-Run Economic Growth**	**608**
25.1	**The Nature of Economic Growth**	609
	Benefits of Economic Growth	610
	Costs of Economic Growth	613
	Sources of Economic Growth	614
25.2	**Economic Growth: Basic Relationships**	616
	A Long-Run Analysis	616
	Investment, Saving, and Growth	617
	The "Neoclassical" Growth Model	621
25.3	**Economic Growth: Advanced Theories**	627
	Endogenous Technological Change	627
	Increasing Marginal Returns	630
25.4	**Are There Limits to Growth?**	632
	Resource Exhaustion	632
	Environmental Degradation	633
	Conclusion	635
Summary		636
Key Concepts		637
Study Exercises		637

PART 10
Money, Banking, and Monetary Policy   **641**

Chapter 26	**Money and Banking**	**641**
26.1	**The Nature of Money**	642
	What Is Money?	642
	The Origins of Money	643
	Modern Money: Deposit Money	648

26.2	**The Canadian Banking System**	650
	The Bank of Canada	650
	Commercial Banks in Canada	653
	Commercial Banks' Reserves	655
26.3	**Money Creation by the Banking System**	658
	Some Simplifying Assumptions	658
	The Creation of Deposit Money	658
	Excess Reserves and Cash Drains	661
26.4	**The Money Supply**	662
	Kinds of Deposits	663
	Definitions of the Money Supply	663
	Near Money and Money Substitutes	664
	The Role of the Bank of Canada	664
Summary		665
Key Concepts		666
Study Exercises		666

Chapter 27	**Money, Interest Rates, and Economic Activity**	**669**
27.1	**Understanding Bonds**	670
	Present Value and the Interest Rate	670
	Present Value and Market Price	672
	Interest Rates, Bond Prices, and Bond Yields	673
	Bond Riskiness	674
27.2	**The Theory of Money Demand**	675
	Three Reasons for Holding Money	675
	The Determinants of Money Demand	677
	Money Demand: Summing Up	678
27.3	**How Money Affects Aggregate Demand**	679
	Monetary Equilibrium	679
	The Monetary Transmission Mechanism	680
	An Open-Economy Modification	683
	The Slope of the *AD* Curve	685
27.4	**The Strength of Monetary Forces**	686
	The Neutrality of Money	686
	Money and Inflation	688
	The Short-Run Effects of Monetary Policy	690
Summary		693
Key Concepts		694
Study Exercises		694

Chapter 28	**Monetary Policy in Canada**	**698**
28.1	How the Bank of Canada Implements Monetary Policy	699
	Money Supply Versus the Interest Rate	699

The Bank of Canada and the
   Overnight Interest Rate   702
The Money Supply Is Endogenous   703
Expansionary and Contractionary
   Monetary Policies   706

28.2   **Inflation Targeting**   706
Why Target Inflation?   707
Inflation Targeting and the
   Output Gap   708
Inflation Targeting as a Stabilizing
   Policy   709
Complications in Inflation Targeting   709

28.3   **Long and Variable Lags**   712
What Are the Lags in Monetary
   Policy?   712
Destabilizing Policy?   713
Communications Difficulties   715

28.4   **Four Decades of Canadian
   Monetary Policy**   716
Economic Recovery: 1983–1987   717
Rising Inflation: 1987–1990   718
Inflation Targeting: 1991–2000   719
Inflation Targeting: 2001–2007   720
Financial Crisis and Recession:
   2007–2010   721
Slow Economic Recovery:
   2011–Present   723

Summary   724
Key Concepts   725
Study Exercises   726

PART 11
Macroeconomic Problems and Policies   729

Chapter 29   Inflation and Disinflation   729
29.1   **Adding Inflation to the Model**   731
Why Wages Change   731
From Wages to Prices   733
Constant Inflation   734

29.2   **Shocks and Policy Responses**   736
Demand Shocks   737
Supply Shocks   738
Accelerating Inflation   740
Inflation as a Monetary Phenomenon   741

29.3   **Reducing Inflation**   744
The Process of Disinflation   744
The Cost of Disinflation   746
Conclusion   747

Summary   748
Key Concepts   749
Study Exercises   749

**Chapter 30   Unemployment Fluctuations and
the NAIRU**   752
30.1   **Employment and Unemployment**   753
Changes in Employment   753
Changes in Unemployment   754
Flows in the Labour Market   755
Measurement Problems   755
Consequences of Unemployment   758

30.2   **Unemployment Fluctuations**   759
Market-Clearing Theories   759
Non-Market-Clearing Theories   761

30.3   **What Determines the NAIRU?**   765
Frictional Unemployment   765
Structural Unemployment   766
The Frictional–Structural
   Distinction   768
Why Does the NAIRU
   Change?   768

30.4   **Reducing Unemployment**   771
Cyclical Unemployment   771
Frictional Unemployment   772
Structural Unemployment   772
Conclusion   774

Summary   774
Key Concepts   775
Study Exercises   775

Chapter 31   Government Debt and Deficits   779
31.1   **Facts and Definitions**   780
The Government's Budget
   Constraint   780
Deficits and Debt in Canada   782

31.2   **Two Analytical Issues**   784
The Stance of Fiscal Policy   784
Debt Dynamics   788

31.3   **The Effects of Government Debt
   and Deficits**   790
Do Deficits Crowd Out Private
   Activity?   791
Do Deficits Harm Future
   Generations?   793
Does Government Debt Hamper
   Economic Policy?   794

31.4   **Formal Fiscal Rules**   796
Annually Balanced Budgets   796
Cyclically Balanced Budgets   797
Maintaining a Prudent Debt-to-GDP
   Ratio   797

Summary   798
Key Concepts   799
Study Exercises   799

PART 12

Canada in the Global Economy   **803**

Chapter 32   The Gains from International Trade   803
32.1   The Gains from Trade   804
       Interpersonal, Interregional, and
         International Trade   805
       Illustrating the Gains from Trade   806
       The Gains from Trade with
         Variable Costs   811
       Sources of Comparative Advantage   814
32.2   The Determination of Trade Patterns   816
       The Law of One Price   817
       The Pattern of Foreign Trade   818
       Is Comparative Advantage Obsolete?   819
       The Terms of Trade   821
Summary   824
Key Concepts   824
Study Exercises   825

Chapter 33   Trade Policy   828
33.1   Free Trade or Protection?   829
       The Case for Free Trade   829
       The Case for Protection   830
       Invalid Arguments for Protection   833
33.2   Methods of Protection   836
       Tariffs   837
       Import Quotas   839
       Tariffs Versus Quotas: An
         Application   839
       Trade-Remedy Laws and
         Non-Tariff Barriers   840
33.3   Current Trade Policy   842
       The GATT and the WTO   842
       Regional Trade Agreements   842
       Trade Creation and Trade Diversion   843
       The North American Free Trade
         Agreement   844
Summary   848
Key Concepts   849
Study Exercises   849

**Chapter 34   Exchange Rates and the Balance
               of Payments   852**
34.1   The Balance of Payments   853
       The Current Account   854
       The Capital Account   854
       The Balance of Payments Must
         Balance   855
       There Can't Be a Balance of
         Payments Deficit!   857
       Summary   857
34.2   The Foreign-Exchange Market   859
       The Exchange Rate   859
       The Supply of Foreign Exchange   860
       The Demand for Foreign Exchange   862
34.3   The Determination of Exchange
         Rates   863
       Flexible Exchange Rates   864
       Fixed Exchange Rates   865
       Changes in Flexible Exchange Rates   865
       Structural Changes   870
34.4   Three Policy Issues   871
       Current Account Deficits
         and Surpluses   871
       Is There a "Correct" Value for the
         Canadian Dollar?   876
       Should Canada Have a Fixed
         Exchange Rate?   879
Summary   884
Key Concepts   885
Study Exercises   885

Mathematical Notes   M-1
Timeline of Great Economists   T-1
Index   I-1

List of Boxes

Applying Economic Concepts

1-1   The Opportunity Cost of Your University Degree   6
2-1   Where Economists Work   29
3-1   Why Apples but Not iPhones?   63
19-1   The Terminology of Business Cycles   465
19-2   How the CPI Is Constructed   472
20-1   Value Added Through Stages of Production   487
20-2   Calculating Nominal and Real GDP   499
21-1   The Simple Multiplier: A Numerical Example   528
22-1   How Large Is Canada's Simple Multiplier?   546
25-1   What Does Productivity Growth Really Look Like?   611
25-2   A Case Against Economic Growth   614
25-3   Climate Change and Economic Growth   634
26-1   Are Cryptocurrencies Really Money?   649
26-2   Confidence and Risk in Canadian Banking   657
27-1   Understanding Bond Prices and Bond Yields   676

27-2   Three Propositions About Money Neutrality   688
28-1   What Determines the Amount of Currency in Circulation?   705
29-1   Is Deflation a Problem?   736
30-1   Stocks and Flows in the Canadian Labour Market   756
30-2   Wage Flexibility and the Rise of the "Gig" Economy   764
31-1   The Continuing Greek Tragedy of Debt Dynamics   790
32-1   Two Examples of Absolute and Comparative Advantage   812
32-2   Comparative Advantage and Global Supply Chains   820
33-1   Canadian Wine: A Free-Trade Success Story   847
34-1   A Student's Balance of Payments with the Rest of the World   858
34-2   Fixed Exchange Rates and Foreign-Exchange Reserves   866

Lessons from History

23-1   The 1997–1998 Asian Crisis and the Canadian Economy   574
24-1   Fiscal Policy in the Great Depression   598
25-1   Should Workers Be Afraid of Technological Change?   626
26-1   Hyperinflation and the Value of Money   644

28-1   Two Views on the Role of Money in the Great Depression   714
33-1   Donald Trump, Tariff Wars, and Stark Lessons from the Great Depression   836
34-1   Donald Trump: Modern-Day Mercantilist   873

Extensions in Theory

3-1   The Distinction Between Stocks and Flows   51
20-1   Arbitrary Decisions in National Income Accounting   496
21-1   The Theory of the Consumption Function   511
21-2   The Algebra of the Simple Multiplier   530

24-1   The Phillips Curve and the Adjustment Process   586
29-1   The Phillips Curve and Inflation Expectations   742
32-1   The Gains from Trade More Generally   810

To the Instructor

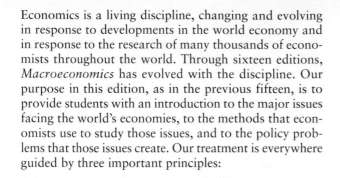

Economics is a living discipline, changing and evolving in response to developments in the world economy and in response to the research of many thousands of economists throughout the world. Through sixteen editions, *Macroeconomics* has evolved with the discipline. Our purpose in this edition, as in the previous fifteen, is to provide students with an introduction to the major issues facing the world's economies, to the methods that economists use to study those issues, and to the policy problems that those issues create. Our treatment is everywhere guided by three important principles:

1. Economics is *scientific,* in the sense that it progresses through the systematic confrontation of theory by evidence. Neither theory nor data alone can tell us much about the world, but combined they tell us a great deal.

2. Economics is *relevant* and it should be seen by students to be so. An understanding of economic theory combined with knowledge about the economy produces many important insights about economic policy. Although we stress these insights, we are also careful to point out cases in which too little is known to support strong statements about public policy. Appreciating what is not known is as important as learning what is known.

3. We strive always to be *honest* with our readers. Although we know that economics is not always easy, we do not approve of glossing over difficult bits of analysis without letting readers see what is happening and what has been assumed. We take whatever space is needed to explain why economists draw their conclusions, rather than just asserting the conclusions. We also take pains to avoid simplifying matters so much that students would have to unlearn what they have been taught if they continue their study beyond the introductory course. In short, we have tried to follow Albert Einstein's advice:

   Everything should be made as simple as possible, but not simpler.

CURRENT ECONOMIC ISSUES

In writing the sixteenth edition of *Macroeconomics,* we have tried to reflect the major economic issues that we face in the early twenty-first century.

Living Standards and Economic Growth

One of the most fundamental economic issues is the determination of overall living standards. Adam Smith wondered why some countries become wealthy while others remain poor. Though we have learned much about this topic in the 240 years since Adam Smith's landmark work, economists recognize that there is still much we do not know.

Technological change plays a central role in our discussion of long-run economic growth in Chapter 25. We explore not only the traditional channels of saving, investment, and population growth, but also the more recent economic theories that emphasize the importance of increasing returns and endogenous growth.

We are convinced that no other introductory economics textbook places as much emphasis on technological change and economic growth as we do in this book. Given the importance of continuing growth in living standards and understanding where that growth comes from, we believe this emphasis is appropriate. We hope you agree.

Financial Crisis, Recession, and Recovery

The collapse of U.S. housing prices in 2007 led to a global financial crisis the likes of which had not been witnessed in a century, and perhaps longer. A deep recession, experienced in many countries, followed quickly on its heels. These dramatic events reawakened many people to two essential facts about economics. First, modern economies *can and do* go into recession. This essential fact had perhaps been forgotten by many who had become complacent after more than two decades of economic prosperity. Second, financial markets are crucial to the operation of modern economies. Like an electricity system, the details of financial markets are a mystery to most people, and the system itself is often ignored when it is functioning properly. But when financial markets cease to work smoothly and interest rates rise while credit flows decline, we are all reminded of their importance. In this sense, the financial crisis of 2007–2008 was like a global power failure for the world economy.

The financial crisis had important macro consequences. It affected the Canadian banking system, as discussed in Chapter 26, and led to some aggressive actions by the Bank of Canada, as discussed in Chapter 28. Moreover, as the global financial crisis led to a deep recession worldwide, Canadian fiscal policy was forced to respond, as we review in Chapters 24 and 31. Finally, as has happened several times throughout history, the recession raised the threat of protectionist policies, as we examine in Chapter 33.

Globalization

Enormous changes have occurred throughout the world over the last few decades. Flows of trade and investment between countries have risen so dramatically that it is now common to speak of the "globalization" of the world economy. Today it is no longer possible to study any economy without taking into account developments in the rest of the world.

Throughout its history, Canada has been a trading nation, and our policies relating to international trade have often been at the centre of political debates. International trade shows up in many parts of this textbook, but it is the exclusive focus of two chapters. Chapter 32 discusses the theory of the gains from trade; Chapter 33 explores trade policy, with an emphasis on NAFTA and the WTO.

With globalization and the international trade of goods and assets come fluctuations in exchange rates. In recent years there have been substantial changes in the Canada–U.S. exchange rate—a 15 percent depreciation followed the Asian economic crisis in 1997–1998 and also the 2014–2015 period, which saw a major decline in the world price of oil. An even greater appreciation occurred in the 2002–2008 period. Such volatility in exchange rates complicates the conduct of economic policy. In Chapters 28 and 29 we explore how the exchange rate fits into the design and operation of Canada's monetary policy. In Chapter 34 we examine the debate between fixed and flexible exchange rates.

The forces of globalization are with us to stay. In this sixteenth edition of *Macroeconomics*, we have done our best to ensure that students are made aware of the world outside Canada and how events elsewhere in the world affect the Canadian economy.

The Role of Government

Between 1980 and 2008, the political winds shifted in Canada, the United States, and many other countries. Political parties that previously advocated a greater role for government in the economy argued the benefits of limited government. But the political winds shifted again with the arrival of the financial crisis and global recession in 2008, which led governments the world over to take some unprecedented actions. Many soon argued that we were observing the "end of laissez-faire" and

witnessing the return of "big government." But was that really true?

Has the *fundamental* role of government changed significantly over the past 35 years? In order to understand the role of government in the economy, students must understand the benefits of free markets as well as the situations that cause markets to fail. They must also understand that governments often intervene in the economy for reasons related more to equity than to efficiency.

In this sixteenth edition of *Macroeconomics,* we continue to incorporate the discussion of government policy as often as possible. Here are but a few of the many examples that we explore:

- fiscal policy (in Chapters 22 and 24)
- policies related to the economy's long-run growth rate (in Chapter 25)
- monetary policy (in Chapters 27, 28, and 29)
- policies that affect the economy's long-run unemployment rate (in Chapter 30)
- the importance of debt and deficits (in Chapter 31)
- trade policies and the threat of "tariff wars" (in Chapter 33)
- policies related to the exchange rate (in Chapter 34)

THE BOOK

Economic growth, financial crisis and recession, globalization, and the role of government are pressing issues of the day. Much of our study of economic principles and the Canadian economy has been shaped by these issues. In addition to specific coverage of growth and internationally oriented topics, growth and globalization appear naturally throughout the book in the treatment of many topics once thought to be entirely "domestic."

Most chapters of *Macroeconomics* contain some discussion of economic policy. We have two main goals in mind when we present these discussions:

1. We aim to give students practice in using economic theory, because applying theory is both a wonderfully effective teaching method and a reliable test of students' grasp of theory.

2. We want to introduce students to the major policy issues of the day and to let them discover that few policy debates are as "black and white" as they often appear in the press.

Both goals reflect our view that students should see economics as relevant and useful in helping us to understand and deal with the world around us.

Structure and Coverage

Our treatment of macroeconomics is divided into six parts. We make a clear distinction between the economy in the short run and the economy in the long run, and we get quickly to the material on long-run economic growth. Students are confronted with issues of long-run economic growth *before* they are introduced to issues of money and banking. Given the importance of economic growth in driving overall living standards, we believe this is an appropriate ordering of the material, but for those who prefer to discuss money before thinking about economic growth, the order can be easily switched without any loss of continuity.

The first macro chapter, Chapter 19, introduces readers to the central macro variables, what they mean, and why they are important. The discussion of national income accounting in Chapter 20 provides a thorough treatment of the distinction between real and nominal GDP, the GDP deflator, and a discussion of what measures of national income *do not measure* and whether these omissions really matter.

Part 8 develops the core short-run model of the macro economy, beginning with the fixed-price (Keynesian Cross) model in Chapters 21 and 22 and then moving on to the *AD/AS* model in Chapter 23. Chapter 21 uses a closed economy model with no government to explain the process of national-income determination and the nature of the multiplier. Chapter 22 extends the setting to include international trade and government spending and taxation. Chapter 23 rounds out our discussion of the short run with the *AD/AS* framework, discussing the importance of both aggregate demand and aggregate supply shocks. We place the Keynesian Cross before the *AD/AS* model to show that there is no mystery about where the *AD* curve comes from and why it is downward sloping; the *AD* curve is derived directly from the Keynesian Cross model. In contrast, books that begin their analysis with the *AD/AS* model are inevitably less clear about where the model comes from. We lament the growing tendency to omit the Keynesian Cross from introductory macroeconomics textbooks; we believe the model has much to offer students in terms of economic insights.

Part 9 begins in Chapter 24 by showing how the short-run model evolves toward the long run through the adjustment of factor prices—what we often call the Phillips curve. We introduce potential output as an "anchor" to which real GDP returns following *AD* or *AS* shocks. This chapter also addresses issues in fiscal policy, including the important distinction between automatic stabilizers and discretionary fiscal stabilization policy. Our treatment of long-run growth in Chapter 25, which we regard as one of the most important issues facing

Canada and the world today, goes well beyond the treatment in most introductory texts.

Part 10 focuses on the role of money and financial systems. Chapter 26 discusses the nature of money, various components of the money supply, the commercial banking system, and the Bank of Canada. In Chapter 27 we offer a detailed discussion of the link between the money market and other economic variables such as interest rates, the exchange rate, national income, and the price level. In Chapter 28 we discuss the Bank of Canada's monetary policy, including a detailed discussion of inflation targeting. The chapter ends with a review of Canadian monetary policy over the past 40 years.

Part 11 deals with some of today's most pressing macroeconomic policy issues. It contains separate chapters on inflation, unemployment, and government budget deficits. Chapter 29 on inflation examines the central role of expectations in determining inflation and the importance of credibility on the part of the central bank. Chapter 30 on unemployment examines the determinants of frictional and structural unemployment and discusses likely reasons for changes in the NAIRU. Chapter 31 on budget deficits stresses the importance of a country's debt-to-GDP ratio and also the effect of budget deficits on long-term economic growth.

Virtually every macroeconomic chapter contains at least some discussion of international issues. However, the final part of *Macroeconomics* focuses primarily on international economics. Chapter 32 gives the basic treatment of international trade, developing both the traditional theory of static comparative advantage and newer theories based on imperfect competition and dynamic comparative advantage. Chapter 33 discusses both the positive and normative aspects of trade policy, as well as the WTO and NAFTA. Chapter 34 introduces the balance of payments and examines exchange-rate determination. Here we also discuss three important policy issues: the desirability of current-account deficits or surpluses, whether there is a "right" value for the Canadian exchange rate, and the costs and benefits of Canada's adopting a fixed exchange rate.

We hope you find this menu both attractive and challenging; we hope students find the material stimulating and enlightening. Many of the messages of economics are complex—if economic understanding were only a matter of common sense and simple observation, there would be no need for professional economists and no need for textbooks like this one. To understand economics, one must work hard. Working at this book should help readers gain a better understanding of the world around them and of the policy problems faced by all levels of government. Furthermore, in today's globalized world, the return to education is large. We like to think that we have contributed in some small part to the understanding that increased investment in human capital by the next generation is necessary to restore incomes to the rapid growth paths that so benefited our parents and our peers. Perhaps we may even contribute to some income-enhancing accumulation of human capital by some of our readers.

SUBSTANTIVE CHANGES TO THIS EDITION

We have revised and updated the entire text with guidance from feedback from both users and nonusers of the previous editions of this book. We have strived very hard to improve the teachability and readability of the book. We have focused the discussions so that each major point is emphasized as clearly as possible, without distracting the reader with nonessential points. As in recent editions, we have kept all core material in the main part of the text. Three types of boxes (Applying Economic Concepts, Lessons from History, and Extensions in Theory) are used to show examples or extensions that can be skipped without fear of missing an essential concept. But we think it would be a shame to skip too many of them, as there are many interesting examples and policy discussions in these boxes.

What follows is a brief listing of the main changes that we have made to the textbook.

Microeconomics Introduction

In Chapter 1, we have added accelerating technological change and rising protectionism to the initial list of economic challenges. We have also rewritten the simple example of the choice between two products; we now use a city planner with a fixed budget, choosing between repairing roads and building new bike paths. We have improved the discussion of how marginal benefits and marginal costs are used to make decisions. In Chapter 3, we have rewritten the discussion of some of the shifters of demand curves, and have added changes in weather as one important factor shifting supply curves.

Macroeconomics

Part 7: An Introduction to Macroeconomics

We have rewritten the introduction to this first macro chapter, hopefully providing a clearer motivation for studying the topic. In Chapter 20, we have added a new figure and explanation to understand the different growth paths of real and nominal GDP. We have also added a brief discussion of measures of "social well-being" in the chapter's final section.

Part 8: The Economy in the Short Run

We have rewritten the introduction to Chapter 21 to better lay out the logical flow of ideas in these crucial macro theory chapters. In Chapter 22 we have clarified the linkage between net exports and aggregate demand, and have added the Canada–U.S. economic relationship as an example of how changes in foreign income affect Canadian exports. In the chapter's section on fiscal policy, we have added a new diagram to show the impact of changes in government purchases and changes in the net tax rate on the *AE* function. In Chapter 23 we have clarified the explanation of how a change in the price level affects net exports. We have also rewritten the discussion of the various kinds of shocks that lead to a shift of the *AS* curve.

Part 9: The Economy in the Long Run

When addressing the economy's adjustment process in Chapter 24, we have added a new section on the strength of the Phillips Curve dynamics, asking whether the output gap still drives wages changes. We show Canadian data in a new figure and provide some explanation for why this relationship may have weakened in recent years. We have also completely rewritten the section on fiscal policy and growth, with an attempt to simplify the central message that the nature of fiscal policies may impact both the level and growth rate of potential GDP.

Part 10: Money, Banking, and Monetary Policy

Chapter 26 addresses the nature of money. In this discussion, we have added a new box that asks whether cryptocurrencies such as Bitcoin should really be considered money. (Spoiler alert: They shouldn't be—yet!). We have added a new box on the Canadian banking system and how regulations in that sector play an important role in providing both stability and confidence. In Chapter 27, we have clarified the discussions of bonds, monetary equilibrium, and money neutrality. We have updated the policy discussion in Chapter 28 to include the impact of NAFTA negotiations on the level of economic uncertainty and the policy stance of the Bank of Canada.

Part 11: Macroeconomic Problems and Policies

Chapter 29 on inflation and disinflation has had no major changes, although several small modifications should improve the overall flow. In the discussion of unemployment in Chapter 30, we have rewritten the discussion of long-term employment relationships and why they are an important reason for wage rigidity. This leads to a new box on the "gig economy," why it is happening, and what it likely means for the overall amount of wage flexibility. Chapter 31 addresses government debt and deficits and remains largely unchanged from the previous edition, although we have added the 2018–2019 fiscal year as a numerical example to illustrate the calculation of the primary budget deficit (surplus).

Part 12: Canada in the Global Economy

We address the gains from international trade in Chapter 32. We have clarified the discussions of the determination of exports and imports in a competitive market. In Chapter 33 on trade policy, the views and policy actions of U.S. President Trump now figure prominently in several places. In our discussion of how protection might improve a country's terms of trade, we have added the example of Chinese tariffs on imported automobiles; we also use China as an example of a country that uses the "infant industry" argument for some trade protection. When discussing "tariff wars," we now discuss President Trump's 2018 tariffs on steel and aluminum. This leads to a box on tariff wars in history, which has been expanded to include a discussion of recent U.S. trade policy. The section on NAFTA has been updated, and we have added a discussion about the importance of integrated supply chains between the three NAFTA countries, especially in the auto sector. This leads to a new section examining the current political threat to NAFTA from the U.S. administration.

In Chapter 34 on exchange rates and the balance of payments, we have rewritten the box on fixed exchange rates, removing the discussion of Thailand and adding a new discussion and figure to explain the case of China's pegged exchange-rate regime and also the changes in its foreign-exchange reserves. The box on mercantilism has been reframed around President Trump's views on trade deficits. In our discussion of current account deficits, we now add the example of a government budget deficit as a possible cause.

* * *

If you are moved to write to us (and we hope that you will be!), please do. You can send any comments or questions regarding the text (or any of the supplementary material, such as the *Instructor's Manual*, the *TestGen*, or the web-based MyLab Economics to:

christopher.ragan@mcgill.ca

To the Student

Welcome to what is most likely your first book about economics! You are about to encounter what is for most people a new way of thinking, which often causes people to see things differently than they did before. But learning a new way of thinking is not always easy, and you should expect some hard work ahead. We do our best to be as clear and logical as possible and to illustrate our arguments whenever possible with current and interesting examples.

You must develop your own technique for studying, but the following suggestions may prove helpful. Begin by carefully considering the Learning Objectives at the beginning of a chapter. Read the chapter itself relatively quickly in order to get the general idea of the argument. At this first reading, you may want to skip the boxes and any footnotes. Then, after reading the Summary and the Key Concepts (at the end of each chapter), reread the chapter more slowly, making sure that you understand each step of the argument.

With respect to the figures and tables, be sure you understand how the conclusions that are stated in boldface at the beginning of each caption have been reached. You should be prepared to spend time on difficult sections; occasionally, you may spend an hour on only a few pages. Paper and pencil are indispensable equipment in your reading. It is best to follow a difficult argument by building your own diagram while the argument unfolds rather than by relying on the finished diagram as it appears in the book.

The end-of-chapter Study Exercises require you to practise using some of the concepts that you learned in the chapter. These will be excellent preparation for your exams. To provide you with immediate feedback, we have posted Solutions to Selected Study Exercises on MyLab Economics (www.pearson.com/mylab). We strongly advise that you should seek to understand economics, not to memorize it.

The red numbers in square brackets in the text refer to a series of mathematical notes that are found starting on page M-1 at the end of the book. For those of you who like mathematics or prefer mathematical argument to verbal or geometric exposition, these may prove useful. Others may disregard them.

In this edition of the book, we have incorporated many elements to help you review material and prepare for examinations.

We encourage you to make use of MyLab Economics that accompanies this book (www.pearson.com/mylab) at the outset of your studies. MyLab Economics contains a wealth of valuable resources to help you. MyLab Economics provides Solutions to Selected Study Exercises. It also includes many additional practice questions, some of which are modelled on Study Exercises in the book. You can also find an electronic version of the textbook.

Over the years, the book has benefited greatly from comments and suggestions we have received from students. Please feel free to send your comments to christopher.ragan@mcgill.ca. Good luck, and we hope you enjoy your course in economics!

Acknowledgements

It would be impossible to acknowledge here by name all the teachers, colleagues, and students who contributed to the development and improvement of this book over its previous fifteen editions. Hundreds of users have written to us with specific suggestions, and much of the credit for the improvement of the book over the years belongs to them. We can no longer list them individually but we thank them all sincerely.

For the development of this sixteenth edition, we are grateful to the many people who offered informal suggestions. We would also like to thank the following instructors who provided us with formal reviews of the textbook and the MyLab Economics. Their observations and recommendations were extremely helpful.

- Medoune Seck, CEGEP John Abbott College
- Paul T. Dickinson, McGill University
- Mark Raymond, Saint Mary's University
- Cheryl Jenkins, John Abbott College
- Kevin Richter, Douglas College
- Fulton Tom, Langara College
- Mayssun El-Attar Vilalta, McGill University
- Michael Barber, Queen's University
- Michael Batu, University of Windsor
- Catherine Boulatoff, Dalhousie University
- Suzanna Fromm, BCIT
- Cheryl Roberts, Vancouver School of Economics and Vantage College
- Sinisa Vujovic, Kwantlen Polytechnic University

We would like to express our thanks to the many people at Pearson Canada involved in the development and production of this textbook. We would especially like to thank three individuals with whom we worked closely. Kimberley Veevers (Executive Portfolio Manager); Toni Chahley (Content Developer); Spencer Snell (Marketing Manager) all showed their professionalism, dedication, and enthusiasm in guiding this book through the publication and marketing processes. We would also like to thank the many sales representatives who work to bring this book to professors across the country. These individuals have been a pleasure to work with each step along the way, and we are deeply grateful for their presence and their participation and are delighted to consider them friends as well as professional colleagues.

Our thanks also to the many people at Pearson with whom we work less closely but who nonetheless toil behind the scenes to produce this book, including Andrea Falkenberg, Pippa Kennard, Leanne Rancourt, and Anthony Leung.

Thanks also to Cat Haggert for copyediting, and to Leanne Rancourt for proofreading, both of which provided an invaluable service with their attention to detail.

In short, we realize that there is a great deal more involved in producing a book than *just* the writing. Without the efforts of all of these dedicated professionals, this textbook simply would not exist. Our sincere thanks to all of you.

Thanks also to James Ryan for his detailed and diligent work in assembling the necessary data for updating this sixteenth edition.

Finally, Ingrid Kristjanson and I have been partners in life for over 30 years and partners in this textbook venture since we began work on the 9th edition in 1995. Without her participation, the quality and efficiency of this project would suffer greatly. Ingrid also plays a leading role in the improvement, rewriting, and expansion of the electronic Testbank. With her involvement, the lengthy revision of the textbook and its supplements continues to be an enriching and pleasant experience.

Christopher Ragan

About the Author

Chris Ragan received his B.A. in economics from the University of Victoria, his M.A. from Queen's University, and his Ph.D. from the Massachusetts Institute of Technology in Cambridge, Massachusetts, in 1990. He then joined the Department of Economics at McGill University in Montreal, where he has taught graduate courses in macroeconomics and international finance and undergraduate courses in macroeconomic theory and policy, current economic issues, and financial crises. Over the years he has taught principles of economics (micro and macro) to thousands of students at McGill and maintains a reputation on campus as being "super-excited" about economics. In 2007, Chris Ragan was awarded the Noel Fieldhouse Teaching Award from McGill for teaching excellence.

In 2017, he was appointed as the inaugural Director of McGill's Max Bell School of Public Policy. In that capacity, he will be designing a new Master of Public Policy (MPP) program as well as the many other research and outreach elements included in leading policy schools.

Professor Ragan's research focuses mainly on the design and implementation of macroeconomic policy in Canada. He has been privileged to serve the federal government in Ottawa as Special Advisor to the Governor of the Bank of Canada, the Clifford Clark Visiting Economist at the Department of Finance, and most recently as a member of the Advisory Council on Economic Growth. He currently serves as the chair of Canada's Ecofiscal Commission, a five-year project of independent economists and advisors to promote the greater use of pollution pricing in the Canadian economy.

Chris Ragan used the third edition of this textbook as an undergraduate student in 1981 and joined Richard Lipsey as a co-author in 1997 for the book's ninth edition. For several editions, Lipsey and Ragan worked diligently to maintain the book's reputation as the clearest and most comprehensive introductory economics textbook in Canada. Although Chris Ragan is now the sole listed author, this sixteenth edition still owes much to the dedication of previous authors, including Richard Lipsey, Douglas Purvis, and Gordon Sparks.

1 Economic Issues and Concepts

CHAPTER OUTLINE	LEARNING OBJECTIVES (LO)
	After studying this chapter you will be able to
1.1 WHAT IS ECONOMICS?	1 explain the importance of scarcity, choice, and opportunity cost, and how each is illustrated by the production possibilities boundary.
1.2 THE COMPLEXITY OF MODERN ECONOMIES	2 view the market economy as self-organizing in the sense that order emerges from a large number of decentralized decisions.
1.3 IS THERE AN ALTERNATIVE TO THE MARKET ECONOMY?	3 explain how specialization gives rise to the need for trade, and how trade is facilitated by money.
	4 explain the importance of maximizing and marginal decisions.
	5 describe how all actual economies are mixed economies, having elements of free markets, tradition, and government intervention.

MANY of the challenges we face in Canada and around the world are primarily economic. Others that appear to be mainly environmental, social, or political usually have a significant economic dimension. Wars and civil unrest throughout history have often had economic roots, with antagonists competing for control over vital resources; global climate change is a phenomenon that engages the attention of the scientific and environmental communities, but the economic implications of both the problem and its solutions will be tremendous; population aging in Canada and other developed countries will have consequences for the structure of our societies, but it will also have significant economic effects; and the existence of poverty, whether in Canada or in the much poorer nations of the world, most certainly has economic causes and consequences. We begin by discussing several issues that are currently of pressing concern, both inside and outside of Canada. Then, we'll move on to acquiring the knowledge and tools we need to better understand these and many other issues.

Productivity Growth Productivity growth lies at the heart of the long-term increase in average living standards. Productivity is a measure of how much output (or income) is produced by one hour of work effort, and it has been rising gradually over the past century. In recent years, however, productivity growth has been slowing in Canada, and economists have been examining the cause of the slowdown and also examining what policies, if any, might reverse this trend. If your living standards are to improve over your lifetime as much as your grandparents' did over theirs, Canada's rate of productivity growth will need to increase significantly.

Population Aging The average age of the Canadian population is steadily rising, due both to a long-term decline in fertility and to an increase in average life-expectancy. This population aging has two important economic effects. First, since people eventually retire as they approach their "golden years," there will be a decline in the growth rate of Canada's labour force. As a result, some firms and industries will find it more difficult to find workers, and wages will likely rise. Second, since our publicly funded healthcare system tends to spend much more on seniors than it does on younger Canadians, there will be a significant increase in public health-care spending that will put difficult demands on governments' fiscal positions. This same demographic problem is being encountered in most developed countries.

Climate Change Climate change is a global phenomenon that has important implications for most nations on Earth. The long-term increase in the emission of greenhouse gases—caused largely from the burning of fossil fuels such as oil, coal, and natural gas—has led to an accumulation of these gases in the atmosphere and is contributing to a long-term increase in Earth's average temperature. The rise in temperature is leading to the melting of polar ice caps, a slow increase in sea level, a creeping expansion of the world's great deserts, reductions in agricultural productivity, and significant changes in global weather patterns—including a greater frequency of extreme events such as floods, droughts, and hurricanes. Global climate change presents a challenge for the design of better economic policy, aimed at reducing greenhouse-gas emissions without unduly slowing the growth of material living standards. Climate change also presents a long-term challenge as to how we will adapt to the changes that are already happening.

Accelerating Technological Change Over the past half century, the digitization of information has created revolutionary changes in technology, from the evolution of hand-held computers with enormous capabilities to the development of artificial intelligence whereby machines are able to learn. Nanotechnology and 3D printing are just two examples that are likely to lead to products and services we can barely imagine today. Such technological change is an important driver of our long-run prosperity—but it also creates enormous disruptions in product markets and labour markets. Some businesses will find it difficult to compete against rivals with more advanced technology and will be forced to adapt or go out of business. Some workers may find their jobs replaced by machines and will be forced to retrain to find acceptable employment, perhaps in another city or province. Such "disruptive technologies" also create challenges for government policy: How can we reap the benefits of these new developments while ensuring that our citizens continue to have satisfying work at thriving businesses?

Rising Protectionism   Canada is a small nation that relies significantly on trade with the rest of the world for its prosperity. We sell our lumber and oil and beef to the world, as we do our engineering and legal and financial services. As consumers we buy a wide variety of products from beyond our borders, including coffee, leather shoes, and fine wine; our firms also buy many inputs from abroad, including machine tools, software, and specialized raw materials. In short, international trade has long been crucial to Canada's economic prosperity. In recent years, however, many countries have been becoming more "protectionist" in their policies—meaning that they are less willing to open their domestic markets to other countries' products. Past experience across many countries and over many years has shown that protectionism tends to lead to less international trade and also less global production and income. Small, trade-reliant countries like Canada have much to fear from rising protectionism elsewhere.

Growing Income Inequality   In Canada and most other developed countries, the past three decades have seen a rise in income inequality. Particularly dramatic has been the increase in the share of national income going to the richest 1 percent of individuals, all while the incomes of those in the "middle classes" have grown very slowly. The causes of this rising inequality are hotly debated among economists, but most agree that the nature and pace of technological change and the growing ability of firms to locate their production facilities in lower-wage developing countries are contributing factors. There is also considerable debate regarding what government actions could be taken to slow or reverse the increase in income inequality, and whether the benefits of those actions in terms of reduced inequality would be justified by the associated costs.

These six issues are only a small sample of the many economic issues that confront Canada and other countries. To understand any of them it is necessary to have a basic understanding of economics—how markets work, how prices are determined, in what sense markets sometimes fail to work well, and how government policy can be used to improve outcomes. These are the main topics of this book. There is a lot to learn, and not many weeks in your college or university course. So, let's get started at the very beginning.

▌ 1.1   What Is Economics?

The issues described in the introduction would not matter much if we lived in an economy of such plenty that there was always enough to fully satisfy everyone's wants. If we could always get all the things we wanted, it wouldn't be so important to be more productive in our work. Rapid growth in health-care spending would not be such a problem if governments had no limits on what they could spend. And rising protectionism would not be so threatening if Canada did not rely on the income earned by selling our many exported products to other countries. But such an economy with unlimited products and income is impossible. Why?

The short answer is because we live in a world of *scarcity*. Compared with the desires of individuals for things such as better food, clothing, housing, education, clean water and health care, the existing supplies of resources are clearly inadequate. They are sufficient to produce only a small fraction of the goods and services that we desire.

This scarcity gives rise to the basic economic problem of choice. If we cannot have everything we want, we must choose what we will and will not have.

One definition of *economics* comes from the great economist Alfred Marshall (1842–1924), who we will encounter at several points in this book: "Economics is a study of mankind in the ordinary business of life." A more informative definition is:

> **Economics is the study of the use of scarce resources to satisfy unlimited human wants.**

Scarcity is inevitable and is central to all economies and all economic problems. What are society's resources? Why is scarcity inevitable? What are the consequences of scarcity?

Resources

A society's resources are often divided into the three broad categories of land, labour, and capital. *Land* includes all natural endowments, such as arable land, forests, lakes, crude oil, and minerals. *Labour* includes all mental and physical human resources, including entrepreneurial capacity and management skills. *Capital* includes all manufactured aids to production, such as tools, machinery, and buildings. Economists call such resources **factors of production** because they are used to produce the things that people desire. We divide what is produced into goods and services. **Goods** are tangible (e.g., cars and shoes), and **services** are intangible (e.g., legal advice and education). People use goods and services to satisfy their wants. The act of making them is called **production**, and the act of using them is called **consumption**.

factors of production Resources used to produce goods and services; frequently divided into the basic categories of land, labour, and capital.

goods Tangible products, such as cars or shoes.

services Intangible products, such as legal services and education.

production The act of making goods or services.

consumption The act of using goods or services to satisfy wants.

Scarcity and Choice

For almost all of the world's 7.6 billion people, scarcity is real and ever-present. As we said earlier, relative to our desires, existing resources are inadequate; there are enough to produce only a fraction of the goods and services that we want.

But aren't the developed nations rich enough that scarcity is no longer a problem? After all, they are "affluent" societies. Whatever affluence may mean, however, it does not mean the end of the problem of scarcity. Canadian families that earn $75 000 per year, approximately the median after-tax income for a Canadian family in 2019 but a princely amount by *world* standards, have no trouble spending it on things that seem useful to them, and they would certainly have no trouble convincing you that their resources are scarce relative to their desires.

Because resources are scarce, all societies face the problem of deciding what to produce and how much each person will consume. Societies differ in who makes the choices and how they are made, but the need to choose is common to all. Just as scarcity implies the need for choice, so choice implies the existence of cost. A decision to have more of one thing is necessarily a decision to have less of some other thing. The *cost* of the more of one thing is the amount of the other thing we must give up in order to get it.

> **Scarcity implies that choices must be made, and making choices implies the existence of costs.**

Opportunity Cost   To see how choice implies cost, we look first at an example of a single decision maker and then at an example for the country as a whole. Both examples involve precisely the same fundamental principles.

Consider Susan, a senior planner who works for a small Canadian city. She is allocated a budget of $12 million for the year and must decide how to allocate it between two activities—repairing existing roads and building new bicycle paths. Repairing roads costs $1 million per kilometre repaired; new bicycle paths cost $500 000 per kilometre to build.

The choices that Susan and her planning department face are illustrated in Figure 1-1. The amount of new bicycle path is shown in kilometres along the horizontal axis. The kilometres of road repair is shown along the vertical axis. The downward-sloping line is Susan's *budget line*—it shows the various combinations of the two activities that use up the full budget of $12 million. Since it is possible to build fractions of a kilometre of bicycle path as well as repair fractions of a kilometre of road, all points along the budget line are *attainable* combinations of the two activities. Any combination outside the budget line—such as point *a*—is *unattainable*; the total cost of this combination requires more than the available budget.

In this setting, Susan and her colleagues need to make a difficult decision. How should the available funds be allocated between the two alternatives? To decide, they will need to compare the benefits of road repair to the benefits from building new bicycle paths. But they will also need to think about costs. For this discussion, we will focus only on the issue of costs.

What is the cost of an extra kilometre of road repair in this situation? One simple answer is that the cost is $1 million. An alternative and more revealing answer is that the cost of an extra kilometre of road repair is the two kilometres of new bicycle path that must be given up to get it. In fact, in this case we say that two kilometres of bicycle path is the *opportunity cost* of one kilometre of road repair.

opportunity cost The value of the next best alternative that is forgone when one alternative is chosen.

> Every time a choice is made, opportunity costs are incurred.

Opportunity Cost Is a Ratio   As simple as it may seem, the idea of opportunity cost is one of the central insights of economics. Here is a precise definition: The **opportunity cost** of choosing any one alternative is the value of the next best alternative that is given up. That is, it is the cost measured in terms of other goods and services that could have been obtained instead. This concept of cost involves a simple ratio, as we can see in our example in Figure 1-1. Suppose Susan had initially determined that the best use of her full budget was to choose point *b*—12 kilometres of new bicycle path and 6 kilometres of road repair. After new information regarding the dire state of some roads is considered, however, the

FIGURE 1-1   Choosing Between Road Repair and New Bicycle Paths

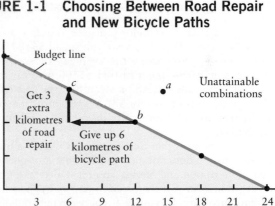

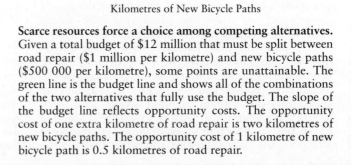

Scarce resources force a choice among competing alternatives. Given a total budget of $12 million that must be split between road repair ($1 million per kilometre) and new bicycle paths ($500 000 per kilometre), some points are unattainable. The green line is the budget line and shows all of the combinations of the two alternatives that fully use the budget. The slope of the budget line reflects opportunity costs. The opportunity cost of one extra kilometre of road repair is two kilometres of new bicycle paths. The opportunity cost of 1 kilometre of new bicycle path is 0.5 kilometres of road repair.

decision is made to choose point *c*—with more road repair and fewer kilometres of bicycle path. The movement from point *b* to point *c* involves a cost: six kilometres of bicycle path must be given up in order to get three extra kilometres of road repair. Each extra kilometre of road repair "costs" two kilometres of new bicycle path (6 ÷ 3 = 2).

Notice that the opportunity costs of the two activities are *inverses* of one another. From Figure 1-1 we see that the opportunity cost of one extra kilometre of road repair is two kilometres of new bicycle path. It is also true that the opportunity cost of one extra kilometre of bicycle path is 0.5 kilometre of road repair. Note that 0.5 is the slope of the green budget line.

The concept of opportunity cost is pervasive in economics. Whenever choices are limited by scarce resources, the decision to have more of one thing implies that we must give up something else. See *Applying Economic Concepts 1-1* for an example of opportunity cost that should seem quite familiar to you: the opportunity cost of getting a university degree.

APPLYING ECONOMIC CONCEPTS 1-1

The Opportunity Cost of Your University Degree

The opportunity cost of choosing one thing is what must be given up as the best alternative. Computing the opportunity cost of a college or university education is a good example to illustrate which factors are included in the computation of opportunity cost. You may also be surprised to learn how expensive your university degree really is!*

Suppose that a bachelor's degree requires four years of study and that each year you spend $6500 for tuition fees—approximately the average at Canadian universities in 2019—and a further $1500 per year for books and materials. Does this mean that the cost of a university education is only $32 000? Unfortunately not; the true cost of a university degree to a student is much higher.

The key point is that the opportunity cost of a university education does not include just the out-of-pocket expenses on tuition and books. You must also take into consideration *what you are forced to give up* by choosing to attend university. Of course, if you were not studying you could have done any one of a number of things, but the relevant one is *the one you would have chosen instead*—your best alternative to attending university.

Suppose your best alternative to attending university was to get a job. In this case, the opportunity cost of your university degree must include the earnings that you would have received had you taken that job. Suppose your (after-tax) annual earnings would have been $25 000 per year, for a total of $100 000 if you had stayed at that job for four years. To the direct expenses of $32 000, we must therefore add $100 000 for the

earnings that you gave up by not taking a job. This brings the true cost of your university degree—the opportunity cost—up to $132 000.

Notice that the cost of food, lodging, clothing, and other living expenses did not enter the calculation of the opportunity cost in this example. The living expenses must be incurred in either case—whether you attend university or get a job.

If the opportunity cost of a degree is so high, why do students choose to go to university? Maybe students simply enjoy learning and are prepared to incur the high cost to be in the university environment. Or maybe they believe that a university degree will significantly increase their future earning potential. In Chapter 14 we will see that this is true. In this case, they are giving up four years of earnings at one salary so that they can invest in building their skills in the hope of enjoying many more years in the future at a considerably higher salary.

Whatever the reason for attending college or university, the recognition that a post-secondary degree is very expensive should convince students to make the best use of their time while they are there. Read on!

_____

*This box considers only the cost *to the student* of a university degree. For reasons that will be discussed in detail in Part 6 of this book, provincial governments heavily subsidize post-secondary education in Canada. Because of this subsidy, the cost *to society* of a university degree is generally much higher than the cost to an individual student.

The nature of Susan's planning decision to allocate a set budget between two activities seems relatively straightforward—although we should not underestimate how tough such decisions actually are in practice. But now consider a bigger problem, one where scarcity and choice still play a central role. Instead of a situation where a single decision maker is allocating dollars of spending, our next situation relates to how a country as a whole allocates its scarce resources—its land, labour, and capital—between the production of various goods and services.

Production Possibilities Boundary

In particular, consider the choice that any country must face between producing goods for final consumption (such as food and clothing) and goods for investment purposes used to increase future production (such as machines and factories). If resources are fully and efficiently employed it is not possible to have more of *both* consumption and investment goods. As the country devotes more resources to producing consumption goods it must take resources away from producing investment goods. The opportunity cost of the extra consumption goods is the value of the investment goods forgone.

The choice is illustrated in Figure 1-2. Because resources are scarce, some combinations—those that would require more than the total available supply of resources for their production—cannot be attained. The negatively sloped curve on the graph divides the combinations that can be attained from those that cannot. Points above and to the right of this curve cannot be attained because there are not enough resources, points below and to the left of the curve can be attained without using all of the available resources, and points on the curve can be attained only if all the available resources are used efficiently. The curve is called the **production possibilities boundary**. (Sometimes "boundary" is replaced with "curve" or "frontier.") It has a negative slope because when all resources are being used efficiently, producing more of one good requires producing less of others.

FIGURE 1-2 A Production Possibilities Boundary

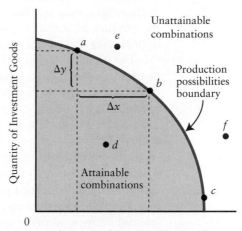

The negatively sloped boundary shows the combinations that are attainable when all resources are used efficiently. The production possibilities boundary separates the attainable combinations of goods, such as *a, b, c,* and *d,* from unattainable combinations, such as *e* and *f.* Points *a, b,* and *c* represent full and efficient use of society's resources. Point *d* represents either inefficient use of resources or failure to use all the available resources. If production changes from point *a* to point *b,* an opportunity cost is involved. The opportunity cost of producing Δx more consumption goods is the necessary reduction in the production of investment goods equal to Δy.

production possibilities boundary A curve showing which alternative combinations of output can be attained if all available resources are used efficiently; it is the boundary between attainable and unattainable output combinations.

A production possibilities boundary illustrates three concepts: scarcity, choice, and opportunity cost. Scarcity is indicated by the unattainable combinations outside the boundary; choice, by the need to choose among the alternative attainable points along the boundary; and opportunity cost, by the negative slope of the boundary.

The shape of the production possibilities boundary in Figure 1-2 implies that an increasing amount of consumption goods must be given up to achieve equal successive increases in the production of investment goods. This shape, referred to as *concave* to the origin, indicates that the opportunity cost of either good increases as we increase the amount of it that is produced. A straight-line boundary would indicate that the opportunity cost of one good stays constant, no matter how much of it is produced.

The concave shape in Figure 1-2 is the way economists usually draw a country's production possibilities boundary. The shape occurs because each factor of production is not equally useful in producing all goods. To see why differences among factors of production are so important, suppose we begin at point *c* in Figure 1-2, where most resources are devoted to the production of consumption goods, and then consider gradually shifting more and more resources toward the production of investment goods. We might begin by shifting the use of iron ore and other raw materials. These resources may not be very well suited to producing consumption goods (like food) but may be essential for producing tools, machinery, and factories. This shift of resources will therefore lead to only a small reduction in the output of consumption goods but a substantial increase in the output of investment goods. Thus, the opportunity cost of producing more units of investment goods, which is equal to the forgone consumption goods, is small. But as we shift more and more resources toward the production of investment goods, and therefore move along the production possibilities boundary toward point *a*, we must shift more and more resources that are actually quite well suited to the production of consumption goods, like arable agricultural land. As we produce more and more investment goods (by devoting more and more resources to producing them), the amount of consumption goods that must be forgone to produce one *extra* unit of investment goods rises. That is, the opportunity cost of producing investment goods rises as more of them are produced.

Four Key Economic Problems

Modern economies involve millions of complex production and consumption activities. Despite this complexity, the basic decisions that must be made are not very different from those that were made in ancient and primitive economies in which people worked with few tools and bartered with their neighbours. In all cases, scarcity, choice, and opportunity cost play crucial roles. Whatever the economic system, whether modern or ancient or complex or primitive, there are four key economic problems.

1. What Is Produced and How?   This question concerns the *allocation* of scarce resources among alternative uses. This **resource allocation** determines the quantities of various goods that are produced. For example, the choice to produce 3 bridges, 16 airplanes, and 2 million bushels of wheat means choosing a particular allocation of resources among the industries or regions producing the goods. What determines which goods are produced and which ones are not?

Is there some combination of the production of goods that is "better" than others? If so, should governments try to alter the pattern of production in this direction?

2. What Is Consumed and by Whom?   Economists seek to understand what determines the distribution of a nation's total output among its people. Who gets a lot, who gets a little, and why? Should governments care about this *distribution* of consumption and, if so, what tools do they have to alter it?

resource allocation The allocation of an economy's scarce resources among alternative uses.

If production takes place on the country's production possibilities boundary, then how about consumption? Will the economy consume exactly the same goods that it produces? Or will the country's ability to trade with other countries permit the economy to consume a different combination of goods?

3. Why Are Resources Sometimes Idle? Sometimes large numbers of workers are unemployed. At the same time, the managers and owners of businesses and factories could choose to produce more goods and services. For some reason, however, these resources—land, labour, and capital—lie idle. Thus, in terms of Figure 1-2, the economy sometimes operates inside its production possibilities boundary.

Why are resources sometimes idle? Should governments worry about such idle resources, or is there some reason to believe that such occasional idleness is necessary for a well-functioning economy?

4. Is Productive Capacity Growing? The capacity to produce goods and services grows rapidly in some countries, grows slowly in others, and actually declines in others. Growth in a country's productive capacity can be represented by an outward shift of the production possibilities boundary, as shown in Figure 1-3. If an economy's capacity to produce goods and services is growing, some combinations that are unattainable today will become attainable in the future. What are the determinants of such growth and can governments do anything to influence them?

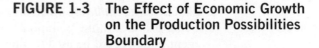

FIGURE 1-3 The Effect of Economic Growth on the Production Possibilities Boundary

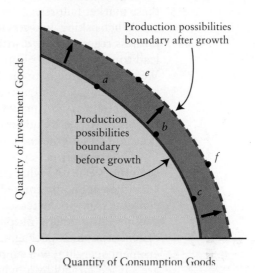

Economic growth shifts the boundary outward and makes it possible to produce more of all products. Before growth in productive capacity, points *a, b,* and *c* were on the production possibilities boundary and points *e* and *f* were unattainable. After growth, points *e* and *f* and many other previously unattainable combinations are attainable.

Microeconomics and Macroeconomics

Questions relating to what is produced and how, and what is consumed and by whom, fall within the realm of microeconomics. **Microeconomics** is the study of the causes and consequences of the allocation of resources as it is affected by the workings of the price system and government policies that seek to influence it. Questions relating to the idleness of resources and the growth of the economy's productive capacity fall within the realm of macroeconomics. **Macroeconomics** is the study of the determination of economic aggregates, such as total output, total employment, and the rate of economic growth.

microeconomics The study of the causes and consequences of the allocation of resources as it is affected by the workings of the price system.

macroeconomics The study of the determination of economic aggregates such as total output, employment, and growth.

Economics and Government Policy

The design and effectiveness of government policy matter for each of our four key economic problems. When asking what combination of goods and services is produced in the economy, and whether some combinations might be better than others, government policy enters the discussion. In later chapters we will examine situations called *market failures,* which arise when free markets lead to too much of some goods being produced (like pollution) and too little of others (like national parks). Government policy could be used to alter the allocation of the economy's resources to correct these market failures.

When asking who gets to consume the economy's output, it is natural to discuss the *fairness* regarding the distribution of consumption across individuals. Do free markets lead to fair outcomes? Can we even decide objectively what is fair and what is unfair? We will see throughout this book that many government policies are designed with fairness in mind. We will also encounter an ongoing debate about how much the government should try to improve the fairness of market outcomes. Some argue that it is reasonable to do so; others argue that attempts to improve fairness often lead to reductions in market efficiency that impose large costs on society.

Government policy is also part of the discussion of why a nation's resources are sometimes idle and what can be done to reduce such idleness. For example, when the Canadian economy entered a major global recession in 2009, the federal and provincial governments increased their spending significantly in an attempt to dampen the decline in aggregate output that was then occurring. Some critics argue that such "fiscal stimulus" packages cannot increase overall output, since the increase in government spending will simply displace private spending. Others argue that recessions are caused largely by a reduction in private spending, and that an increase in government spending can be an effective replacement to sustain the level of economic activity. Such debates lie at the heart of macroeconomic policy, and we have much to say about them in this book.

Finally, government policy also figures prominently in discussions about the determinants of economic growth. Can specific policies lead to an increase in the availability of resources or to the more efficient use of our existing resources? If so, are the benefits in terms of greater production and consumption worth the costs of the resources inevitably involved in the implementation of the policies? We will have much to say about the determinants of economic growth at several points in this book.

1.2 The Complexity of Modern Economies

If you want a litre of milk, you go to your local grocery store and buy it. When the grocer needs more milk, he orders it from the wholesaler, who in turn gets it from the dairy, which in turn gets it from the dairy farmer. The dairy farmer buys cattle feed and electric milking machines, and he gets power to run all his equipment by putting a plug into a wall outlet where the electricity is supplied as he needs it. The milking machines are made from parts manufactured in several different places in Canada, the United States, and overseas. The parts themselves are made from materials produced in a dozen or more countries.

As it is with the milk you drink, so it is with everything else that you buy. When you go to a store, or shop online, what you want is normally available. Those who make these products find that all the required components and materials are available when they need them—even though these things typically come from many different parts of the world and are made by many people who have no direct dealings with one another.

Your own transactions are only a small part of the remarkably complex set of transactions that takes place every day in a modern economy. Shipments arrive daily at our ports, railway terminals, and airports. These shipments include raw materials, such as iron ore, logs, and oil; parts, such as automobile engines, transistors, and circuit boards; tools, such as screwdrivers, lathes, and digging equipment; perishables, such as fresh flowers, coffee beans, and fruit; and all kinds of manufactured goods, such as washing machines, computers, and smartphones. Trains and trucks move these goods among thousands of different destinations within Canada. Some go directly to consumers. Others are used by local firms to manufacture their products—some of which will be sold domestically and others exported to other countries. Remarkably, no one is actually *organizing* all of this economic activity.

The Nature of Market Economies

An *economy* is a system in which scarce resources—labour, land, and capital—are allocated among competing uses. Let's consider how this all happens in a market economy.

Self-Organizing   Early in the development of modern economics, thoughtful observers wondered how such a complex set of decisions and transactions gets organized. Who coordinates the whole set of efforts? Who makes sure that all the activities fit together, providing jobs to produce the things that people want and delivering those things to where they are wanted? The answer, as we said above, is nobody!

A great insight of early economists was that an economy based on free-market transactions is *self-organizing*.

A market economy is self-organizing in the sense that when individual consumers and producers act independently to pursue their own self-interests, the collective outcome is coordinated—there is a "spontaneous economic order." In that order, millions of transactions and activities fit together to produce the things that people want within the constraints set by the resources that are available to the nation.

The great Scottish economist and political philosopher Adam Smith (1723–1790),[1] who was the first to develop this insight fully, put it this way:

It is not from the benevolence of the butcher, the brewer, or the baker, that we expect our dinner, but from their regard to their own interest. We address ourselves, not to their humanity but to their self-love, and never talk to them of our own necessities but of their advantages.[2]

---

[1] Throughout this book, we encounter many great economists from the past whose ideas shaped the discipline of economics. At the back of the book you will find a timeline that begins in the 1600s. It contains brief discussions of many of these thinkers and places them in their historical context.

[2] *An Inquiry Into the Nature and Causes of the Wealth of Nations*, Volume 1.

North Wind Picture Archives/Alamy Stock Photo

Adam Smith wrote An Inquiry into the Nature and Causes of the Wealth of Nations *in 1776. Now referred to by most people simply as* The Wealth of Nations, *it is considered to be the beginning of modern economics.*

Smith is not saying that benevolence is unimportant. Indeed, he praises it in many other passages of his book. He is saying, however, that the massive number of economic interactions that characterize a modern economy are not all motivated by benevolence. Although benevolence does motivate some of our actions, often the very dramatic ones, the vast majority of our everyday actions are motivated by self-interest. Self-interest is therefore the foundation of economic order.

Efficiency   Another great insight, which was hinted at by Smith and fully developed over the next century and a half, was that this spontaneously generated economic order is relatively *efficient*. Loosely speaking, efficiency means that the resources available to the nation are organized so as to produce the various goods and services that people want to purchase and to produce them with the least possible amount of resources.

An economy organized by free markets behaves almost as if it were guided by "an invisible hand," in Smith's now-famous words. This does not literally mean that a supernatural presence runs a market economy. Instead it refers to the relatively efficient order that emerges spontaneously out of the many independent decisions made by those who produce, sell, and buy goods and services. The key to explaining this market behaviour is that these decision makers all respond to the same set of prices, which are determined in markets that respond to overall conditions of national scarcity or plenty. Much of this book is devoted to a detailed elaboration of how this market order is generated and how efficiently that job is done.

That free markets usually generate relatively efficient outcomes does not mean that they are *always* efficient or that everyone views the outcomes as desirable or even *fair*. Free markets sometimes fail to produce efficient outcomes, and these failures often provide a motivation for government intervention. In addition, many market outcomes may be efficient but perceived by many to be quite unfair. For example, we will see that an efficiently operating labour market may nonetheless lead to large differentials in wages, with some individuals receiving low incomes while others receive enormous incomes. So, while a central aspect of economics is the study of how markets allocate resources efficiently, much emphasis is also placed on what happens when markets fail in various ways.

Self-Interest and Incentives   Lying at the heart of modern economies are *self-interest* and *incentives*. Individuals generally pursue their own self-interest, buying and selling what seems best for them and their families. They purchase products that they want rather than those they dislike, and they buy them when it makes sense given their time and financial constraints. Similarly, they sell products, including their own labour services, in an attempt to improve their own economic situation.

When making such decisions about what to buy or sell and at what prices, people respond to incentives. Sellers usually want to sell more when prices are high because by doing so they will be able to afford more of the things they want. Similarly, buyers usually want to buy more when prices are low because by doing so they are better able to use their scarce resources to acquire the many things they desire.

With self-interested buyers and sellers responding to incentives when determining what they want to buy and sell, the overall market prices and quantities are determined by their collective interactions. Changes in their preferences or productive abilities lead to changes in their desired transactions and thus to fluctuations in market prices and quantities.

Of course, individuals are not motivated *only* by self-interest. For most people, love, faith, compassion, and generosity play important roles in their lives, especially at certain times. Behavioural economists devote their research to better understanding how these motivations influence individuals' economic behaviour. But none of this detracts from the importance of understanding the crucial role played in a modern economy by incentives and self-interest.

The Decision Makers and Their Choices

Three types of decision makers operate in any economy. The first is *consumers*. Sometimes we think of consumers as being individuals and sometimes we think in terms of families or households. Consumers purchase various kinds of goods and services with their income; they usually earn their income by selling their labour services to their employers.

The second type of decision maker is *producers*. Producers may be firms that are interested in earning profits or they may be non-profit or charitable organizations. In any case, producers hire workers, purchase or rent various kinds of material inputs and supplies, and then produce and sell their products. In the cases of charitable organizations, their products are often distributed for free.

The third type of decision maker is *government*. Like producers, governments hire workers, purchase or rent material and supplies, and produce goods and services. Unlike most producers, however, governments usually provide their goods and services at no direct cost to the final user; their operations are financed not by revenue from the sale of their products but instead by the taxes they collect from individual consumers and producers. In addition to producing and providing many goods and services, governments create and enforce laws and design and implement regulations that must be followed by consumers and producers.

How Are Decisions Made?   How do consumers, producers, and governments make decisions? We will be examining how and why governments make decisions in detail throughout this book, so we will leave that until later. For now, let's focus on how consumers and producers make their decisions. Economists usually assume that consumers' and producers' decisions are both "maximizing" and "marginal." What does this mean?

Maximizing Decisions.   Economists usually assume that consumers and producers make their decisions in an attempt to do as well as possible for themselves—this is what we mean by self-interest. In the jargon of economics, people are assumed to be *maximizers*. When individuals decide how much of their labour services to sell to producers and how many products to buy from them, they are assumed to make choices designed to maximize their well-being, or *utility*. When producers decide how much labour to hire and how many goods to produce, they are assumed to make choices designed to maximize their *profits*. We explore the details of utility maximization and profit maximization in later chapters.

Marginal Decisions.   Firms and consumers who are trying to maximize usually need to weigh the costs and benefits of their decisions *at the margin*. For example, when you consider buying a new shirt, you know the *marginal cost* of the shirt—that is, how much you must pay to get that one extra shirt. And you need to compare that marginal cost to the *marginal benefit* you will receive—the *extra* satisfaction you get from having that shirt. If you are trying to maximize your utility, you will buy the new shirt only if you think the benefit to you in terms of extra utility exceeds the extra cost. In other words, you buy the shirt only if you think the *marginal* benefit exceeds the *marginal* cost.

Similarly, a producer attempting to maximize its profits and considering whether to hire an extra worker must determine the *marginal cost* of the worker—the extra wages that must be paid—and compare it to the *marginal benefit* of the worker—the increase in sales revenues the extra worker will generate. A producer interested in maximizing its profit will hire the extra worker only if the benefit in terms of extra revenue exceeds the cost in terms of extra wages.

Maximizing consumers and producers make marginal decisions to achieve their objectives; they decide whether they will be made better off by buying or selling a little more or a little less of any given product.

FIGURE 1-4   The Circular Flow of Income and Expenditure

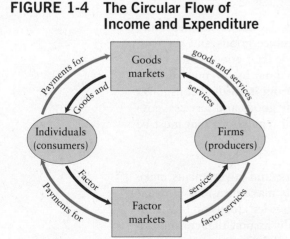

The red line shows the flow of goods and services; the blue line shows the payments made to purchase these. Factor services flow from individuals who own the factors (including their own labour) through factor markets to firms that use them to make goods and services. These goods and services then flow through goods markets to those who consume them. Money payments flow from firms to individuals through factor markets. These payments become the income of individuals. When they spend this income buying goods and services, money flows through goods markets to generate income for producers.

The Flow of Income and Expenditure   Figure 1-4 shows the basic decision makers and the flows of income and expenditure they set up. Individuals own factors of production. They sell the services of these factors to producers and receive payments in return. These are their incomes. Producers use the factor services they buy to make goods and services. They sell these to individuals, receiving payments in return. These are the incomes of producers. These basic flows of income and expenditure pass through markets. Individuals sell the services of the factor they own in what are collectively called *factor markets*. When you get a part-time job during university, you are participating in the factor market—in this case, a market for labour. Producers sell their outputs of goods and services in what are collectively called *goods markets*. When you purchase a haircut, an airplane ticket, or a new pair of shoes, for example, you are participating as a consumer in the goods market.

The prices that are determined in these markets determine the incomes that are earned. People who get high prices for their factor services earn high incomes; those who get low prices earn low incomes. The *distribution of income* refers to how the nation's total income is distributed among its citizens. This is largely determined by the price that each type of factor service receives in factor markets.

Production and Trade

Individual producers decide which goods to produce and how to produce them. Production is a very complex process in any modern economy. For example, a typical car manufacturer assembles a product out of thousands of individual parts. It makes some of these parts itself. Most are subcontracted to parts manufacturers, and many of the major parts manufacturers subcontract some of their work to smaller firms. The same is true for most other products you can imagine purchasing. Such complex production displays two characteristics noted long ago by Adam Smith—*specialization* and the *division of labour*.

Specialization   In ancient hunter–gatherer societies and in modern subsistence economies, most people make most of the things they need for themselves. However, from the time that people first engaged in settled agriculture and then began to live in towns, people have specialized in doing particular jobs. Artisan, soldier, priest, and government official were some of the earliest specialized occupations. Economists call this allocation of different jobs to different people the **specialization of labour**. There are two fundamental reasons why specialization is extraordinarily efficient compared with universal self-sufficiency.

specialization of labour The specialization of individual workers in the production of particular goods or services.

First, individual abilities differ, and specialization allows individuals to do what they can do relatively well while leaving everything else to be done by others. The economy's total production is greater when people specialize than when they all try to be self-sufficient. This is true for individuals, but it is also true for entire countries, and it is one of the most fundamental principles in economics: the principle of *comparative advantage*. A much fuller discussion of comparative advantage is found in Chapter 32, where we discuss the gains from international trade.

The second reason why specialization is more efficient than self-sufficiency concerns improvements in people's abilities that occur *because* they specialize. A person who concentrates on one activity becomes better at it as they gain experience through their own successes and failures. If you watch an experienced electrician or plumber at work, you will see that they are much better at their jobs than a "handyman" who only does this kind of work occasionally. This is due to their *learning by doing* and it is an important form of knowledge acquisition.

The Division of Labour   Throughout most of history each artisan who specialized in making some product made the whole of that product. But over the last several hundred years, many technical advances have made it efficient to organize production methods into large-scale firms organized around what is called the **division of labour**. This term refers to specialization *within* the production process of a particular product. For example, in mass-production car manufacturing facilities, work is divided into highly specialized tasks by using specialized machinery and robotics. Each worker repeatedly does one or a few small tasks that represents only a small fraction of those necessary to produce any one product.

division of labour The breaking up of a production process into a series of specialized tasks, each done by a different worker.

Money and Trade   People who specialize in doing only one thing must satisfy most of their wants by consuming things made by other people. In early societies the exchange of goods and services took place by simple mutual agreement among neighbours. Over time, however, trading became centred on particular gathering places called markets. For example, the French markets or trade fairs of Champagne were known throughout

Europe as early as the eleventh century. Even now, many small towns in Canada have regular market days. Today, however, the term "market" has a much broader meaning, referring to any institutions that allow buyers and sellers to transact with each other, which could be by meeting physically or by trading over the Internet. Also, we use the term "market economy" to refer to a society in which people specialize in productive activities and meet most of their material wants through voluntary market transactions with other people.

Specialization must be accompanied by trade. People who produce only one thing must trade most of it with other people to obtain all the other things they want.

barter An economic system in which goods and services are traded directly for other goods and services.

Early trading was by means of **barter**, the trading of goods directly for other goods. But barter is costly in terms of time spent searching out satisfactory exchanges. If a farmer has wheat but wants a hammer, he must find someone who has a hammer and wants wheat. A successful barter transaction thus requires what is called a *double coincidence of wants*.

Money eliminates the cumbersome system of barter by separating the transactions involved in the exchange of products. If a farmer has wheat and wants a hammer, she merely has to find someone who wants wheat. The farmer takes money in exchange. Then she finds a person who wants to sell a hammer and gives up the money for the hammer.

Money greatly facilitates trade, which itself facilitates specialization.

Money now seems like such a simple and obvious thing, but it was an enormously important invention. By facilitating trade and specialization, money has played a central role in driving economic growth and prosperity over hundreds of years. We will have much to say about money (especially in the macroeconomics half of this textbook), including how the commercial banking system and the central bank can influence the amount of money circulating in the economy.

Mario Aguilar/Shutterstock

The revolution in shipping and in computer technology has drastically reduced communication and transportation costs. This reduction in costs lies at the heart of globalization.

Globalization   Market economies constantly change, largely as a result of the development of new technologies and the new patterns of production and trade that result. Over the past several decades, many of these changes have come under the heading of *globalization*, a term often used loosely to mean the increased importance of international trade.

Though international trade dates back thousands of years, what is new in the last several decades is the globalization of manufacturing. Assembly of a product may take place in the most industrialized countries, but the hundreds of component parts are manufactured in dozens of different countries and delivered to the assembly plant "just in time" for assembly.

Two major causes of globalization are the rapid reduction in transportation costs and the revolution in information technology that have occurred in the past 50 years. The cost of moving products around the world fell greatly over the last half of the twentieth century because of containerization and the increasing size of ships. Our ability to transmit and analyze data increased even more dramatically, while the costs of doing so fell sharply. For example, today $1000 buys an ultra-slim tablet or laptop computer that has the same computing power as a "mainframe" computer that in 1970 cost $10 million and filled a large room. This revolution in information and communication technology has made it possible to coordinate economic transactions around the world in ways that were difficult and costly 50 years ago and quite impossible 100 years ago.

> **Through the ongoing process of globalization, national economies are ever more linked to the global economy.**

Globalization comes with challenges, however. As Canadian firms relocate production facilities to countries where costs are lower, domestic workers are laid off and must search for new jobs, perhaps needing retraining in the process. The location of production facilities in countries with lower environmental or human-rights records raises difficult questions about the standards that should be followed by Canadian-owned firms in foreign lands. And firms often use the threat of relocation in an attempt to extract financial assistance from governments, placing those governments in difficult positions. These concerns have led in recent years to "anti-globalization protests" that have raised awareness of some of the costs associated with the process of globalization. The same concerns have also led to the rise of protectionist policies in some countries, as we mentioned in the introduction to this chapter. We have more to say about these issues in Chapters 33 and 34.

1.3 Is There an Alternative to the Market Economy?

In this chapter we have discussed the elements of an economy based on free-market transactions—what we call a *market economy*. Are there alternatives to this type of economy? To answer this question we first need to identify various types of economic systems.

Types of Economic Systems

It is helpful to distinguish three pure types of economies, called *traditional, command,* and *free-market economies*. These economies differ in the way in which economic decisions are coordinated. But no actual economy fits neatly into one of these three categories—all real economies contain some elements of each type.

Traditional Economies   A **traditional economy** is one in which behaviour is based primarily on tradition, custom, and habit. Young men follow their fathers' occupations. Women do what their mothers did. There is little change in the pattern of goods produced from year to year, other than those imposed by the vagaries of nature. The techniques of production also follow traditional patterns, except when the effects of an occasional new invention are felt. Finally, production is allocated among the members according to long-established traditions.

   Such a system works best in an unchanging environment. Under such static conditions, a system that does not continually require people to make choices can prove effective in meeting economic and social needs.

traditional economy An economy in which behaviour is based mostly on tradition.

Traditional systems were common in earlier times. The feudal system, under which most people in medieval Europe lived, was a largely traditional society. Peasants, artisans, and most others living in villages inherited their positions in that society. They also usually inherited their specific jobs, which they handled in traditional ways.

Command Economies   In command economies, economic behaviour is determined by some central authority, usually the government, or perhaps a dictator, which makes most of the necessary decisions on what to produce, how to produce it, and who gets to consume which products and in what quantities. Such economies are characterized by the *centralization* of decision making. Because centralized decision makers usually create elaborate and complex plans for the behaviour that they want to impose, the terms **command economy** and *centrally planned economy* are usually used synonymously.

command economy An economy in which most economic decisions are made by a central planning authority.

The sheer quantity of data required for the central planning of an entire modern economy is enormous, and the task of analyzing it to produce a fully integrated plan can hardly be exaggerated. Moreover, the plan must be continually modified to take account not only of current data but also of future trends in labour and resource supplies and technological developments. This is a notoriously difficult exercise, not least because of the unavailability of all essential, accurate, and up-to-date information.

Until about 40 years ago, more than one-third of the world's population lived in countries that relied heavily on central planning. Today, after the collapse of the Soviet Union and the rapid expansion of markets in China, the number of such countries is small. Even in countries in which central planning is the proclaimed system, as in Cuba and North Korea, increasing amounts of market determination are gradually being permitted.

Free-Market Economies   In the third type of economic system, the decisions about resource allocation are made without any central direction. Instead, they result from innumerable independent decisions made by individual producers and consumers. Such a system is known as a **free-market economy** or, more simply, a *market economy*. In such an economy, decisions relating to the basic economic issues are *decentralized*. Despite the absence of a central plan, these many decentralized decisions are nonetheless coordinated. The main coordinating device is the set of market-determined prices—which is why free-market systems are often called *price systems*.

free-market economy An economy in which most economic decisions are made by private households and firms.

In a pure market economy, all these decisions are made by buyers and sellers acting through unhindered markets. The government provides the background of defining property rights and protecting citizens against foreign and domestic enemies but, beyond that, markets determine all resource allocation and income distribution.

Mixed Economies   Economies that are fully traditional or fully centrally planned or wholly free-market are pure types that are useful for studying basic principles. When we look in detail at any actual economy, however, we discover that its economic behaviour is the result of some mixture of central control and market determination, with a certain amount of traditional behaviour as well.

mixed economy An economy in which some economic decisions are made by firms and households and some by the government.

In practice, every economy is a mixed economy in the sense that it combines significant elements of all three systems in determining economic behaviour.

Furthermore, within any economy, the degree of the mix varies from sector to sector. For example, in some planned economies, the command principle was used more often to determine behaviour in heavy-goods industries, such as steel, than in agriculture. Farmers were often given substantial freedom to produce and sell what they wanted in response to varying market prices.

When economists speak of a particular economy as being centrally planned, we mean only that the degree of the mix is weighted heavily toward the command principle. When we speak of one as being a market economy, we mean only that the degree of the mix is weighted heavily toward decentralized decision making.

Although no country offers an example of either system working alone, some economies, such as those of Canada, the United States, France, and Japan, rely much more heavily on market decisions than others, such as the economies of China, North Korea, and Cuba. Yet even in Canada, the command principle has some sway. Crown corporations, legislated minimum wages, rules and regulations for environmental protection, quotas on some agricultural outputs, and restrictions on the import of some items are just a few examples of how the government plays an active role in the economy.

The Great Debate

As we saw earlier, in 1776 Adam Smith was one of the first people to analyze the operation of markets, and he stressed the relative efficiency of free-market economies. A century later, another great economist and political philosopher, Karl Marx (1818–1883), argued that although free-market economies would indeed be successful in producing high levels of output, they could not be relied on to ensure that this output would be fairly distributed among citizens. He argued the benefits of a centrally planned system in which the government could ensure a more equitable distribution of output.

Beginning with the Soviet Union in the early 1920s, many nations adopted systems in which conscious government central planning replaced the operation of the free market. For almost a century, a great debate then raged on the relative merits of command economies versus market economies. Along with the Soviet Union, the countries of Eastern Europe and China were command economies for much of the twentieth century. Canada, the United States, and most of the countries of Western Europe were, and still are, primarily market economies. The apparent successes of the Soviet Union and China in the 1950s and 1960s, including the ability to mobilize considerable resources into heavy industries, suggested to many observers that the command principle was at least as good for organizing economic behaviour as the market principle. Over the long run, however, planned economies proved to be a failure of such disastrous proportions that they seriously depressed the living standards of their citizens.

During the last decade of the twentieth century, most of the world's centrally planned economies began the difficult transition back toward freer markets. These transitions occurred at different paces in different countries, but in most cases the initial few years were characterized by significant declines in output and employment.

Karl Marx argued that free-market economies could not be relied on to ensure an equitable distribution of income. He advocated a system of central planning in which government owns most of the means of production.

Thirty years later, however, most of the "transition" economies are experiencing growth rates above the ones they had in their final years as centrally planned economies. Living standards are on the rise.

The large-scale failure of central planning suggests the superiority of decentralized markets over centrally planned ones as mechanisms for allocating an economy's scarce resources. Put another way, it demonstrates the superiority of mixed economies with substantial elements of market determination over fully planned command economies. However, it does *not* demonstrate, as some observers have asserted, the superiority of completely free-market economies over mixed economies.

There is no guarantee that completely free markets will, on their own, handle such urgent matters as controlling pollution, providing public goods (like national defence), or preventing financial crises, such as occurred in 2008 in most of the developed countries. Indeed, as we will see in later chapters, much economic theory is devoted to explaining why free markets often *fail* to do these things. Mixed economies, with significant elements of government intervention, are needed to do these jobs.

Furthermore, acceptance of the free market over central planning does not provide an excuse to ignore a country's pressing social issues. Acceptance of the benefits of the free market still leaves plenty of scope to debate the most appropriate levels and types of government policies directed at achieving specific social goals. It follows that there is still considerable room for disagreement about the degree of the mix of market and government determination in any modern mixed economy—room enough to accommodate such divergent views as could be expressed by conservative, liberal, and modern social democratic parties.

So, the first answer to the question about the existence of an alternative to the market economy is no: There is no *practical* alternative to a mixed system with major reliance on markets but some government presence in most aspects of the economy. The second answer is yes: Within the framework of a mixed economy there are substantial alternatives among many different and complex mixes of free-market and government determination of economic life.

Government in the Modern Mixed Economy

Market economies in today's advanced industrial countries are based primarily on voluntary transactions between individual buyers and sellers. Private individuals have the right to buy and sell what they want, to accept or refuse work that is offered to them, and to move where they want when they want. However, some of the most important institutions in our societies govern the transactions between buyers and sellers.

> **Key institutions are private property and freedom of contract, both of which must be maintained by active government policies. The government creates laws of ownership and contract and then provides the institutions, such as police and courts, to enforce these laws.**

In modern mixed economies, governments go well beyond these important basic functions. They intervene in market transactions to correct what economists call *market failures*. These are well-defined situations in which free markets do not work well. Some products, called *public goods*, are usually not provided at all by markets because their use cannot usually be restricted to those who pay for them. Defence and police protection are examples of public goods. In other cases, private producers or consumers impose costs called *externalities* on those who have no say in the transaction. This is the case when factories pollute the air and rivers. The public is harmed but plays no part in the transaction. In yet other cases, financial institutions, such as banks, mortgage companies, and investment houses, may indulge in risky activities that threaten the health of the entire economic system. These market failures explain why governments sometimes intervene to alter the allocation of resources.

Also, important issues of *equity* arise from letting free markets determine people's incomes. Some people lose their jobs because firms are reorganizing to become more efficient in the face of new technologies. Others keep their jobs, but the market places so little value on their services that they face economic deprivation. The old and the chronically ill may suffer if their past circumstances did not allow them to save enough to support themselves. For many reasons of this sort, almost everyone accepts some government intervention to redistribute income toward individuals or families with fewer resources.

These are some of the reasons all modern economies are mixed economies. Throughout most of the twentieth century in advanced industrial societies, the mix had been shifting toward more and more government participation in decisions about the allocation of resources and the distribution of income. Starting in the early 1980s, a worldwide movement began to reduce the degree of government participation in economies. Following the global financial crisis in 2008, however, there was movement back toward a greater involvement of government in the economy. These shifts in the market/government mix, and the reasons for them, are some of the major issues that will be studied in this book.

SUMMARY

1.1 What Is Economics?

LO 1

- Scarcity is a fundamental problem faced by all economies. Not enough resources are available to produce all the goods and services that people would like to consume.
- Scarcity makes it necessary to choose. All societies must have a mechanism for choosing what goods and services will be produced and in what quantities.
- The concept of opportunity cost emphasizes the problem of scarcity and choice by measuring the cost of obtaining a unit of one product in terms of the number of units of other products that could have been obtained instead.

- A production possibilities boundary shows all the combinations of goods that can be produced by an economy whose resources are fully and efficiently employed. Movement from one point to another along the boundary requires a reallocation of resources.
- Four basic questions must be answered in all economies: What is produced and how? What is consumed and by whom? Why are resources sometimes idle? Is productive capacity growing?
- Issues of government policy enter into discussions of all four questions.

1.2 The Complexity of Modern Economies

LO 2, 3, 4

- A market economy is self-organizing in the sense that when individual consumers and producers act independently to pursue their own self-interest, the collective outcome is coordinated.

- Incentives and self-interest play a central role for all groups of decision makers: consumers, producers, and governments.

- Individual consumers are assumed to make their decisions in an effort to maximize their well-being or utility. Producers' decisions are assumed to be designed to maximize their profits.
- The interaction of consumers and producers through goods and factor markets is illustrated by the circular flow of income and expenditure.

- Modern economies are based on specialization and the division of labour, which necessitate the exchange (trading) of goods and services. Exchange takes place in markets and is facilitated by the use of money.
- Driven by the ongoing revolution in transportation and communications technology, the world economy has been rapidly globalizing for several decades.

1.3 Is There an Alternative to the Market Economy?   LO 5

- We can distinguish three pure types of economies: traditional, command, and free-market. In practice, all economies are mixed economies.
- By the late 1980s, most countries with centrally planned economies had failed to produce minimally acceptable living standards for their citizens. These countries are now moving toward greater market determination and less state command in their economies.

- Governments play an important role in modern mixed economies. They create and enforce important background institutions such as private property and freedom of contract. They intervene to correct market failures. They also redistribute income in the interests of equity.

KEY CONCEPTS

Resources
Scarcity and the need for choice
Choice and opportunity cost
Production possibilities boundary
The self-organizing economy

Incentives and self-interest
Maximizing and marginal decisions
Specialization
The division of labour
Trade and money

Globalization
Traditional economies
Command economies
Free-market economies
Mixed economies

STUDY EXERCISES

MyLab Economics Make the grade with MyLab Economics™: All Study Exercises can be found on MyLab Economics™. You can practise them as often as you want, and many feature step-by-step guided instructions to help you find the right answer.

FILL-IN-THE-BLANK

1 Fill in the blanks to make the following statements correct.

a. The three general categories of any economy's resources are _____, _____, and _____. Economists refer to these resources as the _____ of production.

b. When we use any resource, the benefit given up by not using it in its best alternative way is known as the _____ of that resource.

c. The concepts of scarcity, choice, and opportunity cost can be illustrated by a curve known as the _____.

d. When looking at a production possibilities boundary, any point that is outside the boundary demonstrates _____. The _____ slope of the production possibilities boundary demonstrates _____.

e. A straight-line production possibilities boundary (PPB) indicates that the opportunity cost of each good is _____, no matter how much of that good is produced. A PPB that is concave to the origin indicates that a(n) _____ amount of one good must be given up to produce more of the other good.

f. Consider an economy producing two goods, A and B, with a PPB that is concave to the origin. As the economy produces more of good A and less of good B, its opportunity cost of producing A _____.

2 Fill in the blanks to make the following statements correct.

   a. An important insight by early economists was that an economy based on free-market transactions is _____-organizing. Adam Smith developed the idea that _____, not benevolence, is the foundation of economic order.

   b. Self-interested buyers and sellers respond to _____.

   c. The three types of decision makers in any economy are _____, _____, and _____.

   d. Consumers are assumed to make decisions that will _____ their utility. Producers are assumed to make decisions that will _____ their profit.

   e. Consumers and producers are assumed to weigh the costs and benefits of their decisions at the _____. For example, for a consumer, the benefit of buying "one more" unit of a good must outweigh the _____ of buying that unit.

3 Fill in the blanks to make the following statements correct.

   a. The allocation of different jobs to different people is referred to as the _____ of labour. The specialization within the production process of a particular product is referred to as the _____ of labour.

   b. When people specialize in their activities, it becomes necessary for them to _____ to obtain most of the things they need or want.

   c. Trade is facilitated by _____ because it eliminates the cumbersome system of barter.

   d. The rapid reduction in both transportation and communication costs has greatly contributed to the _____ of the world economy.

REVIEW

4 Explain the three economic concepts illustrated by the production possibilities boundary.

5 Explain why a technological improvement in the production of one good means that a country can now produce more of *other* goods than it did previously. Hint: Draw a country's production possibilities boundary to help answer this question.

6 In this chapter we used a simple idea of a production possibilities boundary to illustrate the concepts of scarcity, choice, and opportunity cost. We assumed there were only two goods—call them *X* and *Y*. But we all know that any economy produces many more than just two goods. Explain why the insights illustrated in Figure 1-2 are more general, and why the assumption of only two goods is a useful one.

7 Imagine a hypothetical world in which *all* Canadian families had $80 000 of after-tax income.

   a. In such a world, would poverty exist in Canada?

   b. In such a world, would scarcity exist in Canada?

   c. Explain the difference between poverty and scarcity.

8 What is the difference between microeconomics and macroeconomics?

9 For each of the following situations, explain how a change in the stated "price" is likely to affect your incentives regarding the stated decision.

   a. the price of ski-lift tickets; your decision to purchase a ski-lift ticket

   b. the hourly wage for your weekend job; the decision to not work and go skiing on the weekend instead

   c. the fine for speeding; your decision to speed on the highway

   d. the weight of your course grade attached to an assignment; your decision to work hard on that assignment

   e. the level of tuition fees at your college or university; your decision to attend that college or university

10 State and explain two reasons why the specialization of labour is more efficient than universal self-sufficiency.

11 Consider the market for doctors' services. In what way has this market taken advantage of the specialization of labour?

12 List the four main types of economic systems and their main attributes.

13 Comment on the following statement: "One of the mysteries of semantics is why the government-managed economies ever came to be called planned and the market economies unplanned. It is the former that are in chronic chaos, in which buyers stand in line hoping to buy some toilet paper or soap. It is the latter that are in reasonable equilibrium—where if you want a bar of soap or a steak or a shirt or a car, you can go to the store and find that the item is magically there for you to buy. It is the liberal economies that reflect a highly sophisticated planning system, and the government-managed economies that are primitive and unplanned."

PROBLEMS

14 Consider your decision whether to go skiing for the weekend. Suppose transportation, lift tickets, and accommodation for the weekend cost $300. Suppose also that restaurant food for the weekend will cost $75. Finally, suppose you have a weekend job that you will have to miss if you go skiing, which pays you $120 (after tax) for the one weekend day that you work. What is the opportunity cost of going skiing? Do you need any other information before computing the opportunity cost?

15 Suppose you own an outdoor recreation company and you want to purchase all-terrain vehicles (ATVs) for your summer business and snowmobiles for your winter business. Your budget for new vehicles this year is $240 000. ATVs cost $8000 each and snowmobiles cost $12 000 each.

a. Draw the budget line for your purchase of new vehicles.
b. What is the opportunity cost of one ATV?
c. What is the opportunity cost of one snowmobile?
d. Does the opportunity cost of one ATV depend on how many you purchase? Why or why not?

16 Suppose one factory produces residential windows and doors. The following scenarios describe various straight-line production possibilities boundaries for this factory. Each scenario describes the numbers of doors that could be produced in one day if all the factory's resources were devoted to producing doors and the number of windows that could be produced in one day if all the factory's resources were devoted to producing windows. For each scenario, calculate the opportunity cost to the factory owner of producing one extra door.

a. 1000 windows; 250 doors
b. 500 windows; 500 doors
c. 1200 windows; 400 doors
d. 942 windows; 697 doors
e. 450 doors; 600 windows

17 Suppose you and a friend are stranded on an island and must gather firewood and catch fish to survive. Through experience, you know that if each of you spends an entire day on either activity, the result is given in the following table:

	Fish	Firewood (bundles)
You	6	3
Your friend	8	2

a. What is the opportunity cost for you to gather an additional bundle of firewood? What is your friend's opportunity cost of gathering an extra bundle of firewood?
b. Assuming that you and your friend specialize, what allocation of tasks maximizes total output for your one day of joint effort?
c. Suppose you both decide to work for two days according to the allocation in part (b). What is the total amount of output? What would it have been had you chosen the reverse allocation of tasks?

18 Consider an economy that produces only food and clothing. Its production possibilities boundary is shown below.

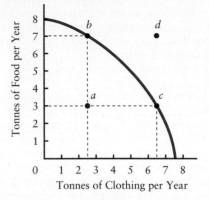

a. If the economy is at point *a*, how many tonnes of clothing and how many tonnes of food are being produced? At point *b*? At point *c*?
b. What do we know about the use of resources when the economy is at point *a*? At point *b*? At point *c*?
c. If the economy is at point *b*, what is the opportunity cost of producing one more tonne of food? What is the opportunity cost of producing one more tonne of clothing?
d. What do we know about the use of resources at point *d*? How would it be possible for the economy to produce at point *d*?

19 Consider an economy called Choiceland that has 250 workers and produces only two goods, X and Y. Labour is the only factor of production, but some workers are better suited to producing X than Y (and vice versa). The table below shows the maximum levels of output of each good possible from various levels of labour input.

Number of Workers Producing X	Annual Production of X	Number of Workers Producing Y	Annual Production of Y
0	0	250	1300
50	20	200	1200
100	45	150	900
150	60	100	600
200	70	50	350
250	75	0	0

a. Draw the production possibilities boundary for Choiceland on a scale diagram, with the production of X on the horizontal axis and the production of Y on the vertical axis.

b. Compute the opportunity cost of producing an extra 15 units of X if the economy is initially producing 45 units of X and 900 units of Y. How does this compare to the opportunity cost if the economy were initially producing 60 units of X and 600 units of Y?

c. If Choiceland is producing 40 units of X and 600 units of Y, what is the opportunity cost of producing an extra 20 units of X?

d. Suppose now that the technology associated with producing good Y improves, so that the maximum level of Y that can be produced from any given level of labour input increases by 10 percent. Explain (or show in a diagram) what happens to the production possibilities curve.

20 For each of the following events, describe the likely effect on the country's production possibilities boundary (PPB). Start with a PPB like the one shown and draw the likely change. In each case, specify the appropriate labels for both axes in the diagram.

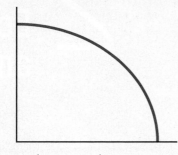

a. Suppose the country has a 10-year civil war that destroys much of its infrastructure.

b. Suppose a small country produces only food and clothing. A new agricultural technology is then introduced that doubles the amount of food that can be produced per year.

c. Suppose a small country produces only food and clothing. An earthquake destroys many of the clothing factories, but the ability to produce food is unaffected.

d. The country admits approximately 250 000 immigrants *each year*, many of whom join the labour force.

2 Economic Theories, Data, and Graphs

CHAPTER OUTLINE	LEARNING OBJECTIVES (LO)
	After studying this chapter, you will be able to
2.1 POSITIVE AND NORMATIVE STATEMENTS	1 distinguish between positive and normative statements.
2.2 BUILDING AND TESTING ECONOMIC THEORIES	2 explain why and how economists use theories to help them understand the economy.
	3 understand the interaction between economic theories and empirical observation.
2.3 ECONOMIC DATA	4 identify several types of economic data, including index numbers, time-series and cross-sectional data, and scatter diagrams.
2.4 GRAPHING ECONOMIC THEORIES	5 recognize the slope of a line on a graph relating two variables as the "marginal response" of one variable to a change in the other.

IF you follow the news, whether online, TV, newspaper, or radio, you are likely to hear the views of economists being discussed—about debt crises, unemployment, income inequality, attempts to reform the healthcare system, environmental policy, changes to corporate income-tax rates, or a myriad of other issues. Where do economists' opinions come from? Are they supported by hard evidence, and if so, why do economists sometimes disagree with each other over important issues?

Economics is a social science, and in this chapter we explore what it means to be "scientific" in the study of economics. Along the way we will learn much about theories, predictions, data, testing, and graphing—economists use all of these tools and techniques in their attempt to understand the economic world. We begin with the important distinction between positive and normative statements.

▌2.1 Positive and Normative Statements

Economists give two broad types of advice, called *normative* and *positive*. For example, they sometimes advise that the government ought to try harder to reduce unemployment. When they say such things, they are giving normative advice; in this case, they are making judgments about the importance of unemployment and the value in the government addressing it. Advice that depends on a value judgment is normative—it tells others what they *ought* to do.

Another type of advice is illustrated by the statement "If the government wants to reduce unemployment, reducing employment insurance benefits is an effective way of doing so." This is positive advice. It does not rely on a judgment about the value of reducing unemployment. Instead, the expert is saying, "If this is what you want to do, here is a way to do it."

Normative statements depend on value judgments and cannot be evaluated solely by a recourse to facts. In contrast, **positive statements** do not involve value judgments. They are statements about matters of fact, and so disagreements about them are appropriately dealt with by an appeal to evidence. The distinction between positive and normative is fundamental to scientific progress. Much of the success of modern science depends on the ability of scientists to separate their views on *what does happen* in the world from their views on *what they would like to happen*. For example, until the eighteenth century almost everyone believed that Earth was only a few thousand years old. Evidence then began to accumulate that Earth was billions of years old. This evidence was hard for most people to accept, since it ran counter to a literal reading of many religious texts. Many did not want to believe the evidence. Nevertheless, scientists, many of whom were religious, continued their research because they refused to allow their feelings about what they wanted to believe to affect their scientific search for the truth. Eventually, all scientists and most members of the public came to accept that Earth is about 4.5 billion years old.

> **Distinguishing what is actually true from what we would like to be true requires distinguishing between positive and normative statements.**

Examples of both types of statements are given in Table 2-1. All five positive statements in the table are assertions about the nature of the world in which we live. In contrast, the five normative statements involve value judgments. Notice two things about the positive/normative distinction. First, positive statements need not be true. Statement C is almost certainly false, and yet it is positive, not normative. Second, the inclusion of a value judgment in a statement does not necessarily make the statement itself normative. Statement D is a positive statement about the value judgments that people hold. We could conduct a survey to check if people really do prefer low unemployment to low inflation. We could ask them and we could observe how they voted. There is no need for the economist to rely on a value judgment to check the validity of the statement itself.

We leave you to analyze the remaining eight statements to decide precisely why each is either positive or normative. Remember to apply the two tests. First, is the statement only about actual or alleged facts? If so, it is a positive one. Second, are value judgments necessary to assess the truth of the statement? If so, it is normative.

normative statement A statement about what ought to be; it is based on a value judgment.

positive statement A statement about what actually is, was, or will be; it is not based on a value judgment.

TABLE 2-1   Positive and Normative Statements

Positive	Normative
A Raising interest rates encourages people to save.	F People should be encouraged to save.
B High rates of income tax encourage people to evade paying taxes.	G Governments should design taxes so that people cannot avoid paying them.
C Lowering the price of cigarettes leads people to smoke less.	H The government should raise the tax on cigarettes to discourage people from smoking.
D The majority of the population would prefer a policy that reduced unemployment to one that reduced inflation.	I Unemployment is a more important social problem than inflation.
E Government financial assistance to commercial banks is ineffective at preventing job losses.	J Government should not spend taxpayers' money on supporting commercial banks.

Disagreements Among Economists

Economists often disagree with one another in public discussions, frequently because of poor communication. They often fail to define their terms or their points of reference clearly, and so they end up "arguing past" each other, with the only certain result being that the audience is left confused.

Economists often disagree with one another in the media or at conferences, but their debates are more often about normative issues than positive ones.

Another source of disagreement stems from some economists' failure to acknowledge the full state of their ignorance. There are many points on which the evidence is far from conclusive. In such cases, a responsible economist makes clear the extent to which his or her view is based on judgments about the relevant (and uncertain) facts.

Many other public disagreements are based on the positive/normative distinction. Different economists have different values, and these normative views play a large part in most discussions of public policy. Many economists stress the importance of individual responsibility and argue, for example, that lower employment insurance benefits would be desirable because people would have a greater incentive to search for a job. Other economists stress the need for a generous "social safety net" and argue that higher employment insurance benefits are desirable because human hardship would be reduced. In such debates, and there are many in economics, it is the responsibility of the economist to state clearly what part of the proffered advice is normative and what part is positive.

Because the world is complex and because few issues can be settled beyond any doubt, economists rarely agree unanimously on an issue. Nevertheless, there is an impressive amount of agreement on many aspects of how the economy works and what happens when governments intervene to alter its workings. A survey published in the *American Economic Review,* perhaps the most influential economics journal, showed

APPLYING ECONOMIC CONCEPTS 2-1

Where Economists Work

This chapter discusses the theoretical and empirical tools that economists use. After reading this material, you might wonder where economists find jobs and what kind of work they actually do. The skills of economists are demanded in many parts of the economy by governments, private businesses and Crown corporations, non-profit organizations, and universities.

In Ottawa and the provincial and territorial capitals, economists are hired in most government departments to analyze the effects of government policies and to design ways to improve those policies. At Finance Canada, economists design and analyze the income-tax system and the effects of current spending programs. At Environment and Climate Change Canada, they help design and evaluate policies aimed at reducing greenhouse-gas emissions and water pollution. At Innovation, Science and Economic Development Canada, they study the sources of productivity growth and design policies to encourage innovation in the private sector. At the Bank of Canada, economists research the link between interest rates, the aggregate demand for goods and services, and the rate of increase in prices. They also monitor developments in the global economy and their effects on the Canadian economy. Statistics Canada employs many economists to design methods of collecting and analyzing data covering all aspects of Canadian society.

The analysis of economic policies also takes place in independent research organizations, often called "think tanks." The C.D. Howe Institute in Toronto is one of Canada's best-known think tanks, and it regularly publishes papers on topics ranging from monetary policy and the state of public pensions to the effects of immigration and the challenges in reforming Canada's policies for foreign development assistance. Other think tanks include the Institute for Research on Public Policy, the Canadian Centre for Policy Alternatives, the Fraser

Institute, the Centre for the Study of Living Standards, and the Conference Board of Canada. All of these independent and non-profit organizations hire economists to study economic issues and then write and edit the economic publications that address them.

Private and public (Crown) corporations in many sectors of the economy also hire economists in a variety of positions. Economists at Canadian Pacific Railway monitor how changes in world commodity prices will lead to changes in Canadian resource production and thus to changes in the demand for their rail transport services. Economists at Manitoba Hydro study the link between economic growth and electricity demand to help the firm with its long-run investment decisions. Those at Export Development Canada examine how economic and political risks in various countries influence the demand for the products of Canadian exporters. Economists at Bombardier are hired to determine how ongoing negotiations within the World Trade Organization will affect tariff levels in various countries and how these changes will affect the demand for Bombardier trains and airplanes.

Finally, many economists are hired by universities all over the world to teach students like you and to conduct research on a wide variety of economic topics. Some of this research is theoretical and some is empirical, using data to test economic theories. Other academic economists focus their research on the design and implementation of better economic policy, and often spend considerable time interacting with the economists employed by government departments.

Training in economics provides useful analytical skills that are valuable for learning about the workings of a complex economic world. There is no shortage of demand for people who can think clearly and analytically about economic issues. This course could well be the start of a great career for you. Study hard!

strong agreement among economists on many propositions, including "Rent control leads to a housing shortage" (85 percent yes), "Tariffs usually reduce economic welfare" (93 percent yes), and "A minimum wage increases unemployment among young workers" (79 percent yes). Notice that all these are positive rather than normative statements. Other examples of these areas of agreement will be found in many places throughout this book.

Whether they agree or disagree with one another, economists are in demand in many sectors of the economy. See *Applying Economic Concepts 2-1* for a discussion of the many organizations that employ economists.

2.2 Building and Testing Economic Theories

The economic world is complex. Many things are changing at the same time, and it is usually difficult to distinguish cause from effect. By examining data carefully, however, regularities and trends can be detected. To better understand these patterns in the data, economists develop *theories*, which they sometimes call *models*. Theories are used to both explain events that have already happened and to help predict events that might happen in the future.

What Are Theories?

Theories are constructed to explain things. For example, economists may seek to explain what determines the quantity of eggs bought and sold in a particular month in Manitoba and the price at which they are sold. Or they may seek to explain what determines the quantity of oil bought and sold around the world on a particular day and the price at which it is traded. As part of the answer to such questions, economists have developed theories of demand and supply—theories that we will study in detail in the next three chapters. These and all other theories are distinguished by their *variables, assumptions,* and *predictions.*

variable Any well-defined item, such as the price or quantity of a commodity, that can take on various specific values.

Variables The basic elements of any theory are its variables. A **variable** is a well-defined item, such as a price or a quantity, that can take on different possible values.

In a theory of the egg market, the variable *quantity of eggs* might be defined as the number of cartons of 12 Grade A large eggs. The variable *price of eggs* is the amount of money that must be given up to purchase each carton of eggs. The particular values taken by those two variables might be 20 000 cartons per week at a price of $2.60 in July 2017, 18 000 cartons per week at a price of $2.75 in July 2018, and 19 500 cartons per week at a price of $2.95 in July 2019.

There are two broad categories of variables that are important in any theory. An **endogenous variable** is one whose value is determined within the theory. An **exogenous variable** influences the endogenous variables but is itself determined outside the theory. To illustrate the difference, the price of eggs and the quantity of eggs are endogenous variables in our theory of the egg market—our theory is designed to explain them. The state of the weather, however, is an exogenous variable. It may well affect the number of eggs consumers demand or producers supply, but we can safely assume that the state of the weather is not influenced by the market for eggs.

endogenous variable A variable that is explained within a theory. Sometimes called an *induced variable* or a *dependent variable.*

exogenous variable A variable that is determined outside the theory. Sometimes called an *autonomous variable* or an *independent variable.*

Assumptions A theory's assumptions concern motives, directions of causation, and the conditions under which the theory is meant to apply.

Motives. The economic theories we study in this book make the fundamental assumption that everyone pursues his or her own self-interest when making economic decisions. Individuals are assumed to strive to maximize their *utility,* while firms are assumed to try to maximize their *profits.* Not only are they assumed to know what they want, but we also assume that they know how to go about getting it within the constraints they face.

Direction of Causation. When economists assume that one variable is related to another, they are usually assuming some causal link between the two. Consider a theory about the market for wheat, for example. When the amount of wheat that producers want to supply is assumed to increase when the weather improves, the causation runs from the weather to the supply of wheat. Producers supply more wheat *because* the growing conditions improve; they are not assumed to experience better weather as a result of their increased supply of wheat.

Conditions of Application.   Assumptions are often used to specify the conditions under which a theory is meant to hold. For example, a theory that assumes there is "no government" usually does not mean literally the absence of government but only that the theory is meant to apply when governments are not significantly affecting the situation being studied.

Although assumptions are an essential part of all theories, students are often concerned about those that seem unrealistic. An example will illustrate some of the issues involved. Much of the theory that we are going to study in this book uses the assumption that owners of firms attempt to make as much money as they can—that is, to maximize their profits. The assumption of profit maximization allows economists to make predictions about the behaviour of firms, such as "firms will supply more output if the market price increases."

Profit maximization may seem like a rather crude assumption. Surely, for example, the managers of firms sometimes choose to protect the environment rather than pursue certain highly polluting but profitable opportunities. Does this not discredit the assumption of profit maximization by showing it to be unrealistic?

The answer is no; to make successful predictions, the theory does not require that managers be solely and unwaveringly motivated by the desire to maximize profits at all times. All that is required is that profits be a sufficiently important consideration that a theory based on the assumption of profit maximization will lead to explanations and predictions that are substantially correct. It is not always appropriate to criticize a theory because its assumptions seem unrealistic. A good theory abstracts in a useful way; a poor theory does not. If a theory has ignored some genuinely important factors, its predictions will usually be contradicted by the evidence.

All theory is an abstraction from reality. If it were not, it would merely duplicate the world in all its complexity and would add little to our understanding of it.

Predictions   A theory's predictions are the propositions that can be deduced from it. They are often called *hypotheses*. For example, a prediction from a theory of the global oil market is that a rise in the world price for oil will lead Canadian oil producers to produce and supply more oil. Another prediction in the same market is that a decision by the members of the OPEC cartel to reduce their annual output of oil will lead to an increase in the world price. The economic logic behind such predictions will be explained in several chapters of this book; for now we can proceed to see how economists *test* such predictions or hypotheses.

Testing Theories

A theory is tested by confronting its predictions with empirical evidence. For example, is an improvement in the weather *actually* followed by an increase in wheat production? Or, is an increase in the world price of oil *actually* followed by an increase in oil production by Canadian producers? A theory ceases to be useful when it cannot predict better than an alternative theory. When a theory consistently fails to predict better than an available alternative, it is either modified or replaced. Figure 2-1 illustrates the interaction between theory and empirical observation that occurs in economics.

> **The scientific approach is central to the study of economics: Empirical observation leads to the construction of theories, theories generate specific predictions, and the predictions are tested by more detailed empirical observation.**

Statistical Analysis   Most theories generate a prediction of the form "If *X* occurs, then *Y* will also happen." A specific example is "If national income rises, the level of

FIGURE 2-1   **The Interaction Between Theory and Empirical Observation**

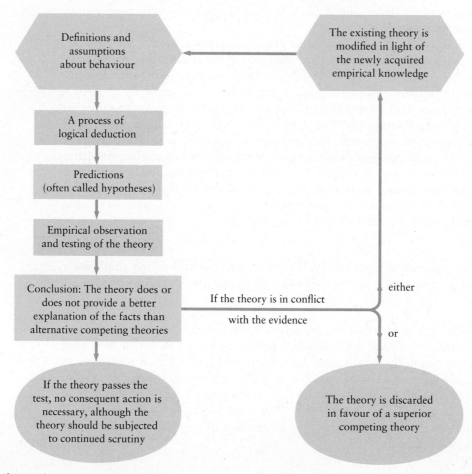

Theory and observation are in continuous interaction. Starting (at the top left) with the assumptions of a theory and the definitions of relevant terms, the theorist deduces by logical analysis everything that is implied by the assumptions. These implications are the predictions or the hypotheses of the theory. The theory is then tested by confronting its predictions with evidence. If the theory is in conflict with facts, it will usually be amended to make it consistent with those facts (thereby making it a better theory), or it will be discarded, to be replaced by a superior theory. The process then begins again: The new or amended theory is subjected first to logical analysis and then to empirical testing.

employment will rise." Another is "If the price of eggs declines, consumers will purchase more eggs." Statistical analysis can be used to test such predictions. In practice, the same data can be used simultaneously to test whether a relationship exists between X and Y and, if it does exist, to provide an estimate of the magnitude of that relationship.

Because economics is primarily a non-laboratory science, it lacks the controlled experiments central to such sciences as physics and chemistry. Economics must therefore use millions of uncontrolled "experiments" that are going on every day in the marketplace. Households are deciding what to purchase given changing prices and incomes, firms are deciding what to produce and how, and governments are involved in the economy through their various taxes, subsidies, and regulations. Because all these activities can be observed and recorded, a mass of data is continually being produced by the economy.

The variables that interest economists—such as the level of employment, the price of a laptop, and the output of automobiles—are generally influenced by many forces that vary simultaneously. If economists are to test their theories about relations among specific variables, they must use statistical techniques designed for situations in which other things *cannot* be held constant. Fortunately, such techniques exist, although their application is usually neither simple nor straightforward.

Later in this chapter we provide a discussion of some graphical techniques for describing data and displaying some of the more obvious relationships. Further examination of data involves techniques studied in elementary statistics courses. More advanced courses in econometrics deal with the array of techniques designed to test economic hypotheses and to measure economic relations in the complex circumstances in which economic evidence is often generated.

Correlation Versus Causation   Suppose you want to test your theory's prediction that "If X increases, Y will also increase." You are looking for a *causal* relationship from X to Y, because a change in X is predicted to *cause* a change in Y. When you look at the data, suppose you find that X and Y are positively correlated—that is, when X rises, Y also tends to rise (and vice versa). Is your theory supported? It might appear that way, but there is a potential problem.

A finding that X and Y are positively correlated means only that X and Y tend to move together. This correlation is *consistent* with the theory that X causes Y, but it is *not* direct evidence of this causal relationship. The causality may be in the opposite direction—from Y to X. Or X and Y may have no direct causal connection; their movements may instead be jointly caused by movements in some third variable, Z.

Here is an example. Suppose your theory predicts that individuals who get more education will earn higher incomes as a result—the causality in this theory runs from education to income. In the data, suppose we find that education and income are positively correlated (as they are). This should not, however, be taken as direct evidence for the causal prediction that more education causes higher income. The data are certainly consistent with that theory, but they are also consistent with others. For example, individuals who grow up in higher-income households may "buy" more education, just as they buy more clothes or entertainment. In this case, income causes education, rather than the other way around. Another possibility is that education and income are positively correlated because the personal characteristics that lead people to become more educated—ability and motivation—are the same characteristics that lead to high incomes. In this case, the *causal* relationship runs from personal characteristics to both income and education.

Most economic predictions involve causality. Economists must take care when testing predictions to distinguish between correlation and causation. Correlation can establish that the data are consistent with the theory; establishing causation usually requires more advanced statistical techniques.

2.3 Economic Data

Economists use real-world observations to test their theories. For example, did the amount that people saved last year rise—as the theory predicts it should have—when a large tax cut increased their after-tax incomes? To test this prediction we need reliable data for people's incomes and their savings.

Political scientists, sociologists, anthropologists, and psychologists often collect the data they use to formulate and test their theories themselves. Economists are unusual among social scientists in mainly using data collected by others, often government statistical agencies. In economics there is a division of labour between collecting data and using them to test theories. The advantage is that economists do not need to spend much of their scarce research time collecting the data they use. The disadvantage is that they are often not as well informed about the limitations of the data collected by others as they would be if they had collected the data themselves.

index number A measure of some variable, conventionally expressed relative to a base period, which is assigned the value 100.

After data are collected, they can be displayed in various ways, many of which we will see later in this chapter. They can be laid out in tables. They can be displayed in various types of graphs. And when we are interested in relative movements rather than absolute ones, the data can be expressed in *index numbers*. We begin with a discussion of index numbers.

Index Numbers

Economists frequently look at data on prices or quantities and explore how specific variables change over time. For example, they may be interested in comparing the time paths of output in two industries: steel and newsprint. The problem is that it may be difficult to compare the time paths of the two different variables if we just look at the "raw" data.

Table 2-2 shows some hypothetical data for the volume of output in the steel and newsprint industries. Because the two variables are measured in different units, it is not immediately clear which of the two variables is more volatile or which, if either, has an upward or a downward trend.

It is easier to compare the two paths if we focus on *relative* rather than *absolute* changes. One way to do this is to construct some **index numbers**.

TABLE 2-2 Volume of Steel and Newsprint Output

Year	Volume of Steel (thousands of tonnes)	Volume of Newsprint (thousands of rolls)
2010	200	3200
2011	210	3100
2012	225	3000
2013	215	3200
2014	250	3100
2015	220	3300
2016	265	3100
2017	225	3300
2018	255	3100
2019	230	3200
2020	245	3000

Comparing the time paths of two data series is difficult when absolute numbers are used. Since steel output and newsprint output have quite different absolute numbers, it is difficult to detect which time series is more volatile.

TABLE 2-3   Constructing Index Numbers

	Steel			Newsprint		
Year	Procedure		Index	Procedure		Index
2010	$(200/200) \times 100$	=	100.0	$(3200/3200) \times 100$	=	100.0
2011	$(210/200) \times 100$	=	105.0	$(3100/3200) \times 100$	=	96.9
2012	$(225/200) \times 100$	=	112.5	$(3000/3200) \times 100$	=	93.8
2013	$(215/200) \times 100$	=	107.5	$(3200/3200) \times 100$	=	100.0
2014	$(250/200) \times 100$	=	125.0	$(3100/3200) \times 100$	=	96.9
2015	$(220/200) \times 100$	=	110.0	$(3300/3200) \times 100$	=	103.1
2016	$(265/200) \times 100$	=	132.5	$(3100/3200) \times 100$	=	96.9
2017	$(225/200) \times 100$	=	112.5	$(3300/3200) \times 100$	=	103.1
2018	$(255/200) \times 100$	=	127.5	$(3100/3200) \times 100$	=	96.9
2019	$(230/200) \times 100$	=	115.0	$(3200/3200) \times 100$	=	100.0
2020	$(245/200) \times 100$	=	122.5	$(3000/3200) \times 100$	=	93.8

Index numbers are calculated by dividing the value in the given year by the value in the base year and multiplying the result by 100. The 2020 index number for steel tells us that steel output in 2020 was 22.5 percent greater than in the base year, 2010. The 2020 index number for newsprint tells us that newsprint output in 2020 was 93.8 percent of the output in the base year, 2010.

How to Build an Index Number   We start by taking the value of the variable at some point in time as the "base" with which the values in other periods will be compared. We call this the *base period*. In the present example, we choose 2010 as the base year for both series. We then take the output in each subsequent year, called the "given year," divide it by the output in the base year, and then multiply the result by 100. This gives us an index number for the output of steel and a separate index number for the output of newsprint. For each index number, the value of output in the base year is equal to 100. The details of the calculations are shown in Table 2-3.

An index number simply expresses the value of some variable in any given year as a percentage of its value in the base year. For example, the 2020 index of steel output of 122.5 tells us that steel output in 2020 was 22.5 percent greater than in 2010. In contrast, the 2020 index for newsprint output of 93.8 tells us that newsprint output in 2020 was only 93.8 percent of the output in 2010—that is, output was 6.2 percent lower in 2020 than in 2010. The results in Table 2-3 allow us to compare the relative fluctuations in the two series. It is apparent from the values in the table that the output of steel has shown significantly more percentage variability than has the output of newsprint. This is also clear in Figure 2-2.

The formula of any index number is

$$\text{Value of index in any given period} = \frac{\text{Absolute value in given period}}{\text{Absolute value in base period}} \times 100$$

Care must be taken, however, when using index numbers. The index number always tells you the percentage change compared with the base year, but when

FIGURE 2-2 Index Values for Steel and Newsprint Output

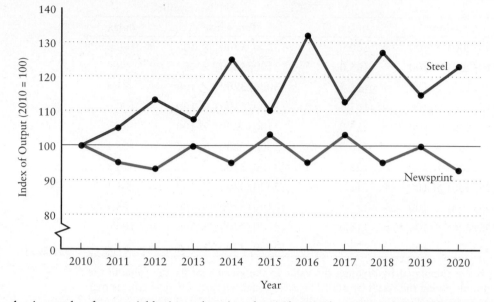

Comparing the time paths of two variables is much easier when index numbers are used. Since both index numbers are equal to 100 in the base year, relative volatility and trends become clear. Steel output is clearly more volatile in percentage terms than newsprint output. Steel output also has an upward trend, whereas newsprint output appears to have little or no trend.

comparing an index number across non-base years, the percentage change in the index number is *not* given by the absolute difference in the values of the index number. For example, if you want to know how much steel output changed from 2014 to 2016, we know from Table 2-3 that the index number for steel output increased from 125.0 to 132.5. But this is not an increase of 7.5 percent. The *percentage* increase in steel output is computed as $(132.5 - 125.0)/125.0 = 7.5/125.0 = 0.06$, or 6 percent.

More Complex Index Numbers Perhaps the most famous index number used by economists is the index of average prices—the Consumer Price Index (CPI). This is a price index of the *average* price paid by consumers for the typical collection of goods and services that they buy. The inclusion of the word "average," however, makes the CPI a more complex index number than the ones we have constructed here.

With what you have just learned, you could construct separate index numbers for the price of beef, the price of bus tickets, and the price of Internet packages. But to get the Consumer Price Index, we need to take the *average* of these separate price indexes (plus thousands of others for the goods and services we have ignored here). But it cannot be a simple average. Instead, it must be a *weighted* average, in which the weight assigned to each price index reflects the relative importance of that good in the typical consumer's basket of goods and services. For example, since the typical consumer spends a tiny fraction of income on sardines but a much larger fraction of income on housing, the weight on the "sardines" price index in the CPI is very small and the weight on the "housing" price index is very large. The result is that even huge swings in the price of sardines have negligible effects on the CPI, whereas much more modest changes in the price of housing have noticeable effects on the CPI.

We will spend much more time discussing the Consumer Price Index when we study macroeconomics beginning in Chapter 19. For now, keep in mind the usefulness of the simple index numbers we have constructed here. They allow us to compare the time paths of different variables.

Graphing Economic Data

A single economic variable, such as unemployment, national income, or the average price of a house, can come in two basic forms.

FIGURE 2-3   A Cross-Sectional Graph of Average House Prices for 10 Canadian Provinces, 2018

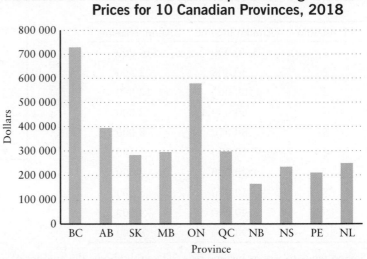

(*Source:* Adapted from MLS® Statistics © 2018 The Canadian Real Estate Association; www.crca.ca/housing-market-stats/national-price-map)

Cross-Sectional and Time-Series Data   The first is called **cross-sectional data**, which means a number of different observations on one variable all taken in different places at the same point in time. Figure 2-3 shows an example. The variable in the figure is the average selling price of a house in each of the 10 Canadian provinces in March 2018. The second type of data is called **time-series data**. It refers to observations of one variable at successive points in time. The data in Figure 2-4 show the unemployment rate for Canada from 1978 to 2018. Note in Figures 2-3 and 2-4 that in each case the figure is showing the behaviour of a *single* economic variable.

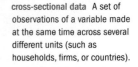

cross-sectional data A set of observations of a variable made at the same time across several different units (such as households, firms, or countries).

time-series data A set of observations of a variable made at successive periods of time.

FIGURE 2-4   A Time-Series Graph of the Canadian Unemployment Rate, 1978–2018

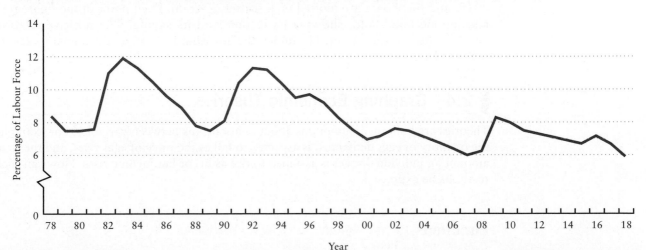

(*Source:* Annual average of monthly, seasonally adjusted data from Statistics Canada, CANSIM Table 282-0087; both sexes, 15 years and over)

FIGURE 2-5   A Scatter Diagram of Household Income and Saving in 2019

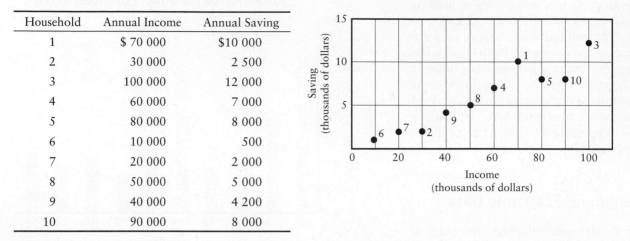

Household	Annual Income	Annual Saving
1	$ 70 000	$10 000
2	30 000	2 500
3	100 000	12 000
4	60 000	7 000
5	80 000	8 000
6	10 000	500
7	20 000	2 000
8	50 000	5 000
9	40 000	4 200
10	90 000	8 000

Saving tends to rise as income rises. The table shows the amount of income earned by 10 (hypothetical) households together with the amount they saved during the same year. The scatter diagram plots the income and saving for the 10 households listed in the table. The number on each dot refers to the household in the corresponding row of the table.

scatter diagram A graph showing two variables, one measured on the horizontal and the other on the vertical axis. Each point represents the values of the variables for a particular unit of observation.

Scatter Diagrams   Another way data can be presented is in a **scatter diagram**. It is designed to show the relation between two different variables. To plot a scatter diagram, values of one variable are measured on the horizontal axis and values of the second variable are measured on the vertical axis. Any point on the diagram relates a specific value of one variable to a corresponding specific value of the other.

The data plotted on a scatter diagram may be either cross-sectional data or time-series data. An example of the former is shown in Figure 2-5. The table in the figure shows hypothetical data for the income and saving of 10 households during 2019, and these data are plotted on a scatter diagram. Each point in the figure represents one household, showing its income and its saving. The positive relation between the two stands out. The higher the household's income, the higher its saving tends to be.

2.4   Graphing Economic Theories

Theories are built on assumptions about relationships between variables. For example, the quantity of eggs demanded is assumed to fall as the price of eggs rises, and the total amount an individual saves is assumed to rise as his or her income rises. How can such relations be expressed?

Functions

When one variable, X, is related to another variable, Y, in such a way that to every value of X there is only one possible value of Y, we say that Y is a *function* of X. When we write this relation down, we are expressing a *functional relation* between the two variables, and we write $Y = f(X)$ where f is the function that relates X and Y.

Here is a specific but hypothetical example. Consider the relation between an individual's annual wage income, which we denote by the symbol W (for wage income), and the amount that person spends on goods and services during the year, which we denote by the symbol C (for consumption). Any particular example of the relation between C and W can be expressed several ways: in words, in a table, in a mathematical equation, or in a graph.

Words.   When income is zero, the person will spend $800 a year (either by borrowing the money or by spending past savings), and for every extra $1 of income the person will increase spending by 80 cents.

Table.   This table shows selected values of the person's income and consumption.

Annual Income	Consumption	Reference Letter
$ 0	$ 800	p
2 500	2 800	q
5 000	4 800	r
7 500	6 800	s
10 000	8 800	t

Mathematical Equation. $C = \$800 + 0.8W$ is the equation of the relation just described in words and displayed in the table. As a check, you can first see that when W is zero, C is $800. Further, you can see that every time W increases by $1, the level of C increases by 0.8($1), which is 80 cents.

Graph.   Figure 2-6 shows the points from the preceding table and the line representing the equation given in the previous paragraph. Comparison of the values on the graph with the values in the table, and with the values derived from the equation just stated, shows that these are alternative expressions of the same relation between C and W.

Graphing Functions

Different functions have different graphs, and we will see many of these in subsequent chapters. Figure 2-6 is an example of a relation in which the two variables move together. When income goes up, consumption goes up. In such a relation the two variables are *positively related* to each other.

Figure 2-7 is an example of variables that move in opposite directions. As the amount spent on pollution reduction goes up, the amount of remaining pollution goes down. In such a relation the two variables are *negatively related* to each other.

Both of these graphs are straight lines. In such cases the variables are *linearly related* to each other (either positively or negatively).

FIGURE 2-6   Income and Consumption

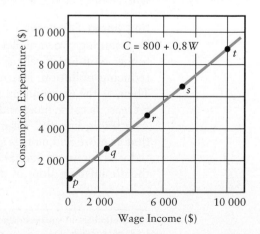

FIGURE 2-7 Linear Pollution Reduction

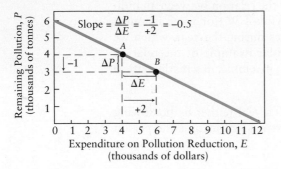

Slope $= \dfrac{\Delta P}{\Delta E} = \dfrac{-1}{+2} = -0.5$

Pollution as a linear function of clean-up expenditure. Between points A and B it costs $2000 to reduce pollution by 1000 tonnes. The cost of pollution reduction is the same elsewhere on the line. The slope of the line, –0.5, indicates that any $1 expenditure on pollution clean-up reduces the amount of pollution by 0.5 tonnes.

The Slope of a Straight Line Slopes are important in economics. They show you how much one variable changes as the other changes. The slope is defined as the amount of change in the variable measured on the vertical axis per unit change in the variable measured on the horizontal axis. In the case of Figure 2-7 it tells us how many tonnes of pollution, symbolized by P, are removed per dollar spent on reducing pollution, symbolized by E. Consider moving from point A to point B in the figure. If we spend $2000 more on clean-up, we reduce pollution by 1000 tonnes. This is 0.5 tonnes per dollar spent. On the graph the extra $2000 is indicated by ΔE, the arrow indicating that E rises by 2000. The 1000 tonnes of pollution reduction is indicated by ΔP, the arrow showing that pollution falls by 1000. (The Greek uppercase letter delta, Δ, stands for "the change in.") To get the amount of pollution reduction per dollar of expenditure, we merely divide one by the other. In symbols this is $\Delta P / \Delta E$.

If we let X stand for whatever variable is measured on the horizontal axis and Y for whatever variable is measured on the vertical axis, the slope of a straight line is $\Delta Y / \Delta X$. [1][1]

The equation of the line in Figure 2-7 can be computed in two steps. First, note that when $E = 0$, the amount of remaining pollution, P, is equal to 6 (thousand tonnes). Thus, the line meets the vertical axis ($E = 0$) when $P = 6$. Second, we have already seen that the slope of the line, $\Delta P / \Delta E$, is equal to -0.5, which means that for every one-unit increase in E, P falls by 0.5 unit. We can thus state the equation of the line as

$$P = 6 - (0.5)E$$

where both P and E are expressed as thousands of units (tonnes and dollars, respectively).

Non-linear Functions Although it is sometimes convenient to simplify the situation by assuming two variables to be linearly related, this is seldom the case over their whole range. Non-linear relations are much more common than linear ones. In the case of reducing pollution, it is usually quite cheap to eliminate the first units of pollution. Then, as the environment gets cleaner and cleaner, the cost of further clean-up tends to increase because more and more sophisticated and expensive methods need to be used. As a result, Figure 2-8 is more realistic than Figure 2-7. Inspection of Figure 2-8 shows that as more and more is spent on reducing pollution, the amount of pollution actually reduced for an additional $1 of expenditure gets smaller and smaller. This is shown by the diminishing slope of the curve as we move rightward along it. For example, as we

---

[1] Red numbers in square brackets indicate mathematical notes that are found in a separate section at the back of the book.

FIGURE 2-8   Non-linear Pollution Reduction

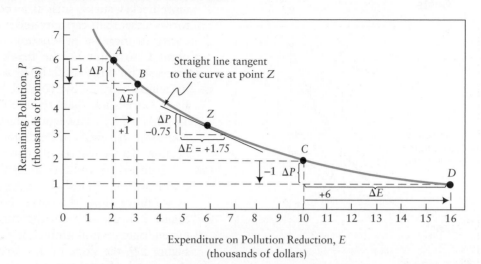

Pollution as a non-linear function of clean-up expenditure. The slope of the curve changes as we move along it. Between points *A* and *B*, it costs $1000 to reduce pollution by 1000 tonnes. Between points *C* and *D*, it costs $6000 to reduce pollution by 1000 tonnes. At point *Z*, the slope of the curve is equal to the slope of the straight line tangent to the curve at point *Z*. The slope of the tangent line is −0.75/1.75 = −0.43.

move from point *A* to point *B*, an increase in expenditure of $1000 is required to reduce pollution by 1000 tonnes. Thus, each tonne of pollution reduction costs $1. But as we move from point *C* (where we have already reduced pollution considerably) to point *D*, an extra $6000 must be spent in order to reduce pollution by 1000 tonnes. At that point, each tonne of pollution reduction therefore costs $6.

Economists call the change in pollution when a bit more or a bit less is spent on clean-up the *marginal* change. The figure shows that the slope of the curve at each point measures this marginal change. It also shows that in the type of curve illustrated, the marginal change per dollar spent is diminishing as we spend more on pollution reduction. There is always a payoff to more expenditure over the range shown in the figure, but the payoff diminishes as more is spent. This relation can be described as *diminishing marginal response*. We will see such relations many times in what follows, so we emphasize now that diminishing marginal response does not mean that the *total* response is diminishing. In Figure 2-8, the total amount of pollution continues to fall as more and more is spent on clean-up. But diminishing marginal response does mean that the amount of pollution reduced per dollar of expenditure gets less and less as the total expenditure rises.

Figure 2-9 shows a graph in which the marginal response is increasing. The graph shows the relationship between annual production costs and annual output for a firm that makes hockey sticks. Notice that the more sticks produced annually, the higher the firm's total costs. This is shown by the positive slope of the line. Notice also that as more and more hockey sticks are produced, the extra amount that the firm must pay to produce each extra stick rises. For example, as the firm moves from point *A* to point *B*, annual costs rise by $30 000 in order to increase its annual output by 10 000 hockey sticks. Each

FIGURE 2-9 Increasing Marginal Production Costs

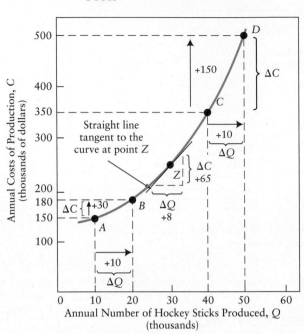

Marginal costs typically increase as annual output rises. From point A to point B, an extra annual output of 10 000 hockey sticks increases annual costs by $30 000. Each extra stick costs $3. From point C to point D, an extra output of 10 000 hockey sticks increases annual costs by $150 000. Each extra hockey stick then costs $15. This is a case of increasing marginal cost. At point Z, the slope of the curve is equal to the slope of the straight line tangent to the curve at point Z. The slope of the tangent line is $65/8 = 8.13$.

extra stick costs $3 ($30 000/10 000 = $3). But when the firm is already producing many more hockey sticks, such as at point C, its factory is closer to its capacity and it becomes more costly to increase production. Moving from point C to point D, the firm's annual costs increase by $150 000 in order to increase its annual output by 10 000 hockey sticks. Each extra stick then costs $15 ($150 000/ 10 000 = $15). This figure illustrates a case of *increasing marginal cost,* a characteristic of production that we will see often in this book.

Figures 2-8 and 2-9 show that with non-linear functions the slope of the curve changes as we move along the curve. For example, in Figure 2-8, the slope of the curve falls as the expenditure on pollution clean-up increases. In Figure 2-9, the slope of the curve increases as the volume of production increases.

In Figure 2-9, it is clear that the curve is steeper between points C and D than it is between points A and B. But how do we measure the slope of a curved line at any specific point? The answer is that we use the slope of a straight line *tangent to that curve* at the point that interests us. For example, in Figure 2-8, if we want to know the slope of the curve at point Z, we draw a straight line that touches the curve *only* at point Z; this is a tangent line. The slope of this line is $-0.75/1.75 = -0.43$. Similarly, in Figure 2-9, the slope of the curve at point Z is given by the slope of the straight line tangent to the curve at point Z. The slope of this line is $65/8 = 8.13$.

> **For non-linear functions, the slope of the curve changes as X changes. Therefore, the marginal response of Y to a change in X depends on the value of X.**

Functions with a Minimum or a Maximum So far, all the graphs we have shown have had either a positive or a negative slope over their entire range. But many relations change directions as the independent variable increases. For example, consider a firm that is attempting to maximize its profits and is trying to determine how much output to produce. The firm may find that its unit production costs are lower than the market price of the good, and so it can increase its profit by producing more. But as it increases its level of production, the firm's unit costs may be driven up because the capacity of the factory is being approached. Eventually, the firm may find that extra output will actually cost so much that its profits are *reduced.* This is a relationship that we will study in detail in later chapters, and it is illustrated in Figure 2-10. Notice that when profits are maximized at point A, the slope of the curve is zero (because a tangent to the curve at point A is horizontal), and so the *marginal response* of profits to output is zero.

Now consider an example of a function with a minimum. You probably know that when you drive a car, the fuel consumption per kilometre depends on your speed. Driving very slowly uses a lot of fuel per kilometre travelled. Driving very fast also uses a lot of fuel per kilometre travelled. The best fuel efficiency—the lowest fuel consumption per kilometre travelled—occurs at a speed of approximately 95 kilometres per hour. The relationship between speed and fuel consumption is shown in Figure 2-11 and illustrates a function with a minimum. Note that, once again, at point A the slope of the curve is zero (because a tangent to the curve at point A is horizontal), and so the *marginal response* of fuel consumption to speed is zero.

At either a minimum or a maximum of a function, the slope of the curve is zero. Therefore, at the minimum or maximum the marginal response of Y to a change in X is zero.

FIGURE 2-10 **Profits as a Function of Output**

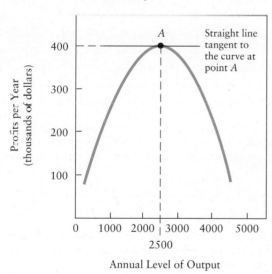

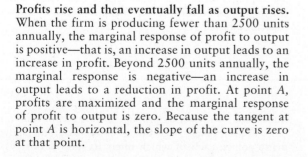

FIGURE 2-11 **Average Fuel Consumption as a Function of Speed**

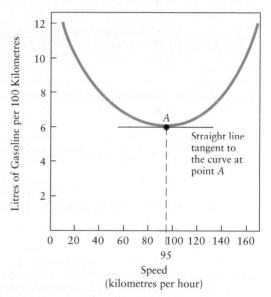

Profits rise and then eventually fall as output rises. When the firm is producing fewer than 2500 units annually, the marginal response of profit to output is positive—that is, an increase in output leads to an increase in profit. Beyond 2500 units annually, the marginal response is negative—an increase in output leads to a reduction in profit. At point A, profits are maximized and the marginal response of profit to output is zero. Because the tangent at point A is horizontal, the slope of the curve is zero at that point.

Average fuel consumption falls and then rises as speed increases. Average fuel consumption in litres per kilometre travelled is minimized at point A at a speed of approximately 95 kilometres per hour (km/h). At speeds less than 95 km/h, the marginal response is negative—that is, an increase in speed reduces fuel consumption per kilometre. At speeds above 95 km/h, the marginal response is positive—an increase in speed increases fuel consumption per kilometre. At 95 km/h, the marginal response is zero and fuel consumption per kilometre is minimized.

A Final Word

We have done much in this chapter. We began by examining the important difference between positive and normative statements. We then discussed why economists develop theories (or models) to help them understand economic events in the real world. We have also discussed how they test their theories and how there is a continual back-and-forth process between empirical testing of predictions and refining the theory. Finally, we devoted considerable time and space to exploring the many ways that data can be displayed in graphs and how economists use graphs to illustrate their theories.

Students are sometimes intimidated when first confronted with graphing economic variables, but keep in mind that the graphing and the math we use in the remainder of this book are no more difficult than what you learned in high school. As we introduce some basic economic theory in the next chapters, you will encounter many graphs (and a little algebra). The best way to get comfortable with economic graphs is to practise drawing them for yourself and to make sure you understand the variables you are graphing and the relationships between them. A graph allows us to see a visual representation of the economic theory we are learning about and to visualize what happens when one or more of our variables changes. A good graph can be worth a thousand words!

SUMMARY

2.1 Positive and Normative Statements

LO 1

- A key to the success of scientific inquiry lies in separating positive statements about the way the world works from normative statements about how one would like the world to work.

- Normative statements involve value judgments and cannot be disproven. Positive statements, at least in principle, can be disproven with an appeal to evidence.

2.2 Building and Testing Economic Theories

LO 2, 3

- Theories (sometimes called models) are designed to explain and predict what we see. A theory consists of a set of definitions of the variables to be discussed, a set of assumptions about how the variables behave, and the conditions under which the theory is meant to apply.
- A theory provides predictions of the type "If one event occurs, then another event will also occur."
- Theories are tested by checking their predictions against evidence. In economics, testing is almost always done using the data produced by the world of ordinary events.

- Economists make use of statistical analysis when testing their theories. They must take care to make the distinction between correlation and causation.
- The progress of any science lies in finding better explanations of events than are now available. Thus, in any developing science, one must expect to discard some existing theories and replace them with demonstrably superior alternatives.

2.3 Economic Data

LO 4

- Index numbers express economic series in relative form. Values in each period are expressed in relation to the value in the base period, which is given a value of 100.
- Economic data can be graphed in three different ways. Cross-sectional graphs show observations taken at the same time. Time-series graphs show observations on one variable taken over time. Scatter diagrams show many points, each of which refers to specific observations on two different variables.

2.4 Graphing Economic Theories

- A functional relation can be expressed in words, in a table giving specific values, in a mathematical equation, or in a graph.
- A graph of two variables has a positive slope when they both increase or decrease together and a negative slope when they move in opposite directions.
- The marginal response of a variable gives the amount it changes in response to a change in a second variable.

When the variable is measured on the vertical axis of a diagram, its marginal response at a specific point on the curve is measured by the slope of the line at that point.
- Some functions have a maximum or minimum point. At such points, the marginal response is zero.

KEY CONCEPTS

Positive and normative statements
Theories and models
Variables, assumptions, and
  predictions

Correlation versus causation
Functional relations
Positive and negative relations
  between variables

Positively and negatively sloped curves
Marginal responses
Maximum and minimum values

STUDY EXERCISES

MyLab Economics Make the grade with MyLab Economics™: All Study Exercises can be found on MyLab Economics™. You can practise them as often as you want, and many feature step-by-step guided instructions to help you find the right answer.

FILL-IN-THE-BLANK

1 Fill in the blanks to make the following statements correct.

a. Economists have designed _____ to better explain and predict the behaviour we observe in the world around us.

b. A variable, such as price or quantity, that is determined within a theory is known as a(n) _____ variable. A variable that is determined outside the theory is known as a(n) _____ variable.

c. When, based on a theory, we claim that "If A occurs, then B will follow," we are making a _____ that can then be tested by _____ observation.

d. If we observe that when variable A decreases, variable B also decreases, we can say that the two variables are _____. We cannot necessarily say that there is a _____ relationship between A and B.

e. An important assumption that is made in economics is that individuals and firms pursue their own _____. We assume that individuals seek to maximize their _____ and firms seek to maximize their _____.

2 Fill in the blanks to make the following statements correct.

a. It is difficult to compare two or more data series when absolute numbers and different units are used. For that reason we construct _____ numbers in order to compare _____ changes.

b. To construct an index number for computer prices over time, we divide the _____ in the given period by the _____ in the base period and multiply by 100.

c. The best way to display and compare the national income in each of the 10 largest economies in the world is a _____ graph.

d. The best way to display data showing national income and investment spending across 50 countries for 2018 is a _____ diagram.

e. The best way to display national income in Canada over the last 25 years is a _____ graph.

3 Fill in the blanks to make the following statements correct.

a. On a graph with Y on the vertical axis and X on the horizontal axis, the slope of a straight line is calculated as _____.

b. In the equation $Y = 500 + 4X$, the vertical intercept is _____, Y and X are _____ related to each other, and the slope of this linear function is _____.

c. In the equation $Y = 12 - 0.2X$, the vertical intercept is _____, Y and X are _____ related to each other, and the slope of this linear function is _____.

d. For a non-linear function, the slope of the curve at any specific point is measured as the slope of a straight line drawn _____ to that point.

e. On a graph of a non-linear function with either a minimum or a maximum point, the slope at the minimum or maximum is _____, meaning that the marginal response to a change in the independent variable is _____.

REVIEW

4 Determine whether each of the following statements is positive or normative.

a. The government should impose stricter regulations on the banking sector to avoid future financial crises.
b. Financial aid to developing countries has no impact on per capita GDP in those countries.
c. Tuition fee increases at Canadian universities lead to reduced access for low-income students.
d. It is unfair that Canadians have universal access to health care but not to dental care.
e. Canadians currently have too much personal debt.

5 In the following examples, identify the exogenous (or independent) variable and the endogenous (or dependent) variable.

a. The amount of rainfall on the Canadian prairies determines the amount of wheat produced in Canada.
b. When the world price of coffee increases, there is a change in the price of a cup of coffee at Tim Hortons.
c. If student loans were no longer available, there would be fewer students attending university.
d. An increase in the tax on gasoline leads people to drive more fuel-efficient vehicles.

6 Suppose that an examination of data reveals a positive correlation between the demand for new homes and the price of lumber. Which of the following conclusions can be correctly inferred from the existence of this correlation? Why?

a. An increase in the demand for homes causes an increase in the price of lumber.
b. The observed correlation is consistent with a theory that an increase in demand for new homes causes an increase in the price of lumber.

PROBLEMS

7 Suppose you want to create a price index for the price of a particular physics textbook over 10 years in your university bookstore. The price of the book on September 1 of each year is as follows:

Year	Price ($)	Year	Price ($)
2009	85	2015	120
2010	87	2016	125
2011	94	2017	127
2012	104	2018	127
2013	110	2019	130
2014	112		

a. The base year is 2009. Construct a physics textbook price index.
b. What is the percentage increase in the price of the book between the base year and 2014?
c. What is the percentage increase in the price of the book from 2016 to 2019?
d. Are the data listed above time-series or cross-sectional data? Explain why.

8 Suppose you want to create a price index for the price of a personal pizza across several Canadian university campuses, as of March 1, 2019. The data are as follows:

University	Price per Pizza
Dalhousie	$6.50
Laval	5.95
McGill	6.00
Queen's	8.00
Waterloo	7.50
Manitoba	5.50
Saskatchewan	5.75
Calgary	6.25
UBC	7.25
Victoria	7.00

a. Using Calgary as the "base university," construct the Canadian university pizza price index.
b. At which university is pizza the most expensive, and by what percentage is the price higher than in Calgary?
c. At which university is pizza the least expensive, and by what percentage is the price lower than in Calgary?
d. Are the data listed above time-series or cross-sectional data? Explain why.

9 According to Statistics Canada, Canada's exports and imports of energy (combined totals of fossil fuels, hydro, and nuclear, all measured in petajoules) over a five-year period were as follows:

	Exports	Imports
2012	11 225	3706
2013	11 687	3550
2014	11 821	3262
2015	12 219	3447
2016	12 507	3659

a. Using 2012 as the base year, construct index numbers for each of exports and imports.
b. Were exports or imports more volatile over this time period? Explain how you know.
c. Using your constructed index numbers, what was the percentage change in exports and imports from 2014 to 2016?

10 Suppose we divide Canada into three regions: the West, the Centre, and the East. Each region has an unemployment rate, defined as the number of people unemployed, expressed as a fraction of that region's labour force. The table that follows shows each region's unemployment rate and the size of its labour force.

Region	Unemployment Rate	Labour Force
West	5.5%	5.3 million
Centre	7.2%	8.4 million
East	12.5%	3.5 million

a. Compute an unemployment rate for Canada using a simple average of the rates in the three regions. Is this the "right" unemployment rate for Canada as a whole? Explain why or why not.
b. Now compute an unemployment rate for Canada using weights that reflect the size of that region's labour force as a proportion of the overall Canadian labour force. Explain the difference in this unemployment rate from the one in part (a). Is this a "better" measure of Canadian unemployment? Explain why.

11 Use the appropriate graph—time-series, cross-sectional, or scatter diagram—to illustrate the economic data provided in each part below.

a. The Canadian-dollar price of one U.S. dollar (the "exchange rate") in 2017:

January	1.319	July	1.269
February	1.311	August	1.261
March	1.339	September	1.228
April	1.344	October	1.261
May	1.361	November	1.277
June	1.330	December	1.277

b. A comparison of average household expenditures across provinces in 2016:

British Columbia	$85 845
Alberta	106 514
Saskatchewan	89 354
Manitoba	79 633
Ontario	88 953
Quebec	70 853
New Brunswick	67 933
Nova Scotia	73 879
Prince Edward Island	68 278
Newfoundland and Labrador	79 831

c. Per capita growth rates of real GDP and investment rates for various countries, averaged over the period 1950–2009:

Country	Average Growth Rate (% per year)	Average Investment Rate (% of GDP)
Canada	2.0	18.2
Austria	3.1	22.0
Japan	4.0	26.6
United States	1.9	18.1
United Kingdom	2.0	14.5
Spain	3.4	23.0
Norway	2.8	27.4
South Korea	5.1	27.2
Iceland	2.7	28.0

12 Use the following figure to answer the questions below.

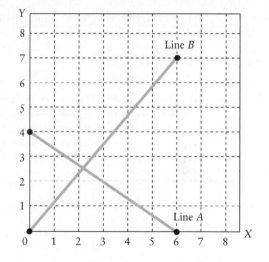

a. Is the slope of Line A positive or negative? Line B?
b. Calculate the slope of Line A. Write the equation describing the line in the form $Y = mX + b$, where m is the slope of the line and b is a constant term.
c. Calculate the slope of Line B. Write the equation describing the line in the form $Y = mX + b$, where m is the slope of the line and b is a constant term.

13 Suppose the relationship between the government's tax revenue (T) and national income (Y) is represented by the following equation: $T = 10 + 0.25Y$. Plot this relationship on a scale diagram, with Y on the horizontal axis and T on the vertical axis. Interpret the equation.

14 The following questions will provide practice working with simple linear functions. All questions refer to a coordinate graph with the variable X on the horizontal axis and the variable Y on the vertical axis.

a. If two points on a straight line are $(X = 3, Y = 2)$ and $(X = 12, Y = 5)$, what is the slope of the line?

b. If point A is at $(X = 20, Y = 20)$ and point B is at $(X = 10, Y = 40)$, what is the slope of the straight line joining points A and B?

c. What is the slope of the function described by $Y = 12\,000 - 0.5X$?

d. What is the slope of a line described by $Y = 6.5X$?

e. What is the slope of a line described by $Y = 27 + 3.2X$?

f. What is the Y-intercept of the function $Y = 1000 + mX$?

g. What is the Y-intercept of the function $Y = -100 + 10X$?

h. What is the X-intercept of the function $Y = 10 - 0.1X$?

15 Suppose ABC Corp. spends \$100 000 per year on some basic level of advertising, regardless of its revenues. In addition, the company spends 15 percent of each dollar of revenue on extra advertising. Write a mathematical equation that describes the functional relation between advertising (A) and revenue (R).

16 Consider the following three specific functions for a functional relation between X and Y:

i) $Y = 50 + 2X$

ii) $Y = 50 + 2X + 0.05X^2$

iii) $Y = 50 + 2X - 0.05X^2$

a. For the values of X of 0, 10, 20, 30, 40, and 50, plot X and Y on a scale diagram for each specific function. Connect these points with a smooth line.

b. For each function, state whether the slope of the line is constant, increasing, or decreasing as the value of X increases.

c. Describe for each function how the marginal change in Y depends on the value of X.

17 For each of the functional relations listed below, plot the relations on a scale diagram (with X on the horizontal axis and Y on the vertical axis) and compute the slope of the line.

a. $Y = 10 + 3X$

b. $Y = 20 + 4X$

c. $Y = 30 + 5X$

d. $Y = 10 + 5X$

18 Draw three graphs in which the dependent variable increases at an increasing rate, at a constant rate, and at a diminishing rate. Then draw three graphs in which it decreases at an increasing, constant, and diminishing rate. State a real relation that each of these graphs might describe, other than the ones given in the text of this chapter.

19 The figure below shows a monthly cost curve for the production of Good X.

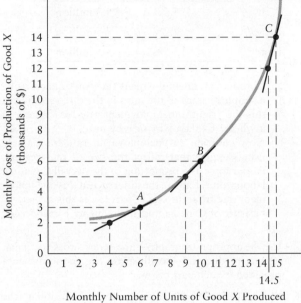

Monthly Number of Units of Good X Produced (thousands)

a. Calculate the slope of this non-linear function at points A, B, and C.

b. Is the marginal response of the cost of production of Good X to the change in the quantity produced of Good X increasing or decreasing?

c. Is the slope of this function increasing or decreasing as the volume of production increases?

3

Demand, Supply, and Price

CHAPTER OUTLINE	LEARNING OBJECTIVES (LO)
	After studying this chapter, you will be able to
3.1 DEMAND	**1** list the factors that determine the quantity demanded of a good.
	2 distinguish between a shift of the demand curve and a movement along the demand curve.
3.2 SUPPLY	**3** list the factors that determine the quantity supplied of a good.
	4 distinguish between a shift of the supply curve and a movement along the supply curve.
3.3 THE DETERMINATION OF PRICE	**5** explain the forces that drive market price to equilibrium, and how equilibrium price and quantity are affected by changes in demand and supply.

WE are now ready to study the important question of how markets work. To do so we will develop a simple model of demand and supply. And though there is much more to economics than just demand and supply, this simple model is our essential starting point for understanding how a market economy functions.

We start with how the demand for any product is determined. After doing the same for supply, we put demand and supply together to see how they interact. Finally, we see how market prices and quantities are determined, and how changes in various exogenous variables affect the market outcomes.

As we will see throughout this book, the concepts of demand and supply help us to understand the price system's successes and failures and the consequences of many government policies.

This chapter deals with the basic elements of demand, supply, and price. In the next two chapters we use the theory of demand and supply to discuss such issues as the effects of gasoline taxes, legislated minimum wages, rent controls, and the burden of payroll taxes.

▌3.1 Demand

What determines the demand for any given product? How will Canadian consumers respond to the next sudden change in the price of gasoline or coffee? What is the impact on the demand for kale once consumers decide it is the latest superfood? We start by developing a theory to explain the demand for some typical product.

Quantity Demanded

quantity demanded The amount of a good or service that consumers want to purchase during some time period.

The total amount of any particular good or service that consumers want to purchase during some time period is called the **quantity demanded** of that product. It is important to notice two things about this concept.

First, quantity demanded is a *desired* quantity. It is the amount that consumers want to purchase when faced with a particular price of the product, other products' prices, their incomes, their tastes, and everything else that might matter. It may be different from the amount that consumers actually succeed in purchasing. If sufficient quantities are not available, the amount that consumers want to purchase may exceed the amount they actually purchase. (For example, you may try to buy an airline ticket for reading week only to find that all flights are already sold out.) To distinguish these two concepts, the term *quantity demanded* is used to refer to desired purchases, and such phrases as *quantity bought* or *quantity exchanged* are used to refer to actual purchases.

Second, quantity demanded refers to a *flow* of purchases, expressed as so much per period of time: 1 million units per day, 7 million per week, or 365 million per year. For example, being told that the quantity of new cars demanded (at current prices) in Canada is 50 000 means nothing unless you are also told the period of time involved. For a country as large as Canada, 50 000 cars demanded per day would be an enormous rate of demand, whereas 50 000 per year would be a very small rate of demand. The important distinction between *stocks* and *flows* is discussed in *Extensions in Theory 3-1*.

The total amount of some product that consumers in the relevant market want to buy during a given time period is influenced by the following important variables: [2]

- Product's own price
- Consumers' income
- Prices of other products
- Consumers' tastes
- Population
- Significant changes in weather

We will discuss the separate effects of each of these variables later in the chapter. For now, we focus on the effects of changes in the product's own price. But how do we analyze the distinct effect of changes in this one variable when all variables are likely to be changing at once? Since this is difficult to do, we consider the influence of the variables one at a time. To do this in our theory, we hold all variables constant except the product's own price. Then we let the product's price vary and study how its change affects quantity demanded. We can do the same for each of the other variables in turn, and in this way we can come to understand the importance of each variable.

Holding all other variables constant is often described by the expressions "other things being equal," "other things given," or the equivalent Latin phrase, *ceteris paribus*.

EXTENSIONS IN THEORY 3-1

The Distinction Between Stocks and Flows

An important conceptual issue that arises frequently in economics is the distinction between *stock* and *flow* variables. Economic theories use both, and it takes a little practice to keep them straight.

As noted in the text, a flow variable has a time dimension—it is so much *per unit of time*. For example, the quantity of Grade A large eggs purchased in Edmonton is a flow variable. No useful information is conveyed if we are told that the number purchased was 2000 dozen eggs unless we are also told the period of time over which these purchases occurred. Two thousand dozen eggs per hour would indicate a much more active market in eggs than would 2000 dozen eggs per month.

In contrast, a stock variable is a variable whose value has meaning *at a point in time*. Thus, the number of eggs in the egg producer's warehouse on a particular day—for example, 10 000 dozen eggs on September 3, 2019—is a stock variable. All those eggs are there at one time, and they remain there until something happens to change the stock held in the warehouse.

The terminology of stocks and flows can be understood using an analogy to a bathtub. At any moment, the tub holds so much water. This is the *stock*, and it can be measured in terms of the volume of water, say, 100 litres. There might also be water flowing into the tub from the tap; this *flow* is measured as so much water per unit time, say, 10 litres per minute.

The distinction between stocks and flows is important. Failure to keep them straight is a common source of error. Note, for example, that a stock variable and a flow variable cannot be added together without specifying some time period for which the flow persists. We cannot add the stock of 100 litres of water in the tub to the flow of 10 litres per minute to get 110 litres. The new stock of water will depend on how long the flow persists; if it lasts for 20 minutes, the new stock will be 300 litres; if the flow persists for 60 minutes, the new stock will be 700 litres (or the tub will overflow!).

The amount of income earned is a flow; it is so much per year or per month or per hour. The amount of a consumer's expenditure is also a flow—so much spent per week or per month or per year. The amount of money in a bank account (earned, perhaps, in the past but unspent) is a stock—just so many thousands of dollars. The key test is always whether a time dimension is required to give the variable meaning.

When economists speak of the influence of the price of gasoline on the quantity of gasoline demanded, *ceteris paribus*, they refer to what a change in the price of gasoline would do to the quantity of gasoline demanded *if all other variables that influence the demand for gasoline did not change*.

Quantity Demanded and Price[1]

We are interested in studying the relationship between the quantity demanded of a product and that product's price. We therefore hold all other influences constant and ask, "How will the quantity demanded of a product change as its own price changes?"

A basic economic hypothesis is that the price of a product and the quantity demanded are related *negatively*, other things being equal. That is, the lower the price, the higher the quantity demanded; the higher the price, the lower the quantity demanded.

---

[1] In this chapter we explore a product's demand curve for the market as a whole—what we often call the *market demand curve*. In Chapter 6 we discuss how this market demand curve is derived by adding up, or *aggregating*, the demands of different individuals.

REDPIXEL.PL/Shutterstock

Changes in prices lead most consumers to alter their choices. For example, as prices for hotel rooms fall, vacationers may be more likely to take weekend trips.

The great British economist Alfred Marshall (1842–1924) called this fundamental relation the "law of demand." In Chapter 6, we will derive the law of demand as a prediction that follows from more basic assumptions about the behaviour of individual consumers. For now, let's simply explore why this relationship seems reasonable.

Products are used to satisfy desires and needs, and there is almost always more than one product that will satisfy any desire or need. Hunger may be alleviated by eating meat or vegetables; a desire for green vegetables can be satisfied by broccoli or spinach. The desire for a vacation may be satisfied by a trip to the ocean or to the mountains; the need to get there may be satisfied by different airlines, a bus, a car, or a train. For any general desire or need, there are almost always many different products that will satisfy it.

Now consider what happens if income, tastes, population, and the prices of all other products remain constant and the price of only one product changes. As the price goes up, that product becomes an increasingly expensive means of satisfying a desire. Many consumers will decide to switch wholly or partly to other products. Some consumers will stop buying it altogether, others will buy smaller amounts, and still others may continue to buy the same quantity. But the overall effect is that less will be demanded of the product whose price has risen. For example, as meat becomes more expensive, some consumers will switch to meat substitutes; others may forgo meat at some meals and eat less meat at others. Taken together as a group, consumers will want to buy less meat when its price rises.

Conversely, as the price goes down, the product becomes a cheaper way of satisfying a desire. Households will demand more of it as they substitute away from other products whose prices have not fallen. For example, if the price of tomatoes falls, many shoppers will buy more tomatoes and less of other vegetables.

Demand Schedules and Demand Curves

demand schedule A table showing the relationship between quantity demanded and the price of a product, other things being equal.

A **demand schedule** is one way of showing the relationship between quantity demanded and the price of a product, other things being equal. It is a table showing the quantity demanded at various prices.

The table in Figure 3-1 shows a hypothetical demand schedule for apples.[2] It lists the quantity of apples that would be demanded at various prices, given the assumption that all other variables are held constant. The table gives the quantities demanded for five selected prices, but in fact a separate quantity would be demanded at every possible price.

---

[2] We realize that apples are not a very exciting product to discuss, and many students wonder why we do not instead use cellphones, restaurant meals, or cars as our hypothetical example. The model of demand and supply, however, best applies to products that are demanded by many consumers and supplied by many producers, each of which offers for sale a virtually identical ("homogeneous") version of the product. For this reason, we have chosen a simple agricultural product, but we could have illustrated the same principles with beef, wheat, copper, newsprint, oil, and a whole host of what economists call "commodities."

FIGURE 3-1   The Demand for Apples

A Demand Schedule for Apples

Reference Point	Price ($ per bushel)	Quantity Demanded (thousands of bushels per year)
U	20	110
V	40	85
W	60	65
X	80	50
Y	100	40

A Demand Curve for Apples

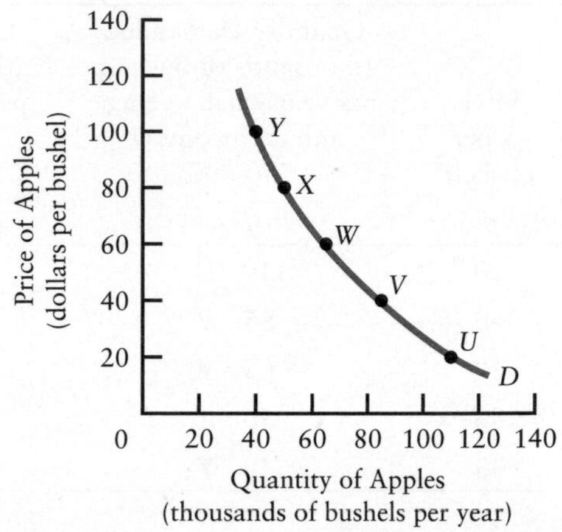

Both the table and the graph show the total quantity of apples that would be demanded at various prices, *ceteris paribus.* For example, row W indicates that if the price of apples were $60 per bushel, consumers would desire to purchase 65 000 bushels of apples per year, holding constant the values of the other variables that affect quantity demanded. The demand curve, labelled D, relates quantity of apples demanded to the price of apples; its negative slope indicates that quantity demanded increases as price falls.

A second method of showing the relationship between quantity demanded and price is to draw a graph. The five price–quantity combinations shown in the table are plotted in Figure 3-1. Price is plotted on the vertical axis, and the quantity demanded is plotted on the horizontal axis.

The curve drawn through these points is called a **demand curve**. It shows the quantity that consumers would like to buy at each price. The negative slope of the curve indicates that the quantity demanded increases as the price falls. Each point on the demand curve indicates a single price–quantity combination. The demand curve as a whole shows something more.

> **demand curve** The graphical representation of the relationship between quantity demanded and the price of a product, other things being equal.

The demand curve represents the relationship between quantity demanded and price, other things being equal; its negative slope indicates that quantity demanded increases when price decreases.

When economists speak of *demand* in a particular market, they are referring not just to the particular quantity being demanded at the moment (i.e., not just to one point on the demand curve) but to the entire demand curve—to the relationship between desired purchases and all the possible prices of the product.

The term **demand** therefore refers to the entire relationship between the quantity demanded of a product and the price of that product. In contrast, a single point on a demand schedule or curve is the quantity demanded at that point. This distinction between "demand" and "quantity demanded" is an extremely important one and we will examine it more closely later in this chapter.

> **demand** The entire relationship between the quantity of a product that buyers want to purchase and the price of that product, other things being equal.

FIGURE 3-2 An Increase in the Demand for Apples

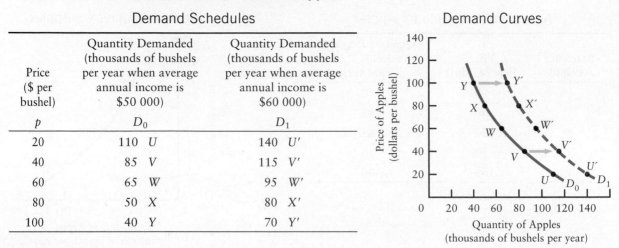

Demand Schedules

Price ($ per bushel)	Quantity Demanded (thousands of bushels per year when average annual income is $50 000)		Quantity Demanded (thousands of bushels per year when average annual income is $60 000)	
p	D_0		D_1	
20	110	U	140	U'
40	85	V	115	V'
60	65	W	95	W'
80	50	X	80	X'
100	40	Y	70	Y'

An increase in annual household income increases the quantity demanded at each price (for all normal goods). This is shown by the rightward shift in the demand curve, from D_0 to D_1. When average income rises from $50 000 to $60 000 per year, quantity demanded at a price of $60 per bushel rises from 65 000 bushels per year to 95 000 bushels per year. A similar rise occurs at every other price.

Shifts in the Demand Curve   A demand curve is drawn with the assumption that everything except the product's own price is being held constant. But what if other things change, as they often do? For example, consider an increase in average household income while the price of apples remains constant. If consumers spend some of their extra income on apples, the new quantity demanded cannot be represented by a point on the original demand curve. It must be represented on a new demand curve that is to the right of the old curve. Thus, a rise in income that causes more apples to be demanded *at each price* shifts the demand curve for apples to the right, as shown in Figure 3-2. This shift illustrates the operation of an important general rule.

> **A change in any of the variables (other than the product's own price) that affect the quantity demanded will shift the demand curve to a new position.**

A demand curve can shift to the right or to the left, and the difference is crucial. In the first case, more is desired at each price—the demand curve shifts rightward so that each price corresponds to a higher quantity than it did before. This is an *increase* in demand. In the second case, less is desired at each price—the demand curve shifts leftward so that each price corresponds to a lower quantity than it did before. This is a *decrease* in demand. Figure 3-3 shows increases and decreases in demand, and the associated shifts in the demand curve.

Let's now consider five important causes of shifts in the demand curve.

1. Consumers' Income.   If *average* income rises, consumers as a group can be expected to desire more of most products, other things being equal. We therefore expect that a rise in average consumer income shifts the demand curve for most products to the right—an increase in demand. Such a shift is shown in Figure 3-2.

Goods for which the quantity demanded increases when income rises are called *normal goods*. This term reflects economists' empirical finding that the demand for most products increases when income rises.

Exceptions exist, however, especially for individual consumers. Goods for which quantity demanded falls when income rises are called *inferior goods*. Some consumers, for example, may demand fewer rides on public transit (and more taxi rides) as their income rises. In this case, public transit would be an inferior good for these consumers. We will say more about normal and inferior goods in Chapter 4.

2. Prices of Other Goods. We saw that a product's demand curve has a negative slope because, *ceteris paribus*, the lower the price of the product, the cheaper it is relative to other products that can satisfy the same needs or desires. We call such products **substitutes in consumption.** If the price of apples goes down but the price of oranges remains fixed, then apples have become cheaper relative to oranges and the quantity demanded of apples will therefore rise.

But suppose instead that the price of oranges rises while the price of apples is unchanged. In this case, apples have again become cheaper relative to oranges, and so we still expect consumers to substitute away from oranges and toward apples. The increase in the price of oranges—a substitute—leads to an increase in the quantity demanded for apples at each price—a rightward shift of the demand curve.

Complements in consumption are products that tend to be used jointly. Cars and gasoline are complements; so are golf clubs and golf balls, and airplane flights to Calgary and ski-lift tickets in Banff. Because complements tend to be consumed together, a fall in the price of one will increase the quantity demanded of *both* products. Thus, a fall in the price of a complement for a product will shift that product's demand curve to the right. More will be demanded at each price. For example, a fall in the price of airplane trips to Calgary will lead to a rise in the demand for ski-lift tickets in Banff, even though the price of those lift tickets is unchanged. (The demand curve for ski-lift tickets will shift to the right.)

3. Consumers' Tastes. Tastes have a powerful effect on people's desired purchases. A change in tastes may be long-lasting, such as the shift from typewriters to computers, or it may be a short-lived fad as is common with many electronic games. In either case, a change in tastes in favour of a product shifts the demand curve to the right. More will be demanded at each price. Of course, a change in tastes against some product has the opposite effect and shifts the demand curve to the left.

4. Population. If there is an increase in population with purchasing power, the demands for all the products purchased by the new people will rise. Thus, we expect that an increase in population will shift the demand curves for most products to the right, indicating that more will be demanded at each price.

5. Significant Changes in Weather. The demands for some products are affected by dramatic changes in the weather. During winter, for example, a cold snap will lead to

FIGURE 3-3   Shifts in the Demand Curve

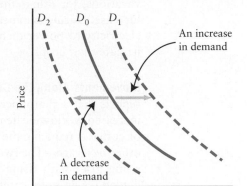

A rightward shift in the demand curve from D_0 to D_1 indicates an increase in demand; a leftward shift from D_0 to D_2 indicates a decrease in demand. An increase in demand means that more is demanded at each price. A decrease in demand means that less is demanded at each price.

substitutes in consumption
Goods that can be used in place of another good to satisfy similar needs or desires.

complements in consumption
Goods that tend to be consumed together.

increases in demand for electricity, natural gas, and other energy sources used to heat homes and buildings. More snowfall will increase the demand by some people for ski vacations; for others their demand for beach vacations in southern destinations will increase. During summer, a hot spell increases the demand for air conditioners and the electricity to power them, and a dry spell will increase farmers' demand for water to irrigate their crops.

Movements Along the Curve Versus Shifts of the Whole Curve   Suppose a news story reports that a sharp increase in the world price of coffee beans has been caused by an increased worldwide demand for coffee. Then the next day we read that the rising price of coffee is reducing the typical consumer's purchases of coffee, as shoppers switch to other beverages. The two stories appear to contradict each other. The first associates a rising price with rising demand; the second associates a rising price with declining demand. Can both statements be true? The answer is yes—because the two statements actually refer to different things. The first describes a shift in the demand curve; the second describes a movement along the demand curve in response to a change in price.

Consider first the statement that the increase in the price of coffee has been caused by an increased demand for coffee. This statement refers to a shift in the demand curve for coffee—in this case, a shift to the right, indicating more coffee demanded at each price. This shift, as we will see later in this chapter, will lead to an increase in the price of coffee.

Now consider the second statement—that less coffee is being bought because of its rise in price. This refers to a movement along the *new* demand curve and reflects a change between two specific quantities demanded, one before the price increased and one afterward.

Possible explanations for the two stories are as follows:

1. A rise in population and income in coffee-drinking countries shifts the demand curve for coffee to the right. This, in turn, raises the price of coffee (for reasons we will soon study in detail). This was the first news story.

2. The rising price of coffee is causing many individual households to cut back on their coffee purchases. The cutback is represented by an upward movement to the left along the *new* demand curve for coffee. This was the second news story.

To prevent the type of confusion caused by our two news stories, economists use a specialized vocabulary to distinguish between shifts of demand curves and movements along demand curves.

We have seen that "demand" refers to the *entire* demand curve, whereas "quantity demanded" refers to a particular *point* on the demand curve. Economists reserve the term **change in demand** to describe a change in the quantity demanded at *every* price. That is, a change in demand refers to a shift of the entire demand curve. The term **change in quantity demanded** refers to a movement from one point on a demand curve to another point, either on the same demand curve or on a new one.

change in demand A change in the quantity demanded at each possible price of the product, represented by a shift in the whole demand curve.

change in quantity demanded A change in the specific quantity of the good demanded, represented by a change from one point on a demand curve to another point, either on the original demand curve or on a new one.

A change in quantity demanded can result from a shift in the demand curve with the price constant, from a movement along a given demand curve due to a change in the price, or from a combination of the two. [3]

We consider these three possibilities in turn.

An increase in demand means that the whole demand curve shifts to the right; at any given price, an increase in demand causes an increase in quantity demanded. For example, in Figure 3-2 the shift in the demand curve for apples from D_0 to D_1 represents an increase in demand, and at a price of $40 per bushel, quantity demanded increases from 85 000 bushels to 115 000 bushels, as indicated by the move from V to V'.

A movement up and to the left along a demand curve represents a reduction in quantity demand in response to a higher price. For example, in Figure 3-2, with the demand for apples given by the curve D_1, an increase in price from $40 to $60 per bushel causes a movement along D_1 from V' to W', and quantity demanded decreases from 115 000 bushels to 95 000 bushels.

When there is a change in demand *and* a change in the price, the overall change in quantity demanded is the net effect of the shift in the demand curve and the movement along the new demand curve. Figure 3-4 shows the combined effect of an increase in demand, shown by a rightward shift in the whole demand curve, and an upward movement to the left along the new demand curve caused by an increase in price. The increase in demand causes an increase in quantity demanded at the initial price, whereas the

FIGURE 3-4   Shifts of and Movements Along the Demand Curve

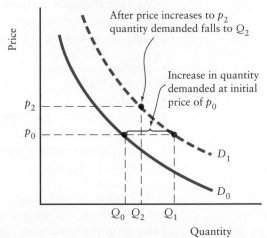

An increase in demand means that the demand curve shifts to the right, and hence quantity demanded is higher at each price. A rise in price causes a movement upward and to the left along the demand curve, and hence quantity demanded falls. The demand curve is originally D_0 and price is p_0, which means that quantity demanded is Q_0. Suppose demand increases to D_1, which means that at any particular price, there is a larger quantity demanded; for example, at p_0, quantity demanded is now Q_1. Now suppose the price rises above p_0. This causes a movement up and to the left along D_1, and quantity demanded falls below Q_1. As the figure is drawn, the quantity demanded at the new price p_2 is less than Q_1 but greater than Q_0. So in this case the combined effect of the increase in demand and the rise in price is an increase in quantity demanded from Q_0 to Q_2.

movement along the new demand curve causes a decrease in the quantity demanded. Whether quantity demanded rises or falls overall depends on the relative magnitudes of these two changes.

3.2   Supply

What determines the supply of any given product? Why do Canadian oil producers extract and sell more oil when the price of oil increases? Why do Canadian cattle ranchers raise and sell more beef when the price of cattle feed falls? We start by developing a theory designed to explain the supply of some typical product.

Quantity Supplied

The amount of some good or service that producers want to sell in some time period is called the **quantity supplied** of that product. Quantity supplied is a flow; it is so much

quantity supplied The amount of a good or service that producers want to sell during some time period.

per unit of time. Note also that quantity supplied is the amount that producers are willing to offer for sale; it is not necessarily the amount that they succeed in selling, which is expressed by *quantity sold* or *quantity exchanged.*

As a general rule, any event that makes production of a specific product more profitable will lead firms to supply more of it. The quantity supplied of a product is influenced by the following key variables: [4]

- Product's own price
- Prices of inputs
- Technology
- Government taxes or subsidies
- Prices of other products
- Significant changes in weather
- Number of suppliers

The situation with supply is the same as that with demand: There are several influencing variables, and we will not get far if we try to discover what happens when they all change at the same time. Again, we use the convenient *ceteris paribus* assumption to study the influence of the variables one at a time.

Quantity Supplied and Price

We begin by holding all other variables constant and ask, "How do we expect the total quantity of a product supplied to vary with its own price?"

> A basic economic hypothesis is that the price of the product and the quantity supplied are related *positively,* other things being equal. That is, the higher the product's own price, the more its producers will supply; the lower the price, the less its producers will supply.

In later chapters we will derive this hypothesis as a prediction from more basic assumptions about the behaviour of individual profit-maximizing firms. For now we simply note that as the product's price rises, producing and selling this product becomes a more profitable activity. Firms interested in increasing their profit will therefore choose to increase their supply of the product.

Supply Schedules and Supply Curves

supply schedule A table showing the relationship between quantity supplied and the price of a product, other things being equal.

supply curve The graphical representation of the relationship between quantity supplied and the price of a product, other things being equal.

The general relationship just discussed can be illustrated by a **supply schedule,** which shows the relationship between quantity supplied of a product and the price of the product, other things being equal. The table in Figure 3-5 presents a hypothetical supply schedule for apples. A **supply curve,** the graphical representation of the supply schedule, is also illustrated in Figure 3-5. Each point on the supply curve represents a specific price–quantity combination; however, the whole curve shows something more.

FIGURE 3-5 The Supply of Apples

A Supply Schedule for Apples

Reference Point	Price ($ per bushel)	Quantity Supplied (thousands of bushels per year)
u	20	20
v	40	45
w	60	65
x	80	80
y	100	95

A Supply Curve for Apples

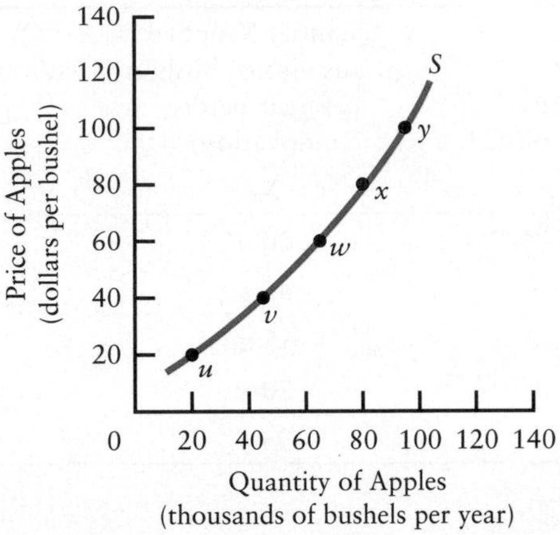

Both the table and the graph show the quantities that producers want to sell at various prices, *ceteris paribus*. For example, row w indicates that if the price of apples were $60 per bushel, producers would want to sell 65 000 bushels per year. The supply curve, labelled S, relates quantity of apples supplied to the price of apples; its positive slope indicates that quantity supplied increases as price increases.

The supply curve represents the relationship between quantity supplied and price, other things being equal; its positive slope indicates that quantity supplied increases when price increases.

When economists make statements about the conditions of *supply*, they are not referring just to the particular quantity being supplied at the moment—that is, not to just one point on the supply curve. Instead, they are referring to the entire supply curve, to the complete relationship between desired sales and all possible prices of the product. **Supply** refers to the entire relationship between the quantity supplied of a product and the price of that product, other things being equal. A single point on the supply curve refers to the *quantity supplied* at that price.

Shifts in the Supply Curve   A shift in the supply curve means that at each price there is a change in the quantity supplied. An increase in the quantity supplied at each price is shown in Figure 3-6. This change appears as a rightward shift in the supply curve. In contrast, a decrease in the quantity supplied at each price would appear as a leftward shift. For supply, as for demand, there is an important general rule:

A change in any of the variables (other than the product's own price) that affect the quantity supplied will shift the supply curve to a new position.

Let's now consider six possible causes of shifts in supply curves.

1. Prices of Inputs.   All things that a firm uses to make its products, such as materials, labour, and machines, are called the firm's *inputs*. Other things being equal, the higher

supply The entire relationship between the quantity of some good or service that producers wish to sell and the price of that product, other things being equal.

FIGURE 3-6 An Increase in the Supply of Apples

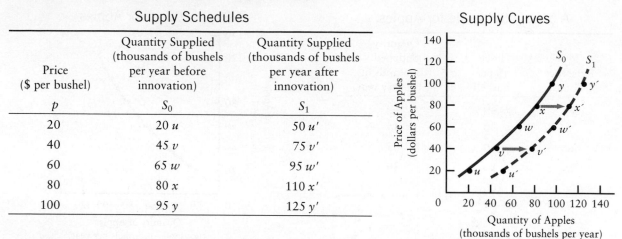

Price ($ per bushel)	Quantity Supplied (thousands of bushels per year before innovation)	Quantity Supplied (thousands of bushels per year after innovation)
p	S_0	S_1
20	20 u	50 u'
40	45 v	75 v'
60	65 w	95 w'
80	80 x	110 x'
100	95 y	125 y'

A cost-saving innovation increases the quantity supplied at each price. This is shown by the rightward shift in the supply curve, from S_0 to S_1. As a result of a cost-saving innovation, the quantity that is supplied at a price of $100 per bushel rises from 95 000 to 125 000 bushels per year. A similar rise occurs at every price.

the price of any input used to make a product, the less profit there will be from making that product. We expect, therefore, that the higher the price of any input used by a firm, the less the firm will produce and offer for sale at any given price of the product. A rise in the price of inputs reduces profitability and therefore shifts the supply curve for the product to the left; a fall in the price of inputs makes production more profitable and therefore shifts the supply curve to the right.

2. Technology.   At any given time, what is produced and how it is produced depend on the state of technology and knowledge. Over time, however, technology changes. The enormous increase in production per worker that has been going on in industrial societies for over 200 years is due largely to improved methods of production. The Industrial Revolution is more than a historical event; it is a present reality. Today, advances in technology are causing revolutionary increases in our ability to produce new products and services. Nanotechnology, 3D printing, cloud computing, robotics, and artificial intelligence are all examples of technologies that are both reducing the costs of producing existing goods and also increasing the range of products we are able to produce. These changes in the state of knowledge cause shifts in supply curves.

Any technological innovation that decreases the amount of inputs needed per unit of output reduces production costs and hence increases the profits that can be earned at any given price of the product. Because increased profitability leads to increased willingness to produce, this technological change shifts the supply curve to the right.

3. Government Taxes or Subsidies.   We have seen that anything increasing firms' costs will shift the supply curve to the left, and anything decreasing firms' costs will shift the supply curve to the right. As we will see in later chapters, governments often levy special taxes on the production of specific goods, such as gasoline, cigarettes, and alcohol. These taxes make the production and sale of these goods less profitable. The result is that the supply curve shifts to the left.

For other products, governments often subsidize producers—that is, they pay producers a specific amount for each unit of the good produced. This often occurs in agricultural markets, especially in the United States and the European Union. In such situations, the subsidy increases the profitability of production and shifts the supply curve to the right. For example, environmental concerns have led the U.S. and Canadian governments in recent years to provide subsidies for the production of biofuels. These subsidies have caused the supply curve for biofuels to shift to the right.

4. Prices of Other Products.   Changes in the price of one product may lead to changes in the supply of some other product because the two products are either *substitutes* or *complements* in the production process.

A prairie farmer, for example, can plant his field in wheat or oats. If the market price of oats falls, thus making oat production less profitable, the farmer will be more inclined to plant wheat. In this case, wheat and oats are said to be *substitutes* in production—for every extra hectare planted in one crop, one fewer hectare can be planted in the other. In this example, a reduction in the price of oats leads to an increase in the supply of wheat.

An excellent example in which two products are *complements* in production is oil and natural gas, which are often found together below Earth's surface. If the market price of oil rises, producers will do more drilling and increase their production of oil. But as more oil wells are drilled, the usual outcome is that more of *both* natural gas and oil are discovered and then produced. Thus, the rise in the price of oil leads to an increase in the supply of the complementary product—natural gas.

5. Significant Changes in Weather.   Especially in the agricultural sector, significant changes in the weather can lead to changes in supply. Drought, excessive rain, or flooding can all massively reduce the supply of wheat and other crops growing in temperate climates. In tropical locations, hurricanes can wipe out a coffee or banana crop, and a cold snap or frost can decimate the supply of fruit.

Dramatic weather events can also reduce supply in industrial sectors. Multiple hurricanes in the summer and fall of 2017 caused massive damage to a wide range of industrial facilities in Florida, Puerto Rico, and several Caribbean islands. In the summer of 2016 a massive wildfire destroyed large parts of Fort McMurray, Alberta, and forced the temporary closure of oil sands production facilities.

6. Number of Suppliers.   For given prices and technology, the total amount of any product supplied depends on the number of firms producing that product and offering it for sale. If profits are being earned by current firms, then more firms will choose to enter this industry and begin producing. The effect of this increase in the number of suppliers is to shift the supply curve to the right. Similarly, if the existing firms are losing money, they will eventually leave the industry; such a reduction in the number of suppliers shifts the supply curve to the left. In Chapter 9 we will see this entry and exit of firms as an important part of the long-run adjustment process in industries.

Movements Along the Curve Versus Shifts of the Whole Curve   As with demand, it is important to distinguish movements along supply curves from shifts of the whole curve. Economists reserve the term **change in supply** to describe a shift of the whole supply curve—that is, a change in the quantity that will be supplied at every price. The term **change in quantity supplied** refers to a movement from one point on a supply curve to another point, either on the same supply curve or on a new one. In other words, an

change in supply A change in the quantity supplied at each possible price of the product, represented by a shift in the whole supply curve.

change in quantity supplied A change in the specific quantity supplied, represented by a change from one point on a supply curve to another point, either on the original supply curve or on a new one.

increase in supply means that the whole supply curve has shifted to the right, so that the quantity supplied at any given price has increased; a movement up and to the right along a supply curve indicates an increase in the quantity supplied in response to an increase in the price of the product.

> **A change in quantity supplied can result from a change in supply with the price constant, a movement along a given supply curve because of a change in the price, or a combination of the two.**

An exercise you might find useful is to construct a diagram similar to Figure 3-4, emphasizing the difference between a shift of the supply curve and a movement along the supply curve.

▌3.3 The Determination of Price

So far we have considered demand and supply separately. We now come to a key question: How do the two forces of demand and supply interact to determine the actual price and quantity? Before considering this question, you should know that the demand-and-supply model does *not* apply to all markets. See *Applying Economic Concepts 3-1* for a discussion of why the model in this chapter applies well to apples (and many other "commodities") but not to many more interesting products, such as iPhones (and a whole range of "differentiated" products).

The Concept of a Market

Originally, the term *market* designated a physical place where products were bought and sold. We still use the term this way to describe such places as Granville Island Market in Vancouver, Kensington Market in Toronto, or Jean Talon Market in Montreal. Once developed, however, theories of market behaviour were easily extended to cover products, such as wheat or oil, that can be purchased anywhere in the world at a price that tends to be uniform the world over. Today we can also buy and sell most consumer products in markets that exist online. The idea that a *market* must be a single geographic location where consumers can go to buy something became obsolete long ago.

market Any situation in which buyers and sellers can negotiate the exchange of goods or services.

For present purposes, a **market** may be defined as existing in any situation (such as a physical place or an electronic medium) in which buyers and sellers negotiate the exchange of goods or services.

Individual markets differ in the degree of *competition* among the various buyers and sellers. In the next few chapters we will examine markets in which the number of buyers and sellers is sufficiently large that no one of them has any appreciable influence on the market price. This is a rough definition of what economists call *perfectly competitive markets*. Starting in Chapter 10, we will consider the behaviour of markets in which there are small numbers of either sellers or buyers. But our initial theory of markets, based on the interaction of demand and supply, will be a very good description of the markets for such things as wheat, pork, newsprint, coffee, copper, oil, and many other commodities.

APPLYING ECONOMIC CONCEPTS 3-1

Why Apples but Not iPhones?

The demand-and-supply model that we have developed in this chapter does *not* apply to the markets for all goods and services, and there is a good reason why our example throughout the chapter has been apples and not, for example, iPhones, cars, brand-name clothing, or even textbooks. Three conditions must be satisfied in order for a market to be well described by the demand-and-supply model.

1. There must be a large number of consumers of the product, each one small relative to the size of the market.

2. There must be a large number of producers of the product, each one small relative to the size of the market.

3. Producers must be selling identical or "homogeneous" versions of the product.

The first assumption ensures that no single consumer is large enough to influence the market price through their buying actions. This is satisfied in most markets, although there are important exceptions. For example, Canadian provincial governments are dominant purchasers of prescription drugs in Canada, and their *market power* tends to keep prices below what they would otherwise be.

The second assumption ensures that no single producer is large enough to influence the market price through their selling actions. There are many markets in which this is not true. For example, DeBeers controls the sale of a large fraction of the world's rough diamonds, and thus it can alter the market price through

its sales restrictions. Hydro-Québec is the sole producer of electricity in the province of Quebec and sets the price that consumers pay. In contrast, most producers of fruits and vegetables are very small relative to the size of the market and have no ability to influence the market price.

The third assumption ensures that there will be a single price in the market because producers have no ability to *differentiate* their product from those of other producers. This condition is satisfied in many markets for commodities—steel, aluminum, copper, wheat, oil, natural gas, lumber, newsprint, beef, pork, etc. But it is *not* satisfied in the markets for many consumer products such as smartphones and other electronic devices, cars and motorcycles, clothing, and fast food and other restaurant meals. In these cases, each producer sells a different version of the product and often spends considerable advertising resources trying to convince consumers to purchase their version. In these markets, differentiated products sell at different prices.

When *all three* conditions are satisfied, economists use the demand-and-supply model to explain the determination of market price and quantity. This model has proven to be very successful in explaining outcomes in markets such as oil, steel, copper, wheat, soybeans, beef, pork, newsprint, lumber, foreign currencies, financial assets like stocks and bonds—and apples!

So be careful when you try to apply the demand-and-supply model. It works very well in describing the events in many markets, but not so well for others. Later chapters in this book will examine the more complex markets for which we need a more advanced model.

Market Equilibrium

The table in Figure 3-7 brings together the demand and supply schedules from Figures 3-1 and 3-5. The quantities of apples demanded and supplied at each price can now be compared.

There is only one price, $60 per bushel, at which the quantity of apples demanded equals the quantity supplied. At prices less than $60 per bushel, there is a shortage of apples because the quantity demanded exceeds the quantity supplied. This is a situation of **excess demand**. At prices greater than $60 per bushel, there is a surplus of apples because the quantity supplied exceeds the quantity demanded. This is a situation of **excess supply**. This same story can also be told in graphical terms. The quantities demanded and supplied at any price can be read off the two curves;

excess demand A situation in which, at the given price, quantity demanded exceeds quantity supplied.

excess supply A situation in which, at the given price, quantity supplied exceeds quantity demanded.

FIGURE 3-7 The Equilibrium Price of Apples

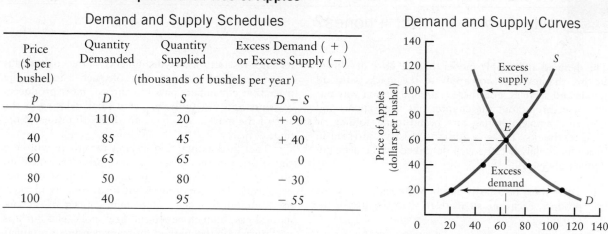

Demand and Supply Schedules

Price ($ per bushel)	Quantity Demanded	Quantity Supplied	Excess Demand (+) or Excess Supply (−)
	(thousands of bushels per year)		
p	*D*	*S*	*D − S*
20	110	20	+ 90
40	85	45	+ 40
60	65	65	0
80	50	80	− 30
100	40	95	− 55

The equilibrium price corresponds to the intersection of the demand and supply curves. At any price above $60, there is excess supply and thus downward pressure on price. At any price below $60, there is excess demand and thus upward pressure on price. Only at a price of $60 is there no pressure for price to change. Equilibrium occurs at point *E*, at a price of $60 per bushel and quantity exchanged equal to 65 000 bushels.

the excess supply or excess demand is shown by the horizontal distance between the curves at each price.

To examine the determination of market price, let's suppose first that the price is $100 per bushel. At this price, 95 000 bushels are offered for sale, but only 40 000 bushels are demanded. There is an excess supply of 55 000 bushels per year. Apple sellers are then likely to cut their prices to get rid of this surplus. And purchasers, observing the stock of unsold apples, will begin to offer less money for the product. In other words, *excess supply causes downward pressure on price.*

Now consider the price of $20 per bushel. At this price, there is excess demand. The 20 000 bushels produced each year are snapped up quickly, and 90 000 bushels of desired purchases cannot be made. Rivalry between would-be purchasers may lead them to offer more than the prevailing price to outbid other purchasers. Also, sellers may begin to ask a higher price for the quantities that they do have to sell. In other words, *excess demand causes upward pressure on price.*

Finally, consider the price of $60. At this price, producers want to sell 65 000 bushels per year, and purchasers want to buy that same quantity. There is neither a shortage nor a surplus of apples. There are no unsatisfied buyers to bid the price up, nor are there unsatisfied sellers to force the price down. Once the price of $60 has been reached, therefore, there will be no tendency for it to change.

Equilibrium implies a state of rest, or balance, between opposing forces. The **equilibrium price** is the one toward which the actual market price will tend. Once established, it will persist until it is disturbed by some change in market conditions that shifts the demand curve, the supply curve, or both.

equilibrium price The price at which quantity demanded equals quantity supplied. Also called the *market-clearing price.*

The price at which the quantity demanded equals the quantity supplied is called the equilibrium price, or the market-clearing price. [5]

Any price at which the market does not "clear"—that is, quantity demanded does not equal quantity supplied—is called a **disequilibrium price**. Whenever there is either excess demand or excess supply in a market, that market is said to be in a state of **disequilibrium**, and the market price will be changing.

Figure 3-7 makes it clear that the equilibrium price occurs where the demand and supply curves intersect. Below that price, there is excess demand and hence upward pressure on the existing price. Above that price, there is excess supply and hence downward pressure on the existing price.[3]

> **disequilibrium price** A price at which quantity demanded does not equal quantity supplied.

> **disequilibrium** A situation in a market in which there is excess demand or excess supply.

Changes in Market Equilibrium

Changes in any of the variables, other than price, that influence quantity demanded or supplied will cause a shift in the demand curve, the supply curve, or both. There are four possible shifts: an increase in demand (a rightward shift in the demand curve), a decrease in demand (a leftward shift in the demand curve), an increase in supply (a rightward shift in the supply curve), and a decrease in supply (a leftward shift in the supply curve).

To discover the effects of each of the possible curve shifts, we use the method known as **comparative statics**.[4] With this method, we derive predictions about how the *endogenous* variables (equilibrium price and quantity) will change following a change in a single *exogenous* variable (the variables whose changes cause shifts in the demand and supply curves). We start from a position of equilibrium and then introduce the change to be studied. We then determine the new equilibrium position and compare it with the original one. The difference between the two positions of equilibrium must result from the change that was introduced, because everything else has been held constant.

The changes caused by each of the four possible curve shifts are shown in Figure 3-8. Study the figure carefully. Previously, we had given the axes specific labels, but because it is now intended to apply to any product, the horizontal axis is simply labelled "Quantity." This means quantity per period in whatever units output is measured. "Price," the vertical axis, means the price measured as dollars per unit of quantity for the same product.

> **comparative statics** The derivation of predictions by analyzing the effect of a change in a single exogenous variable on the equilibrium.

Commodities & Futures					
	Price (US$)	Chg		Price (US$)	Chg
Crude Oil	68.82	0.10	Lumber	412.10	−3.10
Natural Gas	2.887	−0.03	Cocoa	2346.00	−18.00
Heating Oil	2.2187	0.0109	Corn	346.00	−2.50
Gold	1,214.80	1.50	Soybeans	847.50	−7.75
Silver	14.935	0.034	Oat	259.00	−4.75
Copper	2.7295	0.0065	Coffee	1.0575	0.0105
Platinum	800.60	11.20	Live Cattle	108.00	1.75
Palladium	938.60	19.40	Lean Hogs	54.75	2.975

Many commodities like those listed here are actively traded in international markets and their equilibrium prices fluctuate daily.

Source: Based on the data from "Commodities & Futures," TMX Money, https://web.tmxmoney.com/futures.php?locale=EN. Accessed August 27, 2018.

---

[3] When economists graph a demand (or supply) curve, they put the variable to be explained (the dependent variable) on the horizontal axis and the explanatory variable (the independent variable) on the vertical axis. This is "backward" to what is usually done in mathematics. The rational explanation of what is now economists' odd practice is buried in the history of economics and dates back to Alfred Marshall's *Principles of Economics* (1890) [6]. For better or worse, Marshall's scheme is now used by all economists, although mathematicians never fail to wonder at this example of the odd ways of economists.

[4] The term *static* is used because we are not concerned with the actual path by which the market goes from the first equilibrium position to the second, or with the time taken to reach the second equilibrium. Analysis of these movements would be described as dynamic analysis.

FIGURE 3-8 Shifts in Demand and Supply Curves

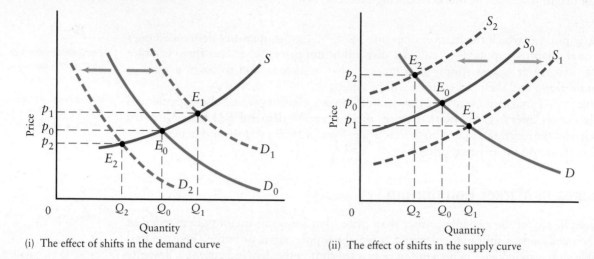

(i) The effect of shifts in the demand curve

(ii) The effect of shifts in the supply curve

Shifts in either demand or supply curves will generally lead to changes in equilibrium price and quantity. In part (i), suppose the original demand and supply curves are D_0 and S, which intersect to produce equilibrium at E_0, with a price of p_0 and a quantity of Q_0. An increase in demand shifts the demand curve to D_1, taking the new equilibrium to E_1. Price rises to p_1 and quantity rises to Q_1. Starting at E_0, a decrease in demand shifts the demand curve to D_2, taking the new equilibrium to E_2. Price falls to p_2 and quantity falls to Q_2.

In part (ii), the original demand and supply curves are D and S_0, which intersect to produce equilibrium at E_0, with a price of p_0 and a quantity of Q_0. An increase in supply shifts the supply curve to S_1, taking the new equilibrium to E_1. Price falls to p_1 and quantity rises to Q_1. Starting at E_0, a decrease in supply shifts the supply curve from S_0 to S_2, taking the new equilibrium to E_2. Price rises to p_2 and quantity falls to Q_2.

The effects of the four possible curve shifts are as follows:

1. An increase in demand causes an increase in both the equilibrium price and the equilibrium quantity exchanged.

2. A decrease in demand causes a decrease in both the equilibrium price and the equilibrium quantity exchanged.

3. An increase in supply causes a decrease in the equilibrium price and an increase in the equilibrium quantity exchanged.

4. A decrease in supply causes an increase in the equilibrium price and a decrease in the equilibrium quantity exchanged.

Demonstrations of these effects are given in the caption to Figure 3-8. The intuitive reasoning behind each is as follows:

1. **An increase in demand (the demand curve shifts to the right).** An increase in demand creates a shortage at the initial equilibrium price, and the unsatisfied buyers bid up the price. This rise in price causes a larger quantity to be supplied, with the result that at the new equilibrium more is exchanged at a higher price.

2. **A decrease in demand (the demand curve shifts to the left).** A decrease in demand creates a surplus at the initial equilibrium price, and the unsuccessful sellers bid the

price down. As a result, less of the product is supplied and offered for sale. At the new equilibrium, both price and quantity exchanged are lower than they were originally.

3. **An increase in supply (the supply curve shifts to the right).** An increase in supply creates a surplus at the initial equilibrium price, and the unsuccessful suppliers force the price down. This drop in price increases the quantity demanded, and the new equilibrium is at a lower price and a higher quantity exchanged.

4. **A decrease in supply (the supply curve shifts to the left).** A decrease in supply creates a shortage at the initial equilibrium price that causes the price to be bid up. This rise in price reduces the quantity demanded, and the new equilibrium is at a higher price and a lower quantity exchanged.

Note that in each of these four examples, a change in some exogenous variable has caused one of the curves to *shift*, and then in response to this shift, there has been a *movement along* the other curve toward the new equilibrium point. Both endogenous variables, price and quantity, adjust in response to the change in the exogenous variable.

By using the tools we have learned in this chapter, we can link many real-world events that cause demand or supply curves to shift and thus lead to changes in market prices and quantities. For example, economic growth in rapidly developing countries like China and India leads to increases in global demand for a wide range of products such as steel, cement, copper, and glass. *Ceteris paribus,* this economic growth will increase the equilibrium prices of these products. For another example, consider the rapid development of hydraulic fracturing ("fracking") in the United States. In recent years, use of this technology has led to an enormous increase in the supply of natural gas in the North American market, which, *ceteris paribus,* has caused a decrease in the equilibrium price.

It is worth noting that real-world demand and supply shifts are often not isolated events. More realistic is that one event causes a shift in the demand curve while some other event occurring at the same time causes a shift in the supply curve. For example, an increase in Calgary's population may lead to an increase in demand for residential accommodation while, at the same time, increased construction of condos and houses increases the supply. If these demand and supply shifts occur at the same time and are of the same magnitude, there may be no noticeable effect on the equilibrium price (although equilibrium quantity would increase).

Readers are referred to several Study Exercises at the end of this chapter to work through examples of demand and supply shifts and the predicted effects on equilibrium price and quantity.

A Numerical Example

Changes in market equilibrium can also be examined by using a simple algebraic model. For example, consider the (hypothetical) wholesale market for potatoes in Atlantic Canada in 2019. The price is the dollar price per crate and the quantity is the number of crates (in thousands). The demand and supply curves are:

$$Q^D = 100 - 3p$$
$$Q^S = 20 + 2p$$

Notice that the many things shifting the demand curve (such as income, tastes, etc.) are not explicitly shown in the demand equation. Instead, their effect is already represented in the constant term of 100. The demand equation shows that for every $1 increase in the price, quantity demanded falls by three (thousand) crates per year. Similarly, the many things shifting the supply curve are not shown explicitly, but their effect is shown inside the constant term of 20. From the supply equation it is clear that each $1 increase in the price leads to an increase in quantity supplied of two (thousand) crates per year.

In order to determine the market equilibrium, we need to find the single price at which $Q^D = Q^S$. By setting $Q^D = Q^S$, we get:

$$100 - 3p = 20 + 2p$$

which can be rewritten to get:

$$80 = 5p$$
$$\Rightarrow p = 16$$

The equilibrium price for potatoes is therefore $16 per crate. To find the equilibrium quantity, we substitute this price into either the demand or supply equation. Using either equation, we get

$$Q^D = 100 - 3(16) = 52 \quad \text{or} \quad Q^S = 20 + 2(16) = 52$$

So the equilibrium quantity of potatoes in Atlantic Canada in 2019 is 52 (thousand) crates. Readers are directed to the Study Exercises at the end of this chapter to work through other algebraic and numerical examples of market equilibrium.

Relative Prices

The theory we have developed explains how individual prices are determined by the forces of demand and supply. To facilitate matters, we have made *ceteris paribus* assumptions. Specifically, we have assumed the constancy of all prices except the one we are studying. This assumption forces us to make the distinction between *absolute* prices and *relative* prices.

The price of a product is the amount of money that must be spent to acquire one unit of that product. This is called the **absolute price** or *money price*. A **relative price** is the ratio of two absolute prices; it expresses the price of one good in terms of (relative to) another.

We have been reminded several times that what matters for demand and supply is the price of the product in question *relative to the prices of other products*; that is, what matters is the relative price. For example, if the price of carrots rises while the prices of other vegetables are constant, we expect consumers to reduce their quantity demanded of carrots as they substitute toward the consumption of other vegetables. In this case, the *relative* price of carrots has increased. But if the prices of carrots and all other vegetables are rising at the same rate, the relative price of carrots is constant. In this case we expect no substitution to take place between carrots and other vegetables.

The same thing is true on the supply side of the market. If the price of carrots increases while all other prices are constant, we expect producers to grow and supply more carrots because it is more profitable to do so. In contrast, if all prices increased together, *relative* prices would be unchanged and we would expect no particular change in the quantity of carrots supplied.

absolute price The amount of money that must be spent to acquire one unit of a product. Also called *money price*.

relative price The ratio of the money price of one product to the money price of another product; that is, a ratio of two absolute prices.

In microeconomics, whenever we refer to a change in the price of one product, we mean a change in that product's relative price, that is, a change in the price of that product relative to the prices of all other goods. The demand and supply of specific products depends on their *relative*, not absolute, prices.

SUMMARY

3.1 Demand

- The amount of a product that consumers want to purchase is called *quantity demanded*. It is a flow expressed as so much per period of time. It is determined by tastes, income, the product's own price, the prices of other products, population, and the weather.
- The relationship between quantity demanded and price is represented graphically by a demand curve that shows how much will be demanded at each market price. Quantity demanded is assumed to increase as the price of the product falls, other things held constant. Thus, demand curves are negatively sloped.

- A shift in a demand curve represents a change in the quantity demanded at each price and is referred to as a *change in demand*.
- An increase in demand means the demand curve shifts to the right; a decrease in demand means the demand curve shifts to the left.
- It is important to make the distinction between a movement along a demand curve (caused by a change in the product's price) and a shift of a demand curve (caused by a change in any of the other determinants of demand).

3.2 Supply

- The amount of a good that producers wish to sell is called *quantity supplied*. It is a flow expressed as so much per period of time. It depends on the product's own price, the costs of inputs, the number of suppliers, government taxes or subsidies, the state of technology, the weather, and prices of other products.
- The relationship between quantity supplied and price is represented graphically by a supply curve that shows how much will be supplied at each market price. Quantity supplied is assumed to increase as the price of the product increases, other things held constant. Thus, supply curves are positively sloped.

- A shift in the supply curve indicates a change in the quantity supplied at each price and is referred to as a *change in supply*.
- An increase in supply means the supply curve shifts to the right; a decrease in supply means the supply curve shifts to the left.
- It is important to make the distinction between a movement along a supply curve (caused by a change in the product's price) and a shift of a supply curve (caused by a change in any of the other determinants of supply).

3.3 The Determination of Price

- The *equilibrium price* is the price at which the quantity demanded equals the quantity supplied. At any price below equilibrium, there will be excess demand; at any price above equilibrium, there will be excess supply. Graphically, equilibrium occurs where the demand and supply curves intersect.
- Price rises when there is excess demand and falls when there is excess supply. Thus, the actual market price will be pushed toward the equilibrium price. When it is reached, there will be neither excess demand nor excess supply, and the price will not change until either the supply curve or the demand curve shifts.
- By using the method of *comparative statics,* we can determine the effects of a shift in either demand or supply. An increase in demand raises both equilibrium price and equilibrium quantity; a decrease in demand lowers both. An increase in supply raises equilibrium quantity but lowers equilibrium price; a decrease in supply lowers equilibrium quantity but raises equilibrium price.
- The absolute price of a product is its price in terms of money; its relative price is its price in relation to other products.
- The demand and supply of specific products depend on their relative, not absolute, prices.

KEY CONCEPTS

Stock and flow
  variables
Ceteris paribus or "other things
  being equal"
Quantity demanded
Demand curve

Change in quantity demanded
  versus change in demand
Quantity supplied
Supply curve
Change in quantity supplied
  versus change in supply

Equilibrium price and
  quantity
Disequilibrium
Comparative statics
Relative and absolute
  prices

STUDY EXERCISES

MyLab Economics Make the grade with MyLab Economics™: All Study Exercises can be found on MyLab Economics™. You can practise them as often as you want, and many feature step-by-step guided instructions to help you find the right answer.

FILL-IN-THE-BLANK

1 Fill in the blanks to make the following statements correct.

a. The term quantity demanded refers to _____ purchases by consumers, whereas quantity exchanged refers to _____ purchases by consumers.

b. Quantity demanded refers to the quantity of widgets demanded per period of _____. "The quantity demanded of widgets is 1000 units" is not meaningful unless we know the _____ period over which the 1000 units are demanded. Quantity demanded is a _____ variable.

c. A demand curve represents the relationship between _____ and _____, *ceteris paribus*. The negative slope indicates that when the price decreases, quantity demanded _____.

d. Five important causes of shifts in the demand curve are:

- _____
- _____
- _____
- _____
- _____

e. The Latin phrase meaning "other things being equal" is _____. When we want to study the effects of changes in one variable at a time, we hold all other variables _____.

2 Fill in the blanks to make the following statements correct.

a. The term quantity supplied refers to _____ sales by producers, whereas quantity exchanged refers to _____ sales by producers.

b. Quantity supplied refers to the quantity of widgets supplied per period of _____. "The quantity supplied of widgets is 1000 units" is not meaningful unless we know the _____ period over which the 1000 units are supplied. Quantity supplied is a _____ variable.

c. A supply curve represents the relationship between _____ and _____, *ceteris paribus*. The positive slope indicates that when the price increases, quantity supplied _____.

d. Six important causes of shifts in the supply curve are:

- _____
- _____
- _____
- _____
- _____
- _____

3 Fill in the blanks to complete the statements about a supply-and-demand model, as applied in the following situations.

a. Consider the market for cement in Toronto. If, *ceteris paribus,* half the producers in this market shut down, the _____ curve for cement will shift to the _____, indicating a(n) _____ in _____.

b. Consider the market for Canadian softwood lumber (a normal good). If, *ceteris paribus,* average incomes in both Canada and the United States rise over several years, the _____ curve for lumber will shift to the _____, indicating a(n) _____ in _____.

c. Consider the market for Quebec artisanal cheeses. If, *ceteris paribus,* the price of imported cheeses from France rises significantly, the _____ curve for Quebec cheeses will shift to the _____, indicating a(n) _____ in _____.

d. Consider the market for milk in the United States. If, *ceteris paribus,* the U.S. government decreases subsidies to dairy farmers, the _____ curve for milk will shift to the _____, indicating a(n) _____ in _____.

e. Consider the world market for shipping containers. If, *ceteris paribus,* the price of steel (a major input) rises, the _____ curve for shipping containers will shift to the _____, indicating a(n) _____ in _____.

f. Consider the market for hot dog buns. If, *ceteris paribus,* the price of wieners doubles, the _____ curve for hot dog buns will shift to the _____, indicating a(n) _____ in _____.

4 Fill in the blanks to make the following statements correct.

a. *Ceteris paribus,* the price of a product and the quantity demanded are related _____.

b. *Ceteris paribus,* the price of a product and the quantity supplied are related _____.

c. At any price above the equilibrium price there will be excess _____. At any price below the equilibrium price there will be excess _____.

d. The equilibrium price is the price at which quantity demanded _____ quantity supplied.

e. An increase in demand for some product will usually cause its equilibrium price to _____ and also cause an increase in _____.

f. A decrease in the supply of some product will usually cause its equilibrium price to _____ and also cause a decrease in _____.

REVIEW

5 Classify the effect of each of the following as (i) a change in the demand for fish or (ii) a change in the quantity of fish demanded. Illustrate each diagrammatically.

a. The government of Canada closes the Atlantic cod fishery.

b. People buy less fish because of a rise in fish prices.

c. The Catholic Church relaxes its ban on eating meat on Fridays.

d. The price of beef falls and, as a result, consumers buy more beef and less fish.

e. Fears of mercury poisoning lead locals to shun fish caught in nearby lakes.

f. It is generally alleged that eating fish is better for one's health than eating meat.

6 Are the following two observations inconsistent?

a. Rising demand for housing causes prices of new homes to soar.

b. Many families refuse to buy homes as prices become prohibitive for them.

7 Consider households' demand for chicken. For each of the events listed below, state and explain the likely

effect on the demand for chicken. How would each event be illustrated in a diagram?

a. A medical study reports that eating chicken reduces the likelihood of suffering from particular types of heart problems.

b. A widespread bovine disease leads to an increase in the price of beef.

c. Average household income increases.

8 Consider the world supply of cocoa beans, the main input in the production of chocolate. For each of the events listed below, state and explain the likely effect on the supply of cocoa beans. How would each event be illustrated in a diagram?

a. Ideal growing conditions lead to a bumper crop of cocoa beans in Ivory Coast, the largest supplier of cocoa beans.

b. A dramatic rise in the world price of coffee beans. Assume that farmers growing cocoa beans can easily grow coffee beans instead.

c. Wages for farm labour in cocoa-growing regions rises.

d. Farmers in various parts of the world see profits being earned by cocoa farmers and choose to enter this industry.

9 For each of the following statements, determine whether there has been a change in supply or a change in quantity supplied. Draw a demand-and-supply diagram for each situation to show either a movement along the supply curve or a shift of the supply curve.

a. The price of Canadian-grown peaches skyrockets during an unusually cold summer that reduces the size of the peach harvest.

b. An increase in income leads to an increase in the price of family-restaurant meals and to an increase in their sales.

c. Technological improvements in electronic publishing lead to price reductions for e-books and an increase in e-book sales.

d. A low-carb diet becomes popular and leads to a reduction in the price of bread and less bread being sold.

10 Early in 2011, the world price of copper reached a record high of over $10 000 per tonne. Two events appeared to lie behind this high price. First, China's rapid economic growth and the massive building of infrastructure. Second, an explosion closed a major Chilean port used for shipping a substantial fraction of the world's copper output. Use a demand-and-supply diagram to illustrate these events in the copper market, and explain how each event shifts either the demand curve or the supply curve.

11 There has been rapid growth in the demand for the green leafy vegetable kale in recent years, as consumers learned of its health benefits. The demand curve has shifted significantly rightward. However, the price of a bunch of kale in the grocery store has been fairly stable. Draw a demand-and-supply diagram showing the market for kale, and explain how the price of kale could remain stable in the face of such an enormous growth in demand. (Hint: There are two possible scenarios in which the equilibrium price does not change.)

12 Consider the world market for wheat, in which Russia is a large producer. Suppose there is a major failure in Russia's wheat crop because of a severe drought. Explain the likely effect on the equilibrium price and quantity in the world wheat market. Also explain why Canadian wheat farmers certainly benefit from Russia's drought. The following diagrams provide a starting point for your analysis.

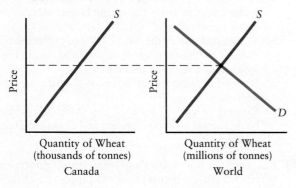

Quantity of Wheat
(thousands of tonnes)
Canada

Quantity of Wheat
(millions of tonnes)
World

PROBLEMS

13 The following table shows hypothetical demand schedules for sugar for three separate months. To help make the distinction between changes in demand and changes in quantity demanded, choose the wording to make each of the following statements correct.

	Quantity Demanded for Sugar (in kilograms)		
Price/kg	October	November	December
$1.50	11 000	10 500	13 000
1.75	10 000	9 500	12 000
2.00	9 000	8 500	11 000
2.25	8 000	7 500	10 000
2.50	7 000	6 500	9 000
2.75	6 000	5 500	8 000
3.00	5 000	4 500	7 000
3.25	4 000	3 500	6 000
3.50	3 000	2 500	5 000

a. When the price of sugar rises from $2.50 to $3.00 in the month of October there is a(n) (*increase/decrease*) in (*demand for/quantity demanded of*) sugar of 2000 kg.
b. We can say that the demand curve for sugar in December shifted (*to the right/to the left*) of November's demand curve. This represents a(n) (*increase/decrease*) in demand for sugar.
c. An increase in the demand for sugar means that quantity demanded at each price has (*increased/decreased*), while a decrease in demand for sugar means that quantity demanded at each price has (*increased/decreased*).
d. In the month of December, a price change for sugar from $3.50 to $2.75 per kilogram would mean a change in (*demand for/quantity demanded of*) sugar of 3000 kg.
e. Plot the three demand schedules on a graph and label each demand curve to indicate whether it is the demand for October, November, or December.

14 The following supply and demand schedules describe a hypothetical Canadian market for potash.

Price ($ per tonne)	Quantity Supplied (million tonnes)	Quantity Demanded (million tonnes)
280	8.5	12.5
300	9.0	11.0
320	9.5	9.5
340	10.0	8.0
360	10.5	6.5
380	11.0	5.0

a. What is the equilibrium price of potash?
b. How much potash would actually be purchased if the price were $280 per tonne?
c. How much potash would actually be sold if the price were $360 per tonne?
d. At a price of $280 per tonne, is there excess supply or demand? If so, how much?
e. At a price of $360 per tonne, is there excess supply or demand? If so, how much?
f. If the price is $280 per tonne, describe the forces that will cause the price to change.
g. If the price is $360 per tonne, describe the forces that will cause the price to change.

15 The following diagram describes the hypothetical demand and supply for canned tuna in Canada in 2019.

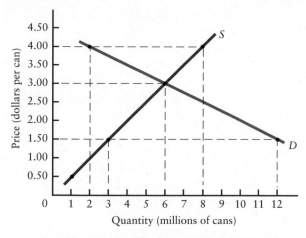

a. Suppose the price of a can of tuna is $4.00. What is the quantity demanded? What is the quantity supplied? At this price, is there a shortage or a surplus? By what amount?
b. Suppose the price of a can of tuna is $1.50. What is the quantity demanded? What is the quantity supplied? At this price, is there a shortage or a surplus? By what amount?
c. What is the equilibrium price and quantity in this market?

16 Consider the world market for a particular quality of coffee beans. The following table shows the demand and supply schedules for this market.

Price (per kilogram)	Quantity Demanded	Quantity Supplied
	(millions of kilograms per year)	
$2.00	28	10
$2.40	26	12
$2.60	24	15
$3.50	19.5	19.5
$3.90	17	22
$4.30	14.5	23.5

a. Plot the demand and supply schedules on a diagram.
b. Identify the amount of excess demand or supply associated with each price.
c. Identify the equilibrium price in this market.
d. Suppose that a collection of national governments were somehow able to set a minimum price for coffee equal to $3.90 per kilogram. Explain the outcome in the world coffee market.

17 Assume you have the following information for the global market for agricultural commodity X. For each scenario, use demand and supply analysis to provide a likely explanation for the change in market equilibrium. The prices are per bushel and the quantities are millions of bushels.

Scenario	August 2018	August 2019
a.	$p^* = \$142\ Q^* = 315$	$p^* = \$180\ Q^* = 315$
b.	$p^* = \$142\ Q^* = 315$	$p^* = \$128\ Q^* = 360$
c.	$p^* = \$142\ Q^* = 315$	$p^* = \$135\ Q^* = 275$
d.	$p^* = \$142\ Q^* = 315$	$p^* = \$142\ Q^* = 400$

18 This question requires you to solve a supply-and-demand model algebraically. Letting p be the price of the product, suppose the demand and supply functions for some product are given by

$$Q^D = 100 - 3p$$
$$Q^S = 10 + 2p$$

a. Plot both the demand curve and the supply curve.
b. What is the condition for equilibrium in this market?
c. By imposing the condition for equilibrium, solve for the equilibrium price.
d. Substitute the equilibrium price into either the demand or the supply function to solve for the equilibrium quantity. Check to make sure you get the same answer whether you use the demand function or the supply function.
e. Now suppose there is an increase in demand so that the new demand function is given by

$$Q^D = 180 - 3p$$

Compute the new equilibrium price and quantity. Is your result consistent with the "law" of demand?
f. Now suppose that with the new demand curve in place, there is an increase in supply so that the new supply function is given by $Q^S = 90 + 2p$. Compute the new equilibrium price and quantity.

19 Find the equilibrium price and quantity for each of the following pairs of demand and supply functions.

a. $Q^D = 10 - 2p$ $Q^S = 5 + 3p$
b. $Q^D = 1270 - 10p$ $Q^S = 1000 + 20p$
c. $Q^D = 100 - 0.25p$ $Q^S = 40 + 0.25p$
d. $Q^D = 6000 - 0.2p$ $Q^S = 4000 + 0.8p$
e. $Q^D = 10\ 000 - 100p$ $Q^S = 100p$

19

What Macroeconomics Is All About

CHAPTER OUTLINE	LEARNING OBJECTIVES (LO)
	After studying this chapter you will be able to
19.1 **KEY MACROECONOMIC VARIABLES**	1 define the key macroeconomic variables: national income, unemployment, productivity, inflation, interest rates, exchange rates, and net exports.
19.2 **GROWTH VERSUS FLUCTUATIONS**	2 understand that most macroeconomic issues are about either long-run growth or short-run fluctuations, and that government policy is relevant for both.

WHEREVER you get your news, it is almost impossible to avoid stories about the economy. Nearly every day there is some announcement about a change in the unemployment rate, a new forecast of economic growth, how a government policy will impact its budget deficit, or how stock-market fluctuations are causing central banks to adjust interest rates.

Nearly everyone cares about some aspect of these economic events. Workers are anxious to avoid the unemployment that comes with recessions and to share in the rising income that is brought about by productivity growth. Firms are concerned about how interest rates, changes in exchange rates, and foreign competition affect their profits. Consumers want to know how changes in interest rates affect mortgage payments and how changes in exchange rates affect the prices of the goods they purchase. Pensioners worry that inflation may erode the purchasing power of their fixed dollar incomes. Governments worry about budget deficits and about whether policies to reduce them will be unpopular with voters.

This chapter provides an introduction to many of these issues, including the many macroeconomic variables that we measure and track over time, what they mean, and how their fluctuations affect the lives of ordinary people.

macroeconomics The study of the determination of economic aggregates, such as total output, total employment, the price level, and the rate of economic growth.

Macroeconomics is the study of the behaviour and performance of the economy as a whole. Whereas the detail that occurs in individual markets is the concern of microeconomics, macroeconomics is concerned with the behaviour of economic *aggregates* and *averages*, such as total output, total investment, total exports, and the price level, and with how they may be influenced by government policy. Their behaviour results from activities in many different markets and from the combined behaviour of millions of different decision makers.

In return for suppressing some valuable detail about individual markets, studying macroeconomics allows us to view the big picture. When aggregate output rises, the output of many commodities and the incomes of many people rise with it. When the unemployment rate rises, many workers lose their jobs. When significant disruptions occur in the credit markets, interest rates rise and borrowers find it more difficult to finance their desired purchases. Such movements in economic aggregates matter for most individuals because they influence the health of the industries in which they work. Macroeconomic issues matter to people's lives, which explains their prominence in the news and public discussions, and why we study macroeconomics.

It will become clear as we proceed through this chapter (and later ones) that macroeconomists consider two different aspects of the economy. They think about the *short-run* behaviour of macroeconomic variables, such as output, employment, and inflation, and about how government policy can influence these variables. This concerns, among other things, the study of *business cycles*. They also examine the long-run behaviour of the same variables, especially the long-run path of aggregate output. This is the study of *economic growth* and is concerned with explaining how investment and technological change affect our material living standards over long periods of time.

A full understanding of macroeconomics requires understanding the nature of short-run fluctuations as well as the nature of long-run economic growth.

19.1 Key Macroeconomic Variables

In this chapter, we introduce several important macroeconomic variables, with an emphasis on what they mean and why they matter for our well-being. Here and in Chapter 20 we also explain how the key macroeconomic variables are measured. The remainder of this book is about the causes and consequences of changes in each of these variables, the many ways in which they interact, and the effects they have on our well-being.

National Product and National Income

The most comprehensive measure of a nation's overall level of economic activity is the value of its total production of goods and services, called *national product*, or sometimes just called *output*.

One of the most important ideas in economics is that the production of goods and services generates income.

As a matter of convention, economists define their terms so that, for the nation as a whole, all of the economic value that is produced ultimately belongs to someone in the form of an income claim on that value. For example, if a firm produces $100 worth of ice cream, that $100 becomes income for the firm's workers, the firm's suppliers of material inputs, and the firm's owners. The value of national product is *by definition* equal to the value of national income.

There are several related measures of a nation's total output and total income. Their various definitions, and the relationships among them, are discussed in detail in the next chapter. In this chapter, we use the generic term *national income* to refer to both the value of total output and the value of the income claims generated by the production of that output.

National Income: Aggregation   To measure national income we add up the *values* of the many different goods and services produced. We cannot add tonnes of steel to loaves of bread, but we can add the dollar value of steel production to the dollar value of bread production. We begin by multiplying the number of units of each good produced by the price at which each unit is sold. This yields a dollar value of production for each good. We then sum these values across all the different goods and services produced in the economy to give us the quantity of total output, or national income, *measured in dollars*. This is usually called **nominal national income**.

A change in nominal national income can be caused by a change in either the physical quantities or the prices at which they are sold. To determine the extent to which any change is due to quantities or to prices, economists calculate **real national income**. This measures the value of individual outputs, not at current prices, but at a set of prices that prevailed in some base period.

Nominal national income is often referred to as *current-dollar national income*. Real national income is often called *constant-dollar national income*. Real national income tells us the value of current output measured at constant prices—the sum of the quantities valued at prices that prevailed in the base period. Since prices are held constant when computing real national income, changes in real national income from one year to another reflect *only* changes in quantities. Comparing real national incomes of different years therefore provides a measure of the change in the quantity of output that has occurred during the intervening period.

National Income: Recent History   One of the most commonly used measures of national income is called *gross domestic product* (*GDP*). GDP can be measured in either real or nominal terms; we focus here on real GDP. The details of its calculation will be discussed in Chapter 20.

Part (i) of Figure 19-1 shows real national income produced by the Canadian economy since 1965; part (ii) shows its annual percentage change over the same period. Canadian GDP shows two kinds of movement. The major movement is a positive trend that increased real output by approximately four times since 1965. This is what economists refer to as *long-term economic growth*.

A second feature of real GDP that is less evident in part (i) is *short-term fluctuations* around the trend. Overall growth so dominates the real GDP series that the fluctuations are hardly visible in part (i) of Figure 19-1. However, as can be seen in part (ii), the growth of GDP has never been smooth. In most years, GDP increases, but in 1982, 1991, and 2009, GDP actually decreased, as shown by the negative rate of growth in the figure. Periods in which real GDP actually falls are called **recessions**.

nominal national income Total national income measured in current dollars. Also called *current-dollar national income*.

real national income National income measured in constant (base-period) dollars. It changes only when quantities change.

recession A fall in the level of real GDP. Often defined precisely as two consecutive quarters of negative growth in real GDP.

FIGURE 19-1   Growth and Fluctuations in Real GDP, 1965–2017

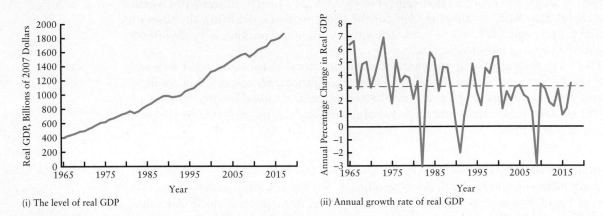

(i) The level of real GDP   (ii) Annual growth rate of real GDP

Real GDP measures the quantity of total output produced by the nation's economy during a year. Real GDP is plotted in part (i). With only a few interruptions, it has risen steadily since 1965, demonstrating the long-term growth of the Canadian economy. Short-term fluctuations are obscured by the long-term trend in part (i) but are highlighted in part (ii). The growth rate fluctuates considerably from year to year. The long-term upward trend in part (i) reflects the positive average annual growth rate of 3.1 percent in part (ii), shown by the dashed line.

(*Source:* Based on Statistics Canada, CANSIM database, Table 380-0106, Gross Domestic Product. www.statcan.gc.ca.)

business cycle Fluctuations of real national income around its trend value that follow a more or less wavelike pattern.

The **business cycle** refers to this continual ebb and flow of business activity that occurs around the long-term trend. For example, a single cycle will usually include an interval of quickly growing output, followed by an interval of slowly growing or even falling output. The entire cycle may last for several years. No two business cycles are exactly the same—variations occur in duration and magnitude. Some expansions are long and drawn out. Others come to an end before high employment and industrial capacity are reached. Nonetheless, fluctuations are similar enough that it is useful to identify common factors, as is done in *Applying Economic Concepts 19-1*.

Potential Output and the Output Gap   National output (or income) represents what the economy *actually* produces. An important related concept is the level of output the economy would produce if all resources—land, labour, and capital—were fully employed.[1] This concept is usually called **potential output**. The value of potential output must be estimated using statistical techniques, whereas the value of actual output can be measured directly. For this reason, there is often disagreement among researchers regarding the level of potential output, owing to their different estimation approaches. In terms of notation, we use Y to denote the economy's actual output and Y^* to denote potential output.

potential output (Y^*) The real GDP that the economy would produce if its productive resources were fully employed. Also called *potential GDP*.

output gap Actual output minus potential output, $Y - Y^*$.

The **output gap** measures the difference between potential output and actual output, and is computed as $Y - Y^*$. When actual output is less than potential output ($Y < Y^*$), the gap measures the market value of goods and services that are not

---

[1] *Full employment* refers to a situation in which the factor markets display neither excess demand nor excess supply. We say more about full employment shortly.

APPLYING ECONOMIC CONCEPTS 19-1

The Terminology of Business Cycles

The accompanying figure shows a stylized business cycle, with real GDP fluctuating around a steadily rising level of potential GDP—the economy's normal capacity to produce output. We begin our discussion of terminology with a trough.

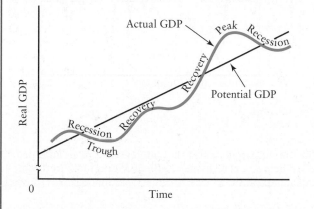

A *trough* is characterized by unemployed resources and a level of output that is low in relation to the economy's capacity to produce. There is a substantial amount of unused productive capacity. Business profits are low; for some individual companies, they are negative. Confidence about economic prospects in the immediate future is lacking, and, as a result, many firms are unwilling to risk making new investments.

The process of *recovery* moves the economy out of a trough. The characteristics of a recovery are many: rundown or obsolete equipment is replaced; employment, income, and consumer spending all begin to rise; and

expectations become more favourable. Investments that once seemed risky may be undertaken as firms become more optimistic about future business prospects. Production can be increased with relative ease merely by re-employing the existing unused capacity and unemployed labour.

Eventually the recovery comes to a *peak* at the top of the cycle. At the peak, existing capacity is used to a high degree; labour shortages may develop, particularly in categories of key skills, and shortages of essential raw materials are likely. As shortages develop, costs begin to rise, but because prices rise also, business remains profitable.

Peaks are eventually followed by slowdowns in economic activity. Sometimes this is just a slowing of the increase in income, while at other times the slowdown turns into a *recession*. A recession, or contraction, is a downturn in economic activity. Common usage defines a recession as a fall in real GDP for two successive quarters. As output falls, so do employment and household incomes. Profits drop, and some firms encounter financial difficulties. Investments that looked profitable with the expectation of continually rising income now appear unprofitable. It may not even be worth replacing capital equipment as it wears out because unused capacity is increasing steadily. In historical discussions, a recession that is deep and long lasting is often called a *depression*, such as the Great Depression in the early 1930s, during which aggregate output fell by 30 percent and the unemployment rate increased to 20 percent!

These terms are non-technical but descriptive: The entire falling half of the business cycle is often called a *slump*, and the entire rising half is often called a *boom*.

produced because the economy's resources are not fully employed. When Y is less than Y^*, the output gap is called a **recessionary gap**. When actual output exceeds potential output ($Y > Y^*$), the gap measures the market value of production in excess of what the economy can produce on a sustained basis. Y can exceed Y^* because workers may work longer hours than normal or factories may operate an extra shift. When Y exceeds Y^* there is often upward pressure on wages and prices, and thus we say the output gap is an **inflationary gap**.

Figure 19-2 shows the path of potential GDP since 1985. The upward trend reflects the growth in the productive capacity of the Canadian economy over this period, caused by increases in the labour force, capital stock, and the level of technological knowledge. The figure also shows actual GDP (reproduced from Figure 19-1), which has kept approximately in step with potential GDP. The distance between the two, which is the output gap, is plotted in part (ii) of Figure 19-2. Fluctuations in economic activity are apparent from fluctuations in the size of the output gap.

recessionary gap A situation in which actual output is less than potential output, $Y < Y^*$.

inflationary gap A situation in which actual output exceeds potential output, $Y > Y^*$.

FIGURE 19-2   Potential GDP and the Output Gap, 1985–2017

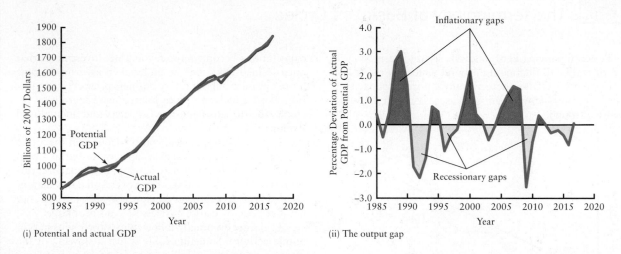

(i) Potential and actual GDP   (ii) The output gap

Potential and actual GDP both display an upward trend. The output gap measures the difference between an economy's potential output and its actual output; the gap is expressed here as a percentage of potential output. Since 1985, potential and actual GDP have almost doubled. The output gap in part (ii) shows clear fluctuations. Shaded areas show inflationary and recessionary gaps.

(*Source:* Real GDP based on Statistics Canada, CANSIM database, Table 380-0106; output gap based on www.bankofcanada.ca.)

Why National Income Matters   National income is an important measure of economic performance. Short-run movements in the business cycle receive the most attention in politics and in the press, but most economists agree that long-term growth—as reflected by the growth of *potential GDP*—is in many ways the more important of the two.

Recessions are associated with unemployment and lost output. When actual GDP is below potential GDP, economic waste and human suffering result from the failure to fully employ the economy's resources. Booms, although associated with high employment and high output, can bring problems of their own. When actual GDP exceeds potential GDP, inflationary pressure usually ensues, causing concern for any government committed to keeping inflation low.

The long-run trend in real *per capita* national income is an important determinant of improvements in a society's overall standard of living. When income per person grows, each generation can expect, on average, to be better off than preceding ones. For example, over the period shown in Figure 19-1, per capita income has grown at an average rate of about 1.5 percent per year. Even at such a modest growth rate, the average person's lifetime income will be about *twice* that of his or her grandparents.

Although economic growth makes people materially better off *on average*, it does not necessarily make *every* individual better off—the benefits of growth are never shared equally by all members of the population. For example, if growth involves significant changes in the structure of the economy, such as a shift away from agriculture and toward manufacturing (as happened in the first part of the twentieth century), or away from manufacturing and toward services (as has been happening for a few decades), then these changes will reduce some people's material living standards for extended periods of time.

Employment, Unemployment, and the Labour Force

National income and employment are closely related. If more output is to be produced, either more workers must be used in production or existing workers must produce more. The first change means a rise in employment; the second means a rise in output per person employed, which is a rise in *productivity*. In the short run, changes in productivity tend to be very small; most short-run changes in output are accomplished by changes in employment. Over the long run, however, changes in both productivity and employment are significant.

Employment denotes the number of adult workers (defined in Canada as workers aged 15 and over) who have jobs. **Unemployment** denotes the number of adult workers who are not employed but who are actively searching for a job. The **labour force** is the total number of people who are either employed or unemployed. The **unemployment rate** is the number of unemployed people expressed as a fraction of the labour force:

$$\text{Unemployment rate} = \frac{\text{Number of people unemployed}}{\text{Number of people in the labour force}} \times 100 \text{ percent}$$

The number of people unemployed in Canada is estimated from the Labour Force Survey conducted each month by Statistics Canada. People who are currently without a job but who say they have searched actively for one during the sample period are recorded as unemployed.

employment The number of persons 15 years of age or older who have jobs.

unemployment The number of persons 15 years of age or older who are not employed and are actively searching for a job.

labour force The number of persons employed plus the number of persons unemployed.

unemployment rate Unemployment expressed as a percentage of the labour force.

Frictional, Structural, and Cyclical Unemployment   When the economy is at potential GDP, economists say there is *full employment*. But for two reasons there will still be some unemployment even when the economy is at potential GDP.

First, there is a constant turnover of individuals in given jobs and a constant change in job opportunities. New people enter the workforce; some people quit their jobs; others are fired. It may take some time for these people to find jobs. So at any point in time, there is unemployment caused by the normal turnover of labour. Such unemployment is called *frictional unemployment*.

Second, because the economy is constantly adapting to shocks of various kinds, at any moment there will always be some mismatch between the characteristics of the labour force and the characteristics of the available jobs. The mismatch may occur, for example, because labour does not currently have the skills that are in demand or because labour is not in the region of the country where the demand is located. This is a mismatch between the *structure* of the supplies of labour and the *structure* of the demands for labour. Such unemployment is therefore called *structural unemployment*.

There is always some frictional unemployment due to natural turnover in the labour market, and some structural unemployment due to mismatch between jobs and workers. As a result, some unemployment exists even when the economy is at "full employment."

Full employment is said to occur when the *only* unemployment is frictional and structural, a situation that corresponds to actual GDP being equal to potential GDP. When actual GDP does not equal potential GDP, the economy is not at full employment.

In these situations there is some *cyclical* unemployment. Cyclical unemployment rises and falls with the ebb and flow of the business cycle.

Unemployment also has *seasonal* fluctuations. For example, workers employed in the fishing industry often are unemployed during the winter, and ski instructors may be unemployed in the summer. Because these seasonal fluctuations are relatively regular and easy to predict, Statistics Canada *seasonally adjusts* the unemployment statistics to remove these fluctuations, thereby revealing more clearly the cyclical and trend movements in the data. For example, suppose that, on average, the Canadian unemployment rate increases by 0.3 percentage points in December. Statistics Canada would then adjust the December unemployment rate so that it shows an increase only if the increase in the *unadjusted* rate exceeds 0.3 percentage points. In this way, the seasonally adjusted December unemployment rate is reported to increase only if unemployment rises by more than its normal seasonal increase. All the unemployment (and other macroeconomic) data shown in this book are seasonally adjusted.

Employment and Unemployment: Recent History Figure 19-3 shows the trends in the labour force, employment, and unemployment since 1960. Despite booms and slumps, employment has grown roughly in line with the growth in the labour force. Although the long-term trend dominates the employment data, the figure also shows that the short-term fluctuations in the unemployment rate have been substantial. The unemployment

FIGURE 19-3   Labour Force, Employment, and Unemployment, 1960–2018

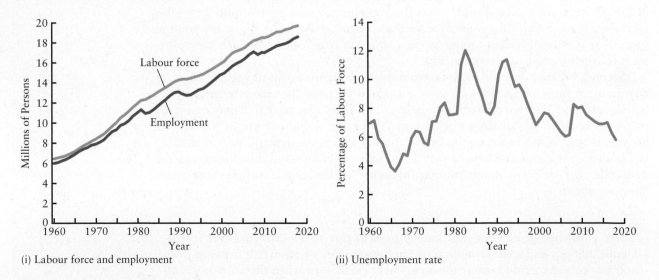

(i) Labour force and employment   (ii) Unemployment rate

The labour force and employment have grown since 1960 with only a few interruptions. The unemployment rate responds to the cyclical behaviour of the economy. The labour force and the level of employment in Canada have both tripled since 1960. Booms are associated with a low unemployment rate and slumps with a high unemployment rate.

(*Source:* Based on data from Statistics Canada's CANSIM database, Table 282-0002, Labour Force Survey estimates.)

rate has been as low as 3.4 percent in 1966 and as high as 12 percent during the deep recession of 1982.

Why Unemployment Matters   The social significance of unemployment is enormous because it involves economic waste and human suffering. Human effort is the least durable of economic commodities. If a fully employed economy has 18 million people who are willing to work, their services must either be used this year or wasted. When only 16 million people are actually employed, one year's potential output of 2 million workers is lost forever. Such a waste of potential output is cause for concern.

The loss of income associated with unemployment is clearly harmful to individuals. In some cases, the loss of income pushes people into poverty. But this lost income does not capture the full cost of unemployment. A person's spirit can be broken by a long period of unsuccessfully searching for work. Research has shown that crime, mental illness, and general social unrest tend to be associated with long-term unemployment.

In the not-so-distant past, only personal savings, private charity, or help from friends and relatives stood between the unemployed and starvation. Today, employment insurance and social assistance ("welfare") have created a safety net, particularly when unemployment is for short periods, as is most often the case in Canada. However, when an economic slump lasts long enough, some unfortunate people exhaust their employment insurance and lose part of that safety net. Short-term unemployment can be a feasible though difficult adjustment for many; long-term unemployment can be a disaster.

Productivity

Figure 19-1 shows that Canadian real GDP has increased relatively steadily for many years, reflecting steady growth in the country's productive capacity. This long-run growth has had three general sources. First, as shown in Figure 19-3, the level of employment has increased significantly. Rising employment generally results from a rising population, but at times is also explained by an increase in the proportion of the population that chooses to participate in the labour force. Second, Canada's stock of physical capital—the buildings, factories, and machines used to produce output—has increased more or less steadily over time. Third, *productivity* in Canada has increased in almost every year since 1960.

Productivity is a measure of the amount of output that the economy produces per unit of input. Since there are many inputs to production—land, labour, and capital—we can have several different measures of productivity. One commonly used measure is **labour productivity**, which is the amount of real GDP produced per unit of labour employed. The amount of labour employed can be measured either as the total number of employed workers or by the total number of hours worked.

labour productivity The level of real GDP divided by the level of employment (or total hours worked).

Productivity: Recent History   Figure 19-4 shows two measures of Canadian labour productivity since 1976. The first is the amount of real GDP per employed worker (expressed in thousands of 2007 dollars). In 2017, real GDP per employed worker was $100 175. The second measure shows the amount of real GDP per *hour worked* (expressed in 2007 dollars). In 2017, real GDP per hour worked was $58.17.

FIGURE 19-4   Canadian Labour Productivity, 1976–2017

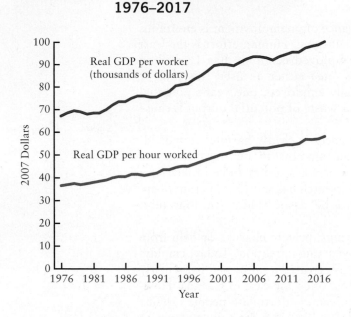

The second is a more accurate measure of productivity because the average number of hours worked per employed worker changes over time. In addition to fluctuating over the business cycle, it has shown a long-term decline, from about 1820 hours per year in 1976 to about 1720 hours per year in 2017. The second measure of productivity takes account of these changes in hours worked, whereas the first measure does not.

One pattern is immediately apparent for both measures of productivity. There has been a significant increase in labour productivity over the past four decades. Real GDP per employed worker increased by 49 percent from 1976 to 2017, an annual average growth rate of 0.98 percent. Real GDP per hour worked increased by 59 percent over the same period, an annual average growth rate of 1.1 percent.

Rising labour productivity is an important contributor to rising material living standards. The figure shows two measures of labour productivity: real GDP per employed worker and real GDP per hour worked. The first is expressed in *thousands* of 2007 dollars per worker and has increased at an average annual rate of 0.98 percent. The second is expressed in 2007 dollars per hour and has grown at the annual rate of 1.1 percent.

(*Source:* Based on data from Statistics Canada's CANSIM database. Real GDP: Table 380-0106. Total weekly hours worked: Table 282-0028. Employment: Table 282-0002.)

Why Productivity Matters   Productivity growth is the single largest cause of rising material living standards over long periods of time. Over periods of a few years, changes in average real incomes have more to do with the ebb and flow of the business cycle than with changes in productivity; increases in employment during an economic recovery and reductions in employment during recessions explain much of the short-run movements in average real incomes. As is clear from Figure 19-1, however, these short-run fluctuations are dwarfed over the long term by the steady upward trend in real GDP—an upward trend that comes in large part from rising productivity.

Why is the real income for an average Canadian this year so much greater than it was for the average Canadian 50 or 100 years ago? Most of the answer lies in the fact that the Canadian worker today is vastly more productive than was his or her counterpart in the distant past. This greater productivity comes partly from the better physical capital with which Canadians now work and partly from their greater skills. The higher productivity for today's workers explains why their *real incomes* (the purchasing power of their earnings) are so much higher than for workers in the past.

The close connection between productivity growth and rising material living standards explains the importance that is now placed on understanding the determinants of productivity growth. It is a very active area of economic research, but there are still many unanswered questions. In Chapter 25 we address the process of long-run growth in real GDP and explore the determinants of productivity growth.

Inflation and the Price Level

Inflation means that prices of goods and services are going up, *on average*. If you are a typical reader of this book, inflation has not been very noticeable during your lifetime. When your parents were your age, however, high inflation was a major economic problem. (Some countries have had their economies almost ruined by very high inflation, called *hyperinflation*. We will say more about this in Chapter 26.)

For studying inflation, there are two related but different concepts that are sometimes confused, and it is important to get them straight. The first is the **price level**, which refers to the average level of all prices in the economy and is given by the symbol P. The second is the rate of **inflation**, which is the rate at which the price level is rising.

To measure the price level, the economic statisticians at Statistics Canada construct a *price index*, which averages the prices of various goods and services according to how important they are. The best-known price index in Canada is the **Consumer Price Index (CPI)**, which measures the average price of the goods and services bought by the typical Canadian household. *Applying Economic Concepts 19-2* shows how a price index such as the CPI is constructed.

As we saw in Chapter 2, a price index is a pure number—it does not have any units. Yet as we all know, prices in Canada are expressed in dollars. When we construct a price index, the units (dollars) are eliminated because the price index shows the price of a basket of goods at some specific time *relative to the price of the same basket of goods in some base period*. Currently, the base year for Statistics Canada's calculation of the CPI is 2002, which means that the price of the basket of goods is set to be 100 in 2002. If the CPI in December 2017 is computed to be 131.7, the meaning is that the price of the basket of goods is 31.7 percent higher in 2017 than in 2002.

> **price level** The average level of all prices in the economy, expressed as an index number.

> **inflation** A rise in the average level of all prices (the price level).

> **Consumer Price Index (CPI)** An index of the average prices of goods and services commonly bought by households.

Since the price level is measured with an index number, its value at any specific time has meaning only when it is compared with its value at some other time.

By allowing us to compare the general price level at different times, a price index, such as the CPI, also allows us to measure the rate of inflation. For example, the value of the CPI in April 2018 was 133.8 and in April 2017 it was 130.4. The *rate of inflation* during that one-year period, expressed in percentage terms, is equal to the change in the price level divided by the initial price level, times 100:

$$\text{Rate of inflation} = \frac{133.8 - 130.4}{130.4} \times 100 \text{ percent}$$

$$= 2.6 \text{ percent}$$

Inflation: Recent History   The rate of inflation in Canada is currently around 2 percent per year and has been near that level since the early 1990s. But during the 1970s and 1980s inflation in Canada was both high and unpredictable from year to year. It was a serious macroeconomic problem.

Figure 19-5 shows the CPI and the inflation rate (measured by the annual rate of change in the CPI) from 1960 to 2018. What can we learn from this figure? First, we learn that the price level has not fallen at all since 1960 (in fact, the last time it fell was in 1953, and even then it fell only slightly). The cumulative effect of this sequence of repeated increases in the price level is quite dramatic: By 2018, the price level was more

APPLYING ECONOMIC CONCEPTS 19-2

How the CPI Is Constructed

Although the details are somewhat more complicated, the basic idea behind the Consumer Price Index is straightforward, as is illustrated by the following hypothetical example.

Suppose we want to discover what has happened to the overall cost of living for typical university students. Assume that a survey of student behaviour in 2009 shows that the average university student consumed only three goods—pizza, coffee, and photocopying—and spent a total of $200 a month on these items, as shown in Table 1.

TABLE 1   Expenditure Behaviour in 2009

Product	Price	Quantity per Month	Expenditure per Month
Photocopies	$0.10 per sheet	140 sheets	$14.00
Pizza	8.00 per pizza	15 pizzas	120.00
Coffee	0.75 per cup	88 cups	66.00
Total expenditure			$200.00

By 2019 in this example, the price of photocopying has fallen to 5 cents per copy, the price of pizza has increased to $9.00, and the price of coffee has increased to $1.00. What has happened to the cost of living over this 10-year period? In order to find out, we calculate the cost of purchasing the 2009 bundle of goods at the prices that prevailed in 2019, as shown in Table 2.

The total expenditure required to purchase the bundle of goods that cost $200.00 in 2009 has risen to $230.00. The increase in required expenditure is $30.00, which is a 15 percent increase over the original $200.00.

If we define 2009 as the base year for the "student price index" and assign an index value of 100 to the cost of the average student's expenditure in that year, the value of the index in 2019 is 115. Thus, goods and services that cost $100.00 in the base year cost $115.00 in 2019, exactly what is implied by Table 2.

TABLE 2   2009 Expenditure Behaviour at 2019 Prices

Product	Price	Quantity per Month	Expenditure per Month
Photocopies	$0.05 per sheet	140 sheets	$7.00
Pizza	9.00 per pizza	15 pizzas	135.00
Coffee	1.00 per cup	88 cups	88.00
Total expenditure			$230.00

The Consumer Price Index, as constructed by Statistics Canada, is built on exactly the same principles as the preceding example. In the case of the CPI, many thousands of consumers are surveyed, and the prices of thousands of products are monitored, but the basic method is the same:

1. Survey the consumption behaviour of consumers.
2. Calculate the cost of the goods and services purchased by the average consumer in the year in which the original survey was done. Define this as the base period of the index.
3. Calculate the cost of purchasing the same bundle of goods and services in other years.
4. Divide the result of Step 3 (in each year) by the result of Step 2, and multiply by 100. The result is the value of the CPI for each year.

The CPI is not a perfect measure of the cost of living because it does not automatically account for ongoing quality improvements or for changes in consumers' expenditure patterns. Changes of this type require the underlying survey of consumer expenditure to be updated from time to time to make sure that the expenditure patterns in the survey more closely match consumers' actual expenditure patterns.

than six times as high as it was in 1960. In other words, you now pay more than $6 for what cost $1 in 1960. The second thing we learn is that, although the price level appears in the figure to be smoothly increasing, the rate of inflation is actually quite volatile. The increases in the inflation rate into double-digit levels in 1974 and 1979 were associated with major increases in the world prices of oil and foodstuffs and with loose monetary policy. The declines in inflation in the early 1980s and 1990s were delayed responses to major recessions, which were themselves brought about to a large extent by policy actions designed to reduce the existing inflation. (We will say much more about this in Chapters 28 and 29.)

Why Inflation Matters   Money is the universal yardstick in our economy. This does not mean that we care only about money—it means simply that we measure *economic values* in terms of money, and we use money to conduct our economic affairs. Things as diverse as wages, share values in the stock market, the value of a house, and a university's financial endowment are all stated in terms of money. We value money, however, not for itself but for what we can purchase with it. The terms **purchasing power of money** and *real value of money* refer to the amount of goods and services that can be purchased with a given amount of money. The purchasing power of money is negatively related to the price level. For example, if the price level doubles, a dollar will buy only half as much, whereas if the price level halves, a dollar will buy twice as much. Inflation reduces the real value of anything whose *nominal value* is *fixed* in dollar terms. Thus, the real value of a $20 bill, a savings account, or the balance that is owed on a student loan is reduced by inflation.

> **Inflation reduces the purchasing power of money. It also reduces the real value of any sum fixed in nominal (dollar) terms.**

When analyzing the effects of inflation, economists usually make the distinction between *anticipated* and *unanticipated* inflation. If households and firms fully anticipate inflation over the coming year, they will be able to adjust many nominal prices and wages so as to maintain their real values. In this case, inflation will have fewer real effects on the economy than if it comes unexpectedly. For example, if both workers and firms expect 2 percent inflation over the coming year, they can agree to increase nominal wages by 2 percent, thus leaving wages constant in real terms.

Unanticipated inflation, on the other hand, generally leads to more changes in the real value of prices and wages. Suppose workers and firms expect 2 percent inflation

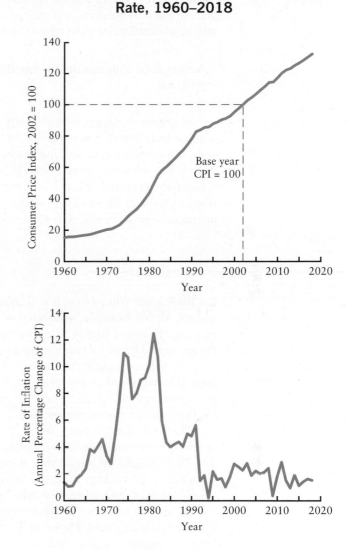

FIGURE 19-5   The Price Level and the Inflation Rate, 1960–2018

The rate of inflation measures the annual rate of increase in the price level. The trend in the price level has been upward over the past half-century. The rate of inflation has varied from almost 0 to more than 12 percent since 1960.

(*Source:* Based on data from Statistics Canada's CANSIM database, Table 326-0020, monthly seasonally adjusted consumer price index. The figures shown are annual averages of the monthly data.)

purchasing power of money The amount of goods and services that can be purchased with a unit of money.

and they increase nominal wages accordingly. If actual inflation ends up being 5 percent, real wages will be reduced and the quantities of labour demanded by firms and supplied by workers will change. As a result, the economy's allocation of resources will be affected more than when the inflation is correctly anticipated.

> **Anticipated inflation has a smaller effect on the economy than unanticipated inflation.**

In reality, inflation is rarely fully anticipated or fully unanticipated. Usually there is some inflation that is expected but also some that comes as a surprise. As a result, some adjustments in wages and prices are made by firms, workers, and consumers, but not all the adjustments that would be required to leave the economy's allocation of resources unaffected. We will see later, in our discussions of monetary policy and inflation in Chapters 28 and 29, how the distinction between anticipated and unanticipated inflation helps us to understand the costs associated with *reducing* inflation.

Interest Rates

If a bank lends you money, it will charge you *interest* for the privilege of borrowing the money. If, for example, you borrow $1000 today, repayable in one year's time, you may also be asked to pay $6.67 per month in interest. This makes $80 in interest over the year, which can be expressed as an interest rate of 8 percent per annum.

The **interest rate** is the price that is paid to borrow money for a stated period of time. It is expressed as a percentage amount per year per dollar borrowed. For example, an interest rate of 8 percent per year means that the borrower must pay 8 cents per year for every dollar that is borrowed.

There are many interest rates. A bank will lend money to a large business customer at a lower rate than it will lend money to you—there is a lower risk of not being repaid. The rate charged on a loan that is not to be repaid for a long time will usually differ from the rate on a loan that is to be repaid quickly.

When economists speak of "the" interest rate, they mean a rate that is typical of all the various interest rates in the economy. Dealing with only one interest rate suppresses much interesting detail. However, because interest rates usually rise and fall together, at least for major changes, following the movement of one rate allows us to consider changes in the general level of interest rates. The *prime interest rate*, the rate that banks charge to their best business customers, is noteworthy because when the prime rate changes, most other rates change in the same direction. Another high-profile interest rate is the *bank rate*, the interest rate that the Bank of Canada (Canada's central bank) charges on short-term loans to commercial banks such as the Royal Bank or the Bank of Montreal. The interest rate that the Canadian government pays on its short-term borrowing is also a rate that garners considerable attention.

Interest Rates and Inflation   How does inflation affect interest rates? To begin developing an answer, imagine that your friend lends you $100 and that the loan is repayable in one year. The amount you pay her for making this loan, measured in dollar terms, is determined by the **nominal interest rate**. If you pay her $108 in one year's time, $100 will be repayment of the amount of the loan (which is called the *principal*) and $8 will be payment of the interest. In this case, the nominal interest rate is 8 percent per year.

interest rate The price paid per dollar borrowed per period of time, expressed either as a proportion (e.g., 0.06) or as a percentage (e.g., 6 percent).

nominal interest rate The price paid per dollar borrowed per period of time.

How much purchasing power has your friend gained or lost by making this loan? The answer depends on what happens to the price level during the year. The more the price level rises, the worse off your friend will be and the better the transaction will be for you. This result occurs because the more the price level rises, the less valuable are the dollars that you use to repay the loan. The **real interest rate** measures the return on a loan in terms of purchasing power.

If the price level remains constant over the year, the real rate of interest your friend earns would also be 8 percent, because she can buy 8 percent more goods and services with the $108 you repay her than with the $100 she lent you. However, if the price level rises by 8 percent, the real rate of interest would be zero because the $108 you repay her buys the same quantity of goods as the $100 she originally gave up. If she is unlucky enough to lend money at 8 percent in a year in which prices rise by 10 percent, the real rate of interest she earns is −2 percent. The repayment of $108 will purchase 2 percent fewer goods and services than the original loan of $100.

> **real interest rate** The nominal rate of interest adjusted for the change in the purchasing power of money. Equal to the nominal interest rate minus the rate of inflation.

The burden of borrowing depends on the real, not the nominal, rate of interest.

For example, a nominal interest rate of 8 percent combined with a 2 percent rate of inflation (a real rate of 6 percent) is a much greater real burden on borrowers than a nominal rate of 16 percent combined with a 14 percent rate of inflation (a real rate of 2 percent). Figure 19 6 shows the nominal and real interest rates paid on short-term government borrowing since 1965.

Why Interest Rates Matter Changes in real interest rates affect the standard of living of savers and borrowers. Many retirees, for example, rely on interest earnings from their stock of accumulated assets to provide much of their income, and thus benefit when real interest rates rise. In contrast, borrowers are made better off with low real interest rates. This point was dramatically illustrated during the 1970s when homeowners who had long-term fixed-rate mortgages benefited tremendously from several years of high and largely unanticipated inflation, which resulted in *negative* real interest rates (see Figure 19-6).

Interest rates also matter for the economy as a whole. As we will see in Chapter 21, real interest rates are an important determinant of the level of investment by firms. Changes in real interest rates lead to changes in the

FIGURE 19-6 Real and Nominal Interest Rates, 1965–2018

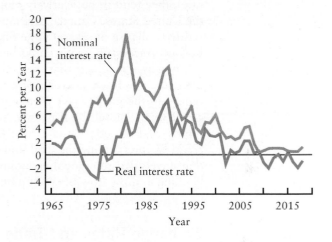

The real interest rate has been less than the nominal interest rate over the past five decades due to the presence of inflation. The data for the nominal interest rate show the average rate on three-month Treasury bills in each year since 1965. The real interest rate is calculated as the nominal interest rate minus the actual rate of inflation over the same period. Through the early 1970s, the real interest rate was negative, indicating that the inflation rate exceeded the nominal interest rate. The 1980s saw real interest rates rise as high as 8 percent. Since then, real rates have declined again to levels closer to the long-term historical average. With the onset of the major global recession in 2008, both real and nominal interest rates fell below their long-term averages.

(*Source:* Based on nominal interest rate: 3-month Treasury bill rate, Statistics Canada, CANSIM database, Table 176-0043. Real interest rate is based on Statistics Canada, Table 326-0020.)

cost of borrowing and thus to changes in firms' investment plans. Such changes in the level of desired investment have important consequences for the level of economic activity. We will see in Chapters 27 and 28 how the Bank of Canada influences interest rates as part of its objective of controlling inflation.

Interest Rates and "Credit Flows"   A loan represents a flow of credit between lenders and borrowers, with the interest rate representing the price of this credit. Credit is essential to the healthy functioning of a modern economy. Most firms require credit at some point—to finance the construction of a factory, to purchase inventories of intermediate inputs, or to continue paying their workers in a regular fashion even though their revenues may arrive at irregular intervals. Most households also require credit at various times—to finance the purchase of a home or car or to finance a child's university education.

Banks play a crucial role in the economy by *intermediating* between those households and firms that have available funds and those households and firms that require funds. In other words, banks play a key role in "making the credit market"—in channelling the funds from those who have them to those who need them.

During normal times, these credit markets function very smoothly and most of us notice little about them. While there are fluctuations in the price of credit (the interest rate), they tend to be relatively modest. In the fall of 2008, however, credit markets in the United States, Canada, and most other countries were thrown into turmoil by the sudden collapse of several large financial institutions, mainly in the United States and Europe. As a result, many banks became reluctant to lend to any but the safest borrowers, mostly out of fear that the borrowers would go bankrupt before they could repay the loan. The flows of credit slowed sharply and market interest rates spiked upward, reflecting the greater risk premium required by lenders. The reduction in the flow of credit was soon felt by firms who needed credit in order to finance material or labour inputs, and the effect was a reduction in production and employment. This *financial crisis*, by interrupting the vital flows of credit, was an important cause of the recession that enveloped the global economy in late 2008 and through 2009. We will discuss banking and the flow of credit in more detail in Chapter 26.

Exchange Rates and Trade Flows

Two important variables reflecting the importance of the global economy to Canada are the *exchange rate* and *trade flows*.

The Exchange Rate   If you are going on a holiday to France, you will need euros to pay for your purchases. Many of the larger banks, as well as any foreign-exchange office, will make the necessary exchange of currencies for you; they will sell you euros in return for your Canadian dollars. If you get 0.66 euros for each dollar that you give up, the two currencies are trading at a rate of 1 dollar = 0.66 euros or, expressed another way, 1 euro = 1.52 dollars. This was, in fact, the actual rate of exchange between the Canadian dollar and the euro in June of 2018.

As our example shows, the exchange rate can be defined either as dollars per euro or euros per dollar. In this book we adopt the convention of defining the **exchange rate** between the Canadian dollar and any foreign currency as the number of Canadian dollars required to purchase one unit of foreign currency.

exchange rate The number of units of domestic currency required to purchase one unit of foreign currency.

The exchange rate is the number of Canadian dollars required to purchase one unit of foreign currency.[2]

The term **foreign exchange** refers to foreign currencies or claims on foreign currencies, such as bank deposits, cheques, and promissory notes, that are payable in foreign money. The **foreign-exchange market** is the market in which currencies are traded—at a price expressed by the exchange rate.

Depreciation and Appreciation A rise in the exchange rate means that it takes *more* Canadian dollars to purchase one unit of foreign currency—this is a **depreciation** of the Canadian dollar. Conversely, a fall in the exchange rate means that it takes *fewer* Canadian dollars to purchase one unit of foreign currency—this is an **appreciation** of the dollar.

Figure 19-7 shows the path of the Canadian–U.S. exchange rate since 1970. Since more than 75 percent of Canada's trade is with the United States, this is the exchange rate most often discussed and analyzed in Canada. In countries with trade more evenly spread across several trading partners, more attention is paid to what is called a *trade-weighted exchange rate*—this is a weighted-average exchange rate between the home country and its trading partners, where the weights reflect each partner's share in the home country's total trade. In Canada, the path of such a trade-weighted exchange rate is virtually identical to the Canadian–U.S. exchange rate shown in Figure 19-7, reflecting the very large proportion of total Canadian trade with the United States.

As we will see in later chapters, both domestic policy and external events have important effects on the Canadian exchange rate. For example, most economists believe that the appreciation of the Canadian dollar between 1986 and 1992 was caused in part by the Bank of Canada's efforts to reduce the rate of inflation. The Bank's policy was controversial at the time, not least because of the effect it had on the exchange rate and the many export-oriented firms that were harmed by Canada's strong dollar. We examine the link between monetary policy and exchange rates in detail in Chapters 27 and 28.

FIGURE 19-7 Canadian–U.S. Dollar Exchange Rate, 1970–2018

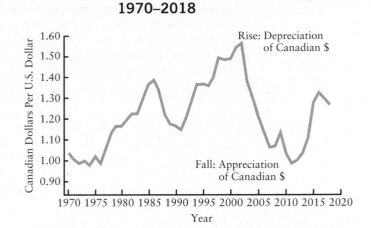

The **Canadian–U.S. exchange rate has been quite volatile over the past four decades.** The Canadian-dollar price of one U.S. dollar increased from just over $1 in the early 1970s to over $1.55 in 2002, a long-term depreciation of the Canadian dollar. By 2012 the Canadian dollar had appreciated and it again cost about $1 to purchase one U.S. dollar. Between 2012 and 2018, the Canadian dollar depreciated against the U.S. dollar again, by about 25 percent.

(*Source:* Based on annual average of monthly data, Statistics Canada, CANSIM database, Table 176-0084.)

foreign exchange Foreign currencies that are traded on the foreign-exchange market.

foreign-exchange market The market in which different national currencies are traded.

depreciation A rise in the exchange rate—it takes more units of domestic currency to purchase one unit of foreign currency.

appreciation A fall in the exchange rate—it takes fewer units of domestic currency to purchase one unit of foreign currency.

---

[2] The media often use a reverse definition of the exchange rate—the number of units of foreign currency that can be purchased with one Canadian dollar. It is up to the student, then, to examine carefully the definition that is being used by a particular writer or speaker. In this book the exchange rate is defined as the number of Canadian dollars required to purchase one unit of foreign currency because this measure emphasizes that foreign currency, like any other good or service, has a price in terms of Canadian dollars. In this case, the price has a special name—the exchange rate.

The depreciation of the Canadian dollar in the late 1990s is thought by most economists to have resulted from a nearly 30 percent decline in the world prices of commodities, many of which are important Canadian exports. The appreciation of the Canadian dollar during the 2002–2012 period was associated with sharp increases in commodity prices. In both cases, the commodity prices were being driven by changes in global economic growth, illustrating the important point that events in faraway lands can have dramatic effects on the Canadian exchange rate. We examine the link between world commodity prices and the Canadian exchange rate in Chapter 34.

Trade Flows: Exports and Imports   Canada has long been a trading nation, buying many goods and services from other countries—Canada's *imports*—and also selling many goods and services to other countries—Canada's *exports*. Figure 19-8 shows the dollar value of Canada's exports, imports, and *net exports* since 1970. Net exports are the difference between exports and imports and are often called the *trade balance*.

FIGURE 19-8   Canadian Imports, Exports, and Net Exports, 1970–2017

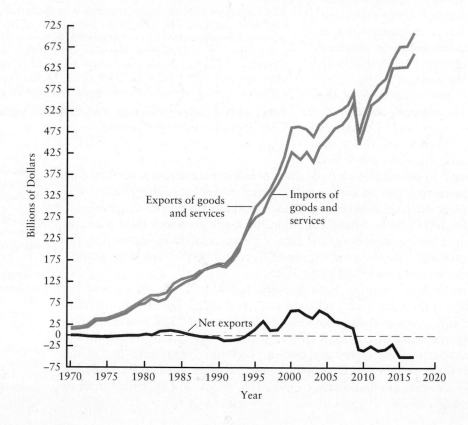

Though imports and exports have increased dramatically over the past four decades, the trade balance has remained roughly in balance. The nominal values of imports and exports rose steadily over the past few decades because of both price increases and quantity increases. The growth of trade increased sharply after the early 1990s. The trade balance—net exports—is usually close to zero.

(*Source:* Based on Statistics Canada, CANSIM database, Table 380-0064.)

Canadian exports and imports have increased fairly closely in step with each other over the past 45 years. The trade balance has therefore fluctuated mildly over the years, but it has stayed relatively small, especially when viewed as a proportion of total GDP.

Also apparent in Figure 19-8 is that Canadian trade flows (both imports and exports) began to grow more quickly after 1990. The increased importance of international trade is largely due to the Canada–U.S. Free Trade Agreement, which began in 1989, and to the North American Free Trade Agreement (which added Mexico), which began in 1994. Note also the sharp decline in both exports and imports in 2009–2010, a result of the global economic recession that occurred at that time.

In Chapters 32 and 33 we will examine the details of why international trade is beneficial for the countries who engage in it, and also some of the challenges created for individual workers and firms exposed to the pressures of international competition. We will also examine trade *policy*, with an emphasis on NAFTA, the future of which was called into question after newly elected U.S. President Donald Trump promised to re-negotiate the agreement during 2018.

19.2 Growth Versus Fluctuations

This chapter has provided a quick tour through macroeconomics and has introduced you to many important macroeconomic issues. If you take a few moments to flip again through the figures in this chapter, you will notice that most of the macroeconomic variables that we discussed are characterized by both *long-run trends* and *short-run fluctuations*.

Figure 19-1, which shows the path of real GDP, provides an excellent example of both characteristics. The figure shows that real GDP has increased by over four times since 1965—this is substantial *economic growth*. The figure also shows considerable year-to-year *fluctuations* in the growth rate of GDP.

An important theme in this book is that a full understanding of macroeconomics requires an understanding of both long-run growth and short-run fluctuations. As we proceed through this book, we will see that these two characteristics of modern economies have different sources and explanations. And that the government's macroeconomic policies have roles to play in both.

Long-Term Economic Growth

Both total output and output per person have risen for many decades in most industrial countries. These long-term trends have meant rising average living standards. Although long-term growth gets less attention in the media than current economic developments, it has considerably more importance for a society's living standards from decade to decade and from generation to generation.

There is considerable debate regarding the ability of government policy to influence the economy's long-run rate of growth. Some economists believe that a policy designed to keep inflation low and stable will contribute to the economy's growth. Some, however, believe there are dangers from having inflation too low—that a moderate inflation rate is more conducive to growth than a very low inflation rate.

Many economists also believe that when governments spend less than they raise in tax revenue—and thus have a budget surplus—the reduced need for borrowing drives down interest rates and stimulates investment by the private sector. Such increases in investment imply a higher stock of physical capital available for future production and thus an increase in economic growth. Do government budget surpluses increase future growth? Or do budget surpluses have no effect at all on the economy's future ability to produce? We address this important debate in Chapter 31.

There is also growing debate about whether economic growth generates excessive costs in terms of resource depletion and environmental damage. Many economists think that with appropriate policies we can have continued growth without damaging the environment; others argue that our long-term future is only sustainable with an intentional *reduction* in the size of the economy. We explore this contentious issue further in Chapter 25.

Finally, there is active debate regarding the appropriate role of the government in developing new technologies. Some economists believe that the private sector, left on its own, can produce inventions and innovation that will guarantee a satisfactory rate of long-term growth. Others point out that almost all of the major new technologies of the last 75 years were initially supported by public funds: The electronic computer was the creation of governments in the Second World War, miniaturized equipment came from the race to the moon, the Internet came from military communications research, the U.S. software industry was created by the U.S. Department of Defense, much of the early work on biotechnology came out of publicly funded research laboratories in universities and government institutions, and so on. The debate about the place of government in helping to foster inventions and innovations of truly fundamental technologies is an ongoing and highly important one.

Short-Term Fluctuations

Short-run fluctuations in economic activity, like the ones shown in part (ii) of Figure 19-1, lead economists to study the causes of *business cycles*. What caused the Great Depression in the 1930s, when almost one-fifth of the Canadian labour force was out of work and massive unemployment plagued all major industrial countries? Why did the Canadian economy begin a significant recession in 1990–1991, from which recovery was initially very gradual? What explains why, by 2007, the Canadian unemployment rate was lower than it had been in more than 30 years? What caused the deep worldwide recession that began in 2008?

Understanding business cycles requires an understanding of monetary policy—the Bank of Canada's policy with respect to the quantity of money that it makes available to the whole economy. Most economists agree that the increase in inflation in the 1970s and early 1980s was related to monetary policy, though they also agree that other events were partly responsible. When the Bank of Canada implemented a policy in the early 1990s designed to reduce inflation, was it merely a coincidence that a significant recession followed? Most economists think not, though they also think that the slowdown in the U.S. economy was an important contributor to Canada's recession. Chapters 28 and 29 focus on how the Bank of Canada uses its policy to influence the level of economic activity.

Government budget deficits and surpluses also enter the discussion of business cycles. Some economists think that, in recessionary years, the government ought to increase spending (and reduce taxes) in an effort to stimulate economic activity. Similarly, they believe that spending should be slowed or taxes should be raised to slow down a booming economy. Indeed, several government policies, from income taxation to employment insurance, are designed to mitigate the short-term fluctuations in national income. Other economists believe that the government cannot successfully "fine-tune" the economy by making frequent changes in spending and taxing because our knowledge of how the economy works is imperfect and because such policies tend to be imprecise. We address these issues in Chapters 22, 23, and 24.

What Lies Ahead?

There is much work to be done before any of these interesting policy debates can be discussed in more detail. Like firms that invest now to increase their production in the future, the next few chapters of this book will be an investment for you—an investment in understanding basic macro theory. The payoff will come when you are able to use a coherent model of the economy to analyze and debate some of the key macro issues of the day.

We begin in Chapter 20 by discussing the measurement of GDP. National income accounting is not exciting but is essential to a complete understanding of the chapters that follow. We then proceed to build a simple model of the economy to highlight some key macroeconomic relationships. As we proceed through the book, we modify the model, step by step, making it ever more realistic. With each step we take, more of today's controversial policy issues come within the grasp of our understanding. We hope that by the time you get to the end of the book, you will have developed some of the thrill for analyzing macroeconomic issues that we feel. Good luck, and enjoy the journey!

SUMMARY

19.1 Key Macroeconomic Variables   LO 1

- The value of the total production of goods and services in a country is called its national product. Because production of output generates income in the form of claims on that output, the total is also referred to as national income. One of the most commonly used measures of national income is gross domestic product (GDP).
- Potential output is the level of output produced when factors of production are fully employed. The output gap is the difference between actual and potential output.
- The unemployment rate is the percentage of the labour force not employed and actively searching for a job. The labour force and employment have both grown steadily for the past half-century. The unemployment rate fluctuates considerably from year to year. Unemployment imposes serious costs in the form of economic waste and human suffering.
- Labour productivity is measured as real GDP per employed worker (or per hour of work). It is an important determinant of material living standards.

- The price level is measured by a price index, which measures the cost of purchasing a set of goods in one year relative to the cost of the same goods in a base year. The inflation rate measures the rate of change of the price level. For almost 25 years, the annual inflation rate in Canada has been close to 2 percent.
- The interest rate is the price that is paid to borrow money for a stated period and is expressed as a percentage amount per dollar borrowed. The nominal interest rate is this price expressed in money terms; the real interest rate is this price expressed in terms of purchasing power.
- The flow of credit—borrowing and lending—is very important in a modern economy. Disruptions in the flow of credit can lead to increases in interest rates and reductions in economic activity.
- The exchange rate is the number of Canadian dollars needed to purchase one unit of foreign currency. A rise in the exchange rate is a depreciation of the Canadian dollar; a fall in the exchange rate is an appreciation of the Canadian dollar.

19.2 Growth Versus Fluctuations

- Most macroeconomic variables have both long-run trends and short-run fluctuations. The sources of the two types of movements are different.

- Important questions for macroeconomics involve the role of policy in influencing long-run growth as well as short-run fluctuations.

KEY CONCEPTS

National product and national income
Real and nominal national income
Potential and actual output
The output gap
Employment, unemployment, and the labour force

Full employment
Frictional, structural, and cyclical unemployment
Labour productivity
The price level and the rate of inflation

Real and nominal interest rates
Interest rates and credit
The exchange rate
Depreciation and appreciation of the Canadian dollar
Exports, imports, and the trade balance

STUDY EXERCISES

MyLab Economics Make the grade with MyLab Economics™: All Study Exercises can be found on MyLab Economics™. You can practise them as often as you want, and many feature step-by-step guided instructions to help you find the right answer.

FILL-IN-THE-BLANK

❶ Fill in the blanks to make the following statements correct.

a. The value of total production of goods and services in Canada is called its _____. National _____ and national _____ are equal because all production generates a claim on its value in the form of income.

b. In measuring Canada's total output, it would be meaningless to add together all goods and services produced during one year (i.e., 50 000 trucks plus 14 million dozen eggs plus 100 million haircuts, etc.). Instead, total output is measured in _____.

c. The difference between nominal national income and real national income is that with the latter, _____ are held constant to enable us to see changes in _____.

d. If all of Canada's resources—its land, labour, and capital—are "fully employed," then we say that Canada is producing its _____.

e. The output gap measures the difference between _____ and _____. During booms, _____ is greater than _____; during recessions, _____ is less than _____.

❷ Fill in the blanks to make the following statements correct.

a. The labour force includes people who are _____ and people who are _____. The unemployment rate is expressed as the number of people who are _____ as a percentage of people in the _____.

b. At any point in time, some people are unemployed because of the normal turnover of labour (new entrants to the labour force, job leavers, and job seekers). This unemployment is referred to as _____. Some people are unemployed because their skills do not match the skills necessary for the available jobs. This unemployment is referred to as _____.

c. Suppose 2002 is the base year in which the price of a basket of goods is set to be 100. If the price of the same basket of goods in 2019 is 137, then we can say that the price level is _____ and that the price of the basket of goods has increased by _____ percent between 2002 and 2019.

d. Canada's CPI in 2016 was 128.4 and in 2017 was 130.4. The rate of inflation during that one-year period was _____ percent.

e. The price that is paid to borrow money for a stated period of time is known as the _____.

f. The real interest rate is equal to the nominal interest rate _____ the rate of inflation.

g. The number of Canadian dollars required to purchase one unit of foreign currency is the _____ between the Canadian dollar and that foreign currency.

h. A(n) _____ in the exchange rate reflects a depreciation of the Canadian dollar; a(n) _____ in the exchange rate reflects an appreciation of the Canadian dollar.

REVIEW

❸ As explained in the text, the unemployment rate is defined as:

Unemployment rate =

$$\frac{\text{Number of people unemployed}}{\text{Number of people in the labour force}} \times 100 \text{ percent}$$

a. Explain why people may decide to join the labour force during booms.
b. From part (a), explain why the unemployment rate might rise during a boom, even when the level of employment is also rising.
c. During a recession, suppose unemployed workers leave the labour force because they are discouraged about their inability to find a job. What happens to the unemployment rate?
d. "A declining unemployment rate is a clear positive sign for the economy." Comment.

❹ Consider an imaginary 10-year period over which output per person falls, but GDP increases. How can this happen? Do you think this is likely to be good for the economy?

❺ When the Canadian dollar depreciates in foreign-exchange markets, many people view this as "good" for the Canadian economy. Who is likely to be harmed by and who is likely to benefit from a depreciation of the Canadian dollar?

PROBLEMS

❻ Consider the macroeconomic data shown below for a hypothetical country's economy.

Year	Real GDP Actual (billions of $)	Real GDP Potential (billions of $)	Output Gap (% of potential)	Unemployment Rate (% of labour force)
2011	1168	1188	—	11.1
2012	1184	1196	—	10.2
2013	1197	1205	—	9.1
2014	1211	1215	—	8.3
2015	1225	1225	—	7.6
2016	1240	1236	—	7.3
2017	1253	1247	—	7.1
2018	1262	1258	—	7.3
2019	1270	1270	—	7.6

a. Compute the output gap for each year and express it as a percentage of potential output.
b. Explain how GDP can exceed potential GDP.

c. Does real GDP ever fall in the time period shown? What do economists call such periods?
d. What is the unemployment rate when this economy is at "full employment"? What kind of unemployment exists at this time?

❼ With the information provided, determine the unemployment rate for each of these hypothetical economies.

a. Labour force = 20 million; number of people unemployed = 1.5 million; population = 30 million.
b. Number of people employed = 14 million; labour force = 16 million.
c. Number of people unemployed = 900 000; number of people employed = 2.25 million.
d. Labour force = 8.2 million; number of people unemployed = 500 000; population = 13.5 million.

❽ The table below shows data over several years for a country's real GDP, the number of full-time employed workers (E), and the annual average number of hours worked per worker (H).

Year	Real GDP	Full-time Employed Workers (E)	Number of Hours Worked per Worker (H)	$\frac{\text{GDP}}{\text{E}}$	$\frac{\text{GDP}}{\text{E} \times \text{H}}$
1	$500 billion	13.0 million	2000		
5	$575 billion	13.6 million	1965		
10	$660 billion	14.3 million	1930		
15	$760 billion	15.0 million	1900		

a. For each of the four years, compute real GDP per worker—a standard measure of labour productivity.
b. For each year, compute a slightly more complex measure of labour productivity—real GDP per hour worked.
c. For the 15-year period, compute the total percentage change for real GDP and both measures of productivity.
d. Explain why the two measures of productivity grow at different rates over the 15-year period.
e. Explain which measure is likely to be a more accurate indication of productivity, and why.

9 Consider the data shown below for the Canadian Consumer Price Index (CPI), drawn from the Bank of Canada's website.

Year	CPI (2002 = 100)	CPI Inflation (% change from previous year)
2008	114.1	2.4
2009	114.4	—
2010	—	1.8
2011	119.9	2.9
2012	121.6	—
2013	—	1.2
2014	125.7	—
2015	126.6	—
2016	—	1.4
2017	130.4	—
2018	—	1.5

a. Compute the missing data in the table.
b. Do average prices ever fall in the time period shown? In which year do prices come closest to being stable?
c. Across which two consecutive years is the rate of inflation closest to being stable?
d. In a diagram with the price level on the vertical axis and time on the horizontal axis, illustrate the difference between a situation in which the price level is stable and a situation in which the rate of inflation is stable.

10 The data below show the nominal interest rate and the inflation rate for several developed economies as reported in *The Economist* in February 2018.

Country	Nominal Interest Rate (on 10-year government bonds)	Inflation Rate (% change in CPI from previous year)	Real Interest Rate
Australia	2.82	1.9	—
Canada	2.36	1.9	—
Euro area	0.70	1.3	—
Japan	0.07	1.1	—
Switzerland	0.15	0.8	—
U.K.	1.59	3.0	—
U.S.A.	2.79	2.1	—

a. Compute the real interest rate for each country, assuming that people expected the inflation rate at the time to persist.
b. If you were a lender, in which country would you have wanted to lend in February 2018? Explain.
c. If you were a borrower, in which country would you have wanted to borrow in February 2018? Explain.

11 Consider the following data drawn from *The Economist*. Recall that the Canadian exchange rate is the number of Canadian dollars needed to purchase one unit of some foreign currency.

Currency	Cdn Dollar Exchange Rate	
	February 2018	February 2017
U.S. dollar	1.25	1.31
Japanese yen	0.011	0.012
British pound	1.74	1.64
Swedish krona	0.16	0.15
Euro	1.54	1.41

a. Which currencies appreciated relative to the Canadian dollar from February 2017 to February 2018?
b. Which currencies depreciated relative to the Canadian dollar from February 2017 to February 2018?
c. Using the information provided in the table, can you tell whether the euro depreciated or appreciated *against the U.S. dollar* from February 2017 to February 2018? Explain.

20 The Measurement of National Income

CHAPTER OUTLINE

20.1 NATIONAL OUTPUT AND VALUE ADDED

20.2 NATIONAL INCOME ACCOUNTING: THE BASICS

20.3 NATIONAL INCOME ACCOUNTING: SOME FURTHER ISSUES

LEARNING OBJECTIVES (LO)

After studying this chapter you will be able to

1 see how the concept of value added solves the problem of "double counting" when measuring national income.

2 explain how GDP is measured from the expenditure side and from the income side.

3 explain the difference between real and nominal GDP.

4 discuss the many important omissions from official measures of GDP.

5 understand why real per capita GDP is a good measure of average material living standards but an incomplete measure of overall well-being.

THIS chapter provides a detailed look at the measurement of national income. Once we know more precisely what is being measured and how it is measured, we will be ready to build a macroeconomic model to explain the determination of national income. Understanding how national income is measured is an important part of understanding how and why it changes. Indeed, this is a general rule of all economics and all science: Before using any data, it is essential to understand how those data are developed and what they measure.

20.1   National Output and Value Added

The central topic of macroeconomics is the overall level of economic activity—aggregate output and the income that is generated by its production. We start by asking: What do we mean by output?

This question may seem odd. Surely your local bakery knows what it produces. And if Air Canada or Imperial Oil or Bombardier does not know its own output, what does it know? If each firm knows the value of its total output, the national income statisticians simply have to add up each separate output value to get the nation's output—or is it really that simple?

Obtaining a total for the nation's output is not that simple because one firm's output is often another firm's input. The local baker uses flour that is the output of the flour milling company; the flour milling company, in turn, uses wheat that is the farmer's output. What is true for bread is true for most goods and services.

Production occurs in stages: Some firms produce outputs that are used as inputs by other firms, and these other firms, in turn, produce outputs that are used as inputs by yet other firms.

If we merely added up the market values of all outputs of all firms, we would obtain a total greatly in excess of the value of the economy's actual output. Consider the example of wheat, flour, and bread. If we added the total value of the output of the wheat farmer, the flour mill, and the baker, we would be counting the value of the wheat three times, the value of the milled flour twice, and the value of the bread once.

The error that would arise in estimating the nation's output by adding all sales of all firms is called *double counting*. "Multiple counting" would actually be a better term, because if we added up the values of all sales, the same output would be counted every time that it was sold by one firm to another. The problem of double counting could in principle be solved by distinguishing between two types of output. **Intermediate goods** are outputs of some firms that are used as inputs by other firms. **Final goods** are products that are not used as inputs by other firms, at least not in the period of time under consideration.

If firms' sales could be easily divided into sales of final goods and sales of intermediate goods, then measuring total output would be straightforward. It would simply be obtained by summing the value of all *final* goods produced by firms. However, when Stelco sells steel to the Ford Motor Company, it does not care, and usually does not know, whether the steel is for final use (say, construction of a warehouse that will not be sold by Ford) or for use as part of an automobile that will be sold again. Even in our earlier example of bread, a bakery cannot be sure that its sales are for final use, for the bread may be further "processed" by a restaurant prior to its final sale to a customer. In general, it is extremely difficult if not impossible to successfully distinguish final from intermediate goods. The problem of double counting must therefore be resolved in some other manner.

To avoid double counting, economists use the concept of **value added**, which is the amount of value that firms and workers add to their products over and above the costs of purchased intermediate goods. An individual firm's value added is

$$\text{Value added} = \text{Sales revenue} - \text{Cost of intermediate goods}$$

intermediate goods All outputs that are used as inputs by other producers in a further stage of production.

final goods Goods that are not used as inputs by other firms but are produced to be sold for consumption, investment, government, or export during the period under consideration.

value added The value of a firm's output minus the value of the inputs that it purchases from other firms.

Consider an example of a steel mill. A steel mill's value added is the revenue it earns from selling the steel it produces minus the cost of the ore that it buys from the mining company, the cost of the electricity and fuel oil that it uses, and the costs of all other inputs that it buys from other firms.

We have said that a firm's value added equals its sales revenue minus the cost of intermediate goods *purchased from other firms*. Payments made to factors of production, such as the wages paid to workers or the profits paid to owners, are not purchases from other firms and hence are not subtracted from the firm's revenue when computing value added. But since the firm's revenue must be fully exhausted by the cost of intermediate goods *plus* all payments to factors of production, it follows that value added is exactly equal to the sum of these factor payments.[1]

Value added = Payments owed to the firm's factors of production

Value added is the correct measure of each firm's contribution to total output—the amount of market value that is produced by that firm and its workers.

The firm's value added is therefore the *net value* of its output. It is this net value that is the firm's contribution to the nation's total output, representing the firm's own efforts that add to the value of what it takes in as inputs. The concept of value added is further illustrated in *Applying Economic Concepts 20-1*. In this simple example, as in

APPLYING ECONOMIC CONCEPTS 20-1
Value Added Through Stages of Production

Because the output of one firm often becomes the input of other firms, the total value of goods sold by all firms greatly exceeds the value of the output of final products. This general principle is illustrated by a simple example in which a mining company starts from scratch and produces iron ore valued at $1000; this firm's value added is $1000. The mining company then sells the iron ore to a different firm that produces steel valued at $1500. The steel producer's value added is $500 because the value of the goods is increased by $500 as a result of the firm's

activities. Finally, the steel producer sells the steel to a metal fabricator who transforms the steel into folding chairs valued at $1800; the metal fabricator's value added is $300.

We find the value of the final goods, $1800, either by counting only the sales of the last firm or by taking the sum of the values added by each firm. This value is much smaller than the $4300 that we would obtain if we merely added up the market value of the output sold by each firm.

Transactions at Three Different Stages of Production

	Mining Company	Steel Producer	Metal Fabricator	All Firms	
A. Purchases from other firms	$ 0	$1000	$1500	$2500	Total interfirm sales
B. Payments to factors of production	1000	500	300	1800	Total value added
A + B = value of product	$1000	$1500	$1800	$4300	Total value of all sales

---

[1] We are ignoring here the role of indirect taxes, such as provincial sales taxes or the federal Goods and Services Tax (GST). Such taxes are included in the market value of a firm's output, but these taxes are remitted to the government and do not represent a payment to factors of production.

all more complex cases, the value of the nation's total output is obtained by summing all the individual values added.

The sum of all values added in an economy is a measure of the economy's total output.

20.2   National Income Accounting: The Basics

The measures of national income that are used in Canada derive from an accounting system called the National Income and Expenditure Accounts (NIEA), which are produced by Statistics Canada. These accounts are not simply collections of economic data. They have a logical structure, based on the important idea of the circular flow of income, which you first saw in Chapter 1 and which is shown again in Figure 20-1. The figure shows the overall flows of national income and expenditure and also how government, the financial system, and foreign countries enter the flows. The key point from the circular flow is as follows:

The value of domestic output (value added) is equal to the value of the expenditure on that output and is also equal to the total income claims generated by producing that output.

The circular flow of income suggests three different ways of measuring national income. The first is simply to add up the value of all goods and services produced in the economy. This requires the concept of value added, which we discussed in the previous section. The remaining two approaches correspond to the two "sides" of the circular flow of income and are the ones most commonly used by Statistics Canada and other countries' national statistical agencies. One approach is to add up the total flow of *expenditure* on final domestic output; the other is to add up the total flow of *income* generated by domestic production. All three measures yield the same total, which is called **gross domestic product (GDP)**. When GDP is calculated by adding up total expenditure for each of the main components of final output, the result is called *GDP on the expenditure side*. When GDP is calculated by adding up all the income claims generated by the act of production, it is called *GDP on the income side*.

The conventions of double-entry bookkeeping require that the value of all production must be accounted for by a claim that someone has to that value. Thus, the two values calculated from the income and the expenditure sides are identical conceptually and differ in practice only because of errors of measurement. Any discrepancy arising from such errors is then reconciled so that one common total is given as *the* measure of GDP. Both calculations are of interest, however, because each gives a different and useful breakdown. Also, having these two independent ways of measuring the same quantity provides a useful check on statistical procedures and on errors in measurement.

gross domestic product (GDP) The total value of goods and services produced in the economy during a given period.

FIGURE 20-1   The Circular Flow of Expenditure and Income

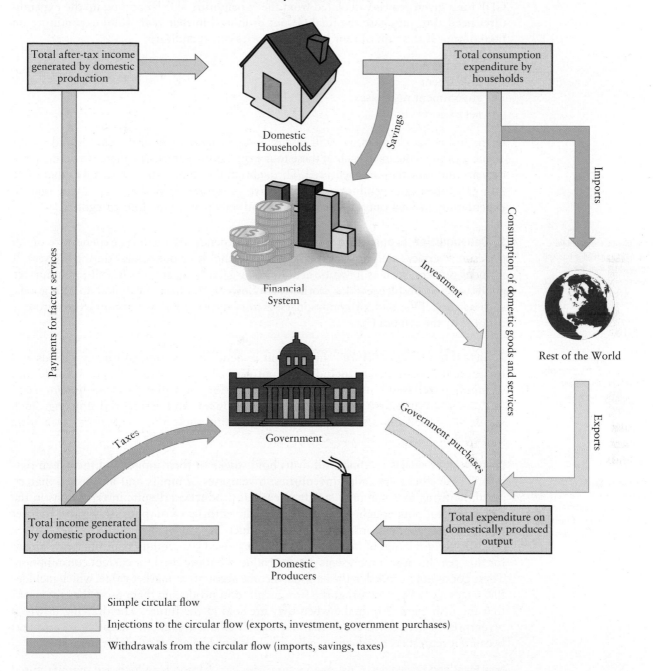

Simple circular flow

Injections to the circular flow (exports, investment, government purchases)

Withdrawals from the circular flow (imports, savings, taxes)

National income is equal to national product. Their flows are shown by the circular flow of income and expenditure. Consider first only the red lines. In this case, the flow would be a simple circle from households to producers and back to households. Now add the blue and green lines. The blue lines represent *injections* to the circular flow (exports, investment, and government purchases), while the green lines represent *withdrawals* from the circular flow (imports, saving, and taxes). Injections and withdrawals complicate the picture but do not change the basic relationship: Domestic production creates an income claim on the value of that production. When all the income claims are correctly added up, they must equal the total value of production.

GDP from the Expenditure Side

GDP for a given year is calculated from the expenditure side by adding up the expenditures needed to purchase the final output produced in that year. Total expenditure on final output is the sum of four broad categories of expenditure:

- consumption
- investment
- government purchases
- net exports

In the following chapters, we will discuss in considerable detail the causes and consequences of movements in each of these four expenditure categories. Here we define what they are and how they are measured. Throughout, it is important to remember that these four categories of expenditure are exhaustive—they are *defined* in such a way that all expenditure on final output falls into one (and only one) of the four categories.

1. Consumption Expenditure　Consumption expenditure includes expenditure on all goods and services sold to their final users (households or businesses) during the year. It includes services, such as haircuts, dental care, legal advice, and phone bills; non-durable goods, such as fresh vegetables, clothing, cut flowers, and fresh meat; and durable goods, such as cars, TVs, and air conditioners. *Actual* measured consumption expenditure is denoted by the symbol C_a.

2. Investment Expenditure　Investment expenditure is expenditure on goods *not* for present consumption, including inventories of goods made but not yet sold and of inputs purchased but not yet used in production; new plant and equipment, such as factories, computers, machines, and warehouses; and residential housing. Such goods are called *investment goods*. Let's examine these three categories in a little more detail.

Changes in Inventories.　Almost all firms hold stocks of their inputs and their own outputs. These stocks are called **inventories**. Inventories of inputs and unfinished materials allow firms to maintain a steady stream of production despite interruptions in the deliveries of inputs bought from other firms. Inventories of outputs allow firms to meet orders despite fluctuations in the rate of production.

　　The accumulation of inventories during any given year counts as positive investment for that year because it represents goods produced but not used for current consumption. These goods are included in the national income accounts at market value, which includes the wages and other costs that the firm incurred in producing them as well as the profit that the firm expects to make when they are sold in the future. The drawing down of inventories, often called *decumulation*, counts as disinvestment (negative investment) because it represents a reduction in the stock of finished goods available to be sold.

New Plant and Equipment.　All production uses capital goods, which are manufactured aids to production, such as tools, machines, computers, vehicles, office buildings, and factories. The economy's total quantity of capital goods accumulated through past production is called the **capital stock**. This is often called "plant and equipment," although the term refers to any manufactured aid to production used by firms. Adding to the existing stock of capital goods is an act of investment and is called *business fixed investment*, often shortened to **fixed investment**.

---

consumption expenditure Expenditure on all goods and services for final use. Represented by the symbol C.

investment expenditure Expenditure on the production of goods not for present consumption. Represented by the symbol I.

inventories Stocks of raw materials, goods in process, and finished goods held by firms to mitigate the effect of short-term fluctuations in production or sales.

capital stock The aggregate quantity of capital goods.

fixed investment The creation of new plant and equipment.

New Residential Housing.   A house or an apartment building is a durable asset that yields its utility over a long period of time. Because such an asset meets the definition of investment that we gave earlier, housing construction—the building of a *new* house—is counted as investment expenditure rather than as consumption expenditure. However, when an individual purchases an existing house from a builder or from another individual, the ownership of an existing asset is simply transferred, and the transaction is not part of national income. Only when a new house is built does it appear as residential investment in the national accounts.

Gross and Net Investment.   The total investment that occurs in the economy is called *gross investment*. Gross investment is divided into two parts: replacement investment and net investment. Replacement investment is the amount of investment required to replace that part of the capital stock that loses its value through wear and tear; this loss in value is called **depreciation**. Net investment is equal to gross investment minus depreciation:

$$\text{Net investment} = \text{Gross investment} - \text{Depreciation}$$

> **depreciation** The amount by which the capital stock is depleted through the production process.

When net investment is positive, the economy's capital stock is growing. If net investment is negative—which rarely happens—the economy's capital stock is shrinking.

Total Investment.   The production of new investment goods is part of the nation's total current output, and their production creates income whether the goods produced are a part of net investment or are merely replacement investment. Thus, all of gross investment is included in the calculation of national income.

Total annual investment for the economy is the sum during the year of the *changes* in inventories, the *additions* to the stock of plant and equipment, and *new* construction of residential housing units. *Actual* total investment expenditure is denoted by the symbol I_a.

3. Government Purchases

When governments provide goods and services such as street-cleaning and firefighting, they are adding to the sum total of valuable output in the economy. The same is true when governments pay public servants to design and implement social programs or soldiers to fight overseas. All **government purchases** of goods and services are included as part of national expenditure.[2] *Actual* government purchases of goods and services are denoted G_a.

> **government purchases** All government expenditure on currently produced goods and services, exclusive of government transfer payments. Represented by the symbol *G*.

Cost Versus Market Value.   Government output is typically valued at cost rather than at market value. In many cases, there is really no choice. What, for example, is the market value of the law courts or of police protection or of the economic analysis done by economists at the Department of Finance? No one knows. But since we do know what it costs the government to provide these services, we value them at their cost of production.

Although valuing at cost is the only possible way to measure many government activities, it does have

Unsold merchandise becomes part of firms' inventories. In national income accounting, an increase in firms' inventories is one part of total investment.

---

[2] Government purchases are divided into *current* expenditure and *investment* expenditure, depending on the durability of the good or service. Payments of salaries, for example, are current expenditures; construction of new government buildings, in contrast, are investment expenditures. See Table 20-1 for recent data.

one curious consequence. If, because of an increase in productivity, one civil servant now does what two used to do, and the displaced worker shifts to the private sector, the government's measured contribution to national income will fall (but the private sector's contribution will rise). Conversely, if two workers now do what one worker used to do, the government's contribution will rise. Both changes could occur even though what the government actually produced did not change. This is an inevitable but curious consequence of measuring the value of the government's output by the cost of producing it.

Government Purchases Versus Government Expenditure.   Only government *purchases* of currently produced goods and services are included as part of GDP. As a result, a great deal of government spending does *not* count as part of GDP. For example, when the government makes payments to a retired person through the Canada Pension Plan, there is no market transaction involved as the government is not purchasing any currently produced goods or services from the retiree. The payment itself does not add to total output. The same is true of payments for employment insurance and welfare, and interest on the national debt (which transfers income from taxpayers to holders of government bonds). These are examples of **transfer payments**, which are government expenditures that are not made in return for currently produced goods and services. They are not a part of expenditure on the nation's total output and are therefore not included in GDP. (Of course, the recipients of transfer payments often choose to spend their money on consumption goods. Such expenditure then counts in the same way as any other consumption expenditure.)

4. Net Exports   The fourth category of aggregate expenditure arises from foreign trade. **Imports** are domestic expenditure on foreign-produced goods and services; **exports** are foreign expenditure on domestically produced goods and services.

Exports.   If Canadian firms sell goods to German households, the goods are part of German consumption expenditure but constitute expenditure *on Canadian output*. Indeed, all goods and services produced in Canada and sold to foreigners must be counted as part of Canadian production and income; they are produced in Canada, and they create incomes for the Canadian residents who produce them. They are not purchased by Canadian residents, however, so they are not included as part of C_a, I_a, or G_a. Therefore, to arrive at the total value of expenditure *on Canadian output*, it is necessary to add in the value of Canadian exports of goods and services. The value of actual exports is denoted X_a.

Imports.   If you buy a car that was made in Japan, only a small part of that value will represent expenditure on Canadian production. Some of it represents payment for the services of the Canadian dealers and for transportation; the rest is expenditure on Japanese products. If you take your next vacation in Italy, much of your expenditure will be on goods and services produced in Italy and thus will contribute to Italian GDP rather than to Canadian GDP.

Similarly, when a Canadian firm makes an investment expenditure on a machine that was made partly with imported raw materials, only part of the expenditure is on Canadian production; the rest is expenditure on foreign production. The same is true for government expenditure on such things as roads and dams; some of the expenditure is for imported materials, and only part of it is for domestically produced goods and services. The same is also true for exports, most of which use some imported inputs in their production process.

transfer payments Payments to an individual or institution not made in exchange for a good or service.

imports The value of all goods and services purchased from firms, households, or governments in other countries.

exports The value of all domestically produced goods and services sold to firms, households, and governments in other countries.

Consumption, investment, government purchases, and exports all have an import content. To arrive at total expenditure *on Canadian products*, we need to subtract from total Canadian expenditure the economy's total expenditure on imports. The value of actual imports is given the symbol IM_a.

It is customary to group actual imports and actual exports together as **net exports**. Net exports are defined as total exports minus total imports $(X_a - IM_a)$, which is also denoted NX_a. When the value of Canadian exports exceeds the value of Canadian imports, net exports are positive. When the value of imports exceeds the value of exports, net exports are negative.

Total Expenditures   Recall, as shown in the circular flow of income in Figure 20-1, that the value of domestic production is equal to the value of total expenditure *on domestically produced output*. We have explained the four separate components of expenditure; it is now time to put them all together.

Gross domestic product measured from the expenditure side is equal to the sum of these four major expenditure categories. In terms of a simple equation, we have

$$GDP = C_a + I_a + G_a + (X_a - IM_a)$$

These data are shown in Table 20-1 for Canada in 2017, including some data on the expenditure in the various subcategories.

> Measured from the expenditure side, GDP is equal to the total expenditure on domestically produced output. GDP is equal to $C_a + I_a + G_a + NX_a$.

TABLE 20-1   GDP from the Expenditure Side, 2017

Category	Billions of Dollars	Percent of GDP
Consumption (C)		
Durable goods	161.6	
Semi-durable goods	85.0	
Non-durable goods	284.2	
Services	707.9	
	1238.7	57.8
Investment (I)		
Plant and equipment	208.2	
Residential structures	164.8	
Inventories	15.1	
Other	36.6	
	424.7	19.8
Government Purchases (G)		
Current expenditure	446.6	
Investment	83.5	
	530.1	24.7
Net Exports (X − IM)		
Exports of goods and services	662.3	
Imports of goods and services	−711.3	
	−49.0	−2.3
Statistical Discrepancy	−0.1	0.0
Total GDP	**2144.4**	**100.0**

GDP measured from the expenditure side of the national accounts gives the size of the major components of aggregate expenditure.

(*Source:* Based on Statistics Canada, "Gross Domestic Product, Expenditure based, 2017," CANSIM database, Table 380-0064. Available at www.statcan.gc.ca.)

net exports The value of total exports minus the value of total imports. Represented by the symbol *NX*.

GDP from the Income Side

As we said earlier, the conventions of national income accounting ensure that the production of a nation's output generates income *exactly* equal to the value of that production. Labour must be employed, land must be rented, and capital must be used. The calculation of GDP from the income side involves adding up factor incomes and other claims on the value of output until all of that value is accounted for.

1. Factor Incomes   National income accountants distinguish three main components of factor incomes: wages and salaries, interest, and business profits (which includes rent received by property owners).

Wages and Salaries. Wages and salaries are the payment for the services of labour and they include all *pre-tax* labour earnings: take-home pay, income taxes withheld, employment-insurance contributions, pension-fund contributions, and other employee benefits. In total, wages and salaries represent the part of the value of production that is paid to labour.

Interest. Interest includes interest that is earned on bank deposits, interest that is earned on loans to firms, and miscellaneous other investment income (but excludes interest income earned from loans to Canadian governments).[3]

Business Profits. Some profits are paid out as *dividends* to owners of firms; the rest are held by firms and are called *retained earnings*. Both dividends and retained earnings are included in the calculation of factor incomes. For accounting purposes, total profits include corporate profits, incomes of unincorporated businesses (mainly small businesses, farmers, partnerships, and professionals), rent paid on land and buildings, and profits of government business enterprises and Crown corporations (such as Canada Post and Export Development Canada).

Profits and interest together represent the payment for the use of capital—interest for borrowed capital and profits for capital contributed by the owners of firms.

Net Domestic Income. The sum of wages and salaries, interest, and profits is called *net domestic income at factor cost*. It is "net" because it excludes the value of output that is used as replacement investment. It is "domestic income" because it is the income accruing to domestic factors of production. It is "at factor cost" because it represents only that part of the value of final output that accrues to factors in the form of payments due to them for their services. As we will see next, some part of the value of final output does not accrue to the factors at all.

2. Non-factor Payments Every time a consumer spends $10 on some item, some part of this $10 expenditure *does not* get paid as income to factors of production. This shortfall is due to the presence of indirect taxes and depreciation.

Indirect Taxes and Subsidies. An important claim on the market value of output arises out of indirect taxes, which are taxes on the production and sale of goods and services. In Canada, the most important indirect taxes are provincial sales taxes, excise taxes on specific products, and the federal Goods and Services Tax (GST).

For example, if a good's market price of $10.00 includes 60 cents in provincial sales taxes and 50 cents in federal GST, only $8.90 is available as income to factors of production. Governments are claiming $1.10 of the $10.00 market value of the good. Adding up income claims to determine GDP therefore necessitates including the portion of the total market value of output that goes to governments in the form of indirect taxes.

---

[3] The treatment of interest in the national accounts is a little odd. Interest paid by the government is considered a transfer payment, whereas interest paid by private households or firms is treated as expenditure (and its receipt is counted as a factor payment). This is only one example of arbitrary decisions in national income accounting. Others are discussed in *Extensions in Theory 20-1* on page 496.

Sometimes the government gives subsidies to firms, which act like negative taxes. When these occur, it is necessary to *subtract* their value, since they allow factor incomes to *exceed* the market value of output. For example, suppose a municipal bus company spends $150 000 providing bus rides and covers its costs by selling $140 000 in fares and obtaining a $10 000 subsidy from the local government. The total income that the company will generate from its production is $150 000, but the total market value of its output is only $140 000, with the difference made up by the subsidy. To get from total factor income to the market value of its total output, we must subtract the amount of the subsidy.

Hence, the value of indirect taxes (net of subsidies) must be added to net domestic income in order to compute GDP from the income side.

Depreciation. Some portion of current output replaces worn out physical capital—depreciation. As we said earlier, depreciation is the loss in the value of physical capital generated by wear and tear during the production process. It is part of gross profits, but because it is needed to compensate for capital used up in the process of production, it is not part of net profits. Hence, depreciation must be added to net domestic income in order to compute GDP from the income side.

Total National Income   The various components of the income side of the GDP in the Canadian economy in 2017 are shown in Table 20-2. Note that one of the terms in the table is called *statistical discrepancy*, a term that appears with equal magnitude but opposite sign in Table 20-1. This is a "fudge factor" to make sure that the independent measures of income and expenditure come to the same total. Statistical discrepancy is a clear indication that national income accounting is not error-free. Although national income and national expenditure are conceptually identical, in practice both are measured with slight error.

> From the income side, GDP is the sum of factor incomes *plus* indirect taxes (net of subsidies) *plus* depreciation.

We have now seen the two commonly used methods for computing a country's national income. Both are correct and give us the same measure of GDP, but each gives us some different additional information. For some questions, such as what will be the likely future path of the nation's capital stock, it is useful to know the relative importance of consumption and investment. In this case, the expenditure approach for computing GDP provides some of the necessary information. For other questions, such as what is

TABLE 20-2   GDP from the Income Side, 2017

Category	Billions of Dollars	Percent of GDP
Factor Incomes		
Wages, salaries, and supplementary income	1084.2	50.6
Interest and other investment income	187.9	8.8
Business profits (including rent)	273.7	12.8
Net Domestic Income at Factor Cost	**1545.8**	**72.1**
Non-factor Payments		
Depreciation	356.3	16.6
Indirect taxes less subsidies	242.2	11.3
Statistical Discrepancy	0.1	0.0
Total	**2144.4**	**100.0**

GDP measured from the income side of the national accounts gives the sizes of the major components of the income generated by producing the nation's output.

(*Source:* Based on Statistics Canada, "Gross Domestic Product, Income based, 2017," CANSIM database, Table 380-0063. Available at www.statcan.gc.ca.)

EXTENSIONS IN THEORY 20-1

Arbitrary Decisions in National Income Accounting

National income accounting uses many arbitrary decisions. For example, goods that are finished and held in inventories are valued at market value, thereby anticipating their sale, even though the actual selling price may not be known. In the case of a Ford in a dealer's showroom, this practice may be justified because the *value* of this Ford is perhaps virtually the same as that of an identical Ford that has just been sold to a customer. However, what is the correct market value of a half-finished house or an unfinished novel? Accountants arbitrarily treat goods in process at cost (rather than at market value) if the goods are being made by firms. They ignore completely the value of the unfinished novel. The arbitrary nature of these decisions is inevitable: Because people must arrive at some practical compromise between consistent definitions and measurable magnitudes, any decision will be somewhat arbitrary.

Such arbitrary decisions surely affect the size of measured GDP. But does it matter? The surprising answer, for many purposes, is no. It is wrong to think that just because a statistical measure is imperfect (as all statistical measures are) it is useless. Simple measures often give estimates that are quite accurate, and substantial improvements in sophistication may make only trivial improvements in these estimates.

In 2017, for example, Canadian GDP was measured as $2144.4 billion. It is certain that the market value of all production in Canada in that year was neither $500 billion nor $3000 billion, but it might well have been $1900 billion or $2300 billion had different measures been defined with different arbitrary decisions built in. Similarly, Canadian per capita GDP is about three times the Mexican per capita GDP and is about 20 percent less than U.S. per capita GDP. Other measures might differ, but it is unlikely that any measure would reveal the Mexican per capita GDP to be higher than Canada's, or Canada's to be significantly above that of the United States.

happening to the distribution of income between labour and capital, we need information about the composition of factor incomes. In this case, a useful starting point would be to examine GDP from the income side.

Measuring national income is not problem-free. As in any accounting exercise, many arbitrary rules must be used. Some of them seem odd, but the important thing is that these rules be used consistently over time. Comparisons of GDP over time will then reflect genuine changes in economic activity, which is the primary objective. *Extensions in Theory 20-1* discusses the issue of arbitrariness in national income accounting.

20.3 National Income Accounting: Some Further Issues

Now that we have examined the basics of national income accounting, we are ready to explore some more detailed issues. We discuss the distinction between real and nominal GDP, the major omissions from measured GDP, and the connection between GDP and "living standards."

Real and Nominal GDP

In Chapter 19, we distinguished between real and nominal measures of aggregate output. When we add up dollar values of outputs, expenditures, or incomes, we end up with what are called *nominal values*. Nominal GDP increased by 209.5 percent between 1990 and 2017. If we want to compare *real* GDP in 2017 to that in 1990,

FIGURE 20-2 Nominal and Real GDP in Canada, 1985–2017 (billions of dollars)

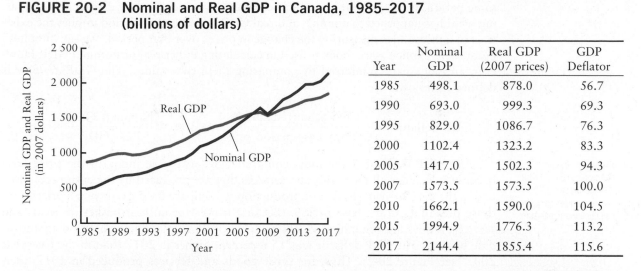

Year	Nominal GDP	Real GDP (2007 prices)	GDP Deflator
1985	498.1	878.0	56.7
1990	693.0	999.3	69.3
1995	829.0	1086.7	76.3
2000	1102.4	1323.2	83.3
2005	1417.0	1502.3	94.3
2007	1573.5	1573.5	100.0
2010	1662.1	1590.0	104.5
2015	1994.9	1776.3	113.2
2017	2144.4	1855.4	115.6

Nominal GDP tells us about the money value of output; real GDP tells us about the quantity of physical output. Nominal GDP gives the total value of output in any year, valued at the prices of that year. Real GDP gives the total value of output in any year, *valued at prices from some base year*, in this case 2007. The comparison of real and nominal GDP implicitly defines a price index, changes in which reveal changes in the (average) prices of goods produced domestically. Note that in 2007, nominal GDP equals real GDP (measured in 2007 prices), and thus the GDP deflator equals 100.

(*Source:* Based on Statistics Canada, CANSIM database, Table 380-0064. Available at www.statcan.gc.ca.)

we need to determine how much of that nominal increase was due to increases in prices and how much was due to increases in quantities produced. Although there are many possible ways of doing this, the underlying principle is always the same: The value of output in each period is computed by using a common set of *base-period prices*. When this is done, economists say that real output is measured in *constant dollars*.

> Total GDP valued at current prices is called *nominal* GDP. GDP valued at base-period prices is called *real* GDP.

Any change in nominal GDP reflects the combined effects of changes in quantities and changes in prices. However, when real income is measured over different periods by using a common set of base-period prices, changes in real income reflect only changes in quantities. Figure 20-2 shows the growth of real and nominal GDP since 1985. Note that nominal GDP grows faster over the period because both prices and quantities are increasing. Real GDP, in contrast, grows more slowly because the effect of increasing prices has been removed; we are thus able to see the growth in GDP due solely to increases in the underlying quantities. Nominal and real GDP are the same in 2007, which is the base year for the data in Figure 20-2.

The GDP Deflator If nominal and real GDP change by different amounts over a given time period, then prices must have changed over that period. For example, if nominal

GDP has increased by 6 percent and real GDP has increased by only 4 percent over the same period, we know that average prices must have increased by 2 percent. Comparing what has happened to nominal and real GDP over the same period implies the existence of a price index measuring the change in prices over that period. We say "implies" because no explicit price index is used in calculating either real or nominal GDP. However, an index can be inferred by comparing these two values. The *GDP deflator* is defined as follows:

$$\text{GDP deflator} = \frac{\text{GDP at current prices}}{\text{GDP at base-period prices}} \times 100 = \frac{\text{Nominal GDP}}{\text{Real GDP}} \times 100$$

GDP deflator An index number derived by dividing nominal GDP by real GDP. Its change measures the average change in price of all the items in the GDP.

The **GDP deflator** is the most comprehensive available index of the price level because it includes all the goods and services that are produced by the entire economy. It uses the current year's basket of production to compare the current year's prices with those prevailing in the base period. (Because it uses the current basket of goods and services, it does not run into the CPI's problem of sometimes being based on an out-of-date basket.) The GDP deflator was 15.6 percent higher in 2017 than in the base year 2007 (see Figure 20-2). Thus, for those goods and services produced in 2017, their average price increased by 15.6 percent over the previous 10 years. *Applying Economic Concepts 20-2* illustrates the calculation of real and nominal GDP and the GDP deflator for a simple hypothetical economy that produces only wheat and steel.

As we have said, a change in nominal GDP can be split into the change of prices and the change of quantities. For example, from the data in Figure 20-2 we can calculate that in 2017, Canadian nominal GDP was 209.5 percent higher than in 1990. This increase was due to a 66.8 percent increase in prices (as calculated by the percentage change in the GDP deflator) and a 85.6 percent increase in real GDP.[4]

GDP Deflator Versus the CPI   An important point about the GDP deflator is that it does not necessarily change in line with changes in the CPI. The two price indices are measuring different things. Movements in the CPI measure the change in the average price of consumer goods, whereas movements in the GDP deflator reflect the change in the average price of goods produced in Canada. Changes in the world price of coffee, for example, would have a larger effect on the CPI than on the GDP deflator, since Canadians drink a lot of coffee but no coffee is produced here. Conversely, a change in the world price of wheat is likely to have a bigger effect on the GDP deflator than on the CPI, since most of Canada's considerable production of wheat is exported to other countries, thus leaving a relatively small fraction to appear in the Canadian basket of consumer products.

Changes in the GDP deflator and Consumer Price Index (CPI) similarly reflect overall inflationary trends. Changes in relative prices, however, may lead the two price indices to move in different ways.

---

[4] For large percentage changes in price and quantity, the nominal percentage change is not exactly equal to the sum of the price and the quantity changes; generally, the relationship is multiplicative. In this case, prices and quantities are, respectively, 1.668 and 1.856 times their original values. Thus, nominal GDP is $(1.668) \times (1.856) = 3.095$ times its original value, which is an increase of 209.5 percent. For small percentage changes, the sum is a very good approximation of the multiplicative change. For example, if prices grow by 2 percent and quantities by 3 percent, the nominal change is $(1.02) \times (1.03) = 1.0506$, which is very close to 1.05, an increase of 5 percent.

APPLYING ECONOMIC CONCEPTS 20-2

Calculating Nominal and Real GDP

To see what is involved in calculating nominal GDP, real GDP, and the GDP deflator, an example may be helpful. Consider a simple hypothetical economy that produces only two commodities, wheat and steel.

Table 1 gives the basic data for output and prices in the economy for two years.

TABLE 1   Data for a Hypothetical Economy

| | Quantity Produced | | Prices | |
	Wheat (bushels)	Steel (tonnes)	Wheat ($/bushel)	Steel ($/tonne)
Year 1	100	20	10	50
Year 2	110	16	12	55

Table 2 shows nominal GDP, calculated by adding the dollar values of wheat output and of steel output for each year. In year 1, the values of both wheat and steel production were $1000, so nominal GDP was $2000. In year 2, wheat output rose to $1320, and steel output fell to $880. Since the rise in the value of wheat was greater than the fall in the value of steel, nominal GDP rose by $200.

TABLE 2   Calculation of Nominal GDP

Year 1: (100 × $10) + (20 × $50) = $2000
Year 2: (110 × $12) + (16 × $55) = $2200

Table 3 shows real GDP, calculated by valuing output in each year *at year-2 prices*; that is, year 2 is used as the base year. In year 2, wheat output rose, but steel output fell. If we use year-2 prices, the fall in the value of steel output between years 1 and 2 exceeded the rise in the value of wheat output, and so real GDP fell.

TABLE 3   Calculation of Real GDP Using Year-2 Prices

Year 1: (100 × $12) + (20 × $55) = $2300
Year 2: (110 × $12) + (16 × $55) = $2200

In Table 4, the ratio of nominal to real GDP is calculated for each year and multiplied by 100. This ratio implicitly measures the change in prices over the period in question and is called the *GDP deflator*. The deflator shows that average prices increased by 15 percent between year 1 and year 2.

TABLE 4   Calculation of the GDP Deflator

Year 1: (2000/2300) × 100 = 86.96
Year 2: (2200/2200) × 100 = 100.00

Throughout this box we have used year 2 as the base year, but we could just as easily have used year 1. The changes we would have computed in real GDP and the deflator would have been very similar—but not identical—to the ones we did compute using year 2 as the base year. The choice of base year matters because of different *relative* prices in the different years (note that the price of steel relative to the price of wheat is lower in year 2 than in year 1). Put simply, with different relative prices in different years, the various output changes are weighted differently depending on which prices we use, and thus the *aggregate* measure of real GDP changes by different amounts. (If you want to understand this point in more detail, try doing Study Exercise 12.)

How do we choose the "right" base year? As with many other elements of national income accounting, there is some arbitrariness in the choice. There is no "right" year. The important thing is not which year to use—the important thing is to be clear about which year you are using and then, for a given set of comparisons, to be sure that you are consistent in your choice. In recent years, Statistics Canada has avoided this problem by using "chain weighting," a technique that essentially uses an average over several measures, each one corresponding to a different base year.

Omissions from GDP

Gross domestic product is an excellent measure of the economic activity flowing through organized markets in a given year. But much economic activity takes place outside the markets that the national income accountants survey. Although these activities are not typically included in the measure of GDP, they nevertheless use real resources and generate incomes.

Cascade Creatives/Shutterstock

Consuming marijuana was legalized in Canada in 2018. As a result, production and consumption that was once unrecorded will now be recorded in official data on national income.

Illegal Activities   GDP does not measure illegal activities, even though many of them are ordinary business activities that produce goods and services sold in markets and that generate factor incomes. Many forms of illegal gambling, prostitution, and drug trade are in this category. To gain an accurate measure of the total demand for factors of production, of total marketable output, or of total incomes generated, we should include these activities, whether or not they are legal. The omission of illegal activities is no trivial matter: The drug trade alone is a multi-billion-dollar business.

In 2018, the production and consumption of marijuana became legal, though regulated by provincial governments. These market transactions, once ignored by national income accountants, are now formally included in GDP data. The result will likely be an increase in *measured* GDP, although at least some of this income will not reflect a rise in genuine economic activity.

Note that some illegal activities do get included in national income measures, although they are generally misclassified by industry. The income is included because people sometimes report their illegally earned income as part of their earnings from legal activities. They do this to avoid the fate of Al Capone, the famous Chicago gangster in the 1920s and 1930s, who, having avoided conviction on many more serious charges, was finally caught and imprisoned for income-tax evasion.

The Underground Economy   A significant omission from GDP is the so-called underground economy. The transactions that occur in the underground economy are perfectly legal in themselves; the only illegality involved is that such transactions are not reported for tax purposes. Because such transactions go unreported, they are omitted from GDP. One example of this is the carpenter who repairs a leak in your roof and takes payment in cash (and does not report it as income) in an effort to avoid taxation.

The growth of the underground economy is facilitated by the rising importance of services in the nation's total output. It is much easier for a carpenter to pass unnoticed by government authorities than it is for a manufacturing establishment. Estimates of the value of income earned in the underground economy run from 2 percent to 15 percent of GDP. In some countries, the figures are even higher. The Italian underground economy, for example, has been estimated at close to 25 percent of that country's GDP.

Home Production, Volunteering, and Leisure   Sometimes genuine economic activity occurs but is not associated with a market transaction. Consider three general types of such *non-market activities*, all of which are excluded from measurements of GDP.

If a homeowner hires a firm to do some landscaping, the value of the landscaping enters into GDP (as long as the landscaper records the transaction and declares the income); if the homeowner does the landscaping herself, the value of the landscaping is omitted from GDP because there is no recorded market transaction. Such production of goods and services in the home is called *home production* and includes all of the "ordinary" work that is required to keep a household functioning, such as cooking, cleaning, shopping, and doing laundry.

Other non-market activities include voluntary work, such as canvassing for a political party or coaching a local hockey team. Both home production and volunteer activities clearly add to economic well-being, and both use economic resources. Yet neither is included in official measures of national income since they are non-market activities.

Another extremely important non-market activity is *leisure*. If a lawyer voluntarily chooses to reduce her time at work from 2400 hours to 2200 hours per year, measured national income will fall by the lawyer's wage rate times 200 hours. Yet the value to the lawyer of the 200 hours of new leisure enjoyed outside of the marketplace presumably exceeds the lost wages (otherwise she would not have chosen to reduce her work effort by 200 hours), so total economic well-being has increased even though measured GDP has fallen. Over the years, one of the most important ways in which economic growth has benefited people is by permitting increased amounts of leisure. Because the leisure time is not marketed, its value does not show up in measures of national income. We will say more about leisure shortly, as it is an important aspect of our "living standards" not captured by GDP.

Economic "Bads"   When a coal-burning electric power plant sends sulphur dioxide into the atmosphere, leading to acid rain and environmental damage, the value of the electricity sold is included as part of GDP, but the value of the damage done by the acid rain is not deducted. Similarly, the gasoline that we use in our cars is part of national income when it is produced, but the environmental damage done by burning that gasoline is not deducted. To the extent that economic growth brings with it increases in pollution, congestion, and other disamenities of modern living, measurements of national income will overstate the improvement in living standards. Such measures capture the increased output of goods and services, but they fail to account for the increased output of "bads" that generally accompany economic growth.

The extraction, refining, and transportation of oil are all included as goods and services in measures of GDP. But the environmental damage inflicted by an oil spill—an economic "bad"—is not included in any measure of GDP.

Do the Omissions Matter?   Should our current measure of GDP be modified to deal with these omissions? Changing the formal GDP measure to include illegal activities and home production and leisure would be extremely difficult, if not impossible. Not only would it be very costly to get accurate measurements of the level of these activities, but in the cases of home production and leisure there are no prices associated with the "transactions."

Including economic "bads" in the measure of GDP would be possible but doing so would fundamentally change the nature of the measurement such that it would no longer give an accurate measure of the level of economic activity. Damage to the environment is certainly important, but addressing that problem does not require including it in a measure of economic activity.

The current approach to measuring GDP continues to be used for three reasons. First, as we have just said, correcting the major omissions in the measure would be difficult if not impossible. Second, even though the *level* of measured GDP in any given year may be inaccurate, the *change* in GDP from one year to the next is a good indication of the *changes* in economic activity (as long as the omissions are themselves not changing a lot from one year to the next).

The third reason is that policymakers need to measure the amount of market output in the economy in order to design policies to control inflation and set tax rates. To do so, they need to know the flow of money payments made to produce and purchase Canadian output. Modified measures that included non-market activities would distort these figures and likely lead to policy errors.

That the conventional measure of GDP continues to be used is not to say that economists and policymakers are not concerned about the imperfections and omissions. Statistics Canada is constantly striving to improve the measurement of GDP, while at the same time there is a recognition that some problems in measurement will probably always exist.

GDP and Living Standards

We have said that GDP does a good job of measuring the flow of economic activity during a given time period. But we have also said that many things are omitted from this measure, some of which represent beneficial economic activity and some of which represent economic "bads." These observations lead to the obvious question: To what extent does GDP provide a useful measure of our living standards?

The answer depends on what we mean by "living standards." For many people, this term refers to our *purchasing power* or *real income*. When GDP rises, do we experience a rise in our average real incomes? Not necessarily. The *average* level of real income in the economy is best measured by real GDP *per person*, but this does not necessarily rise whenever real GDP rises. If real GDP rises because more people become employed, real GDP per person may not rise. However, if real GDP rises because the existing labour force becomes more productive, then average real incomes will also rise. This explains why most economists believe that productivity growth is such an important determinant of living standards.

To many people, however, the term "living standards" is much broader than simply real per capita income—it includes such important but intangible things as religious and political freedom, the quality of local community life, environmental sustainability, the distribution of income, and our ability to prevent and treat illness and disease. And since measures of real GDP omit many of these intangible things that contribute positively to our overall well-being, it is not even clear that changes in real per capita GDP accurately reflect changes in this broader concept of living standards. For example, greater productivity may lead to an increase in real per capita income and thus to a rise in our average *material* living standards, but if this change also leads to greater environmental damage or greater inequality in the distribution of income, some people may argue that while our material living standards have increased, our overall well-being has declined.

Changes in real per capita income are a good measure of average material living standards. But material living standards are only part of what most people consider their overall well-being.

In recent years, researchers have been developing broad indexes of "social well-being" that go well beyond per capita real income. One measure, the *Canadian Index of Wellbeing*, tracks movements in eight categories of variables, including education, environmental performance, and leisure. From 1994 to 2014, while real per capita GDP increased by 38 percent, the index of well-being rose by only 9.9 percent. Time spent on leisure and cultural activities fell considerably during this period, helping to explain the relatively poor performance of the index.

Note that broad indexes of this type are inevitably controversial. While we might all agree that our living standards depend on more than just our real income, it is almost impossible to agree on the list of other important factors and to their relative importance. For example, is increased leisure more or less important than a cleaner environment? And how does each compare in importance to a rise in democratic engagement?

Despite such methodological debates, researchers continue to develop and examine measures of well-being that go beyond real per capita GDP.

SUMMARY

20.1 National Output and Value Added

LO 1

- Each firm's contribution to total output is equal to its value added, which is the value of the firm's output minus the values of all intermediate goods and services that it uses. The sum of all the values added produced in an economy is the economy's total output, which is called gross domestic product (GDP).

20.2 National Income Accounting: The Basics

LO 2

- Based on the circular flow of income, there are two commonly used ways to compute national income. One is to add up total expenditure on domestic output. The other is to add up the total income generated by domestic production. By standard accounting conventions, these two aggregations define the same total.

- From the expenditure side of the national accounts,

$$GDP = C_a + I_a + G_a + (X_a - IM_a)$$

- C_a comprises consumption expenditures of businesses and households. I_a is investment in inventory accumulation, plant and equipment, and new residential construction. G_a is government purchases of goods and services. $(X_a - IM_a)$ represents net exports of goods and services.

- GDP measured from the income side = wages and salaries + interest + profits + depreciation + (indirect taxes − subsidies).

20.3 National Income Accounting: Some Further Issues

LO 3, 4, 5

- Real measures of national income reflect changes in real quantities. Nominal measures of national income reflect changes in both prices and quantities. Any change in nominal income can be split into a change in quantities and a change in prices.

- The comparison of nominal and real GDP yields the implicit GDP price deflator, an index of the average price of all goods and services produced in the economy.

- GDP must be interpreted with its limitations in mind. GDP excludes production resulting from activities that are illegal, that take place in the underground economy, or that do not pass through markets.

- Notwithstanding its limitations, GDP remains an important measure of the total economic activity that passes through the nation's markets. Recorded *changes* in GDP will generally do an accurate job of measuring *changes* in economic activity.

- Real per capita GDP is a good measure of average material living standards. But because GDP omits many intangible things that contribute positively to our quality of life, GDP-based measures miss important parts of our overall well-being.

KEY TERMS

Intermediate and final goods
Value added
GDP as the sum of all values added
GDP from the expenditure side

GDP from the income side
Nominal and real GDP
GDP deflator

Omissions from GDP
Per capita GDP and productivity
Living standards and GDP

STUDY EXERCISES

MyLab Economics Make the grade with MyLab Economics™: All Study Exercises can be found on MyLab Economics™. You can practise them as often as you want, and many feature step-by-step guided instructions to help you find the right answer.

FILL-IN-THE-BLANK

❶ Fill in the blanks to make the following statements correct.

a. If, when measuring Canada's national output, we add the market values of all firms' outputs in Canada, then we are committing the error of _____. Such an amount would greatly _____ the economy's actual output.

b. To avoid double counting in measuring national income, statisticians use the concept of _____. Each firm's _____ is the value of its output minus the costs of _____ that it purchases from other firms.

c. There are two methods to compute national income: (1) add up total _____ on domestic output; and (2) add up total _____ generated by producing that output. The first measure is called GDP from the _____ side; the second measure is called GDP from the _____ side. The values calculated by the two methods are _____, other than errors of measurement.

d. If we measure GDP from the expenditure side, we are adding four broad categories of expenditure: _____, _____, _____, and _____. As an equation it is written as GDP = _____.

e. If we measure GDP from the income side, we are adding three main components of factor incomes: _____, _____, and _____. To these items we must add non-factor payments of _____ and _____.

❷ Fill in the blanks to make the following statements correct.

a. If nominal GDP increases by 35 percent over a 10-year period, then it is unclear how much of this increase is due to increases in _____ and how much is due to increases in _____. To overcome this problem, we look at GDP valued at _____ prices and we refer to this measure as _____ national income.

b. GDP divided by total population gives us a measure of _____.

c. GDP divided by the number of employed persons in Canada gives us a measure of labour _____.

REVIEW

❸ In measuring GDP from the expenditure side (GDP = $C_a + I_a + G_a + NX_a$), which of the following expenditures are included and within which of the four categories?

a. expenditures on automobiles by consumers
b. expenditures on automobiles by firms
c. expenditures on new machinery by Canadian-owned forest companies located in Canada
d. expenditures on new machinery by Canadian-owned forest companies located in the United States
e. expenditures on new machinery by U.S.-owned forest companies located in Canada
f. reductions in business inventories
g. purchases of second-hand cars and trucks

h. the hiring of economic consultants by the Manitoba government

i. the purchase of Canadian-produced software by a firm in Japan

4 A company's wages and salaries are part of its value added. Suppose, however, that the cleaning and machinery maintenance that its own employees used to do are now contracted out to specialist firms who come in to do the same work more cheaply.

a. What happens to the company's value added when it "contracts out" such work?

b. What happens to value added in the economy as a whole?

5 As we saw in the text, the expenditure approach to measuring GDP shows that

$$GDP = C_a + I_a + G_a + NX_a$$

a. Is this equation a *causal* relationship, suggesting that an increase in any one of the right-hand-side terms *causes* an increase in GDP?

b. It is common to hear commentators suggest that an increase in imports reduces Canadian GDP. Is this true?

6 For each of the following events, describe the likely effect on real GDP in Canada.

a. A major ice storm in Quebec damages homes and thus increases the demand for building materials.

b. A flood on the Red River destroys the annual barley crop on hundreds of thousands of acres of Manitoba farmland.

c. In a near-perfect growing season, Saskatchewan's wheat crop increases by 20 percent above normal levels.

d. A 50 percent decline in the world price of oil in 2014–2015 causes Alberta-based oil producers to decrease their oil production (measured in barrels) by 3 percent.

e. A large new hospital complex is built in Montreal in 2014.

f. The building of a larger arena in Toronto increases the demand for Maple Leafs tickets by Torontonians.

g. The building of a larger arena in Toronto increases the demand for Maple Leafs tickets by residents of Buffalo, New York.

7 Would inflation, as measured by the rate of change in the GDP deflator, ever be different from inflation as measured by the rate of change in the Consumer Price Index? Would it ever be the same? Explain.

8 In 2015, the United Nations ranked Norway first on the Human Development Index—a ranking of the "quality of life" in many countries. Yet Norway was *not* ranked first in terms of real per capita GDP. Explain how the two rankings can be different.

PROBLEMS

9 For each of the following situations, determine the *value added* for Canadian national income.

a. A Canadian farmer pays $100 for seeds to grow organic beets, which she sells to a produce distributor for $1000. The distributor sells the beets to a restaurant for $1300, who then sells $2500 worth of beet salads.

b. A mining firm uses $1 million worth of purchased inputs to extract bauxite, which it sells to an aluminum company for $2 million. The aluminum company sells $2.8 million worth of aluminum to a door manufacturer who sells $4 million worth of finished doors to a big-box retailer who sells them to the public for $6 million.

c. A Canadian retailer imports $400 000 worth of toys from China and sells them for $1 million.

10 The list below provides some national income figures for the country of Econoland. All figures are in millions of dollars.

Wages and salaries	5000
Interest income	200
Personal consumption	3900
Personal saving	1100
Personal income taxes	200
Business profits	465
Indirect taxes	175
Subsidies	30
Government purchases	1000
Exports	350
Imports	390
Net private investment	950
Depreciation	150

a. Using the expenditure approach, what is the value of GDP for Econoland?

b. Using the income approach, what is the value of GDP?

c. What is the value of net domestic income at factor cost?

11 The table below shows data for real and nominal GDP for a hypothetical economy over several years.

Year	Nominal GDP (billions of $)	Real GDP (billions of 2013 $)	GDP Deflator
2014	775.3	798.4	—
2015	814.1	838.6	—
2016	862.9	862.9	—
2017	901.5	882.5	—
2018	951.3	920.6	—
2019	998.8	950.5	—

a. Compute the GDP deflator for each year.
b. Compute the total percentage change in nominal GDP from 2014 to 2019. How much of this change was due to increases in prices and how much was due to changes in quantities?

12 Consider the following data for a hypothetical economy that produces two goods, milk and honey.

	Quantity Produced		Prices	
	Milk (litres)	Honey (kg)	Milk ($/litre)	Honey ($/kg)
Year 1	100	40	2	6
Year 2	120	25	3	6

a. Compute nominal GDP for each year in this economy.
b. Using year 1 as the base year, compute real GDP for each year. What is the percentage change in real GDP from year 1 to year 2?
c. Using year 1 as the base year, compute the GDP deflator for each year. What is the percentage change in the GDP deflator from year 1 to year 2?
d. Now compute the GDP deflator for each year, using year 2 as the base year.
e. Explain why the measures of real GDP growth (and growth in the deflator) depend on the choice of base year.

21 The Simplest Short-Run Macro Model

CHAPTER OUTLINE	LEARNING OBJECTIVES (LO)
	After studying this chapter you will be able to
21.1 DESIRED AGGREGATE EXPENDITURE	**1** explain the difference between desired and actual expenditure.
	2 identify the determinants of desired consumption and desired investment.
21.2 EQUILIBRIUM NATIONAL INCOME	**3** understand the meaning of equilibrium national income.
21.3 CHANGES IN EQUILIBRIUM NATIONAL INCOME	**4** explain how a change in desired expenditure affects equilibrium income through the "simple multiplier."

IN Chapters 19 and 20 we introduced some important macroeconomic variables, and we looked at how they have behaved over recent decades. But we did not explain how any of these variables are determined. For example, we now know what real GDP is and how it is measured, but we do not yet know what makes it rise or fall over time. We are now going to start the hard work of learning what determines real GDP, the price level, the rate of unemployment, and other important macro variables.

In the next few chapters we will build a simplified model of the macro economy that will give us the analytical tools we need to study the determination of these macro variables. Our initial goal in Chapters 21 and 22 is to build the simplest version of the model with which we can examine how real GDP is determined in the *short run*.[1] In reality, real GDP and the price level are determined simultaneously, but we are going to begin by studying these two variables one at a time, and so will start with the important assumption that the *price level is constant*. As we proceed into Chapter 23 we will make the model more realistic by removing this assumption, which will allow us to see how real GDP and the price level are determined together. When we get to Chapter 24 we will make the model even more realistic (and complex) to allow

---

[1] Readers who have studied microeconomics are familiar with a different concept of the short run. In microeconomics, the short run varies industry by industry and corresponds to the period of time for which there are one or more *fixed* factors of production. In macroeconomics, the short run refers to a period of time during which prices and wages have not fully adjusted to various shocks. We say much more about this adjustment process in later chapters.

us to better understand how the various interconnecting parts of the macro economy fit together.

We are now ready to take the first step in building our simple macro model, which is to examine the expenditure decisions of households and firms. In particular, what determines the amount that households and firms *desire* to spend, as opposed to how much they *actually* spend? Understanding why this difference matters is where we start our discussion.

█ 21.1 Desired Aggregate Expenditure

In Chapter 20, we discussed how national income statisticians divide *actual* GDP into its expenditure components: consumption, investment, government purchases, and net exports. In this chapter and the next, we are concerned with a different concept. It is variously called *desired* or *planned* expenditure. Of course, most people would like to spend virtually unlimited amounts, if only they had the resources. Desired expenditure does not refer, however, to what people would like to do under imaginary circumstances; it refers to what people desire to spend out of the resources they actually have. Recall from Chapter 20 that the *actual* values of the various categories of expenditure are indicated by C_a, I_a, G_a, and $(X_a - IM_a)$. Economists use the same letters without the subscript "*a*" to indicate the *desired* expenditure in the same categories: C, I, G, and $(X - IM)$.

Everyone makes expenditure decisions. Fortunately, it is unnecessary for our purposes to look at each of the millions of such individual decisions. Instead, it is sufficient to consider four main groups of decision makers: domestic households, firms, governments, and foreign purchasers of domestically produced commodities. The sum of their *desired* expenditures on domestically produced output is called **desired aggregate expenditure** (*AE*):

$$AE = C + I + G + (X - IM)$$

Desired expenditure need not equal actual expenditure, either in total or in any individual category. For example, firms might not plan to invest in inventory accumulation this year but might do so unintentionally if sales are unexpectedly low—the unsold goods that pile up on their shelves are undesired inventory accumulation. In this case, actual investment expenditure, I_a, will exceed desired investment expenditure, I.

> National income accounts measure *actual* expenditures in each of the four expenditure categories. Our model of the macro economy deals with both *actual* and *desired* expenditures.

You may be wondering why the distinction between desired and actual expenditure is so important. The answer will become clear in the next section, where we discuss the concept of *equilibrium* national income, which involves the relationship between desired and actual expenditure. For now, in the remainder of this section we examine the consumption (*C*) and investment (*I*) components of desired aggregate expenditure. Before we begin, however, it is necessary to understand the distinction between autonomous and induced expenditure, and to establish some important simplifications.

desired aggregate expenditure (*AE*) The sum of desired or planned spending on domestic output by households, firms, governments, and foreigners.

Autonomous Versus Induced Expenditure.   Components of aggregate expenditure that do *not* depend on national income are called **autonomous expenditures**. Autonomous expenditures can and do change, but such changes do not occur systematically in response to changes in national income. Components of aggregate expenditure that *do* change systematically in response to changes in national income are called **induced expenditures**. As we will see, the induced response of desired aggregate expenditure to a change in national income plays a key role in the determination of equilibrium national income.

Important Simplifications.   Our goal in this chapter is to develop the simplest possible model of national income determination. We begin by making three simplifying assumptions:

- there is no trade with other countries—that is, the economy we are studying is a **closed economy;**
- there is no government—and hence no taxes; and
- the price level is constant.

These extreme assumptions serve a vital purpose. As we will soon see, the presence of government and foreign trade is *not* essential to understanding the basic principles of national income determination. By simplifying the model as much as possible, we are better able to understand its structure and therefore how more complex versions of the model work. In following chapters we will complicate our simple macro model by adding government and international trade and then by removing the assumption of a fixed price level. The result will be a more complex but also more realistic model of the macro economy.

Desired Consumption Expenditure

The amount of income households receive after deducting what they pay in taxes is called disposable income. In our simple model with no government and no taxation, disposable income, Y_D, is equal to national income, Y. We define **saving** as all disposable income that is not spent on consumption.

> **By definition, there are only two possible uses of disposable income—consumption and saving. When the household decides how much to put to one use, it has automatically decided how much to put to the other use.**

Figure 21-1 shows the time series for real per capita consumption and disposable income in Canada since 1981. It is clear that the two variables tend to move together over time, although the relationship is not exact. The vertical distance between the two lines is the amount of saving done by households, and the figure shows that household saving as a share of disposable income has been declining over this period. In the early 1980s, household saving was roughly 10 percent of disposable income, whereas by 2017 saving had virtually disappeared. What determines the amount of their disposable income that households decide to consume and the amount they decide to save? The factors that influence this decision are summarized in the *consumption function* and the *saving function.*

autonomous expenditure Elements of expenditure that do not change systematically with national income.

induced expenditure Any component of expenditure that is systematically related to national income.

closed economy An economy that has no foreign trade in goods, services, or assets.

saving All disposable income that is not spent on consumption.

FIGURE 21-1 Consumption and Disposable Income in Canada, 1981–2017

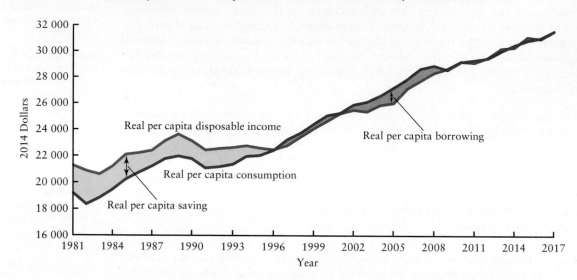

Per capita consumption and disposable income move broadly together over time. The relationship between consumption and disposable income is not exact, but they clearly move broadly together. The vertical distance between the lines is household saving, which as a share of income has been declining since 1981. In years when consumption exceeds disposable income, Canadians are borrowing or selling accumulated assets.

(*Source:* Based on author's calculations using data from Statistics Canada, CANSIM database. Population: Table 051-0001; Consumer Price Index: Table 326-0020; Consumption and Disposable Income: Table 380-0072.)

consumption function The relationship between desired consumption expenditure and all the variables that determine it. In the simplest case, it is the relationship between desired consumption expenditure and disposable income.

The Consumption Function The **consumption function** relates the total desired consumption expenditures of all households to the several factors that determine it. In our macro model, the key factors influencing desired consumption are assumed to be

- disposable income
- wealth
- interest rates
- expectations about the future

In building our simple macro model, we emphasize the role of disposable income in influencing desired consumption; however, as we will see later, changes in the other variables are also important.

That desired consumption is related to disposable income should not be surprising. As income rises, households naturally want to spend more, both now and in the future. For example, if a household's monthly disposable income permanently increases from $3000 to $3500, its monthly consumption will also increase, but probably by less than the full $500 increase. The remainder will be added to its monthly saving—assets that will accumulate and be available to finance future vacations, education, home purchases, or retirement.

> Holding constant other determinants of desired consumption, an increase in disposable income is assumed to lead to an increase in desired consumption.

The consumption function—the assumed relationship between desired consumption and disposable income—has an interesting history in economics. *Extensions in Theory 21-1*

EXTENSIONS IN THEORY 21-1

The Theory of the Consumption Function

Though it may seem natural to assume that a household's current consumption depends largely on its current disposable income, much debate and research has surrounded the issue of how to model consumption behaviour. To see what is involved, consider two quite different—and rather extreme—households.

The first household is short-sighted and spends everything it receives and puts nothing aside for the future. When some overtime work results in a large paycheque, the members of the household go out and spend it. When it is hard to find work, the household's paycheque is small and its members reduce their expenditures. This household's monthly expenditure is therefore exactly equal to its current monthly disposable income.

The second household is forward-looking. Its members think about the future as much as the present and make plans that stretch over their lifetimes. They put money aside for retirement and for the occasional rainy day when disposable income may fall temporarily. An unexpected windfall of income will be saved. An unexpected shortfall of income will be cushioned by spending some of the accumulated savings that were put aside for just such a rainy day. In short, this household's monthly expenditure will be closely related to the average monthly income it expects over its lifetime—the household's *permanent* income. Fluctuations in its current monthly income will have little effect on its current consumption expenditure. Economists refer to this behaviour as *consumption smoothing*.

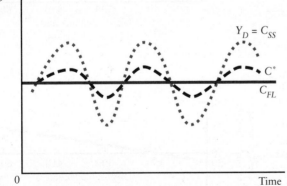

The figure shows the difference between our two sample households, short-sighted and forward-looking, and how their respective consumption expenditure is related to their current disposable income. We assume that disposable income, Y_D, fluctuates over time. C_{SS} is the consumption path of the short-sighted household and is the same as the path of disposable income. C_{FL} is the consumption path for the forward-looking household and is flat.

John Maynard Keynes (1883–1946), the famous English economist who developed much of the basic theory of macroeconomics, populated his theory with households whose current consumption expenditure depended mostly on their current income. But these households are not as extreme as the short-sighted households we just discussed. Keynes did not assume that households *never* saved. He simply assumed that their current level of expenditure and saving depended on their current level of income, as we do in this book. To this day, a consumption function based on this assumption is called a *Keynesian consumption function*.

In the 1950s, two U.S. economists, Franco Modigliani and Milton Friedman, both of whom were subsequently awarded Nobel Prizes in economics, analyzed the behaviour of forward-looking households. Their theories, which Modigliani called the *life-cycle theory* and Friedman called the *permanent-income theory*, explain some observed consumer behaviour that cannot be explained by the simplest Keynesian consumption function.

The differences between the theories of Keynes, on the one hand, and Friedman and Modigliani on the other are not as great as they might seem at first. To see why, let us return to our two imaginary households.

Even the extremely short-sighted household may be able to do some consumption smoothing in the face of income fluctuations. Most households have some money in the bank and some ability to borrow, even if it is just from friends and relatives. As a result, every change in income need not be matched by an equal change in consumption expenditures.

In contrast, although the forward-looking household wants to smooth its pattern of consumption, it may not have the borrowing capacity to do so. Its bank may not be willing to lend money for consumption when the security consists of nothing more than the *expectation* that the household's income will be higher in later years. As a result, the household's consumption expenditure may fluctuate with its current income more than it would want.

The foregoing discussion suggests that the consumption expenditure of both types of households will fluctuate to some extent with their current disposable incomes and to some extent with their expectations of future disposable income. Moreover, in any economy there will be households of both types, and aggregate consumption will be determined by a mix of the two types. The consumption behaviour for the *average* household in such an economy is shown in the figure as the path C^*. The consumption function we use in our simple macro model is of this type: Desired consumption rises and falls in response to changes in disposable income.

discusses consumption behaviour in two hypothetical households and illustrates a debate regarding the importance of *current* disposable income in determining consumption. As the discussion shows, however, our simple assumption that desired consumption is positively related to current disposable income is a good approximation of the behaviour of the *average* household and therefore is suitable for a simple macro model.

Part (i) of Figure 21-2 illustrates a hypothetical consumption function. The first two columns of the table show the value of desired consumption (C) associated with each value of disposable income (Y_D). There is clearly a positive relationship. The figure plots these points and connects them with a smooth line. In this hypothetical economy, the equation of the consumption function is

$$C = 30 + 0.8Y_D$$

In words, this equation says that if disposable income is zero, desired aggregate consumption will be $30 billion, and that for every one-dollar increase in Y_D, desired consumption rises by 80 cents.

FIGURE 21-2 The Consumption and Saving Functions

Disposable Income (Y_D)	Desired Consumption (C)	Desired Saving (S)	APC = C/Y_D	ΔY_D	ΔC	MPC = $\Delta C/\Delta Y_D$
0	30	−30	—			
				30	24	0.8
30	54	−24	1.80			
				120	96	0.8
150	150	0	1.00			
				150	120	0.8
300	270	30	0.90			
				150	120	0.8
450	390	60	0.87			
				75	60	0.8
525	450	75	0.86			
				75	60	0.8
600	510	90	0.85			

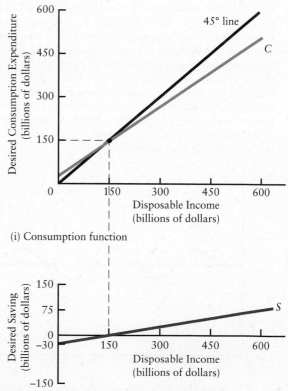

(i) Consumption function

(ii) Saving function

Both desired consumption and desired saving are assumed to rise as disposable income rises. Line C in part (i) of the figure relates desired consumption expenditure to disposable income by plotting the data from the second column of the accompanying table. The consumption function cuts the 45° line at the "break even" level of disposable income, where $C = Y_D$. Note that the level of autonomous consumption is $30 billion; even with zero disposable income, consumers have this amount of desired consumption. The slope of the consumption function is equal to the marginal propensity to consume, which is shown in the table to be 0.8.

The relationship between desired saving and disposable income is shown in part (ii) by line S, which plots the data from the third column of the table. The vertical distance between C and the 45° line in part (i) is by definition the height of S in part (ii); that is, any given level of disposable income must be either consumed or saved. Note that the level of autonomous saving is −$30 billion.

The $30 billion is said to be *autonomous* consumption because it is autonomous (or independent) of the level of income. Autonomous consumption is greater than zero because households are assumed to have some desired consumption even if there is no disposable income. The $0.8Y_D$ is called *induced* consumption because it is induced (or brought about) by a change in income. In part (i) of Figure 21-2, the autonomous part of desired consumption is the vertical intercept of the consumption function. The induced part of consumption occurs as disposable income changes and we move along the consumption function.

We now go on to examine the properties of the consumption function in more detail.

Average and Marginal Propensities to Consume.   To discuss the consumption function concisely, economists use two technical expressions.

The **average propensity to consume (APC)** is the proportion of disposable income that households want to consume. It is equal to desired consumption expenditure divided by disposable income:

$$APC = C/Y_D$$

The fourth column of the table in Figure 21-2 shows the APC calculated from the data in the table. Note that with this consumption function the APC falls as disposable income rises.

The **marginal propensity to consume (MPC)** tells us how much of one additional dollar of income gets spent on consumption. It is equal to the *change* in desired consumption divided by the *change* in disposable income that brings it about:

$$MPC = \Delta C/\Delta Y_D$$

where the Greek letter Δ, delta, means "a change in." The last column of the table in Figure 21-2 shows the MPC that corresponds to the data in the table. Note that in this simple example, the MPC is constant and equal to 0.8. [28]

The Slope of the Consumption Function.   The consumption function shown in Figure 21-2 has a slope of $\Delta C/\Delta Y_D$, which is, by definition, the marginal propensity to consume. The positive slope of the consumption function shows that the MPC is positive; increases in disposable income lead to increases in desired consumption expenditure. The *constant* slope of the consumption function shows that the MPC is the same at any level of disposable income.

The Break-Even Level of Income.   Figure 21-2, part (i), also shows a 45° line, showing all the points where desired consumption equals disposable income. The consumption function intersects this 45° line when income is $150 billion; this is called the "break-even" level of income. When disposable income is less than $150 billion, desired consumption exceeds disposable income. In this case, desired saving must be negative; households are financing their consumption either by spending out of their accumulated saving or by borrowing funds. When disposable income is greater than $150 billion, desired consumption is less than disposable income and so desired saving is positive; households are paying back debt or accumulating assets. At the break-even level of disposable income, desired consumption exactly equals disposable income and so desired saving is zero.

The Saving Function   Households decide how much to consume and how much to save. As we have said, this is only a single decision—how to divide their disposable

average propensity to consume (APC) Desired consumption divided by the level of disposable income.

marginal propensity to consume (MPC) The change in desired consumption divided by the change in disposable income that brought it about.

income between consumption and saving. Therefore, once we know the relationship between desired consumption and disposable income, we automatically know the relationship between desired saving and disposable income.

There are two saving concepts that are exactly parallel to the consumption concepts of *APC* and *MPC*. The **average propensity to save (APS)** is the proportion of disposable income that households want to save, computed by dividing desired saving by disposable income:

$$APS = S/Y_D$$

The **marginal propensity to save (MPS)** relates the change in desired saving to the change in disposable income that brought it about:

$$MPS = \Delta S/\Delta Y_D$$

There is a simple relationship between the saving and the consumption propensities. *APC* and *APS* must sum to 1, and *MPC* and *MPS* must also sum to 1. Because all disposable income is either spent or saved, it follows that the fractions of income consumed and saved must account for all income (*APC* + *APS* = 1). It also follows that the fractions of any *increment* to income consumed and saved must account for all of that increment (*MPC* + *MPS* = 1). [29]

Look back at the table in Figure 21-2 and calculate *APC* and *APS* for yourself by computing C/Y_D and S/Y_D for each row in the table. You will notice that the sum of *APC* and *APS* is *always* 1. Similarly, calculate *MPC* and *MPS* by computing $\Delta C/\Delta Y_D$ and $\Delta S/\Delta Y_D$ for each row in the table. You will also notice that *MPC* and *MPS* *always* sum to 1.

Part (ii) of Figure 21-2 shows the saving function in our simple model. Notice that it is positively sloped, indicating that increases in disposable income lead to an increase in desired saving. Note also that the amount of desired saving is always equal to the vertical distance between the consumption function and the 45° line. When desired consumption exceeds income, desired saving is negative; when desired consumption is less than income, desired saving is positive.

Shifts of the Consumption Function

Earlier we said that desired consumption is assumed to depend on four things—disposable income, wealth, interest rates, and households' expectations about the future. In Figure 21-2, we illustrate the most important relationship—between desired consumption and disposable income (while holding the other determinants constant). In this diagram, changes in disposable income lead to *movements along* the consumption function. Changes in the other three factors will lead to *shifts of* the consumption function. Let's see why.

A Change in Household Wealth.   Household wealth is the value of all accumulated assets minus accumulated debts. The most common types of household assets are savings accounts, mutual funds, portfolios of stocks or bonds, Registered Retirement Savings Plans (RRSPs), and the ownership of homes and cars. The most common household debts are home mortgages, car loans, and outstanding lines of credit from banks (including credit-card debt).

What happens to desired consumption if household wealth increases even while disposable income is unchanged? Suppose, for example, that a rising stock market (a "bull" market) leads to an increase in aggregate household wealth. To the extent that this increase in wealth is expected to persist, less current income needs to be saved for

---

average propensity to save (APS) Desired saving divided by disposable income.

marginal propensity to save (MPS) The change in desired saving divided by the change in disposable income that brought it about.

the future, and households will therefore tend to spend a larger fraction of their current income. The consumption function will shift up, and the saving function down, as shown in Figure 21-3. Current estimates based on research from the International Monetary Fund suggest that an increase in aggregate Canadian wealth of $1 billion leads to an increase in desired aggregate consumption of approximately $50 million.

An increase in household wealth shifts the consumption function up at any level of disposable income; a decrease in wealth shifts the consumption function down.

A Change in Interest Rates. Household consumption can be divided into consumption of *durable* and *non-durable* goods. Durable goods are goods that deliver benefits for several years, such as cars and household appliances. Non-durable goods are consumption goods that deliver benefits to households for only short periods of time, such as groceries, restaurant meals, and clothing. Since many durable goods are also expensive, many of them are purchased on credit—that is, households borrow in order to finance their purchases.

The cost of borrowing, as we discussed in Chapter 19, is the interest rate. A fall in the interest rate reduces the cost of borrowing and generally leads to an increase in desired consumption expenditure, especially of durable goods. That is, for any given level of disposable income, a fall in the interest rate leads to an increase in desired consumption; the consumption function shifts up and the saving function shifts down, as shown in Figure 21-3.

A fall in interest rates usually leads to an increase in desired aggregate consumption at any level of disposable income; the consumption function shifts up. A rise in interest rates shifts the consumption function down.[2]

FIGURE 21-3   Shifts in the Consumption Function

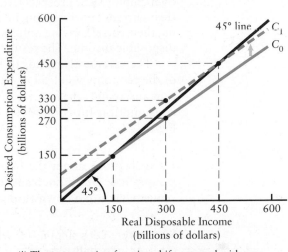

(i) The consumption function shifts upward with an increase in wealth, a decrease in interest rates, or an increase in optimism about the future

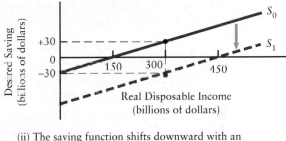

(ii) The saving function shifts downward with an increase in wealth, a decrease in interest rates, or an increase in optimism about the future

Changes in wealth, interest rates, or expectations about the future shift the consumption function. In part (i), line C_0 reproduces the consumption function from part (i) of Figure 21-2. The consumption function then shifts up by $60 billion, so with disposable income of $300 billion, for example, desired consumption rises from $270 billion to $330 billion.

The saving function in part (ii) shifts down by $60 billion, from S_0 to S_1. At a disposable income of $300 billion, for example, desired saving falls from $30 billion to −$30 billion.

---

[2] This is the *substitution* effect of a reduction in the interest rate, which induces all consumers to spend more when the interest rate falls (and less when it rises). The *income* effect of a change in the interest rate works in the opposite direction for creditors and debtors. Since these income effects tend to cancel out in the aggregate economy, they are ignored here.

A Change in Expectations.   Households' expectations about the future are important in determining their desired consumption. Suppose, for example, that large numbers of households become pessimistic about the future state of the economy and about their own employment prospects. In many cases, these fears will lead households to increase their current desired saving in anticipation of rough economic times ahead. But increasing their current saving implies a reduction in current consumption at any given level of disposable income. The result will be a downward shift in the consumption function.

The reverse also tends to be true. Favourable expectations about the future state of the economy will lead many households to increase their current desired consumption and reduce their current desired saving. The result will be an upward shift in the consumption function and a downward shift in the saving function, as shown in Figure 21-3.

Expectations about the future state of the economy often influence desired consumption. Optimism leads to an upward shift in the consumption function; pessimism leads to a downward shift in the consumption function.

Summary   Let's summarize what we have learned so far about the consumption function. As you will soon see, it will play a crucial role in our simple macroeconomic model. The main points are as follows:

1. Desired consumption is assumed to be positively related to disposable income. In a graph, this relationship is shown by the positive slope of the consumption function, which is equal to the marginal propensity to consume (*MPC*).

2. There are both *autonomous* and *induced* components of desired consumption. A movement along the consumption function shows changes in consumption *induced* by changes in disposable income. A shift of the consumption function shows changes in *autonomous* consumption.

3. An increase in household wealth, a fall in interest rates, or greater optimism about the future are all assumed to lead to an increase in desired consumption and thus an upward shift of the consumption function.

4. All disposable income is either consumed or saved. Therefore, there is a saving function associated with the consumption function. Any event that causes the consumption function to shift must also cause the saving function to shift by an equal amount in the opposite direction.

Desired Investment Expenditure

Our simple macroeconomic model includes only consumption and investment expenditure. Having spent considerable time discussing desired consumption, we are now ready to examine the determinants of desired investment. Recall from Chapter 20 the three categories of investment:

- inventory accumulation
- residential construction
- new plant and equipment

Investment expenditure is the most volatile component of GDP, and changes in investment are strongly associated with aggregate economic fluctuations. As shown in Figure 21-4, total investment in Canada fluctuates around an average of about 19 percent of GDP. In each of the last three recessions (1982, 1991, and 2009), investment as a share of GDP fell by between three and five percentage points. In contrast, consumption, government purchases, and net exports are much smoother over the business cycle, each typically changing by less than one percentage point. An important part of our understanding of business cycles will therefore rely on our understanding of the fluctuations in investment.

What explains such fluctuations? Here we examine three important determinants of desired investment expenditure:

- the real interest rate
- changes in the level of sales
- business confidence

Let's now examine these in turn.

FIGURE 21-4   The Volatility of Investment, 1981–2017

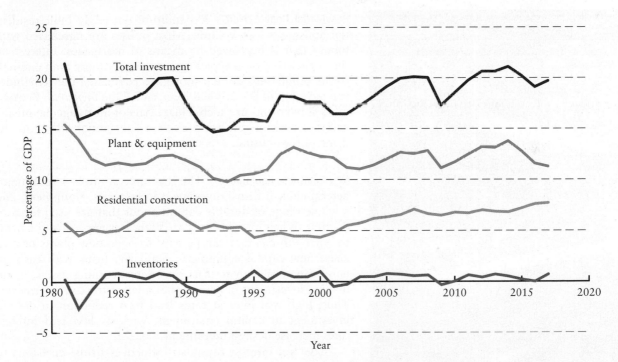

The major components of investment fluctuate considerably as a share of GDP. The recessions of 1982, 1991, and 2009 are evident from the reductions in all components of investment. These data exclude investment by government and non-profit institutions, which combined are quite stable and amount to about 4 percent of GDP.

(*Source:* Based on author's calculations using data from Statistics Canada's CANSIM database: Table 380-0064.)

Investment and the Real Interest Rate   The real interest rate represents the real opportunity cost of using money (either borrowed money or retained earnings) for investment purposes. A rise in the real interest rate therefore reduces the amount of desired investment expenditure. This relationship is most easily understood if we separate investment into its three components: inventories, residential construction, and new plant and equipment.

Inventories.   Changes in inventories represent only a small percentage of private investment in a typical year. As shown by the bottom line in Figure 21-4, inventory investment has been between −2 percent and 2 percent of GDP over the past 35 years. (Inventory investment of −2 percent in a year means that inventories *fall* by 2 percent of GDP.) But the average amount of inventory investment is not an adequate measure of its importance. Since inventory investment is quite volatile, it has an important influence on fluctuations in investment expenditure.

When a firm ties up funds in inventories, those same funds cannot be used elsewhere to earn income. As an alternative to holding inventories, the firm could lend the money out at the going rate of interest. Hence, the higher the real rate of interest, the higher the opportunity cost of holding an inventory of a given size. Other things being equal, the higher the opportunity cost, the smaller the inventories that will be desired.

The largest part of investment by firms is in new plant and equipment, such as this expansion of a pulp mill in British Columbia.

Lloyd Sutton/Alamy Stock Photo

Residential Construction.   Expenditure on newly built residential housing is also volatile. Most houses are purchased with money that is borrowed by means of mortgages. Interest on the borrowed money typically accounts for more than one-half of the purchaser's annual mortgage payments; the remainder is repayment of the original loan, called the *principal*. Because interest payments are such a large part of mortgage payments, variations in interest rates exert a substantial effect on the demand for housing.

New Plant and Equipment.   The real interest rate is also a major determinant of firms' investment in factories, equipment, and a whole range of durable capital goods that are used for production. When interest rates are high, it is expensive for firms to borrow funds that can be used to build new plants or purchase new capital equipment. Similarly, firms with cash on hand can earn high returns on interest-earning assets, again making investment in new capital a less attractive alternative. Thus, high real interest rates lead to a reduction in desired investment in capital equipment, whereas low real interest rates increase desired investment.

The real interest rate also influences firms' decisions to conduct expensive research activities to develop new products or processes. In Figure 21-4, firms' investment in "intellectual property" products (the result of research activities) is included in the "plant and equipment" category and typically represents about one-sixth of that category or about 2 percent of GDP.

The real interest rate reflects the opportunity cost associated with investment, whether in inventories, residential construction, or new plant and equipment. The higher the real interest rate, the higher the opportunity cost and thus the lower the amount of desired investment.

Investment and Changes in Sales   Firms hold inventories to meet unexpected changes in sales and production, and they usually have a target level of inventories that depends on their normal level of sales. Because the size of inventories is related to the level of sales, the *change* in inventories (which is part of current investment) is related to the *change* in the level of sales.

For example, suppose a firm wants to hold inventories equal to 10 percent of its monthly sales. If normal monthly sales are $100 000, it will want to hold inventories valued at $10 000. If monthly sales increase to $110 000 and persist at that level, it will want to increase its inventories to $11 000. Over the period during which its stock of inventories is being increased, there will be a total of $1000 of new inventory investment.

> The higher the level of sales, the larger the desired stock of inventories. Changes in the rate of sales therefore cause temporary bouts of investment (or disinvestment) in inventories.

Changes in sales have similar effects on investment in plant and equipment. For example, if there is a general increase in consumers' demand for products that is expected to persist and that cannot be met by existing capacity, investment in new plant and equipment will be needed. Once the new plants have been built and put into operation, however, the rate of new investment will fall.

Investment and Business Confidence   When a firm invests today, it increases its *future* capacity to produce output. If it can sell the new output profitably, the investment will prove to be a good one. If the new output does not generate profits, the investment will have been a bad one. When it undertakes an investment, the firm does not know if it will turn out well or badly—it is betting on a favourable future that cannot be known with certainty.

When firms expect good times ahead, they will want to invest now so that they have a larger productive capacity in the future ready to satisfy the greater demand. When they expect bad times ahead, they will not invest because they expect no payoff from doing so.

> Investment depends on firms' expectations about the future state of the economy. Optimism about the future leads to more desired investment; pessimism leads to less desired investment.

Investment as Autonomous Expenditure   We have seen that desired investment is influenced by many things, and a complete discussion of the determination of national

FIGURE 21-5 Desired Investment as Autonomous Expenditure

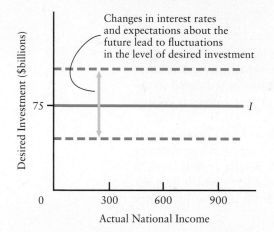

In this simple macro model, desired investment is assumed to be autonomous with respect to current national income. In this example, the level of desired investment is $75 billion. However, changes in interest rates or business confidence will lead to upward or downward shifts in the investment function.

income is not possible without including all of these factors.

For the moment, however, our goal is to build the *simplest* model of the macro economy in which we can examine the interaction of actual national income and desired aggregate expenditure. To build this simple model, we begin by treating desired investment as *autonomous*—that is, we assume it to be unaffected by changes in national income. Figure 21-5 shows the investment function as a horizontal line.

We are making the assumption that desired investment is *autonomous* with respect to national income, *not* that it is constant. It is important that aggregate investment be able to change in our model since in reality investment is the most volatile of the components of aggregate expenditure. As we will soon see, shocks to firms' investment behaviour that cause upward or downward shifts in the investment function are important explanations for fluctuations in national income. The assumption that desired investment is autonomous, and that the I function is therefore horizontal in Figure 21-5, is mainly for simplification. However, this assumption does reflect the fact that investment is an act undertaken by firms for *future* benefit, and thus the *current* level of GDP is unlikely to have a significant effect on desired investment.

The Aggregate Expenditure Function

aggregate expenditure (*AE*) function The function that relates desired aggregate expenditure to actual national income.

The **aggregate expenditure (*AE*) function** relates the level of desired aggregate expenditure to the level of actual national income. (In both cases we mean *real* as opposed to *nominal* variables.) In the simplified economy of this chapter without government and international trade, there is no G or $(X - IM)$ in our function. Desired aggregate expenditure is thus equal to desired consumption plus desired investment, $C + I$.

$$AE = C + I$$

The table in Figure 21-6 shows how the AE function can be calculated, given the consumption function from Figure 21-2 and the investment function from Figure 21-5. The AE function is constructed by vertically summing the C function and the I function, thus showing desired total spending at each level of national income. In this specific case, all of desired investment expenditure is autonomous, as is the $30 billion of consumption that would be desired if national income were equal to zero. Total autonomous expenditure is therefore $105 billion. Induced expenditure is just equal to induced consumption, which is equal to the MPC times disposable income ($0.8 \times Y_D$). Furthermore, since our simple model has no government and no taxes, disposable income, Y_D, is equal to national income, Y. Hence, desired aggregate expenditure can be written as

$$AE = \$105 \text{ billion} + (0.8)Y$$

The Marginal Propensity to Spend   The fraction of any increment to national income that people spend on purchasing domestic output is called the economy's **marginal propensity to spend**. The marginal propensity to spend is measured by the change in desired aggregate expenditure divided by the change in national income that brings it about, or $\Delta AE/\Delta Y$. This is the slope of the aggregate expenditure function. In this book, the marginal propensity to spend is denoted by the symbol z, which is a number greater than zero and less than 1. For the example given in Figure 21-6, the marginal propensity to spend is 0.8. If national income increases by a dollar, there will be an induced increase in desired consumption equal to 80 cents.

marginal propensity to spend The change in desired aggregate expenditure on domestic output divided by the change in national income that brought it about.

> The marginal propensity to spend is the amount of extra total expenditure induced when national income rises by $1, whereas the marginal propensity to consume is the amount of extra consumption induced when households' disposable income rises by $1.

In the simple model of this chapter, however, the marginal propensity to spend is equal to the marginal propensity to consume because consumption is the only kind of expenditure that is assumed to vary with national income. In later chapters, when we add government and international trade to the model, the marginal propensity to spend will differ from the marginal propensity to consume. Both here and in later chapters, it is the more general measure—the marginal propensity to spend—that is important for determining equilibrium national income.

FIGURE 21-6   The Aggregate Expenditure Function

National Income (Y)	Desired Consumption (C = 30 + 0.8 × Y)	Desired Investment (I = 75)	Desired Aggregate Expenditure (AE = C + I)
30	54	75	129
150	150	75	225
300	270	75	345
450	390	75	465
525	450	75	525
600	510	75	585
900	750	75	825

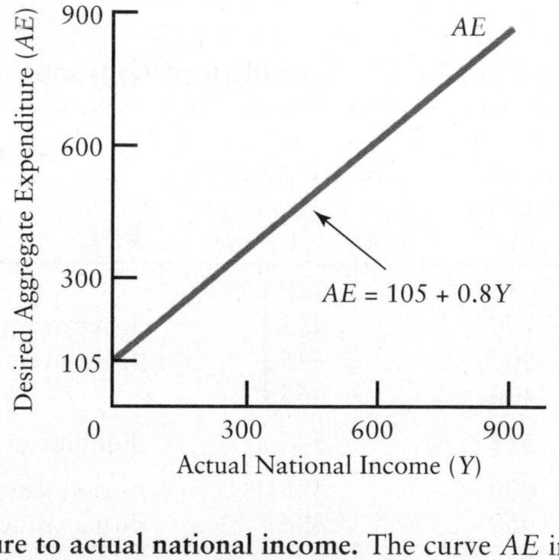

The aggregate expenditure function relates desired aggregate expenditure to actual national income. The curve AE in the figure plots the data from the first and last columns of the accompanying table. Its intercept, which in this case is $105 billion, shows the sum of autonomous consumption and autonomous investment. The slope of AE is equal to the marginal propensity to spend, which in this simple economy is just the marginal propensity to consume.

▌21.2 Equilibrium National Income

We have constructed an *AE* function that combines the spending plans of households and firms. The function shows, for any given level of *actual* national income, the level of *desired* aggregate spending. We are now ready to see what determines the *equilibrium* level of national income. When something is in equilibrium, there is no tendency for it to change. Any conditions required for something to be in equilibrium are called *equilibrium conditions*. We will see that the distinction between desired and actual expenditure is central to understanding the equilibrium conditions for national income.

A "Demand-Determined" Equilibrium

In this chapter and the next, we make an important assumption that influences the nature of equilibrium. In particular, we assume that firms are able and willing to produce any amount of output that is demanded of them and that changes in their production levels do not require a change in their product prices. In this setting, we say that output is *demand determined*. This is an extreme assumption because normally when firms increase their output and move upward along their individual supply curves they would require a higher price for their product. For now, however, we are assuming that this change in product price does not happen. We will relax this assumption in Chapter 23, but until then the assumption of demand-determined output (and stable prices) allows us to more easily understand how our macro model works.

Table 21-1 illustrates the determination of equilibrium national income for our simple model economy. Suppose firms are producing a final output of $300 billion, and thus *actual* national income is also $300 billion. According to the table, at this level of actual national income, *desired* aggregate expenditure is $345 billion. If firms persist in producing a current output of only $300 billion in the face of desired aggregate expenditure of $345 billion, one of two things will happen.

One possibility is that households and firms will be unable to spend the extra $45 billion that they would like to spend, so lines or waiting lists of unsatisfied customers will appear. These shortages will send a signal to firms that they could increase their sales if they increased their production. When the firms do increase their production, actual national income rises.

A more realistic possibility is that all spenders will spend everything that they wanted to spend and there will be no lineups of unsatisfied customers. Since desired expenditure exceeds the actual amount of output, this is possible only if some sales come from the producers' accumulated inventories. In our example, the fulfillment of plans to purchase $345 billion worth of goods in the face of a current output of only $300 billion will reduce inventories by $45 billion. As long as inventories last, more goods can be sold than are currently being produced. But since firms want to maintain a certain level of inventories, they will eventually increase their

TABLE 21-1   Equilibrium National Income

Actual National Income (Y)	Desired Aggregate Expenditure (AE = C + I)	Effect
30	129 ⎤	
150	225 ⎥	Inventories are falling;
300	345 ⎥	firms increase output
450	465 ⎦	
525	525	Equilibrium income
600	585 ⎤	Inventories are rising;
900	825 ⎦	firms reduce output

National income is in equilibrium when desired aggregate expenditure equals actual national income. The data are from Figure 21-6.

production in order to replenish their inventories. Once again, the consequence of each individual firm's decision to increase production is an increase in actual national income.

For any level of national income at which desired aggregate expenditure exceeds actual income, there will be pressure for actual national income to rise.

Next consider the $900 billion level of actual national income in Table 21-1. At this level of output, desired expenditure on domestically produced goods is only $825 billion. If firms persist in producing $900 billion worth of goods, $75 billion worth must remain unsold. Therefore, inventories must rise. However, firms will not allow inventories of unsold goods to rise indefinitely; sooner or later, they will reduce the level of output to the level of sales. When they reduce their level of output, national income will fall.

Changes in firms' accumulated inventories often signal changes in desired aggregate expenditure and eventually induce firms to change their production decisions.

For any level of income at which desired aggregate expenditure is less than actual income, there will be pressure for national income to fall.

Finally, look at the national income level of $525 billion in Table 21-1. At this level, and only at this level, desired aggregate expenditure is equal to actual national income. Purchasers can fulfill their spending plans without causing inventories to change. There is no incentive for firms to alter output. Because the amount that people want to purchase is equal to what is actually being produced, output and income will remain steady; they are in equilibrium.

Equilibrium: Desired *AE* = Actual *Y*

We have just worked through the logic of the equilibrium in our simple macro model. If desired aggregate expenditure is above actual GDP, firms' decisions to increase output will push up GDP. If desired aggregate expenditure is below actual GDP, firms' decisions to reduce output will push GDP down. These forces in the economy suggest a straightforward *equilibrium condition* in this model:

The equilibrium level of national income occurs where desired aggregate expenditure equals actual national income.

In algebraic terms, the *equilibrium condition* for our simple macro model is

$$AE = Y$$

As we will now see, the combination of our *AE* function and this condition will determine the equilibrium level of national income.

Consider Figure 21-7. The line labelled $AE = C + I$ graphs the specific aggregate expenditure function that we have been working with throughout this chapter. The line

FIGURE 21-7 Equilibrium National Income

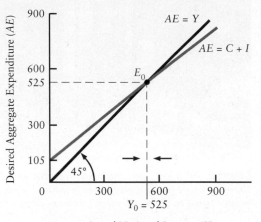

Equilibrium national income is that level of national income where desired aggregate expenditure equals actual national income. If actual national income is below Y_0, desired aggregate expenditure will exceed national income, and output will rise. If actual national income is above Y_0, desired aggregate expenditure will be less than national income, and production will fall. Only when national income is equal to Y_0 will the economy be in equilibrium, as shown at E_0.

labelled $AE = Y$ graphs the equilibrium condition that desired aggregate expenditure equals actual national income. For obvious reasons, this equilibrium condition is often referred to as the 45° line.

Graphically, equilibrium occurs at the level of income at which the AE line intersects the 45° line. This is the level of income at which desired aggregate expenditure is just equal to actual national income. In Figure 21-7, the equilibrium level of national income is Y_0.

To understand how Figure 21-7 illustrates economic behaviour, consider some level of national income (GDP) below Y_0. At this level of income, the AE curve lies above the 45° line, indicating that desired spending exceeds actual output. The vertical distance between AE and the 45° line reflects the size of this excess demand. As we said earlier, this excess demand will induce firms to increase their production. Conversely, at any level of income above Y_0, the AE curve is below the 45° line, indicating that desired spending is less than actual output. The vertical distance between the curves in this case shows the size of the excess supply, which will induce firms to reduce their production. Only when national income equals Y_0 is desired spending equal to actual output, thus providing firms with no incentive to change their production.

Now that we have explained the meaning of equilibrium national income, we will go on to examine the various forces that can *change* this equilibrium. We will then be well on our way to understanding some of the sources of short-run fluctuations in real GDP.

▌21.3 Changes in Equilibrium National Income

Figure 21-7 shows that the equilibrium level of national income occurs where the AE function intersects the 45° line. Through the adjustment in firms' inventories and production levels, the level of actual national income will adjust until this equilibrium level is achieved. Because the position of the AE function is key to determining equilibrium national income, you should not be surprised to hear that *shifts* in the AE function are key to explaining why the equilibrium level of national income changes.

Shifts of the *AE* Function

The AE function shifts when one of its components shifts—that is, when there is a shift in the consumption function or in the investment function. As we have already mentioned, both the consumption function and the investment function will shift if there is a change in interest rates or expectations of the future state of the economy. A change in household wealth is an additional reason for the consumption function to shift. Let's first consider what happens when there is an upward shift in the AE function, and then do the same for a downward shift.

Upward Shifts in the *AE* Function   Suppose households experience an increase in wealth and thus increase their desired consumption at each level of income. Or suppose firms' expectations of higher future sales lead them to increase their planned investment. What is the effect of such events on national income?

Because any increase in autonomous expenditure shifts the entire AE function upward, the same analysis applies to each of the changes mentioned. Two types of shifts in AE can occur. First, if the same increase in expenditure occurs at all levels of income, the AE function shifts parallel to itself, as shown in part (i) of Figure 21-8. Second, if there is an increase in the marginal propensity to spend, the AE function becomes steeper, as shown in part (ii) of Figure 21-8.

FIGURE 21-8   Shifts in the Aggregate Expenditure Function

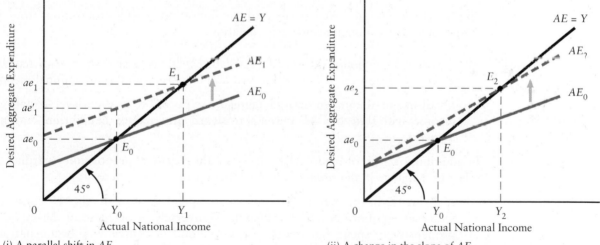

(i) A parallel shift in AE (ii) A change in the slope of AE

Upward shifts in the *AE* function increase equilibrium income; downward shifts decrease equilibrium income. In parts (i) and (ii), the AE function is initially AE_0 with equilibrium national income equal to Y_0.

In part (i), a parallel upward shift in the AE curve from AE_0 to AE_1 reflects an equal increase in desired expenditure at each level of national income. For example, at Y_0, desired expenditure rises from ae_0 to ae'_1 and therefore exceeds actual national income. A new equilibrium is reached at E_1, where income is Y_1. The increase in desired expenditure from ae'_1 to ae_1, represented by a movement along AE_1, is an induced response to the increase in income from Y_0 to Y_1.

In part (ii), a non-parallel upward shift in the AE curve from AE_0 to AE_2 reflects an increase in the marginal propensity to spend. This leads to an increase in equilibrium national income. A new equilibrium is reached at E_2, where national income is equal to Y_2.

Changes in household wealth, such as those created by large and persistent swings in stock-market values, lead to changes in households' desired consumption expenditure, thus changing the equilibrium level of national income.

Figure 21-8 shows that either kind of upward shift in the *AE* function increases equilibrium national income. After the shift in the *AE* curve, income is no longer in equilibrium at its original level because at that level desired aggregate expenditure exceeds actual national income. Given this excess demand, firms' inventories are being depleted and firms respond by increasing production. Equilibrium national income rises to the higher level indicated by the intersection of the *new AE* curve with the 45° line.

Downward Shifts in the *AE* Function   What happens to national income if there is a decrease in the amount of consumption or investment expenditure desired at each level of income? These changes shift the *AE* function downward, as shown in Figure 21-8 by the movement from the dashed *AE* curve to the solid *AE* curve. An equal reduction in desired expenditure at all levels of income shifts *AE* parallel to itself. A fall in the marginal propensity to spend out of national income reduces the slope of the *AE* function. In both cases, the equilibrium level of national income decreases; the new equilibrium is found at the intersection of the 45° line and the *new AE* curve.

The Results Restated   We have derived two important general propositions from our simple model of national income determination:

1. A rise in the amount of desired aggregate expenditure at each level of national income will shift the *AE* curve upward and increase equilibrium national income.

2. A fall in the amount of desired aggregate expenditure at each level of national income will shift the *AE* curve downward and reduce equilibrium national income.

In addition, part (ii) of Figure 21-8 suggests a third general proposition regarding the effect of a change in the *slope* of the *AE* function:

3. An increase in the marginal propensity to spend, z, steepens the *AE* curve and increases equilibrium national income. Conversely, a decrease in the marginal propensity to spend flattens the *AE* curve and decreases equilibrium national income.

The Multiplier

We have learned how specific changes in the *AE* function cause equilibrium national income to rise or fall. We would now like to understand what determines the *size* of the change in national income. A measure of the magnitude of such changes is provided by the *multiplier*. A change in autonomous expenditure increases equilibrium national income by a *multiple* of the initial change in autonomous expenditure. That is, the change in national income is *larger than* the initial change in desired expenditure.

The multiplier is the change in equilibrium national income divided by the change in autonomous expenditure that brought it about. In the simple macro model, the multiplier is greater than 1.[3]

The Logic of the Multiplier   To see why the multiplier is greater than 1 in this model, consider a simple example of an increase in investment expenditure. Imagine what would happen to national income if Kimberley-Clark decided to spend an additional $500 million per year on the construction of new paper mills. Initially, the construction of the paper mills would create $500 million worth of new national income and a corresponding amount of income for households and firms who produce the goods and services on which the initial $500 million is spent. But this is not the end of the story. The increase in national income of $500 million would cause an induced increase in desired consumption.

Electricians, masons, carpenters, and others—who gain new income directly from the building of the paper mills—will spend some of it on food, clothing, entertainment, cars, TVs, and other goods and services. When output expands to meet this demand, new incomes will be created for workers and firms in the industries that produce these goods and services. When they, in turn, spend their newly earned incomes, output will rise further. More income will be created, and more expenditure will be induced. Indeed, at this stage, we might wonder whether the increases in income will ever come to an end. To deal with this concern, we need to consider the multiplier in somewhat more precise terms.

Let total autonomous expenditure be denoted by A. Now consider an increase in autonomous expenditure of ΔA, which in our example is $500 million per year. Remember that ΔA stands for any increase in autonomous expenditure; this could be an increase in investment or in the autonomous component of consumption. The AE function shifts upward by ΔA. National income is no longer in equilibrium because desired aggregate expenditure now exceeds actual national income. Equilibrium is restored by a *movement along* the new AE curve.

The **simple multiplier** measures the change in equilibrium national income that occurs in response to a change in autonomous expenditure when the price level is constant. We refer to it as "simple" because we have simplified the situation by assuming that the price level is fixed. Figure 21-9 illustrates the simple multiplier and makes clear that, since ΔY

simple multiplier The ratio of the change in equilibrium national income to the change in autonomous expenditure that brought it about, calculated for a constant price level.

FIGURE 21-9   The Simple Multiplier

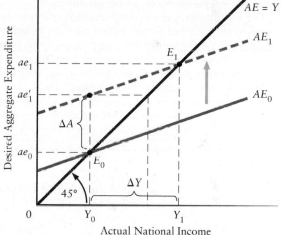

An increase in autonomous aggregate expenditure increases equilibrium national income by a multiple of the initial increase. The initial equilibrium is at E_0, where AE_0 intersects the 45° line. At this point, desired aggregate expenditure, ae_0, is equal to actual national income, Y_0. An increase in autonomous expenditure of ΔA then shifts the AE function upward to AE_1.

Equilibrium occurs when income rises to Y_1. Here desired expenditure, ae_1, equals national income, Y_1. The increase in desired expenditure from ae'_1 to ae_1 represents the induced increase in expenditure that occurs as national income rises. Because ΔY is greater than ΔA, the simple multiplier is greater than one ($\Delta Y/\Delta A > 1$).

---

[3] In this chapter and the next, we assume that firms can readily change their output in response to changes in demand (perhaps because there is some unemployed labour and capital). This assumption of *demand-determined output* is central to the result of a multiplier being greater than 1. We relax this assumption in later chapters.

APPLYING ECONOMIC CONCEPTS 21-1

The Simple Multiplier: A Numerical Example

Consider an economy that has a marginal propensity to spend out of national income of 0.80. Suppose an increase in business confidence leads many firms to increase their investment in new capital equipment. Specifically, suppose annual desired investment increases by $1 billion. National income initially rises by $1 billion, but that is not the end of it. The factors of production that received the first $1 billion spend $800 million. This second round of spending generates $800 million of new production and income. This new income, in turn, induces $640 million of third-round spending, and so it continues, with each successive round of new production and income generating 80 percent as much in new expenditure. Each additional round of expenditure creates new production and income and yet another round of expenditure.

The table carries the process through 10 rounds. Students with sufficient patience (and no faith in mathematics!) may compute as many rounds in the process as they want; they will find that the sum of the rounds of expenditures approaches a limit of $5 billion, which is five times the initial increase in expenditure. [30]

Notice that most of the total change in national income occurs in the first few rounds. Of the total change of $5 billion, 68 percent ($3.4 billion) occurs after only five rounds of activity. By the end of the tenth round, 89 percent ($4.5 billion) of the total change has taken place.

Round of Spending	Increase in Expenditure	Cumulative Total
	(millions of dollars)	
1 (initial increase)	1000.0	1000.0
2	800.0	1800.0
3	640.0	2440.0
4	512.0	2952.0
5	409.6	3361.6
6	327.7	3689.3
7	262.1	3951.4
8	209.7	4161.1
9	167.8	4328.9
10	134.2	4463.1
11 to 20 combined	479.3	4942.4
All others	57.6	5000.0

is greater then ΔA, it is greater than 1. *Applying Economic Concepts 21-1* provides a numerical example.

The Size of the Simple Multiplier The size of the simple multiplier depends on the slope of the *AE* function—that is, on the marginal propensity to spend, *z*.

As shown in Figure 21-10, a high marginal propensity to spend means a steep *AE* curve. The expenditure induced by any increase in income is large, with the result that the overall increase in *Y* caused by the upward shift of the *AE* curve is also large. By contrast, a low marginal propensity to spend means a relatively flat *AE* curve. The expenditure induced by any increase in income is small, and the overall rise in *Y* is not much larger than the shift in the *AE* curve that brought it about.

The larger the marginal propensity to spend, the steeper the *AE* function and thus the larger the simple multiplier.

We can derive the precise value of the simple multiplier by using elementary algebra. (The formal derivation is given in *Extensions in Theory 21-2*.) The result is

$$\text{Simple multiplier} = \frac{\Delta Y}{\Delta A} = \frac{1}{1 - z}$$

FIGURE 21-10 The Size of the Simple Multiplier

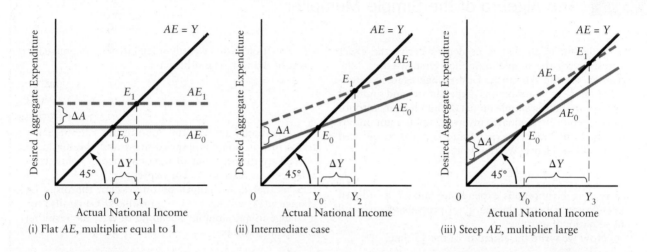

(i) Flat *AE*, multiplier equal to 1   (ii) Intermediate case   (iii) Steep *AE*, multiplier large

The larger the marginal propensity to spend out of national income (z), the steeper is the *AE* curve and the larger is the simple multiplier. In each part of the figure, the initial *AE* function is AE_0, equilibrium is at E_0, with income Y_0. The *AE* curve then shifts upward to AE_1 as a result of an increase in autonomous expenditure of ΔA. ΔA is the same in each part. The new equilibrium in each case is at E_1.

In part (i), the *AE* function is horizontal, indicating a marginal propensity to spend of zero ($z = 0$). The change in equilibrium income ΔY is only the increase in autonomous expenditure because there is no induced expenditure by the people who receive the initial increase in income. The simple multiplier is then equal to 1, its minimum possible value.

In part (ii), the *AE* curve slopes upward but is still relatively flat (z is low). The increase in equilibrium national income to Y_2 is only slightly greater than the increase in autonomous expenditure that brought it about. The simple multiplier is slightly greater than 1.

In part (iii), the *AE* function is quite steep (z is high). Now the increase in equilibrium income to Y_3 is much larger than the increase in autonomous expenditure that brought it about. The simple multiplier is much larger than 1.

For the simple model we have developed in this chapter, $z = 0.8$ and so the simple multiplier $= 1/(1 - 0.8) = 1/0.2 = 5$. In this model, therefore, a \$1 billion increase in autonomous expenditure leads to a \$5 billion increase in equilibrium national income.

Recall that z is the marginal propensity to spend out of national income and is between zero and 1. The smallest simple multiplier occurs when z equals zero. In this case, $(1 - z)$ equals 1 and so the multiplier equals 1. On the other hand, if z is very close to 1, $(1 - z)$ is close to zero and so the multiplier becomes very large. The relationship between the slope of the *AE* function (z) and the size of the multiplier is shown in Figure 21-10.

Economic Fluctuations as Self-Fulfilling Prophecies

Expectations about the future play an important role in macroeconomics. We said earlier that households' and firms' expectations about the future state of the economy influence desired consumption and desired investment. But as we have just seen,

EXTENSIONS IN THEORY 21-2

The Algebra of the Simple Multiplier

Basic algebra is all that is needed to derive the exact expression for the simple multiplier. First, we derive the equation for the AE curve. Desired aggregate expenditure comprises autonomous expenditure and induced expenditure. In the simple model of this chapter, autonomous expenditure is equal to investment plus autonomous consumption. Induced expenditure is equal to induced consumption. Hence, we can write

$$AE = A + zY \qquad [1]$$

where A is autonomous expenditure and zY is induced expenditure, z being the marginal propensity to spend out of national income.

Now we write the equation of the 45° line,

$$AE = Y \qquad [2]$$

which states the equilibrium condition that desired aggregate expenditure equals actual national income. Equation 1 and 2 are two equations with two unknowns, AE and Y. To solve them, we substitute Equation 1 into Equation 2 to obtain

$$Y = A + zY \qquad [3]$$

Equation 3 can be easily solved to get Y expressed in terms of A and z. The solution is

$$Y = \frac{A}{1 - z} \qquad [4]$$

Equation 4 tells us the equilibrium value of Y in terms of autonomous expenditures and the marginal propensity to spend out of national income. Now consider a $1 increase in A. The expression $Y = A/(1 - z)$ tells us that if A changes by one dollar, the resulting change in Y will be $1/(1 - z)$ dollars. Generally, for a change in autonomous spending of ΔA, the resulting change in Y will be

$$\Delta Y = \frac{\Delta A}{1 - z} \qquad [5]$$

Dividing through by ΔA gives the value of the multiplier:

$$\text{Simple multiplier} = \frac{\Delta Y}{\Delta A} = \frac{1}{1 - z} \qquad [6]$$

changes in desired aggregate expenditure will, through the multiplier process, lead to changes in national income. This link between expectations and national income suggests that expectations of a healthy economy can actually produce a healthy economy—what economists call a *self-fulfilling prophecy*.

Imagine a situation in which many firms begin to feel optimistic about future economic prospects. This optimism may lead them to increase their desired investment, thus shifting up the economy's AE function. As we have seen, however, any upward shift in the AE function will lead to an increase in national income. Such "good" economic times will then be seen by firms to have justified their initial optimism. Many firms in such a situation may take pride in their ability to predict the future—but this would be misplaced pride. The truth of the matter is that if enough firms are optimistic and take actions based on that optimism, their actions will *create* the economic situation that they expected.

Now imagine the opposite situation, in which many firms begin to feel pessimistic about future economic conditions. This pessimism may lead them to scale down or cancel planned investment projects. Such a decline in planned investment would shift the AE function down and lead to a decrease in national income. The "bad" economic times will then be seen by the firms as justification for their initial pessimism, and many will take pride in their predictive powers. But again their pride would be misplaced; the truth is that sufficient pessimism on the part of firms will tend to *create* the conditions that they expected.

The aggregate consequences of pessimism on the part of both firms and consumers were an important contributing factor to the global recession that started in late 2008.

In many countries, including Canada, the events surrounding the financial crisis of 2008–2009 led to a shattering of economic optimism. Measures of business and consumer confidence fell by more than had been observed in decades, and this decline in confidence partly explained the large declines in investment and household consumption that occurred at the time and lasted for more than a year. A significant global recession followed. As we will see in later chapters, governments took actions to replace this drop in private-sector demand with increases in government spending.

SUMMARY

21.1 Desired Aggregate Expenditure

LO 1, 2

- Desired aggregate expenditure (AE) is equal to desired consumption plus desired investment plus desired government purchases plus desired net exports. It is the amount that economic agents want to spend on purchasing domestic output.

$$AE = C + I + G + (X - IM)$$

- The relationship between disposable income and desired consumption is called the consumption function. The constant term in the consumption function is autonomous expenditure. The part of consumption that responds to income is called induced expenditure.
- A change in disposable income leads to a change in desired consumption and desired saving. The

responsiveness of these changes is measured by the marginal propensity to consume (MPC) and the marginal propensity to save (MPS), both of which are positive and sum to 1, indicating that all disposable income is either consumed or saved.

- Changes in wealth, interest rates, or expectations about the future lead to a change in autonomous consumption. As a result, the consumption function shifts.
- Firms' desired investment depends on real interest rates, changes in sales, and business confidence. In our simplest model of the economy, investment is treated as autonomous with respect to changes in national income.

21.2 Equilibrium National Income

LO 3

- Equilibrium national income is defined as that level of national income at which desired aggregate expenditure equals actual national income, $AE = Y$.
- At incomes above equilibrium, desired expenditure is less than national income. In this case, inventories accumulate and firms will eventually reduce output. At incomes below equilibrium, desired expenditure

exceeds national income. In this case, inventories are depleted and firms will eventually increase output.

- Equilibrium national income is represented graphically by the point at which the aggregate expenditure (AE) curve cuts the 45° line—that is, where desired aggregate expenditure equals actual national income.

21.3 Changes in Equilibrium National Income

LO 4

- Equilibrium national income is increased by a rise in either autonomous consumption or autonomous investment expenditure. Equilibrium national income is reduced by a fall in these desired expenditures.
- The magnitude of the effect on national income of shifts in autonomous expenditure is given by the multiplier. It is defined as $\Delta Y / \Delta A$, where ΔA is the change in autonomous expenditure.
- The simple multiplier is the multiplier when the price level is constant. The simple multiplier =

$\Delta Y / \Delta A = 1/(1 - z)$, where z is the marginal propensity to spend out of national income. The larger is z, the larger is the simple multiplier.

- Expectations play an important role in the determination of national income. Optimism can lead households and firms to increase desired expenditure, which, through the multiplier process, leads to increases in national income. Pessimism can similarly lead to decreases in desired expenditure and national income.

KEY CONCEPTS

Desired versus actual expenditure
The consumption function
Average and marginal propensities to consume
Average and marginal propensities to save

The aggregate expenditure (AE) function
Marginal propensity to spend
Equilibrium national income
Effect on national income of shifts in the AE curve

The simple multiplier
The size of the simple multiplier and slope of the AE curve

STUDY EXERCISES

MyLab Economics **Make the grade with MyLab Economics™: All Study Exercises can be found on MyLab Economics™. You can practise them as often as you want, and many feature step-by-step guided instructions to help you find the right answer.**

FILL-IN-THE-BLANK

❶ Fill in the blanks to make the following statements correct.

a. The equation for *actual* national income from the expenditure side is written as GDP = _____.

b. The equation for *desired* aggregate expenditure is written as AE = _____.

c. National income accounts measure _____ expenditures in four broad categories. National income theory deals with _____ expenditure in the same four categories.

d. The equation for a simple consumption function is written as $C = a + bY$. The letter a represents the _____ part of consumption. The letters bY represent the _____ part of consumption. When graphing a consumption function, the vertical intercept is given by the letter _____, and the slope of the function is given by the letter _____.

e. In the simple macro model of this chapter, all investment is treated as _____ expenditure, meaning that it is unaffected by changes in national income.

f. The aggregate expenditure function in the simple macro model of this chapter is written as AE = _____ and is graphed with _____ on the vertical axis and _____ on the horizontal axis.

g. An example of an aggregate expenditure function is $AE = \$47$ billion $+ 0.92Y$. Autonomous expenditure is _____ and the marginal propensity to spend out of national income is _____. In the simple model in this chapter, the marginal propensity to spend is the same as the marginal propensity to consume because _____.

❷ Fill in the blanks to make the following statements correct.

a. If actual national income is $200 billion and desired aggregate expenditure is $180 billion, inventories may begin to _____, firms will _____ the level of output, and national income will _____.

b. If actual national income is $200 billion and desired aggregate expenditure is $214 billion, inventories may begin to _____, firms will _____ the level of output, and national income will _____.

c. If households experience an increase in wealth that leads to an increase in desired consumption, the AE curve will shift _____. Equilibrium national income will _____ to the level indicated by the intersection of the AE curve with the _____ line.

d. When autonomous desired expenditure increases by $10 billion, national income will increase by _____ than $10 billion. The magnitude of the change in national income is measured by the _____.

e. The larger is the marginal propensity to spend, the _____ is the multiplier. Where z is the marginal propensity to spend, the multiplier is equal to _____.

REVIEW

❸ Relate the following newspaper headlines to shifts in the C, S, I, and AE functions and to changes in equilibrium national income.

a. "Revival of consumer confidence leads to increased spending."

b. "High mortgage rates discourage new house purchases."

c. "Concern over future leads to a reduction in inventories."

d. "Accelerated depreciation allowances in the new federal budget set off boom on equipment purchases."

e. "Consumers spend as stock market soars."

4 In the chapter we explained the difference between *desired* expenditures and *actual* expenditures.

a. Is national income accounting based on desired or actual expenditures? Explain.

b. Suppose there were a sudden decrease in desired autonomous consumption expenditure. Explain why this would likely be followed by an equally sudden increase in *actual* investment in inventories.

c. Illustrate the event from part (b) in a 45°-line diagram.

5 Consider the following diagram of the AE function and the 45° line.

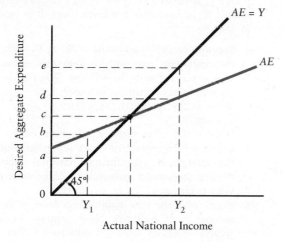

Actual National Income

a. Suppose the level of actual national income is Y_1. What is the level of desired aggregate expenditure? Is it greater or less than actual output? Are inventories being depleted or accumulated?

b. If actual income is Y_1, explain the process by which national income changes toward equilibrium.

c. Suppose the level of actual national income is Y_2. What is the level of desired aggregate expenditure? Is it greater or less than actual output? Are inventories being depleted or accumulated?

d. If actual income is Y_2, explain the process by which national income changes toward equilibrium.

6 The "Paradox of Thrift" is a famous idea in macroeconomics—one that we will discuss in later chapters. The basic idea is that if every household in the economy increases its level of desired saving, the level of

national income will fall and they will end up saving no more than they were initially. Use the model and diagrams of this chapter to show how an (autonomous) increase in desired saving would reduce equilibrium income and lead to no change in actual aggregate saving.

7 In the simple model of this chapter, aggregate investment was assumed to be autonomous with respect to national income. The simple multiplier was $1/(1 - z)$, where z was the marginal propensity to spend. And with autonomous investment, the marginal propensity to spend is simply the marginal propensity to consume.

But now suppose firms' investment is *not* completely autonomous. That is, suppose that $I = \bar{I} + \beta Y$, where $\bar{I}$ is autonomous investment and β is the "marginal propensity to invest" ($\beta > 0$). Explain how this modification to the simple model changes the simple multiplier, and why.

PROBLEMS

8 Consider the following table showing aggregate consumption expenditures and disposable income. All values are expressed in billions of constant dollars.

Disposable Income (Y_D)	Desired Consumption (C)	APC = C/Y_D	MPC = $\Delta C/\Delta Y_D$
0	150	—	
100	225	—	—
200	300	—	—
300	375	—	—
400	450	—	—
500	525	—	—
600	600	—	—
700	675	—	—
800	750	—	—

a. Compute the average propensity to consume for each level of income and fill in the table.

b. Compute the marginal propensity to consume for each successive change in income and fill in the table.

c. Write down the equation for this consumption function.

d. Plot the consumption function on a scale diagram. What is its slope?

9 This question relates to desired saving and is based on the table in Study Exercise 8.

a. Compute desired saving at each level of disposable income. Plot the saving function on a scale diagram. What is its slope?

b. Show algebraically that the average propensity to save plus the average propensity to consume must equal 1.

c. Write down the equation for this saving function.

10 Consider a simple model like the one developed in this chapter. The following equations show the levels of desired consumption and desired investment:

$$C = 500 + 0.9Y$$
$$I = 100$$

Y	C	I	AE
0	—	—	—
2 000	—	—	—
4 000	—	—	—
6 000	—	—	—
8 000	—	—	—
10 000	—	—	—

a. Complete the table above.

b. What is autonomous expenditure in this simple model?

c. Notice the notation used here for income, Y, which represents national income, as opposed to Y_D, which represents disposable income. Explain why the two terms are interchangeable in this model.

d. What is the equilibrium level of national income in this model? Why?

11 Suppose you are given the following information for an economy without government spending, exports, or imports. C is desired consumption, I is desired investment, and Y is national income. C and I are given by

$$C = 1400 + 0.8Y$$
$$I = 400$$

a. What is the equation for the aggregate expenditure (AE) function?

b. Applying the equilibrium condition that $Y = AE$, determine the level of equilibrium national income.

c. Using your answer from part (b), determine the values of consumption, saving, and investment when the economy is in equilibrium.

12 For each of the following aggregate expenditure (AE) functions, identify the marginal propensity to spend (z) and calculate the simple multiplier.

a. $AE = 150 + 0.4Y$
b. $AE = 900 + 0.62Y$
c. $AE = 6250 + 0.92Y$
d. $AE = 457 + 0.57Y$
e. $AE = 500 + 0.2Y$
f. $AE = 1000 + 0.35Y$
g. Explain why the simple multiplier is larger when z is larger, independent of the value of autonomous expenditure.

13 Consider an economy characterized by the following equations:

$$C = 500 + 0.75Y + 0.05W$$
$$I = 150$$

where C is desired consumption, I is desired investment, W is household wealth, and Y is national income.

a. Suppose wealth is constant at $W = 10\ 000$. Draw the aggregate expenditure function on a scale diagram along with the 45° line. What is the equilibrium level of national income?

b. What is the marginal propensity to spend in this economy?

c. What is the value of the simple multiplier?

d. Using your answer from part (c), what would be the change in equilibrium national income if desired investment increased to 250? Show this in your diagram.

e. Begin with the new equilibrium level of national income from part (d). Now suppose household wealth increases from 10 000 to 15 000. What happens to the AE function and by how much does national income change?

22

Adding Government and Trade to the Simple Macro Model

CHAPTER OUTLINE	LEARNING OBJECTIVES (LO)
	After studying this chapter you will be able to
22.1 INTRODUCING GOVERNMENT	**1** understand how government purchases and tax revenues relate to national income.
22.2 INTRODUCING FOREIGN TRADE	**2** explain how exports and imports relate to national income.
22.3 EQUILIBRIUM NATIONAL INCOME	**3** determine equilibrium in our macro model with government and foreign trade.
22.4 CHANGES IN EQUILIBRIUM NATIONAL INCOME	**4** explain why the introduction of government and foreign trade in the macro model reduces the value of the simple multiplier.
	5 describe how government can use fiscal policy to influence the level of national income.
22.5 DEMAND-DETERMINED OUTPUT	**6** understand why output is demand determined in our simple macro model.

IN Chapter 21, we developed a simple short-run model of national income determination in a closed economy with a constant price level. In this chapter, we add government and foreign trade to that model. In Chapter 23, we will expand the model further to allow for a changing price level.

Adding government to the model allows us to understand how the government's use of its taxing and spending powers can affect the level of national income. Adding foreign trade allows us to examine some ways in which external events affect the Canadian economy. Fortunately, the key elements of the previous chapter's model are unchanged even after government and foreign trade are incorporated.

22.1 Introducing Government

fiscal policy The use of the government's tax and spending policies to achieve government objectives.

A government's **fiscal policy** is defined by its plans for taxes and spending. Our discussion of fiscal policy begins in this chapter; we go into more detail in Chapter 24 and again in Chapter 31. Before getting to the details of fiscal policy, however, we need to see how the presence of government spending and taxation can be incorporated into our simple macro model. We consider each in turn.

Government Purchases

In Chapter 20, we distinguished between government *purchases of goods and services* and government *transfer payments*. The distinction bears repeating here. When the government hires a public servant, buys office supplies, purchases fuel for the Canadian Armed Forces, or commissions a study by consultants, it is adding directly to the demands for the economy's current output of goods and services. Hence, desired government purchases, G, are part of aggregate desired expenditure.

The other part of government spending, transfer payments, also affects desired aggregate expenditure but only indirectly. Consider welfare or employment-insurance benefits, for example. These government expenditures place no direct demand on the nation's production of goods and services since they merely transfer funds to the recipients. The same is true of government transfers to firms, which often take the form of subsidies. However, when individuals or firms spend some of these payments on consumption or investment, their spending is part of aggregate expenditure. Thus, government transfer payments do affect aggregate expenditure but only through the effect these transfers have on households' and firms' spending.

In our macro model we make the simple assumption that the level of government purchases, G, is autonomous with respect to the level of national income. That is, we assume that G does not automatically change just because GDP changes. We then view any change in G as a result of a government policy decision. (The government's transfer payments generally *do change* as GDP rises or falls, but it is G that is part of desired aggregate expenditure.)

Net Tax Revenues

Taxes reduce disposable income relative to national income (GDP). In contrast, transfer payments raise disposable income relative to national income. For the purpose of calculating the effect of government policy on desired consumption expenditure, it is the net effect of the two that matters.

net tax revenue Total tax revenue minus transfer payments, denoted T.

Net tax revenue is defined as total tax revenue received by the government minus total transfer payments made by the government, and it is denoted T. (For the remainder of this chapter, the term "taxes" means "net taxes" unless stated otherwise.) Because transfer payments are smaller than total tax revenues, net tax revenues are positive. In our macro model, we assume that net tax revenues vary directly with the level of national income. As GDP rises, a tax system with given tax rates will yield more net revenue. For example, when GDP rises, households and firms will pay more income tax in total even though the tax *rates* are unchanged. In addition, when GDP rises, the government generally reduces its transfers to households and firms. We will use the following simple form for government net tax revenues, T:

$$T = tY$$

where Y is GDP and t is the **net tax rate**—the increase in net tax revenue generated when GDP increases by \$1.

It may be tempting to think of t as the income-tax rate, but note that we are representing in a simple way what in reality is a complex tax-and-transfer structure that includes, in addition to several different types of financial transfers to households and firms, the personal income tax, the corporate income tax, the GST, provincial sales tax, and property taxes. For that reason, t is not the rate on one specific type of tax. It is the amount by which total government tax revenues (net of transfers) change when national income changes.

net tax rate The increase in net tax revenue generated when national income rises by one dollar.

The Budget Balance

The *budget balance* is the difference between total government revenue and total government expenditure; equivalently, it equals net tax revenue minus government purchases, $T - G$. When net revenues exceed purchases, the government has a **budget surplus**. When purchases exceed net revenues, the government has a **budget deficit**. When the two amounts are equal, the government has a *balanced budget*.

When the government has a budget deficit, it must borrow the excess of spending over revenues. It does this by issuing additional *government debt* in the form of bonds or Treasury bills. When the government has a budget surplus, it uses the excess revenue to buy back outstanding government debt. Budget deficits and government debt are the principal topics of Chapter 31.

budget surplus Any excess of current revenue over current expenditure.

budget deficit Any shortfall of current revenue below current expenditure.

Provincial and Municipal Governments

Many people are surprised to learn that the combined activities of the many Canadian provincial and municipal governments account for *more* purchases of goods and services than does the federal government. The federal government raises about the same amount of tax revenue as do the provincial and municipal governments combined, but it transfers a considerable amount of its revenue to the provinces and also makes significant transfers to households, especially in the form of elderly support and employment insurance.

> **When measuring the overall contribution of government purchases to desired aggregate expenditure, all levels of government must be included.**

As we proceed through this chapter discussing the role of government in the determination of national income, think of "the government" as the combination of all levels of government—federal, provincial, territorial, and municipal.

Summary

How does the presence of government affect our simple macro model? Let's summarize:

1. All levels of government add directly to desired aggregate expenditure through their purchases of goods and services, G. Later in this chapter when we are constructing the aggregate expenditure (AE) function for our model, we will include G and we will treat it as autonomous expenditure.

2. Governments also collect tax revenue and make transfer payments. Net tax revenues are denoted T and are positively related to national income. Since T does not represent expenditure on goods and services, it is not included directly in the AE function. T will enter the AE function *indirectly*, however, through its effect on disposable income (Y_D) and consumption. Recall that $Y_D = Y - T$ and that desired consumption is assumed to depend on Y_D.

22.2 Introducing Foreign Trade

Canada imports all kinds of goods and services, from French wine and Italian shoes to Swiss financial and American architectural services. Canada also exports a variety of goods and services, including timber, nickel, automobiles, engineering services, computer software, flight simulators, and commuter jets. U.S.–Canadian trade is the largest two-way flow of trade between any two countries in the world today. Of all the goods and services produced in Canada in a given year, roughly a third are exported. A similar value of goods and services is imported into Canada every year.

To see how foreign trade is incorporated into our macro model, we need to see how exports (X) and imports (IM) affect desired aggregate expenditure (AE). Recall that AE is desired expenditures on *domestically produced goods and services*. Exports are purchases by foreigners of Canadian products and so are a component of AE. In contrast, imports are expenditures by Canadians on goods and services *produced elsewhere* and thus must be subtracted from total expenditures to determine AE. It is therefore *net exports* ($X - IM$) that appears in our macro model as part of AE.

Net Exports

marginal propensity to import The increase in import expenditures induced by a $1 increase in national income. Denoted by m.

Exports depend on spending decisions made by foreign households and firms that purchase Canadian products. Typically, Canada's exports will not change as a result of changes in Canadian national income. We therefore treat exports, X, as autonomous expenditure.

Canada's imports, however, depend on the spending decisions of Canadian households and firms. Almost all consumption goods have an import content. Canadian-made cars, for example, use large quantities of imported components in their manufacture. Canadian-made clothes most often use imported cotton or wool. And most restaurant meals contain some imported fruits, vegetables, or meats. Hence, as consumption rises, imports will also increase. Because consumption rises with national income, we also get a positive relationship between imports and national income (GDP). In our macro model, we use the following simple form for desired imports:

$$IM = mY$$

where Y is GDP and m is the **marginal propensity to import**, the amount that desired imports rise when national income rises by $1.

International trade is very important for the Canadian economy. More than $2.5 billion worth of goods and services flows across the Canada–U.S. border every day, much of it in trucks like these.

Andy Clark/Reuters

In our model, net exports can be described by the following equation:

$$NX = X - mY$$

Since exports are autonomous with respect to Y but imports are positively related to Y, we see that *net exports* are negatively related to national income. This negative relationship is called the *net export function*. Data for a hypothetical economy with autonomous exports and with imports that are 10 percent of national income ($m = 0.1$) are illustrated in Figure 22-1. In this example, exports form the autonomous component and imports form the induced component of desired net exports.

Shifts in the Net Export Function

Any given net export function is drawn under the assumption that everything affecting net exports, except domestic national income, remains constant. The two major influences that are held constant when we draw the NX function are foreign national income and international relative prices. If either one changes, the NX function will shift. Notice that anything affecting Canadian exports will shift the NX function parallel to itself, upward if exports increase and downward if exports decrease. Also notice that anything affecting the marginal propensity to import will change the *slope* of the NX function. Let's now explore some of these changes in detail.

Changes in Foreign Income An increase in foreign income, other things being equal, will lead to an increase in the quantity of Canadian products demanded by foreign countries—that is, to an increase in Canadian exports. This change causes the X curve in Figure 22-1 to shift upward and therefore the NX function also to shift upward, parallel to its original position. A fall in foreign income leads to a reduction in Canadian exports and thus to a parallel downward shift in the NX function.

Due to the size and proximity of the United States, it should not be surprising that Canada's exports are highly sensitive to changes in U.S. GDP. As a result, Canadian policymakers closely monitor developments in the U.S. economy. Booms in the United States generally lead to increases in Canadian exports; economic slumps in the United States usually lead to a slowdown in Canada's exports. Through this trade "linkage," economic conditions in the two countries are connected.

FIGURE 22-1 The Net Export Function

Actual National Income (Y)	Desired Exports (X)	Desired Imports ($IM = 0.1Y$)	Net Exports ($NX = X - IM$)
0	72	0	72
300	72	30	42
600	72	60	12
720	72	72	0
900	72	90	−18

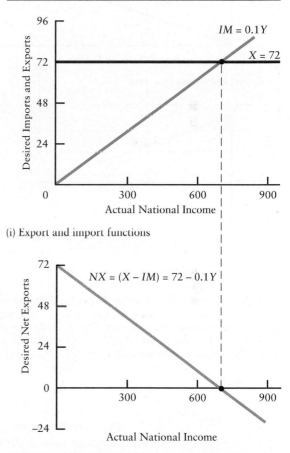

(i) Export and import functions

(ii) Net export function

Net exports fall as national income rises. The data are hypothetical. In part (i), desired exports are constant at $72 billion while desired imports rise with national income; the marginal propensity to import is assumed to be 0.10. Therefore, net exports, shown in part (ii), decline with national income. The slope of the import function in part (i) is equal to the marginal propensity to import. The slope of the net export function in part (ii) is the *negative* of the marginal propensity to import.

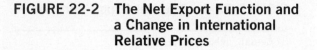

FIGURE 22-2   The Net Export Function and a Change in International Relative Prices

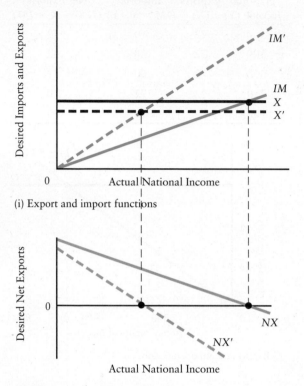

(i) Export and import functions

(ii) Net export function

Changes in international relative prices shift the NX function. A rise in Canadian prices relative to foreign prices lowers desired exports from X to X' and raises the import function from IM to IM'. This shifts the net export function downward from NX to NX'. A fall in Canadian prices (relative to foreign prices) has the opposite effect.

Changes in foreign GDP, especially in the United States, are an important determinant of Canada's exports.

Changes in International Relative Prices   Any change in the prices of Canadian products *relative* to the prices of foreign products will cause both imports and exports to change. These changes will shift the NX function.

Consider what happens with a rise in Canadian prices relative to those in foreign countries. The increase in Canadian prices means that foreigners now see Canadian goods as more expensive relative both to goods produced in their own country and to goods imported from countries other than Canada. As a result, foreigners will purchase fewer Canadian products and so the value of Canadian exports will fall.[1] The X curve shifts down in Figure 22-2. Similarly, Canadians will see imports from foreign countries become cheaper relative to the prices of Canadian-made goods. As a result, they will shift their expenditures toward foreign goods and away from Canadian goods. That is, the marginal propensity to import (m) will rise, and so the IM curve will rotate up. The combination of these two effects is that the net export function shifts downward and becomes steeper, as shown in Figure 22-2.

A fall in Canadian prices relative to foreign prices would have the opposite effect, shifting the X function up and the IM function down, and thus rotating the NX function up.

A rise in Canadian prices relative to those in other countries reduces Canadian net exports at any level of national income. A fall in Canadian prices increases net exports at any level of national income.

The most important cause of a change in international relative prices is a change in the exchange rate. A *depreciation* of the Canadian dollar means that foreigners must pay less of their money to buy one Canadian dollar, and Canadian residents must pay more Canadian dollars to buy a unit of any foreign currency. As a result, the price of foreign goods in terms of Canadian dollars rises, and the price of Canadian goods in terms of foreign currency falls. This reduction in the relative price of Canadian goods will cause a shift in expenditure away from foreign goods and toward Canadian goods. Canadian residents will import less at each level of Canadian national income, and

---

[1] The rise in Canadian prices leads to a reduction in the quantity of Canadian goods demanded by foreigners. But in order for the *value* of Canadian exports to fall, the price elasticity of demand for Canadian exports must exceed 1 (so that the quantity reduction dominates the price increase). Throughout this book, we make this assumption.

foreigners will buy more Canadian exports. The net export function thus shifts upward and becomes flatter.

An example may help to clarify the argument. Suppose something causes the Canadian dollar to depreciate relative to the euro (the common currency used in most of the European Union). The depreciation of the Canadian dollar leads Canadians to switch away from French wines and German cars, purchasing instead more B.C. wine and Ontario-made cars. This reduction in the marginal propensity to import (m) is shown by a downward rotation of the IM curve. The depreciation of the Canadian dollar relative to the euro also stimulates Canadian exports. Quebec furniture and Maritime vacations now appear cheaper to Europeans than previously, and so their expenditure on such Canadian goods increases. This increase in Canadian exports is shown by a parallel upward shift in the X curve. The overall effect is that the net export function shifts up and becomes flatter.

A Word of Caution About Prices and Exchange Rates   It is important to keep in mind that our macro model so far treats prices and exchange rates as *exogenous* variables. That is, though we can discuss what happens if they change, we do not yet explain where these changes come from. Of course, in the actual economy the price level and the exchange rate are key macroeconomic variables whose changes we want to understand. In the next chapter, the price level will be *endogenous* in our model and we can therefore consider why it changes. In Chapter 34, we explain in detail what causes the exchange rate to change. For now, however, the price level and the exchange rate are exogenous variables—we can explain what happens in our model *if* they change but we cannot use the current version of our model to explain *why* they change.

Summary

How does the presence of foreign trade modify our basic model? Let's summarize:

1. Foreign firms and households purchase Canadian-made products. Changes in foreign income and international relative prices will affect Canadian exports (X), but we assume that X is autonomous with respect to Canadian national income. When we construct the economy's aggregate expenditure (AE) function, we will include X since it represents expenditure on domestically produced goods and services.

2. All components of domestic expenditure (C, I, and G) include some import content. Since C is positively related to national income, imports (IM) are also related positively to national income. When we construct the economy's AE function, which shows the desired aggregate expenditure on *domestic* products, we will *subtract* IM because these expenditures are on foreign products.

▌22.3 Equilibrium National Income

As in Chapter 21, equilibrium national income is the level of income at which desired aggregate expenditure equals actual national income. The addition of government and net exports changes the calculations that we must make but does not alter the equilibrium concept or the basic workings of the model.

Adding Taxes to the Consumption Function

Recall that disposable income is equal to national income minus net taxes, $Y_D = Y - T$. We take several steps to determine the relationship between consumption and national income in the presence of taxes.

1. First, assume that the net tax rate, t, is 10 percent, so that net tax revenues are 10 percent of national income (GDP):

$$T = (0.1)Y$$

2. Disposable income must therefore be 90 percent of national income:

$$Y_D = Y - T$$
$$= Y - (0.1)Y$$
$$= (0.9)Y$$

3. The consumption function we used last chapter is given as

$$C = 30 + (0.8)Y_D$$

which tells us that the MPC out of disposable income is 0.8.

4. We can now substitute $(0.9)Y$ for Y_D in the consumption function. By doing so, we get

$$C = 30 + (0.8)(0.9)Y$$
$$\Rightarrow C = 30 + (0.72)Y$$

So, we can express desired consumption as a function of Y_D or as a *different* function of Y. In this example, 0.72 is equal to the MPC times $(1 - t)$, where t is the net tax rate. Whereas 0.8 is the marginal propensity to consume out of *disposable* income, 0.72 is the marginal propensity to consume out of *national* income.

In the presence of taxes, the marginal propensity to consume out of national income is less than the marginal propensity to consume out of disposable income.

The *AE* Function

In Chapter 21, The only components of desired aggregate expenditure were consumption and investment. We now add government purchases and net exports. The separate components in their general form are

$C = c + MPC \times Y_D$	consumption
I	investment
G	government purchases
$T = tY$	net tax revenues
X	exports
$IM = mY$	imports

Our first step in constructing the AE function is to express desired consumption in terms of national income. By using the four steps from above, we write desired consumption as

$$C = c + MPC(1 - t)Y$$

where c is autonomous consumption and MPC is the marginal propensity to consume out of disposable income. Now we sum the four components of desired aggregate expenditure:

$$AE = C + I + G + (X - IM)$$
$$= c + MPC(1 - t)Y + I + G + (X - mY)$$
$$AE = \underbrace{[c + I + G + X]}_{\substack{\text{Autonomous} \\ \text{expenditure}}} + \underbrace{[MPC(1 - t) - m]Y}_{\substack{\text{Induced} \\ \text{expenditure}}}$$

In this last equation, we can see the distinction between autonomous aggregate expenditure and induced aggregate expenditure. The first square bracket brings together all the autonomous parts of expenditure. The second square bracket brings together all the parts of expenditure that change when national income changes—the induced part of consumption and imports. The term in the second square bracket is the marginal propensity to spend out of national income—how much total desired spending on domestically produced output changes when national income changes by $1.

Figure 22-3 graphs the AE function for our hypothetical economy in which we assume that desired investment is $75 billion and the level of government purchases is

FIGURE 22-3   The Aggregate Expenditure Function

The aggregate expenditure function is the sum of desired consumption, investment, government purchases, and net export expenditures. The autonomous components of desired aggregate expenditure are desired investment, desired government purchases, desired exports, and the autonomous part of desired consumption. These sum to $228 billion in the given example, and this sum is the vertical intercept of the AE curve. The induced component is $[MPC(1 - t) - m]Y$, which in our example is equal to $[0.8(0.9) - 0.1]Y = 0.62Y$.

The equation for the AE function is $AE = 228 + 0.62Y$. The slope of the AE function, $\Delta AE/\Delta Y$, is 0.62, indicating that a $1 increase in Y leads to a 62-cent increase in desired expenditure. This is the marginal propensity to spend out of national income. The equilibrium level of national income is $600 billion, the level of Y where the AE function intersects the 45° line.

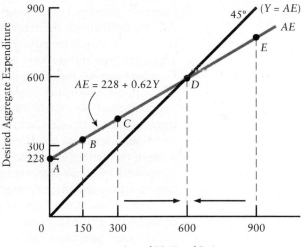

Point	Actual National Income (Y)	Desired Consumption (C = 30 + 0.72Y)	Desired Investment (I = 75)	Desired Government Purchases (G = 51)	Desired Net Exports (X − IM = 72 − 0.1Y)	Desired Aggregate Expenditure (AE = C + I + G + X − IM)
A	0	30	75	51	72	228
B	150	138	75	51	57	321
C	300	246	75	51	42	414
D	600	462	75	51	12	600
E	900	678	75	51	−18	786

$51 billion. The slope of the *AE* function is the marginal propensity to spend out of national income and is equal to $MPC(1 - t) - m$.

Note that, unlike in Chapter 21, the marginal propensity to spend out of national income (z) is not simply equal to the marginal propensity to consume (MPC). To illustrate why, suppose national income rises by $1 and the response to this is governed by the relationships in Figure 22-3. Because 10 cents is collected by the government as net taxes, 90 cents becomes disposable income, and 80 percent of this amount (72 cents) is spent on consumption. However, 10 cents of all expenditure goes to imports, so expenditure on *domestic* goods rises by only 62 cents. Hence, z, the marginal propensity to spend, is 0.62. In algebraic terms,

$$z = MPC(1 - t) - m$$
$$= (0.8)(1 - 0.1) - 0.1$$
$$= 0.72 - 0.1$$
$$= 0.62$$

Equilibrium National Income

As in Chapter 21, we are maintaining our assumption that firms are able and willing to produce whatever level of output is demanded of them at a constant price level. With this assumption that output is *demand determined*, the equilibrium level of national income is that level of national income where desired aggregate expenditure (along the *AE* function) equals the actual level of national income. As was also true in Chapter 21, the 45° line shows the *equilibrium condition*—the collection of points where $Y = AE$. Thus, the equilibrium level of national income in Figure 22-3 is $600 billion at point *D*, where the *AE* function intersects the 45° line.

Suppose national income is less than its equilibrium amount. The forces leading back to equilibrium are exactly the same as those described in Chapter 21. When households, firms, foreign demanders, and governments try to spend at their desired amounts, they will try to purchase more goods and services than the economy is currently producing. Hence, some of the desired expenditure must either be frustrated or take the form of purchases of inventories of goods that were produced in the past. As firms see their inventories being depleted, they will increase production, thereby increasing the level of national income.

The opposite sequence of events occurs when national income is greater than its equilibrium amount. Now the total of desired household consumption, investment, government purchases, and net foreign demand on the economy's production is less than national output. Firms will notice that they are unable to sell all their output. Their inventories will be rising, and sooner or later they will seek to reduce the level of output until it equals the level of sales. When they do, national income will fall.

Only when national income is equal to desired aggregate expenditure ($600 billion in Figure 22-3) is there no pressure for output to change. Desired consumption, investment, government purchases, and net exports just add up to national output.

22.4 Changes in Equilibrium National Income

Changes in any of the components of desired aggregate expenditure will cause changes in equilibrium national income (GDP). In Chapter 21, we investigated the consequences of shifts in the consumption function and in the investment function. Here we take a first look at fiscal policy—the effects of changes in government spending and taxation.

We also consider changes in desired exports and imports. First, we explain why the simple multiplier is reduced by the presence of taxes and imports.

The Multiplier with Taxes and Imports

In Chapter 21, we saw that the *simple multiplier*, the amount by which equilibrium real GDP changes when autonomous expenditure changes by $1, was equal to $1/(1 - z)$, where z is the marginal propensity to spend out of national income. In the simple model of Chapter 21, with no government and no international trade, z was simply the marginal propensity to consume out of disposable income. But in the more complex model of this chapter, which contains both government and foreign trade, we have seen that the marginal propensity to spend out of national income is slightly more complicated.

> The presence of imports and taxes reduces the marginal propensity to spend out of national income and therefore reduces the value of the simple multiplier.

Let's be more specific. In Chapter 21, the marginal propensity to spend, z, was just equal to the marginal propensity to consume. Let ΔY be the change in equilibrium national income brought about by a change in autonomous spending, ΔA. In this case we have the following relationships:

Without Government and Foreign Trade:

$$z = MPC$$

$$\text{Simple multiplier} = \frac{\Delta Y}{\Delta A} = \frac{1}{1 - z}$$

$$= \frac{1}{1 - MPC}$$

In our example from that chapter, the MPC was 0.8, and so the simple multiplier was equal to 5:

$$\text{Simple multiplier} = 1/(1 - 0.8) = 1/0.2 = 5$$

In our expanded model with government and foreign trade, the marginal propensity to spend out of national income must take account of the presence of net taxes and imports, both of which reduce the value of z.

With Government and Foreign Trade:

$$z = MPC(1 - t) - m$$

$$\text{Simple multiplier} = \frac{\Delta Y}{\Delta A} = \frac{1}{1 - z}$$

$$= \frac{1}{1 - [MPC(1 - t) - m]}$$

APPLYING ECONOMIC CONCEPTS 22-1

How Large Is Canada's Simple Multiplier?

In our macro model, the "simple multiplier" expresses the overall change in equilibrium national income resulting from an increase in desired autonomous spending. To the extent that increases in output are only possible in the short run by increasing the level of employment, the multiplier can also tell us something about the total change in employment that will result from an initial increase in spending. And this is the way we usually hear about the effects of the multiplier in the media.

Imagine you hear a news story about a recent announcement by the government to increase its annual spending by $5 billion on the repairs of highways and bridges. Rather than claiming that the $5 billion increase in spending will lead to an overall increase in national income larger than $5 billion, the politician making the announcement is likely to speak in terms of the number of jobs "created" in the economy as a result of the new government spending. For example, the minister of finance might claim that this new spending will *directly* create 5000 new jobs and that an additional 10 000 new jobs will be created *indirectly*. With such a claim, the politician

In our example in this chapter, $MPC = 0.8$, $t = 0.1$, and $m = 0.1$. This makes the simple multiplier equal to 2.63:

$$\text{Simple multiplier} = 1/\{1 - [0.8(1 - 0.1) - 0.1]\}$$
$$= 1/[1 - (0.72 - 0.1)]$$
$$= 1/(1 - 0.62) = 1/0.38 = 2.63$$

What is the central point? When we introduce government and foreign trade to our macro model, the simple multiplier becomes smaller. Since some of any increase in national income goes to taxes and imports, the induced increase in desired expenditure on domestically produced goods is reduced. (The *AE* curve is flatter.) The result is that, in response to any change in autonomous expenditure, the overall change in equilibrium GDP is smaller.

> **The higher is the marginal propensity to import, the lower is the simple multiplier. The higher is the net tax rate, the lower is the simple multiplier.**

Applying Economic Concepts 22-1 examines what the size of the simple multiplier is likely to be in the Canadian economy. You may be surprised at the result!

Net Exports

Earlier in this chapter, we discussed the determinants of desired exports and desired imports. As with the other elements of aggregate expenditure, changes in desired

appears to believe that the simple multiplier is equal to 3—the total increase in employment (and output) will be three times the direct increase. Is a simple multiplier of 3 a realistic estimate for Canada?

In the simple model we have developed in this chapter, we have used values for key parameters that are simple to work with but not necessarily realistic. In particular, we assumed values of t and m that are well below their actual values. To find a realistic estimate for the multiplier in Canada, we need to use more realistic values for the net tax rate (t) and the marginal propensity to import (m). In Canada a reasonable value for t is 0.25, the approximate share of combined government net taxation in GDP. Imports into Canada are close to 35 percent of GDP, and so $m = 0.35$ is a reasonable value. If we use these more realistic values for t and m, and continue the reasonable assumption that the marginal propensity to consume out of disposable income is 0.8, the implied value of z is

$$z = MPC(1 - t) - m$$
$$= 0.8(1 - 0.25) - 0.35 = 0.25$$

and so the implied value of the simple multiplier is

$$\text{Simple multiplier} = 1/(1 - z) = 1/0.75 = 1.33$$

Two main lessons emerge from this analysis:

1. Net taxes and imports reduce the size of the simple multiplier.

2. Realistic values of t and m in Canada suggest a simple multiplier that is closer to 1 than to 2 and certainly far below the value of 5 that we used in the very simple model of Chapter 21.

So the next time you hear a politician make claims about how new spending plans are likely to have large effects on the level of employment and economic activity, think about what the implied value of the simple multiplier must be in order for the claims to be reasonable. The analysis here suggests that the simple multiplier in Canada is likely to be only moderately greater than 1.*

---

*In the next two chapters we will see that once we allow for a price level that can change over time, the multiplier gets even smaller.

---

exports and desired imports will shift the AE function and, through the multiplier process, cause a change in equilibrium national income.

Generally, exports themselves are autonomous with respect to domestic national income. Foreign demand for Canadian exports depends on foreign income, on foreign and Canadian prices, and on the exchange rate, but it does not depend on Canadian income. Export demand could also change because of a change in foreigners' preferences. Suppose foreign consumers develop a preference for Canadian-made furniture and desire to consume $1 billion more per year of these goods than they had in the past. The result will be a $1 billion increase in X, an upward shift of the AE function by $1 billion, and equilibrium national income will increase by $1 billion times the simple multiplier.

Canadian imports of foreign products depend on Canadian income, international relative prices (including the exchange rate), and on Canadian firms' and households' preferences for foreign products. For example, if Canadian firms decide to adjust their supply chains by purchasing more imported intermediate goods, Canada's marginal propensity to import (m) will rise. The result will be a flattening of the AE curve and a reduction in Canada's equilibrium national income.

Fiscal Policy: Government Spending and Taxation

In Chapter 19 we introduced the concept of potential GDP, the level of GDP that would exist if all factors of production were fully employed. Deviations of actual GDP (Y) from potential GDP (Y^*) usually create problems. When $Y < Y^*$, factor incomes are low and unemployment of factors is high; when $Y > Y^*$, rising costs create inflationary pressures. To reduce these problems, governments often try to *stabilize* the level of real GDP close to Y^*. Any attempt to use government policy in this manner is called **stabilization policy**,

stabilization policy Any policy designed to reduce the economy's cyclical fluctuations and thereby stabilize national income.

and here we focus on stabilization through fiscal policy. In Chapters 24 and 32, we examine some important details about fiscal policy, including why the real-world practice of fiscal policy is more complicated than our simple model suggests.

In our macro model, there are two fiscal policy tools available to government policymakers—the net tax rate (*t*) and government purchases (*G*). A reduction in the net tax rate or an increase in government purchases shifts the *AE* curve upward, setting in motion the multiplier process that tends to increase equilibrium national income. An increase in the net tax rate or a decrease in government purchases shifts the *AE* curve downward and tends to decrease equilibrium income.

Once we know the direction in which the government wants to change national income, the *directions* of the required changes in government purchases or taxation are easy to determine. But the *timing* and *magnitude* of the changes are more difficult issues. The issue of timing is difficult because it takes an uncertain amount of time before fiscal policies have an effect on real GDP. The issue of magnitude is difficult because the level of potential output can only be estimated imperfectly, and so the gap between actual and potential GDP is uncertain.

Let's now examine these two policy tools in more detail.

Changes in Government Purchases   Suppose the government decides to reduce its purchases of all consulting services, thus eliminating $200 million per year in spending. Planned government purchases (*G*) would fall by $200 million, shifting *AE* downward by the same amount. How much would equilibrium income change? This amount can be calculated by using the simple multiplier. Government purchases are part of autonomous expenditure, so a *change* in government purchases of ΔG will lead to a *change* in equilibrium national income equal to the simple multiplier times ΔG. In this example, equilibrium income will fall by $200 million times the simple multiplier. In *Applying Economic Concepts 22-1* we argued that a realistic value for the simple multiplier in Canada is about 1.3. Using this value in our example, the effect of the $200 million reduction in *G* is to reduce equilibrium national income by $260 million.

Increases in government purchases would have the opposite effect. If the government increases its spending by $1 billion on new highways, equilibrium national income will rise by $1 billion times the simple multiplier. The effect of a change in *G* on equilibrium national income is shown in part (i) of Figure 22-4.

Changes in the Net Tax Rate   Recall that the slope of the *AE* function is *z*, the marginal propensity to spend out of national income. As we saw earlier,

$$z = MPC(1 - t) - m$$

A change in the net tax rate will change *z*, rotate the *AE* function, and change the equilibrium level of national income.

Consider first a decrease in tax rates. If the government decreases its net tax rate so that it collects 5 cents less out of every dollar of national income, disposable income rises in relation to national income. Hence, desired consumption also rises at every level of national income. This increase in consumption results in an upward *rotation* of the *AE* curve—that is, an increase in the slope of the curve, as shown in part (ii) of Figure 22-4. The result of this shift will be an increase in equilibrium national income.

A rise in tax rates has the opposite effect. A rise in the net tax rate causes a decrease in disposable income, and hence desired consumption expenditure, at each level of national income. This results in a downward rotation of the *AE* curve, which decreases the level of equilibrium national income.

FIGURE 22-4   The Effects of Fiscal Policy on Equilibrium GDP

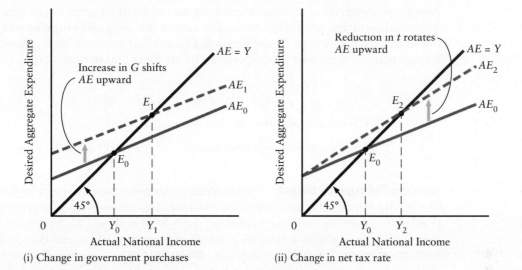

(i) Change in government purchases   (ii) Change in net tax rate

Changes in fiscal policy lead to changes in equilibrium national income. Part (i) shows the effect of a change in government purchases, G. A rise in G causes the AE curve to shift upward in a parallel fashion from AE_0 to AE_1. The change in equilibrium national income equals ΔG times the simple multiplier.

Part (ii) shows the effect of a change in the net tax rate. A reduction in the net tax rate rotates the AE curve upward from AE_0 to AE_2. The new AE curve has a steeper slope because the lower net tax rate withdraws a smaller amount of national income from the desired consumption flow. Equilibrium income rises from Y_0 to Y_2.

Note that when the AE function *rotates*, as happens if anything causes z to change, the simple multiplier is *not* used to tell us about the resulting change in equilibrium national income. The simple multiplier is only used to tell us how much equilibrium national income changes in response to a change in *autonomous* desired spending—that is, in response to a *parallel shift* in the AE function.

22.5 Demand-Determined Output

In this and the preceding chapter, we have discussed the determination of the four categories of aggregate expenditure and have seen how they simultaneously determine equilibrium national income in the short run. An algebraic exposition of the complete model is presented in the appendix to this chapter.

Our macro model is based on three central concepts, and it is worth reviewing them.

Equilibrium National Income   The equilibrium level of national income is the level at which *desired* aggregate expenditure equals *actual* national income ($AE = Y$). If actual national income exceeds desired expenditure, inventories are rising and so firms will eventually reduce production, causing national income to fall. If actual national income is less than desired expenditure, inventories will be falling and so firms will eventually increase production, causing national income to rise.

The Simple Multiplier   The simple multiplier measures the change in equilibrium national income that results from a change in the *autonomous* part of desired aggregate expenditure. The simple multiplier is equal to $1/(1 - z)$, where z is the marginal propensity to spend out of national income. In the model of Chapter 21, in which there is no government and no foreign trade, z is simply the marginal propensity to consume out of disposable income. In our expanded model that contains both government and foreign trade, z is reduced by the presence of net taxes and imports. To review:

$$\text{Simple multiplier} = 1/(1 - z)$$

$$\text{Closed economy with no government: } z = MPC$$

$$\text{Open economy with government: } \quad z = MPC(1 - t) - m$$

Demand-Determined Output   Our model is so far constructed *for a given price level*—that is, the price level is assumed to be constant. This assumption of a given price level is related to another assumption that we have been making. We have been assuming that firms are able and willing to produce any amount of output that is demanded without requiring any change in prices. When this is true, national income depends only on how much is demanded—that is, national income is *demand determined*. Things get more complicated if firms are either unable or unwilling to produce enough to meet all demands without requiring a change in prices. We deal with this possibility in Chapter 23 when we consider *supply-side* influences on national income.

There are two situations in which we might expect national income to be demand determined. First, when there are unemployed resources and firms have excess capacity, firms will often be prepared to provide whatever is demanded from them at unchanged prices. In contrast, if the economy's resources are fully employed and firms have no excess capacity, increases in output may be possible only with higher unit costs, and these cost increases may lead to price increases.

The second situation occurs when firms are *price setters*. Readers who have studied some microeconomics will recognize this term. It means that the firm has the ability to influence the price of its product, either because it is large relative to the market or, more usually, because it sells a product that is *differentiated* to some extent from the products of its competitors. Firms that are price setters often respond to changes in demand by altering their production and sales, at least initially, rather than by adjusting their prices. Only after some time has passed, and the change in demand has persisted, do such firms adjust their prices. This type of behaviour corresponds well to our short-run macro model in which changes in demand initially lead to changes in output (for a given price level).

> Our simple model of national income determination assumes a constant price level. In this model, national income is demand determined.

In the following chapters, we complicate the model by making the price level an *endogenous* variable. In other words, movements in the price level are explained within the model. We do this by considering the *supply side* of the economy—that is, those things that influence the costs at which firms can produce, such as technology and factor prices. When we consider the demand side and the supply side of the economy simultaneously, we will see that changes in desired aggregate expenditure usually cause both prices and real GDP to change.

SUMMARY

22.1 Introducing Government

- Desired government purchases, G, are assumed to be part of autonomous aggregate expenditure. Taxes minus transfer payments are called net taxes and affect aggregate expenditure indirectly through households' disposable income. Taxes reduce disposable income, whereas transfers increase disposable income.

- The budget balance is defined as net tax revenues minus government purchases, $(T - G)$. When $(T - G)$ is positive, there is a budget surplus; when $(T - G)$ is negative, there is a budget deficit.

22.2 Introducing Foreign Trade

- Exports are foreign purchases of Canadian goods, and thus do not depend on Canadian national income. Desired imports are assumed to increase as national income increases. Hence, net exports decrease as national income increases.
- Changes in international relative prices lead to shifts in the net export function. A depreciation of the Canadian

dollar implies that Canadian goods are now cheaper relative to foreign goods. This leads to a rise in exports and a fall in imports, shifting the net export function up. An appreciation of the Canadian dollar has the opposite effect.

22.3 Equilibrium National Income

- As in Chapter 21, national income is in equilibrium when desired aggregate expenditure equals actual national income. The equilibrium condition is

$$Y = AE, \text{ where } AE = C + I + G + (X - IM)$$

- The slope of the AE function in the model with government and foreign trade is $z = MPC(1 - t) - m$, where MPC is the marginal propensity to consume out of disposable income, t is the net tax rate, and m is the marginal propensity to import.

22.4 Changes in Equilibrium National Income

- The presence of taxes and net exports reduces the value of the simple multiplier. With taxes and imports, every increase in national income induces less new spending than in a model with no taxes or imports.
- An increase in government purchases shifts up the AE function and thus increases the equilibrium level of national income. A decrease in the net tax rate makes

the AE function rotate upward and increases the equilibrium level of national income.
- An increase in exports can be caused by an increase in foreign demand for Canadian goods, a fall in the Canadian price level, or a depreciation of the Canadian dollar. An increase in exports shifts the AE function up and increases the equilibrium level of national income.

22.5 Demand-Determined Output

- Our simple model of national income determination is constructed for a given price level. That prices are assumed not to change in response to an increase in desired expenditure reflects a related assumption that output is demand determined.

- Output may be demand determined in two situations: if there are unemployed resources, or if firms are price setters.

KEY CONCEPTS

Taxes, transfers, and net taxes
The budget balance
The net export function
International relative prices

The simple multiplier in an open
economy with government
Fiscal policy

Changes in government purchases
Changes in net tax rates
Demand-determined output

STUDY EXERCISES

MyLab Economics **Make the grade with MyLab Economics™: All Study Exercises can be found on MyLab Economics™. You can practise them as often as you want, and many feature step-by-step guided instructions to help you find the right answer.**

FILL-IN-THE-BLANK

❶ Fill in the blanks to make the following statements correct.

a. In our macro model, government purchases (G) is _____ with respect to national income.
b. G does *not* include _____. Net tax revenue (T) is total tax revenue collected by all governments, *minus* _____.
c. The net tax rate, t, indicates the increase in tax revenues generated when national income increases by _____.
d. T enters the AE function only indirectly through its effect on _____ in the consumption function.
e. If G is larger than T, there is a budget _____. If G is smaller than T, there is a budget _____. The budget is in balance when _____.

❷ Fill in the blanks to make the following statements correct.

a. In our macro model exports (X) are _____ with respect to domestic national income, but the X function will *shift* in response to changes in _____ and _____.
b. The marginal propensity to import (m) indicates the increase in desired _____ when national income rises by _____.
c. The equation for the net export function (NX) is _____. As national income rises, imports _____; NX is therefore _____ related to national income.
d. If Canadian prices rise relative to those in other countries, then imports will _____, and the net export function will shift _____. If Canadian prices fall relative to those in other countries, imports will _____, and the net export function will shift _____.

❸ Fill in the blanks to make the following statements correct.

a. With the addition of government and foreign trade to our simple macro model, the marginal propensity to spend out of national income is _____ than the marginal propensity to consume out of disposable income.
b. Consider the following equation: $z = MPC(1 - t) - m$. The term t represents _____. The term m represents _____. The term z represents _____.
c. The marginal propensity to spend out of national income is less than the marginal propensity to consume out of disposable income because some national income is collected as _____ and some national income is spent on _____.
d. If there is no government and no foreign trade, the simple multiplier can be written as _____, where $z = $ _____. With government and foreign trade, we have $z = $ _____.
e. In comparison to a model with no government and foreign trade, once we add taxes and imports, the value of the simple multiplier is _____. As a result, the effect on equilibrium national income of a change in autonomous expenditure will be _____ in the presence of taxes and imports.

❹ Fill in the blanks to make the following statements correct.

a. Our simple macro model in Chapters 21 and 22 has made an important assumption that the price level is _____. We say that output, or national income, is _____ determined.
b. The assumption that the price level is _____ implies that firms are willing and able to produce any amount of output that is demanded without _____. In this case, national income depends only on how much is _____. We are not yet considering _____-side influences on national income.

REVIEW

5 Classify each of the following government activities as either government purchases or transfers.

a. Welfare payments for the poor
b. Payments to teachers in public schools
c. Payments to teachers at a military college
d. Payments to hospitals and physicians
e. Public vaccination programs
f. Old Age Security payments to the elderly

6 In Chapter 20 we examined how national income was *measured*. By using the expenditure approach, we showed that GDP is always equal to the sum of consumption, investment, government purchases, and net exports. In Chapters 21 and 22 we examined the *determination* of national income. We showed that equilibrium national income occurs when actual national income equals the sum of desired consumption, investment, government purchases, and net exports.

a. Does this mean that national income is always at its equilibrium level?
b. Explain the important difference between "actual" and "desired" expenditures.

7 Each of the following headlines describes an event that will have an effect on desired aggregate expenditure. What will be the effect on equilibrium national income? In each case, describe how the event would be illustrated in the diagram with *AE* and the 45° line.

a. "Minister takes an axe to the armed forces budget."
b. "Russia agrees to buy more Canadian wheat."
c. "High-tech firms to cut capital outlays."
d. "Finance minister pledges to cut income-tax rates."
e. "U.S. imposes import restrictions on Canadian lumber."
f. "Booming Chinese economy expands market for Canadian coal."
g. "Weak dollar spurs exports from Ontario manufacturers."
h. "Prime minister promises burst of infrastructure spending."

8 Suppose the Canadian economy is facing a major global recession, and the minister of finance presents a plan to stimulate the economy.

a. Describe the basic fiscal tools at his disposal.
b. Using the model from this chapter, explain the effect on GDP from an increase in *G* by $5 billion.
c. Using the model from this chapter, explain the effect on GDP from a tax rebate equal in value to $5 billion.
d. Can you offer one reason why the minister of finance might choose to emphasize increases in government spending rather than tax reductions in a federal budget in an effort to increase national income?

PROBLEMS

9 Consider the following table showing national income and government net tax revenues in billions of dollars. Assume that the level of government purchases is constant at $155 billion.

Actual National Income (Y)	Net Tax Revenues (T)	Budget Balance ($T - G$)
100	45	—
200	70	—
300	95	—
400	120	—
500	145	—
600	170	—
700	195	—
800	220	—

a. Compute the government's budget balance for each level of national income and fill in the table.
b. Suppose that net taxes are given by T, where $T = t_0 + t_1 Y$. Using the data in the table, determine the values of t_0 and t_1.
c. What is the interpretation of t_0?
d. What is the interpretation of t_1?
e. Suppose the government decides to increase the level of its purchases of goods and services by $15 billion. What happens to the budget balance for any level of national income?

10 Consider the following table showing national income and imports in billions of dollars. Assume that the level of exports is constant at $300 billion.

Actual National Income (Y)	Imports (IM)	Net Exports ($X - IM$)
100	85	—
200	120	—
300	155	—
400	190	—
500	225	—
600	260	—
700	295	—
800	330	—

a. Compute the level of net exports for each level of national income and fill in the table.
b. Plot the net export function on a scale diagram. Explain why it is downward sloping.
c. Suppose desired imports are given by $IM = m_0 + m_1 Y$. Using the data in the table, determine the values of m_0 and m_1.

d. What is the interpretation of m_0?

e. What is the interpretation of m_1?

f. Suppose that a major trading partner experiences a significant recession. Explain how this affects the net export function in your diagram.

⓫ The economy of Sunrise Island has the following features:

- fixed price level
- no foreign trade
- autonomous desired investment (I) of $20 billion
- autonomous government purchases (G) of $30 billion
- autonomous desired consumption (C) of $15 billion
- marginal propensity to consume out of disposable income of 0.75
- net tax rate of 0.20 of national income

a. Write an equation expressing consumption as a function of disposable income.

b. Write an equation expressing net tax revenues as a function of national income.

c. Write an equation expressing disposable income as a function of national income.

d. Write an equation expressing consumption as a function of national income.

e. Write an equation for the AE function.

f. What is the marginal propensity to spend out of national income?

g. Calculate the simple multiplier for Sunrise Island.

⓬ This question requires you to solve a macro model algebraically. Reading the appendix to this chapter will help you to answer this question. But, just in case, we lead you through it step by step. The equations for the model are as follows:

i) $C = c + MPC \times Y_D$ consumption
ii) $I = I_0$ investment
iii) $G = G_0$ government purchases
iv) $T = tY$ net tax revenue
v) $X = X_0$ exports
vi) $IM = mY$ imports

a. Step 1: Recall that $Y_D = Y - T$. By using this fact, substitute the tax function into the consumption function and derive the relationship between desired consumption and national income.

b. Step 2: Sum the four components of desired aggregate expenditure (C, I, G, NX). This is the aggregate expenditure (AE) function. Collect the autonomous terms separately from the induced terms.

c. Step 3: Recall the equilibrium condition, $Y = AE$. Form the equation $Y = AE$, where AE is your expression for the AE function from part (b). (Your autonomous terms can be collectively labelled A and the terms that represent the marginal propensity to spend can be labelled z.)

d. Step 4: Now collect terms and solve for Y. This is the equilibrium value of national income.

e. Step 5: Suppose the level of autonomous expenditure, which we could call A, rises by ΔA. What is the effect on the level of equilibrium national income?

⓭ The following diagram shows desired aggregate expenditure for the economy of Sunset Island. The AE curve assumes a net tax rate (t) of 10 percent, autonomous exports of $25 billion, and a marginal propensity to import (m) of 15 percent.

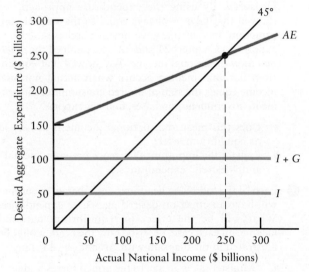

a. What is the level of desired investment expenditure (I)?

b. What is the level of government purchases (G)?

c. What is the autonomous portion of consumption?

d. What is total autonomous expenditure?

e. Starting from equilibrium national income of $250 billion, suppose government purchases decreased by $25 billion. Describe the effect on the AE curve and on equilibrium national income.

f. Starting from equilibrium national income of $250 billion, suppose the net tax rate increased from 10 percent to 30 percent of national income. Describe the effect on the AE curve and on equilibrium national income.

g. Starting from equilibrium national income of $250 billion, suppose investment increased by $50 billion. Describe the effect on the AE curve and on equilibrium national income.

h. Starting from equilibrium national income of $250 billion, suppose the marginal propensity to import fell from 15 percent to 5 percent of national income. Describe the effect on the AE curve and on equilibrium national income.

⓮ The following table shows alternative hypothetical economies and the relevant values for the marginal propensity to consume out of disposable income (MPC), the net tax rate (t), and the marginal propensity to import, m.

Economy	MPC	t	m	z	Simple Multiplier $1/(1-z)$
A	0.75	0.2	0.15	—	—
B	0.75	0.2	0.30	—	—
C	0.75	0.4	0.30	—	—
D	0.90	0.4	0.30	—	—

a. Recall that z, the marginal propensity to spend out of national income, is given by the simple expression $z = MPC(1 - t) - m$. By using this expression, compute z for each of the economies and fill in the table.

b. Compare Economies A and B (they differ only by the value of m). Which one has the larger multiplier? Explain why the size of the multiplier depends on m.

c. Compare Economies B and C (they differ only by the value of t). Which one has the larger multiplier? Explain why the size of the multiplier depends on t.

d. Compare Economies C and D (they differ only by the value of MPC). Which one has the larger multiplier? Explain why the size of the multiplier depends on MPC.

⓯ This question repeats the exercise of Study Exercise 12, but for specific numerical values. The equations of the model are

$$C = 50 + 0.7Y_D \qquad T = (0.2)Y$$

$$I = 75 \qquad X = 50$$

$$G = 100 \qquad IM = (0.15)Y$$

a. Compute the AE function and plot it in a diagram. What is total autonomous expenditure?

b. What is the slope of the AE function?

c. Compute the equilibrium level of national income.

d. Suppose X rises from 50 to 100. How does this affect the level of national income?

e. What is the simple multiplier in this model?

An Algebraic Exposition of the Simple Macro Model

We start with the definition of desired aggregate expenditure:

$$AE = C + I + G + (X - IM) \quad [1]$$

For each component of AE, we write down a behavioural function:

$$C = a + bY_D \text{ (consumption function)} \quad [2]$$

$$I = I_0 \text{ (autonomous investment)} \quad [3]$$

$$G = G_0 \text{ (autonomous government purchases)} \quad [4]$$

$$X = X_0 \text{ (autonomous exports)} \quad [5]$$

$$IM = mY \text{ (imports)} \quad [6]$$

where a is autonomous consumption spending, b is the marginal propensity to consume, and m is the marginal propensity to import. Obviously, the "behavioural" functions for investment, government purchases, and exports are very simple: These are all assumed to be independent of the level of national income.

Before deriving aggregate expenditure, we need to determine the relationship between national income (Y) and disposable income (Y_D), because it is Y_D that determines desired consumption expenditure. Y_D is defined as income after net taxes. In Chapter 22 we examined a very simple linear tax of the form

$$T = tY \quad [7]$$

Taxes must be subtracted from national income to obtain disposable income:

$$Y_D = Y - tY = Y(1 - t) \quad [8]$$

Substituting Equation 8 into the consumption function allows us to write consumption as a function of national income.

$$C = a + b(1 - t)Y \quad [9]$$

Now we can add up all the components of desired aggregate expenditure, substituting Equations 3, 4, 5, 6, and 9 into Equation 1:

$$AE = a + b(1 - t)Y + I_0 + G_0 + X_0 - mY \quad [10]$$

Equation 10 is the AE function, which shows desired aggregate expenditure as a function of actual national income.

In equilibrium, desired aggregate expenditure must equal actual national income:

$$AE = Y \quad [11]$$

Equation 11 is the equilibrium condition for our model. It is the equation of the 45° line in the figures in this chapter.

To solve for the equilibrium level of national income, we want to solve for the level of Y that satisfies both Equation 10 and 11. That is, solve for the level of Y that is determined by the intersection of the AE curve and the 45° line. Substitute Equation 11 into Equation 10:

$$Y = a + b(1 - t)Y + I_0 + G_0 + X_0 - mY \quad [12]$$

Group all the terms in Y on the right-hand side, and subtract them from both sides:

$$Y = Y[b(1 - t) - m] + a + I_0 + G_0 + X_0 \quad [13]$$

$$Y - Y[b(1 - t) - m] = a + I_0 + G_0 + X_0 \quad [14]$$

Notice that $[b(1 - t) - m]$ is exactly the marginal propensity to spend out of national income, defined earlier as z. When national income goes up by one dollar, only $1 - t$ dollars go into disposable income, and only b of that is spent on consumption. Additionally, m is spent on imports, which are not expenditures on domestic national income. Hence $[b(1 - t) - m]$ is spent on domestic output.

Substituting z for $[b(1 - t) - m]$ and solving Equation 14 for equilibrium Y yields

$$Y = \frac{a + I_0 + G_0 + X_0}{1 - z} \quad [15]$$

Notice that the numerator of Equation 15 is total autonomous expenditure, which we call A. Hence, Equation 15 can be rewritten as

$$Y = \frac{A}{1 - z} \quad [16]$$

Notice also that if autonomous expenditure rises by some amount ΔA, Y will rise by $\Delta A/(1 - z)$. So, the simple multiplier is $1/(1 - z)$.

The Algebra Illustrated

The numerical example that was carried through Chapters 21 and 22 can be used to illustrate the preceding exposition. In that example, the behavioural equations are

$$C = 30 + 0.8Y_D \qquad [17]$$

$$I = 75 \qquad [18]$$

$$G = 51 \qquad [19]$$

$$X - IM = 72 - 0.1Y \qquad [20]$$

$$T = 0.1Y \qquad [21]$$

From Equation 8, disposable income is given by $Y(1 - t) = 0.9Y$. Substituting this into Equation 17 yields

$$C = 30 + 0.72Y$$

as in Equation 9.

Now, recalling that in equilibrium $AE = Y$, we add up all the components of AE and set the sum equal to Y, as in Equation 12:

$$Y = 30 + 0.72Y + 75 + 51 + 72 - 0.1Y \quad [22]$$

Collecting terms yields

$$Y = 228 + 0.62Y$$

Subtracting $0.62Y$ from both sides gives

$$0.38Y = 228$$

and dividing through by 0.38, we have

$$Y = \frac{228}{0.38} = 600$$

This can also be derived by using Equation 16. Autonomous expenditure is 228, and z, the marginal propensity to spend out of national income, is 0.62. Thus, from Equation 16, equilibrium income is $228/(1 - 0.62) = 600$, which is exactly the equilibrium we obtained in Figure 22-3.

23

Real GDP and the Price Level in the Short Run

CHAPTER OUTLINE	LEARNING OBJECTIVES (LO)

After studying this chapter you will be able to

23.1 THE DEMAND SIDE OF THE ECONOMY

1 explain why an exogenous change in the price level shifts the *AE* curve and changes the equilibrium level of real GDP.

2 derive the aggregate demand (*AD*) curve and understand what causes it to shift.

23.2 THE SUPPLY SIDE OF THE ECONOMY

3 describe the meaning of the aggregate supply (*AS*) curve and understand why it shifts when technology or factor prices change.

23.3 MACROECONOMIC EQUILIBRIUM

4 explain how *AD* and *AS* shocks affect equilibrium real GDP and the price level.

IN Chapters 21 and 22, we developed a simple model of national income determination. We saw that changes in wealth, interest rates, the government's fiscal policies, or expectations about the future lead to changes in desired aggregate expenditure. Through the multiplier process, such changes in desired expenditure cause equilibrium real GDP to change.

The simple model in Chapters 21 and 22 had a constant price level. We assumed that firms were prepared to provide more output when it was demanded without requiring an increase in prices. In this sense, we said that real GDP was *demand determined*.

The actual economy, however, does not have a constant price level. Rather than assuming it is constant, we would like to understand what causes it to change. We therefore expand our model to make the price

level an *endogenous* variable—one whose changes are explained within the model.

We make the transition to a variable price level in three steps. First, we study the consequences for national income of *exogenous* changes in the price level—changes that happen for reasons that are not explained by our model of the economy. We ask how changes in the price level affect desired aggregate expenditure. That is, we examine the *demand side* of the economy. Second, we examine the *supply side* of the economy by exploring the relationship among the price level, the prices of factor inputs, and the level of output producers would like to supply. Finally, we examine the concept of *macroeconomic equilibrium* that combines both the demand and the supply sides to determine the price level and real GDP simultaneously.

23.1 The Demand Side of the Economy

Consider the macro model in Chapter 22 in which the price level is assumed to be constant. What would happen to equilibrium GDP in that model if the price level changed for some reason? To find out, we need to understand how an exogenous change in the price level affects desired aggregate expenditure.

Exogenous Changes in the Price Level

The *AE* curve shifts in response to a change in the price level—a change, that is, in the average price of all the goods and services in the economy. This shift occurs because a change in the price level affects desired consumption expenditures and desired net exports. These are the changes on which we will focus in this chapter. In later chapters, we will see that changes in the price level will also change interest rates and thus shift the *AE* curve for an additional reason.

Changes in Consumption   You might think it is obvious that a fall in the price level leads to an increase in desired consumption for the simple reason that the demand curves for most individual products are negatively sloped. As we will see in a few pages, however, this logic is incorrect in the context of a macroeconomic model—our focus here is on the *aggregate* price level rather than on the prices of individual products. The relationship between the price level and desired consumption has to do with how changes in the price level lead to changes in household *wealth* and thus to changes in desired spending.

Much of the private sector's total wealth is held in the form of assets with a fixed nominal value. The most obvious example is money itself. We will discuss money in considerable detail in Chapters 26 and 27, but for now just note that most individuals and businesses hold money in their wallets, in their cash registers, or in their bank accounts. What this money can buy—its real value—depends on the price level. The higher the price level, the fewer goods and services a given amount of money can purchase. For this reason, a rise in the domestic price level lowers the real value of money holdings. Similarly, a reduction in the price level raises the real value of money holdings.

> A rise in the price level lowers the real value of money held by the private sector. A fall in the price level raises the real value of money held by the private sector.

Other examples of assets that have fixed nominal values include government and corporate bonds. The bondholder has lent money to the issuer of the bond and receives a repayment of principal and interest from the issuer when the bond matures. What happens when there is a change in the price level in the intervening period? A rise in the price level means that the repayment to the bondholder is lower in real value than it otherwise would be. This is a decline in wealth for the bondholder.

Changes in the price level cause changes in the real value of cash held by households and firms. This change in wealth leads to changes in the amount of desired consumption expenditure.

However, the issuer of the bond, having made a repayment of lower real value because of the increase in the price level, has experienced an increase in wealth. In dollar terms, the bondholder's reduction in wealth is exactly offset by the issuer's increase in wealth.

> **Changes in the price level change the wealth of bondholders and bond issuers, but because the changes offset each other, there is no change in aggregate wealth.**[1]

In summary, a rise in the price level leads to a reduction in the real value of the private sector's wealth. And as we saw in Chapter 21, a reduction in wealth leads to a decrease in autonomous desired consumption and thus to a downward shift in the *AE* function. A fall in the domestic price level leads to a rise in wealth and desired consumption and thus to an upward shift in the *AE* curve.

Changes in Net Exports When the domestic price level rises (and the exchange rate remains unchanged), Canadian goods become more expensive relative to foreign goods. As we saw in Chapter 22, this change in international relative prices causes Canadian consumers to buy fewer Canadian-made goods, which have now become relatively more expensive, and to buy more foreign goods, which have now become relatively less expensive. At the same time, consumers in other countries buy fewer of the now relatively more expensive Canadian-made goods. We saw in Chapter 22 that these changes reduce net exports and lead to a downward shift in the *AE* curve.

> **A rise in the domestic price level (with a constant exchange rate) reduces net exports and causes a downward shift in the *AE* curve. A fall in the domestic price level increases net exports and causes an upward shift in the *AE* curve.**

Changes in Equilibrium GDP

Because it reduces both desired consumption and desired net exports, an exogenous rise in the price level causes a downward shift in the *AE* curve, as shown in Figure 23-1. When the *AE* curve shifts downward, the equilibrium level of real GDP falls.

Conversely, with a fall in the price level, Canadian goods become relatively cheaper internationally, so net exports rise. Also, the purchasing power of nominal assets increases, so households spend more. The resulting increase in desired expenditure on Canadian goods causes the *AE* curve to shift upward. The equilibrium level of real GDP therefore rises.

A Change of Labels In Chapters 21 and 22 the horizontal axis in our figures was labelled "Actual National Income" because we wanted to emphasize the important difference between *actual* income and *desired* expenditure. Notice in Figure 23-1, however, that we have labelled the horizontal axis "Real GDP." We use GDP rather than *national*

---

[1] If bonds are issued by domestic firms or governments but held by foreigners, the changes in domestic wealth caused by a change in the domestic price level will not completely offset each other. In particular, a rise in the domestic price level will lead to a transfer of wealth away from foreign bondholders and toward domestic bond issuers. This is why bondholders who expect future inflation usually demand higher returns in order to hold bonds. In Canada, most corporate and government bonds are held by Canadian firms or individuals and so we ignore this issue; in many other countries, where much debt is held abroad, the issue is of greater importance.

income, but these have the same meaning. It is still *actual*, as opposed to *desired*, but we leave that off, also for simplicity. Finally, we add *real* because from this chapter onward the price level will be changing and thus it is necessary to distinguish changes in nominal GDP from changes in real GDP.

The Aggregate Demand Curve

We have just seen, using our simple model from Chapters 21 and 22, that the price level and real equilibrium GDP are negatively related to each other. This negative relationship can be shown in an important new concept, the *aggregate demand curve*.

Recall that the *AE* curve is drawn with real GDP on the horizontal axis and desired aggregate expenditure on the vertical axis, and that it is plotted for a *given* price level. We are now going to let the price level vary and keep track of the various equilibrium points that occur as the *AE* function shifts. By doing so we can construct an **aggregate demand (*AD*) curve** that shows the relationship between the price level and the equilibrium level of real GDP. It will be plotted with the price level on the vertical axis and real GDP on the horizontal axis. Because the horizontal axes of both the *AE*

FIGURE 23-1 Desired Aggregate Expenditure and the Price Level

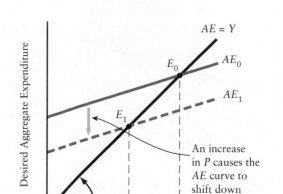

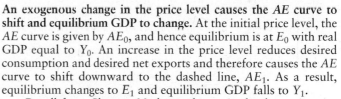

An exogenous change in the price level causes the *AE* curve to shift and equilibrium GDP to change. At the initial price level, the *AE* curve is given by AE_0, and hence equilibrium is at E_0 with real GDP equal to Y_0. An increase in the price level reduces desired consumption and desired net exports and therefore causes the *AE* curve to shift downward to the dashed line, AE_1. As a result, equilibrium changes to E_1 and equilibrium GDP falls to Y_1.

Recall from Chapter 22 that a change in the domestic price level also affects the marginal propensity to import (*m*) and thus the *slope* of the *AE* function. For simplicity, that effect is ignored in this chapter.

and the *AD* curves measure real GDP, the two curves can be placed one above the other so that the levels of GDP on both can be compared directly. This is shown in Figure 23-2.

Now let us derive the *AD* curve. Given a value of the price level, P_0, equilibrium GDP is determined in part (i) of Figure 23-2 at the point where the AE_0 curve crosses the 45° line. The equilibrium level of real GDP is Y_0. Part (ii) of the figure shows the same equilibrium level of GDP, Y_0, plotted against the price level P_0. The equilibrium point in part (i), E_0, corresponds to point E_0 on the *AD* curve in part (ii).

As the price level rises to P_1, the *AE* curve shifts down to AE_1 and the equilibrium level of real GDP falls to Y_1. This determines a second point on the *AD* curve, E_1. At an even higher price level, P_2, the *AE* curve shifts down again and equilibrium real GDP falls to Y_2. This determines a third point on the AD curve.

aggregate demand (*AD*) curve A curve showing combinations of real GDP and the price level that make desired aggregate expenditure equal to actual national income.

For any given price level, the *AD* curve shows the level of real GDP for which desired aggregate expenditure equals actual GDP.

Note that because the *AD* curve relates equilibrium GDP to the price level, changes in the price level that cause *shifts in* the *AE* curve are simply *movements along* the *AD* curve.

FIGURE 23-2 Derivation of the *AD* Curve

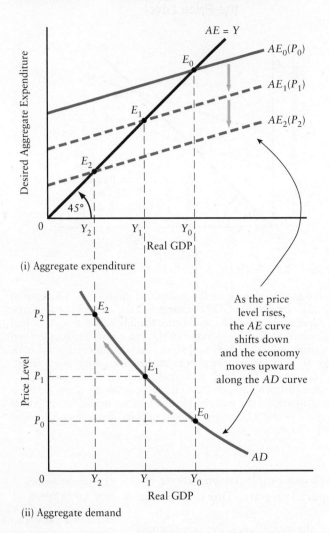

(i) Aggregate expenditure

(ii) Aggregate demand

As the price level rises, the *AE* curve shifts down and the economy moves upward along the *AD* curve

Equilibrium GDP is determined by the *AE* curve for each given price level; the level of equilibrium GDP and its associated price level are then plotted to yield a point on the *AD* curve. When the price level is P_0, the *AE* curve is AE_0, and hence equilibrium GDP is Y_0, as shown in part (i). Plotting Y_0 against P_0 yields the point E_0 on the *AD* curve in part (ii).

An increase in the price level to P_1 causes the *AE* curve to shift downward to AE_1 and causes equilibrium GDP to fall to Y_1. Plotting this new level of GDP against the higher price level yields a second point, E_1, on the *AD* curve. A further increase in the price level to P_2 causes the *AE* curve to shift downward to AE_2, and thus causes equilibrium GDP to fall to Y_2. Plotting P_2 and Y_2 yields a third point, E_2, on the *AD* curve.

A change in the price level causes a *shift* of the *AE* curve but a *movement along* the *AD* curve.

A movement along the *AD* curve thus traces out the response of equilibrium GDP to a change in the price level.[2]

The *AD* Curve Is Not a Micro Demand Curve!

Figure 23-2 provides us with sufficient information to establish that the *AD* curve is negatively sloped.

1. A rise in the price level causes the *AE* curve to shift downward and hence leads to a movement upward and to the left along the *AD* curve, reflecting a fall in the equilibrium level of GDP.

2. A fall in the price level causes the *AE* curve to shift upward and hence leads to a movement downward and to the right along the *AD* curve, reflecting a rise in the equilibrium level of GDP.

What is the underlying economic logic for the negative slope of the *AD* curve? In Chapter 3, we saw that demand curves for individual goods, such as coffee, T-shirts, and cars, are negatively sloped. However, the reasons for the negative slope of the *AD* curve are different from the reasons for the negative slope of individual demand curves used in microeconomics. Why is this the case?

A "micro" demand curve describes a situation in which the price of one product changes *while the prices of all other products and consumers' dollar incomes are constant.* Such an individual demand curve is negatively sloped for two reasons. First, as the price of the product falls, the purchasing power of each consumer's income will rise, and this rise in real income will normally lead to more units of the good being purchased. Second, as the price of the product falls, consumers buy more of that product and fewer of the now relatively more expensive substitutes.

---

[2] Our discussion of Figure 23-2 is for an economy open to international trade, and we have emphasized the reduction of consumption and net exports that occurs in response to a rise in the domestic price level. In a *closed* economy, however, the second effect would be absent, resulting in a steeper *AD* curve than what is shown in Figure 23-2.

The first reason does not apply to the *AD* curve because the dollar value of national income is not being held constant as the price level changes and we move along the *AD* curve. The second reason applies to the *AD* curve but only in a limited way. A change in the price level does not change the *relative* prices of domestic goods and thus does not cause consumers to substitute between them. However, a change in the domestic price level (for a given exchange rate) *does* lead to a change in *international* relative prices and thus to some substitution between domestic and foreign products; this is the link between the price level and net exports that we discussed earlier.

To summarize, the *AD* curve is negatively sloped for two reasons:

1. A fall in the price level leads to a rise in private-sector wealth, which increases desired consumption and thus leads to an increase in equilibrium GDP.

2. A fall in the price level (for a given exchange rate) leads to a rise in net exports and thus leads to an increase in equilibrium GDP.

In later chapters, after we have discussed money, banking, and interest rates in detail, we will introduce a third reason for the negative slope of the *AD* curve.

Shifts in the *AD* Curve   What can cause the *AD* curve to shift? *For a given price level*, any event that leads to a shift of the *AE* curve, and thus a change in equilibrium GDP, will cause the *AD* curve to shift. The event could be a change in any of the autonomous variables that cause the *AE* curve to shift—for example, a change in desired consumption, a change in government purchases, a change in desired investment, or a change in Canada's net exports.

Figure 23-3 shows a shift in the *AD* curve caused by a change in some component of autonomous expenditure. Because the *AD* curve plots equilibrium GDP as a function of the price level, anything that alters equilibrium GDP *at a given price level* must shift the *AD* curve. In other words, any change—other than a change in the price level—that causes the *AE* curve to

FIGURE 23-3   The Simple Multiplier and Shifts in the *AD* Curve

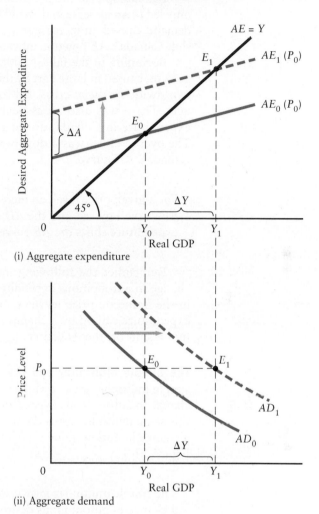

(i) Aggregate expenditure

(ii) Aggregate demand

A change in autonomous expenditure changes equilibrium GDP for any given price level. The simple multiplier measures the resulting horizontal shift in the *AD* curve. The original *AE* curve is AE_0 in part (i). Equilibrium is at E_0, with GDP of Y_0 at price level P_0. This yields point E_0 on the curve AD_0 in part (ii).

The *AE* curve in part (i) then shifts upward from AE_0 to AE_1 because of an increase in autonomous desired expenditure of ΔA. Equilibrium GDP now rises to Y_1, with the price level still constant at P_0. Thus, the *AD* curve in part (ii) shifts to the right to point E_1, indicating the higher equilibrium GDP of Y_1 associated with the same price level P_0. The size of the horizontal shift of the *AD* curve, ΔY, is equal to the simple multiplier times ΔA.

aggregate demand shock Any event that causes a shift in the aggregate demand (*AD*) curve.

shift will also cause the *AD* curve to shift. Such a shift is called an **aggregate demand shock**.

For example, in the 2002–2008 period, strong economic growth in the world economy led to an increase in demand for Canadian-produced raw materials. This increase in demand caused an increase in Canada's net exports. This event, taken by itself, would shift Canada's *AE* function upward and thus would shift Canada's *AD* curve to the right.

Beginning in the fall of 2008, however, a dramatic slowdown in world economic growth, caused in large part by the collapse of the U.S. housing market and the resulting worldwide financial crisis, led to a reduction in foreign demand for Canadian products. There was also an associated reduction in both investment and consumption expenditure in Canada, driven partly by the pessimism that accompanied the crisis. The overall effect was a downward shift in the *AE* curve and thus a leftward shift of Canada's *AD* curve.

> For a given price level, an increase in autonomous aggregate expenditure shifts the *AE* curve upward and the *AD* curve to the right. A fall in autonomous aggregate expenditure shifts the *AE* curve downward and the *AD* curve to the left.

Remember the following important point: In order to shift the *AD* curve, the change in autonomous expenditure must be caused by something *other than* a change in the domestic price level. As we saw earlier in this chapter, a change in aggregate expenditure caused by a change in the domestic price level leads to a movement along (not a shift of) the *AD* curve.

The Simple Multiplier and the *AD* Curve We saw in Chapters 21 and 22 that the simple multiplier measures the size of the change in equilibrium real GDP caused by a change in autonomous expenditure *when the price level is held constant*. It follows that this same multiplier gives the size of the *horizontal shift* in the *AD* curve in response to a change in autonomous expenditure, as illustrated by the movement from E_0 to E_1 in Figure 23-3.

> The simple multiplier measures the horizontal shift in the *AD* curve in response to a change in autonomous desired expenditure.

If the price level remains constant and producers are willing to supply everything that is demanded at that price level, the simple multiplier will also show the change in equilibrium GDP that will occur in response to a change in autonomous expenditure. This mention of producers' willingness to supply output brings us to a discussion of the *supply side* of the economy.

23.2 The Supply Side of the Economy

So far, we have explained how equilibrium real GDP is determined *when the price level is taken as given* and how that equilibrium changes as the price level is changed exogenously. We are now ready to take the important next step: adding an *explanation* for changes in the price level. To do this, we need to take account of the supply decisions of firms.

The Aggregate Supply Curve

Aggregate supply refers to the total output of goods and services that firms would like to produce and sell. The **aggregate supply (AS) curve** relates the price level to the quantity of output that firms would like to produce and sell under two assumptions:

- the state of technology is constant
- the prices of all factors of production are constant

What does the *AS* curve look like, and why?

The Positive Slope of the AS Curve   At their current level of production, firms are incurring some cost per unit of output—what we call their **unit costs**. How will these unit costs change if firms attempt to increase their level of output? The aggregate supply curve is drawn under the assumption that technology and the prices of all factors of production remain constant. This does not, however, mean that firms' unit costs will be constant as they change their output. As output increases, less efficient standby plants may have to be used, and less efficient workers may have to be hired, while existing workers may have to be paid overtime rates for additional work. For these reasons, unit costs tend to rise as output rises, even when technology and input prices are constant. (Readers who have studied microeconomics will recognize the *law of diminishing returns* as one reason that costs may rise in the short run as firms squeeze more output out of a fixed quantity of capital equipment.)

This positive relationship between output and unit costs leads to the positive slope of the *AS* curve, as shown in Figure 23-4. Firms will not be prepared to produce and sell more output unless they are able to charge a higher price sufficient to cover their higher unit costs. This argument applies to *price-taking* firms who sell homogeneous products at market prices beyond their influence. It also applies to *price-setting* firms who sell differentiated products and have some ability to determine the price they charge. In both cases, the fact that unit costs generally rise with output means that firms generally increase their production only if they are able to receive higher prices.

> **The actions of both price-taking and price-setting firms cause the price level and the supply of output to be positively related—the aggregate supply (AS) curve is positively sloped.**

The Increasing Slope of the AS Curve   In Figure 23-4 we see that at low levels of GDP the *AS* curve is relatively flat, but as GDP rises the *AS* curve gets progressively steeper. What explains this shape?

aggregate supply (AS) curve A curve showing the relation between the price level and the quantity of aggregate output supplied, for given technology and factor prices.

unit cost Cost per unit of output, equal to total cost divided by total output.

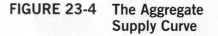

FIGURE 23-4   The Aggregate Supply Curve

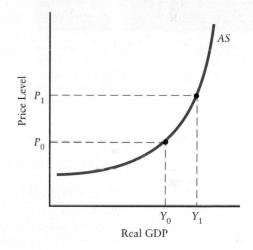

The *AS* curve is positively sloped, indicating that firms will provide more aggregate output only at a higher price level. The *AS* curve is drawn for a given level of technology and factor prices. At price level P_0, firms are prepared to produce and supply output equal to Y_0. An expansion of their output to Y_1 leads to an increase in unit costs, and thus firms are prepared to supply Y_1 only at a higher price level, P_1.

The higher is the level of output, the faster unit costs tend to rise with each extra increment to output. This explains why the *AS* curve becomes steeper as output rises. At low levels of output, firms may have excess capacity and increases in output may not drive up unit costs. In these situations, the *AS* curve would be flat (horizontal).

Charles Phelps Cushing/ClassicStock/Alamy Stock Photo

John Maynard Keynes was the founder of much of modern macroeconomics, and emphasized the importance of aggregate demand in determining the level of economic activity. His name is often identified with the horizontal portion of the AS curve.

When output is low, firms typically have excess capacity—some plant and equipment are idle. When firms have excess capacity, increases in output generate only small increases in unit costs. As a result, only a small increase in the price of their output may be needed to induce them to expand production. Indeed, if firms have enough excess capacity, they may be willing to sell more at their existing prices when the demand for their product increases. In this case, output is truly demand determined and the *AS* curve is horizontal up to the level at which costs begin to rise. The horizontal portion of an *AS* curve is often called the *Keynesian* range of the curve after John Maynard Keynes (1883–1946), who developed his important theory of macroeconomics to explain the nature of equilibrium during times of depressed activity, high unemployment, and excess capacity among firms.

Once output is pushed above normal capacity, however, unit costs tend to rise quite rapidly. Many higher-cost production methods may have to be adopted—such as standby capacity, overtime, and extra shifts. These higher-cost production methods will not be used unless the selling price of the output has risen enough to cover them. The more output is expanded beyond normal capacity, the more unit costs rise and hence the larger is the rise in price that is necessary to induce firms to increase output.

As we will see later in this chapter, the shape of the *AS* curve is crucial for determining how the effect of an aggregate demand shock is divided between a change in the price level and a change in real GDP.

Shifts in the *AS* Curve

Recall that the *AS* curve is drawn for a given state of technology and for a given set of factor prices. Anything that leads to a *change* in these variables will then cause a *shift* in the *AS* curve, indicating that firms require a different price level in order to provide the same level of output.

We begin with a discussion of changes to technology and factor prices that are *exogenous* to our macro model. These changes are referred to as **aggregate supply shocks**.

aggregate supply shock Any shift in the aggregate supply (AS) curve caused by an exogenous force.

Changes in Input Prices When factor prices change, the *AS* curve shifts. If factor prices rise, firms' profits at their current levels of output are reduced. Firms respond to this reduction in profit by 1) maintaining their current level of output, in which case they require an increase in the price level, or 2) reducing their level of output if the price level does not change. In either case, in response to a rise in factor prices, the *AS* curve shifts upward (and to the left). This is a decrease in aggregate supply and is shown in Figure 23-5.

Similarly, a fall in factor prices causes the *AS* curve to shift downward (and to the right). There will be more output supplied at each price level. This is an increase in aggregate supply. A dramatic example of such a reduction in factor prices occurred in 2014 when the world price of oil fell by over 50 percent. In the many countries that use oil as an input in manufacturing and other industries, the *AS* curves shifted to the right.

Changes in Technology   Firms adopt new technologies in order to produce better versions of their products or to produce their existing products at lower costs. For the purposes of our discussion, we define an *improvement* in technology as any change to production methods that reduces unit costs for any given level of output. Improvements in technology reduce unit costs and typically lead to lower prices as competing firms cut prices in attempts to raise their market share. Since the same output can now be sold at lower prices, the *AS* curve shifts downward and to the right. This is an increase in aggregate supply.

A *deterioration* in technology is any change in production methods that raises unit costs for any given level of output. Since firms are unlikely to intentionally adopt new methods that raise their costs, the latter occurrences are rare. However, in industries that rely on specific weather conditions for production—like agriculture—poor weather can be interpreted as a deterioration in technology. A deterioration in technology raises unit costs and causes the *AS* curve to shift upward and to the left, as shown in Figure 23-5.

> A change in factor prices or technology will shift the *AS* curve, because any given output will be supplied at a different price level than previously. **An increase in factor prices or a deterioration in technology shifts the *AS* curve to the left; a decrease in factor prices or an improvement in technology shifts the *AS* curve to the right.**

Before we put the demand-side and the supply-side of our macro model together, we need to say one final thing about our assumption that changes in factor prices are exogenous to our model. In many cases in the real world, changes in factor prices are *endogenous* to the economy—in particular, they change in response to the economy's output gap. We will examine these endogenous changes in detail in Chapter 24 when we discuss how the economy adjusts from the short run to the long run. For the remainder of this chapter, however, we retain the assumption that any change in factor prices (or technology) are *exogenous*. Such aggregate supply shocks play an important role in explaining real-world changes in equilibrium GDP and the price level.

23.3 Macroeconomic Equilibrium

We are now ready to see how both real GDP and the price level are simultaneously determined by the interaction of aggregate demand and aggregate supply.

FIGURE 23-5   Shifts in the *AS* Curve

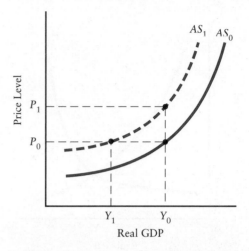

For any given level of output, anything that increases firms' costs will shift the *AS* curve upward (and to the left). Starting from (P_0, Y_0), a rise in input prices or a deterioration in technology would increase firms' unit costs. Firms would be prepared to continue supplying output of Y_0 only at the higher price level P_1. Or, at the initial price level P_0, firms would now be prepared to supply output of only Y_1. In either case, the *AS* curve has shifted up (or to the left) from AS_0 to AS_1. This is called a reduction in aggregate supply.

A fall in input prices or an improvement in technology would cause the *AS* curve to shift down (and to the right). This is an increase in aggregate supply.

For many firms, increases in output will drive up their unit costs. As a result, they will be prepared to supply more output only at a higher price. This behaviour gives rise to an upward-sloping AS curve.

FIGURE 23-6 Macroeconomic Equilibrium

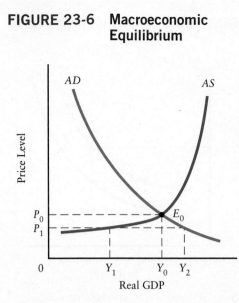

Macroeconomic equilibrium occurs at the intersection of the *AD* and *AS* curves and determines the equilibrium values for real GDP and the price level. Given the *AD* and *AS* curves in the figure, macroeconomic equilibrium only occurs at E_0.

If the price level were equal to P_1, the desired output of firms would be Y_1. However, at P_1, the level of output demanded by the economy's spenders would be Y_2. Hence, when the price level is less than P_0, the desired output of firms will be less than the total output demanded. Conversely, for any price level above P_0, the desired output of firms exceeds the level of output demanded.

The only price level at which the supply decisions of firms are consistent with desired expenditure is P_0. At P_0, firms want to produce Y_0. When they do so, they generate a real GDP of Y_0; when real GDP is Y_0, decision makers want to spend exactly Y_0, thereby purchasing the nation's output. Hence, all decisions are consistent with each other.

The equilibrium values of real GDP and the price level occur at the intersection of the *AD* and *AS* curves, as shown by the pair Y_0 and P_0 that arises at point E_0 in Figure 23-6. The combination of real GDP and price level that is on both the *AD* and the *AS* curves is called a *macroeconomic equilibrium*.

To see why E_0 is the only macroeconomic equilibrium, consider what would occur at either a lower or a higher price level. First, consider the price level P_1. At this price level, total desired expenditure is Y_2, but the economy's firms are only prepared to produce and sell an output of Y_1; there is excess demand for goods and services. Conversely, consider any price level above P_0. At these prices, the amount of output supplied by firms is greater than total desired expenditure; there is excess supply of good and services. Only at the price level P_0 is the desired production of output by firms consistent with desired aggregate expenditure decisions.

> Only at the combination of real GDP and price level given by the intersection of the *AS* and *AD* curves are demand behaviour and supply behaviour consistent.

Macroeconomic equilibrium thus requires that two conditions be satisfied. The first is familiar to us because it comes from Chapters 21 and 22. At the prevailing price level, desired aggregate expenditure must be equal to actual GDP. The *AD* curve is constructed in such a way that this condition holds everywhere along it. The second requirement for macroeconomic equilibrium is introduced by consideration of aggregate supply. At the prevailing price level, firms must want to produce the prevailing level of GDP, no more and no less. This condition is fulfilled everywhere along the *AS* curve. Only where the two curves intersect are both conditions fulfilled simultaneously.

Changes in the Macroeconomic Equilibrium

The aggregate demand and aggregate supply curves can now be used to understand how various shocks to the economy change both real GDP and the price level.

As indicated earlier, a shift in the *AD* curve is called an aggregate demand shock. A rightward shift in the *AD* curve is an increase in aggregate demand; it means that at all price levels, expenditure decisions will now be consistent with a higher level of real GDP. This is called a *positive* shock. Similarly, a leftward shift in the *AD* curve is a decrease in aggregate demand—that is, at all price levels, expenditure decisions will now be consistent with a lower level of real GDP. This is called a *negative* shock.

Also as indicated earlier, a shift in the *AS* curve caused by an exogenous force is called an aggregate supply shock. A rightward shift in the *AS* curve is an increase in aggregate supply; at any given price level, more real GDP will be supplied. This is a *positive* shock. A leftward shift in the *AS* curve is a decrease in aggregate supply; at any given price level, less real GDP will be supplied. This is a *negative* shock.

Aggregate demand and supply shocks are labelled according to their effect on real GDP. Positive shocks increase equilibrium GDP; negative shocks reduce equilibrium GDP.

Aggregate Demand Shocks

Figure 23-7 shows the effects of an increase in aggregate demand—a positive *AD* shock. This increase could have occurred because of, say, increased investment or government purchases, an increase in foreigners' demand for Canadian goods, or an increase in household consumption resulting from a reduction in personal income taxes or an increase in transfer payments. (Remember that each of these events causes the *AE* curve to shift up, and therefore the *AD* curve to shift to the right.) Whatever the cause, the increase in aggregate demand means that more domestic output is demanded at any given price level. As is shown in the figure, the increase in aggregate demand causes both the price level and real GDP to rise in the new macroeconomic equilibrium. Conversely, a decrease in demand causes both the price level and real GDP to fall.

FIGURE 23-7   Aggregate Demand Shocks

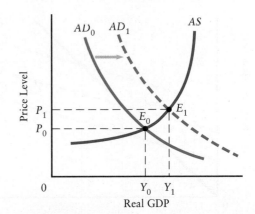

Shifts in aggregate demand cause the price level and real GDP to move in the same direction. An increase in aggregate demand shifts the *AD* curve to the right, from AD_0 to AD_1. Macroeconomic equilibrium moves from E_0 to E_1. The price level rises from P_0 to P_1, and real GDP rises from Y_0 to Y_1, reflecting a movement along the *AS* curve.

Aggregate demand shocks cause the price level and real GDP to change in the same direction; both rise with an increase in aggregate demand, and both fall with a decrease in aggregate demand.

Figure 23-7 shows how the macroeconomic equilibrium changes when there is an aggregate demand shock, but it does not show the complex adjustment going on "behind the scenes." We now examine this adjustment and see how the change in the price level alters the value of the multiplier.

The Multiplier When the Price Level Varies   We saw earlier in this chapter that the simple multiplier gives the size of the horizontal shift in the *AD* curve in response to a change in autonomous expenditure. If the price level remains constant and firms supply all that is demanded at the existing price level (as would be the case with a horizontal *AS* curve), the simple multiplier gives the increase in equilibrium national income.

But what happens in the more usual case in which the *AS* curve slopes upward? As can be seen in Figure 23-7, when the *AS* curve is positively sloped, the change in real GDP caused by a change in autonomous expenditure is no longer equal to the size of the horizontal shift in the *AD* curve. Part of the expansionary impact of an increase in demand is dissipated by a rise in the price level, and only part is transmitted to a rise in

FIGURE 23-8 The Multiplier When the Price Level Varies

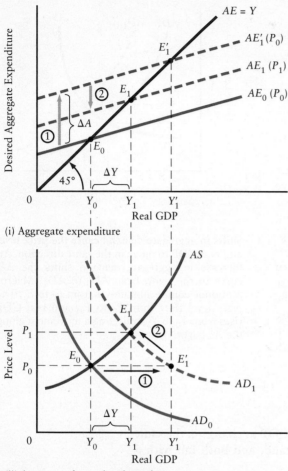

(i) Aggregate expenditure

(ii) Aggregate demand and supply

real GDP. Of course, an increase in output does occur; thus, a multiplier may still be calculated, but its value is not the same as that of the *simple* multiplier.

Why is the multiplier smaller when the AS curve is positively sloped? The answer lies in the behaviour that is summarized by the AE curve. To understand this, it is useful to think of the final change in real GDP as occurring in two stages, as shown in Figure 23-8.

First, with a constant price level, an increase in autonomous expenditure shifts the AE curve upward (from AE_0 to AE'_1). This increase in autonomous expenditure is shown in part (ii) by a shift to the right of the AD curve. The movement marked ① is the horizontal shift of the AD curve and is equal to the simple multiplier times the change in autonomous expenditure. This is the end of the first stage, but is not the end of the whole story.

In the second stage we must take account of the rise in the price level that occurs because of the positive slope of the AS curve. As we saw earlier in this chapter, a rise in the price level, via its effect on net exports and desired consumption, leads to a downward shift in the AE curve (from AE'_1 to AE_1). This second shift of the AE curve partly counteracts the initial rise in real GDP and so reduces the size of the multiplier. The second stage shows up as a downward shift of the AE curve in part (i) of Figure 23-8 and a movement upward and to the left along the new AD curve, as shown by arrow ② in part (ii).

> If an aggregate demand shock leads to a change in the price level, the ultimate change in real GDP will be *less than* what is predicted by the simple multiplier. In other words, a variable price level reduces the value of the multiplier.

The Importance of the Shape of the AS Curve We have now seen that the shape of the AS curve has important implications for how the effects of an aggregate demand shock are divided between changes in real GDP and changes in the price level. Figure 23-9 highlights the price level and GDP effects of aggregate demand shocks by considering these shocks in the presence of an AS curve with three distinct ranges.

An increase in autonomous expenditure causes the AE curve to shift upward, but the rise in the price level causes it to shift part of the way down again. Hence, the multiplier is smaller than when the price level is constant. Originally, equilibrium is at point E_0 in both parts (i) and (ii). Desired aggregate expenditure then shifts by ΔA to AE'_1, shifting the AD curve to AD_1. These shifts are shown by arrow ① in both parts. But the adjustment is not yet complete.

The shift in the AD curve raises the price level to P_1 because the AS curve is positively sloped. The rise in the price level shifts the AE curve down to AE_1, as shown by arrow ② in part (i). This is shown as a movement along the new AD curve, as indicated by arrow ② in part (ii). The new equilibrium is thus at E_1. The amount Y_0Y_1 is ΔY, the actual increase in real GDP. The multiplier, adjusted for the effect of the price increase, is the ratio $\Delta Y/\Delta A$.

Over the *flat* range, which is also called the *Keynesian* range of the *AS* curve, any aggregate demand shock leads to a change in equilibrium GDP but no change in the price level. The price level does not change because firms with excess capacity can adjust their output without generating any change in their unit costs. As seen earlier, the change in output in this case is determined by the size of the simple multiplier.

Over the *intermediate* range, along which the *AS* curve is positively sloped, a shift in the *AD* curve gives rise to appreciable changes in both real GDP and the price level. Because of the increase in the price level, the multiplier in this case is positive, but smaller than the simple multiplier.

Over the *steep* range, very little more can be produced, no matter how large the increase in demand. This range deals with an economy near its physical capacity constraints. Any change in aggregate demand leads to a sharp change in the price level and to little or no change in real GDP. The multiplier in this case is nearly zero.

> The effect of any given shift in aggregate demand will be divided between a change in real output and a change in the price level, depending on the conditions of aggregate supply. The steeper the *AS* curve, the greater the price effect and the smaller the output effect.

FIGURE 23-9 The Effects of Increases in Aggregate Demand

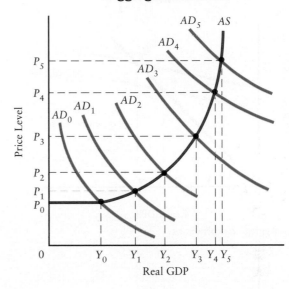

The effect of increases in aggregate demand is divided between increases in real GDP and increases in the price level, depending on the slope of the *AS* curve. Because of the increasing slope of the *AS* curve, increases in aggregate demand up to AD_0 have virtually no impact on the price level. Successive further increases bring larger price increases and relatively smaller output increases. By the time aggregate demand is at AD_4 or AD_5, virtually all of the effect is on the price level.

Reconciliation with Previous Analysis One of the central points of this chapter is that aggregate demand shocks typically lead to changes in *both* the price level and real GDP. Furthermore, in the case of a vertical *AS* curve, aggregate demand shocks will result in no change in real GDP, but only a change in the price level. How do we reconcile this possibility with the analysis of Chapters 21 and 22, where shifts in *AE always* change real GDP? The answer is that each *AE* curve is drawn on the assumption that there is a constant price level. An upward shift in the *AE* curve shifts the *AD* curve to the right. However, a positively sloped *AS* curve means that the price level rises, and this rise shifts the *AE* curve back down, offsetting some of its initial rise. This process was explained in Figure 23-8.

It is instructive to consider an extreme version of Figure 23-8, one with a vertical *AS* curve. If you draw this diagram for yourself, you will note that an increase in autonomous expenditure shifts the *AE* curve upward, indicating an increase in desired expenditure. However, a vertical *AS* curve means that output cannot be expanded to satisfy the increased demand. Instead, the extra demand merely forces prices up, and as prices rise, the *AE* curve shifts down again. The rise in prices continues until the *AE* curve is back to where it started. Thus, the rise in prices offsets the expansionary effect of the original shift and consequently leaves both real aggregate expenditure and equilibrium real GDP unchanged.

FIGURE 23-10   A Negative Aggregate Supply Shock

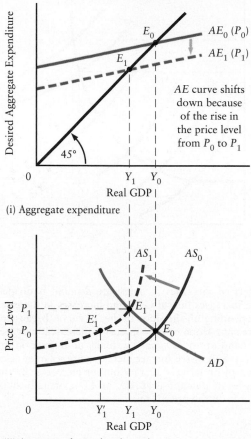

(i) Aggregate expenditure

(ii) Aggregate demand and supply

Aggregate supply shocks cause the price level and real GDP to move in opposite directions. The original equilibrium is at E_0, with GDP of Y_0 appearing in both parts of the figure. The price level is P_0 in part (ii), and at that price level, the desired aggregate expenditure curve is AE_0 in part (i).

A negative aggregate supply shock now shifts the AS curve in part (ii) to AS_1. At the original price level of P_0, firms are willing to supply only Y'_1. The fall in aggregate supply causes a rise in the price level. The new equilibrium is reached at E_1, where the AD curve intersects AS_1. At the new and higher equilibrium price level of P_1, the AE curve has shifted down to AE_1, as shown in part (i).

A vertical AS curve, however, is quite unrealistic. An AS curve shaped something like the one shown in Figure 23-9—that is, relatively flat for low levels of GDP and becoming steeper as GDP rises—is closer to reality.

We now complete our discussion of changes in the macroeconomic equilibrium by discussing supply shocks.

Aggregate Supply Shocks

A negative aggregate supply shock, shown by an upward (or leftward) shift in the AS curve, means that less real output will be supplied at any given price level. A positive aggregate supply shock, shown by a downward (or rightward) shift in the AS curve, means that more real output will be supplied at any given price level.

Figure 23-10 illustrates the effects on the price level and real GDP of a negative aggregate supply shock. This could have occurred because of, say, an increase in the world price of important inputs, such as oil, copper, or iron ore. As can be seen from the figure, following the decrease in aggregate supply, the price level rises and real GDP falls. Conversely, a positive aggregate supply shock leads to an increase in real GDP and a decrease in the price level.

> **Aggregate supply shocks cause the price level and real GDP to change in opposite directions. With an increase in supply, the price level falls and GDP rises; with a decrease in supply, the price level rises and GDP falls.**

Oil-price increases have provided three major examples of negative aggregate supply shocks that affected most countries, the first two during the 1970s and the third between 2002 and 2008. Developed economies are especially responsive to changes in the price of oil because, in addition to being used to produce energy, oil is an input into plastics, chemicals, fertilizers, and many other materials that are widely used in industry.

Massive increases in oil prices occurred during 1973–1974 and 1979–1980, caused by the successful efforts of the OPEC countries to form a cartel and restrict the output of oil. These increases in the price of oil caused leftward shifts in the AS curve in most countries. Real GDP fell while the price level rose, a combination commonly referred to as *stagflation*.

The world price of oil also increased dramatically between 2002 and 2008, the cause of which was rapid growth in the world economy, especially in the large developing economies of China and India. For all countries that use oil as inputs to production, this oil-price increase led to large leftward shifts in their *AS* curves.

Commodity prices have provided an important example of a positive aggregate supply shock. The Southeast Asian countries of Indonesia, Malaysia, Thailand, and South Korea are all significant users of raw materials. When their economies plunged into a major recession in 1997, the world demand for raw materials fell, and the prices of such goods fell as a result. From 1997 to 1998, the average price of raw materials fell by approximately 30 percent. Though these were clearly bad economic times for much of Southeast Asia, the reduction in raw materials prices was a *positive* aggregate supply shock for countries that used raw materials as inputs for production. In countries like Canada, the United States, and most of Western Europe, the *AS* curves shifted to the right.

A Word of Warning

We have discussed the effects of aggregate demand and aggregate supply shocks on the economy's price level and real GDP. Students are sometimes puzzled, however, because some events would appear to be *both* demand and supply shocks. How do we analyze such complicated shocks? For example, when the world price of oil fell by over 50 percent during 2014, this was a *positive supply shock* because oil is an important input to production for many firms. But for Canada, which produces and exports oil, doesn't the decline in the world price of oil also imply a decline in export revenue? And doesn't this imply a *negative demand shock*?

The answer to both questions is yes. A decrease in world oil prices is a positive aggregate supply shock to any country that uses oil as an input (which means most countries). But for those countries that also produce and export oil—like Canada—a decrease in the price of oil causes a reduction in income to domestic oil producers and is thus a negative aggregate demand shock. It is no surprise that the economies of the oil-producing regions of Canada, especially Alberta, Saskatchewan, and Newfoundland and Labrador, were booming during the 2002–2008 period when the price was rising but experienced significant slowdowns after the price of oil fell sharply in 2014.

A complete analysis of the macroeconomic effect on any individual country from a change in world oil prices must consider both a shift of the *AS* curve and, for those countries that produce oil, a shift of the *AD* curve. The equilibrium price level will certainly change, but the overall effect on real GDP will depend on the relative importance of the demand-side and supply-side effects.

Our discussion here has been about the macroeconomic effects of oil-price changes, but the central message is more general:

> Many economic events—especially changes in the world prices of raw materials—cause both aggregate demand and aggregate supply shocks in the same economy. The overall effect on real GDP in that economy depends on the relative importance of the two separate effects.

This general principle should be kept in mind whenever our *AD/AS* model is used to analyze the macro economy. *Lessons from History 23-1* uses our model to interpret the effects of the 1997–1998 Asian economic crisis on the Canadian economy. As you will see in that discussion, the Asian crisis generated both *AD* and *AS* shocks for Canada.

LESSONS FROM HISTORY 23-1

The 1997–1998 Asian Crisis and the Canadian Economy

In the summer of 1997, the currencies of several countries in Southeast Asia plummeted (relative to the U.S. and Canadian dollars) as their central banks were no longer able to "peg" their exchange rates. In Chapter 34 we will discuss how such pegged exchange rates operate. For now, the important point is that, for various reasons, banks, firms, and households in these countries had accumulated a large stock of debt denominated in foreign currencies, especially U.S. dollars. The sudden depreciations of their currencies—in some cases by 70 percent in just a few days—led to dramatic increases in the amount of domestic income required to pay the interest on this debt. Financial institutions went bankrupt, manufacturing firms were unable to access credit, workers were laid off, and economic output fell sharply. By late in 1997, the economies of Malaysia, Indonesia, Thailand, South Korea, and the Philippines were suffering major recessions.

This Asian Crisis had offsetting positive and negative effects on the level of economic activity in Canada. The events in Asia generated both a *negative* aggregate demand shock and a *positive* aggregate supply shock for Canada.

To understand the demand side of the story, we must recognize that these Asian economies are important users of raw materials. When their economies went into recession, their demand for raw materials fell sharply. As a result, average raw materials prices fell by roughly 30 percent between 1997 and 1998. Since raw materials are an important Canadian export, Canadian producers of copper, pork, newsprint, lumber, iron ore, and many other raw materials suffered significantly. In terms of our macroeconomic model, the Asian crisis caused a leftward shift of the Canadian *AD* curve.

The story does not end there. Also important to Canada is the fact that many Canadian firms use raw materials as inputs for their production of car parts, prefabricated houses and trailers, electrical equipment, and so on. A dramatic reduction in the prices of raw materials implies a reduction in costs for these firms. This is a positive aggregate supply shock, and is illustrated by a rightward shift of the Canadian *AS* curve.

What is the overall effect on the Canadian economy? The effect of each shock taken separately is to reduce the price level—so the overall effect is unambiguously a lower price level.* In contrast, the effect on real GDP would appear to be ambiguous since the *AD* shock reduces GDP whereas the *AS* shock increases it. But this is not quite right. Since Canada earns more from its sales of raw materials than it spends on them (that is, Canada is a net exporter of these products), it experiences a decrease in national income when these prices fall. In other words, the net effect of the negative demand shock and the positive supply shock is to reduce Canadian GDP. The figure is therefore drawn with the *AD* shock being larger than the *AS* shock and so the new equilibrium level of GDP, Y_1, is lower than in the initial equilibrium, Y_0.

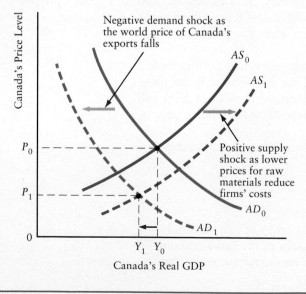

Canada's Real GDP

---

*We are assuming in this analysis that there is no ongoing inflation, so a positive *AS* shock or a negative *AD* shock reduces the price level. A more accurate description for the Canadian economy in 1998, with a small amount of ongoing inflation, is that the price level fell below *what it otherwise would have been*. This appears as a reduction in the rate of inflation.

SUMMARY

23.1 The Demand Side of the Economy

LO 1, 2

- The *AE* curve shows desired aggregate expenditure for each level of GDP at a particular price level. Its intersection with the 45° line determines equilibrium GDP for that price level. Equilibrium GDP thus occurs where desired aggregate expenditure equals actual GDP.
- A change in the price level leads to two effects on aggregate expenditure:
  1. by changing wealth it changes desired consumption
  2. by changing international relative prices it changes desired net exports.

- A rise in the price level shifts the *AE* curve down and reduces equilibrium GDP; a fall in the price level shifts the *AE* curve up and increases equilibrium GDP.
- The *AD* curve plots the equilibrium level of GDP that corresponds to each possible price level. A change in equilibrium GDP following a change in the price level is shown by a movement along the *AD* curve.
- The *AD* curve shifts horizontally when any element of autonomous expenditure changes, and the simple multiplier measures the size of the shift.

23.2 The Supply Side of the Economy

LO 3

- Any aggregate supply (*AS*) curve is drawn for given factor prices and a given state of technology.
- The *AS* curve is usually drawn as an upward-sloping curve, reflecting the assumption that firms' unit costs tend to rise when their output rises.
- At low levels of output, firms' excess capacity may result in a horizontal *AS* curve.

- An improvement in technology or a decrease in factor prices shifts the *AS* curve to the right. This is an increase in aggregate supply.
- A deterioration in technology or an increase in factor prices shifts the *AS* curve to the left. This is a decrease in aggregate supply.

23.3 Macroeconomic Equilibrium

LO 4

- Macroeconomic equilibrium refers to equilibrium values of real GDP and the price level, as determined by the intersection of the *AD* and *AS* curves. Shifts in the *AD* and *AS* curves, called aggregate demand and aggregate supply shocks, change the equilibrium values of real GDP and the price level.
- When the *AS* curve is positively sloped, an aggregate demand shock causes the price level and real GDP to move in the same direction. When the *AS* curve is flat, shifts in the *AD* curve primarily affect real GDP. When the *AS* curve is steep, shifts in the *AD* curve primarily affect the price level.

- With a positively sloped *AS* curve, a demand shock leads to a change in the price level. As a result, the multiplier is smaller than the simple multiplier in Chapter 22.
- An aggregate supply shock moves equilibrium GDP along the *AD* curve, causing the price level and real GDP to move in opposite directions.
- Some events are both aggregate supply and aggregate demand shocks. Changes in the world prices of raw materials, for example, shift the *AS* curve. If the country (like Canada) is also a producer of such raw materials, there will also be a shift in the *AD* curve. The overall effect then depends on the relative sizes of the separate effects.

KEY CONCEPTS

Effects of an exogenous change in the price level
Relationship between the *AE* and *AD* curves

Negative slope of the *AD* curve
Positive slope of the *AS* curve
Macroeconomic equilibrium
Aggregate demand shocks

The multiplier when the price level varies
Aggregate supply shocks

STUDY EXERCISES

MyLab Economics Make the grade with MyLab Economics™: All Study Exercises can be found on MyLab Economics™. You can practise them as often as you want, and many feature step-by-step guided instructions to help you find the right answer.

FILL-IN-THE-BLANK

1 Fill in the blanks to make the following statements correct.

a. In the simple macro model of the previous two chapters, the price level was _____ to the model. In the macro model of this chapter, the price level is _____ to the model.

b. A change in the price level shifts the *AE* curve because the price level change affects desired _____ and desired _____.

c. A rise in the price level causes a(n) _____ in households' wealth, which leads to a(n) _____ in desired consumption, which causes the *AE* curve to shift _____. A fall in the price level causes a(n) _____ in households' wealth, which leads to a(n) _____ in desired consumption, which causes the *AE* curve to shift _____.

d. A rise in the domestic price level causes net exports to _____, which causes the *AE* curve to shift _____. A fall in the domestic price level causes net exports to _____, which causes the *AE* curve to shift _____.

e. Equilibrium GDP is determined by the position of the *AE* function for each given price level. An equilibrium point for a particular price level corresponds to one point on the _____ curve.

f. A rise in the price level causes a downward shift of the _____ curve and a movement upward along the _____ curve.

g. An increase in autonomous expenditure, with no change in the price level, causes the *AE* curve to _____ and causes the *AD* curve to _____.

2 Fill in the blanks to make the following statements correct.

a. The _____ curve relates the price level to the quantity of output that firms would like to produce and sell.

b. Each aggregate supply curve is drawn under the assumption that _____ and _____ remain constant.

c. The aggregate supply curve is upward sloping because firms will produce more output only if prices _____ to offset higher unit costs.

d. The aggregate supply curve is relatively flat when GDP is low (well below potential output) because

firms typically have _____ and are able to expand production with little or no increase in _____.

e. The aggregate supply curve is relatively steep when GDP is high (above potential output) because firms are operating above _____ and _____ are rising rapidly.

f. The aggregate supply curve shifts in response to changes in _____ and changes in _____. These are known as supply _____.

3 Fill in the blanks to make the following statements correct.

a. Macroeconomic equilibrium occurs at the intersection of _____ and _____, and determines equilibrium levels of _____ and _____.

b. If the *AS* curve is upward sloping, a positive *AD* shock will cause the price level to _____ and real GDP to _____. A negative *AD* shock will cause the price level to _____ and real GDP to _____.

c. A positive *AS* shock will cause the price level to _____ and real GDP to _____. A negative *AS* shock will cause the price level to _____ and real GDP to _____.

d. In previous chapters, the simple multiplier measured the change in real GDP in response to a change in autonomous expenditure when the price level was constant. When the price level varies, the multiplier is _____ than the simple multiplier.

e. An increase in autonomous government spending is a(n) _____ *AD* shock, which will initially cause a(n) _____ shift of the *AE* curve and a(n) _____ shift of the *AD* curve. Given an upward-sloping aggregate supply curve, there will be a(n) _____ in the price level, which leads to a partial _____ shift of the *AE* curve.

REVIEW

4 Consider the effects of an exogenous increase in the domestic price level. For each of the assets listed, explain how the change in the price level would affect the wealth of the asset holder. Then explain the effect on *aggregate* (private sector) wealth and the effect on the *AE* curve. The footnote on page 560 will help to answer parts (d) and (e) of this question.

a. Cash holdings
b. Deposits in a bank account
c. A household mortgage
d. A corporate bond that promises to pay the bond-holder $10 000 on January 1, 2025
e. A government bond that promises to pay the holder $10 000 on January 1, 2025

5 Consider the following diagram showing the *AD* curves in two different economies. One economy is Autarkland—it does not trade with the rest of the world (*autarky* is a situation in which a country does not trade with other countries). The other economy is Openland—it exports to and imports from the rest of the world.

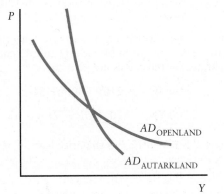

a. Explain why an increase in the domestic price level (for a given exchange rate) reduces net exports in Openland. How would you illustrate this with the *AE* curve in the 45°-line diagram?
b. Explain why the *AD* curve is steeper in Autarkland than in Openland.
c. If there are never any net exports in Autarkland, why isn't the *AD* curve vertical? Explain what other aspect of the economy generates a downward-sloping *AD* curve.

6 For each of the following situations, describe the movement, either *along* the *AS* curve, or the direction of the shift of the *AS* curve.

a. A significant and binding increase in the minimum wage.
b. An increase in labour productivity and no change in wages.
c. An increase in demand for Canada's exports.
d. Advances in artificial intelligence that reduce costs in all service industries.
e. A decrease in business confidence that reduces firms' desired investment.

7 Each of the following events caused a shift in the *AD* or *AS* curve in Canada. Identify which curve was affected and describe the effect on equilibrium real GDP and the price level.

a. OPEC's actions to restrict oil output significantly increased the world price of oil in 1979–1980.
b. World commodity prices increased sharply from 2002 to 2008. Many of these commodities are both produced in Canada and used as important inputs for Canadian firms.
c. The end of the Cold War in 1990 led to large declines in defence spending in many countries (including Canada).
d. The federal government and (many) provincial governments reduced corporate income-tax rates between 2000 and 2015.
e. The federal government increased its level of government purchases (*G*) in 2009 and 2010, amidst a global recession.
f. The beginning of a strong recovery in the United States in 2014 led to a large increase in the demand for many Canadian exports.
g. The world price of oil fell from U.S. $105 per barrel in June 2014 to U.S. $50 in February 2015.
h. The possible cancellation of the North American Free Trade Agreement led many Canadian firms to reduce desired investment in 2017 and 2018.

8 The following diagrams show the *AD* and *AS* curves in two different economies.

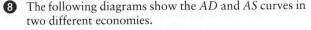
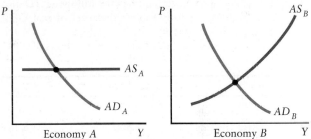

a. Explain what aspect of firms' behaviour might give rise to the horizontal *AS* curve in Economy *A*.
b. Explain what aspect of firms' behaviour gives rise to the upward-sloping *AS* curve in Economy *B*.
c. In which economy is output purely demand determined? Explain.
d. Consider the effects of an increase in autonomous expenditure. Which economy has the larger multiplier? Explain your reasoning.

PROBLEMS

9 Consider the following simplified *AE* function:

$$AE = 350 + 0.8Y + 0.1\,(M/P)$$

where *AE* is desired aggregate expenditure, *Y* is real GDP, *M* is the private sector's *nominal wealth*, and *P* is the price level. Suppose that *M* is constant and equal to 6000.

a. Fill in the table below:

P	M/P	AE
1	6000	950 + 0.8Y
2	—	—
3	—	—
4	—	—
5	—	—
6	—	—

b. Plot each of the AE functions—one for each price level—on the same-scale 45°-line diagram.

c. Compute the level of equilibrium national income (Y) for each of the values of P. For example, when P = 1, AE = 950 + 0.8Y. Thus the equilibrium level of Y is such that Y = 950 + 0.8Y, which implies Y = 4750.

d. Plot the pairs of price level and equilibrium national income on a scale diagram with P on the vertical axis and Y on the horizontal axis. What is this curve you have just constructed?

e. Explain why the expression for AE above makes sense. Why do M and P enter the AE function?

10 The economy of Neverland has the following AD and AS schedules. Denote Y_{AD} as the level of real GDP along the AD curve; let Y_{AS} be the level of real GDP along the AS curve. GDP is shown in billions of 2002 dollars.

Price Level	Y_{AD}	Y_{AS}
90	1100	750
100	1000	825
110	900	900
120	800	975
130	700	1050
140	600	1125

a. Plot the AD and AS curves on a scale diagram.

b. What is the price level and level of real GDP in Neverland's macroeconomic equilibrium?

c. Suppose the price level in Neverland is 100. At this price level, what amount of total output are firms willing to supply? What is desired expenditure? Describe this disequilibrium.

d. Suppose the price level in Neverland is 120. At this price level, what amount of total output are firms willing to supply? What is desired expenditure? Describe this disequilibrium.

e. Now suppose we are at the macro equilibrium determined in part (b) above, but the level of potential output for Neverland is $950 billion. Using the terminology introduced in Chapter 19, what do we call such an output gap?

11 This question involves algebraically solving the system of two equations given by the AD and AS curves. The equations for the curves are given by

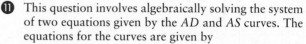

$$AD: Y_{AD} = 710 - 30P + 5G$$

$$AS: Y_{AS} = 10 + 5P - 2P_{OIL}$$

where Y is real GDP, P is the price level, G is the level of government purchases, and P_{OIL} is the world price of oil.

a. Explain the various terms in the AD curve. Explain why G enters positively.

b. What is the value of the simple multiplier? (Hint: Refer back to the caption of Figure 23-3.)

c. Explain the various terms in the AS curve. Explain why the price of oil enters negatively.

d. Solve for the equilibrium value of real GDP and the price level.

e. Using your solution to part (d), what is the effect of a change in G on equilibrium Y and P? Explain.

f. Using your solution to part (d), what is the effect of a change in P_{OIL} on equilibrium Y and P? Explain.

24

From the Short Run to the Long Run: The Adjustment of Factor Prices

CHAPTER OUTLINE	LEARNING OBJECTIVES (LO)
	After studying this chapter you will be able to
24.1 THREE MACROECONOMIC STATES	1 describe the three different macroeconomic states and the underlying assumptions for each one.
24.2 THE ADJUSTMENT PROCESS	2 explain why output gaps cause wages and other factor prices to change.
	3 describe how changes in factor prices affect firms' costs and shift the AS curve.
24.3 AGGREGATE DEMAND AND SUPPLY SHOCKS	4 explain why real GDP gradually returns to potential output following an AD or AS shock.
24.4 FISCAL STABILIZATION POLICY	5 understand why lags and uncertainty place limitations on the use of fiscal stabilization policy.

IN the previous three chapters, we developed a model of the *short-run* determination of equilibrium real GDP and the price level. In this chapter, we discuss how this short-run macroeconomic equilibrium evolves, through an adjustment process in which wages and other factor prices change, into a *long-run* equilibrium,

in which real GDP is equal to potential output, Y^*. In the next chapter we examine theories explaining why Y^* increases over many years—what we call *long-run economic growth*. Before we proceed, however, we will define carefully our assumptions regarding the short run, the adjustment process, and the long run.

24.1 Three Macroeconomic States

Macroeconomic analysis considers three different "states" or spans of time. In the last three chapters, we considered the economy in the short run. In the next chapter we will examine the economy in the long run, when real GDP equals Y^*. In this chapter we explore the details of the crucial adjustment process that takes the economy from its short-run equilibrium to its long-run state. Let's begin by clarifying the assumptions being made in each state.

The Short Run

In Chapters 21, 22, and 23 we developed our macro model in the *short run*. The assumptions of the model in the short run are:

- Factor prices are assumed to be exogenous; they may change, but any change is not explained within the model.
- Technology and factor supplies are assumed to be constant (and therefore Y^* is constant).

With these assumptions, the short-run macroeconomic equilibrium is determined by the intersection of the AD and AS curves, both of which are subject to shocks of various kinds. These shocks cause the level of real GDP to fluctuate around a *constant* level of potential output, Y^*. This version of our macro model is convenient to use when analyzing the economy over short periods. Even though factor prices, technology, and factor supplies are rarely constant in reality, even over short periods of time, the simplifying assumption that they are constant in our short-run model allows us to focus on the important role of AD or AS shocks over this time span.

The Adjustment of Factor Prices

In this chapter we analyze the *adjustment process* that takes the economy from the short run to the long run. The assumptions of our theory of the adjustment process are:

- Factor prices are assumed to adjust in response to output gaps.
- Technology and factor supplies are assumed to be constant (and therefore Y^* is constant).

For the first time, in this chapter we will see why deviations of real GDP from potential output generally cause wages and other factor prices to adjust. We will also see how this adjustment is central to the economy's evolution from its short-run equilibrium to its long-run equilibrium. Note that, as in the short-run version of the model, the adjustment process is assumed to take place with a constant level of potential output.

In reality, neither technology nor factor supplies are constant over time; the level of potential output is continually changing. Our assumption throughout much of this chapter of a constant value for Y^* is thus a simplifying one, allowing us to focus on our theory of the adjustment process that brings the level of real GDP back to potential output.

Our emphasis on the macroeconomic adjustment process is especially useful for examining how the effects of policies differ in the short and long runs. In this chapter's final section, we will contrast the short-run and long-run effects of fiscal policy. We will do the same for monetary policy in Chapters 27 and 28. Understanding the adjustment process is central to understanding the different short-run and long-run implications of policy actions.

The Long Run

In Chapter 25 we examine our macro model in the long run and focus on the process of *economic growth*. The assumptions of the model in the long run are:

- Factor prices are assumed to have fully adjusted to any output gap.
- Technology and factor supplies are assumed to be changing.

The first assumption tells us that, after factor prices have fully adjusted, real GDP will return to the level of potential output. The second assumption implies that the level of potential output is changing (and typically growing). Thus, in the long-run version of our macroeconomic model, our focus is not on the nature of short-run fluctuations in GDP but rather on the nature of *economic growth*—where technological change and the growth of factor supplies play key roles.

The economy is probably never "in" the long run in the sense that factor prices have fully adjusted to all *AD* and *AS* shocks. This is because such shocks are not isolated events but instead events that occur more or less continually. So, before the full adjustment to one shock is complete, another shock occurs and sets the adjustment process in motion again. Nonetheless, the long-run version of our model is very useful for examining some issues. For example, if we want to understand why our children's material standard of living will be significantly greater than our grandparents', we should not focus on short-run *AD* or *AS* shocks or the stabilization policies that may follow; the effects of particular shocks will disappear after a few years. Instead, we will gain more understanding if we abstract from short-run issues and focus on why Y^* increases dramatically over periods of several decades.

Summary

The three states of the economy central to macroeconomic analysis are summarized in Table 24-1. Note for each state the assumptions made regarding factor prices and the

TABLE 24-1   Three Macroeconomic States

	The Short Run	The Adjustment Process	The Long Run
Key Assumptions	Factor prices are exogenous. Technology and factor supplies (and thus Y^*) are constant/exogenous.	Factor prices are flexible/endogenous. Technology and factor supplies (and thus Y^*) are constant/exogenous.	Factor prices are fully adjusted/endogenous. Technology and factor supplies (and thus Y^*) are changing.
What Happens	Real GDP (Y) is determined by aggregate demand and aggregate supply.	Factor prices adjust to output gaps; real GDP eventually returns to Y^*.	Potential GDP (Y^*) usually grows over the long run.
Why We Study This State	To show the effects of *AD* and *AS* shocks on real GDP.	To see how output gaps cause factor prices to change and why real GDP tends to return to Y^*.	To understand the nature of long-run economic growth.

level of potential output and the causes of changes in real GDP. As we proceed through this chapter and the next, you may find it useful to refer back to this table.

You already know from Chapter 23 how the short-run version of our macro model works. And now that you have a sketch of what is meant by the adjustment process and the long run, we are ready to fill in the details. In this chapter we will see how this adjustment process takes the economy from its short-run equilibrium to its long-run equilibrium. To repeat, we assume in this chapter that factor prices adjust in response to output gaps and that potential output (Y^*) is constant.

24.2 The Adjustment Process

We develop our theory of the adjustment process by examining the relationship among output gaps, factor markets, and factor prices. We begin by understanding the broad outline of how the adjustment process works. We then go on to discuss *how well* it works in greater detail.

Potential Output and the Output Gap

Recall from Chapter 19 that *potential output* is the total output that can be produced when all productive resources—land, labour, and capital—are fully employed. When a nation's actual output diverges from its potential output, the difference is called the output gap.

Although growth in potential output has powerful effects from one decade to the next, its change from one *year* to the next is small enough that we ignore it when studying the year-to-year behaviour of real GDP and the price level. In this chapter, therefore, we view variations in the output gap as determined solely by variations in *actual* GDP around a constant level of *potential* GDP.

Figure 24-1 shows real GDP being determined in the short run by the intersection of the *AD* and *AS* curves. Potential output is assumed to be constant, and it is shown by the vertical lines in the two parts of the figure. In part (i), the *AD* and *AS* curves intersect to produce an equilibrium real GDP less than potential output. The result, as we saw in Chapter 19, is called a *recessionary gap* because recessions are often characterized as having GDP below potential output. In part (ii), the *AD* and *AS* curves intersect to produce an equilibrium real GDP above potential output, resulting in what is called an *inflationary gap*. Why an inflationary output gap puts upward pressure on prices will become clear in the ensuing discussion.

Factor Prices and the Output Gap

We make two key assumptions in our macro model regarding factor prices and the output gap. First, when real GDP is above potential output, there will be pressure on factor prices to rise because of a higher than normal demand for factor inputs. Second, when real GDP is below potential output, there will be pressure on factor prices to fall because of a lower than normal demand for factor inputs. These relationships are assumed to hold for the prices of all factors of production, including labour, land, and capital equipment.[1]

---

[1] We also make the simplifying assumption throughout this chapter that the price level is expected to be stable. Otherwise, *expected inflation* would be an additional reason for wages and other factor prices to change.

FIGURE 24-1   Output Gaps in the Short Run

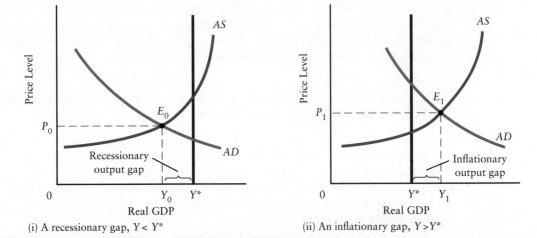

(i) A recessionary gap, $Y < Y^*$ (ii) An inflationary gap, $Y > Y^*$

The output gap is the difference between actual GDP and potential GDP, $Y - Y^*$. Potential output is shown by the vertical line at Y^*. A recessionary gap, shown in part (i), occurs when actual output is less than potential GDP. An inflationary gap, shown in part (ii), occurs when actual output is greater than potential GDP.

Output Above Potential, $Y > Y^*$ Here is the reasoning behind our first assumption. Sometimes the AD and AS curves intersect where real GDP exceeds potential, as illustrated in part (ii) of Figure 24-1. Because firms are producing beyond their normal capacity output, there is an excess demand for all factor inputs, including labour. Labour shortages will emerge in some industries and among many groups of workers. Firms will try to bid workers away from other firms in order to maintain the high levels of output and sales made possible by the boom conditions.

As a result of this excess demand in factor markets, workers will find that they have considerable bargaining power with their employers, and they will put upward pressure on wages. Firms, recognizing that demand for their goods is strong, will be anxious to maintain a high level of output. To prevent their workers from either striking or quitting and moving to other employers, firms will be willing to accede to some of these upward pressures.

> **The boom that is associated with an inflationary gap generates an excess demand for factors that tends to cause wages (and other factor prices) to rise.**

This increase in factor prices will increase firms' unit costs. As unit costs increase, firms will require higher prices in order to supply any given level of output, and the AS curve will therefore shift up. This shift has the effect of reducing equilibrium real GDP and raising the price level. Real GDP moves back toward potential and the inflationary gap begins to close.

In our model, factor prices are assumed to continue to rise as long as some inflationary gap remains. In other words, they will continue rising until the AS curve shifts up to the point where the equilibrium level of GDP is equal to potential GDP. At this point, there is no longer an excess demand for factors, no more pressure for factor prices to rise, firms' costs are stable, and the AS curve stops shifting.

Output Below Potential, $Y < Y^*$ Here is the reasoning behind our second assumption regarding factor prices. Sometimes the AD and AS curves intersect where real GDP is less than potential, as illustrated in part (i) of Figure 24-1. Because firms are producing below their normal capacity output, there is an excess supply of all factor inputs, including labour. There will be labour surpluses in some industries and among some groups of workers. Firms will have below-normal sales and not only will resist upward pressures on wages but also may seek reductions in wages.

> The slump that is associated with a recessionary gap generates an excess supply of factors that tends to cause wages (and other factor prices) to fall.[2]

Such a reduction in factor prices will reduce firms' unit costs. As unit costs fall, firms require a lower price in order to supply any given level of output, and the AS curve therefore shifts down. This shift has the effect of increasing equilibrium real GDP and reducing the price level. Real GDP moves back toward potential and the recessionary gap begins to close.

In our model, wages and other factor prices are assumed to fall as long as some recessionary gap remains. As factor prices fall, the AS curve shifts down, and this process continues until the equilibrium level of GDP is equal to potential output. At this point, there is no longer an excess supply of factors, no more pressure for factor prices to fall, firms' unit costs are stable, and the AS curve stops shifting.

Downward Wage Stickiness   At this stage, we encounter an important asymmetry in the economy's aggregate supply behaviour. Boom conditions (an inflationary gap), along with labour shortages, cause wages and unit costs to rise. The experience of many developed economies, however, suggests that the downward pressures on wages during slumps (recessionary gaps) often do not operate as strongly or as quickly as the upward pressures during booms. Even when wages do fall, they tend to fall more slowly than they would rise in an equally sized inflationary gap. This *downward wage stickiness* implies that the downward shift in the AS curve and the downward pressure on the price level are quite weak.

> Both upward and downward adjustments to wages and unit costs do occur, but there are differences in the speed at which they typically operate. Booms can cause wages to rise rapidly; recessions usually cause wages to fall only slowly.

The Phillips Curve   The factor-price adjustment process that we have been discussing was explored many years ago in a famous study of wages and unemployment in the United Kingdom. Using data from the late nineteenth and early twentieth centuries, when wages were more flexible than they are now, A.W. Phillips observed that wages tended to fall in periods of high unemployment and rise in periods of low unemployment. The resulting negative relationship between unemployment and the rate of change in

---

[2] Because of ongoing inflation and productivity growth, nominal wages rarely fall, even when there is an excess supply of labour. But remember that in this chapter, to allow us to focus on the adjustment process, we are assuming that technology is constant and expected inflation is zero. Thus nominal (and real) wages and other factor prices are assumed to fall when real GDP is below potential output, although perhaps very slowly. With some ongoing inflation in our model, the assumption would be modified so that nominal wages rise less than prices, thus implying a slow reduction in *real* wages.

wages has been called the *Phillips* curve ever since. *Extensions in Theory 24-1* discusses the Phillips curve and its relationship to the *AS* curve.

Inflationary and Recessionary Gaps   Now it should be clear why the output gaps are named as they are. When real GDP exceeds potential GDP in our model, there will normally be rising unit costs, and the *AS* curve will be shifting upward. This will in turn push the price level up and create temporary inflation. The larger the excess of real GDP over potential GDP, the greater the inflationary pressure. The term *inflationary gap* emphasizes this salient feature of the economy when $Y > Y^*$.

When actual output is less than potential output, as we have seen, there will be unemployment of labour and other productive resources. Unit costs will tend to fall slowly, leading to a slow downward shift in the *AS* curve. Hence, the price level will be falling only slowly so that *unemployment* will be the output gap's most obvious result. The term *recessionary gap* emphasizes this salient feature that high rates of unemployment occur when $Y < Y^*$.

Kenneth Summers/Shutterstock

Potential output acts like an anchor for the level of real GDP. Following aggregate demand or supply shocks that push real GDP below or above potential, the adjustment of factor prices brings real GDP back to potential output.

Potential Output as an "Anchor"

We have seen that wages and other factor prices tend to change when output is above or below potential. These changes in factor prices lead to changes in firms' unit costs that shift the *AS* curve and change the equilibrium level of GDP. Moreover, we assumed that this process of factor-price adjustment will continue as long as some output gap remains, coming to a halt only when the equilibrium level of GDP is equal to potential GDP, Y^*. This leads to an important prediction from our macro model:

> Following an *AD* or *AS* shock, the short-run equilibrium level of output may be different from potential output. Any output gap is assumed to cause wages and other factor prices to adjust, eventually bringing the equilibrium level of output back to potential. The level of potential output therefore acts like an "anchor" for the economy.

We now go on to examine our theory of the factor-price adjustment process in greater detail, illustrating it for the cases of positive and negative shocks to aggregate demand and supply. We will also examine this factor-price adjustment process following changes in fiscal policy. The idea that Y^* acts as an "anchor" for the economy will become clear: Shocks of various kinds may cause output to rise above or fall below Y^* in the short run, but the adjustment of factor prices to output gaps ensures that output eventually returns to Y^*.

24.3 Aggregate Demand and Supply Shocks

We can now study the consequences of aggregate demand and aggregate supply shocks in our model, distinguishing between the immediate effects of *AD* and *AS* shocks and the longer-term effects, after factor prices have adjusted fully. It is necessary to examine positive and negative shocks separately because the adjustment of factor prices is not symmetrical for the two cases. Let's begin with demand shocks.

EXTENSIONS IN THEORY 24-1

The Phillips Curve and the Adjustment Process

In the 1950s, Professor A.W. Phillips of the London School of Economics was conducting pioneering research on macroeconomic policy. In his early models, he related the rate of inflation to the difference between actual and potential output. Later he investigated the empirical underpinnings of this equation by studying the relationship between the rate of increase of nominal wages and the level of unemployment. He studied these variables because unemployment data were available as far back as the mid-nineteenth century, whereas very few data on output gaps were available when he did his empirical work. In 1958, he reported that a stable relationship had existed between these two variables for 100 years in the United Kingdom. This relationship came to be known as the **Phillips curve**, which provided an explanation, rooted in empirical observation, of the speed with which wage changes shifted the AS curve by changing firms' unit costs.

In the form in which it became famous, the Phillips curve related wage changes to the level of unemployment, as shown in part (i) of the accompanying figure. But we can express the same information in a slightly different way. Note that unemployment and output gaps are negatively related—a recessionary gap is associated with high unemployment, and an inflationary gap is associated with low unemployment. We can therefore create another Phillips curve that plots wage changes against real GDP, as shown in part (ii). Both figures show the same information.

When output equals Y^* the corresponding unemployment rate is sometimes called the natural rate of unemployment, and is denoted U^*. Inflationary gaps (when $Y > Y^*$ and $U < U^*$) are associated with increases in wages. Recessionary gaps (when $Y < Y^*$ and $U > U^*$) are associated with *decreases* in wages. Thus, a Phillips curve that plots wage changes against real GDP is upward sloping, whereas a Phillips curve that plots wage changes against the unemployment rate is downward sloping. When output is at potential, there is neither upward nor downward pressure on wages (or other factor prices) because there is neither an excess demand nor an excess supply of labour. Hence, the Phillips curve cuts the horizontal axis at Y^* (and at U^*).

Note that the Phillips curve is *not* the same as the AS curve. The AS curve has the *price level* on the vertical axis whereas the Phillips curve has the *rate of change of nominal wages* on the vertical axis. How are the two curves related? The economy's location on the Phillips curve indicates how the AS curve is shifting as a result of the existing output gap.

Part (iii) of the figure shows how the AD/AS diagram relates to the Phillips curve. For example, consider an economy that begins at point A in all three diagrams; there is no output gap and wages, prices, and real GDP are stable. Now, suppose a positive aggregate demand shock causes real GDP to increase to Y_1 (and unemployment to fall to U_1) and thus produces an inflationary gap. The excess demand for labour puts upward pressure on wages and the economy moves along the Phillips curve to point B, where wages begin rising. The increase in wages increases unit costs and causes the AS curve to shift up. Thus, each

Phillips curve Originally, a relationship between the unemployment rate and the rate of change of nominal wages. Now often drawn as a relationship between real GDP and the rate of change of nominal wages.

Positive *AD* Shocks

Suppose the economy starts with a stable price level and real GDP equal to potential GDP, as shown by the initial equilibrium in part (i) of Figure 24-2. Now suppose this situation is disturbed by an increase in autonomous expenditure, perhaps caused by an upturn in business confidence and a resulting boom in investment spending. Figure 24-2(i) shows the effects of this positive aggregate demand shock in raising both the price level and real GDP. The AD curve shifts from AD_0 to AD_1, the economy moves along the AS curve, and real GDP rises above Y^*. An inflationary gap opens up.

We have assumed that an inflationary output gap leads to increases in factor prices, which cause firms' unit costs to rise. The AS curve begins to shift up as firms respond by increasing their output prices. As seen in part (ii) of the figure, the upward shift of the AS curve causes a further rise in the price level, but this time the price rise is associated with a *fall* in output (along the AD_1 curve).

point on the Phillips curve determines the rate at which the *AS* curve is shifting. To complete the example, note that as the *AS* curve shifts up, the level of GDP will fall back toward *Y** and the inflationary gap will begin to close. The economy moves back along the Phillips curve toward point *A*. Wages continue to rise, but the rate at which they are rising slows. When all adjustment is complete, the new equilibrium will be at point *C* in part (iii) of the figure, with output equal to *Y** and the price level and nominal wages higher than initially. On the Phillips curve, the economy will be back at point *A*, where real GDP equals *Y** and wages are stable (but at a higher level than before the demand shock occurred).

Note that the shape of the Phillips curve is not accidental—it reflects the adjustment asymmetry we mentioned in the text. The shape of the Phillips curve

implies that an inflationary gap of a given amount will lead to faster wage increases than an equally sized recessionary gap will lead to wage reductions. In other words, an inflationary gap will cause the *AS* curve to shift up more quickly than a recessionary gap will cause the *AS* curve to shift down.

Finally, you might be wondering what would happen if the Phillips curve were to shift. And what would cause such a shift? As we will see in Chapter 29 when we discuss the phenomenon of sustained inflation, an important cause of shifts of the Phillips curve is changes in firms' and households' *expectations* of future inflation. In this chapter, however, we have assumed expected inflation to be zero. Whether there is expected inflation or not, the Phillips curve describes the factor-price adjustment process that is the focus of this chapter.

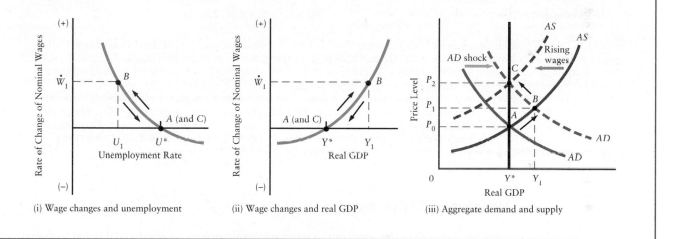

(i) Wage changes and unemployment   (ii) Wage changes and real GDP   (iii) Aggregate demand and supply

The increases in unit costs (and the consequent upward shifts of the *AS* curve) continue until the inflationary gap has been removed—that is, until in part (ii) real GDP returns to *Y**. Only then is there no excess demand for labour and other factors, and only then do factor prices and unit costs, and hence the *AS* curve, stabilize.

The adjustment in wages and other factor prices eventually eliminates any inflationary output gap caused by an *AD* shock; real GDP returns to its potential level.

It is worth remembering here that a key assumption in our macro model is that the level of potential output, *Y**, is constant. This key assumption lies behind the strong result in our model that the adjustment process, once complete, fully reverses any shock's short-run effects on real GDP.

FIGURE 24-2 The Adjustment Process Following a Positive *AD* Shock

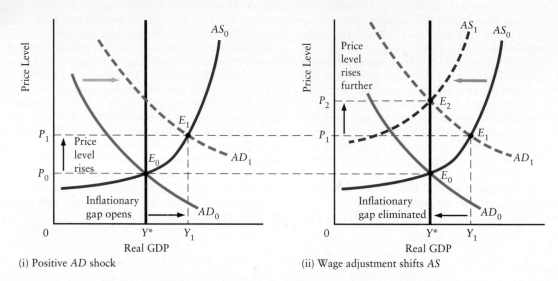

(i) Positive *AD* shock   (ii) Wage adjustment shifts *AS*

A positive *AD* shock first raises prices and output along the *AS* curve. It then induces a shift of the *AS* curve that further raises prices but lowers output along the new *AD* curve. In part (i), the economy is in equilibrium at E_0, at its level of potential output, Y^*, and price level P_0. The *AD* curve then shifts from AD_0 to AD_1. This moves equilibrium to E_1, with income Y_1 and price level P_1, and opens up an inflationary gap.

In part (ii), the inflationary gap results in an increase in wages and other factor prices, which drives up firms' unit costs and shifts the *AS* curve upward. As this happens, output falls and the price level rises along AD_1. Eventually, when the *AS* curve has shifted to AS_1, output is back to Y^* and the inflationary gap has been eliminated. However, the price level has risen to P_2. The eventual effect of the *AD* shock, after all adjustment has occurred, is to raise the price level but leave real GDP unchanged.

Negative *AD* Shocks

Suppose again that the economy starts with stable prices and real GDP equal to potential, as shown in part (i) of Figure 24-3. Now assume there is a *decline* in aggregate demand. This negative *AD* shock might be a reduction in investment expenditure, or perhaps a decline in the world demand for Canadian forest products or automobiles.

The first effects of the decline are a fall in output and some downward adjustment of prices, as shown in part (i) of the figure. As real GDP falls below potential, a recessionary gap is created, and unemployment rises. At this point we must analyze two separate cases. The first occurs when wages and other factor prices fall quickly in response to the excess supply of factors. The second occurs when factor prices fall only slowly.

Flexible Wages   Suppose wages (and other factor prices) fell quickly in response to the recessionary gap. The *AS* curve would therefore shift quickly downward as the lower wages led to reduced unit costs.

As shown in part (ii) of Figure 24-3, as the *AS* curve shifted downward the economy would move along the new *AD* curve, with falling prices and rising output, until real GDP was quickly restored to potential, Y^*. We conclude that if wages were to fall rapidly whenever there was unemployment, the resulting shift in the *AS* curve would quickly eliminate recessionary gaps.

FIGURE 24-3   The Adjustment Process Following a Negative *AD* Shock

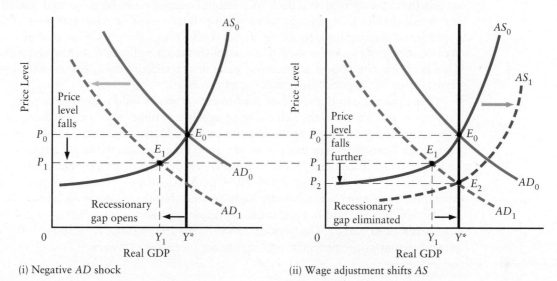

(i) Negative *AD* shock   (ii) Wage adjustment shifts *AS*

A negative *AD* shock first lowers the price level and GDP along the *AS* curve and then induces a (possibly slow) shift of the *AS* curve that further lowers prices but raises output along the new *AD* curve. In part (i), the economy is in equilibrium at E_0, at its level of potential output, Y^*, and price level P_0. The *AD* curve then shifts to AD_1, moving equilibrium to E_1, with income Y_1 and price level P_1, and opens up a recessionary gap.

Part (ii) shows the adjustment back to potential output that occurs from the supply side of the economy. The fall in wages and other factor prices shifts the *AS* curve downward. Real GDP rises, and the price level falls further along the new *AD* curve. Unless factor prices are completely rigid, the *AS* curve eventually reaches AS_1, with equilibrium at E_2. The eventual effect of the negative *AD* shock, after all adjustment has occurred, is to reduce the price level but leave real GDP unchanged.

Flexible wages that fall rapidly in the presence of a recessionary gap provide an automatic adjustment process that pushes the economy back quickly toward potential output.

Sticky Wages   As we noted earlier, the experience of most economies suggests that wages typically do not fall rapidly in response to even large recessionary gaps. It is sometimes said that wages are "sticky" in the downward direction. This does not mean that wages never fall, only that they tend to fall much more slowly in a recessionary gap than they rise in an equally sized inflationary gap. When wages are sticky, the analysis is the same as when wages are flexible, and thus Figure 24-3 tells the correct story. The significant difference, however, is that the *AS* curve shifts more slowly when wages are sticky and thus the adjustment process may not close the recessionary gap for a long time.

If wages are downwardly sticky, the economy's adjustment process is sluggish and thus will not quickly eliminate a recessionary gap.[3]

---

[3] The causes of downward wage stickiness have been hotly debated among macroeconomists for years. We discuss several possible reasons in Chapter 30 when examining the causes of cyclical unemployment.

The weakness of the adjustment process following a negative demand shock does not mean that recessionary gaps must always be prolonged. Rather, this weakness means that speedy recovery back to potential output must be generated mainly from the demand side. This often happens when private-sector demand revives and the *AD* curve starts shifting back to the right. But it also raises the possibility that government *stabilization policy* can be used to accomplish such a rightward shift in the *AD* curve. This is an important and contentious issue in macroeconomics, one to which we will return often throughout the remainder of this book.

The difference in the speed of adjustment of wages (and other factor prices) is the important asymmetry in the behaviour of aggregate supply that we noted earlier in this chapter. This asymmetry helps to explain two key facts about the Canadian economy. First, high unemployment can persist for quite long periods without causing decreases in wages of sufficient magnitude to quickly remove the unemployment. For example, during the 1991–1995 and 2009–2014 periods, output was below potential and unemployment remained relatively high. Second, booms, along with labour shortages and production beyond normal capacity, do not persist for long periods without causing increases in wages. The periods 1988–1990, 1999–2000, and 2004–2007 all displayed output above potential and significant increases in wages.

Aggregate Supply Shocks

We have discussed the economy's adjustment process that returns real GDP to Y^* following an aggregate demand shock. The same adjustment process operates following an aggregate supply shock.

Consider an economy that has a stable price level and real GDP at its potential level, as illustrated by point E_0 in part (i) of Figure 24-4. Suppose there is an increase in the world price of an important input, such as oil. An increase in the price of oil increases unit costs for firms and causes the *AS* curve to shift upward. Real GDP falls and the price level increases—a combination often called *stagflation*. The short-run equilibrium is at point E_1. With the opening of a recessionary gap, the economy's adjustment process comes into play, though sticky wages reduce the speed of this adjustment.

In our macro model, the recessionary gap caused by the negative supply shock causes firms to reduce output and trim their workforce. Some workers are laid off. The excess supply of labour (and other factors) eventually pushes wages down and begins to reverse the initial increase in unit costs caused by the increase in the price of oil. This adjustment is shown in part (ii) of the figure. As wages fall, the *AS* curve shifts back toward its starting point, and real GDP rises back toward its potential level, Y^*. Since our model assumes that Y^* is constant, the reductions in factor prices eventually bring the economy back to its initial point, E_0. Note, however, that *relative* prices will have changed when the economy returns to E_0. The price level is back to P_0, its starting point, but real wages are lower while the relative price of oil is higher.

We leave it to the reader to analyze the adjustment process following a positive aggregate supply shock. The logic of the analysis is exactly the same as illustrated in Figure 24-4, except that the initial shift in the *AS* curve is to the right, creating an inflationary gap.

Exogenous changes in input prices cause the *AS* curve to shift, creating an output gap. The adjustment process then reverses the initial *AS* shift and brings the economy back to potential output and the initial price level.

FIGURE 24-4 The Adjustment Process Following a Negative *AS* Shock

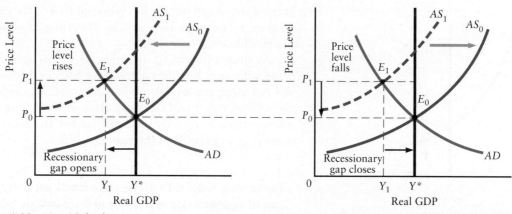

(i) Negative *AS* shock   (ii) Wage adjustment returns *AS* to initial position

A negative *AS* shock caused by an increase in input prices causes real GDP to fall and the price level to rise. The economy's adjustment process then reverses the *AS* shift and eventually returns the economy to its starting point. The economy begins at point E_0 in part (i). The rise in input prices increases firms' unit costs and causes the *AS* curve to shift up to AS_1. Real GDP falls to Y_1 and the price level rises to P_1. A recessionary gap is created. In part (ii), the excess supply of factors associated with the recessionary gap causes wages and other factor prices to fall, possibly slowly. As factor prices fall, unit costs fall and so the *AS* curve shifts back down to AS_0. The eventual effect of the *AS* shock, after all adjustment has occurred, is to leave the price level and real GDP unchanged.

Long-Run Equilibrium

Following any *AD* or *AS* shocks in our model, we have seen that the adjustment of factor prices continues until real GDP returns to Y^*. The economy is said to be in a *long-run equilibrium* when this adjustment process is complete, and there is no longer an output gap. In other words, the economy is in its long-run equilibrium when the intersection of the *AD* and *AS* curves occurs at Y^*.

We also assume in our macro model that the value of Y^* depends only on real variables, such as the labour force, capital stock, and the level of technology. We assume, in particular, that Y^* is independent of nominal variables, such as the price level. The vertical line at Y^* that we have seen in our diagrams is sometimes called a *long-run aggregate supply curve*—the relationship between the price level and the amount of output supplied by firms *after all factor prices have adjusted to output gaps*. This vertical line is also sometimes called a *Classical aggregate supply curve* because the Classical economists were mainly concerned with the behaviour of the economy in long-run equilibrium.[4]

---

[4] The Classical school of economic thought began with Adam Smith (1723–1790) and was developed through the work of David Ricardo (1772–1823), Thomas Malthus (1766–1834), and John Stuart Mill (1806–1873). These economists emphasized the long-run behaviour of the economy. Beginning in the middle of the nineteenth century, Neoclassical economists devoted much time and effort to studying short-term fluctuations. *The General Theory of Employment, Interest and Money* (1936), written by John Maynard Keynes (1883–1946), was in a long tradition of the study of short-term fluctuations. Where Keynes differed from the Neoclassical economists was in approaching the issues from a macroeconomic perspective that emphasized fluctuations in *aggregate* expenditure. Each of the economists mentioned in this footnote, along with several others, is discussed in more detail in the timeline at the back of the book.

FIGURE 24-5   Changes in Long-Run Equilibrium

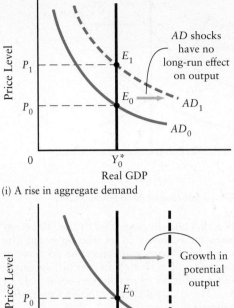

(i) A rise in aggregate demand

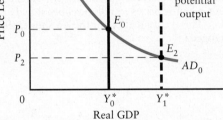

(ii) A rise in potential output

Potential output determines the long-run equilibrium value of real GDP; given Y^*, aggregate demand determines the long-run equilibrium value of the price level. In both parts of the figure, the initial long-run equilibrium is at E_0, so the price level is P_0 and real GDP is Y_0^*.

In part (i), a shift in the AD curve from AD_0 to AD_1 moves the long-run equilibrium from E_0 to E_1. This raises the price level from P_0 to P_1 but leaves real GDP unchanged at Y_0^* in the long run.

In part (ii), an increase in potential output from Y_0^* to Y_1^* moves the long-run equilibrium from E_0 to E_2. This raises real GDP from Y_0^* to Y_1^* and lowers the price level from P_0 to P_2.

Figure 24-5 shows an AD/AS diagram without the usual upward-sloping AS curve. It is useful to omit this curve if our focus is on the state of the economy *after* all factor prices have fully adjusted and output has returned to Y^*. We can use this diagram to examine how shocks affect the economy's long-run equilibrium.

As shown in part (i) of Figure 24-5, any shift in the AD curve will cause a change in the price level in the long run but will not affect the level of potential output, Y^*. In our model, the only way that real GDP can change in the long run (*after* factor prices have fully adjusted) is for the level of Y^* to change, as in part (ii) of the figure.

> **In the long run, real GDP is determined solely by Y^*; the role of aggregate demand is only to determine the price level.**

This strong result—that changes in aggregate demand have no long-run effect on real GDP—follows from the assumption in our macro model that Y^* is independent of the price level and thus unaffected by AD shocks.[5]

We will discuss the long-run behaviour of the economy in detail in Chapter 25. There we examine why Y^* grows over extended periods of time and why this growth is important for determining the ongoing increases in our material living standards.

The Canadian Wage-Adjustment Process: Empirical Evidence

We have been assuming in our macro model that wages rise whenever real GDP is above potential output ($Y > Y^*$) and that wages fall, though perhaps slowly, whenever real GDP is below potential output ($Y < Y^*$). It is worth asking whether this empirical relationship—what we call the Phillips curve—actually exists in Canadian data.

Before we try to answer this question, we must recognize an important difference between our theoretical macro model and the real world. In our macro model we assume that inflation is zero and labour productivity is constant, and so any change in nominal wages creates an equal change in firms' costs. And in our model it is the changes in firms' costs that lead to shifts in the AS curve as part of the wage-adjustment process.

---

[5] Whether short-run fluctuations in real GDP have an effect on the value of Y^* is an important area of research in macroeconomics. In Chapters 27 and 30 we discuss reasons why some short-run changes in real GDP may cause Y^* to change in the same direction.

In reality, however, the changes in firms' costs depend on more than just nominal wages. *Unit labour cost* is a measure of the labour cost required to produce one unit of output. Unit labour costs rise when real wages increase because workers are more expensive; but unit labour costs *fall* when labour productivity increases because workers are able to produce more output per hour. We can compute the annual *change* in unit labour cost by starting with the growth rate of nominal wages and then subtracting the rate of inflation and the growth rate of labour productivity. For example, suppose nominal wages are growing by 5 percent per year, the annual rate of inflation is 2 percent, and labour productivity is rising annually by 1 percent. In this situation, unit labour costs are rising by 2 percent per year ($2 = 5 - 2 - 1$). Only when firms' unit labour costs are rising, as in this numerical example, will the *AS* curve be shifting upward in our macro model.

To examine the empirical validity of the wage-adjustment process (the Phillips curve) with actual Canadian data we should therefore plot a measure of the output gap against a measure of the change in firms' unit labour costs. A positive relationship between these two variables would then be consistent with our model's key assumption, that firms' costs rise when real GDP is above potential output ($Y > Y^*$) and fall when real GDP is below potential output ($Y < Y^*$).

Is this empirical relationship evident in the data? Figure 24-6 is a scatterplot of annual Canadian data from 1991 through 2017, showing the output gap (as a percentage of potential output) on the horizontal axis and the rate of growth of unit labour costs on the vertical axis. But we have also allowed for the slow adjustment of wages and costs; each point in the graph matches up the output gap in any specific year with the change in unit labour costs *two years later*. The graph shows a clear positive relationship between these two macro variables. The black dashed line is the "line of best fit" and has a slope of 0.5, indicating that, on average across this sample period, an increase in the output gap of one percentage point is associated with a faster rise in unit

FIGURE 24-6   The Canadian Phillips Curve, 1991–2017

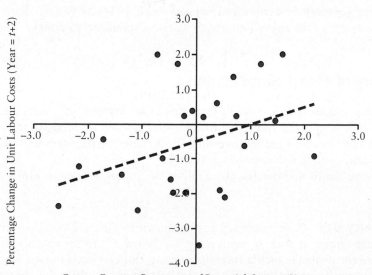

Output Gap as a Percentage of Potential Output (Year = *t*)

Canadian data confirm our macro model's key assumption that positive output gaps tend to drive wages and costs upward while negative output gaps tend to drive wages and costs downward. The scatterplot matches up the output gap in any given year (*t*) with the growth of unit labour costs two years later (*t* + 2). This timing allows for the slow adjustment of wages and costs to output gaps that is typical in actual economies. The change in unit labour costs is measured by the growth rate of nominal wages minus the rate of inflation minus the growth rate of labour productivity.

(*Source:* Author's calculations using data from the Bank of Canada and Statistics Canada.)

labour costs by about half a percentage point after two years. The empirical evidence from Canada is therefore consistent with the central assumption in this chapter—that positive output gaps tend to drive wages (and costs) upward while negative output gaps tend to drive wages (and costs) downward.

24.4 Fiscal Stabilization Policy

In Chapter 22, we briefly examined fiscal policy in our macro model in which output was demand determined and the price level was assumed to be constant. Now that our model is more complete—and also more realistic—we can examine fiscal policy in more detail. We now consider taxation and government spending as tools of fiscal stabilization policy; in Chapter 31, we return to more advanced aspects of fiscal policy.

Fiscal stabilization policy is fundamentally a short-run policy. In response to various shocks that cause changes in real GDP, the government may use various fiscal tools in an attempt to push real GDP back towards potential output. The alternatives to using fiscal stabilization policy are to wait for the recovery of private-sector demand (a shift in the AD curve) or to wait for the economy's adjustment process (a shift in the AS curve) to bring real GDP back to potential. The slower these processes are, the stronger is the justification for government to use its fiscal tools.

There is no doubt that the government can exert a major influence on real GDP. Prime examples are the massive increases in military spending during major wars. Canadian federal expenditure during the Second World War rose from 12.2 percent of GDP in 1939 to 41.8 percent in 1944. At the same time, the unemployment rate fell from 11.4 percent to 1.4 percent. Economists agree that the increase in government spending helped to bring about the rise in output and the associated fall in unemployment. More recently, the Canadian government dramatically increased spending in an effort to dampen the effects of the major global recession that began in late 2008. Most economists agree that this "fiscal stimulus" contributed significantly to real GDP growth in the 2009–2012 period.

In the heyday of "activist" fiscal policy, from about 1945 to about 1970, many economists were convinced that the economy could be stabilized adequately just by varying the size of the government's taxes and expenditures. That day is past. Today, economists are more aware of the many limitations of fiscal stabilization policy.

The Basic Theory of Fiscal Stabilization

In our macroeconomic model, a reduction in tax rates or an increase in government purchases or transfers will shift the AD curve to the right, causing an increase in real GDP. An increase in tax rates or a cut in government purchases or transfers will shift the AD curve to the left, causing a decrease in real GDP.

Let's look in more detail at how fiscal stabilization policy works to close an output gap.

Closing a Recessionary Gap   A recessionary gap is shown in Figure 24-7; the economy's short-run equilibrium is at point E_0 with real GDP below Y^*. In the absence of a recovery in private-sector demand, such a recessionary gap can be closed in two ways. The first involves the economy's adjustment process that we saw previously in this chapter. The excess supply of factors at E_0 will eventually cause wages and other factor prices to fall, shifting the AS curve downward and restoring output to Y^*, as shown in part (i)

FIGURE 24-7 The Closing of a Recessionary Gap

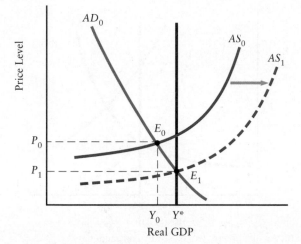 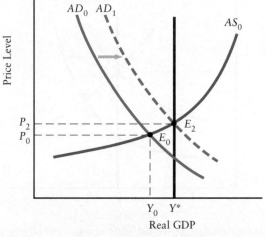

(i) A recessionary gap closed by falling wages and other factor prices

(ii) A recessionary gap closed by expansionary fiscal policy

A recessionary gap may be closed by a (slow) downward shift of the AS curve or an increase in aggregate demand. Initially, equilibrium is at E_0, with real GDP at Y_0 and the price level at P_0. There is a recessionary gap.

As shown in part (i), the gap might be removed by a shift in the AS curve to AS_1, as will eventually happen when wages and other factor prices fall in response to excess supply. The shift in the AS curve causes a movement down and to the right along AD_0 to a new equilibrium at E_1, achieving potential output Y^* and lowering the price level to P_1.

As shown in part (ii), the gap might also be removed by a shift of the AD curve to AD_1, caused by an expansionary fiscal policy (or a recovery of private-sector demand). The shift in the AD curve causes a movement up and to the right along AS_0. This movement shifts the equilibrium to E_2, raising output to Y^* and the price level to P_2.

of the figure. However, because of the downward stickiness of wages, this process may take a long time. Policymakers may not be prepared to wait the time necessary for the recessionary gap to correct itself. The second way to close the recessionary gap involves an active policy choice. The government can use expansionary fiscal policy to shift the AD curve to the right, as shown in part (ii) of the figure. It would do this by reducing tax rates, increasing transfers, or increasing the level of government purchases.

The advantage of using fiscal policy rather than allowing the economy to recover naturally is that it may substantially shorten what might otherwise be a long recession. One disadvantage is that the use of fiscal policy may stimulate the economy just before private-sector spending recovers on its own. As a result, the economy may overshoot its potential output, and an inflationary gap may open up. In this case, fiscal policy that is intended to promote economic stability can actually cause instability.

Closing an Inflationary Gap An inflationary gap is illustrated in Figure 24-8; the economy's short-run equilibrium is at point E_0, with real GDP above Y^*. In the absence of a downward adjustment of private-sector demand, there are two ways such an inflationary gap may be closed. Again, the first involves the economy's adjustment process. Excess demand for factors will cause wages and other factor prices to rise, shifting the AS curve upward and gradually restoring output to Y^*, as shown in part (i) of the figure. Alternatively, the government can use a contractionary fiscal policy to shift the AD

FIGURE 24-8 The Closing of an Inflationary Gap

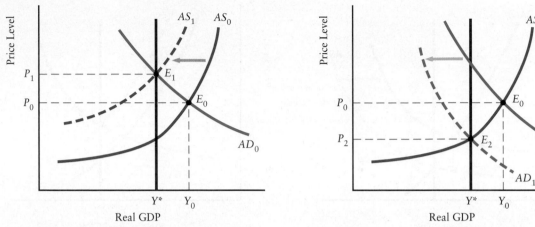

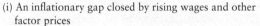

(i) An inflationary gap closed by rising wages and other factor prices

(ii) An inflationary gap closed by contractionary fiscal policy

An inflationary gap may be removed by an upward shift of the *AS* curve or by a leftward shift of the *AD* curve. Initially, equilibrium is at E_0, with real GDP at Y_0 and the price level at P_0. There is an inflationary gap.

As shown in part (i), the gap might be removed by a shift in the *AS* curve to AS_1, as will happen when wages and other factor prices rise in response to the excess demand. The shift in the *AS* curve causes a movement up and to the left along AD_0. This movement establishes a new equilibrium at E_1, reducing output to its potential level Y^* and raising the price level to P_1.

As shown in part (ii), the gap might also be removed by a shift in the *AD* curve to AD_1 caused by a contractionary fiscal policy (or by a reduction of private-sector demand). The shift in the *AD* curve causes a movement down and to the left along AS_0. This movement shifts the equilibrium to E_2, lowering income to Y^* and the price level to P_2.

curve to the left and close the inflationary gap, as shown in part (ii). The government would do this by increasing tax rates, reducing transfers, or reducing its level of purchases.

The advantage of using a contractionary fiscal policy to close the inflationary gap is that it avoids the inflation that would otherwise occur. One disadvantage is that if private-sector expenditures fall for some unrelated reason, the fiscal contraction may end up being too large and real GDP may be pushed below potential, thus opening up a recessionary gap.

This discussion leads to a key proposition:

> When the economy's adjustment process is slow to operate, or produces undesirable side effects such as rising prices, there is a potential stabilization role for fiscal policy.

Fiscal Policy and the Paradox of Thrift Suppose you have a good job but you are sufficiently unsure about your economic future that you decide to increase the fraction of disposable income that you save. Your decision to save more today would not change your current income but these funds would accumulate and be useful in the future if your economic situation changed for the worse. Most people would agree that a decision to increase their saving in these circumstances would be prudent.

But what would happen if *many people* did the same thing at the same time? In our macro model, an increase in the country's total desired saving would shift the *AD* curve to the left and *reduce* the equilibrium level of real GDP in the short run. Thus, frugality on the part of individuals, which may seem to be prudent behaviour for each individual taken separately, ends up reducing the aggregate level of economic activity. This phenomenon is known as the *paradox of thrift*—the paradox being that what may be good for any individual when viewed in isolation ends up being undesirable for the economy as a whole.

The policy implication of this phenomenon is that a major and persistent recession can be battled by encouraging governments, firms, and households to reduce their saving and increase their spending. In times of unemployment and recession, a greater desire to save will only make things worse for the overall economy. This result goes directly against the idea that we should "tighten our belts" when times are tough. The notion that it is not only possible but even *desirable* to spend one's way out of a recession touches a sensitive point with people raised on the belief that success is based on hard work and frugality; as a result, the idea often arouses great hostility.

As is discussed in *Lessons from History 24-1*, the policy implications of the paradox of thrift were not generally understood during the Great Depression of the 1930s. Most governments, faced with depression-induced reductions in tax revenues, reduced their expenditures to balance their budgets. As a result, many economists argue that the fiscal policies at the time actually made things worse for the economy as a whole. When Nobel Prize–winning economist Milton Friedman (many years later) said, "We are all Keynesians now," he was referring to the general acceptance of the view that the government's budget is much more than just the revenue and expenditure statement of a very large organization. Whether we like it or not, the sheer size of the government's budget inevitably makes it a powerful tool for influencing the overall level of economic activity.

Knowledge of the fiscal policy mistakes during the Great Depression led most governments to avoid those same mistakes during the global financial crisis of 2008 and the recession that followed. In a decision that was coordinated across governments of the G20 countries, the Canadian government embarked on a two-year program of fiscal stimulus beginning in 2009. Over these two years, spending increased by approximately $40 billion, most of which was directed at public infrastructure projects. The provincial governments acted similarly, and the fiscal stimulus for all governments combined was about $52 billion, an average of 1.7 percent of GDP in each of the two years.

Short Run Versus Long Run   The paradox of thrift applies to shifts in aggregate demand that have been caused by changes in saving (and spending) behaviour. That is why it applies only in the short run, when the *AD* curve plays an important role in the determination of real GDP.

The paradox of thrift does not apply after factor prices have fully adjusted and the economy has achieved its new long-run equilibrium with real GDP equal to Y^*. Remember from Figure 24-5 that in the long run, aggregate demand does not influence the level of real GDP—output is determined only by the level of potential output, Y^*. In the long run, the more people and government save, the larger is the supply of financial capital available for investment. As we will see in Chapter 25, this increase in the pool of financial capital will reduce interest rates and encourage more investment by firms. The greater rate of investment leads to a higher rate of growth of potential output.

LESSONS FROM HISTORY 24-1

Fiscal Policy in the Great Depression

The Great Depression, which is usually dated as beginning with the massive stock-market crash on October 29, 1929, was perhaps the most dramatic economic event of the twentieth century. As the accompanying figure shows, Canadian real GDP plummeted by almost 30 percent from its peak in 1929 to its low point in 1933. The price level fell beginning in 1930 and declined by about 20 percent over the next five years. The unemployment rate increased from 3 percent of the labour force in 1929 to an unparalleled 19.3 percent four years later. To put these numbers in perspective, by today's standards a very serious recession (like the most recent one in 2008 and 2009) sees real GDP fall by 2 to 3 percent, the unemployment rate rise to 8 to 10 percent, and prices continue rising but perhaps at a slower rate. The economic events of the 1930s certainly deserve to be called the Great Depression.

The Great Depression was not just a catastrophic event that happened exogenously—its depth and duration were made worse by some fundamental mistakes in macro policy. Failure to understand the implication of the paradox of thrift led many countries to adopt disastrous fiscal policies during the Great Depression. In addition, failure to understand the role of automatic stabilizers has led many observers to conclude, erroneously, that fiscal expansion was tried in the Great Depression but failed. Let us see how these two misperceptions are related.

The Paradox of Thrift in Action

In 1932, Canadian Prime Minister R.B. Bennett said, "We are now faced with the real crisis in the history of Canada. To maintain our credit we must practise the most rigid economy and not spend a single cent." His government that year—at the deepest point in the recession—brought down a budget based on the principle of trying to balance revenues and expenditures, and it included *increases* in tax rates.

In the same year, Franklin Roosevelt was elected U.S. president on a platform of fighting the Great Depression with government policies. In his inaugural address he urged, "Our great primary task is to put people to work . . . [This task] can be helped by insistence that the federal, state, and local governments act forthwith on the demand that their costs be drastically reduced . . . ."

Across the Atlantic, King George V told the British House of Commons in 1931, "The present condition of the national finances, in the opinion of His Majesty's ministers, calls for the imposition of additional taxation and for the effecting of economies in public expenditure."

As the paradox of thrift predicts, these policies tended to worsen, rather than cure, the Great Depression.

Interpreting the Deficits in the 1930s

In general, governments can have a budget deficit for two different reasons. First, a government might increase its level of purchases without increasing its tax revenues. Such a *deficit-financed* increase in government spending represents

The paradox of thrift—the idea that an increase in desired saving reduces the level of real GDP—is true only in the short run. In the long run, the path of real GDP is determined by the path of potential output. The increase in saving has the long-run effect of increasing investment and therefore increasing potential output.

Automatic Fiscal Stabilizers

The fiscal policies that we have been discussing are referred to as *discretionary* because the government uses its discretion in changing its taxation or its spending in an attempt to change the level of real GDP. However, even if the government makes no active decisions regarding changes in spending or taxation, the mere existence of the government's tax-and-transfer system will act as an *automatic stabilizer* for the economy. Let's see how this works.

an expansion in aggregate demand. Second, a government might leave its purchases unchanged but have lower tax revenues. If the lower tax revenues are caused by a policy decision to reduce *tax rates*, then this policy also represents an expansion in aggregate demand. But if the decline in tax revenues is caused by a fall in real GDP with unchanged tax rates, the existing budget deficit *does not* represent an expansion in aggregate demand. These distinctions are central to interpreting the budget deficits of the 1930s.

Government budget deficits did increase in the 1930s, but they were not the result of an increase in government expenditures or reductions in tax rates. Rather, they were the result of the fall in tax revenues, brought about by the fall in real GDP as the economy sank into depression. The various governments did not advocate programs of massive deficit-financed spending to increase aggregate demand. Instead, they hoped that a small amount of government spending in addition to numerous policies designed to stabilize prices and to restore confidence would lead to a recovery of private investment expenditure. To have expected a massive revival of private investment expenditure as a result of the puny increase in aggregate demand that was instituted by the federal government now seems hopelessly naïve.

When we judge these policies from the viewpoint of modern macro theory, their failure is no mystery. Indeed, Professor E. Cary Brown of MIT, after a careful study for the United States, concluded, "Fiscal policy seems to have been an unsuccessful recovery device in the thirties—not because it did not work, but because it was not tried." Once the massive, war-geared expenditure of the 1940s began, output responded sharply and

unemployment all but evaporated. A similar pattern occurred in Canada, as seen clearly in the figure.

The performance of the Canadian and U.S. economies from 1930 to 1945 is well explained by the macroeconomic theory that we have developed in the last few chapters. The governments did not effectively use fiscal policy to stabilize their economies. War brought the Depression to an end because war demands made acceptable a level of government expenditure sufficient to remove the recessionary gap. Had the Canadian and American administrations been able to do the same in the early 1930s, it might have ended the waste of the Great Depression many years sooner.

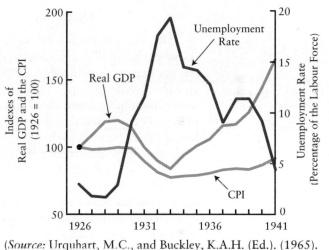

(*Source:* Urquhart, M.C., and Buckley, K.A.H. (Ed.). (1965). *Historical Statistics of Canada*. Toronto: Macmillan.)

Consider a shock that shifts the *AD* curve to the right and thus increases the short-run level of real GDP. As real GDP increases, government tax revenues also increase. In addition, since there are fewer low-income households and unemployed persons requiring assistance, governments make fewer transfer payments to individuals. The rise in net tax revenues (taxes minus transfers) dampens the overall increase in real GDP caused by the initial shock. In other words, the tax-and-transfer system reduces the value of the multiplier and thus acts as an **automatic stabilizer** for the economy. As we saw in Chapter 22, the presence of a tax-and-transfer system reduces the value of the multiplier; any positive demand shock thus leads to a smaller shift in the *AD* curve than would occur in the absence of taxes and transfers.

The same is true in the presence of a negative *AD* shock. As real GDP declines in response to the shock, the reduction in government net tax revenues dampens the overall decline in real GDP.

automatic stabilizers Elements of the tax-and-transfer system that reduce the responsiveness of real GDP to changes in autonomous expenditure.

Even in the absence of discretionary fiscal stabilization policy, the government's tax-and-transfer system provides the economy with an automatic stabilizer.

At the end of Chapter 22 we argued that realistic Canadian values for our model's key parameters are as follows:

- marginal propensity to consume (MPC) = 0.8
- net tax rate (t) = 0.25
- marginal propensity to import (m) = 0.35

The implied value of z, the marginal propensity to spend on national income, is therefore

$$z = MPC(1-t) - m$$
$$= (0.8)(0.75) - 0.35 = 0.25$$

As a result, a realistic value for the simple multiplier in Canada is

$$\text{Simple multiplier} = 1/(1-z) = 1/0.75 = 1.33$$

The lower is the net tax rate, the larger is the simple multiplier and thus the less stable is real GDP in response to shocks to autonomous spending. For example, if the net tax rate were reduced to 20 percent ($t = 0.20$), the value of z would rise to 0.29 and the simple multiplier would rise to $1/(1 - 0.29) = 1/0.71 = 1.41$. The larger multiplier implies that a shock to autonomous expenditure would result in a larger shift in the AD curve and thus a larger total change in GDP—that is, the economy would be less stable. Therefore, whatever benefits might arise from a reduction in the net tax rate, one drawback is that the tax reduction would lead to the economy being less stable following shocks to autonomous expenditure.

The great advantage of automatic fiscal stabilizers is that they are "automatic." As long as the tax-and-transfer system is in place (and there is no sign of its imminent disappearance!), some stability is provided without anyone having to make active decisions about fiscal policy. As we see next, the sorts of decisions required for successful *discretionary* fiscal policy are not simple, and some attempts to provide stability through discretionary fiscal policy may actually reduce the stability of the economy.

Limitations of Discretionary Fiscal Policy

According to our earlier discussion of fiscal stabilization policy, returning the economy to potential output would appear to be a simple matter of changing taxes and government spending, in some combination. Why do so many economists believe that such policies would be "as likely to harm as help"? Part of the answer is that the *practical* use of discretionary fiscal policy is anything but simple.

Decision and Execution Lags   To change fiscal policy requires making changes in taxes and government expenditures. The changes must be agreed on by the Cabinet and passed by Parliament. The political stakes in such changes are generally very large; taxes and spending are called "bread-and-butter issues" precisely because they affect the economic well-being of almost everyone. Even if economists agreed that the economy would be helped by, say, a tax cut, politicians would likely spend a good deal of time debating *whose* taxes should be cut and by *how much*. If the assessment by economists was that an increase in government spending was desirable, the lengthy political debate would then be about what *type* of spending should increase and whether it should focus on particular industries or regions. The delay between the initial recognition of a recessionary or inflationary gap and the enactment of legislation to change fiscal policy, which may be several months long, is called a **decision lag**.

Once policy changes are agreed on, there is still an **execution lag**, adding time between the enactment of the legislation and the implementation of the policy action. Furthermore, once the new policies are in place, it will usually take still more time for their economic consequences to be felt. Because of these lags, it is quite possible that by the time a given policy decision has any impact on the economy, circumstances will have changed such that the policy is no longer appropriate.

The decision lag applies more or less equally to both tax and expenditure policies. The execution lag, however, tends to be considerably longer for expenditure than tax policies. Once Parliament agrees to specific tax changes, the effects can be realized quite soon by individual or corporate taxpayers. For an increase in expenditure, however, new programs may need to be created or infrastructure projects planned and designed before the bulk of the new spending can occur. Even for planned reductions in expenditure, it often takes time to scale down or cancel existing spending programs and to identify the public servants who will be laid off.

> **decision lag** The period of time between perceiving some problem and reaching a decision on what to do about it.
>
> **execution lag** The time it takes to put policies in place after a decision has been made.

Temporary Versus Permanent Tax Changes

Changes in taxation that are known to be temporary are generally less effective than measures that are expected to be permanent. For example, if households know that an announced tax cut will last only a year, they may recognize that the effect on their long-run consumption possibilities is small and may choose to save rather than spend their current increase in disposable income. If so, the effect of the tax cut on aggregate demand will be nil.

In other cases, however, temporary changes in taxes may be quite effective at changing aggregate demand. If the government temporarily increases employment-insurance (EI) benefits to the long-term unemployed, for example, it is quite likely that they will spend a large fraction of the increased benefits and that aggregate demand will increase as a result.

For most tax changes, the following general principle is a useful guide for policy: The more closely household consumption expenditure is related to *lifetime* income rather than to *current* income, the smaller will be the effects on current consumption of tax changes that are known to be of short duration. Or, to use the language that we used when introducing the consumption function in Chapter 21, the more forward-looking households are, the smaller will be the effects of what are perceived to be temporary changes in taxes.

Fine Tuning versus Gross Tuning

Attempts to use discretionary fiscal policy to "fine tune" the economy are fraught with difficulties. **Fine tuning** refers to the use of fiscal (and monetary) policy to offset virtually all fluctuations in private-sector spending so as to keep real GDP at or near its potential level. However, neither economics nor political science has yet advanced far enough to allow policymakers to undo the consequences of every aggregate demand or supply shock. Nevertheless, many economists still argue that when a recessionary gap is large enough and persists for long enough, *gross tuning* may be appropriate. **Gross tuning** refers to the use of fiscal and monetary policy to remove large and persistent output gaps. Other economists believe that fiscal policy should not be used for economic stabilization under any circumstances. Rather, they would argue, tax and spending behaviour should be the

> **fine tuning** The attempt to maintain output at its potential level by means of frequent changes in fiscal or monetary policy.
>
> **gross tuning** The use of macroeconomic policy to stabilize the economy such that large deviations from potential output do not persist for extended periods of time.

outcome of public choices regarding the long-term size and financing of the public sector and should not be altered for short-term considerations. We return to these debates in Chapter 31.

Fiscal Policy and Growth

We have seen how decisions about fiscal policy can affect the level of real GDP and the price level in the short run. In summary, increases in government spending and reductions in tax rates generally lead to an increase in aggregate demand and thus to a rightward shift of the *AD* curve, increasing real GDP. In contrast, reductions in government spending and increases in tax rates generally reduce aggregate demand and thus lead to a leftward shift in the *AD* curve, reducing real GDP. But what are the effects of such fiscal policy actions on the economy's long-run growth rate?

We will examine the process of economic growth in detail in the next chapter. But for now it is worth simply asking how current changes in fiscal policy might have an impact on Y^*, the economy's level of potential GDP. Whatever short-run impacts follow from the fiscal policy, our macro model predicts that the factor-price adjustment process will eventually bring the economy back to Y^*. So, asking about how fiscal policy affects Y^* makes sense if we want to know how fiscal policy affects long-run growth.

We can approach this issue in two parts: the impact of government purchases on Y^* and the impact of taxation on Y^*.

Increases in Government Purchases   Suppose the government chooses to increase its purchases of goods and services. The impact on potential output depends on *which* goods and services are purchased. If the government purchases more weapons for the military or chooses to spend more on salaries for government workers, or purchases new buildings for government departments, it is unlikely to have any effect on the economy's level of potential output. There will be the now-familiar short-run boost to GDP as a consequence of this fiscal policy, but the long-run impact will be nil since Y^* will be unaffected.

In contrast, if the government purchases bridges and ports which can improve our flows of exports and imports, or expands airports which can improve commerce and tourism, or invests in medical research facilities which can develop more effective vaccines, then it is possible that the economy's level of potential GDP will increase as a result of this spending. In this case, in addition to the short-run boost to GDP that occurs in response to this fiscal policy, the positive impact on Y^* implies that even after factor prices have fully adjusted, the economy will return to a *higher value* of Y^*. In this case, the fiscal expansion will have improved the economy's long-run growth.

Reductions in Tax Rates   If the government chooses to reduce tax rates, the effect on Y^* will depend on *which* taxes are reduced. Reductions in personal income-tax rates or the GST rate may have small effects on individuals' incentive to work, thus increasing overall labour supply and the level of potential output. However, economic research suggests that this effect is likely to be very small (unless marginal income-tax rates are very high). In this case, the short-run boost to GDP that follows the tax cuts will be largely reversed as the factor-price adjustment process returns real GDP to a (relatively) unchanged level of Y^*.

Reductions in corporate income-tax rates are more likely to generate an increase in Y^*. By providing an incentive for firms to increase their desired investment, cuts in corporate income-tax rates are likely to increase the economy's capital stock and, through this channel, to increase its long-run growth. In this case, the short-run boost to GDP that is caused by the tax cut is not entirely reversed in the long run; even after factor prices have fully adjusted, the economy will return to a *higher value* of Y^*. In this case, the fiscal expansion will have improved the economy's long-run growth.

This discussion of fiscal policy and long-run growth is a natural place to end this chapter and a natural segue to our next chapter, which examines the process of economic growth in considerable detail.

SUMMARY

24.1 Three Macroeconomic States

LO 1

- The short run in macroeconomics assumes that factor prices are exogenous and technology and factor supplies are constant.
- During the adjustment process, factor prices respond to output gaps; technology and factor supplies are assumed to be constant.

- In the long run, factor prices are assumed to have fully adjusted to output gaps; technology and factor supplies are assumed to change.

24.2 The Adjustment Process

LO 2, 3

- Potential output, Y^*, is the level of real GDP at which all factors of production are fully employed.
- The output gap is the difference between potential output and the actual level of real GDP, the latter determined by the intersection of the AD and AS curves.
- An inflationary gap means that Y is greater than Y^*, and hence there is excess demand in factor markets. As a result, wages and other factor prices rise, causing firms' unit costs to rise. The AS curve shifts upward, and the price level rises.

- A recessionary gap means that Y is less than Y^*, and hence there is excess supply in factor markets. Wages and other factor prices fall but perhaps very slowly. As firms' unit costs fall, the AS curve gradually shifts downward, eventually returning output to potential.
- In our macro model, the level of potential output, Y^*, acts as an "anchor" for the economy. Given the short-run equilibrium as determined by the AD and AS curves, wages and other factor prices will adjust, shifting the AS curve, until output returns to Y^*.

24.3 Aggregate Demand and Supply Shocks

LO 4

- Beginning from a position of potential output, a positive demand shock creates an inflationary gap, causing wages and other factor prices to rise. Firms' unit costs rise, shifting the AS curve upward and bringing output back toward Y^*.
- Beginning from a position of potential output, a negative demand shock creates a recessionary gap. Because factor prices tend to be sticky downward, the adjustment process tends to be slow, and a recessionary gap tends to persist for some time.
- Aggregate supply shocks, such as those caused by changes in the prices of inputs, lead the AS curve to shift, changing real GDP and the price level. But the

economy's adjustment process reverses the shift in AS, tending eventually to bring the economy back to its initial level of output and prices.
- In the short run, macroeconomic equilibrium is determined by the intersection of the AD and AS curves. In the long run, the economy is in equilibrium only when real GDP is equal to potential output. In the long run, the price level is determined by the intersection of the AD curve and the vertical Y^* curve.
- Shocks to the AD or AS curves can change real GDP in the short run. For a shock to have long-run effects, the value of Y^* must be altered.

24.4 Fiscal Stabilization Policy   LO 5

- In our macro model, fiscal policy can be used to stabilize output at Y^*. To remove a recessionary gap, governments can shift AD to the right by cutting taxes or increasing spending. To remove an inflationary gap, governments can adopt the opposite policies.
- In the short run, increases in desired saving on the part of firms, households, and governments lead to reductions in real GDP. This phenomenon is called the paradox of thrift. In the long run, the paradox of thrift does not apply, and increased saving will lead to increased investment and economic growth.
- Because government tax-and-transfer programs tend to reduce the size of the multiplier, they act as automatic stabilizers.

- Discretionary fiscal policy is subject to decision lags and execution lags that limit its ability to take effect quickly.
- Fiscal policy has different effects in the short and long run. In the short run, a fiscal expansion created by an increase in government purchases (G) will increase real GDP. In the long run, the effect on potential output depends on which goods are purchased.
- A fiscal expansion created by a reduction in taxes increases real GDP in the short run. In the long run, if the tax reduction leads to more investment and work effort, there will be a positive effect on potential output.

KEY CONCEPTS

The output gap and factor prices
Inflationary and recessionary gaps
Asymmetry of wage adjustment: flexible and sticky wages
The Phillips curve

Potential output as an "anchor" for the economy
Short-run versus long-run effects of AD and AS shocks
Fiscal stabilization policy

The paradox of thrift
Decision lags and execution lags
Automatic stabilizers
Fine tuning and gross tuning

STUDY EXERCISES

MyLab Economics Make the grade with MyLab Economics™: All Study Exercises can be found on MyLab Economics™. You can practise them as often as you want, and many feature step-by-step guided instructions to help you find the right answer.

FILL-IN-THE-BLANK

1 Fill in the blanks to make the following statements correct.

   a. In our short-run macro model, it is assumed that factor prices are _____ and the level of potential output is _____. Changes in real GDP are caused by fluctuations in _____ and _____.
   b. During the adjustment process highlighted in this chapter, the central assumption is that factor prices are _____ and respond to _____. Potential output is assumed to be _____ and acts as a(n) _____ for real GDP following AD or AS shocks.

2 Fill in the blanks to make the following statements correct.

   a. When actual GDP is higher than potential GDP, we say that there is a(n) _____ gap. When actual GDP is less than potential GDP we say there is a(n) _____ gap.
   b. An inflationary gap leads to excess demand for labour, which causes wages and thus _____ costs to rise. Firms require higher _____ in order to supply any level of output, and so the AS curve shifts _____.

c. A recessionary gap leads to excess supply of labour, which tends to cause wages and thus _____ costs to fall. Firms reduce _____ for any level of output supplied, and so the *AS* curve shifts _____.

d. The downward adjustment of wages in response to a recessionary gap is much _____ than the upward adjustment of wages in response to a(n) _____ gap. Economists refer to this phenomenon as _____.

❸ Fill in the blanks to make the following statements correct.

a. Beginning with output equal to potential, suppose there is a sudden increase in demand for Canadian exports. This is a _____ shock to the Canadian economy, which will result in the _____ curve shifting to the _____ and the opening of a(n) _____ gap. Firms' unit costs will start to _____ and the _____ curve will shift _____. Long-run equilibrium will be restored at _____ output and _____ price level.

b. Beginning with output equal to potential, suppose there is a drop in business confidence and investment falls. This is a _____ shock to the Canadian economy, which shifts the _____ curve to the left and creates a(n) _____ gap. Unit costs will start to _____ and the _____ curve will shift _____. Long-run equilibrium will (slowly) be restored at _____ output and _____ price level.

c. Beginning with output equal to potential, suppose there is a large and sudden increase in the price of electricity. This is a _____ shock to the Canadian economy, which will result in the _____ curve shifting _____ and the opening of a(n) _____ gap. If wages are downwardly sticky the economy's _____ process could be very slow and the _____ will persist for a long time.

d. Beginning with output equal to potential, suppose there is a large and sudden decrease in the price of electricity. This is a _____ shock to the Canadian economy, which will result in the _____ curve shifting _____ and the opening of a(n) _____ gap. Unit costs will start to _____ and the _____ curve will shift _____, restoring equilibrium at _____ output and _____ price level.

❹ Fill in the blanks to make the following statements correct.

a. In the long run, total output is determined only by _____. In the long run, aggregate demand determines the _____.

b. Permanent increases in real GDP are possible only if _____ is increasing.

c. Suppose illiteracy in Canada were eliminated, and the school dropout rate was reduced to zero. The effect would be a permanent _____ in productivity and a(n) _____ in potential output.

d. A reduction in corporate income tax is likely to make _____ more attractive and thus shift the _____ curve to the right. The result is a(n) _____ in the short-run level of real GDP. In the long run, the greater rate of _____ by firms will lead to a greater level of _____.

REVIEW

❺ The following diagram shows two economies, *A* and *B*. Each are in short-run equilibrium at point *E*, where the *AD* and *AS* curves intersect.

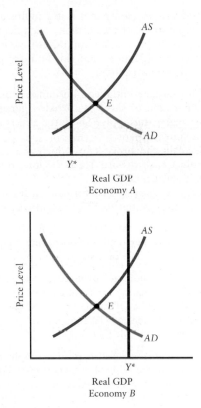

Real GDP
Economy *A*

Real GDP
Economy *B*

a. Explain why in Economy *A* wages and other factor prices will begin to rise, and why this will increase firms' unit costs.

b. Following your answer in part (a), show the effect on the *AS* curve. Explain what happens to real GDP and the price level.

c. Explain why in Economy *B* wages and other factor prices will begin to fall, and why this will decrease firms' unit costs.

d. Following your answer in part (c), show the effect on the *AS* curve. Explain what happens to real GDP and the price level.

❻ Consider an economy that is in equilibrium with output equal to *Y**. There is then a significant reduction in the world's demand for this country's goods.

a. Illustrate the initial equilibrium in a diagram.
b. What kind of shock occurred—aggregate demand or aggregate supply? Show the effects of the shock in your diagram.
c. Explain the process by which the economy will adjust back toward Y^* in the long run. Show this in your diagram.
d. Explain why policymakers may want to use a fiscal expansion to restore output back to Y^* rather than wait for the process you described in part (c). What role does downward wage stickiness play in the policymakers' thinking?

7 Consider an economy that is in equilibrium with output equal to Y^*. There is then a significant reduction in the world price of an important raw material, such as iron ore. (Assume that this country produces no iron ore domestically.)

a. Illustrate the initial equilibrium in a diagram.
b. What kind of shock occurred—aggregate demand or aggregate supply? Show the effects of the shock in your diagram.
c. Explain the process by which the economy will adjust back toward Y^* in the long run. Show this in your diagram.
d. Is there a strong case for using a fiscal contraction to return output to Y^*? Explain why or why not.

8 Between 2006 and 2012, the Canadian government reduced both personal and corporate income taxes. Is this a demand-side or a supply-side policy? Explain.

9 In our discussion of automatic fiscal stabilizers, we argued that income taxes and transfers increased the stability of real GDP in the face of AD and AS shocks. Recall from Chapter 22 that the simple multiplier is given by $1/[1 - MPC(1 - t) - m]$.

a. Explain how the size of the simple multiplier is related to the *slope* of the AD curve. (You may want to review the relationship between the AE curve and the AD curve, as discussed in Chapter 23.)
b. Explain how the slope of the AD curve affects the stability of real GDP in the presence of AS shocks.
c. Now explain how the size of the simple multiplier is related to the size of the *shift* in the AD curve for any given change in autonomous expenditure.
d. For any given AS curve, show how the size of the AD shift affects the stability of real GDP.
e. Finally, explain how the economy's automatic stabilizers depend on the sizes of MPC, t, and m.

10 Which of the following would be automatic stabilizers? Explain why.

a. Employment-insurance payments
b. Cost-of-living escalators in government contracts and pensions
c. Income taxes

d. Free university tuition for unemployed workers after six months of unemployment, provided that they are under 30 years old and have had five or more years of full-time work experience since high school

11 The following diagram shows the AD, AS, and Y^* curves for an economy. Suppose the economy begins at point A. Then the government increases its level of purchases (G).

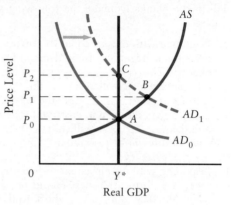

a. Describe the short-run effects of this fiscal expansion.
b. Describe the adjustment process and the new long-run equilibrium for the economy.
c. Has the *composition* of real GDP changed from the initial to the new long-run equilibrium? Explain how you know.
d. Repeat parts (a), (b), and (c) for a fiscal expansion generated by a reduction in the net tax rate.

PROBLEMS

12 The table shows several possible situations for the economy in terms of output gaps and the rate of change of wages. Real GDP is measured in billions of dollars. Assume that potential output is $800 billion.

Situation	Real GDP	Output Gap	Rate of Wage Change	Shift of AS Curve
A	775	—	−2.0%	—
B	785	—	−1.2%	—
C	795	—	−0.2%	—
D	800	—	0.0%	—
E	805	—	1.0%	—
F	815	—	2.4%	—
G	825	—	4.0%	—
H	835	—	5.8%	—

a. Compute the output gap $(Y - Y^*)$ for each situation and fill in the table.
b. Explain why wages rise when output is greater than potential but fall when output is less than potential.
c. For each situation, explain whether the economy's AS curve is shifting up, shifting down, or stationary. Fill in the table.
d. Plot the Phillips curve on a scale diagram for this economy, with the rate of change of nominal wages on the vertical axis and the level of GDP on the horizontal axis. (See *Extensions in Theory 24-1* for a review of the Phillips curve.)

13 The table below shows hypothetical data for five economies. Real GDP is measured in millions of dollars.

	Real GDP	Potential GDP (Y^*)	Output Gap (of Y^*)	Rate of Wage Change
Economy 1	10 050	9100	—	+2.0%
Economy 2	70 000	77 000	—	−0.3%
Economy 3	115 000	130 000	—	−0.5%
Economy 4	4000	3700	—	+1.0%
Economy 5	50 000	50 000	—	0.0%

a. Fill in the missing data. Which economies have an inflationary gap? Which have a recessionary gap?
b. Which economies likely have the most unused capacity? Explain.

c. In which economies are labour and other factors of production in excess demand?
d. Explain why the rate of change of nominal wages is high in Economies 1 and 4, and low in Economies 2 and 3.
e. Assuming that labour productivity is constant, in which economies are unit costs rising? In which are they falling? Explain.

14 Consider the following sets of values for *MPC*, *t*, and *m*, and recall that the simple multiplier is given by $1/[1 - MPC(1 - t) - m]$. Assume the AS curve is upward sloping and identical in each economy.

Economy A: $MPC = 0.84, t = 0.15, m = 0.19$
Economy B: $MPC = 0.84, t = 0.40, m = 0.19$
Economy C: $MPC = 0.93, t = 0.15, m = 0.12$
Economy D: $MPC = 0.75, t = 0.30, m = 0.27$
Economy E: $MPC = 0.75, t = 0.10, m = 0.30$

a. For each economy, calculate the *simple* multiplier.
b. Which economy would experience the largest swings in real GDP in response to a given AD shock? Which would experience the smallest swings?
c. Explain why the change in real GDP in response to an AD shock would *not* be solely determined by the simple multiplier for each of these economies.
d. Compare Economies A and B and explain how the tax-and-transfer system provides greater automatic stabilization in one of the two economies.
e. Explain how the slope of the AS curve would affect the short-run change in real GDP in response to an AD shock.

25

LONG-RUN ECONOMIC GROWTH

CHAPTER OUTLINE

25.1 THE NATURE OF ECONOMIC GROWTH

25.2 ECONOMIC GROWTH: BASIC RELATIONSHIPS

25.3 ECONOMIC GROWTH: ADVANCED THEORIES

25.4 ARE THERE LIMITS TO GROWTH?

LEARNING OBJECTIVES (LO)

After studying this chapter you will be able to

1 discuss the costs and benefits of economic growth.

2 list four important determinants of growth in potential GDP.

3 describe the relationship between investment, saving, and long-run growth.

4 explain the main elements of Neoclassical growth theory in which technological change is exogenous.

5 discuss advanced growth theories based on endogenous technical change and increasing returns.

6 explain why resource exhaustion and environmental degradation may create serious challenges for public policy directed at sustaining economic growth.

ECONOMIC growth is the single most powerful engine for generating long-term increases in living standards. Our material living standards over time depend largely on the growth in real GDP in relation to the growth in population—that is, it depends on the growth of real per capita GDP. Such growth does not necessarily make *everybody* in Canada materially better off in the short term. But it does increase the *average* standard of living over the short term and virtually everyone's in the long term.

What determines the long-run growth rate of per capita GDP in Canada? Is this something beyond our control, or are there government policies that can stimulate economic growth? What are the costs and benefits of those policies?

In this chapter we examine the important issue of economic growth. We will look at the benefits and costs of economic growth and then study various theories to explain how growth happens. Finally, we examine the idea that there may be *limits to growth* imposed by resource exhaustion and environmental degradation.

▌25.1 The Nature of Economic Growth

Economic growth is sought after in the rich, developed economies of Canada, France, and Australia as well as in the much poorer, developing countries of Haiti, Bangladesh, and Vietnam. Governments in all countries view economic growth as an important objective. While the *urgency* for growth is clearly higher in poorer countries than it is in richer ones, the fundamental nature of growth—its causes and consequences—is strikingly similar across all countries. We begin our discussion by examining some Canadian data.

Figure 25-1 shows the paths, since 1960, of three variables in the Canadian economy, each of which relates to long-run economic growth. Each variable is expressed as an index number, which takes a value of 100 in 1960. The first is real GDP, which shows an overall growth from 1960 to 2017 of 500 percent, an average annual growth rate of 3.3 percent. Though real GDP is an accepted measure of the amount of annual economic activity that passes through markets, it does not tell us about changes in average material living standards because it does not take into account the growth in the population—more national income is not necessarily better if more people have to share it. The second variable shown is the index of real *per capita* GDP. It shows an overall growth of 192 percent between 1960 and 2017, an annual average growth rate of 2.0 percent.

FIGURE 25-1 Three Aspects of Economic Growth

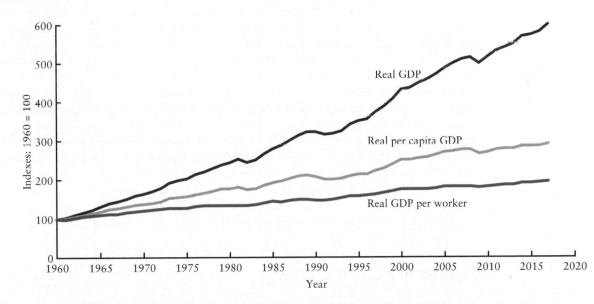

Real GDP, real per capita GDP, and labour productivity have all grown substantially over the past half-century. Each variable shown is an index number with 1960 = 100. Real GDP has grown faster than real per capita GDP because the population has grown. Real per capita GDP has grown faster than real GDP per worker (labour productivity) because the level of employment has grown faster than the population.

(*Source:* Based on data from Statistics Canada, CANSIM database. Real GDP: Table 380-0106. Employment: Series V2091072. Population: Series V2062809.)

TABLE 25-1   The Cumulative Effect of Economic Growth

| | | | Annual Growth Rate | | |
Year	1%	2%	3%	5%	7%
0	100	100	100	100	100
10	111	122	134	163	197
30	135	181	243	432	761
50	165	269	438	1 147	2 946
70	201	400	792	3 043	11 399
100	271	725	1 922	13 150	86 772

Small differences in income growth rates make enormous differences in levels of income over a few decades. Let income be 100 in year 0. At a growth rate of 3 percent per year, it will be 134 in 10 years, 438 after 50 years, and 1922 after a century. Notice the difference between 2 percent and 3 percent growth—even small differences in growth rates make big differences in future income levels.

economic growth Sustained, long-run increases in the level of real GDP.

As we will see in this chapter, one of the most important reasons that per capita GDP increases over many years is growth in *productivity*. The third variable provides one measure of labour productivity; it is an index of real GDP *per employed worker*. Its overall growth from 1960 to 2017 is 95 percent, an average annual growth rate of 1.2 percent; the average Canadian worker produced 90 percent more in 2017 than in 1960. *Applying Economic Concepts 25-1* provides some everyday examples of the sources of productivity growth in specific industries.

The three variables in Figure 25-1 show different aspects of **economic growth**, a term that economists usually reserve for describing sustained or long-run increases in real GDP. This chapter will discuss each of these three aspects of economic growth—real GDP, real per capita GDP, and productivity.

The average annual growth rates shown in Figure 25-1 may seem small, especially those for the measure of productivity. It is important to realize, however, that because these growth rates are sustained for many years, they have a profound influence on material living standards from one generation to the next. Table 25-1 illustrates the cumulative effect of what appear to be very small differences in annual growth rates.

It is useful to know the "rule of 72" to understand the cumulative effects of annual growth rates. For any variable that grows at an annual rate of X percent, that variable will double in approximately 72/X years. [31] For example, if your income grows at 2 percent per year, it will double in 36 years; at an annual rate of 3 percent, it will take only 24 years to double. Another application of the rule of 72 is to determine the *gap* in living standards between countries with different growth rates. If one country grows faster than another, the gap in their respective living standards will widen progressively. If, for example, Canada and France start from the same level of income but Canada grows at 3 percent per year while France grows at 2 percent per year, Canada's income will be twice France's in 72 years. The central lesson from Table 25-1 can be summed up as follows: The longer your time horizon, the more you should care about the economy's long-run growth rate. Small differences in annual growth rates, if sustained for many years, lead to large differences in income levels.

We now examine in more detail the benefits and costs of economic growth.

Benefits of Economic Growth

Economists typically measure average *material* living standards with real per capita GDP.[1] The benefits of long-run growth in per capita GDP may appear obvious. But it is important to distinguish between the increases in average living standards that economic

[1] As we noted in Chapter 20, per capita GDP is a good measure of average *material* living standards because it shows the average person's command over resources. But it is not necessarily a good measure of *well-being*, which is a broader and more subjective measure including such things as income distribution, political and religious freedom, environmental quality, and other things that are not captured by measures of GDP.

APPLYING ECONOMIC CONCEPTS 25-1

What Does Productivity Growth Really Look Like?

The most commonly used measure of productivity is *labour productivity*, defined as the amount of output produced per hour of work, and it can be measured for the aggregate economy or for a particular firm or industry. For the aggregate economy, the appropriate measure of output is real GDP, and labour productivity is then measured as real GDP divided by the total number of hours worked. In 2017, Canadian labour productivity was about $58 per hour (expressed in 2007 dollars); it has been rising at an average annual rate of 1.2 percent since the mid-1970s.

How does labour productivity grow over time? Any new production process or technique that raises output proportionally more than it raises labour input will increase labour productivity. Often the introduction of new physical capital or new techniques allow firms to increase output while *reducing* their use of labour. In this case, labour productivity for the firm might increase significantly. Here are some examples from various industries and occupations:

- Accountants who prepare income-tax forms for their clients have experienced an enormous increase in labour productivity with the use of software packages designed specifically for the task. The software allows a given number of accountants to complete more tax returns per hour of work, thus increasing labour productivity.
- Residential landscaping companies move large amounts of soil, sand, and rock. The development of small and inexpensive diggers and bulldozers vastly increased the amount of work that can be done with a crew of two or three workers, thus dramatically raising labour productivity.
- In modern lumber mills, a computer "reads" each log in three dimensions and then computes how the log can most efficiently be cut into the various regular sizes of cut lumber. Fewer workers are needed to sort the logs and more marketable lumber is produced from a given number of logs because the amount of waste is reduced. Labour productivity rises as a result.
- Doctors who specialize in eye surgery have been greatly aided by the development of precise medical lasers. The equipment is expensive, but allows a

single doctor to perform more surgical procedures per day than was possible only a decade ago, thus increasing labour productivity.

In each of these examples, the use of new and better capital equipment allows the enterprise in question to produce more output with a given number of workers, or the same amount of output with a reduced number of workers. Both are an increase in labour productivity.

How do we get from these specific micro examples back to macroeconomics and the change in real GDP and aggregate labour productivity? If in each example the amount of work is unchanged but output rises, real GDP and aggregate labour productivity will both be higher as a result. If instead each specific output is unchanged but the amount of work is reduced, then we need to recognize that the workers released from these activities are now available to move to other firms and industries. When they begin working elsewhere in the economy, their new production will constitute an increase in real GDP. In this case, total work effort will be back to its original level but real GDP will be higher—an increase in aggregate labour productivity.

Small digging machines like this have replaced the difficult work of individuals with shovels and have significantly increased labour productivity.

growth brings more or less automatically and the reduction in poverty that economic growth makes possible but that may still require active policy to make a reality.

Rising Average Living Standards Economic growth is a powerful means of improving average material living standards. The average Canadian family today earns about

$80 000 per year before taxes. With 2 percent annual growth in its *real* income, that same family will earn $97 520 (in constant dollars) in 10 years' time, an increase in its purchasing power of almost 22 percent. If the annual growth rate is instead 3 percent, its income will rise to $107 513 in 10 years, an increase of over 34 percent.

A family often finds that an increase in its income can lead to changes in the pattern of its consumption—extra money buys important amenities of life and also allows more saving for the future. Similarly, economic growth that raises average income tends to change the whole society's consumption patterns, shifting away from tangible goods such as TVs and furniture and cars and toward services such as vacations, restaurant meals, and financial services. In Canada and other rich, developed countries, services account for roughly 70 percent of aggregate consumption, whereas this ratio is significantly lower in poorer, developing countries.

Another example of how economic growth can improve living standards involves environmental protection. In developing countries, most resources are devoted to providing basic requirements of life, such as food, shelter, and clothing. These countries typically do not have the "luxury" of being concerned about environmental degradation. Some people in richer societies may consider this a short-sighted view, but the fact is that the concerns associated with hunger *today* are much more urgent than the concerns associated with *future* environmental problems. In contrast, richer countries are wealthy enough that they can more easily afford to provide the basic requirements of life *and* devote significant resources to environmental protection. Economic growth provides the higher incomes that often lead to a demand for a cleaner environment, thus leading to higher average levels of well-being that are not directly captured by measures of per capita GDP.

One recent example of this phenomenon can be seen in China, whose government paid almost no attention to environmental protection when the country was very poor. As average income in China has risen in the past 30 years, where it is now well above a subsistence level, concern within China has been growing over the extent of environmental degradation, which in some cases is causing serious human health problems. The Chinese government has been responding with policies to address some of these concerns, and will likely do much more as Chinese prosperity continues to rise.

Addressing Poverty and Income Inequality   Not everyone benefits equally from economic growth, and some may not benefit at all. Many of the poorest members of a society are not in the labour force and do not receive the higher wages and profits that are the primary means by which the gains from growth are distributed. Others, although they *are* in the labour force, may experience wage gains far smaller than average.

In recent years, growing attention has been paid to the fact that the majority of aggregate income growth in many countries, including Canada, has been accruing to the top earners in the income distribution. The result is that, while average per capita incomes have been rising (as shown in Figure 25-1), there has also been a rise in income inequality and also a relative stagnation of incomes for those at or below the middle of the income distribution. Both poverty and income inequality are important challenges for public policy.

A rapid overall growth rate makes the alleviation of poverty and the reduction of income inequality easier to achieve politically. If existing income is to be redistributed through the government's tax or spending policies, someone's standard of living will actually have to be lowered. However, when there is economic growth and when some of the *increment* in income is redistributed (through active government policy), it is possible to reduce income inequalities while simultaneously allowing all incomes to rise. It is much easier for a rapidly growing economy to be generous toward its less fortunate citizens—or neighbours—than it is for a static economy.

Costs of Economic Growth

Economic growth comes with real costs, some of which are more obvious than others. For example, the simple act of producing goods and services necessarily uses resources and causes environmental damage. While these effects may be very small for some products, for others they are significant. As a logical matter, we cannot deny that economic production has negative consequences. Indeed, many of those who advocate *against* continued economic growth do so on the grounds that it depletes our natural resources and leads to excessive environmental degradation.

This debate is important, and continues to gain prominence among academic and government economists. *Applying Economic Concepts 25-2* presents a case against continued economic growth, especially in the developed countries. We take up some of these ideas in this chapter's final section where we examine the extent to which there are *limits to growth*. Here, we address two other costs associated with economic growth: the cost of forgone consumption, and the social costs of the disruption that typically accompanies growth.

Forgone Consumption   In a world of scarcity, almost nothing is free, including economic growth. As we will soon see, long-run increases in real per capita GDP typically result from investment in capital goods as well as in such activities as education and scientific research. Often these investments yield no immediate return in terms of goods and services for consumption; thus, they imply that sacrifices are being made by the current generation of consumers.

> Economic growth, which promises more goods and services tomorrow, is achieved by consuming fewer goods today. This sacrifice of current consumption is an important cost of growth.

For example, suppose an economy's annual growth rate could be permanently increased by one percentage point if investment as a share of GDP increased permanently by four percentage points (and consumption's share fell by four percentage points). If such a reallocation of resources were made, consumption would be lower for several years along the new growth path, and the payoff from faster growth—higher future consumption—would not occur for several years. Lower consumption now and in the near future would be the cost of obtaining higher consumption in the more distant future.

Social Costs   A growing economy is also a changing economy. Part of growth is accounted for by existing firms expanding and producing more output, hiring more workers, and using more equipment and intermediate goods. But another aspect of growth is that existing firms are overtaken and made obsolete by new firms, old products are made obsolete by new products, and existing skills are made obsolete by new skills.

> The process of economic growth renders some machines obsolete and also leaves the skills of some workers obsolete.

APPLYING ECONOMIC CONCEPTS 25-2

A Case Against Economic Growth

Economists have long recognized that economic growth comes with real costs. In recent years, however, some economists have been arguing that the benefits of further growth are outweighed by the costs now being imposed on Earth and its inhabitants. While these arguments are not the mainstream view within the profession, they are increasingly receiving serious attention. This box presents some of their main arguments against continued economic growth.*

Growth Is Not Sustainable

There is overwhelming evidence that the effects on the biosphere of the world's growing economies and population are not sustainable over the long term. Expanding production and consumption of goods and services is causing biodiversity losses, land degradation, scarcities of fresh water, ocean acidification, climate change, and the disruption of the earth's nutrient cycles. This environmental damage will eventually reduce our capacity to continue producing and consuming at current rates.

In addition, the low-cost supplies of fossil fuels on which economic growth has depended for over a century are rapidly being depleted. As supplies diminish, there is a need to introduce new technologies to obtain resources from less accessible locations. Extraction of oil sands, hydraulic fracturing for natural gas, and deep-sea

drilling for oil and gas are examples of new technologies that bring increased environmental impact and risks. This extraction of less accessible and higher-cost fossil fuels highlights the conflict between the need for new supplies of resources to sustain economic growth and the need to reduce our overall burden on the environment.

The ongoing degradation of the planet in pursuit of economic growth also runs counter to the interests of other species that inhabit Earth. Mainstream economics is not well equipped to address this important ethical issue, but it should not be ignored.

Growth May Not Increase Overall Well-Being

Quite apart from whether current growth rates are sustainable, the benefits from continued growth, especially in developed countries, are questionable. Economists have long understood that GDP is a reasonable measure of the level of economic activity and income but that it is not an accurate measure of overall *well-being*.

---

*The author thanks Peter Victor for providing material on which this box is based. For a thorough discussion of the case against economic growth, see Peter Victor, *Managing Without Growth: Slower by Design not Disaster*, Edward Elgar, 2008.

No matter how well trained workers are at age 25, within a decade many will find that their skills are at least partly obsolete. A high growth rate usually requires rapid adjustments in the labour force, which can cause much upset and misery to some of the people affected by it.

It is often argued that costs of this kind are a small price to pay for the great benefits that growth can bring. Even if this is true in the aggregate, these personal costs are borne very unevenly. Indeed, many of the people for whom growth is most costly (in terms of lost jobs or lowered incomes) share least in the fruits that growth brings.

Sources of Economic Growth

Where does economic growth come from? Four major determinants of growth are as follows:

1. *Growth in the labour force.* Growth in population or increases in the fraction of the population that chooses to participate in the labour force cause the labour force to grow.

Other measures that include a range of environmental and social factors suggest that income growth in the developed economies is no longer closely related with greater well-being. People typically attach far more significance to their income in relation to others' incomes than to its absolute level, and it is simply not possible for economic growth to raise everyone's relative income.

In addition, the growing evidence on income and wealth inequality in the developed economies suggests that over the past few decades the lion's share of total income growth has been captured by the highest income earners. The resulting increase in income and wealth inequality has actually led to rising discontent among large parts of the population. So growth in national income, given its current distribution, may actually be causing a reduction rather than an increase in overall well-being.

The Weakness of the Technological Defence

Economists who argue in favour of further economic growth typically note the possibility of increasing GDP even while reducing resource use and environmental damage. They argue that by producing and consuming fewer goods and more services, employing more efficient and improved technologies, and more compact forms of land use, economic growth can continue indefinitely.

Those who argue against further growth see a serious problem with this argument. While it is true that the amount of resources used per dollar of GDP continues to shrink gradually in the developed countries, it is also true that the absolute resource use and absolute environmental damage continue to grow.

Looking to the future, if the world economy grows at a rate of 3 percent per year, after a century the economy will have increased in size by nearly 20 times. To prevent any absolute increase in resource and energy use would require an ambitious twenty-fold improvement in resource and environmental efficiency—a far greater improvement than we have witnessed over the past century.

So the belief that ongoing technological improvement can be consistent with continued economic growth and a reduced impact on Earth's resources and environment is a belief that must be based on extreme—and probably unrealistic—optimism.

Not So Gloomy

Economists arguing against further growth are quick to emphasize that their message is not so gloomy. The good news is that further economic growth in the developed economies isn't necessary for continued prosperity. The benefits of ongoing productivity growth can be taken in the form of reduced work and production, and also by directing effort at reducing our absolute resource use and environmental damage. Making these adjustments will surely require a significant change in most peoples' way of thinking, but there is no reason why they can't be made. Prosperity can continue without economic growth.

---

2. *Growth in human capital.* **Human capital** is the term economists use to refer to the set of skills that workers have; it can increase either through formal education or on-the-job training. Human capital can be thought of as the *quality* of the labour force.

3. *Growth in physical capital.* The stock of physical capital (such as factories, machines, electronic equipment, and transportation and communications facilities) grows only through the process of investment. We include here improvements in the *quality* of physical capital.

4. *Technological improvement.* This is brought about by innovation that introduces new products, new ways of producing existing products, and new forms of organizing economic activity.

The various theories of economic growth that we explore next emphasize these different sources of economic growth. For example, some theories emphasize the role of increases in physical capital in explaining growth; others emphasize the role of increases in human capital; and still others emphasize the importance of technological improvements.

human capital The set of skills workers acquire through formal education and on-the-job training.

25.2 Economic Growth: Basic Relationships

In this section we examine some basic macro relationships regarding long-run economic growth. For many years, these relationships have been central to how economists think about the process of economic growth and the policies that can affect it. With these basic relationships in place, we will then go on to examine more advanced theories on economic growth in the next section.

We begin by studying the relationship among saving, investment, and economic growth. We then examine the precise predictions of what economists call the Neoclassical growth theory. For simplicity, we assume that the economy is closed—there is no trade in goods, services, or assets with the rest of the world.

A Long-Run Analysis

Though our discussion of economic growth will focus on the long-run behaviour of the economy, we can use some of the insights we developed in the short-run version of our macro model. Think back to Chapter 21 when we were building the simplest short-run macro model (with no government or foreign trade). The equilibrium level of real GDP in that model was such that real GDP equals desired consumption plus desired investment:

$$Y = C + I$$

We can rearrange this equilibrium condition to get

$$Y - C = I$$

or

$$S = I$$

which says that at the equilibrium level of real GDP, desired saving equals desired investment. This is just an alternative way to think about exactly the same macro equilibrium.

Recall also that in Chapter 21 we took the real interest rate as given, or *exogenous*. Taking the interest rate (and several other variables) as exogenous, we then determined the equilibrium level of real GDP. For our discussion of economic growth, we will use this same equilibrium condition from Chapter 21 but will "switch" endogenous variables. Instead of the interest rate being exogenous and the model then solving endogenously for real GDP, we impose the long-run restriction that real GDP equals Y^* (reflecting the assumption that all factor-price adjustment has taken place) and then solve endogenously for the equilibrium real interest rate.

> In the short-run macro model, real GDP adjusts to determine equilibrium, in which desired saving equals desired investment. In the model's long-run version, real GDP is equal to Y^* and the real interest rate adjusts to determine equilibrium.

This long-run perspective of our model will tell us a great deal about the relationship among saving, investment, and economic growth—and the interest rate will play an important role.

Investment, Saving, and Growth

We now complicate our model slightly by adding a government sector that purchases goods and services (G) and collects taxes net of transfers (T). National saving is the sum of private saving and public (government) saving. Desired private saving is the difference between disposable income and desired consumption. With real GDP equal to Y^* in the long run, desired private saving is equal to

$$\text{Private saving} = Y^* - T - C$$

Public saving is equal to the combined budget surpluses of the federal, provincial, and municipal governments:

$$\text{Public saving} = T - G$$

National saving is therefore equal to

$$\text{National saving} = NS = (Y^* - T - C) + (T - G)$$

$$\Rightarrow NS = Y^* - C - G$$

For a given level of real GDP in the long run (Y^*), an increase in household consumption or government purchases must imply a reduction in national saving.[2]

Figure 25-2 shows the supply of national saving as a function of the real interest rate. The horizontal axis measures the quantity of national saving, measured in dollars. The real interest rate is shown on the vertical axis. The national saving (NS) curve is upward sloping because, as we first saw in Chapter 21, an increase in the interest rate is assumed to lead households to reduce their current consumption, especially on big ticket items such as cars, furniture, and appliances, that are often purchased on credit. Note also that the NS curve is quite steep, in keeping with empirical evidence suggesting that household consumption responds only modestly to changes in the real interest rate.

Figure 25-2 also shows a downward-sloping investment demand curve, I. As we first saw in Chapter 21, all components of desired investment (plant and equipment, inventories, and residential investment) are negatively related to the real interest rate because, whether the investment is financed by borrowing or by using firms' retained earnings, the real interest rate reflects the opportunity cost of using these funds.

The supply curve for national saving (NS) and the investment demand curve (I) make up the economy's market for financial capital. The NS curve shows the supply of financial capital that comes from households and governments. The I curve shows the

FIGURE 25-2   Investment and Saving in the Long Run

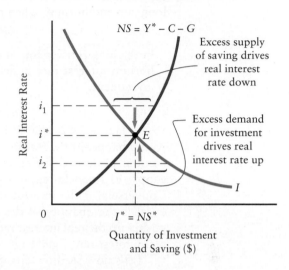

In the long run, the condition that desired national saving equals desired investment determines the equilibrium real interest rate. Investment demand by firms is negatively related to the real interest rate. The supply of national (private plus public) saving is positively related to the real interest rate, since increases in the interest rate lead to a decline in desired consumption (C). Since the analysis applies to the long run, we have assumed that real GDP is equal to Y^*. In the long run, the equilibrium real interest rate is i^*. At this real interest rate, the amount of investment is I^*, which equals the amount of national saving, NS^*.

---

[2] It appears in our NS equation that changes in taxes have no effect on the level of national saving, but this is misleading. Changes in T can affect national saving through an *indirect* effect on C. For example, as we saw in Chapter 24, a reduction in taxes is likely to lead to an increase in consumption spending and therefore to a reduction in national saving (for given values of Y^* and G).

demand for financial capital derived from firms' desired investment in plant, equipment, and residential construction. The interest rate that clears this market for financial capital determines the amount of investment and saving that occur in the economy's long-run equilibrium, when real GDP is equal to Y^*.

> In the long-run version of our macro model, with real GDP equal to Y^*, the equilibrium interest rate is determined where desired national saving equals desired investment.

In Figure 25-2, equilibrium occurs at interest rate i^* where $NS = I$. Imagine what would happen if the real interest rate were above i^* at i_1. At this high interest rate, the amount of desired saving exceeds the amount of desired investment, and this excess supply of financial capital pushes down the price of credit—the real interest rate. Conversely, if the interest rate is below i^* at i_2, the quantity of desired investment exceeds the quantity of desired saving, and this excess demand for financial capital pushes up the real interest rate. Only at point E is the economy in equilibrium, with the real interest rate equal to i^* and desired investment equal to desired saving.

Let's now see how changes in the supply of saving or investment demand lead to changes in the real interest rate and what these changes imply for the economy's long-run economic growth.

An Increase in the Supply of National Saving   Suppose the supply of national saving increases, so that the NS curve shifts to the right, as shown in part (i) of Figure 25-3. This increase in the supply of national saving could happen either because household consumption (C) falls or because government purchases (G) fall (or because T rises, which reduces C). A decline in either C or G means that national saving rises at any real interest rate, and so the NS curve shifts to the right.

The increase in the supply of national saving leads to an excess supply of financial capital and thus to a decline in the real interest rate. As the interest rate falls, firms decide to undertake more investment projects and the economy moves from the initial equilibrium E_0 to the new equilibrium E_1. At the new equilibrium, more of the economy's resources are devoted to investment than before, and thus the country's stock of physical capital is rising at a faster rate. Since growth in the capital stock is an important reason for growth in potential output, we conclude that the higher rate of investment at E_1 leads to a higher growth rate of potential output.

> In the long run, an increase in the supply of national saving reduces the real interest rate and encourages more investment. The higher rate of investment leads to a higher growth rate of potential output.

An Increase in Investment Demand   Now suppose firms' demand for investment increases so that the I curve shifts to the right, as shown in part (ii) of Figure 25-3. The increase in desired investment might be caused by technological improvements that increase the productivity of investment goods or by a government tax incentive aimed at encouraging investment. Whatever its cause, the increase in investment demand creates an excess demand for financial capital and therefore leads to a rise in the real interest rate. The rise in the interest rate encourages households to reduce their current consumption and increase their desired saving. At the new equilibrium, E_1, both the

FIGURE 25-3   Increases in Investment Demand and the Supply of National Saving

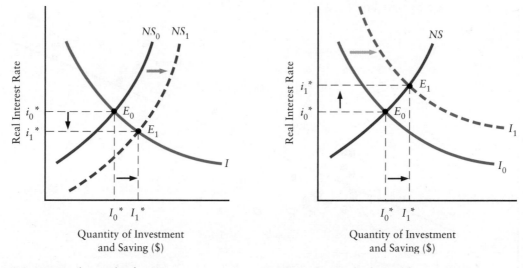

(i) Increase in the supply of saving   (ii) Increase in the demand for investment

Changes in the supply of national saving or the demand for investment will change the equilibrium real interest rate and the rate of growth of potential output. In part (i), the increase in the supply of national saving pushes down the real interest rate and encourages more investment. In part (ii), the increase in the demand for investment pushes up the real interest rate and encourages more saving. In both cases, there is an increase in the equilibrium amount of investment (and saving), and the economy moves from E_0 to E_1; this higher rate of investment means faster growth in the capital stock; it leads to an increase in the economy's long-run rate of growth.

real interest rate and the amount of investment are higher than at the initial equilibrium. The greater investment means faster growth in the economy's capital stock and therefore a higher rate of growth of potential output.

In the long run, an increase in the demand for investment pushes up the real interest rate and encourages more saving by households. The higher rate of saving (and investment) leads to a higher growth rate of potential output.

Summary   In our macro model, which we have now extended to enable us to determine the real interest rate in long-run equilibrium, there is a close relationship among saving, investment, and the rate of economic growth. We can see this relationship most clearly when studying the market for financial capital. Let's summarize our results:

1. In long-run equilibrium, with $Y = Y^*$, the condition that desired national saving equals desired investment determines the equilibrium interest rate in the market for financial capital. This equilibrium also determines the economy's flows of investment and saving.

2. An increase in the supply of national saving will lead to a fall in the real interest rate and thus to an increase in the amount of investment. This is a shift of the NS curve and a movement along the I curve.

FIGURE 25-4 Cross-Country Investment and Growth Rates, 1961–2016

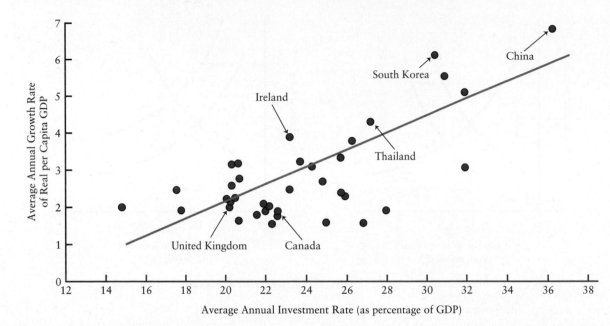

There is a positive relationship between a country's investment rate (as a percentage of GDP) and its growth rate of real per capita GDP. For each of the countries, the annual averages for investment rates and per capita GDP growth rates are computed between 1961 and 2016. Each point represents the average values of these variables for a single country over this period. The straight line is the "line of best fit" between the growth rates and the investment rates. Countries with high investment rates tend to be countries with high rates of economic growth.

(*Source:* Based on author's calculations using data from the World Bank, www.worldbank.org.)

3. An increase in the demand for investment will lead to a rise in the real interest rate and thus to an increase in the amount of national saving. This is a shift of the *I* curve and a movement along the *NS* curve.

4. A shift in either the *NS* or the *I* curve will lead to a change in the equilibrium real interest rate and thus to a change in the amount of the economy's resources devoted to investment. An increase in the equilibrium amount of investment (and saving) implies faster growth of the capital stock and thus a higher growth rate of potential output.

Investment and Growth in Industrialized Countries Our long-run version of the macro model predicts that countries with high rates of investment are also countries with high rates of real GDP growth. To provide evidence in support of this prediction, Figure 25-4 shows data from a large sample of countries between 1961 and 2016. Each point in the figure corresponds to a single country and shows that country's annual average investment rate (as a percentage of GDP) plotted against the annual average growth rate in real per capita GDP. What is clear from the figure is a positive relationship between investment rates and growth rates, as predicted by our macro model.

The "Neoclassical" Growth Model

We have seen the basic relationship between saving, investment, and long-run growth in our macro model. We now examine a *specific* version of this model, one that assumes a particular relationship between the economy's factor inputs, especially labour and capital, and the amount of output produced. This specific model is called the *Neoclassical growth model*; it was developed during the 1950s and 1960s and was refined in later years. It quickly became the primary model used by economists to analyze economic growth, and still has tremendous influence today.

Recall the four sources of economic growth that we discussed in the first section of this chapter. The Neoclassical growth model is based on the idea that these four sources of economic growth can be connected by what is called the **aggregate production function**. This is an expression for the relationship between the total amounts of labour (L) and physical capital (K) employed, the quality of labour's human capital (H), the state of technology (T), and the nation's total level of output (GDP). The aggregate production function can be expressed as

$$\text{GDP} = F_T(L, K, H)$$

It is an *aggregate* production function because it relates the economy's *total* output to the *total* amount of the factors used to produce that output.[3] (Those who have studied microeconomics will recall that a micro production function, such as is discussed in Chapters 7 and 8, relates the output of *one firm* to the factors of production employed by *that firm*.)

The production function above—indicated by F_T—tells us how much GDP will be produced for any given amounts of labour, physical capital, human capital, and a given state of technology. Using the notation F_T is a simple way of indicating that the function relating L, K, and H to GDP depends on the state of technology. For a given state of technology (T), changes in either L, K, or H will lead to changes in GDP. Similarly, for given values of L, K, and H, changes in T will lead to changes in GDP. [32]

Recall that we are assuming throughout this chapter that real GDP is equal to Y^* because we are examining the economy in the long run. Let's now examine the properties of the aggregate production function and the predictions that follow.

Properties of the Aggregate Production Function   The key assumptions of the Neoclassical growth model are that the aggregate production function displays diminishing marginal returns when any one of the factors is increased on its own and constant returns to scale when all factors are increased together (and in the same proportion). To explain the meaning of these concepts more clearly, we will assume for simplicity that human capital and physical capital can be combined into a single variable called capital and that technology is held constant; this allows us to focus on the effects of changes in K and L.

1. Diminishing Marginal Returns.   To begin, suppose the labour force grows while the stock of capital remains constant. More and more people go to work using a fixed quantity of capital. The amount that each new worker adds to total output is called labour's *marginal product*. The **law of diminishing marginal returns** tells us that the employment

aggregate production function The relationship between the total amount of each factor of production employed and total GDP.

law of diminishing marginal returns The hypothesis that if increasing quantities of one factor are applied to a given quantity of other factors, the marginal product of the one factor will eventually decrease.

---

[3] Land (including natural resources such as forests and mineral deposits) is also an important input to the production process. We leave it out of this discussion only for simplicity.

FIGURE 25-5 The Aggregate Production Function and Diminishing Marginal Returns

Production function: GDP $= 4\sqrt{KL}$
$K = 9$

Units of Labour (1)	Units of Output (GDP) (2)	Average Product of Labour (GDP/L) (3)	Marginal Product of Labour (ΔGDP/ΔL) (4)
1	12.0	12.0	
			5.0
2	17.0	8.5	
			3.8
3	20.8	6.9	
			3.2
4	24.0	6.0	
			2.8
5	26.8	5.4	
			2.6
6	29.4	4.9	
			2.5
7	31.9	4.6	
			2.1
8	34.0	4.2	
			2.0
9	36.0	4.0	
			1.9
10	37.9	3.8	

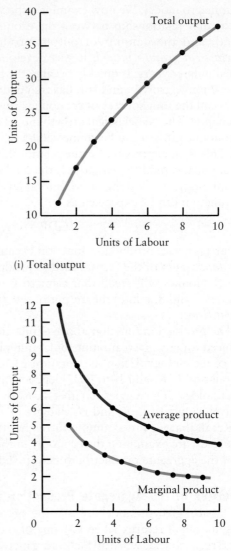

(i) Total output

(ii) Marginal and average product of labour

With one input held constant, the other input has a declining average and marginal product. We have assumed a hypothetical aggregate production function given by GDP $= 4\sqrt{KL}$; we have also assumed that K is constant and equal to 9. Column 2 shows total output as more of the variable factor, labour, is used with a fixed amount of capital. Total output is plotted in part (i) of the figure. Both the average product of labour and the marginal product of labour decline continuously. They are plotted in part (ii) of the figure.

of additional workers (or hours of work) will eventually add less to total output than the previous worker did. A simple production function is shown in Figure 25-5 and the law of diminishing marginal returns is illustrated.

The law of diminishing returns applies to any factor that is varied while the other factors are held constant. Hence, successive amounts of capital added to a fixed supply of labour will also eventually add less and less to GDP.

constant returns to scale A situation in which output increases in proportion to the change in all inputs as the scale of production is increased.

2. Constant Returns to Scale. The other main assumption concerning the aggregate production function is that it displays **constant returns to scale**. Remember that we are

assuming for simplicity that labour and capital are the only two inputs. With constant returns to scale, if L and K both change in an equal proportion, total output will change by that same proportion. For example, if L and K both increase by 10 percent, GDP will also increase by 10 percent. [33]

Economic Growth in the Neoclassical Model   To recap: The Neoclassical growth model assumes that the aggregate production function displays diminishing marginal returns (in both L and K) and also constant returns to scale. What specific predictions follow from these assumptions? Recall the four major sources of growth:

1. Growth in labour force

2. Growth in human capital

3. Growth in physical capital

4. Technological improvement

What does the Neoclassical model predict will happen when each of these elements changes? In this section, we focus on the effects of labour-force growth and the accumulation of physical and human capital (combined), holding constant the level of technology. In the next section, we focus on technological change.

1. Labour-Force Growth.   Over the long term, we can associate labour-force growth with population growth (although in the short term, the labour force can grow if participation rates rise even though the population remains constant). As more labour is used, more output will be produced. For a given stock of capital, however, the law of diminishing marginal returns tells us that each additional unit of labour employed will cause smaller and smaller additions to GDP. With the marginal product and average product of labour falling (with each additional increment to labour), we get an interesting result. Although economic growth continues in the sense that total output is growing, material living standards are actually *falling* because average GDP *per person* is falling (real GDP is growing more slowly than the population). If we are interested in growth in material living standards, however, we are concerned with increasing real GDP per person.

In the Neoclassical growth model with diminishing marginal returns, increases in population (with a fixed stock of capital) lead to increases in GDP but an eventual decline in material living standards.

2. Physical and Human Capital Accumulation.   Consider the accumulation of both physical and human capital. Growth in physical capital occurs whenever there is positive (net) investment in the economy. For example, if Canadian firms produce $300 billion of capital goods this year, and only $40 billion is for the replacement of old, worn-out equipment, then Canada's capital stock increases by $260 billion.

How does human capital accumulate? Human capital has several aspects. One involves improvements in the health and longevity of the population. Of course, these are desired as ends in themselves, but they also have consequences for both the size and the productivity of the labour force. There is no doubt that improvements in the health of workers tend to increase productivity per worker-hour by cutting down on illness, accidents, and absenteeism. A second aspect of human capital concerns specific training and education—from learning to operate a machine or software program to learning

Increases in the amount and quality of physical capital lead to improvements in the productivity of labour. These productivity improvements raise material living standards, as measured by real per capita GDP.

how to be a scientist. Sometimes this increase in human capital occurs through on-the-job training; sometimes it occurs through formal educational programs. Advances in knowledge allow us not only to build more productive physical capital but also to create more effective human capital. Also, the longer a person has been educated, the more adaptable and, hence, the more productive in the long run that person is in the face of new and changing challenges.

The accumulation of capital—either physical or human—affects GDP in a manner similar to population growth. The law of diminishing marginal returns implies that each successive unit of capital will add less to total output than each previous unit of capital.

There is, however, a major contrast with the case of labour-force growth because it is output *per person* that determines material living standards, not output per unit of capital. Thus, for a constant population, increases in the stock of physical or human capital always lead to increases in living standards because output *per person* increases. However, because the increases in capital are subject to diminishing marginal returns, successive additions to the economy's capital stock bring smaller and smaller increases in per capita output.

> **In the Neoclassical model, capital accumulation leads to improvements in material living standards, but because of the law of diminishing marginal returns, these improvements become smaller with each additional increment of capital.**

3. Balanced Growth with Constant Technology. Now consider what happens if labour and capital (both human and physical capital) grow at the same rate. This is what economists call "balanced" growth. In this case, the Neoclassical assumption of constant returns to scale means that GDP grows in proportion to the increases in inputs. For example, if capital and labour both increase by 2 percent per year, then GDP also increases by 2 percent per year. As a result, per capita output (GDP/*L*) remains constant. Thus, balanced growth in labour and capital leads to growth in total GDP but unchanged per capita GDP.

Balanced growth can therefore *not* explain sustained increases in material living standards. Increases in material living standards require *increases* in per capita output.

> **If capital and labour grow at the same rate, GDP will increase. But in the Neoclassical growth model with constant returns to scale, such balanced growth will not lead to increases in per capita output and therefore will not generate improvements in material living standards.**

To summarize, the Neoclassical growth model predicts that growth in the labour force alone leads to declining per capita income, while capital accumulation alone leads to positive but ever-diminishing growth rates of per capita income. Increases in labour and capital together cause an increase in real GDP but leave per capita income unchanged. What we observe in many countries around the world, however, is sustained growth in real per capita incomes. How does the Neoclassical model explain this observation, if not through growth in labour or capital? The answer is technological change, to which we now turn.

The Importance of Technological Change In the Neoclassical growth model, technological change is assumed to be exogenous—that is, it is not explained within the model. This is an important weakness because it means that the theory is unable to explain what is undoubtedly the most important determinant of long-run improvements in living standards. Even though it is exogenous to the model, it is necessary to understand the nature of technological change, the important role it plays in economic growth, and some ways to measure it. In the next section we move beyond the Neoclassical growth model and see some more modern theories designed to explain the sources of technological change.

New knowledge and inventions can contribute markedly to the growth of potential output, even without capital accumulation or labour-force growth. To illustrate this point, suppose the proportion of a society's resources devoted to the production of capital goods is just sufficient to replace capital as it wears out. If the old capital is merely replaced in the same form, the capital stock will be constant, and there will be no increase in the capacity to produce. However, if there is a growth of knowledge so that as old equipment wears out it is replaced by more productive equipment, then productive capacity will be growing.

The increase in productive capacity created by installing new and better capital goods is called **embodied technical change**. This term reflects the idea that technological improvements are contained in the new capital goods. Thus, even if the *quantity* of capital may be unchanged, improvements in its *quality* lead to increases in the economy's productive capacity. Embodied technical change has been enormously important through history and continues to be important today. Consider how the invention of propeller and then jet airplanes has revolutionized transportation over the past 75 years, or how the invention of the electronic computer and satellite transmission has revolutionized communications over an even shorter period. Indeed, once you start thinking about embodied technical change, you see many examples of it around you on a daily basis.

Less obvious but nonetheless important are technical changes that are embodied in *human* capital. These are changes that result from a better-educated, more experienced labour force; better management practices and techniques; improved design, marketing, and organization of business activities; and feedback from user experience leading to product improvement.

New and better microchips enhance the range of capabilities of countless types of physical capital. But such improvements in technology are embodied in the capital stock, making it difficult to estimate the change in technology independently from the change in the capital stock.

Tudor Voinea/Shutterstock

embodied technical change Technical change that is intrinsic to the particular capital goods in use.

> Many innovations are embodied in either physical or human capital. These innovations cause continual changes in the techniques of production and in the nature of what is produced. Embodied technical change leads to increases in potential output even if the amounts of labour and capital are held constant.

LESSONS FROM HISTORY 25-1

Should Workers Be Afraid of Technological Change?

For centuries people have observed that technological change destroys particular jobs and have worried that it will destroy jobs in general. Should they worry?

Technological change *does* destroy particular jobs. When water wheels were used to automate the production of cloth in twelfth-century Europe, there were riots and protests among the workers who lost their jobs. A century ago, 50 percent of the labour force in North America and Europe produced the required food. Today, in high-income countries less than 5 percent of the labour force is needed to feed all their citizens. In other words, out of every 100 jobs that existed in 1900, 50 were in agriculture and 45 of those were destroyed by technological progress over the course of the twentieth century.

Individual workers are therefore right to fear that technological changes may destroy particular jobs. This process of job destruction has been going on for centuries and will undoubtedly continue in the future. Those individuals who cannot retrain for jobs in other industries or regions may suffer reduced wages or employment prospects. This concern is especially acute for older workers who may find retraining difficult or who may find it difficult to convince potential new employers to hire them.

What about the overall level of employment? Do workers need to worry that technological changes will cause widespread unemployment? Just as technological change destroys some jobs, it also creates many new jobs. The displaced agricultural workers did not join the ranks of the permanently unemployed—although some of the older ones may have, their children did not. Instead they, and their children, took jobs in the expanding manufacturing and service industries and helped to produce the mass of new goods and services—such as automobiles, refrigerators, computers, and foreign travel—that have raised living standards over the century.

Worries that technological change will cause general unemployment have been recorded for centuries, but, so far at least, there is no sign that those displaced by technological change (or their children) are being forced into the ranks of the permanently unemployed. Over all of recorded history, technological change has created more jobs than it has destroyed.

How about today? Aren't there good reasons to be more afraid of technological change now than in the past? Modern technologies have two aspects that worry some observers. First, they tend to be *knowledge intensive*. A fairly high degree of literacy and numeracy, as well as familiarity with computers, is needed to work with many of these new technologies. Second, through the process of globalization, unskilled workers in advanced countries have come into competition with unskilled workers everywhere in the world. Both of these forces are decreasing the relative demand for unskilled workers in developed countries and have led to falling relative wages for unskilled workers in countries like Canada. If labour markets are insufficiently flexible, this change in relative demand may also lead to some structural unemployment.

For these reasons, some people blame the high unemployment rates in Europe (and to a lesser extent in Canada) on the new technologies. This is hard to reconcile, however, with the fact that the lowest unemployment rates in the industrialized countries have been recorded in the United States, the most technologically dynamic of all countries. This suggests that the cause of high European unemployment rates may be not enough technological change and too much inflexibility in labour markets rather than too much technological change.

We have been discussing the benefits of technological change in terms of raising overall material living standards. Ever since the Industrial Revolution, however, some workers have feared the effects of technological change. After all, changes in technology are often responsible for workers losing their jobs as employers replace less efficient labour with more efficient equipment. *Lessons from History 25-1* examines the relationship between technological progress and changes in employment.

Can We Measure Technological Change? Technological change is obviously important. You need only look around you at the current products and production methods that did not exist a generation ago, or even a few years ago, to realize how the advance of technology changes our lives. But *how much* does technology change? Unfortunately, technology is not something that is easily measured and so it is very difficult to know just how important it is to the process of economic growth.

In 1957, Robert Solow, an economist at MIT who was awarded the Nobel Prize 30 years later for his research on economic growth, attempted to measure the amount of technical change in the United States. He devised a way to infer from the data (under some assumptions about the aggregate production function) how much of the observed growth in real GDP was due to the growth in labour and capital and how much was due to technical change. His method led to the creation of what is now called the "Solow residual." The Solow residual is the amount of growth in GDP that *cannot* be accounted for by observed growth in the labour force and capital stock. Since Solow was thinking about changes in GDP as having only three possible sources—changes in capital, changes in labour, and changes in technology—the "residual" was naturally interpreted as a measure of technical change.

Today, economists do not view the Solow residual as a precise estimate of the amount of technical change. One reason is that much technical change is known to be embodied in new physical and human capital, as we discussed earlier. Thus, capital accumulation and technological change are inherently connected. For example, imagine a firm that adds to its stock of capital by purchasing two new computers. These new computers embody the latest technology and are more productive than the firm's existing computers. In this case, there has been an increase in the capital stock but there has also been an increase—though not easily measured—in the level of technology. Solow's method would attribute much of the change in (embodied) technology to the change in the capital stock, even though we know that a technological change has also taken place. Thus, in the presence of embodied technical change that gets measured as increases in capital, the Solow residual is, at best, an underestimate of the true amount of technological change.

Despite these problems, the Solow residual is still used by many economists in universities and government, and it often goes by another name—the rate of growth of *total factor productivity (TFP)*.

25.3 Economic Growth: Advanced Theories

Some newer theories of economic growth go beyond the specific Neoclassical growth model and even beyond our more general macro model. These advanced theories are based on more complex assumptions about the nature of technological change and the properties of the aggregate production function. Economic growth is an active area of research in which there is debate over whether these new theories are necessary, or whether the older and established theories do an adequate job of explaining the process of long-term economic growth.

In this section, we give a brief discussion of two strands of this new research—models that emphasize *endogenous technological change* and models based on *increasing marginal returns*.

Endogenous Technological Change

In the Neoclassical growth model, advances in technology increase the amount of output producible from a given level of factor inputs. But such changes are themselves unexplained. The Neoclassical model thus views technological change as *exogenous*.

It has profound effects on economic variables but it is not itself influenced by economic causes. It just happens.

Yet research by many scholars has established that technological change—what we often call *innovation*—is responsive to such economic signals as prices and profits; in other words, it is *endogenous* to the economic system. Though much of the earliest work on this issue was done in Europe, the most influential overall single study was by an American, Nathan Rosenberg, whose 1982 book *Inside the Black Box: Technology and Economics* argued this case in great detail.

Research and development and the innovation necessary to put the results of the R&D into practice are costly and risky activities; firms undertake these activities in the expectation of generating profits. It is not surprising, therefore, that these activities respond to economic incentives. If the price of some particular input, such as petroleum or skilled labour, goes up, R&D and innovating activities may be directed to altering the production function to economize on these expensive inputs. This process is not simply a substitution of less expensive inputs for more expensive ones; rather, it is the *development of new technologies* in response to changes in relative prices.

There are several important implications of the understanding that, to a great extent, growth is achieved through costly, risky, innovative activity that often occurs in response to economic signals.

Learning by Doing The pioneering theorist of innovation, Joseph Schumpeter (1883–1950), developed a model in which innovation flowed in one direction from a pure discovery "upstream," to more applied R&D, then to working machines, and finally to output "downstream."

In contrast, modern research shows that innovation involves a large amount of "learning by doing" at all of its stages. What is learned downstream then modifies what must be done upstream. The best innovation-managing systems encourage such "feedback" from the more applied steps to the purer researchers and from users to designers.

This interaction is illustrated, for example, by the differences that existed for many years between the Japanese automobile manufacturers and their North American competitors in the design and production of new models. North American design was traditionally centralized: Design production teams developed the overall design and then instructed their production sections and asked for bids from parts manufacturers to produce according to specified blueprints. As a result, defects in the original design were often not discovered until production was underway, causing many costly delays and rejection of parts already supplied. In contrast, Japanese firms involved their design and production departments and their parts manufacturers in all stages of the design process. Parts manufacturers were not given specific blueprints for production; instead, they were given general specifications and asked to develop their own detailed designs. As they did so, they learned. They then fed information about the problems they were encountering back to the main designers while the general outlines of the new model were not yet finalized. As a result, the Japanese were able to design a new product faster, at less cost, and with far fewer problems than were the North American firms. Since that time, however, the North American automotive firms have adopted many of these Japanese design and production methods.

Knowledge Transfer The diffusion of technological knowledge from those who have it to those who want it is not costless. We often think that once a production process is developed, it can easily be copied by others. In practice, however, the diffusion of new technological knowledge is not so simple. Firms need research capacity just to adopt the technologies developed by others. Some of the knowledge needed to use a new technology can be learned only through experience by plant managers, technicians, and operators.

For example, research has shown that most industrial technologies require technology-specific organizational skills that cannot be "embodied" in the machines themselves, in instruction books, or in blueprints. The needed knowledge is *tacit* in the sense that it can be acquired only by experience—much like driving a car or playing a video game. Acquiring tacit knowledge requires a deliberate process of building up new skills, work practices, knowledge, and experience.

The fact that diffusion is a costly and time-consuming process explains why new technologies take considerable time to diffuse, first through the economy of the originating country and then through the rest of the world. If diffusion were simple and virtually costless, the puzzle would be why technological knowledge and best industrial practices did not diffuse very quickly. As it is, decades can pass before a new technological process is diffused everywhere that it could be employed.

Market Structure and Innovation   Because it is risky, innovation is encouraged by strong rivalry among firms and discouraged by monopoly practices. Competition among three or four large firms often produces much innovation, but a single firm, especially if it serves a secure home market protected by trade barriers, often seems much less inclined to innovate. The reduction in trade barriers over the past several decades and the increasing globalization of markets as a result of falling transportation and communication costs have increased international competition. Whereas one firm in a national market might have had substantial monopoly power three or four decades ago, today it is more likely to be in intense competition with firms based in other countries. This greater international competition generally leads to more innovation.

An important implication of this idea is that policies that make firms more competitive—either by lowering protective tariffs or by reducing domestic regulations that hamper competition—are likely to have a positive effect on the amount of innovation and thus on an economy's rate of growth of productivity. This is a central conclusion in William Lewis's *The Power of Productivity*, an influential book published in 2004.

Shocks and Innovation   One interesting consequence of endogenous technological change is that shocks that would be unambiguously adverse to an economy operating with fixed technology can sometimes provide a spur to innovation that proves a blessing in disguise. A sharp rise in the price of one input can raise costs and lower the value of output per person for some time. But it may lead to a wave of innovations that reduce the need for this expensive input and, as a side effect, greatly raise productivity.

Sometimes individual firms will respond differently to the same economic signal. Sometimes those that respond by altering technology will do better than those that concentrate their efforts on substituting within the confines of known technology. For example, several years ago when the consumer electronics industry was beset with high costs in both Japan and the United States, some U.S. firms moved their operations abroad to avoid high, rigid labour costs. They continued to use their existing technology and went where labour costs were low enough to make that technology pay. Their Japanese competitors, however, stayed at home. They innovated away most of their labour costs and then built factories in the United States to replace the factories of U.S. firms that had gone abroad!

Increasing Marginal Returns

We saw earlier that the Neoclassical growth model assumes that investment in capital is subject to diminishing marginal returns. Some research suggests, however, the possibility of *increasing returns* that remain for considerable periods of time: As investment in some new geographic area, new product, or new production technology proceeds through time, new increments of investment are often *more* productive than previous increments. The result of such increasing returns is that growth does not necessarily slow down as capital accumulates—it may even speed up.

The sources of such increasing returns fall under the two general categories of *market-development costs* and *knowledge.*

Market-Development Costs   For three reasons there may be important costs associated with the initial development of a market. These costs result in increasing marginal returns to investment.

1. Investment in the early stages of development of a country, province, or town may create new skills and attitudes in the workforce that are then available to all subsequent firms, whose costs are therefore lower than those encountered by the initial firms.

2. Each new firm may find the environment more and more favourable to its investment because of the physical infrastructure that has been created by those who came before.

3. The first investment in a new product will encounter countless production problems that, once overcome, cause fewer problems to subsequent investors.

In each of these examples, the returns to later investment are greater than the returns to the same investment made earlier for the simple reason that the economic environment becomes more fully developed over time. Early firms must incur costs in order to develop various aspects of the market, but some benefits of this development are then reaped by later firms that need not incur these costs. As a result, the investment returns for "followers" can be substantially greater than the investment returns for "pioneers."

The behaviour of customers is also important. When a new product is developed, customers will often resist adopting it, both because they may be conservative and because they know that new products often experience "growing pains." Customers also need time to learn how best to use the new product. Many potential users take the reasonable approach of letting others try a new product, following only after the product's success has been demonstrated. This makes the early stages of innovation especially costly and risky for the firms involved.

The development of the electric car has been expensive for those companies involved at early stages. As a result, there may be significant advantages to other firms who follow the pioneers.

Caradoc/Fotolia

Successive increments of investment associated with an innovation often yield a range of increasing marginal returns as costs that are incurred in earlier investment expenditure provide publicly available knowledge and experience and as customer attitudes and abilities become more receptive to new products.

Knowledge   Many of the newer growth theories shift the emphasis from the economics of goods to the economics of *ideas*. Physical goods, such as factories and machines, exist in one place at one time. This has two consequences. First, when physical goods are used by someone, they cannot be used by someone else. Second, if a given labour force is provided with more and more physical objects to use in production, sooner or later diminishing marginal returns will be encountered.

Ideas have different characteristics. Once someone develops an idea, it is available for use by everyone. For example, if one firm uses a truck, another firm cannot use it at the same time; but one firm's use of a revolutionary design for a new suspension system on a truck does not prevent other firms from using that design as well. (For those who have studied microeconomics, some knowledge has aspects that make it a *public good*, as we discussed in Chapter 16.)

Ideas are also not necessarily subject to diminishing marginal returns. As our knowledge increases, each increment of new knowledge does not inevitably add less to our productive ability than each previous increment. Indeed, the reverse is often the case: One new idea may spawn several additional ideas that build on or extend it in some ways. For example, the discovery of genes and the subsequent work on gene technology has spawned entire biotechnology industries that are revolutionizing aspects of medicine, agriculture, and environmental control.

Ideas produce what is called *knowledge-driven growth*. New knowledge provides the input that allows investment to produce increasing rather than diminishing marginal returns. Because there are no practical limits to human knowledge, there need be no immediate boundaries to finding new ways to produce more output by using less of all inputs.

Neoclassical theories gave economics the name "the dismal science" by emphasizing diminishing marginal returns under conditions of given technology. Advanced growth theories are more optimistic because they emphasize the unlimited potential of knowledge-driven technological change.

Probably the most important contrast between these ideas-based theories and the Neoclassical theory concerns investment and income. In the Neoclassical growth model, diminishing marginal returns to investment imply a limit to the possible increase of per capita GDP. In the advanced theories, investment alone can hold an economy on a "sustained growth path" in which per capita GDP increases without limit, provided that the investment embodies the results of continual advances in technological knowledge.

A computer is a private good because if I own it then you cannot also own it. But the knowledge required to build the computer is a public good. And knowledge, unlike traditional factors of production, is not necessarily subject to the law of diminishing returns.

Sasirin Pamai/Shutterstock

▌25.4   **Are There Limits to Growth?**

Many opponents of growth argue that sustained growth of the world economy is undesirable; some argue that it is impossible. The idea that economic growth is limited by nature is not new. In the early 1970s, a group called the "Club of Rome" published a book entitled *The Limits to Growth*, which focused on the limits to growth arising from the finite supply of natural resources. Extrapolating from the oil shortages and price increases caused by the OPEC cartel, the Club of Rome concluded that industrialized countries faced an imminent absolute limit to growth. Do such limits really exist? We now discuss the two issues of resource exhaustion and environmental degradation.

Resource Exhaustion

The years since the Second World War have seen a rapid acceleration in the consumption of the world's resources, particularly fossil fuels and basic minerals. World population has increased from fewer than 2.5 billion to more than 7.6 billion in that period; this increase alone has intensified the demand for the world's resources. Furthermore, as people attain higher incomes, they generally consume more resources. Thus, not only are there more people in the world, but many of those people are consuming increasing quantities of resources.

Most everyone in the world today would like to achieve a standard of living equal to that of the average Canadian family. Unfortunately, the world's current resources and its present capacity to cope with pollution and environmental degradation are insufficient to accomplish this rise in global living standards with present technology.

Most economists, however, agree that absolute limits to growth, based on the assumptions of constant technology and fixed resources, are not relevant. As emphasized by the growth theories we discussed in the previous section, technology changes continually, as do the available stocks of resources. For example, 75 years ago, few would have thought that the world could produce enough food to feed its present population of 7.6 billion people, let alone the 10 billion at which the population is projected to stabilize sometime later this century. Yet significant advances in agricultural methods make this task now seem feasible. Further, while existing resources are being depleted, new ones are constantly being discovered or developed. One example is the massive expansion in U.S. oil and gas production that has occurred since the late 2000s. The oil and gas reserves currently being exploited were virtually unknown a decade earlier but technological improvements allowed them to be developed to such an extent that the United States is now forecast to be the world's largest oil producer in just a few years.

Another consideration relates to both resource use and technological progress. Along with advances in technological knowledge typically comes an increase in the economy's *resource efficiency*—a reduction in the amount of resources used to produce one unit of output. In Canada, for example, an average dollar of real GDP is currently produced with nearly 40 percent less energy than was the case in 1978, and if we focus just on petroleum use, the reduction is almost 50 percent. More generally, every dollar's worth of real GDP produced in the world has used steadily fewer resources over the past century. Part of this reduction is due to an improvement in the efficiency with which resources are used; part is due to the gradual shift toward the production of services (and away from the production of goods) in world GDP. Improvements in resource efficiency do not eliminate the concerns about resource exhaustion, but they do underline the importance of recognizing the role of technological change when considering limits to economic growth.

Technology is constantly advancing, and many things that seemed impossible a generation ago will be commonplace a generation from now. Such technological advance makes any absolute limits to economic growth less likely.

The development of the Alberta oil sands has significantly increased Canada's oil-production capacity. At the same time, it has raised concerns regarding environmental degradation, including substantial emissions of greenhouse gases.

Yet there is surely cause for concern. Although many barriers can be overcome by technological advances, such achievements are not instantaneous and are certainly not automatic. There is a critical problem of timing: How soon can we discover and put into practice the knowledge required to solve the problems that are made ever more imminent by the growth in the population, the affluence of the rich nations, and the aspirations of the billions who now live in poverty? There is no guarantee that a whole generation will not be caught in transition between technologies, with enormous social and political consequences.

A final point worth noting is that the extent of resource depletion is not something that "just happens." Since natural resources are typically owned by the public, government policy can be used to influence the rate of resource extraction if that objective is deemed to be appropriate. If we fail to protect some key natural resources, it will not be because we lacked the ability or the technology to do so, only that we lacked the political will to make contentious and difficult decisions—decisions that may nonetheless be in our long-run interests.

Environmental Degradation

Another problem associated with economic growth is the generation of pollution and the degradation of our natural environment. Air, water, and soil are polluted by a variety of natural activities, and, for billions of years, the environment has coped with them. Earth's natural processes had little trouble coping with the pollution generated by its 1 billion inhabitants in 1800. But the 7.6 billion people who now exist put such extreme demands on our ecosystems that there are now legitimate concerns about environmental sustainability. Smoke, sewage, chemical waste, hydrocarbon and greenhouse-gas emissions, spent nuclear fuel, and a host of other pollutants threaten to overwhelm Earth's natural regenerative processes.

Conscious management of pollution was unnecessary when the world's population was 1 billion people, but such management has now become a pressing matter.

APPLYING ECONOMIC CONCEPTS 25-3

Climate Change and Economic Growth

There is no doubt that Earth's average surface temperature has been rising over the past century, and that the increase has been unevenly distributed, from less than 1°C near the equator to over 5°C near the poles. As a result of this global warming, the polar ice caps have been melting significantly, the world's deserts have been gradually increasing in size, and extreme weather events are becoming more frequent and severe. The melting of the Antarctic and Greenland ice caps is predicted to cause a significant increase in sea level, with potentially catastrophic effects for the many highly populated island and coastal regions of Asia and Africa. The creeping desertification and changing rainfall patterns are predicted to cause significant reductions in agricultural productivity, especially in the developing countries. The effects of climate change will be felt by people in many countries, but the most dramatic effects are likely to be experienced in the lowest-income countries least prepared to shoulder the burden.

Although the underlying cause of the rising global temperatures is still debated, the bulk of the scientific evidence points to a clear causal link. The burning of fossil fuels leads to the emission of carbon dioxide and other "greenhouse gases," which accumulate in the atmosphere and remain there for many years. This rising atmospheric concentration of gases acts like a greenhouse to lock in the sun's warmth, thus increasing average global temperature.

The world's annual emissions of greenhouse gases have been increasing steadily, broadly in line with the growth of the world economy. In the absence of policies aimed at reducing these emissions, they are predicted to approximately double between today and 2050. Yet the weight of scientific evidence suggests that in order to stabilize the atmospheric concentration of greenhouse gases (at a level well above today's), and thus to stabilize Earth's average temperature (at a level 1° to 2°C above today's average temperature), annual emissions will need to fall by 80 to 90 percent from *current* levels by 2050. Achieving such reductions will likely affect the world's economic growth.

What is the connection between climate change and economic growth? First, modern economic growth is a significant cause of global warming. Since energy is an important input to production for most goods and services, and since the burning of fossil fuels is currently one

Reducing the extent of environmental degradation, however, is different from advocating an "anti-growth" position. To put it differently, there is nothing inconsistent about an economy displaying *both* high rates of economic growth and active environmental protection. As students of microeconomics will recognize, an important part of a policy designed to reduce the extent of environmental degradation is to get polluters (firms and households) to face the full cost of their polluting activities—especially the external costs that their activities impose on society. This often involves levying some form of tax on polluters for every unit of pollution emitted. Although such policies, if stringently enforced, will lead to output reductions in specific industries, they need not lead to reductions in the *overall* level of economic activity. And long-run economic growth is related to growth in the overall level of economic activity, not to the growth of specific industries.

Furthermore, many technological advances reduce the amount of pollution per unit of output and also reduce the costs of dealing with whatever pollution remains. Rich, advanced economies, such as Canada, the United States, and the European Union, create less pollution per dollar of GDP and find it easier to bear the cost of pollution cleanup than do poorer, less technologically advanced economies.

None of this implies that environmental issues are not serious. It is possible that our management of these issues will be sufficiently inadequate that growth will be

of the most efficient ways to produce energy, it is not surprising that a close relationship exists between the growth of real GDP and the growth of greenhouse-gas emissions. But reducing emissions by reducing world GDP is probably both unrealistic and undesirable. As the world's population continues to grow, and the people of the developing world strive to increase their per capita incomes to levels closer to ours, there will inevitably be a rise in global GDP.

A more realistic way to reduce greenhouse-gas emissions is to reduce our reliance on energy and, in particular, our reliance on those forms of energy that release greenhouse gases into the atmosphere. Most economists argue that the most effective policy to reduce the world's emissions of greenhouse gases involves placing a price on the emission of greenhouse gases, either through a direct tax (such as a "carbon tax") or by directly restricting the amount of total emissions and then allowing the distribution of emissions among firms to be determined through the trading of emissions permits (a "cap-and-trade" system). Either policy approach will increase the cost associated with emitting greenhouse gases and thus will create incentives for firms and households to use non-emitting forms of energy. Incentives will also be created for the further development of non-emitting energy sources such as solar, wind, nuclear, and hydroelectricity.

Since these policies will be effective only by imposing costs on firms and households, their use will highlight a second connection between economic growth and climate change. These higher costs will eventually lead to the adoption of cleaner energy systems and thus a reduction of greenhouse-gas emissions. But unless the carbon prices are matched with other growth-enhancing policies, such as reductions in income taxes, the overall effect will likely be a reduction in the rate of economic growth. Over the long term, however, once the economy adjusts to the new and possibly more efficient fuel sources, it is possible that the rate of economic growth would increase.

Policymakers are thus faced with difficult choices. If their objective was to make such choices sensibly, they would first need to estimate the costs to the economy of taking the "business as usual" approach and thus experiencing the predicted changes in the world climate over the next several decades. Then they would need to estimate the costs associated with taking aggressive policy actions designed to dramatically reduce the emission of greenhouse gases. Finally, they would need to choose a policy approach, appropriately weighing the costs of inaction against the costs of action. These would be very difficult decisions to make, partly because of the uncertainty surrounding the impact of any policies and partly because of the considerable political pressures generated by advocates on both sides of the debate.

impaired and our living standards will suffer by significant amounts. If this happens, it will probably *not* be because we lacked the technology or know-how to solve these problems once they were recognized. If we do create environmental disasters, more likely it will be because we failed to respond quickly enough (if at all) to the growing dangers as they were occurring.

Most climate scientists believe, for example, that we may already be too late to reverse the forces leading to global climate change and that significant increases in sea level are now a virtual certainty over the next few decades. However, most agree that there is still time to take actions that could stabilize Earth's climate over the course of this century. Concerted global actions and considerable political will in many countries must be part of the solution. *Applying Economic Concepts 25-3* explores in more detail the problem of climate change caused by greenhouse-gas emissions associated with the burning of fossil fuels.

Conclusion

The world faces many problems. Starvation and poverty are the common lot of citizens in many countries and are not unknown even in such countries as Canada and the United States, where average living standards are very high. Growth has raised the average citizens of advanced countries from poverty to plenty in the course of two centuries—a short time in terms of human history. Further growth is needed if people in developing countries are to escape material poverty, and further growth would also help advanced countries to deal with many of their pressing economic problems.

Rising population and consumption, however, put pressure on the world's natural ecosystems, especially through the many forms of pollution. Further growth can only occur if it is *sustainable* growth that is in turn based on knowledge-driven technological change. Past experience suggests that new technologies will use less of all resources per unit of output. But if they are to dramatically reduce the demands placed on Earth's ecosystems, price and policy incentives will be needed to direct technological change in more environmentally sustainable ways. Just as present technologies are much less polluting than the technologies of a century ago, the technologies of the future need to be made much less polluting than today's.

There is no guarantee that the world will solve the problems of sustainable growth in the time available, but there is nothing in modern growth theory and existing evidence to suggest that such an achievement is impossible.

SUMMARY

25.1 The Nature of Economic Growth

LO 1, 2

- Long-term economic growth refers to sustained increases in potential GDP.
- The cumulative effects of even small differences in growth rates become very large over periods of a decade or more.
- The most important benefit of growth lies in its contribution to raising average material living standards.
- Growth also facilitates the redistribution of income among people.

- The opportunity cost of growth is the reduction of consumption as resources are used instead for investment in capital goods.
- An additional cost of growth is the personal losses to those whose skills are made obsolete by the economic disruption caused by growth.
- There are four major determinants of growth: increases in the labour force; increases in physical capital; increases in human capital; and improvements in technology.

25.2 Economic Growth: Basic Relationships

LO 3

- The long-run relationship among saving, investment, and economic growth is most easily observed in the market for financial capital, in which the real interest rate is determined by the equality of desired investment and desired national saving.
- Increases in the supply of national saving will reduce the interest rate and encourage more investment by firms, thus increasing the rate of growth of potential output.
- Increases in the demand for investment will increase the interest rate and encourage an increase in household saving. The higher saving (and investment) in equilibrium leads to a higher growth rate of potential output.

- The Neoclassical growth model assumes an aggregate production function that displays diminishing marginal returns (when one factor is changed in isolation) and constant returns to scale (when all factors are changed in equal proportions).
- In a balanced growth path in the Neoclassical growth model, the quantity of labour, the quantity of capital, and real GDP all increase at a constant rate. But since per capita output is constant, material living standards are not rising.

- Changes in output that cannot be accounted for by changes in the levels of physical and human capital and in the size of the labour force are called growth in total factor productivity (TFP).

- In the Neoclassical growth model, technological change is assumed to be exogenous—unaffected by the size of the labour force, the size of the capital stock, or the level of economic activity.

25.3 Economic Growth: Advanced Theories

LO 4

- Unlike the Neoclassical growth model, advanced growth theories emphasize endogenous technological change that responds to market signals, such as prices and profits. In addition, shocks that would be adverse in a setting of fixed technology may provide a spur to innovation and result in technological improvements.
- These advanced growth theories also suggest that investment embodying new technologies may be subject to *increasing* rather than diminishing marginal returns.

Investment that embodies a continuing flow of new technologies can explain ongoing growth in per capita incomes caused by capital accumulation—a phenomenon difficult to explain with the Neoclassical growth model.

- New knowledge is an important input to the growth process and, because it is a public good that can be used simultaneously by many, it is not subject to diminishing marginal returns.

25.4 Are There Limits to Growth?

LO 5

- Without ongoing technological change, world living standards could not be raised to those currently existing in the developed nations.
- Rising population and rising real incomes place pressure on resources. Technological improvements, however, lead to less resource use per unit of output produced and also to the discovery and development of new resources.
- Earth's environment could cope naturally with much of human pollution 200 years ago, but the present

population and level of output is so large that pollution has outstripped many of nature's coping mechanisms.

- Although problems associated with environmental degradation have been surmounted in the past, there is no guarantee that the ones now being encountered, such as the effects of climate change, will be effectively addressed by policies before the effects can be reversed.

KEY CONCEPTS

The cumulative nature of growth
Benefits and costs of growth
The market for financial capital and the equilibrium interest rate
Saving, investment, and growth

The Neoclassical growth model
The aggregate production function
Diminishing marginal returns
Constant returns to scale
Balanced growth

Endogenous technical change
Increasing marginal returns to investment
Resource depletion
Environmental degradation

STUDY EXERCISES

MyLab Economics Make the grade with MyLab Economics™: All Study Exercises can be found on MyLab Economics™. You can practise them as often as you want, and many feature step-by-step guided instructions to help you find the right answer.

FILL-IN-THE-BLANK

1 Fill in the blanks to make the following statements correct.

a. Long-run, sustained increases in potential output are called _____.

b. Increases in material living standards occur with increases in real _____.

c. An important cost of economic growth is the sacrifice of current _____ in exchange for investment that raises future _____.

d. Four major determinants of growth examined in this chapter are

- _____
- _____
- _____
- _____

2 In this chapter, we developed a theory of the market for financial capital. Using that theory, fill in the blanks to make the following statements correct.

a. An increase in the real interest rate leads to a(n) _____ in the amount of national saving as households reduce their _____.

b. An increase in the interest rate leads firms to _____ their amount of desired investment.

c. In the long run, with output equal to potential, equilibrium in the market for financial capital determines the interest rate as well as the amount of _____ and _____ in the economy.

d. Following a shift in either the supply of national saving or the demand for investment, there will be a change in both the equilibrium _____ and the amount of _____ in the economy.

e. An increase in the amount of the economy's resources devoted to _____ leads to an increase in the growth rate of _____.

3 Fill in the blanks to make the following statements correct.

a. An important aspect of the Neoclassical growth model is that increases in the supply of one factor, all else held constant, imply eventually _____ marginal returns to that factor.

b. In the Neoclassical growth model, an increase in the labour force (with capital held constant) will _____ total output and _____ the level of per capita output.

c. When a new and better harvesting machine replaces an old harvesting machine on a farm and is more productive than the old one, we say there has been _____ technical change.

d. Some advanced growth theories are based on the assumption that technological change is _____ to the economic system; others are based on the possibility that there are _____ marginal returns to investment.

e. Neoclassical growth theories are pessimistic because they emphasize _____ returns with a given state of _____. Advanced growth theories are more optimistic because they emphasize the unlimited potential of _____.

REVIEW

4 The diagram below shows two paths for aggregate consumption. One grows at a rate of 3 percent per year; the other grows at 4 percent per year but begins at a lower level.

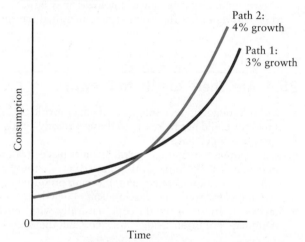

a. Suppose the economy jumps from Path 1 to Path 2 in Year 0 because its rate of capital accumulation increases. What is the opportunity cost in this economy for this increase in capital accumulation?

b. Suppose the economy jumps from Path 1 to Path 2 in Year 0 because its rate of R&D (research and development) expenditures increases. The greater R&D leads to technological improvements that generate the higher growth rate. What is the opportunity cost to this economy for the increase in R&D expenditures?

c. Given the two paths in the diagram, can you offer a way to identify the "break-even" point for making the jump from Path 1 to Path 2? Explain.

5 In this chapter we discussed four major determinants of growth in real output: increases in the labour force, increases in the stock of physical capital, increases in human capital, and improvements in technology.

a. For each of the four determinants, give an example of a government policy that is likely to increase growth.
b. Discuss the likely cost associated with each policy.
c. Does one of your proposed policies appear better (in a cost-benefit sense) than the others? Explain.

6 Consider an economy in the long run with real GDP equal to the level of potential output, Y^*.

a. Draw the diagram of the market for financial capital. Explain the slopes of the investment demand curve and the national saving curve.
b. Suppose the government pursued a fiscal contraction by reducing the level of government purchases. Explain what would happen to the equilibrium interest rate, the amount of investment in the economy, and the long-run growth rate.
c. Now suppose the fiscal contraction occurs by increasing taxes. Explain what effect this would have on the interest rate, investment, and long-run growth rate. (Hint: An increase in taxes is likely to reduce disposable income and thus reduce aggregate consumption.)

7 Consider the market for financial capital and the relationship among saving, investment, and the interest rate. In what follows, assume that the economy is in a long-run equilibrium with $Y = Y^*$.

a. Suppose the government wants to encourage national saving. How could it do this, and what would be the effects of such a policy? Illustrate in a diagram.
b. Suppose instead that the government wants to encourage investment. How might this be accomplished, and what would be the effects? Illustrate in a diagram.
c. It is often heard in public debate that "high interest rates are bad for investment and growth." Is this true?

8 In the early 1970s the Club of Rome, extrapolating from the rates of resource use at the time, predicted that the supply of natural resources (especially oil) would be used up within a few decades. Subsequent events appear to have proven them wrong.

a. What is predicted to happen to the price of oil (and other natural resources) as population and per capita incomes rise?
b. Given your answer to part (a), what is the likely response by firms and consumers who use such resources?
c. Explain why resource exhaustion should, through the workings of the price system, lead to technological developments that reduce the use of the resource.

9 Dr. David Suzuki, an opponent of further economic growth, has argued that despite the fact that "in the twentieth century the list of scientific and technological achievements has been absolutely dazzling, the costs of such progress are so large that negative economic growth may be right for the future." Policies to achieve this include "rigorous reduction of waste, a questioning and distrustful attitude toward technological progress, and braking demands on the globe's resources." Identify some of the benefits and costs of economic growth, and evaluate Suzuki's position. What government policies would be needed to achieve his ends?

PROBLEMS

10 In the text we said that, over many years, small differences in growth rates can have large effects on the level of income. This question will help you understand this important point. Consider an initial value of real GDP equal to Y_0. If real GDP grows at a rate of g percent annually, after N years real GDP will equal $Y_0(1 + g)^N$. Now consider the following table. Let the initial level of GDP in all cases be 100.

	Real GDP with Alternative Growth Rates					
	1%	1.5%	2%	2.5%	3%	3.5%
Year	(1)	(2)	(3)	(4)	(5)	(6)
0	100	100	100	100	100	100
1	—	—	—	—	—	—
3	—	—	—	—	—	—
5	—	—	—	—	—	—
10	—	—	—	—	—	—
20	—	—	—	—	—	—
30	—	—	—	—	—	—
50	—	—	—	—	—	—

a. By using the formula provided above, compute the level of real GDP in column 1 for each year. For example, in Year 1, real GDP will equal $100(1.01)^1 = 101$. For each year, compute the GDP to two decimal places.
b. Now do the same for the rest of the columns.
c. In Year 20, how much larger (in percentage terms) is real GDP in the 3 percent growth case compared with the 1.5 percent growth case?
d. In Year 50, how much larger (in percentage terms) is real GDP in the 3 percent growth case compared with the 1.5 percent growth case?

⓫ The table below shows aggregate values for a hypothetical economy. Real GDP is equal to potential GDP. Figures are billions of dollars.

Potential GDP	950
Net tax revenue	125
Government purchases	140
Desired investment	10
Desired consumption	800

a. What is the level of private saving?
b. What is the level of public saving?
c. What is the level of national saving?
d. Is the interest rate at its equilibrium level? How do you know?

⓬ The Neoclassical growth model is based on the existence of an aggregate production function—showing the relationship between labour (L), capital (K), technology (T), and real GDP (Y). The table below shows various values for L, K, and T. In all cases, the aggregate production function is assumed to take the following form:

$$Y = T \times \sqrt{KL}$$

Labour (L)	Capital (K)	Technology (T)	Real GDP (Y)
10	20	1	—
15	20	1	—
20	20	1	—
25	20	1	—
10	20	1	—
15	30	1	—
20	40	1	—
25	50	1	—
20	20	1	—
20	20	3	—
20	20	4	—
20	20	5	—

a. Compute real GDP for each case and complete the table.
b. In the first part of the table, capital is constant but labour is increasing. What property of the production function is displayed? Explain.
c. In the second part of the table, capital and labour are increasing by the same proportion. What property of the production function is displayed? Explain.
d. What is the source of growth shown in the third part of the table?

26 Money and Banking

CHAPTER OUTLINE	LEARNING OBJECTIVES (LO)

After studying this chapter you will be able to

26.1 THE NATURE OF MONEY

1 describe the various functions of money, and how money has evolved over time.

26.2 THE CANADIAN BANKING SYSTEM

2 see that modern banking systems include both privately owned commercial banks and government-owned central banks.

26.3 MONEY CREATION BY THE BANKING SYSTEM

3 explain how commercial banks create money by taking deposits and making loans.

26.4 THE MONEY SUPPLY

4 describe the various measures of the money supply.

IN the next three chapters, we look at the role of money and monetary policy. The role of money may seem obvious to most readers: Money is what people use to buy things. Yet as we will see, increasing the amount of money circulating in Canada may not make the average Canadian better off in the long run. Although money allows those who have it to buy someone else's output, the total amount of goods and services available for everyone to buy depends on the total output produced, and thus may be unaffected by the total amount of money circulating in the economy. In other words, an increase in the quantity of money may not increase the level of potential real GDP. However, most economists agree that changes in the amount of money have important short-run effects on national income. A complete understanding of money's role in the economy requires that we recognize the distinction between the short run and the long run.

We begin by talking in detail about what money is and how it evolved over the centuries to its current form. We then examine the Canadian banking system, which includes a central bank (the Bank of Canada) and many commercial banks. Finally, we explain the process whereby commercial banks "create" money, seemingly out of thin air. This money creation process will play a central role in our discussion of how money influences the level of economic activity, a topic we begin in the next chapter.

▌26.1 The Nature of Money

What exactly is money? In this section, we describe the functions of money and briefly outline its history.

What Is Money?

medium of exchange Anything that is generally accepted in return for goods and services sold.

Money is any generally accepted **medium of exchange**, which means anything widely accepted in a society in exchange for goods and services. Although its medium-of-exchange role is perhaps its most important one, money also acts as a *store of value* and as a *unit of account*. Different kinds of money vary in their abilities to fulfill these functions.

barter A system in which goods and services are traded directly for other goods and services.

Money as a Medium of Exchange   If there were no money, products would have to be exchanged by barter. **Barter** is the system whereby goods and services are exchanged directly with each other. The major difficulty with barter is that each transaction requires a *double coincidence of wants*: Anyone who specialized in producing one commodity would have to spend a great deal of time searching for satisfactory transactions. For example, the barber who needs his sink repaired would have to find a plumber who wants a haircut. In a world of many different goods and many different people, the effort required to make all transactions by barter would border on the ridiculous. The use of money as a medium of exchange solves this problem. People can sell their output for money and then, in separate transactions, use the money to buy what they want from others.

> The double coincidence of wants is unnecessary when a medium of exchange is used.

By facilitating transactions, money makes possible the benefits of specialization and the division of labour, two concepts we first discussed in Chapter 1. As a result, money greatly contributes to the efficiency of the economic system. Not surprisingly, money has been called one of the great inventions contributing to human freedom and well-being.

To serve as an efficient medium of exchange, money must have a number of characteristics. It must be both easily recognizable and readily acceptable. It must have a high value relative to its weight, because otherwise it would be a nuisance to carry around. It must be divisible, because money that comes only in large denominations is useless for transactions having only a small value. It must also be reasonably durable. (Notice that Canada's polymer "paper" money can easily survive trips through a washing machine!) Finally, it must be difficult, if not impossible, to counterfeit.

Money as a Store of Value   Money is a convenient means of storing purchasing power; goods may be sold today for money and the money may then be stored until it is needed for some future purchase. To be a satisfactory store of value, however, money's purchasing power should be relatively stable over time. Recall from the beginning of Chapter 23 that a rise in the price level causes a decrease in the purchasing power of money. When the price level is stable, the purchasing power of a given sum of money is also stable; when the price level is highly variable, so is the purchasing power of money, and the usefulness of money as a store of value is undermined.

Between the early 1970s and the early 1990s, inflation in Canada was high enough and sufficiently variable to diminish money's usefulness as a store of value. Since 1992, however, inflation has been low and relatively stable, thus increasing money's effectiveness as a store of value. Even Canada's high-inflation experience, however, is very modest compared with that in some other countries, such as Chile in the mid-1970s, Bolivia in the mid-1980s, Argentina, Romania, and Brazil in the early 1990s, and Zimbabwe in the mid-2000s. One of the most infamous experiences of very high inflation—*hyperinflation*—comes from Germany in the early 1920s. This case is discussed in *Lessons from History 26-1*.

Canadian bank notes are money. They serve the function of a medium of exchange and a unit of account. And if the rate of inflation is low, they also serve as a reasonable store of value.

Money as a Unit of Account Money is also used for accounting, and its use for such purpose does not rely on its physical existence. Canadian businesses, governments, and households all record their financial accounts in terms of dollars. Expenditures and receipts and deficits and surpluses are computed in dollar terms even without the immediate presence of physical money.

Indeed, money can be used for accounting purposes even if it has *no* physical existence whatsoever. For instance, a government store in a communist society might say that everyone was allocated so many "dollars" to use each month. Goods could then be assigned prices and each consumer's purchases recorded, the consumer being allowed to buy until the allocated supply of dollars was exhausted. These dollars need have no existence other than as entries in the store's books, yet they would serve as a perfectly satisfactory unit of account. Whether they could also serve as a medium of exchange between individuals depends on whether the store would agree to transfer dollar credits from one customer to another at the customer's request. Canadian banks transfer dollars credited to deposits in this way each time you make a purchase with your ATM or debit card. Thus, a bank deposit can serve as both a unit of account and a medium of exchange.

The Origins of Money

The origins of money go far back in antiquity. Most primitive societies are known to have made some use of it.

Metallic Money All sorts of commodities have been used as money at one time or another, but gold and silver proved to have great advantages. They were precious because their supplies were relatively limited, and they were in constant demand by the wealthy for ornament and decoration. Further, they were easily recognized, they were divisible into extremely small units, and they did not easily wear out. For these reasons, precious metals came to circulate as money and to be used in many transactions.

Before the invention of coins, it was necessary to carry the metals in bulk. When a purchase was made, the requisite quantity of the metal was carefully weighed on a scale.

LESSONS FROM HISTORY 26-1

Hyperinflation and the Value of Money

Hyperinflation is generally defined as inflation that exceeds 50 percent per month. At this rate of inflation, a chocolate bar that costs $1 on January 1 would cost $129.74 by December 31 of the same year. When prices are rising at such rapid rates, is it possible for money to maintain its usefulness as a medium of exchange or as a store of value? Several examples from history have allowed economists to study the role of money during hyperinflation. This historical record is not very reassuring. In a number of instances, prices were rising so quickly that the nation's money ceased to be a satisfactory store of value, even for short periods.

A spectacular example of hyperinflation is the experience of Germany in the period after the First World War. The price index in the accompanying table shows that a typical good purchased for one 100-mark note in July 1923 would cost *10 million* 100-mark notes only three months later! Germany had experienced substantial inflation during the First World War, averaging more than 30 percent per year, but the immediate postwar years of 1920 and 1921 gave no sign of explosive inflation. By the summer of 1922, however, the rate of inflation was extremely high and by November 1923 the German mark was officially repudiated, its value wholly destroyed. How could such a dramatic increase in prices happen?

The main cause was the German government's inability to finance its rising expenditures with tax revenues and its resort to printing new money on a massive scale. As more and more physical money was being spent to purchase the same volume of real goods and services, the rate of inflation soared.

When inflation becomes so high that people lose confidence in the purchasing power of their currency, they rush to spend it. People who have goods become increasingly reluctant to accept the rapidly depreciating money in exchange. The rush to spend money accelerates the increase in prices until people finally become unwilling to accept money on any terms. What was once money ceases to be money. The price system can then be restored only by repudiation of the old monetary unit, its replacement by a new unit, and a complete reform of the country's monetary policy.

About a dozen hyperinflations in world history have been documented, among them the collapse of the continental during the American Revolution in 1776, the ruble during the Russian Revolution in 1917, the drachma during and after the German occupation of Greece in the Second World War, the pengö in Hungary in 1945–1946, the Chinese national currency from 1946 to 1948, the Bolivian peso in 1984–1985, and the Argentinian peso in the early 1990s. Between 2004 and 2009, there was a massive hyperinflation in Zimbabwe—the largest in recorded history. At the height of the hyperinflation in 2008, the *annual* inflation rate was estimated at over 230 million percent!

Every one of these hyperinflations was accompanied by great increases in the money supply; new money was printed to give governments purchasing power that they could not or would not obtain by taxation. Further, every hyperinflation occurred in the midst of a major political upheaval in which serious doubts existed about the stability and the future of the government itself.

Is hyperinflation likely in the absence of civil war, revolution, or collapse of the government? Most economists think not. Further, it is clear that high inflation rates over a period of time do not mean the inevitable or even likely onset of hyperinflation.

Hulton Deutsch/Corbis Historical/Getty Images

During hyperinflation, money loses its value so quickly that people cease to accept it as a means of payment. At that point, money may as well be used for wallpaper.

Date	German Wholesale Price Index (1913 = 1)
January 1913	1
January 1920	13
January 1921	14
January 1922	37
July 1922	101
January 1923	2 785
July 1923	74 800
August 1923	944 000
September 1923	23 900 000
October 1923	7 096 000 000

The invention of coinage eliminated the need to weigh the metal at each transaction, but it created an important role for an authority, usually a king or queen, who made the coins and affixed his or her seal, guaranteeing the amount of precious metal that the coin contained. This was clearly a great convenience, as long as traders knew that they could accept the coin at its "face value." The face value was nothing more than a statement that a certain weight of the precious metal was contained therein.

However, coins often could not be taken at their face value. The practice of clipping a thin slice off the edge of the coin and keeping the valuable metal became common. This, of course, served to undermine the acceptability of coins, even if they were stamped. To get around this problem, the idea arose of minting the coins with a rough edge. The absence of the rough edge would immediately indicate that the coin had been clipped. This practice, called *milling*, survives on Canadian dimes, quarters, and two-dollar coins as an interesting anachronism to remind us that there were days when the market value of the metal in the coin was equal to the face value of the coin.

Canadian quarters are intentionally produced with rough or bumpy edges. Many years ago, such "milling" of coins was useful in preventing individuals from clipping the coins. Today, milling is useful mainly to help the visually impaired distinguish between coins.

Not to be outdone by the cunning of their subjects, some rulers were quick to seize the chance of getting something for nothing. The power to mint coins placed rulers in a position to work a very profitable fraud. They often used some suitable occasion—a marriage, an anniversary, an alliance—to remint the coinage. Subjects would be ordered to bring their coins in to the mint to be melted down and coined afresh with a new stamp. Between the melting down and the recoining, however, the rulers had only to toss some further inexpensive base metal in with the melted coins. This *debasing* of the coinage allowed the ruler to earn a handsome profit by minting more new coins than the number of old ones collected and putting the extras in the royal vault. Through debasement, the amount of money in the economy (but not the amount of gold) had increased.

The eventual result of such debasement was inflation. The subjects had the same number of coins as before and hence could demand the same quantity of goods. When rulers paid their bills, however, the recipients of the extra coins could be expected to spend them. This caused a net increase in demand, which in turn bid up prices. Thus, increasing the money supply by debasing the coinage was a common cause of inflation.

Gresham's Law.   The early experience of currency debasement led to the observation known as **Gresham's Law**, after Sir Thomas Gresham (1519–1579), an advisor to the Elizabethan court, who coined the phrase "bad money drives out good."

Gresham's Law The theory that "bad," or debased, money drives "good," or undebased, money out of circulation.

When Queen Elizabeth I came to the throne of England in the middle of the sixteenth century, the coinage had been severely debased. Seeking to help trade, Elizabeth minted new coins that contained their full face value of gold. However, as fast as she fed these new coins into circulation, they disappeared. Why?

Suppose you possessed one of these new coins and one of the old ones, each with the same face value, and had to make a purchase. What would you do? You would use the debased coin to make the purchase and keep the undebased one; you part with less gold that way. Suppose you wanted to obtain a certain amount of gold bullion by melting down the gold coins (as was frequently done). Which coins would you use? You would use new, undebased coins because it would take more of the debased coins than the new coins to get a given amount of gold bullion. The debased coins (bad money) would thus remain in circulation, and the undebased coins (good money) would disappear into peoples' private hoards—the "bad" money would drive out the "good" money.

Gresham's Law predicts that when two types of money are used side by side, the one with the greater intrinsic value will be driven out of circulation.

Gresham's insights have proven helpful in explaining the experience of a number of modern high-inflation economies. For example, in the 1970s, the rising prices of base metals raised the value of the metallic content in Chilean coins above their face value. Coins quickly disappeared from circulation as the coins were melted down for their metal. Only paper currency remained in circulation and was used even for tiny transactions, such as purchasing a pack of matches. Gresham's law is one reason that modern coins, unlike their historical counterparts, are merely tokens that contain a metallic value that is only a small fraction of their face value.

Paper Money   The next important step in the history of money was the evolution of paper currency. Artisans who worked with gold required secure safes, and the public began to deposit gold with these goldsmiths for safekeeping. Goldsmiths would give their depositors receipts promising to return the gold on demand. When a depositor wanted to make a large purchase, he could go to his goldsmith, reclaim some of his gold, and pay it to the seller of the goods. If the seller had no immediate need for the gold, he would carry it back to the goldsmith for safekeeping.

If people knew the goldsmith to be reliable, there was no need to go through the cumbersome and risky business of physically transferring the gold. The buyer needed only to transfer the goldsmith's receipt to the seller, who would accept it as long as he was confident that the goldsmith would pay over the gold whenever it was needed. This transferring of paper receipts rather than gold was essentially the invention of paper money.[1]

bank notes Paper money issued by commercial banks.

When it first came into being, paper money represented a promise to pay so much gold on demand. In this case, the promise was made first by goldsmiths and later by banks. Such paper money was *backed* by precious metal and was *convertible on demand* into this metal. In the nineteenth century, private banks commonly issued paper money, called **bank notes**, nominally convertible into gold. As with the goldsmiths, each bank issued its own notes, and these notes were convertible into gold at the issuing bank. Thus, in the nineteenth century, bank notes from many different banks circulated side by side, each of them being backed by gold at the bank that issued them.

Bank of Montreal Archives-BMO Financial Group

The development of paper money, such as this bank note issued by The Montreal Bank more than a century ago, was an important step in the evolution of modern, fractional-reserve banking systems. Paper money allowed individuals to avoid the cumbersome transportation of gold when making their daily transactions.

Fractionally Backed Paper Money.   Early on, many goldsmiths and banks discovered that it was not

---

[1] Paper money dates back as far as the T'ang dynasty in China (A.D. 618–907) but first appeared in Europe much later, in the 1660s in Sweden. For a very readable history of the development of money, see Jack Weatherford, *The History of Money*, Three Rivers Press, 1997.

necessary to keep one ounce of gold in the vaults for every claim to one ounce circulating as paper money. At any one time, some of the bank's customers would be withdrawing gold, others would be depositing it, and most would be using the bank's paper notes without any need or desire to convert those notes into gold. As a result, the bank was able to issue more paper money redeemable in gold than the amount of gold that it held in its vaults. This was good business because the extra paper money could be invested profitably in interest-earning loans to households and firms. To this day, banks have many more claims outstanding against them than they actually have in reserves available to pay those claims. We say that such a currency is *fractionally backed* by the reserves.

The major problem with a fractionally backed currency was maintaining its convertibility into the precious metal behind it. The imprudent bank that issued too much paper money would find itself unable to redeem its currency in gold when the demand for gold was even slightly higher than usual. It would then have to suspend payments, and all holders of its notes would suddenly find that the notes were worthless. The prudent bank that kept a reasonable relationship between its note issues and its gold reserves would find that it could meet a normal range of demand for gold without any trouble.

Paper money used to be backed by the value of gold—meaning that it was redeemable for gold. But now money is not redeemable for anything except itself—people hold it because they know that others will accept it as payment for goods and services.

If, for whatever reason, the public lost confidence in the banks and demanded redemption of its currency *en masse*, even the most prudent bank would be unable to honour its promises. The history of nineteenth- and early-twentieth-century banking on both sides of the Atlantic is full of examples of banks that were ruined by "panics," or sudden "runs" on their gold reserves. When these happened, the banks' depositors and the holders of their notes would find themselves with worthless pieces of paper.

Fiat Money   As time went on, currency (notes and coins) issued by private banks became less common, and central banks took control of issuing currency. By the early decades of the twentieth century in the United States and Canada, *only* central banks were permitted by law to issue currency. Originally, the central banks issued currency that was fully convertible into gold. In those days, gold would be brought to the central bank, which would issue currency in the form of "gold certificates" that asserted that the gold was available on demand. The reserves of gold thus set an upper limit on the amount of currency that could circulate in the economy. This practice of backing the currency with gold is known as a **gold standard**.

However, central banks, like private banks before them, could issue more currency than they had in gold because in normal circumstances only a small fraction of the outstanding currency would be presented for payment at any one time. Thus, even though the need to maintain convertibility into gold put some upper limit on note issuance, central banks had substantial discretionary control over the quantity of currency outstanding. For example, if the central bank decided to hold gold reserves equal to at least 20 percent of its outstanding currency, the total amount of currency would be limited to five times the gold reserves. But the central bank would nonetheless have complete discretion in choosing this fraction; the smaller the fraction held in reserves, the larger the supply of paper currency that could be supported with a given stock of gold.

During the period between the First and Second World Wars (1919–1939), almost all the countries of the world abandoned the gold standard; their currencies were thus no longer convertible into gold. Money that is not convertible by law into anything

gold standard A currency standard whereby a country's currency is convertible into gold at a fixed rate of exchange.

fiat money Paper money or coinage that is neither backed by nor convertible into anything else but is decreed by the government to be legal tender.

tangible derives its value only from its general acceptability in exchange. Such **fiat money** is widely acceptable because it is declared by government order, or *fiat*, to be legal tender. *Legal tender* is anything that by law must be accepted when offered either for the purchase of goods or services or to repay a debt.

Today, no country allows its currency to be converted into gold on demand. Gold backing for Canadian currency was eliminated in 1940, although note issues continued to carry the traditional statement "will pay to the bearer on demand" until 1954. Today's Bank of Canada notes simply say, "This note is legal tender." It is, in other words, fiat money pure and simple.[2]

> **If fiat money is generally acceptable, it is a medium of exchange. If its purchasing power remains stable, it is a satisfactory store of value. If both of these things are true, it serves as a satisfactory unit of account. Today, almost all currency is fiat money.**

Many people are disturbed to learn that present-day paper money is neither backed by nor convertible into anything more valuable—that it consists of nothing but pieces of paper (or plastic) whose value derives from common acceptance and from confidence that it will continue to be accepted in the future. Many people believe that their money should be more "substantial" than this. Yet money is, in fact, nothing more than generally acceptable pieces of paper.

Modern Money: Deposit Money

Today's bank customers deposit coins and paper money with the banks for safekeeping, just as in former times they deposited gold. Such a deposit is recorded as a credit to the customer's account and is a liability (a promise to pay) for the commercial bank.

When the customer wants to purchase goods or services, or wants to settle a debt, three options are available. First, the customer can withdraw cash from the bank account and use it to make a transaction. Second, the customer can write a *cheque* to the recipient, who then deposits the cheque in their own bank account. A cheque is simply an order for a *transfer* of funds from the customer's account to the recipient's account, possibly at a different bank. The development of automatic teller machines (ATMs) in the past 30 years has made the cash option more convenient than it was before ATMs existed, and the cheque-writing option was common until quite recently, but is now much less so.

The customer's third option involves an electronic transfer of funds. Like a cheque, although much faster, a purchase using a debit card leads to a transfer of funds from the bank account of the purchaser to the bank account of the seller. Other electronic transfers of funds are also commonly used, such as direct-deposit payments by employers to employees and online payments that individuals can make from their bank accounts to firms for the provision of various services, such as Internet service, credit cards, and telephone service.

deposit money Money held by the public in the form of deposits with commercial banks.

Deposits contained inside bank accounts can easily be used to facilitate transactions, even though they exist only as electronic entries; these are referred to as **deposit money**. As we will see later in this chapter, the value of deposit money in a modern economy far exceeds the value of coins and paper currency in circulation. As in much earlier times, modern banks create more promises to pay (deposits) than they hold as cash in reserve.

---

[2] See *A History of the Canadian Dollar* (written by James Powell and published by the Bank of Canada) for a detailed and very readable discussion of the evolution of Canadian money.

Bank deposits are money. Today, just as in the past, banks create money by issuing more promises to pay (deposits) than they have cash reserves available to pay out.

Another modern form of money is "cryptocurrencies" such as Bitcoin, Ethereum, and Ripple. These technically fascinating currencies are privately controlled, offer considerable privacy to users, and are seen by many as a great investment opportunity. But are they really "money"? *Applying Economic Concepts 26-1* examines this in more detail.

APPLYING ECONOMIC CONCEPTS 26-1

Are Cryptocurrencies Really Money?

A cryptocurrency is a digital currency that uses cryptography to secure its transactions, to control its supply, and to verify transfers as part of a transaction. The supply of cryptocurrencies is controlled through decentralized and private decisions, as opposed to the centralized control of normal currencies by government-owned central banks. Created in 2009, Bitcoin was the first cryptocurrency, and it remains the most prominent. In the past decade, however, many other cryptocurrencies have been introduced.

As we discuss in the text, "money" does not have to take the form of currency issued by a central bank. Money can be any item that satisfies three essential properties: medium of exchange, store of value, and unit of account. By this standard, do cryptocurrencies deserve to be considered money?

There is no doubt that Bitcoin and other cryptocurrencies serve as a *medium of exchange*. Owners of these currencies can store them in their online "wallets" and use them to make purchases with some online retailers. In selected cases, consumers can make in-store transactions by transferring their cryptocurrencies to the participating retailer. But cryptocurrencies are far from being a *generalized* medium of exchange; in other words, the fraction of total transactions that can be made with them is still very small. Cryptocurrencies will not really be considered money until they are much more widely accepted throughout the economy.

For two reasons, only a tiny share of the population chooses to use cryptocurrencies. First, they are technically more complicated than normal currencies. Questions of their source, acceptability, supply, and reliability likely lead many potential users to keep their distance, viewing them as a curiosity rather than as a safe form of money. A second reason is that cryptocurrencies are—so far at least—a poor *store of value*. For example, in January 2017, one bitcoin sold for U.S. $1000. By September of that year its price had increased to U.S. $4800 and then increased again to U.S. $19 000 three months later. By

March 2018, however, the price of one bitcoin had collapsed to below U.S. $10 000. This huge price volatility may offer an exciting investment opportunity for those prepared to take on enormous risk, but it also means that Bitcoin cannot be a reliable store of value—at least not until its price trajectory becomes much more predictable.

Cryptocurrencies could be used as a *unit of account* but they do not yet play this role, likely due to their lack of widespread use. Anyone could choose to express economic values in terms of any given cryptocurrency. For example, they could express the value of a house as 40 bitcoins, a car as 4 bitcoins or a nice dinner for two as two-tenths of a bitcoin. But very few people think this way, for the simple reason that our current unit of account (Canadian dollars) works very well for so many people. As long as the vast majority of us continue to think in terms of dollars (or pounds or euros or yen), cryptocurrencies will not serve as widespread units of account.

Cryptocurrencies are a fascinating technological invention, offering some of the functions of normal currency (including some advantages). If they can prove themselves to be a reliable store of value, they may gain widespread acceptability and use, including as an accounting metric. If this ever happens, they will deserve to be considered "money." Until then, they do not merit such a designation.

Despite the small role being played by cryptocurrencies in modern economies, governments and central banks continue to monitor closely their development and growth. Governments are concerned that cryptocurrencies may greatly facilitate the scale of illegal activities, such as the buying and selling of illegal drugs, and may also permit tax evasion for otherwise legal activities. Central banks are concerned that massive growth in cryptocurrencies may undermine the control of the monetary system, thereby complicating the conduct of monetary policy. While cryptocurrencies remain narrowly used, however, they will unlikely be a serious cause of concern for policymakers.

26.2 The Canadian Banking System

central bank A bank that acts as banker to the commercial banking system and often to the government as well. Usually a government-owned institution that is the sole money-issuing authority.

Two types of institutions make up a modern banking system. The **central bank** is the government-owned and government-operated institution that is the sole money-issuing authority and serves to control the banking system. Through it, the government's monetary policy is conducted. In Canada, the central bank is the Bank of Canada, often called just the Bank.

Financial intermediaries are privately owned institutions that serve the general public. They are called *intermediaries* because they stand between savers, from whom they accept deposits, and borrowers, to whom they make loans. For many years, government regulations created sharp distinctions among the various types of financial intermediaries by limiting the types of transactions in which each could engage. The past three decades have seen a sweeping deregulation of the financial system so that many of these traditional distinctions no longer apply. In this book, we use the term *commercial banks* to extend to all financial intermediaries that accept deposits and create deposit money, including chartered banks, trust companies, credit unions, and caisses populaires.

The Bank of Canada

Many of the world's early central banks were initially private, profit-making institutions that provided services to ordinary banks. Their importance, however, caused them to develop close ties with government. Central banks soon became instruments of the government, though not all of them were publicly owned. The Bank of England, one of the world's oldest and most famous central banks, began to operate as the central bank of England in the seventeenth century, but it was not formally taken over by the government until 1947.

The similarities in the functions performed and the tools used by the world's central banks are much more important than the differences in their organization. Although we give our attention to the operations of the Bank of Canada, its basic functions are similar to those of the Bank of England, the Federal Reserve System in the United States, or the European Central Bank (the sole issuer of the euro).

Organization of the Bank of Canada The Bank of Canada commenced operations on March 11, 1935. It is a Crown corporation; all profits it earns are remitted to the Government of Canada. The responsibility for the Bank's affairs rests with a board of directors composed of the governor, the senior deputy governor, the deputy minister of finance, and 12 directors. The governor is appointed by the directors, with the approval of the federal cabinet, for a seven-year term.

The organization of the Bank of Canada is designed to keep the operation of monetary policy free from day-to-day political influence. The Bank is not responsible to Parliament for

Timothy Hellum/Alamy Stock Photo

The Bank of Canada is located on Wellington Street in Ottawa, across the street from the Parliament Buildings.

its day-to-day behaviour in the way that the department of finance is for the operation of fiscal policy. In this sense, the Bank of Canada has considerable autonomy in the way it carries out monetary policy. But the Bank is not completely independent. The *ultimate* responsibility for the Bank's actions rests with the government, since it is the government that must answer to Parliament. This system is known as "joint responsibility," and it dates back to 1967.

Under the system of joint responsibility, the governor of the Bank and the minister of finance consult regularly. In the case of fundamental disagreement over monetary policy, the minister of finance has the option of issuing an explicit *directive* to the governor and announcing this decision publicly. In such a case (which has not happened since the inception of joint responsibility), the governor would simply carry out the minister's directive or ignore the directive and resign. In the absence of such a directive, however, responsibility for monetary policy rests with the governor of the Bank.

The system of joint responsibility keeps the conduct of monetary policy free from day-to-day political influence while ensuring that the government retains ultimate responsibility for monetary policy.[3]

Basic Functions of the Bank of Canada   A central bank serves three main functions: as a banker for commercial banks, as a bank for the government, and as the regulator of the nation's money supply. The three functions are reflected in Table 26 1, which shows the balance sheet of the Bank of Canada as of December 2017.

1. Banker to the Commercial Banks.   The central bank accepts deposits from commercial banks and will, on order, transfer them to the account of another bank. In this way, the central bank provides the commercial banks with the means of settling debts to other banks. The deposits of the commercial banks with the Bank of Canada—part of their *reserves*—appear in Table 26-1. In December 2017 the banks had $500 million on reserve at the Bank of Canada. Notice that the cash reserves of the commercial banks deposited with the central bank are liabilities of the central bank, because it promises to pay them on demand.

Historically, one of the earliest services provided by central banks was that of "lender of last resort" to the banking system. Central banks would lend money to private banks that had sound investments (such as business loans, home mortgages, and government securities) but were in urgent need of cash. If such banks could not obtain ready cash, they might be forced into insolvency, because they could not meet the demands of their depositors, in spite of their being basically sound. Today's central banks continue to be lenders of last resort. Table 26-1 shows that in December 2017 the Bank of Canada had no outstanding loans to commercial banks, although normally there are small amounts of short-term loans.

During the global financial crisis that began in 2008, the Bank of Canada played a much more active role than usual in supporting financial markets. At that time,

---

[3] This system was motivated by the "Coyne Affair" in 1961, during the Progressive Conservative government of John Diefenbaker. James Coyne, then governor of the Bank of Canada, disagreed with the minister of finance, Donald Fleming, over the conduct of monetary policy and was eventually forced to resign. Louis Rasminsky then accepted the position as governor of the Bank on the condition that the *Bank of Canada Act* be modified to incorporate the idea of joint responsibility. The *Bank of Canada Act* was so amended in 1967. For a discussion of the early history of the Bank of Canada, see George Watts, *The Bank of Canada: Origins and Early History*, Carleton University Press, 1993.

TABLE 26-1 Assets and Liabilities of the Bank of Canada, December 2017 (millions of dollars)

Assets		Liabilities	
Government of Canada securities	100 457.4	Notes in circulation	85 855.9
Advances to commercial banks	0.0	Government of Canada deposits	21 454.2
Net foreign-currency assets	14.6	Deposits of commercial banks (reserves)	500.3
Other assets	10 628.3	Other liabilities and capital	3 289.9
Total	111 100.3	Total	111 100.3

The balance sheet of the Bank of Canada shows that it serves as banker to the commercial banks and to the government of Canada, and as issuer of our currency; it also suggests the Bank's role as regulator of money markets and the money supply. The principal liabilities of the Bank are the basis of the money supply. Bank of Canada notes are currency, and the deposits of the commercial banks give them the reserves they need to create deposit money. The Bank's holdings of Government of Canada securities arise from its operations designed to regulate the money supply.

(*Source:* Adapted from Bank of Canada, *Annual Report 2017.* www.bankofcanada.ca.)

commercial banks around the world dramatically reduced their interbank lending after the failure of some large U.S. and U.K. financial institutions. The reduction in lending reflected heightened uncertainty regarding the credit-worthiness of *all* commercial banks. In response, the Bank of Canada took unprecedented actions designed to keep credit flowing as normally as possible in Canada, including the significant provision of short-term loans to Canadian financial institutions.

2. Banker to the Federal Government.   Governments, too, need to hold their funds in an account into which they can make deposits and on which they can write cheques. The Government of Canada keeps some of its chequing deposits at the Bank of Canada. In December 2017, the federal government had $21.5 billion in deposits at the Bank of Canada (an unusally large amount).

When the government requires more money than it collects in taxes, it needs to borrow, and it does so by issuing government securities in the form of short-term Treasury bills or longer-term bonds. Most are sold directly to financial institutions and large institutional investors, but in most years the Bank of Canada buys some and credits the government's account with a deposit for the amount of the purchase. In December 2017, the Bank of Canada held $100.5 billion in Government of Canada securities. These securities are the Bank of Canada's primary asset, usually representing over 95 percent of the Bank's total assets. It is largely by earning interest on these securities that the Bank of Canada earns a profit every year—a profit that is eventually remitted to the government.

3. Regulator of the Money Supply.   One of the most important functions of a central bank is to regulate the *money supply*. Though we have not yet defined the money supply precisely—and there are several different definitions of the money supply that we will encounter—we will see that most measures of the money supply include currency in circulation plus deposits held at commercial banks. Table 26-1 shows that the vast

majority of the Bank of Canada's liabilities (that is, its promises to pay) are the currency in circulation or the reserves of the commercial banks.[4] These reserves, in turn, underlie the deposits of households and firms—in exactly the same way that in much earlier times the goldsmith's holdings of gold underlay its issue of notes.

By changing its liabilities (currency plus reserves), the Bank of Canada can change the money supply. The Bank can change the levels of its assets and liabilities in many ways and, as its liabilities rise and fall, so does the money supply. In Chapter 28, we will explore in detail how this happens and how it is related to the Bank's decisions regarding monetary policy. At that point we will see how the Bank's holdings of government securities (its largest asset) are closely related to the value of notes in circulation (its largest liability).

Commercial Banks in Canada

All private-sector banks in Canada are referred to as **commercial banks**. Commercial banks have common attributes: They hold deposits for their customers; they permit certain deposits to be transferred electronically or by cheque from an individual account to other accounts in the same or other banks; they invest in government securities (short-term Treasury bills and longer-term bonds); they make loans to households and firms; and they often divide these loans into small pieces and re-package them into securities, each of which contains a diversified collection of many pieces from the original loans—a process called *securitization*.

> **commercial bank** A privately owned, profit-seeking institution that provides a variety of financial services, such as accepting deposits from customers and making loans and other investments.

Banks are not the only financial institutions in the country. Many other privately owned, profit-seeking institutions, such as trust companies and credit unions, accept deposits and grant loans for specific purposes. Many retail stores and credit-card companies also extend credit so that purchases can be made on a buy-now, pay-later basis.

The Provision of Credit   From the perspective of the overall economy, the most important role played by commercial banks is that of *financial intermediary*. Banks borrow (accept deposits) from households and firms that have money that they do not currently need, and they lend (provide credit) to those households and firms that need credit to achieve their objectives. They therefore act as essential *intermediaries* in the credit market.

Credit can be viewed as the lifeblood of a modern economy. Households often require credit to make large purchases, such as home appliances and cars, and they almost always use credit in the form of a mortgage when they buy a house. Without easy access to credit, most of these household purchases would either be delayed by many years or impossible altogether. Firms often require credit to finance their operations. For example, firms often need to pay their workers and pay for their inputs before receiving payment for their output. In addition, firms often finance their capital investments—purchases of equipment or the construction of facilities—with the use of borrowed money. Without easy access to credit, many firms would be unable to conduct their normal business operations and, as a result, the level of economic activity would decline.

This crucial function of banks and other financial institutions—the provision of credit—is easy to overlook when credit markets are functioning smoothly. Like the flow of electricity, we usually take it for granted in our daily activities, only to be reminded of its importance when the next power failure occurs. Similarly, when the

---

[4] Currency is a liability for the central bank because holders of currency can take it back to the central bank and redeem it for . . . currency! In the days of the gold standard, currency was redeemable for gold. Today, it is just redeemable for itself.

credit markets cease to function well, as they did during the global financial crisis of 2008, their importance to the economy becomes clear to all. Indeed, the economic recession that began in the United States in 2008 and quickly spread around the world originated in the failure of some large U.S. and U.K. banks, which in turn led to a reduction in the flow of credit and a rise in interest rates in most countries. The effect on economic activity was quick and significant. A central part of the policy response, in Canada and elsewhere, involved taking actions to ensure that banks and other financial institutions were in a position to extend credit in a normal manner.

Interbank Activities   Commercial banks have a number of interbank cooperative relationships. For example, banks often share loans. Even the biggest bank cannot meet all the credit needs of a giant corporation, and often a group of banks will offer a "pool loan," agreeing on common terms and dividing the loan up into manageable segments. Another form of interbank cooperation is the bank credit card. Visa and MasterCard are the two most widely used credit cards, and each is operated by a group of banks.

Probably the most important form of interbank cooperation is cheque clearing and collection, including the clearing of electronic transfers through debit cards and online banking activities. Bank deposits are an effective medium of exchange only because banks accept each other's cheques and allow funds to be transferred electronically when purchases are made with debit cards and other forms of electronic transfer. If a depositor in the Bank of Montreal writes a cheque to someone who deposits it in an account at CIBC, the Bank of Montreal now owes money to CIBC. This creates a need for the banks to present cheques to each other for payment. The same is true for transactions made electronically.

clearing house An institution in which interbank indebtedness, arising from the transfer of cheques between banks, is computed and offset and net amounts owing are calculated.

Millions of such transactions take place in the course of a day, and they result in an enormous sorting and bookkeeping job. Multibank systems make use of a **clearing house** where interbank debts are settled. At the end of the day, all the transfers (cheque and electronic) from the Bank of Montreal's customers for deposit to CIBC are totalled and set against the total of all the transfers from CIBC's customers for deposit to the Bank of Montreal. It is necessary only to settle the difference between the two sums. Electronic transfers take place immediately, whereas cheques are passed through the clearing house back to the bank on which they were drawn. Both banks are then able to adjust the individual accounts by a set of book entries. An overall transfer between banks is necessary only when there is a net transfer from the customers of one bank to those of another. This is accomplished by a daily transfer of deposits held by the commercial banks with the Bank of Canada.

Banks as Profit Seekers   Banks are private firms that seek to make profits. A commercial bank provides a variety of services to its customers: the convenience of deposits that can be transferred by personal cheque, debit card, or online transaction; a safe and convenient place to earn a modest but guaranteed return on savings; and financial advice and wealth-management services.

Table 26-2 is the combined balance sheet of the chartered banks in Canada. The bulk of any bank's liabilities are deposits owed to its depositors. The principal assets of a bank are the *securities* it owns (including government bonds), which pay interest or dividends, and the interest-earning *loans* it makes to individuals and to businesses, both in Canada and abroad. A bank loan is a liability to the borrower but an asset to the bank.

Commercial banks attract deposits by paying interest to depositors and by providing them with services, such as clearing cheques, automated teller machines, debit cards, and online banking. Banks earn profits by lending and investing money deposited

TABLE 26-2   Consolidated Balance Sheet of the Canadian Chartered Banks, March 2018 (millions of dollars)

Assets		Liabilities	
Reserves (including deposits with Bank of Canada)	40 092	Demand and notice deposits	1 172 163
Government securities	267 598	Term deposits	658 307
Mortgage and non-mortgage loans	2 220 402	Government deposits	17 639
Canadian corporate securities	155 894	Foreign-currency liabilities	2 794 992
Foreign-currency and other assets	2 859 722	Shareholders' equity	319 194
		Other liabilities	581 413
Total	5 543 708	Total	5 543 708

Reserves are only a tiny fraction of deposit liabilities. If all the chartered banks' customers who held demand and notice deposits tried to withdraw them in cash, the banks could not meet this demand without liquidating over $1 trillion of other assets. This would be impossible without assistance from the Bank of Canada.

(*Source:* Adapted from Bank of Canada, *Banking and Financial Statistics,* May 2018, Tables C3 and C4.)

with them for more than they pay their depositors in terms of interest and other services provided. They also earn profits through the wealth-management and investment services they provide to their customers.

Competition for deposits is active among commercial banks and between banks and other financial institutions. Interest paid on deposits, advertising, personal solicitation of accounts, giveaway programs for new deposits to existing accounts, and improved services are all forms of competition for funds.

Commercial Banks' Reserves

Commercial banks keep sufficient cash on hand to be able to meet depositors' day-to-day requirements for cash. As we saw earlier, they also keep deposits at the central bank, which can be readily converted into cash. However, just as the goldsmiths of long ago discovered that only a fraction of the gold they held was ever withdrawn at any given time, and just as banks of long ago discovered that only a small fraction of gold-convertible bank notes were actually converted, so too do modern bankers know that only a small fraction of their total deposits will be withdrawn in cash at any one time.

The reserves needed to ensure that depositors can withdraw their deposits whenever they like will normally be quite small.

In abnormal times, however, nothing short of 100 percent would do the job if the commercial banking system had to stand alone. If a major bank were to fail, it would probably cause a general loss of confidence in the ability of other banks to redeem their

AF archive/Alamy Stock Photo

bank run A situation in which many depositors rush to withdraw their money, possibly leading to a bank's financial collapse.

deposits. The results would then be devastating. Such an event—or even the rumour of it—could lead to a **bank run** as depositors rushed to withdraw their money. Faced with such a panic, banks would have to close until either they had borrowed enough funds or sold enough assets to meet the demand, or the demand subsided. However, banks could not instantly turn their loans into cash because the borrowers would have the money tied up in such things as real estate or business enterprises. Neither could the banks obtain cash by selling their securities to the public because payments to the bank would be made by cheques, which would not provide cash to pay off depositors.

The difficulty of providing sufficient reserves to meet abnormal situations is alleviated by the central bank, which can provide all the reserves that are needed to meet any abnormal situation. It can do this in two ways. First, it can lend reserves directly to commercial banks on the security of assets that are sound but not easy to liquidate quickly, such as interest-earning residential or commercial mortgages. Second, it can enter the open market and buy all the government securities that commercial banks need to sell in order to increase their available cash reserves. Once the public finds that deposits can be turned into cash at their request, any panic would usually subside and any further drain of cash out of commercial banks would cease.

The possibility of a bank run in Canada has been all but eliminated by the provision of deposit insurance by the Canada Deposit Insurance Corporation (CDIC), a federal Crown corporation. The CDIC guarantees that, in the unlikely event of a bank failure, depositors will get their money back, up to a limit of $100 000 per eligible deposit. Most depositors will not rush to withdraw all of their money as long as they are certain they can get it when they need it.

fractional-reserve system A banking system in which commercial banks keep only a fraction of their deposits in cash or on deposit with the central bank.

reserve ratio The fraction of its deposits that a commercial bank actually holds as reserves in the form of cash or deposits with the central bank.

target reserve ratio The fraction of its deposits that a commercial bank ideally wants to hold as reserves.

Target and Excess Reserves   Canada's banks hold reserves against their deposit liabilities for the simple reason that they want to avoid situations in which they cannot satisfy their depositors' demands for cash, and it is costly for them to borrow from other banks or from the Bank of Canada when they run short of reserves. Look again at Table 26-2. Notice that the chartered banks' reserves of $40 billion are 2.1 percent of their *deposit* liabilities of more than $1.8 trillion. Thus, if the holders of even 2.5 percent of deposits demanded cash, the banks would be unable to meet the demand without outside help. Reserves can be as low as they are because, first, banks know that it is very unlikely that even 2.5 percent of their total deposits will be withdrawn at any given time and, second, the banks know that the Bank of Canada will help them out in time of temporary need. The Canadian banking system is thus a **fractional-reserve system**, with commercial banks holding reserves—either as cash or as deposits at the Bank of Canada—of just a tiny fraction of their total deposits.

A bank's **reserve ratio** is the fraction of its deposits that it *actually* holds as reserves at any point in time, either as cash or as deposits with the Bank of Canada. A bank's **target reserve ratio** is the fraction of its deposits it would *ideally* like to hold as reserves. This target reserve ratio will generally not be constant over time. During holiday seasons, for example, banks may choose to hold more reserves because they know, based on past experience, that there will be heavy demands for cash.

The late Jimmy Stewart plays George Bailey in It's a Wonderful Life. *In this scene, Bailey, the owner of a small commercial bank, explains to his panicking customers why they can't all take their money out at the same time. It is a great illustration of the workings of a fractional-reserve banking system.*

At any given time, any commercial bank will probably not be exactly at its target level of reserves. Reserves may be slightly above or slightly below the target, but the commercial bank will take actions to gradually restore its actual reserves toward its target level. Any reserves in excess of the target level are called **excess reserves**. As we will see next, a bank can expand or contract its portfolio of loans to adjust its actual reserves toward its target level. Understanding this process is the key to understanding the "creation" of deposit money.

excess reserves Reserves held by a commercial bank in excess of its target reserves.

One final comment is in order, however, before we examine the process of money creation by the banking system. At the core of any commercial banking system lies both *confidence* and *risk*. Depositors need to have confidence that their money will be safely invested and available when they want it; banks need to recognize the risks involved in lending to households, businesses, and even governments. *Applying Economic Concepts 26-2* examines some of the key Canadian banking regulations designed to maintain confidence and manage risks.

APPLYING ECONOMIC CONCEPTS 26-2

Confidence and Risk in Canadian Banking

Commercial banks play a vital role as *intermediaries* in the credit market. They accept deposits from millions of households and firms who want to save, and then channel those funds to other firms and households who want to borrow. The business model for banks is actually quite simple: Pay a relatively low interest rate on deposits, charge a higher interest rate on loans, and the bank earns a profit based on the *spread* in interest rates.

At the core of the banking system lies both *confidence* and *risk*. The banks' depositors require confidence that they can access their funds when they want and that the bank will not collapse. Without such confidence, few would deposit their money in the bank, and without deposits the bank would not be able to make loans. The loans that the bank makes are inherently risky because firms and households may fail to repay what they owe.

Given the need to maintain confidence in an industry that is inherently about risk-taking, several government regulations apply to Canadian banks (and those in most other countries as well). Examples of such regulations are:

- All Canadian banks are members of the Canadian Deposit Insurance Corporation (CDIC). CDIC is a Crown corporation that uses fees paid by the member banks to provide insurance to depositors against the risk of bank failure. This insurance is central in providing individuals confidence that their deposits are safe (up to a limit of $100 000 per deposit.)
- Banks are limited in the amount of their assets (loans) that can be financed by customer deposits. Some fraction of their assets must be financed by the financial capital provided by the banks' owners; this is known as the bank's required *capital ratio*.

Such restrictions permit the banks' assets to fall in value by a modest amount (as occasionally happens) without leading to insolvency and failure.
- Banks that extend home mortgages to customers are required to purchase mortgage insurance if the value of the loan exceeds 80 percent of the value of the home (i.e., if the borrower's down payment is less than 20 percent). With such insurance, the bank is protected from loss in the event that the borrower defaults on the loan. The bank can purchase mortgage insurance from the Canada Mortgage and Housing Corporation (CMHC), a Crown corporation, or from private-sector insurers.

This is just a small sample of the many regulations that apply to Canadian banks. Given the nature of the industry it is not surprising that many regulations are aimed at promoting confidence and limiting the amount and nature of risks to which banks are exposed.

This aspect of Canadian bank regulation came to the attention of international observers during the global financial crisis of 2008–2009. While several large banks in other developed economies collapsed, and many others required significant government financial assistance in order to avoid collapse, no Canadian banks experienced equivalent strains. Some argue that Canadian bankers have traditionally been more prudent than bankers in other countries; others argue that Canada was just lucky. Most economists agree, however, that Canadian bank regulation prevented some of the extreme risk-taking behaviour that occurred elsewhere and was partly responsible for the better performance of the Canadian banking industry during this period.

26.3   Money Creation by the Banking System

We noted before that the *money supply* includes both currency and deposits at commercial banks. The fractional-reserve system provides the means by which commercial banks create new deposits and thus new money. The process is important for understanding monetary policy, so it is worth examining in some detail.

Some Simplifying Assumptions

To focus on the essential aspects of how commercial banks create money, suppose that banks can invest in only one kind of asset—loans—and they have only one kind of deposit. Two other assumptions are provisional and will be relaxed after we have developed some basic ideas about the creation of money:

1. *No excess reserves.* We assume that all banks choose to lend out any reserves in excess of their target reserves, which we assume are a fixed ratio of total deposits. In our numerical illustration, we will assume that the target reserve ratio is 20 percent (0.20); that is, for every $5 of deposits, the banks want to hold $1 in reserves, investing the rest in new loans.

2. *No cash drain from the banking system.* We also assume that the public holds a fixed absolute amount of the currency in circulation, whatever the level of their bank deposits. Later on we will assume that the amount of currency held by the public grows as total bank deposits grow. This is called a *cash drain*.

The Creation of Deposit Money

A hypothetical balance sheet, with assets and liabilities, is shown for TD Bank (TD) in Table 26-3. TD has assets of $200 of reserves, held partly as cash on hand and partly as deposits with the central bank, and $900 of loans outstanding to its customers. Its liabilities are $100 to investors (owners) who contributed financial capital to start the bank and $1000 to current depositors. The bank's ratio of reserves to deposits is 0.20 (200/1000), exactly equal to its target reserve ratio.

TABLE 26-3   The Initial Balance Sheet of TD

Assets ($)		Liabilities ($)	
Reserves (cash and deposits with the central bank)	200	Deposits	1000
Loans	900	Capital	100
	1100		1100

TD has reserves equal to 20 percent of its deposit liabilities. The commercial bank earns profits by finding profitable investments for much of the money deposited with it. In this balance sheet, loans are its income-earning assets.

What Is a New Deposit?   In what follows, we are interested in knowing how the commercial banking system can "create money" when it receives a new deposit. But what do we mean by a new deposit? By "new," we mean a deposit of cash that is new to the *commercial banking system*. There are three examples:

- First, an individual might immigrate to Canada and bring cash. When that cash is deposited into a commercial bank, it constitutes a new deposit to the Canadian banking system.
- Second, an individual who had some cash stashed under his bed (or in a safety deposit box) has now decided to deposit it into an account at a commercial bank.

- Third is the most interesting but also the most complicated example. If the Bank of Canada were to purchase a government security from an individual or from a firm, it would purchase that asset with a cheque drawn on the Bank of Canada. When the individual or firm deposits the cheque with a commercial bank, it would be a new deposit to the commercial banking system.

The important point to keep in mind here is that the *source* of the new deposit is irrelevant to the process of money creation by the commercial banks. In the discussion that follows, we use the example of the Bank of Canada buying government securities from firms or households as a way of generating a new deposit. But this is not crucial. We use this example because, as we will see in Chapter 28, this is how the Bank of Canada directly alters the level of reserves in the banking system when it chooses to do so. But the general process of money creation we are about to describe applies to *any* new deposit, whatever its source.

The Expansion of Money from a Single New Deposit Suppose the Bank of Canada enters the open market and buys $100 worth of Government of Canada bonds from John Smith. The Bank issues a cheque to Smith, who then deposits the $100 cheque into his account at TD. This $100 is a wholly new deposit for the commercial bank, and it results in a revised balance sheet (Table 26-4). As a result of the new deposit, TD's reserve assets and deposit liabilities have both increased by $100. More important, TD's ratio of reserves to deposits has increased from 0.20 to 0.27 (300/1100). The bank now has $80 in excess reserves; with $1100 in deposits, its target reserves are only $220.

TD can now lend the $80 in excess reserves that it is holding. As it lends the $80, it increases its loan portfolio by $80 but reduces its reserves by the same amount. Table 26-5 shows TD's balance sheet after this new loan is made. Notice that TD has restored its reserve ratio to 20 percent, its target reserve ratio.

So far, of the $100 initial deposited at TD, $20 is held by TD as reserves against the deposit and $80 has been lent out in the system. As a result, other banks have received new deposits of $80 stemming from the loans made by TD; persons receiving payment from those who borrowed the $80 from TD will have deposited those payments in their own banks.

The banks that receive deposits from the proceeds of TD's loan are called second-round banks, third-round banks, and so on. In this case, the second-round banks receive new deposits of $80, and when the cheques clear, they have new reserves of $80. Because they desire to hold only $16 in

TABLE 26-4 TD's Balance Sheet Immediately After a New Deposit of $100

Assets ($)		Liabilities ($)	
Reserves	300	Deposits	1100
Loans	900	Capital	100
	1200		1200

The new deposit raises liabilities and assets by the same amount. Because both reserves and deposits rise by $100, the bank's actual reserve ratio, formerly 0.20, increases to 0.27. The bank now has excess reserves of $80.

TABLE 26-5 TD's Balance Sheet After Making a New Loan of $80

Assets ($)		Liabilities ($)	
Reserves	220	Deposits	1100
Loans	980	Capital	100
	1200		1200

TD converts its excess cash reserves into new loans. The bank keeps $20 as a reserve against the initial new deposit of $100. It lends the remaining $80 to a customer, who writes a cheque to someone who deals with another bank. Comparing Table 26-3 and 26-5 shows that the bank has increased its deposit liabilities by the $100 initially deposited and has increased its assets by $20 of cash reserves and $80 of new loans. It has also restored its target reserve ratio of 0.20.

TABLE 26-6   Changes in the Balance Sheets of Second-Round Banks

Assets ($)		Liabilities ($)	
Reserves	+16	Deposits	+80
Loans	+64		
	+80		+80

Second-round banks receive cash deposits and expand loans. The second-round banks gain new deposits of $80 as a result of the loan granted by TD. These banks keep 20 percent of the cash that they acquire as their reserve against the new deposit, and they can make new loans using the other 80 percent.

TABLE 26-7   The Sequence of Loans and Deposits After a Single New Deposit of $100

Bank	New Deposits	New Loans	Addition to Reserves
TD	100.00	80.00	20.00
2nd-round bank	80.00	64.00	16.00
3rd-round bank	64.00	51.20	12.80
4th-round bank	51.20	40.96	10.24
5th-round bank	40.96	32.77	8.19
6th-round bank	32.77	26.22	6.55
7th-round bank	26.22	20.98	5.24
8th-round bank	20.98	16.78	4.20
9th-round bank	16.78	13.42	3.36
10th-round bank	13.42	10.74	2.68
Total for first 10 rounds	446.33	357.07	89.26
All remaining rounds	53.67	42.93	10.74
Total for banking system	500.00	400.00	100.00

The banking system as a whole can create deposit money whenever it receives new deposits. The table shows the process of the creation of deposit money on the assumptions that all the loans made by one set of banks end up as deposits in another set of banks (the next-round banks), that the target reserve ratio (*v*) is 0.20, and that banks always lend out any excess reserves. With no cash drain to the public, the banking system as a whole eventually increases deposits by 1/*v*, which, in this example, is five times the amount of any increase in reserves that it obtains.

additional reserves to support the new deposits, they have $64 of excess reserves. They now increase their loans by $64. After this money has been spent by the borrowers and has been deposited in other, third-round banks, the balance sheets of the second-round banks will have changed, as in Table 26-6.

The third-round banks now find themselves with $64 of new deposits. Against these they want to hold only $12.80 as reserves, so they have excess reserves of $51.20 that they can immediately lend out. Thus, there begins a long sequence of new deposits, new loans, new deposits, and new loans. These stages are shown in Table 26-7.

The new deposit of $100 to the banking system has led, through the banks' desire to lend their excess reserves, to the creation of new money. After the completion of the process depicted in Table 26-7, the total change in the combined balance sheets of the entire banking system is shown in Table 26-8.

> If *v* is the target reserve ratio, a new deposit to the banking system will increase the total amount of deposits by 1/*v* times the new deposit. [34]

In our example, where *v* = 0.2 and the new deposit equals $100, total deposits in the banking system will eventually increase by (1/0.2) times $100—that is, by $500. In our example in which there was an initial new deposit of $100, this $100 was also the amount by which reserves increased in the banking system as a whole. This is because the entire amount of new cash eventually ends up in reserves held against a much larger volume of new deposits. Identifying a new deposit as the change in reserves in the banking system permits us to state our central result slightly differently.

> With no cash drain from the banking system, a banking system with a target reserve ratio of *v* can change its deposits by 1/*v* times any change in reserves.

Recalling that the Greek letter delta (Δ) means "the change in," we can express this result in a simple equation:

$$\Delta \text{ Deposits} = \frac{\text{New cash deposit}}{v} = \frac{\Delta \text{ Reserves}}{v}$$

The "multiple expansion of deposits" that we have just described applies in reverse to a withdrawal of funds. Deposits of the banking system will fall by $1/v$ times the amount withdrawn from the banking system creating a "multiple contraction of deposits."

Excess Reserves and Cash Drains

The two simplifying assumptions that were made earlier can now be relaxed.

Excess Reserves If banks choose to not lend their excess reserves, the multiple expansion that we discussed will not occur. Go back to Table 26-4. If TD had been content to hold 27 percent of its deposits in reserves, it would have done nothing more. Other things being equal, banks will choose to lend their excess reserves because of the profit motive, but there may be times when they believe that the risk is too great. It is one thing to be offered a good rate of interest on a loan, but if the borrower defaults on the payment of interest and principal, the bank will be the loser. Similarly, if the bank expects interest rates to rise in the future, it may hold off making loans now so that it will have reserves available to make more profitable loans after the interest rate has risen.

> Deposit creation does not happen automatically; it depends on the decisions of bankers. If commercial banks do not choose to lend their excess reserves, there will not be a multiple expansion of deposits.

Recall that we have said that the money supply includes both currency and bank deposits. What we have just seen is that the behaviour of commercial banks is crucial to the process of deposit creation. It follows that the money supply is partly determined by the commercial banks—in response, for example, to changes in national income, interest rates, and expectations of future business conditions.

Cash Drain Until now, we have been assuming that the public holds a fixed amount of cash, so that when deposits were multiplying in the economy, there was no change in the amount of cash held by the public. But now suppose that instead of holding a fixed *number* of dollars, people decide to hold an amount of cash equal to a fixed *fraction* of their bank deposits. An extra $100 that now gets injected into the banking system as a new cash deposit will not all stay in the banking system. As the amount of deposits multiplies, some fraction of those deposits will be added to the cash held by the public. In such a situation, any multiple expansion of bank deposits will be accompanied by what is called a *cash drain* to the public. This cash drain will reduce the multiple expansion of bank deposits in exactly the same way that taxes and imports reduced the value of the simple multiplier in Chapter 22.

In the case of a cash drain, the relationship between the eventual change in deposits and a new injection of cash into the banking system is slightly more complicated. If new cash is injected into the system, it will ultimately show up either as reserves or as cash

TABLE 26-8 Change in the Combined Balance Sheets of All the Banks in the System Following the Multiple Expansion of Deposits

Assets ($)		Liabilities ($)	
Reserves	+100	Deposits	+500
Loans	+400		
	+500		+500

The reserve ratio is returned to 0.20. The entire initial deposit of $100 ends up as additional reserves of the banking system. Therefore, deposits rise by (1/0.2) times the initial deposit—that is, by $500.

held by the public. If c is the ratio of cash to deposits that people want to maintain, the final change in deposits will be given by

$$\Delta \text{ Deposits} = \frac{\text{New cash deposit}}{c + v}$$

For example, suppose again the Bank of Canada were to purchase $100 of government securities from John Smith. As Smith deposits the $100 into his bank account, there is an injection of $100 into the banking system. If commercial banks' target reserve ratio is 20 percent and there is *no* cash drain, the eventual expansion of deposits will be $500 ($\Delta$ Deposits = $100/0.20). But if there is a cash drain of 10 percent, the eventual expansion of deposits will only be $333.33 ($\Delta$ Deposits = $100/(0.10 + 0.20)). [35]

> **The larger is the cash drain from the banking system, the smaller will be the total expansion of deposits created by a new cash deposit.**

Realistic Expansion of Deposits   We have explained the expansion of deposits in the banking system by using reserve-deposit and cash-deposit ratios that are easy to work with but unrealistic for Canada. In particular, we have been assuming a reserve-deposit ratio (v) equal to 20 percent, whereas Table 26-2 shows that Canadian commercial banks hold reserves equal to *roughly 2 percent* of their deposit liabilities. A realistic value for the cash-deposit ratio in Canada is roughly 5 percent—indicating that firms and households hold cash outside the banks equal to 5 percent of the value of their bank deposits. Putting these more realistic values for v and c into our equation, we see that a $100 cash injection (new deposit) to the banking system will eventually lead to a total change in deposits equal to:

$$\frac{\$100}{(c + v)} = \frac{\$100}{(0.02 + 0.05)} = \frac{\$100}{(0.07)} = \$1428.57$$

Therefore, small changes in the amount of cash can lead, through the commercial banks' process of deposit creation, to very large changes in the total level of deposits. Commercial banks really do create a lot of (deposit) money out of thin air!

▎26.4 The Money Supply

Several times in this chapter we have mentioned the *money supply* without ever defining it precisely. But now that you are familiar with the balance sheets of the Bank of Canada and the commercial banking system, and are comfortable with the idea of deposit creation by the commercial banks, we are ready to be more precise about what we mean by the money supply.

money supply The total quantity of money in an economy at a point in time. Also called the *supply of money*.

The total stock of money in the economy at any moment is called the **money supply** or the *supply of money*. Economists use several alternative definitions for the money supply. Each definition includes the amount of currency in circulation *plus* some types of deposit liabilities of the financial institutions.

Money supply = Currency + Bank deposits

The various definitions differ only by which deposit liabilities are included. We begin by looking at the different kinds of deposits.

Kinds of Deposits

Over the past several decades banks have evolved a bewildering array of deposit options. From our point of view, the most important distinction is between deposits that can be readily transferred by cheque, online banking, automatic transfer, or debit card, and those that cannot be so easily transferred. The deposits that are easily transferred are media of exchange; the second type are not.

For many years, the distinction lay between *demand deposits*, which earned little or no interest but were transferable on demand (by cheque), and *savings deposits*, which earned a higher interest return but were not easily transferable. Today, however, it is so easy to transfer funds between almost all accounts that the distinction is almost meaningless. The deposit that is genuinely tied up for a period of time now takes the form of a **term deposit**, which has a specified withdrawal date a minimum of 30 days into the future, and which pays a much reduced interest rate in the event of early withdrawal. Term and other "notice" deposits pay significantly higher interest rates than do regular bank deposits.

term deposit An interest-earning bank deposit, subject to notice before withdrawal. Also called a *notice deposit*.

Non-bank financial institutions, such as asset-management firms, now offer *money-market mutual funds* and *money-market deposit accounts*. These accounts earn higher interest and are chequable, although some are subject to minimum withdrawal restrictions and others to prior notice of withdrawal.

> **The long-standing distinction between money and other highly liquid assets used to be that, narrowly defined, money was a medium of exchange that did not earn interest, whereas other liquid assets earned interest but were not media of exchange. Today, this distinction has almost completely disappeared.**

Definitions of the Money Supply

Different definitions of the money supply include different types of deposits. Until recently, a common definition of the money supply used by the Bank of Canada was called M1, which included currency in circulation plus demand (chequable) deposits held at the chartered banks. But M1 did not include similar deposits at other financial institutions or any non-chequable term or notice deposits. With the changing nature of deposits, it is now more common to use broader measures of the money supply. Two commonly used measures in Canada today are M2 and M2+. **M2** includes currency in circulation plus demand and notice deposits at the chartered banks; **M2+** includes M2 plus similar deposits at other financial institutions (trust and mortgage-loan companies, credit unions and caisses populaires) and holdings of money-market mutual funds. Table 26-9 shows the composition of M2 and M2+ in Canada as of February 2018.

M2 Currency plus demand and notice deposits at the chartered banks.

M2+ M2 plus similar deposits at other financial institutions.

The Bank of Canada computes other measures of the money supply even broader than M2+. These are referred to as M2++, M3, and so on, where each measure is broader than the previous one, meaning that it includes more types of financial assets. For example, M2++ includes M2+ plus holdings of Canada Savings Bonds and non-money-market funds. In general, the broader the measure of the money supply, the more the concept of money being measured includes assets that do not serve as a direct medium of exchange but do serve the store-of-value function and can be converted into a medium of exchange.

TABLE 26-9 M2 and M2+ in Canada, February 2018 (millions of dollars)

Currency	82 697
Demand Deposits (chequable)	
Personal	286 386
Non-personal	497 454
Notice Deposits (non-chequable)	
Personal	670 418
Non-personal	53 481
Adjustment	−4 453
M2	**1 585 983**
Deposits at:	
Trust and mortgage-loan companies	18 400
Credit unions and caisses populaires	311 925
Money-market mutual funds	22 321
Other	53 007
M2+	**1 991 636**

M2 and M2+ are two commonly used measures of the money supply in Canada. M2 includes demand (chequable) and notice (non-chequable) deposits at the chartered banks; M2+ adds similar deposits at other financial institutions. These deposits all serve the medium-of-exchange function of money. Still broader measures (like M2++ and M3) include financial assets that best serve the store-of-value function but can readily be converted into a medium of exchange.

(*Source*: Adapted from Bank of Canada, *Weekly Financial Statistics*, May 2018.)

near money Liquid assets that are easily convertible into money without risk of significant loss of value. They can be used as short-term stores of value but are not themselves media of exchange.

money substitute Something that serves as a medium of exchange but is not a store of value.

Near Money and Money Substitutes

Recall our early discussion of money as a medium of exchange and as a store of value. In arriving at empirical measures of money, we must consider some assets that do not perform one or both of these roles perfectly. This brings us to the concepts of *near money* and *money substitutes*.

Assets that adequately fulfill the store-of-value function and are readily converted into a medium of exchange but are not themselves a medium of exchange are sometimes called **near money**. Term deposits are a good example of near money. When you have a term deposit, you know exactly how much purchasing power you hold and, given modern banking practices, you can turn your deposit into a medium of exchange—cash or a demand deposit—at a moment's notice (though you may pay a penalty in the form of reduced interest if you withdraw the funds before the end of the specified term).

So why doesn't everyone keep his or her money in such deposits instead of in demand deposits or currency? The answer is that the inconvenience of continually shifting money back and forth may outweigh the interest that can be earned. One week's interest on $100 (at 5 percent per year) is only about 10 cents, and not worth the hassle for most people. For money that will be needed soon, it would hardly pay to shift it to a term deposit.

Things that serve as media of exchange but are not a store of value are sometimes called **money substitutes**. Credit cards are a prime example. With a credit card, many transactions can be made without either cash, a debit card, or a cheque. The credit card serves the short-run function of a medium of exchange by allowing you to make purchases, even though you have no cash or bank deposit currently in your possession. But this is only temporary; money remains the final medium of exchange for these transactions when the credit-card bill is paid.

The Role of the Bank of Canada

In this chapter, we have seen that the commercial banking system, when presented with a new deposit, can create a multiple expansion of bank deposits. This shows how the reserves of the banking system are systematically related to the money supply. In Chapter 28 we will see the details of how the Bank of Canada conducts its monetary policy and how its actions influence the total amount of reserves in the banking system. At that point we will have a more complete picture of the connection among the Bank's monetary policy, reserves in the banking system, and the overall money supply.

Recall that in the previous chapter we examined how in the long run, with real GDP equal to Y^*, the real interest rate was determined by desired saving and desired investment. In the next chapter, we return to the short-run version of our macro model (in which real GDP is not assumed to equal Y^*) but add money to that model explicitly. There we will see how the interaction of money demand and money supply determines the equilibrium interest rate in the short run. We will also see how changes in the money market lead to changes in desired aggregate expenditure and real GDP. In Chapter 28 we examine the details of the Bank of Canada's monetary policy, with an emphasis on its current policy regime of *inflation targeting*.

SUMMARY

26.1 The Nature of Money

LO 1

- Money is anything that serves as a medium of exchange, a store of value, and a unit of account.
- Money arose because of the inconvenience of barter, and it developed in stages: from precious metal to metal coinage, to paper money convertible to precious metals, to token coinage and paper money fractionally backed by precious metals, to fiat money, and to deposit money.

26.2 The Canadian Banking System

LO 2

- The banking system in Canada consists of two main elements: the Bank of Canada (the central bank) and the commercial banks.
- The Bank of Canada is a government-owned corporation that is responsible for the day-to-day conduct of monetary policy. Though the Bank has considerable autonomy in its policy decisions, ultimate responsibility for monetary policy resides with the government.
- Commercial banks and other financial institutions play a key role as intermediaries in the credit market.

- Significant interruptions in the flow of credit usually lead to increases in interest rates and reductions in the level of economic activity.
- Commercial banks are profit-seeking institutions that allow their customers to transfer deposits from one bank to another by means of cheques or electronic transfer. They create deposit money as a by-product of their commercial operations of making loans and other investments.

26.3 Money Creation by the Banking System

LO 3

- Because most customers are content to pay by cheque or debit card rather than with cash, banks need only small reserves to back their deposit liabilities. It is this *fractional-reserve aspect* of the banking system that enables commercial banks to create deposit money.
- When the banking system receives a new cash deposit, it can create new deposits equal to some multiple of this amount. For a target reserve ratio of v and a cash-deposit ratio of c, the total change in deposits following a new cash deposit is

$$\Delta \text{ Deposits} = \frac{\text{New cash deposit}}{c + v}$$

26.4 The Money Supply

LO 4

- The money supply—the stock of money in an economy at a specific moment—can be defined in various ways. M2 includes currency plus demand and notice deposits at the chartered banks. M2+ includes M2 plus deposits at non-bank financial institutions and money-market mutual funds.

- Near money includes interest-earning assets that are convertible into money on a dollar-for-dollar basis but that are not currently a medium of exchange. Money substitutes are things such as credit cards that serve as a medium of exchange but are not money.

KEY CONCEPTS

Medium of exchange, store of value, and unit of account

Fully backed, fractionally backed, and fiat money

The banking system and the Bank of Canada

Target reserve ratio and excess reserves

The creation of deposit money

Demand and term deposits

The money supply

Near money and money substitutes

STUDY EXERCISES

MyLab Economics Make the grade with MyLab Economics™: All Study Exercises can be found on MyLab Economics™. You can practise them as often as you want, and many feature step-by-step guided instructions to help you find the right answer.

FILL-IN-THE-BLANK

1 Fill in the blanks to make the following statements correct.

a. Money serves three functions: _____, _____, and _____.

b. Suppose children at a summer camp are each given a credit of $20 at the snack shop, where purchases are recorded but no cash is exchanged. This is an example of money as a(n) _____ and a(n) _____.

c. Paper money and coins that are not convertible into anything with intrinsic value, but are declared by the government to be legal tender, are known as _____.

d. The Bank of Canada has three main functions in the Canadian economy:
   • _____
   • _____
   • _____

e. Canada has a(n) _____ reserve banking system, in which commercial banks keep only a fraction of their total deposits in reserves. A commercial bank has a(n) _____ ratio that governs what it attempts to keep as reserves.

2 Fill in the blanks to make the following statements correct. Answer these questions in the sequence given.

a. Suppose the Bank of Canada purchases a $1000 bond from Bob's Financial Firm, and Bob's deposits its cheque at the CIBC. This is a(n) _____ deposit to the banking system and will allow the commercial banks to _____.

b. Continuing on from part (a), if the CIBC has a target reserve ratio of 5 percent, it will keep _____ dollars as reserves and will lend _____ dollars.

c. Assuming there is no cash drain from the banking system, the ultimate effect is a(n) _____ in deposits in the banking system of _____ × $1000 = _____.

d. Suppose the Bank of Canada sells a $1000 bond to Bob's Financial Firm, and Bob's pays for that bond with a cheque drawn on its account at the CIBC. This is a(n) _____ of funds from the banking system and will cause the commercial banks to _____.

e. If the CIBC pays the $1000 from its reserves, its reserve ratio will then be _____ its target rate of 5 percent. If CIBC keeps its reserves at the new level, its deposits must fall by an additional _____ to restore the 5 percent target reserve ratio.

3 Fill in the blanks to make the following statements correct.

a. There are multiple measures of the money supply in Canada because, in addition to currency in circulation, there are many different types of bank _____.

b. The distinctions in the measures of the money supply generally reflect the different ability to convert funds from the deposit into _____.

c. The most general definition of the money supply is the sum of _____ and _____.

d. A term deposit at a bank does not fulfill the _____ role of money. However, it can be easily converted into a deposit that does fulfill this role. For this reason, a term deposit is referred to as _____.

e. A credit card can serve as a medium of exchange, but it is not a _____. For this reason, credit cards are referred to as a _____.

REVIEW

4 Which of the following items can be considered money in the Canadian economy? Explain your answers by discussing the three functions of money—medium of exchange, store of value, and unit of account.

  a. A Canadian $100 bill
  b. A Visa credit card
  c. A well-known painting by Robert Bateman
  d. The balance in an interest-earning savings account
  e. A U.S. Treasury bill payable in three months
  f. A share of Canadian Tire stock
  g. A $1 bill of Canadian Tire money

5 Suppose that on January 1, 2017, a household had $300 000, which it wanted to hold for use one year later. Calculate, by using resources available online or in your university library, which of the following would have been the best store of value over that period.

  a. The (Canadian) dollar
  b. Stocks whose prices moved with the Toronto Stock Exchange (S&P/TSX) index
  c. A Government of Canada 5.75 percent bond coming due in 2029
  d. Gold
  e. A house whose value changed with the average house price in Canada

6 During 2011, after the worst of the global financial crisis was over, the governor of the Bank of Canada expressed concern that the commercial banks were still "hoarding" cash rather than extending a more appropriate volume of loans. Why might the banks do this, and what is the implication for the money supply?

PROBLEMS

7 Sunshine Bank has the following list of entries on its balance sheet. All figures are in millions of dollars.

Mortgage loans	2100
Cash reserves	630
Shareholders' equity	600
Foreign currency reserves	6000
Government deposits	180
Deposits at the Bank of Canada	150
Demand deposits	4500
Notice (term) deposits	3600

  a. Draw the balance sheet for Sunshine Bank and record the entries appropriately in the asset or liability column.
  b. What are total assets and liabilities for this commercial bank?
  c. What is the bank's actual reserve ratio?

8 The table below shows the balance sheet for the Regal Bank, a hypothetical commercial bank. Assume that the Regal Bank has achieved its target reserve ratio.

Balance Sheet: Regal Bank			
Assets		Liabilities	
Reserves	$200	Deposits	$4000
Loans	$4200	Capital	$400

  a. What is the Regal Bank's target reserve ratio?
  b. What is the value of the owners' investment in the bank?
  c. Suppose someone makes a new deposit to the Regal Bank of $100. Draw a new balance sheet showing the *immediate* effect of the new deposit. What is the Regal Bank's new reserve ratio?
  d. Suppose instead that someone *withdraws* $100 cash from the Regal Bank. Show the new balance sheet and the new reserve ratio.

9 Consider a new deposit to the Canadian banking system of $1000. Suppose all commercial banks have a target reserve ratio of 10 percent and there is no cash drain. The following table shows how deposits, reserves, and loans change as the new deposit permits the banks to "create" money.

Round	Δ Deposits	Δ Reserves	Δ Loans
First	$1000	$100	$900
Second	——	——	——
Third	——	——	——
Fourth	——	——	——
Fifth	——	——	——

  a. The first round has been completed in the table. Now, recalling that the new loans in the first round become the new deposits in the second round, complete the second round in the table.
  b. By using the same approach, complete the entire table.
  c. You have now completed the first five rounds of the deposit-creation process. What is the total change in deposits *so far* as a result of the single new deposit of $1000?
  d. This deposit-creation process could go on forever, but it would still have a *finite* sum. In the text, we showed that the eventual total change in deposits is equal to $1/v$ times the new deposit, where v is the target reserve ratio. What is the eventual total change in deposits in this case?
  e. What is the eventual total change in reserves? What is the eventual change in loans?

⑩ Consider a withdrawal of $5000 from the Canadian banking system. Suppose all commercial banks have a target reserve ratio of 8 percent and there is no cash drain.

  a. Using a table like that shown in the previous question, show the change in deposits, reserves, and loans for the first three "rounds" of activity.
  b. Compute the eventual total change in deposits, reserves, and loans.

⑪ Consider an individual who immigrates to Canada and deposits $3000 in Canadian currency into the Canadian banking system. Suppose all commercial banks have a target reserve ratio of 10 percent and individuals choose to hold cash equal to 10 percent of their bank deposits.

  a. In the text, we showed that the eventual total change in deposits is equal to $1/(v + c)$ times the new deposit, where v is the target reserve ratio and c is the ratio of cash to deposits. What is the eventual total change in deposits in this case?
  b. What is the eventual total change in reserves?
  c. What is the eventual total change in loans?

⑫ Consider an individual who moves to Canada and brings with him $40 000 in Canadian currency, which he deposits in a Canadian bank. For each of the cases below, compute the overall change in deposits and reserves in the Canadian banking system as a result of this new deposit.

  a. 10 percent target reserve ratio, no cash drain, no excess reserves
  b. 10 percent target reserve ratio, 5 percent cash drain, no excess reserves
  c. 10 percent target reserve ratio, 5 percent cash drain, 5 percent excess reserves

⑬ This question is intended to illustrate the similarity between the simple income-expenditure multiplier from Chapters 21 and 22 and the deposit multiplier that we examined in this chapter.

  a. Recalling the macro model of Chapters 21 and 22, suppose the marginal propensity to spend out of GDP, z, is 0.6. If autonomous spending increases by

$1000, fill in the table below. (Hint: You might want to re-read *Applying Economic Concepts 21-1*.)

Round	ΔAE	ΔY
First	$1000	$1000
Second	——	——
Third	——	——
Fourth	——	——
Fifth	——	——

  b. The sum of the values in the third column should be

$$\Delta Y = \$1000 + z\,\$1000$$
$$+ z^2\,\$1000 + z^3\,\$1000 + \ldots$$

What is the total change in GDP (after an infinite number of rounds)?

  c. Now consider the process of deposit creation from this chapter. Consider a new deposit of $1000 and a target reserve ratio, v, of 0.25 (with no cash drain). Fill in the following table:

Round	Δ Deposits	Δ Reserves	Δ Loans
First	$1000	$250	$750
Second	——	——	——
Third	——	——	——
Fourth	——	——	——
Fifth	——	——	——

  d. The sum of the values in the first column should be

$$\Delta \text{ Deposits} = \$1000 + (1 - v)\$1000 +$$
$$(1 - v)^2\,\$1000 + (1 - v)^3\,\$1000 + \ldots$$

What is the total change in deposits (after an infinite number of rounds)?

  e. Explain why taxes and imports for the simple multiplier in Chapter 21 are similar to a reserve ratio for the deposit multiplier in this chapter.

27 Money, Interest Rates, and Economic Activity

CHAPTER OUTLINE	LEARNING OBJECTIVES (LO)
	After studying this chapter you will be able to
27.1 UNDERSTANDING BONDS	**1** explain why the price of a bond is inversely related to the market interest rate.
27.2 THE THEORY OF MONEY DEMAND	**2** describe how the demand for money depends on the interest rate, the price level, and real GDP.
27.3 HOW MONEY AFFECTS AGGREGATE DEMAND	**3** explain how monetary equilibrium determines the interest rate in the short run.
	4 describe the monetary transmission mechanism.
27.4 THE STRENGTH OF MONETARY FORCES	**5** understand the difference between the short-run and long-run effects of changes in the money supply.
	6 describe the conditions under which changes in the money supply are most effective in the short run.

IN Chapter 26, we learned how the commercial banking system multiplies a given amount of reserves into deposit money and thus influences the nation's money supply. We also learned that because the Bank of Canada can influence the amount of commercial-bank reserves, it too has an influence on the money supply. What we have not yet discussed, however, is *how* the Bank influences the amount of reserves. We will leave that discussion until the next chapter, when we examine Canadian monetary policy. For now, just think of the nation's money supply as being determined jointly by the actions of the Bank of Canada and the commercial banking system.

In this chapter, we will look at the important role money plays in the economy. Developing a theory to explain how money affects interest rates, real GDP, and the price level requires a few steps. First, understanding the role of money requires an understanding of the interaction of money supply and money demand. To examine the nature of money demand, we begin by examining how households decide to divide their total holdings of assets between money and bonds (which here are any interest-earning assets). Once that is done, we put money supply and money demand together to examine *monetary equilibrium*. Only then can we ask how changes in the supply of money or in the demand for money affect the economy in the short run—interest rates, real GDP, and the price level. We begin with a discussion of the relationship between bond prices and interest rates.

▌ 27.1 Understanding Bonds

At any moment, households and businesses have a stock of financial wealth that they hold in several forms. Some of it is money in the bank or cash in a wallet or vault. Some may be in *Treasury bills* and *bonds*, which are IOUs issued by the government or corporations. Some may be in *equity*, meaning ownership shares of a company.

To simplify our discussion, we will group financial wealth into just two categories, which we call "money" and "bonds." By money we mean all assets that serve as a medium of exchange—that is, paper money, coins, and bank deposits that can be transferred on demand by cheque or electronic means. By bonds we mean all other forms of financial wealth; this includes interest-earning financial assets and claims on real capital (equity). This simplification is useful because it emphasizes the important distinction between interest-earning and non-interest-earning assets, a distinction that is central for understanding the demand for money.

Before discussing how individuals and businesses decide to divide their assets between money and bonds, we need to make sure we understand what bonds are and how they are priced. This requires an understanding of *present value*.

Economists often simplify the analysis of financial assets by considering only two types of assets—non-interest-bearing "money" and interest-bearing "bonds."

Present Value and the Interest Rate

present value (PV) The value now of one or more payments or receipts made in the future; often referred to as *discounted present value*.

A bond is a financial asset that promises to make one or more payments at specified dates in the future. The **present value** (*PV*) of any asset refers to the value now of the future payments that the asset offers. Present value depends on the market interest rate because when we calculate present value, the interest rate is used to *discount* the value of the future payments to obtain their *present* value. Let's consider two examples to illustrate the concept of present value.

A Single Payment One Year Hence We start with the simplest case. What is the value *now* of a bond that will return a single payment of $100 in one year's time?

Suppose the market interest rate is 5 percent. Now ask how much you would have to lend out at that interest rate today in order to have $100 a year from now. If we use *PV* to stand for this unknown amount, we can write $PV \times (1.05) = \$100$. Thus, $PV = \$100/1.05 = \$95.24$.[1] This tells us that the present value of $100 receivable in one year's time is $95.24; if you lend out $95.24 for one year at 5 percent interest you

---

[1] Notice that in this type of formula, the interest rate is expressed as a decimal fraction where, for example, 5 percent is expressed as 0.05, so $1 + i = 1.05$.

will get back the original $95.24 that you lent (the principal) plus $4.76 in interest, which makes $100.

We can generalize this relationship with a simple equation. If R_1 is the amount we receive one year from now and i is the annual interest rate, the present value of R_1 is

$$PV = \frac{R_1}{1 + i}$$

If the interest rate is 7 percent ($i = 0.07$) and the bond pays $100 in one year ($R_1 = \$100$), the present value of that bond is $PV = \$100/1.07 = \$93.46$. Notice that, when compared with the previous numerical example, the higher market interest rate leads to a lower present value. The future payment of $100 gets discounted at a higher rate and so is worth less at the present time.

A Sequence of Future Payments   Now consider a more complicated case, but one that is actually more typical. Many bonds promise to make "coupon" payments every year and then return the face value of the bond at the end of the term of the loan. For example, imagine a three-year bond that promises to repay the face value of $1000 in three years, but will also pay a 10 percent coupon payment of $100 at the end of each of the three years that the bond is held. How much is this bond worth now? We can compute the present value of this bond by adding together the present values of each of the payments. If the market interest rate is 7 percent, the present value of this bond is

$$PV = \frac{\$100}{1.07} + \frac{\$100}{(1.07)^2} + \frac{\$1100}{(1.07)^3}$$

The first term is the value today of receiving $100 one year from now. The second term is the value today of receiving the second $100 payment two years from now. Note that we discount this second payment twice—once from Year 2 to Year 1, and once again from Year 1 to now—and thus the denominator shows an interest rate of 7 percent *compounded* for two years. Finally, the third term shows the value today of the $1100 repayment ($1000 of face value plus $100 of coupon payment) three years from now. The present value of this bond is

$$PV = \$93.46 + \$87.34 + \$897.93$$
$$= \$1078.73$$

In general, any asset that promises to make a sequence of payments for T periods into the future of $R_1, R_2, \ldots$, and so on, up to R_T has a present value given by

$$PV = \frac{R_1}{1 + i} + \frac{R_2}{(1 + i)^2} + \cdots + \frac{R_T}{(1 + i)^T}$$

It is useful to try another example. Let's continue with the case in which the bond repays its face value of $1000 three years from now and makes three $100 coupon payments at the end of each year the bond is held. But this time we assume the market interest rate is 9 percent. In this case, the present value of the bond is

$$PV = \frac{\$100}{1.09} + \frac{\$100}{(1.09)^2} + \frac{\$1100}{(1.09)^3}$$
$$= \$91.74 + \$84.17 + \$849.40$$
$$= \$1025.31$$

Notice that when the market interest rate is 9 percent, the present value of the bond is lower than the present value of the same bond when the market interest rate is 7 percent. The higher interest rate implies that any future payments are discounted at a higher rate and thus have a lower present value.

A General Relationship   There are many types of bonds. Some make no coupon payments and only a single payment (the "face value") at some point in the future. This is the case for short-term government bonds called *Treasury bills*. Other bonds, typically longer-term government or corporate bonds, make regular coupon payments as well as a final payment of the bond's face value. Though there are many types of bonds, they all have one thing in common: They promise to make some payment or sequence of payments in the future. Because bonds make payments in the future, their present value is negatively related to the market interest rate.

> **The present value of any bond that promises one or more future payments is negatively related to the market interest rate.**

Present Value and Market Price

Even well after they are first issued by the original borrower, most bonds are traded in financial markets in which there are large numbers of both buyers and sellers. The present value of a bond is important because it establishes the price at which a bond will be exchanged in the financial markets.

> **The present value of a bond is the most someone would be willing to pay now to own the bond's future stream of payments.[2]**

To understand this concept, let us return to our example of a bond that promises to pay $100 one year from now. When the interest rate is 5 percent, the present value of this bond is $95.24. To see why this is the maximum that anyone would pay for this bond, suppose that some sellers offer to sell the bond at some other price, say, $98. If, instead of paying this amount for the bond, a potential buyer lends $98 out at 5 percent interest, he or she would have at the end of one year more than the $100 that the bond will produce. (At 5 percent interest, $98 yields $4.90 in interest, which when added to the principal makes $102.90.) Clearly, no well-informed individual would pay $98—or, by the same reasoning, any sum in excess of $95.24—for the bond. Thus, at any price above the bond's present value, the lack of demand for that bond will cause its price to fall.

Now suppose the bond is offered for sale at a price less than $95.24, say, $90. A potential buyer could borrow $90 to buy the bond and at an interest rate of 5 percent would pay $4.50 in interest on the loan. At the end of the year, the bond yields $100. When this is used to repay the $90 loan and the $4.50 in interest, $5.50 is left as profit. Clearly, it would be worthwhile for someone to buy the bond at the price of $90 or, by

---

[2] We ignore for now the possibility that the issuer of the bond will default and thereby fail to make some or all of the future payments. If such a risk does exist, it will reduce the expected present value of the bond and thus reduce the price that buyers will be prepared to pay. We address bond riskiness shortly.

the same argument, at any price less than $95.24. Thus, at any price below the bond's present value, the abundance of demand for that bond will cause its price to rise.

This discussion should make clear that the present value of an asset determines its equilibrium market price. If the market price of any asset is greater than the present value of its income stream, no one will want to buy it, and the resulting excess supply will push down the market price. If the market price is below its present value, there will be a rush to buy it, and the resulting excess demand will push up the market price. When the bond's market price is exactly equal to its present value, there is no pressure for the price to change.

The equilibrium market price of any bond is determined by the present value of the income stream that it produces.

Interest Rates, Bond Prices, and Bond Yields

We now have two relationships that can be put together to tell us about the link between the market interest rate and bond prices. Let's restate these two relationships:

1. The present value of any given bond is negatively related to the market interest rate.

2. A bond's equilibrium market price will be equal to its present value.

Putting these two relationships together, we come to a key relationship:

An increase in the market interest rate leads to a fall in the price of any given bond. A decrease in the market interest rate leads to an increase in the price of any given bond.

Remember that a bond is a financial investment for the purchaser. The cost of the investment is the price of the bond, and the return on the investment is the sequence of future payments. Thus, for a given sequence of future payments, a lower bond price implies a higher rate of return on the bond, or a higher *bond yield*.[3]

To illustrate the yield on a bond, consider a simple example of a bond that promises to pay $1000 two years from now. If you purchase this bond for $857.34, your return on your investment will be 8 percent per year because $857.34 compounded for two years at 8 percent will yield $1000 in two years.

$$\$857.34 \times (1.08)^2 = \$1000$$

In other words, your yield on the bond will be 8 percent per year.

Notice that we are making a distinction between the concept of the *yield* on a bond and the *market interest rate*. The yield on any specific bond is a function of that bond's sequence of payments and its purchase price. The market interest rate is the rate at which you can borrow or lend money in the credit market.

---

[3] Note the important distinction between a bond's *coupon rate* and its *yield*. The former is an explicit and unchanging characteristic of any given bond; it is the fraction of the bond's face value the purchaser receives in regular payments. The latter is the overall rate of return a purchaser earns by buying the bond and holding it to maturity. The yield is inversely related to the bond's purchase price, which adjusts in response to changes in the market interest rate.

Although they are logically distinct from each other, there is a close relationship between the market interest rate and bond yields. A rise in the market interest rate will lead to a decline in the present value of any bond and thus to a decline in its equilibrium price. As the bond price falls, its yield naturally rises. Thus, we see that market interest rates and bond yields tend to move in the same direction.

> An increase in the market interest rate will reduce bond prices and increase bond yields. A reduction in the market interest rate will increase bond prices and reduce bond yields. Therefore, market interest rates and bond yields tend to move together.

Because of this close relationship between bond yields and market interest rates, economists discussing the role of money in the macroeconomy typically refer to "the" interest rate—or perhaps to "interest rates" in general—rather than to any specific interest rate among the many different rates corresponding to the many different financial assets. Since these rates all tend to rise or fall together, it is a very useful simplification to refer only to "the" interest rate, meaning the rate of return that can be earned by holding interest-earning assets rather than money.

Bond Riskiness

We have been discussing present values and bond prices under the assumption that the bond is *risk free*—that is, that the coupon payments and the repayment of principal are absolutely certain. In reality, however, there is some chance that bond issuers will be unable to make some or all of these payments. In the face of this possibility, purchasers of bonds reduce the price they are prepared to pay by an amount that reflects the likelihood of non-repayment.

It follows that not all changes in bond yields are caused by changes in market interest rates. Sometimes the yields on specific bonds change because of a change in their perceived *riskiness*. For example, if some event increases the likelihood that a specific corporate bond issuer will soon go bankrupt, bond purchasers will revise downward the *expected* present value of the issuer's bonds. As a result, the demand for the bond will fall and its equilibrium price will decline. As the price falls, the bond's yield will rise—the higher bond yield now reflecting the greater riskiness of the bond.

> An increase in the riskiness of any bond leads to a decline in its *expected* present value and thus to a decline in the bond's price. The lower bond price implies a higher bond yield.

For the past several years, holders of Greek government bonds have demanded higher yields to reflect the perceived likelihood that the Greek government would default on some or all of its debt.

It is rare in Canada that government bonds are perceived as risky, but in recent years some bonds issued by some southern European countries have been viewed as high-risk assets, and this riskiness has been reflected in high bond yields. In general, however, since governments have the power to collect revenue through taxation, it is unusual for a government bond to be viewed as a risky asset. More usual at any given time is specific corporations that are believed to be in precarious financial situations and thus their bonds are perceived to be risky assets. As a result, there are often very high yields (low bond prices) on specific corporate bonds. *Applying Economic Concepts 27-1* discusses the relationship among bond prices, bond yields, riskiness, and *term to maturity* of government and corporate bonds.

▌27.2 The Theory of Money Demand

Our discussion of bonds, bond prices, and interest rates leads us to a theory that explains how individuals and businesses allocate their current stock of financial wealth between "bonds" and "money." A decision to hold more bonds is at the same time a decision to hold less money, and the decision to hold more money is a decision to hold fewer bonds. We can therefore build our theory by considering the desire to hold bonds or by considering the desire to hold money. We follow the tradition among economists by focusing on the desire to hold money. The amount of money that everyone (collectively) wants to hold at any time is called the **demand for money**.

demand for money The total amount of money that the public wants to hold for all purposes.

Three Reasons for Holding Money

Why do firms and households hold money? Our theory offers three reasons. First, households and firms hold money in order to carry out transactions. Economists call this the *transactions demand* for money. You carry money in your pocket or keep it in a chequing account in order to have it readily available for your upcoming transactions; it would be very inconvenient to have to sell bonds or withdraw money from your mutual fund or GIC (guaranteed investment certificate) every time you wanted to spend. Similarly, firms are continually making expenditures on intermediate inputs and payments to labour, and they keep money available in their chequing accounts to pay these expenses.

A second and related reason firms and households hold money is that they are uncertain about when some expenditures will be necessary, and they hold money as a precaution to avoid the problems associated with missing a transaction. This is referred to as the *precautionary demand* for money. For example, you might keep cash on hand because you might need to take an unplanned taxi ride during a rainstorm, or you keep a buffer of $500 in your chequing account for unexpected car repairs; a small business may hold cash because of the possibility that it might need the emergency services of a tradesperson, such as a plumber or an electrician. In the days before the widespread use of ATMs, the precautionary demand for actual cash was quite large, since to be caught on a weekend or away from home without sufficient cash could be a serious matter. Today, this motive for holding cash is less important.

The third reason for holding money applies more to large businesses and to professional money managers than to individuals because it involves *speculating* about how interest rates are likely to change in the future. Economists call this the *speculative demand* for money. To understand this reason for holding money, recall what we said earlier about the negative relationship between market interest rates and bond prices. If interest rates are expected to rise in the future, bond prices will be expected to fall. Whenever bond prices fall, bondholders experience a decline in the value of their bond holdings. The expectation of increases in *future* interest rates will therefore lead to the

APPLYING ECONOMIC CONCEPTS 27-1

Understanding Bond Prices and Bond Yields

Millions of bonds are traded every day, and they differ in terms of the issuer, price, yield, riskiness, and term to maturity. We focus here on how to understand these bond characteristics.

How to Read the Bond Tables

The accompanying table shows seven bond listings just as they appeared on www.globeinvestor.com on June 11, 2018. The five columns are as follows:

1. **Issuer.** This is the issuer of the bond—that is, the borrower of the money. The first five bonds shown are issued by the Government of Canada. The last two are issued by large private-sector firms.

2. **Coupon.** This is the coupon rate—the annual rate of interest that the bond pays before it matures. For example, a 6 percent coupon rate means that the bondholder (the lender) will receive 6 percent of the face value of the bond every year until the bond matures.

3. **Maturity.** This is when the bond matures and the face value is repaid to the bondholder. All debt obligations are then fulfilled.

4. **Price.** This is the market price of the bond (on June 11, 2018), expressed as the price per $100 of face value. For example, a price of $112.47 would mean that for every $100 of face value, the purchaser must pay $112.47. When the price is greater than $100, we say there is a *premium*; when the price is less than $100, we say the bond is selling at a *discount*.

5. **Yield.** This is the rate of return earned by the bondholder if the bond is bought at the *current* price and held to maturity, earning all regular coupon payments.

Issuer	Coupon (%)	Maturity	Price ($)	Yield (%)
1. Canada	9.75	June 1, 2021	144.25	0.70
2. Canada	3.25	June 1, 2021	112.47	0.70
3. Canada	9.0	June 1, 2025	167.25	1.11
4. Canada	5.75	June 1, 2033	158.43	1.76
5. Canada	3.50	Dec. 1, 2045	136.15	1.89
6. Capital Desjardins Inc.	5.54	June 1, 2021	100.01	5.54
7. Loblaw	8.75	Nov. 23, 2033	142.52	5.06

Bond Prices and Yields

Three general patterns can be seen in the table. First, for a given issuer and maturity, there is a positive relationship between the bond price and the coupon rate. Rows 1 and 2, for example, show two bonds, both issued by the Government of Canada and maturing at the same date in 2021. The common issuer suggests a common risk of non-repayment, which in this case is very low. The first bond has a 9.75 percent coupon whereas the second has a 3.25 percent coupon. Not surprisingly, the higher coupon payments make the first bond a more attractive asset and thus its market price is higher—$144.25 as compared with $112.47. Note, however, that the implied yield on the two bonds is identical. If this weren't the case, demand would shift toward the high-yield (low-price) bond, driving down the yield (increasing the price) until the two yields were the same.

Second, for a given bond issuer, there is a positive relationship between the bond yield and the term to maturity. This is shown in the first five rows, as yields rise from 0.7 percent on bonds maturing in three years (from the date of the listing) to 1.89 percent on bonds maturing in 30 years' time. This positive relationship is often referred to as the *yield curve* or the *term structure of interest rates*. The higher yields on longer-term bonds reflect what is often called a *term premium*—the higher yield that bondholders must be paid in order to induce them to have their money tied up for longer periods of time.

Third, for a given term to maturity, there is a positive relationship between the bond yield and the perceived riskiness of the bond issuer. Compare rows 2 and 6, for example. Both bonds have identical maturity dates in 2021, but one is issued by the Government of Canada while the other is issued by Capital Desjardins Inc. Though it is almost impossible for the Government of Canada to go bankrupt and almost inconceivable that it would default on its debt, it is certainly possible for Capital Desjardins to do so. This difference explains the difference in yields. The same is true between rows 4 and 7, where the more than three-percentage-point yield difference is attributable to the higher likelihood of default by Loblaw than by the Canadian government.

If you run your eyes down the bond tables, you will easily see those corporations viewed by the market as being risky borrowers because the yields on their bonds will be higher—often dramatically so—than the yields on similar-maturity government bonds. For example, in the fall of 2015, when some European banks were experiencing difficulty, the bonds issued by the Royal Bank of Scotland were selling at such a discount that the implied annual yield was more than 18 percent. Such high yields represent a great investment opportunity only if you are prepared to take the associated risk. Beware!

holding of more money (and fewer bonds) *now* as financial managers adjust their portfolios in order to preserve their values.

The Determinants of Money Demand

We have just seen three reasons why firms and households hold money. We now want to examine which key macroeconomic variables affect the *amount* of money that is demanded in our macro model. We focus on three: the interest rate, the level of real GDP, and the price level.

The Interest Rate   No matter what benefits households or firms receive from holding money, there is also a cost. The cost of holding money is the income that *could have been earned* if that wealth were instead held in the form of interest-earning bonds. This is the *opportunity cost* of holding money. In our macro model, we assume that an increase in the interest rate leads firms and households to reduce their desired money holdings. Conversely, a reduction in the interest rate means that holding money is less costly, and so firms and households are assumed to increase their desired money holdings.

> Other things being equal, the demand for money is assumed to be negatively related to the interest rate.[4]

This negative relationship between interest rates and desired money holdings is shown in Figure 27-1 and is drawn as the money demand (M_D) curve. Remember that the decision to hold money is also the decision *not* to hold bonds, and so movements along the M_D curve imply the substitution of assets between money and bonds. For example, as the interest rate declines, bonds become a less attractive asset and money becomes more attractive, so firms and households substitute away from bonds and toward money.

FIGURE 27-1   **Money Demand as a Function of the Interest Rate, Real GDP, and the Price Level**

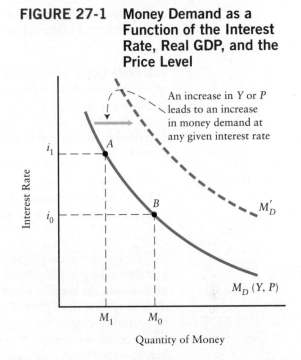

The quantity of money demanded is assumed to be negatively related to the interest rate and positively related to real GDP and the price level. The negative slope of the M_D curve comes from the choice between holding money and holding bonds. A fall in the interest rate from i_1 to i_0 reduces the opportunity cost of holding money because the rate of return on bonds declines. Thus, the decision to hold more money (the movement from A to B as the interest rate falls) is the "flip side" of the decision to hold fewer bonds.

We show the initial money demand curve as $M_D(Y, P)$, indicating that the curve is drawn for given values of Y and P. Increases in Y or P shift the M_D curve to the right; decreases in Y or P shift the M_D curve to the left.

Real GDP   As we said earlier, an important reason for holding money is to make transactions. Not surprisingly, the number of transactions that firms and households collectively want to make is positively related to the level of income and production in the economy—that is, to the level of real GDP. This positive relationship between real GDP and desired money holdings is shown in Figure 27-1 by a rightward shift of the M_D curve to M'_D. At any given interest rate, an increase in Y is assumed to generate more transactions and thus greater desired money holdings.

---

[4] The opportunity cost of holding money is the interest that could have been earned on bonds—this is the nominal interest rate. In the presence of expected inflation, we must distinguish between the nominal and real interest rates. In this chapter we assume, however, that expected inflation is zero, and so we simply speak of "the" interest rate. We discuss inflation in detail in Chapter 29.

> The demand for money is assumed to be positively related to real GDP (for any given interest rate). When real GDP increases, the M_D curve shifts to the right.

The Price Level   An increase in the price level leads to an increase in the *dollar* value of transactions even if there is no change in the *real* value of transactions. That is, as P rises, households and firms will need to hold more money in order to carry out an unchanged real value of transactions. This positive relationship between the price level and desired money holdings is also shown in Figure 27-1 as a rightward shift of the M_D curve to M'_D.

> The demand for money is assumed to be positively related to the price level (for any given interest rate). When the price level increases, the M_D curve shifts to the right.

We can be more precise than just saying there is a positive relationship between P and desired money holdings. Suppose, for example, that Y and i are constant but that all prices in the economy increase by 10 percent. Since Y is unchanged, the *real* value of desired transactions should also be unchanged. Furthermore, since i is unchanged, the opportunity cost of holding money is constant. Therefore, in order to make the same transactions as before, households and firms must not just hold more money than before—they must hold precisely 10 percent more. For this reason, economists usually assume that if real GDP and the interest rate are constant, the demand for money is *proportional* to the price level.

Money Demand: Summing Up

We have discussed the theory of why firms and households hold money, and we have examined the relationship between desired money holding and three macroeconomic variables. Since the demand for money reflects firms' and households' preference to hold their wealth in the form of a *liquid* asset (money) rather than a less liquid asset (bonds), economists sometimes refer to the money demand function as a *liquidity preference* function. We can summarize our assumptions regarding money demand with the following algebraic statement:

$$M_D = M_D(\overset{-}{i}, \overset{+}{Y}, \overset{+}{P})$$

This equation says that the amount of money firms and households want to hold at any given time is a function of three variables; the sign above each variable indicates whether that variable positively or negatively affects desired money holding. Our central assumptions are as follows:

1. An increase in the interest rate increases the opportunity cost of holding money and leads to a reduction in the quantity of money demanded.

2. An increase in real GDP increases the volume of transactions and leads to an increase in the quantity of money demanded.

3. An increase in the price level increases the dollar value of a given volume of transactions and leads to an increase in the quantity of money demanded.

Remember that money demand is also related to bond demand. Firms and households must decide at any time how to divide their financial assets between money and bonds. Therefore, our statements here about money demand apply in reverse to the demand for bonds. For example, in Figure 27-1, a movement down the M_D curve from point A to point B indicates that firms and households are deciding to hold more money and fewer bonds as the interest rate falls. In other words, the movement from A to B involves a substitution away from holding bonds and toward holding money.

27.3 How Money Affects Aggregate Demand

So far, this chapter has been devoted to understanding bonds and how they relate to the demand for money. In the previous chapter we examined the supply of money. We are now ready to put these two sides of the money market together to develop a theory of how interest rates are determined in the short run. You may recall, however, that we already developed in Chapter 25 a theory of how interest rates are determined. But remember that Chapter 25 was a discussion of long-run economic growth, and real GDP was assumed to be equal to Y^* throughout that discussion. What we do in this chapter and the next is return to the short-run version of our macro model but make it more complete by adding money and interest rates explicitly. We will see how changes in money demand and money supply can cause real GDP and interest rates to diverge for short periods of time from their long-run values.

We begin by examining the concept of *monetary equilibrium*—the theory of how interest rates are determined in the short run by the interaction of money demand and money supply. We then explore what economists call the *monetary transmission mechanism*—the chain of events that takes us from changes in the interest rate, through to changes in desired aggregate expenditure, to changes in the level of real GDP and the price level.

Monetary Equilibrium

Figure 27-2 illustrates what economists call the "money market." The money supply (M_S) curve is vertical, indicating that it is assumed to be independent of the interest rate. The money supply increases (M_S shifts to the right) if the central bank increases reserves in the banking system or if the commercial banks decide to lend out a larger fraction of those reserves. The money supply decreases (M_S shifts to the left) if the central bank decreases reserves in the banking system or if the commercial banks decide to reduce their lending. The money demand (M_D) curve is

FIGURE 27-2   Monetary Equilibrium

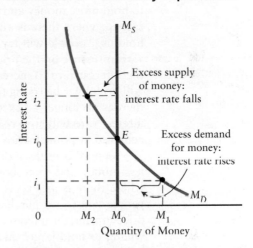

The interest rate rises when there is an excess demand for money and falls when there is an excess supply of money. The fixed quantity of money M_0 is shown by the vertical supply curve M_S. The money supply is determined by the behaviour of the central bank as well as the commercial banks (as we saw in Chapter 26). The demand for money is given by M_D; its negative slope indicates that a fall in the rate of interest causes the quantity of money demanded to increase. Monetary equilibrium is at E, with a rate of interest of i_0.

If the interest rate is i_1, there will be an excess demand for money of M_0M_1. Bonds will be offered for sale in an attempt to increase money holdings. This will force the rate of interest up to i_0 (the price of bonds falls), at which point the quantity of money demanded is equal to the fixed available quantity of M_0.

If the interest rate is i_2, there will be an excess supply of money M_2M_0. Bonds will be demanded in return for excess money balances. This will force the rate of interest down to i_0 (the price of bonds rises), at which point the quantity of money demanded is equal to the fixed supply of M_0.

downward sloping, indicating that firms and households decide to hold more money (and fewer bonds) when the interest rate falls.

Monetary equilibrium occurs when the quantity of money demanded equals the quantity of money supplied. In Chapter 3, we saw that in a competitive market for some product, the price will adjust to establish equilibrium. In the money market, the interest rate is the "price" that adjusts to bring about equilibrium.

When a single household or firm finds that it would like to hold more money (and fewer bonds) it can sell some bonds and add the cash proceeds to its money holdings. If the preference instead is to hold less money, bonds can be purchased. Such adjustments in money and bond holdings for an individual household or firm can easily be made and will have a negligible effect on the economy. But what happens if *all* households and firms try to make this kind of adjustment at the same time? It is this aggregate behaviour that determines how the economy's monetary equilibrium is achieved. Let's consider two separate situations.

First, consider a disequilibrium situation in which firms and households would like to hold more money and fewer bonds. This situation is shown in Figure 27-2 at interest rate i_1, where there is an excess demand for money. In order to increase their money holdings, people will try to sell some bonds. This excess supply of bonds puts downward pressure on the price of bonds which, as we saw earlier in the chapter, will cause the interest rate to increase. Eventually, the interest rate will rise enough that people will no longer be trying to add to their money balances by selling bonds. At that point, there is no longer an excess demand for money (or an excess supply of bonds) and the interest rate will stop rising. In Figure 27-2, the monetary equilibrium will have been achieved at point E with the interest rate i_0.

Second, consider a disequilibrium in which firms and households would like to hold less money and more bonds. This situation is shown in Figure 27-2 at interest rate i_2, where there is an excess supply of money. In order to decrease their money holdings, people will try to purchase more bonds; this excess demand for bonds will push bond prices up and the interest rate down. As the interest rate falls, households and firms become willing to hold larger quantities of money. The interest rate falls until firms and households stop trying to convert bonds into money. In other words, it continues until everyone is content to hold the existing supply of money and bonds, as at point E in Figure 27-2.

> **Monetary equilibrium occurs when the interest rate is such that the quantity of money demanded equals the quantity of money supplied.**

The theory of interest-rate determination depicted in Figure 27-2 is often called the *liquidity preference theory of interest*. This name reflects the fact that when there are only two financial assets, a demand to hold money (rather than bonds) is a demand for the more liquid of the two assets—a preference for liquidity. The theory determines how the interest rate fluctuates in the short term as people seek to achieve *portfolio balance*, given fixed supplies of both money and bonds.

The Monetary Transmission Mechanism

The connection between changes in the demand for and supply of money and the level of aggregate demand is called the **monetary transmission mechanism**. It operates in three stages:

monetary equilibrium The situation in which the quantity of money demanded equals the quantity of money supplied.

monetary transmission mechanism The channels by which a change in the demand for or supply of money leads to a shift of the aggregate demand curve.

1. Changes in the demand for money or the supply of money cause a change in the equilibrium interest rate in the short run.

2. The change in the equilibrium interest rate leads to a change in desired investment and consumption expenditure (and net exports in an open economy). Desired aggregate expenditure therefore changes.

3. The change in desired aggregate expenditure leads to a shift in the *AD* curve and thus to short-run changes in real GDP and the price level.

Let's examine these three stages in more detail.

1. A Change in the Equilibrium Interest Rate   The interest rate will change if the equilibrium depicted in Figure 27-2 is disturbed by a change in either the supply of money or the demand for money. For example, as shown in part (i) of Figure 27-3, we see the following sequence of events when there is an increase in the supply of money but no change in the money demand curve:

$\uparrow$ money supply $\Rightarrow$ excess supply of money at initial interest rate

$\Rightarrow$ firms and households buy bonds

$\Rightarrow \uparrow$ bond prices

$\Rightarrow \downarrow$ equilibrium interest rate

FIGURE 27-3   A Change in the Equilibrium Interest Rate

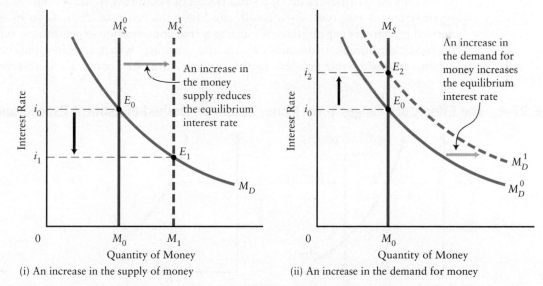

(i) An increase in the supply of money   (ii) An increase in the demand for money

Changes in the supply of money or in the demand for money cause the equilibrium interest rate to change. In both parts of the figure, the money supply is shown by the vertical curve M_S, and the demand for money is shown by the negatively sloped curve M_D. The initial monetary equilibrium is at E_0, with corresponding interest rate i_0. In part (i), an increase in the money supply causes M_S^0 to shift to M_S^1. The new equilibrium is at E_1, where the equilibrium interest rate has fallen to i_1. In part (ii), an increase in the demand for money shifts M_D^0 to M_D^1. The new monetary equilibrium occurs at E_2, and the equilibrium interest rate increases to i_2.

Note that the original increase in the supply of money could be caused either by the central bank increasing the reserves in the banking system or by the commercial banks lending out a higher fraction of their existing reserves.

As shown in part (ii) of Figure 27-3, an increase in the demand for money, with an unchanged supply of money, leads to the following sequence of events:

$\uparrow$ money demand $\Rightarrow$ excess demand for money at initial interest rate

$\Rightarrow$ firms and households sell bonds

$\Rightarrow \downarrow$ bond prices

$\Rightarrow \uparrow$ equilibrium interest rate

The original increase in the demand for money could be caused by an increase in real GDP or by an increase in the price level. It could also be caused by an increase in the perceived riskiness of bonds, which would lead to a preference to hold money rather than bonds.

> **Changes in either the demand for or the supply of money cause changes in the short-run equilibrium interest rate.**

2. A Change in Desired Investment and Consumption The second link in the monetary transmission mechanism relates interest rates to desired investment and consumption expenditure. We saw in Chapter 21 that desired investment, which includes expenditure on inventory accumulation, residential construction, and business fixed investment, responds to changes in the interest rate. Other things being equal, a decrease in the interest rate reduces the opportunity cost of borrowing or using retained earnings for investment purposes. As a result, the lower interest rate leads to an increase in desired investment expenditure. We also saw that consumption expenditures, especially on big-ticket durable items such as cars and furniture, which are often purchased on credit, are negatively related to the interest rate. In Figure 27-4, this negative

FIGURE 27-4 The Effects of Changes in the Money Supply on Desired Investment Expenditure

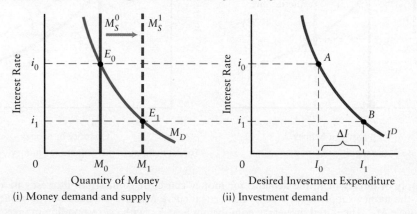

(i) Money demand and supply (ii) Investment demand

Increases in the money supply reduce the equilibrium interest rate and increase desired investment expenditure. In part (i), monetary equilibrium is at E_0, with a quantity of money of M_0 and an interest rate of i_0. The corresponding level of desired investment is I_0 (point A) in part (ii). An increase in the money supply to M_1 reduces the equilibrium interest rate to i_1 and increases investment expenditure by ΔI to I_1 (point B).

relationship between desired expenditure and the interest rate is labelled I^D for investment demand, reflecting the fact that investment is the *most* interest-sensitive part of expenditure.

The first two links in the monetary transmission mechanism are shown in Figure 27-4.[5] Although the analysis in Figure 27-4 illustrates a change in the money supply, remember that the transmission mechanism can also be set in motion by a change in the demand for money. In part (i), we see that an increase in the money supply reduces the short-run equilibrium interest rate. In part (ii), we see that the lower interest rate leads to an increase in desired investment (and consumption) expenditure.

3. A Change in Aggregate Demand

The third link in our theory of the monetary transmission mechanism is from changes in desired expenditure to shifts in the *AE* function and in the *AD* curve. This is familiar ground. In Chapter 23, we saw that a shift in the aggregate expenditure curve (caused by something *other than* a change in the price level) leads to a shift in the *AD* curve. This situation is shown again in Figure 27-5.

> **An increase in the money supply causes a reduction in the interest rate and an increase in desired aggregate expenditure; it therefore causes a rightward shift of the *AD* curve. A decrease in the money supply causes an increase in the interest rate and a decrease in desired aggregate expenditure; it therefore causes a leftward shift of the *AD* curve.**

The entire monetary transmission mechanism is summarized in Figure 27-6 for the case of a shock to the money market that reduces the short-run equilibrium interest rate. Either an increase in money supply or a decrease in money demand will reduce the interest rate, increase desired investment expenditure, and increase aggregate demand.

An Open-Economy Modification

So far, the emphasis in our discussion of the monetary transmission mechanism has been on the effect that a change in the interest rate has on desired investment and desired consumption. In an open economy, however, where financial capital flows

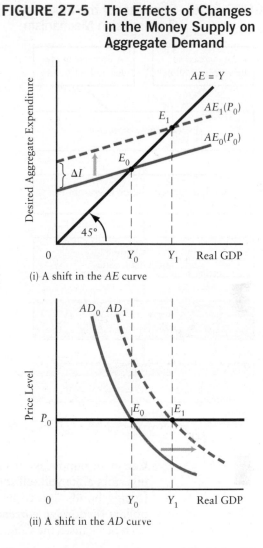

FIGURE 27-5   The Effects of Changes in the Money Supply on Aggregate Demand

(i) A shift in the *AE* curve

(ii) A shift in the *AD* curve

Changes in the money supply cause shifts in the *AE* and *AD* functions. In Figure 27-4, an increase in the money supply increased desired investment expenditure by ΔI. In part (i) of this figure, the *AE* function shifts up by ΔI. At any given price level P_0, equilibrium GDP rises from Y_0 to Y_1, as shown by the rightward shift in the *AD* curve in part (ii). The magnitude of the *AD* shift is equal to ΔI times the simple multiplier.

---

[5] In part (i) of Figure 27-4, it is the *nominal* interest rate—the rate of return on bonds—that affects money demand. In part (ii), however, it is the *real* interest rate that influences desired investment expenditure. It is therefore worth emphasizing that we are continuing with the assumption in this chapter that inflation is expected to be zero, and thus the nominal and real interest rates are the same. This assumption allows us to use the same vertical axis in the two parts of the figure.

FIGURE 27-6 **Summary of the Monetary Transmission Mechanism**

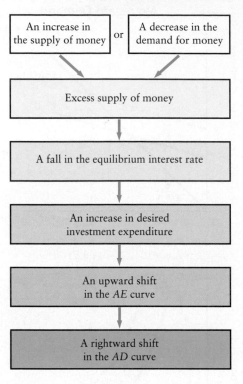

easily across international borders, the monetary transmission mechanism is a little more complex.

Financial capital is very mobile across countries. Bondholders, either in Canada or abroad, are able to substitute among Canadian bonds, U.S. bonds, German bonds, and bonds from almost any country you can think of. Bonds from different countries are generally not *perfect* substitutes for each other because the varying amounts of political and economic instability imply that different levels of *risk* are associated with different bonds. But bonds from similar countries—Canada and the United States, for example—are often viewed as very close substitutes.

The ability of bondholders to substitute easily between bonds from different countries implies that monetary disturbances that cause changes in interest rates often lead to international flows of financial capital, which in turn cause changes in exchange rates and changes in exports and imports.

To understand how capital mobility adds a second channel to the monetary transmission mechanism, consider an example. Suppose the Bank of Canada decides to increase the money supply by increasing reserves in the banking system. As shown in part (i) of Figure 27-4, the increase in money supply reduces the interest rate and increases desired investment expenditure. This is the first channel of the monetary transmission mechanism. But the story does not end there.

The reduction in Canadian interest rates also makes Canadian bonds less attractive assets relative to foreign bonds. Canadian and foreign investors alike will sell some of their Canadian bonds and buy more of the high-return foreign bonds. But to buy foreign bonds, it is necessary first to exchange Canadian dollars for foreign currency. The desire to sell Canadian dollars and purchase foreign currency causes the Canadian dollar to depreciate relative to other currencies.

> **An increase in the Canadian money supply reduces Canadian interest rates and leads to an outflow of financial capital. This capital outflow causes the Canadian dollar to depreciate.**

As the Canadian dollar depreciates, however, Canadian goods and services become less expensive relative to those from other countries. As we first saw in Chapter 22, this change in international relative prices causes households and firms—both in Canada and abroad—to substitute away from foreign goods and toward Canadian goods. Imports fall and exports rise.

So the overall effect of the increase in the Canadian money supply is not just a fall in Canadian interest rates and an increase in investment. Because of the international mobility of financial capital, the low Canadian interest rates also lead to a capital outflow, a depreciation of the Canadian dollar, and an increase in Canadian net exports. This increase in net exports *strengthens* the positive impact on aggregate demand already coming from the increase in desired investment.

This complete open-economy monetary transmission mechanism is shown in Figure 27-7. This figure is based on Figure 27-6, but simply adds the second channel of the transmission mechanism that works through capital mobility, exchange rates, and net exports.

> In an open economy with capital mobility, an increase in the money supply is predicted to cause an increase in aggregate demand for two reasons. First, the reduction in interest rates causes an increase in investment. Second, the lower interest rate causes a capital outflow, a currency depreciation, and a rise in net exports.

Our example has been that of an increase in the money supply. A *decrease* in the money supply has the opposite effect, but the logic of the mechanism is the same. A reduction in the Canadian money supply raises Canadian interest rates and reduces desired investment expenditure. The higher Canadian interest rates attract foreign financial capital as bondholders sell low-return foreign bonds and purchase high-return Canadian bonds. This action increases the demand for Canadian dollars in the foreign-exchange market and thus causes the Canadian dollar to appreciate. Finally, the appreciation of the Canadian dollar increases Canadians' imports of foreign goods and reduces Canadian exports to other countries. Canadian net exports fall. The reduction in both desired investment and net exports causes the *AE* curve to shift down and the *AD* curve to shift to the left.

FIGURE 27-7 The Open-Economy Monetary Transmission Mechanism

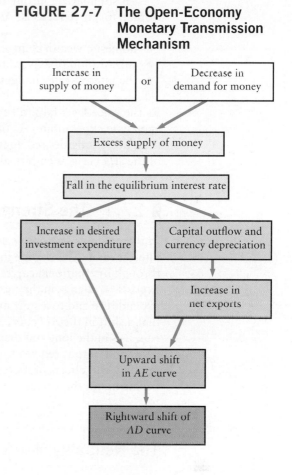

The Slope of the *AD* Curve

We can now use our theory of the monetary transmission mechanism to add to the explanation of the negative slope of the *AD* curve. In Chapter 23, we mentioned two reasons for its negative slope: a change in the price level causes a change in wealth and also causes a substitution between domestic and foreign goods. A third effect operates through interest rates, and works as follows. A rise in the price level raises the money value of transactions and thus leads to an increase in the demand for money. For a given supply of money (a vertical M_S curve), the increase in money demand means that the M_D curve shifts to the right, raising the equilibrium interest rate. The higher interest rate then leads to a reduction in desired investment expenditure. We therefore have a third reason that the price level and the level of aggregate demand are negatively related.

To summarize, in our more complete macro model, the *AD* curve is downward sloping for three reasons. As the domestic price level changes:

- domestic wealth changes
- substitution of expenditure occurs between domestic and foreign products
- the interest rate changes, which leads to changes in investment and net exports

As the price level falls, all three effects work in the same direction, increasing desired aggregate expenditure. As the price level rises, the three effects work in the same direction, decreasing desired aggregate expenditure. The third reason for the negative slope of the *AD* curve is empirically the most important of the three.

▍27.4 The Strength of Monetary Forces

In the previous section we saw that a change in the money supply leads to a change in interest rates. The change in interest rates, in turn, leads to changes in investment and, through international capital flows and changes in the exchange rate, to changes in net exports. A change in the money supply therefore leads to a change in desired aggregate expenditure and to a shift in the *AD* curve. From our analysis in Chapter 24, we know that a shift in the *AD* curve will lead to different effects in the short run and in the long run. It is in the long run that factor prices fully adjust to excess demands or excess supplies, and output returns to the level of potential output, Y^*. Let's begin by examining the long-run effects of increases in the money supply, and then turn to a long-standing debate about the strength of monetary forces in the short run.

The Neutrality of Money

Starting from a long-run equilibrium in our macro model with real GDP equal to Y^*, any *AD* or *AS* shock that creates an output gap sets in place an adjustment process that will eventually close that gap and return real GDP to Y^*. The operation of this adjustment process following an increase in the money supply is illustrated in Figure 27-8. In the figure, the only long-run effect of the shift in the *AD* curve is a change in the price level; there is no long-run effect on real GDP or any other real economic variable. This result is referred to as **long-run money neutrality**; that is, Y^* is unaffected by changes in the supply of money.

long-run money neutrality The idea that a change in the supply of money has no long-run effect on any real variables; it affects only the price level.

The Classical Dichotomy   Many eighteenth- and nineteenth-century economists developed theories of the economy's long-run equilibrium and emphasized the neutrality of money. They argued that the "monetary side" of the economy was independent from the "real side" in the long run. This belief came to be referred to as the *Classical dichotomy*. In the long run, relative prices, real GDP, employment, investment, and all other real economic variables were assumed to be determined by real factors, such as firms' technologies and consumers' preferences. The absolute level of money prices was then determined by the monetary side of the economy, where the money supply determined the price level. In macro models that contain this dichotomy, the long-run effect of a change in the money supply is a change in the price level, with no changes to any real economic variables.

The concept of money neutrality is interpreted differently by different people. Our definition above, which emphasizes the independence of Y^* from the country's money supply, is probably the most commonly used definition today, but there are others as well. *Applying Economic Concepts 27-2* examines the concept of money neutrality as it relates to changes in the denominations of a country's paper currency.

> **Money is neutral in the long run if a change in the money supply has no long-run effect on the level of potential GDP or any other real variables. Much empirical evidence is consistent with long-run money neutrality, although the proposition is often debated.**

Hysteresis Effects The proposition of long-run money neutrality is debatable. Though it is a common assumption in many macroeconomic models, there are good reasons to think that changes in a country's money supply may have effects on Y^* and thus have long-run effects on real GDP. Here we examine what is called *hysteresis*—the possibility that short-run changes in real GDP caused by changes in the money supply may have an influence on Y^*.

One possible reason for hysteresis relates to firms' use of borrowed funds to finance their investment expenditures. As we have seen in this chapter, changes in the country's money supply will lead to changes in the interest rate and thus in desired investment. The increased investment will cause a short-run increase in aggregate demand and thus in real GDP. But depending on the *nature* of the firms' investment decisions, there may also be a long-run impact. For example, if firms' investments in capital equipment or research and development lead to improvements in the state of knowledge and technology, there will likely be a permanent effect on the level of potential output. In this case, the short-run change in investment will generate a long-run change in Y^*.

Another reason for hysteresis is the effect on human capital that often accompanies prolonged unemployment. Consider a reduction in the money supply that raises interest rates, reduces real GDP, and increases the unemployment rate. If wages and other factor prices are slow to adjust, some individuals will experience long spells of unemployment. Prolonged lack of work for even experienced workers may cause their skills to deteriorate. If the recession lasts long enough, some

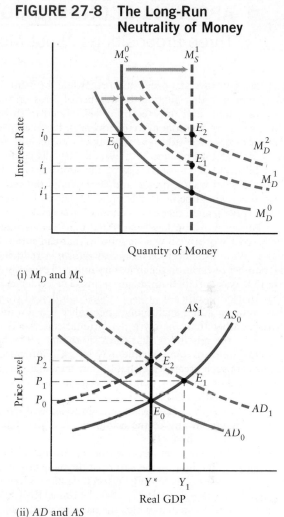

FIGURE 27-8 The Long-Run Neutrality of Money

(i) M_D and M_S

(ii) AD and AS

Money is neutral in the long run if the only long-run effect of an increase in the money supply is a higher price level. The economy begins in long-run equilibrium at E_0 in both diagrams, with real GDP equal to Y^* and the price level equal to P_0. An increase in the money supply from M_S^0 to M_S^1 reduces interest rates immediately to i_1' and stimulates aggregate demand, thus shifting the aggregate demand curve from AD_0 to AD_1. As real GDP and the price level increase, the demand for money increases to M_D^1, thus pushing i_1' up to i_1. The point E_1 in part (i) therefore corresponds to E_1 in part (ii). Since real GDP is now above Y^*, wages and other factor prices start to increase, thus shifting the AS curve upward. The adjustment process continues until Y is back to Y^* and the price level has increased to P_2. In the new long-run equilibrium, the higher price level (with unchanged Y^*) has increased money demand to M_D^2, thus restoring the interest rate to its initial level, i_0.

APPLYING ECONOMIC CONCEPTS 27-2

Three Propositions About Money Neutrality

The least controversial proposition regarding the neutrality of money is that altering the number of zeros on the monetary unit, and on everything else stated in those units, will have no economic consequences. For example, if an extra zero were added to all Bank of Canada notes—so that all $5 bills became $50 bills, all $10 bills became $100 bills, and so on—and the same adjustment was made to all nominal wages, prices, and contracts in the economy, there would be no effects on real GDP, real wages, relative prices, and other real economic variables.*

This proposition has been tested many times since the Second World War, when countries that had suffered major inflations undertook *monetary reform* by reducing the number of zeros on the monetary unit and everything else that was specified in money terms. The evidence is clear that no significant or lasting effects followed from these reforms. That such money neutrality is a testable theory, rather than merely a definitional statement, is shown by the possibility that for a short time after the monetary reforms some people may be so ill informed, and others such creatures of habit, that they make mistakes based on assuming that the new money is the same as the old. Although some such behaviour probably occurred, it was not significant enough to show up as a sudden change in any of the economic data that have been collected in these cases.

A slightly stronger proposition regarding money neutrality is that altering the nature of the monetary unit will have no real economic effects. Such a change occurred, for example, in 1971, when the United Kingdom changed from a system in which the basic monetary unit, the pound sterling, was composed of 240 pence to its

current system which contains 100 pence. Another example is Ireland's 1999 conversion from the punt, which contained 240 pence, to the euro, which contains 100 cents. In these cases there were some alterations in real behaviour immediately after the change was made, as many people were confused by the new units. Once again, however, these changes were neither important enough nor long-lasting enough to show up in the macroeconomic data.

These two propositions regarding the neutrality of money are important because they emphasize the nominal nature of money and the important distinction between nominal and real values. It would be unusual indeed if multiplying all nominal values in the economy by the same scalar had any real effect other than some temporary confusion. For this reason, these two propositions are accepted by virtually all economists and central bankers.

The stronger and more controversial proposition regarding money neutrality is the one discussed in the text—that the economy's level of potential output and thus its long-run equilibrium is unaffected by changes in the supply of money. This assumption is common in many macroeconomic models but, as we argue in the text, there are good reasons to think that monetary policy may have effects on Y^* and thus have long-run effects on real GDP.

---

*Of course, there would be some real effects from such an adjustment, including the level of inconvenience associated with using paper money with larger denominations (which would be enormous if we added many zeros rather than just one to all existing bills and prices).

---

individuals may eventually become "unemployable," even after the aggregate economy recovers. In this case, the fall in the level of real GDP, if prolonged, leads through hysteresis effects to a fall in the level of Y^*.

> **Some short-run changes in GDP may be associated with changes in investment or employment that cause long-lasting effects on Y^*. In these situations, the proposition of long-run money neutrality is called into question.**

Money and Inflation

Whether or not money is neutral in the long run, it is certainly closely related to the price level. As we observed in Chapter 26 (in *Applying Economic Concepts 26-1*), there have been many examples throughout history of countries experiencing dramatic increases in the money supply and equally dramatic increases in the price level.

The close connection between money growth and inflation does not hold just in the dramatic examples; it is a connection that applies in the long run to most if not all economies. Figure 27-9 shows a scatter plot of inflation and money growth for a large sample of countries between 1978 and 2017. The vertical axis measures each country's average annual inflation rate. The horizontal axis measures each country's average annual growth rate of the money supply. Each point in the figure represents the rates of inflation and money supply growth for one country averaged over the sample period. As is clear in the figure, there is a strong positive correlation between the growth rate of the money supply and the rate of inflation, as reflected by the tight bunching of points around the upward-sloping line. This line is the statistical "line of best fit" between money supply growth and inflation. Its slope is 0.87, indicating that two countries that differ in their money growth rates by 10 percent will, on average, differ in their inflation rates by 8.7 percent.

FIGURE 27-9   Inflation and Money Growth Across Many Countries, 1978–2017

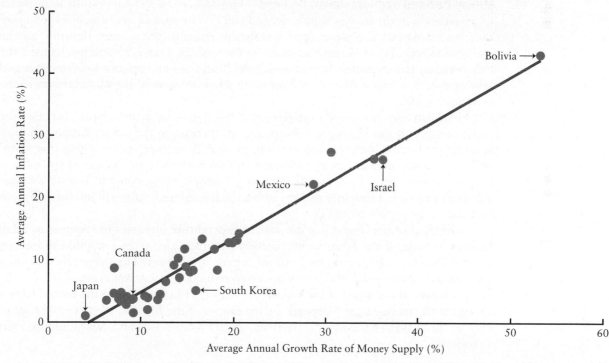

Countries with higher inflation rates tend to be countries with higher rates of growth of the money supply. This figure plots long-run data for many countries. Each point shows the average annual inflation rate and the average annual growth rate of the money supply for a specific country for the 1978–2017 period. For all countries, the inflation data refer to the rate of change of the Consumer Price Index; the money supply data refer to the growth rate of M2. The positive relationship between inflation and money supply growth (with a slope of the best-fit line very close to 1) is consistent with the proposition of long-run money neutrality.

(*Source:* Based on author's calculations using data from the World Bank. Go to www.worldbank.org and look for "world development indicators and global development finance.")

Across many countries over long periods of time, the rate of inflation and the growth rate of the money supply are highly correlated.

The Short-Run Effects of Monetary Policy

monetary policy A central bank's decisions regarding the money supply and interest rates used in its efforts to influence aggregate demand.

A central bank's **monetary policy** is the set of decisions it makes regarding the determination of the money supply in its efforts to influence real GDP and the price level. We will examine the Bank of Canada's approach to monetary policy in detail in the next chapter. For now, we can examine how aspects of money demand and investment demand determine the *effectiveness* of monetary policy.

In our macro model, money is clearly not neutral in the short run. We have seen that a change in the money supply shifts the AD curve and hence alters the short-run equilibrium level of real GDP. For a given AS curve, the short-run effect of a change in the money supply on real GDP and the price level is determined by the extent of the shift of the AD curve. What determines how much the AD curve shifts?

Money Demand and Investment Demand How much the AD curve shifts in response to an increase in the money supply depends on the amount of investment expenditure that is stimulated. The increase in investment expenditure in turn depends on the strength of two of the linkages that make up the monetary transmission mechanism: the link between money supply and interest rates, and the link between interest rates and investment.[6] Let's look more closely at these separate parts of the monetary transmission mechanism.

First, consider how much interest rates fall when the central bank increases the money supply. If the M_D curve is steep, a given increase in the money supply will lead to a large reduction in the equilibrium interest rate. A steep M_D curve means that firms' and households' desired money holding is not very sensitive to changes in the interest rate, so interest rates have to fall a lot to get people to be content to hold a larger amount of money. The flatter the M_D curve, the less interest rates will fall for any given increase in the supply of money.

Second, consider how much investment expenditure increases in response to a fall in interest rates. If the I^D curve is relatively flat, then any given reduction in interest rates will lead to a large increase in firms' desired investment. The steeper the I^D curve, the less investment will increase for any given reduction in interest rates.

It follows that the size of the shift of the AD curve in response to the central bank's change in the money supply depends on the shapes of the M_D and I^D curves. The influence of the shapes of the two curves is shown in Figure 27-10 and can be summarized as follows:

1. The steeper the M_D curve, the more interest rates will change in response to a given change in the money supply.

2. The flatter the I^D curve, the more investment expenditure will change in response to a given change in the interest rate, and hence the larger the shift in the AD curve.

---

[6] As we saw earlier in the chapter, the consumption of durable goods is also sensitive to changes in the interest rate. In this section, however, we simplify by focusing only on the behaviour of desired investment.

FIGURE 27-10   Two Views on the Strength of Monetary Policy

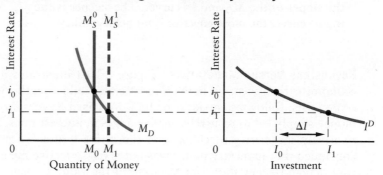

(i) Monetarist view: Changes in the money supply are effective

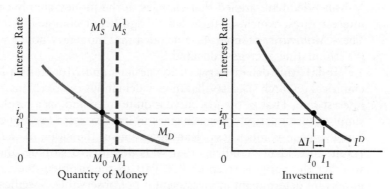

(ii) Keynesian view: Changes in the money supply are ineffective

The effect of a change in the money supply on aggregate demand depends on the slopes of the M_D and I^D curves. Initially, in parts (i) and (ii), the money supply is M_S^0, and the economy has an interest rate of i_0 and investment expenditure of I_0. The central bank then expands the money supply from M_S^0 to M_S^1. The rate of interest thus falls from i_0 to i_1, as shown in each of the left panels. This causes an increase in investment expenditure of ΔI, from I_0 to I_1, as shown in each of the right panels.

In part (i), the demand for money is relatively insensitive to the interest rate, so the increase in the money supply leads to a large fall in the interest rate. Further, desired investment expenditure is highly interest sensitive, so the large fall in interest rates also leads to a large increase in investment expenditure. In this case, the change in the money supply will be very effective in stimulating aggregate demand.

In part (ii), the demand for money is more sensitive to the interest rate, so the increase in the money supply leads to only a small fall in the interest rate. Further, desired investment expenditure is much less sensitive to the interest rate, and so the small fall in interest rates leads to only a small increase in investment expenditure. In this case, the change in the money supply will be less effective in stimulating aggregate demand.

The combination that produces the largest shift in the AD curve for a given change in the money supply is a steep M_D curve and a flat I^D curve. This combination is illustrated in part (i) of Figure 27-10. It makes monetary policy relatively effective as a means of influencing real GDP in the short run. The combination that produces the smallest shift in the AD curve is a flat M_D curve and a steep I^D curve. This combination is illustrated in part (ii) of Figure 27-10. It makes monetary policy relatively ineffective in the short run.

The ability of monetary policy to induce short-run changes in real GDP depends on the slopes of the M_D and I^D curves. The steeper is the M_D curve, and the flatter is the I^D curve, the more effective is monetary policy.

Keynesians Versus Monetarists Figure 27-10 illustrates a famous debate among economists that occurred in the three decades following the Second World War. Some economists, following the ideas of John Maynard Keynes, argued that changes in the money supply led to relatively small changes in interest rates, and that investment was relatively insensitive to changes in the interest rate. These *Keynesian* economists concluded that monetary policy was not a very effective method of stimulating aggregate demand—they therefore emphasized the value of using fiscal policy (as Keynes himself had argued during the Great Depression). Another group of economists, led by Milton Friedman, argued that changes in the money supply caused sharp changes in interest rates, which, in turn, led to significant changes in investment expenditure. These *Monetarist* economists concluded that monetary policy was a very effective tool for stimulating aggregate demand.[7]

Today, this debate between Keynesians and Monetarists is over. A great deal of empirical research suggests that money demand is relatively insensitive to changes in the interest rate. That is, the M_D curve is quite steep and, as a result, changes in the money supply cause relatively large changes in interest rates (as argued by the Monetarists). The evidence is much less clear, however, on the slope of the I^D curve. Though the empirical evidence confirms that I^D is downward sloping, there is no consensus on whether the curve is steep or flat. Part of the problem facing researchers is that an important determinant of investment is not observable. Specifically, firms' expectations about the future cannot easily be measured. Keynes famously referred to the "animal spirits" of firms, the pessimism or optimism which have such a significant effect on their investment decisions. The non-observability of this variable makes it very difficult to estimate precisely the relationship between interest rates and investment. Another problem is that the I^D curve is an aggregation of a number of different investment demands (plant, equipment, inventories, new housing, and durable consumer goods), each subject to different influences. While each type of investment is responsive to changes in the interest rate, their individual differences make it difficult to estimate the responsiveness of *aggregate* desired investment (I^D) to changes in the interest rate.

Though empirical research over the years has largely filled the gaps in our knowledge, there is still plenty of debate about the effectiveness and the appropriate objectives of monetary policy. Some economists argue that monetary policy should be directed only to achieving a desired path of the price level, with little or no attention being paid to fluctuations in real GDP. Others argue that monetary policy should attempt to offset the largest and most persistent shocks that hit the economy, while maintaining a long-run focus on the behaviour of the price level. Yet others argue that short-run fluctuations in real GDP and employment are so important that monetary policy ought to place much less emphasis on the price level and instead be actively engaged in reducing the economy's fluctuations in the face of all but the smallest and most transient shocks.

---

[7] Monetarists argued that monetary policy was very effective for stimulating aggregate demand but they *did not* advocate an "activist" monetary policy. One of their concerns was that monetary forces were so strong that an activist monetary policy would potentially destabilize the economy. We address these issues in Chapter 28.

In the next chapter we examine the details of how monetary policy is conducted in Canada. For several reasons, the real-world practice of monetary policy is more complex than it appears in this chapter. But as we will see, the Bank of Canada's system of *inflation targeting* can be viewed as a means of providing both short-run stabilization and a long-run focus on the behaviour of the price level.

SUMMARY

27.1 Understanding Bonds

LO 1

- The present value of any bond that promises to pay some sequence of payments in the future is negatively related to the market interest rate. A bond's present value determines its market price. Thus, there is a negative relationship between the market interest rate and the price of a bond.
- The yield on a bond is the rate of return the bondholder receives, having bought the bond at its purchase price

and then receiving the entire stream of future payments the bond offers. For a given stream of future payments, a lower purchase price implies a higher bond yield.
- An increase in the perceived riskiness of bonds leads to a reduction in bond prices and thus an increase in bond yields.

27.2 The Theory of Money Demand

LO 2

- In our macro model, households and firms are assumed to divide their financial assets between interest-bearing "bonds" and non-interest-bearing "money." They hold money to facilitate both expected and unexpected transactions, and also to protect against the possibility of a decline in bond prices (a rise in interest rates).
- The opportunity cost of holding money is the interest that would have been earned if bonds had been held instead.
- Households' and firms' desired money holdings are assumed to be influenced by three key macroeconomic variables:

1. Increases in the interest rate reduce desired money holdings.
2. Increases in real GDP increase desired money holdings.
3. Increases in the price level increase desired money holdings.
- These relationships are captured in the M_D curve, which is drawn as a negative relationship between interest rates (i) and desired money holding (M_D). Increases in real GDP (Y) or the price level (P) lead to a rightward shift of this M_D curve.

27.3 How Money Affects Aggregrate Demand

LO 3, 4

- In the short run, the interest rate is determined by the interaction of money supply and money demand. Monetary equilibrium is established when the interest rate is such that the quantity of money supplied is equal to the quantity of money demanded.
- A change in the money supply (coming from the central bank or the commercial banking system) or in the demand for money (coming from a change in Y or P) will lead to a change in the equilibrium interest rate. This is the first stage of the monetary transmission mechanism.

- The second stage of the monetary transmission mechanism is that any change in the interest rate leads to a change in desired investment and consumption expenditure. In an open economy with capital mobility, the change in the interest rate leads to capital flows, changes in the exchange rate, and changes in net exports.
- The third stage of the monetary transmission mechanism is that any change in desired investment, consumption, or net exports leads to a shift in the aggregate demand (AD) curve, and thus to a change in real GDP and the price level.

27.4 The Strength of Monetary Forces

- Changes in the money supply have different effects on the economy in the short run and in the long run.
- Money is said to be neutral in the long run if a change in the money supply leads to no changes in the long-run level of real GDP (or other real variables).
- In the long run, after wages and other factor prices have fully adjusted to any output gaps, real GDP returns to potential output, Y^*. If Y^* is unaffected by the change in the money supply, there will be no long-run effect from the monetary shock.

- There is a strong positive correlation between the rate of money growth and the rate of inflation across countries when viewed over the long run.
- In the short run, the effects of a change in the money supply depend on the shape of the M_D and I^D curves in our macro model. The steeper the M_D curve and the flatter the I^D curve, the more effective changes in the money supply will be in causing short-run changes in real GDP.

KEY CONCEPTS

The interest rate and present value
Interest rates, bond prices, and bond yields
Reasons for holding money

The money demand (M_D) function
Monetary equilibrium
The monetary transmission mechanism
The investment demand (I^D) function

Effects of changes in the money supply
Neutrality and non-neutrality of money
Hysteresis
Keynesians and Monetarists

STUDY EXERCISES

MyLab Economics Make the grade with MyLab Economics™: All Study Exercises can be found on MyLab Economics™. You can practise them as often as you want, and many feature step-by-step guided instructions to help you find the right answer.

FILL-IN-THE-BLANK

❶ Fill in the blanks to make the following statements correctly reflect the theory developed in this chapter.

a. Monetary equilibrium occurs when the quantity of _____ equals the quantity of _____. Monetary equilibrium determines the _____.

b. When there is an excess supply of money, households and firms will attempt to _____ bonds. This action will cause the price of bonds to _____ and the interest rate to _____.

c. When there is an excess demand for money, households and firms will attempt to _____ bonds. This action will cause the price of bonds to _____ and the interest rate to _____.

d. The _____ _____ _____ refers to the three stages that link the money market to aggregate demand. The first link is between monetary equilibrium and the _____; the second link is between the _____ and desired _____; the third link is between desired _____ and _____.

e. Suppose the economy is in equilibrium and then the Bank of Canada increases the money supply. The first effect will be an excess _____ of/for money, which will then lead to a(n) _____ in

the interest rate, which will in turn lead to a(n) _____ in desired investment.

f. Suppose the economy is in equilibrium and the Bank of Canada decreases the money supply. The first effect will be an excess _____ of/for money, which will lead to a _____ in the interest rate, which will in turn lead to a(n) _____ in desired investment.

g. Through the monetary transmission mechanism, a rightward shift of the AD curve can be caused by a(n) _____ in the money supply; a leftward shift of the AD curve can be caused by a(n) _____ in the money supply.

h. In an open economy with capital mobility, an increase in the money supply causes interest rates to _____, which leads to a capital outflow. This causes a(n) _____ of the Canadian dollar and thus to a(n) _____ in net exports, which leads the AD curve to shift _____.

❷ Fill in the blanks to make the following statements correctly reflect the theory developed in this chapter.

a. If money is neutral in the long run, then changes in the money supply have no effect on _____ in the long run.

b. If the demand for money is not very sensitive to changes in the interest rate, then the M_D curve will be relatively _____. An increase in the money supply will lead to a(n) _____ reduction in the interest rate.

c. If the demand for money is very sensitive to changes in the interest rate, then the M_D curve will be relatively _____. An increase in the money supply will lead to a(n) _____ reduction in the interest rate.

d. A relatively flat investment demand curve means that a change in the interest rate will have a(n) _____ effect on _____, which leads to a relatively large shift in the _____ curve.

e. A relatively steep investment demand curve means that a change in the interest rate will have a(n) _____ effect on _____, which leads to a relatively small shift in the _____ curve.

f. Changes in the money supply will have the largest effect on the position of the AD curve when the M_D curve is relatively _____ and the I^D curve is relatively _____.

REVIEW

❸ What motives for holding money—transactions, precautionary, or speculative—do you think explain the following holdings? Explain.

a. Currency in the cash register of the local grocery store at the start of each working day.

b. Money to meet Queen's University's biweekly payroll deposited in the local bank.

c. A household tries to keep a "buffer" of $1000 in its savings account.

d. An investor, fearing a rise in interest rates, sells her bonds for cash.

e. You carry $20 in your pocket even though you have no planned expenditures.

❹ The diagram below shows the demand for money and the supply of money.

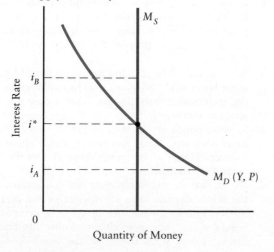

a. Explain why the M_D function is downward sloping.

b. Suppose the interest rate is at i_A. Explain how firms and households attempt to satisfy their excess demand for money. What is the effect of their actions?

c. Suppose the interest rate is at i_B. Explain how firms and households attempt to dispose of their excess supply of money. What is the effect of their actions?

d. Now suppose there is an increase in the transactions demand for money (perhaps because of growth in real GDP). Beginning at i^*, explain what happens in the money market. How is this shown in the diagram?

❺ The following diagrams show the monetary equilibrium and the demand for investment. The economy begins with money supply M_S, money demand M_D, and investment demand I^D. The interest rate is i_0 and desired investment is I_0.

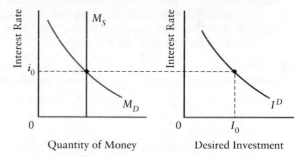

a. Beginning at the initial equilibrium, suppose the Bank of Canada increases the money supply. What happens in the money market, and what happens to desired investment expenditure?

b. Beginning in the initial equilibrium, suppose there is a reduction in the demand for money (caused, perhaps, by bonds becoming more attractive to firms and households). What happens in the money market, and what happens to desired investment expenditure?

c. Explain why an increase in money supply can have the same effects on desired investment expenditure as a reduction in money demand.

❻ In the text we discussed why, in an open economy with international capital mobility, there is a second part to the monetary transmission mechanism. (It may be useful to review Figure 27-7 when answering this question.)

a. Explain why an increase in Canada's money supply makes Canadian and foreign investors shift their portfolios away from Canadian bonds and toward foreign bonds.

b. Explain why this portfolio adjustment leads to a depreciation of the Canadian dollar.

c. Why would such a depreciation of the Canadian dollar lead to an increase in Canada's net exports?

d. Now suppose that the Bank of Canada does not change its policy at all, but the Federal Reserve (the U.S. central bank) increases the U.S. money supply. What is the likely effect on Canada? Explain.

7 In the text we discussed the historical debate between Keynesians and Monetarists regarding the effectiveness of monetary policy in changing real GDP (see Figure 27-10 to review). Using the same sort of diagram, discuss two conditions in which a change in the money supply would have *no* short-run effect on real GDP.

8 In 2008, at a time when many developed economies were close to full employment, stock markets in Canada and many other countries experienced very large declines. These declines occurred largely in response to the failure of several large U.S. and European banks and the resulting disruption in global financial markets.

a. Explain how such stock-market declines affect wealth and thus are likely to affect the *AD* curve.
b. If the central banks attempt to keep output close to *Y**, what will they likely do in response? Explain.
c. Did the Bank of Canada act as predicted in part (b)? Explain how you know.

9 Consider the effects of events in the U.S. economy on the Canadian economy and on Canadian monetary policy.

a. If a serious recession begins in the United States, what is the likely effect on Canadian aggregate demand? Explain.
b. If Canadian real GDP was equal to *Y** before the U.S. recession began, what would be the likely response by the Bank of Canada?
c. Given the mobility of financial capital across international boundaries, what is the likely effect on Canadian aggregate demand from a policy by the U.S. Federal Reserve that reduces U.S. interest rates?
d. Given your answer to part (c), explain why Canadian monetary policy might sometimes appear to "mirror" U.S. monetary policy even though the Bank of Canada is wholly independent from the U.S. Federal Reserve.

PROBLEMS

10 The following table shows the stream of income produced by several different assets. In each case, P_1, P_2, and P_3 are the payments made by the asset in Years 1, 2, and 3.

Asset	Market Interest Rate (i)	P_1	P_2	P_3	Present Value
Treasury Bill	4%	$1000	$0	$0	—
Bond	3%	$0	$0	$5000	—
Bond	5%	$200	$200	$200	—
Stock	6%	$50	$40	$60	—

a. For each asset, compute the asset's present value. (Note that the market interest rate, i, is not the same in each situation.)
b. Explain why the market price for each asset is expected to be the asset's present value.

11 Consider a bond that promises to make coupon payments of $100 one year from now and $100 two years from now, and to repay the principal of $1000 three years from now. Suppose also that the market interest rate is 8 percent per year, and that no perceived risk is associated with the bond.

a. Compute the present value of this bond.
b. Suppose the bond is being offered for $995. Would you buy the bond at that price? What do you expect to happen to the bond price in the very near future?
c. Suppose the bond is instead being offered at a price of $950. Would you buy the bond at that price? Do you expect the bond price to change in the near future?
d. If the price of the bond is equal to its computed present value from part (a), what is the implied bond yield?
e. Explain why bond yields and the market interest rate tend to move together so that economists can then usefully refer to "the" interest rate.

12 The table below provides information for six different bonds: current market price (P), the face value of the bond (V), and the number of years before the bond matures (N).

Bond Number	Market Price (P)	Face Value (V)	Years to Maturity (N)
1a	$926	$1000	1
1b	$850	$1000	1
2a	$1270	$2000	5
2b	$838	$2000	5
3a	$1760	$5000	10
3b	$684	$5000	10

a. In each case, compute the bond's yield, assuming that you buy the bond at its current market price and hold the bond until it matures. There are no coupons. If x is the bond's yield, then $P(1 + x)^N = V$.
b. Suppose bonds 1a, 2a, and 3a are all issued by the same borrower. Can you offer an explanation for the relationship between the bond yields and the terms to maturity?
c. Suppose bonds 1b, 2b, and 3b are all issued by the same borrower. What can you conclude about the riskiness of the "a" borrower versus that of the "b" borrower? Explain.
d. Notice that the market interest rate is not shown in the table. Explain why knowledge of the market interest rate is unnecessary in order to compute a bond's yield, once you already know the bond's market price. What aspect of the bond does the market interest rate influence, if anything?

13 The figure below shows an economy that begins in long-run equilibrium with money supply at $350 billion and real GDP equal to Y^* at $1200 billion. The money demand curve is M_D^0, the aggregate demand curve is AD_0, the aggregate supply curve is AS_0, and the price level is equal to 100. Assume that Y^* is unaffected by changes in the nation's money supply (i.e., there is no hysteresis).

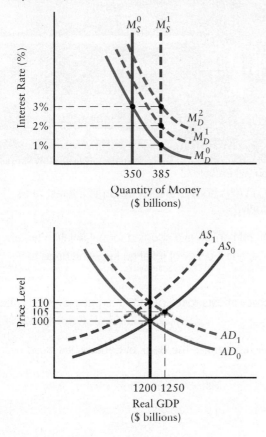

Quantity of Money
($ billions)

Real GDP
($ billions)

a. Suppose the central bank increases the money supply to $385 billion. What is the initial effect of the central bank's action before any changes in the price level and real GDP occur?

b. Once the economy's short-run adjustments have occurred, what are the levels of real GDP, the price level, and the interest rate? Explain which curves are shifting, and why.

c. In the short-run equilibrium from part (b), what output gap exists, if any? What starts happening to factor prices, and why?

d. Describe the economy's adjustment process to its new long-run equilibrium. What curves are shifting, and why?

e. After wages and other factor prices have fully adjusted, what are the new levels of real GDP, the price level, and the interest rate?

f. Was the increase in the money supply neutral in the short run? Explain.

g. Was the increase in the money supply neutral in the long run? Explain. What has been the long-run change in the *real* money supply?

28 Monetary Policy in Canada

CHAPTER OUTLINE	LEARNING OBJECTIVES (LO)
	After studying this chapter you will be able to
28.1 HOW THE BANK OF CANADA IMPLEMENTS MONETARY POLICY	**1** explain why the Bank of Canada chooses to directly target interest rates rather than the money supply.
28.2 INFLATION TARGETING	**2** understand why many central banks have adopted formal inflation targets.
	3 explain how the Bank of Canada's policy of inflation targeting helps to stabilize the economy.
28.3 LONG AND VARIABLE LAGS	**4** describe why monetary policy affects real GDP and the price level only after long time lags.
28.4 FOUR DECADES OF CANADIAN MONETARY POLICY	**5** discuss the main economic challenges the Bank of Canada has faced over the past four decades.

IN the previous two chapters we learned about money and its importance for the economy. In Chapter 26 we saw how commercial banks, through their activities of accepting deposits and extending loans, create deposit money. These bank deposits, together with the currency in circulation, make up the nation's money supply. In Chapter 27 we examined the variables that influence households' and firms' money demand. We then put money demand together with money supply to examine how interest rates are determined in the short run in monetary equilibrium. Finally, we examined the monetary transmission mechanism—the chain of cause-and-effect events describing how changes in money demand or supply

lead to changes in interest rates, aggregate demand, real GDP, and the price level.

Chapters 26 and 27 presented a general view of the role of money in the economy. What is still missing is a detailed account of how the Bank of Canada conducts its monetary policy.

We begin this chapter by describing some technical details about how the Bank influences the monetary equilibrium and thereby sets in motion the monetary transmission mechanism. We then discuss the Bank's current system of inflation targeting and how this system helps to stabilize the economy. Finally, we discuss some limitations for monetary policy and some of the Bank's major policy challenges over the past 40 years.

28.1 How the Bank of Canada Implements Monetary Policy

The monetary transmission mechanism describes how changes in the demand for or supply of money cause changes in the interest rate, which then lead to changes in aggregate demand, real GDP, and the price level. But how does the Bank of Canada influence the money market and thereby implement its monetary policy?

As we saw in Chapter 26, the money supply is the sum of currency in circulation and total bank deposits. Because the commercial banks control the process of deposit creation, and deposits are one component of money, the Bank of Canada cannot directly *set* the money supply. As we will soon see, the Bank of Canada is also unable to directly *set* interest rates. In the following discussion, therefore, we speak of the Bank "targeting" the money supply or interest rates rather than "setting" them directly.

Money Supply Versus the Interest Rate

In general, any central bank has two alternative approaches for implementing its monetary policy—it can choose to target the money supply or it can choose to target the interest rate. These two approaches are illustrated in Figure 28-1, which shows money demand, money supply, and the equilibrium interest rate. For any given M_D curve, the central bank must choose one approach or the other; it cannot target *both* the money

FIGURE 28-1   Two Approaches to the Implementation of Monetary Policy

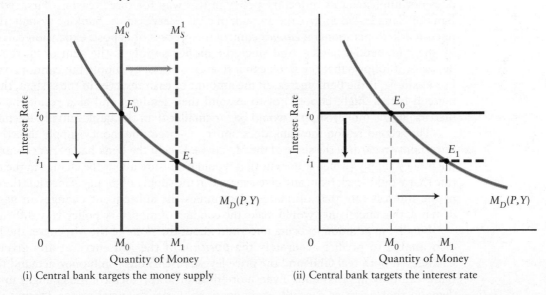

(i) Central bank targets the money supply   (ii) Central bank targets the interest rate

Monetary policy can be implemented either by targeting the money supply directly or by targeting the interest rate directly—but not both. In part (i), the Bank of Canada could attempt to shift the M_S curve directly and thereby change the equilibrium interest rate. But because the Bank cannot directly control the money supply, and because the slope and position of the M_D curve are uncertain, this is an ineffective way to conduct monetary policy. The Bank's chosen method is illustrated in part (ii), in which it targets the interest rate directly. It then accommodates the resulting change in money demand through its open-market operations.

supply and the interest rate independently. If it chooses to target the money supply, monetary equilibrium will determine the interest rate. Alternatively, if the central bank targets the interest rate, the money supply must adjust to accommodate the movement along the M_D curve.

> **Monetary policy can be implemented either by targeting the money supply or by targeting the interest rate. But for a given M_D curve, both cannot be targeted independently.**

Part (i) of Figure 28-1 shows how the Bank of Canada could attempt to shift the M_S curve directly, by changing the amount of currency in circulation in the economy. It could do this by buying or selling government securities in the financial markets—transactions called *open-market operations*. For example, by using currency to buy $100 000 of government bonds from a willing seller, the Bank of Canada would increase the amount of cash reserves in the banking system by $100 000. As we saw in Chapter 26, commercial banks would then be able to lend out these new reserves and thereby increase the amount of deposit money in the economy. The combined effect of the new reserves and the new deposit money would be an increase in the money supply and thus a shift of the M_S curve to the right. For a given M_D curve, this increase in money supply would lead to a reduction in the equilibrium interest rate and, through the various parts of the transmission mechanism, to an eventual increase in aggregate demand.

Why the Bank of Canada Does Not Target the Money Supply The Bank of Canada does not implement its monetary policy in this way for three reasons. First, while the Bank of Canada *can* control the amount of cash reserves in the banking system (through open-market operations) it *cannot* control the process of deposit expansion carried out by the commercial banks. And since the money supply is the sum of currency and deposits, it follows that the Bank can influence the money supply but cannot *control* it. For example, if the Bank increased the amount of cash reserves in the system, the commercial banks might choose not to expand their lending, and as a result the overall increase in the money supply would be far smaller than the Bank initially intended.

The second reason the Bank does not try to target the money supply directly is the uncertainty regarding the slope of the M_D curve. Even if the Bank had perfect control over the money supply (which it does not), it would be unsure about the change in the interest rate that would result from any given change in the supply of money. Since it is the change in the interest rate that ultimately determines the subsequent changes in aggregate demand, this uncertainty would make the conduct of monetary policy very difficult.

Finally, in addition to being uncertain about the *slope* of the M_D curve, the Bank is also unable to predict accurately the *position* of the M_D curve at any given time. Changes in both real GDP and the price level cause changes in money demand that the Bank can only approximate. Even more difficult to predict are the changes in money demand that occur as a result of innovations in the financial sector. During the late 1970s and early 1980s, for example, the creation of new types of bank deposits led to unprecedented and unpredicted changes in money demand, as people transferred funds between bank accounts of different types. More recently, such unpredictable transfers have increased in the era of internet banking, making money demand even harder to predict. Unpredictable fluctuations in the demand for money make a monetary policy based on the direct control of the money supply difficult to implement.

In summary, the disadvantages of conducting monetary policy by targeting the money supply are as follows:

1. The Bank of Canada cannot control the process of deposit creation.

2. There is uncertainty regarding the slope of the M_D curve.

3. There is uncertainty regarding the position of the M_D curve.

If the Bank of Canada chose to target the money supply, it would have little control over the resulting interest rate, which is the key link between the Bank's actions and aggregate demand. It therefore chooses *not* to implement its monetary policy in this way.

Why the Bank of Canada Targets the Interest Rate   The alternative approach to implementing monetary policy is to target the interest rate directly. This is the approach used by most central banks, including the Bank of Canada. As part (ii) of Figure 28-1 shows, if the Bank can directly change the interest rate, the result will be a change in the quantity of money demanded. In order for this new interest rate to be consistent with monetary equilibrium, the Bank must *accommodate* the change in the amount of money demanded—that is, it must alter the supply of money in order to satisfy the change in desired money holdings by firms and households (we will see shortly how this occurs).

Why does the Bank of Canada choose to implement its monetary policy in this manner? Let's consider the advantages. First, while the Bank cannot control the money supply for the reasons we have just discussed, it *is* able to almost completely control a particular interest rate. (We will see shortly which rate it targets and how it does so.) Second, the Bank's uncertainty about the slope and position of the M_D curve is not a problem when the Bank chooses instead to target the interest rate directly. If the Bank ascertains that a lower interest rate is necessary in order to achieve its policy objectives, it can act directly to reduce the interest rate. Any uncertainty about the M_D curve then implies uncertainty about the ultimate change in the quantity of money, but it is the interest rate that matters, through the transmission mechanism, for determining the level of aggregate demand.

Finally, the Bank can more easily *communicate* its policy actions to the public by targeting the interest rate than by targeting the money supply or the level of reserves in the banking system. Changes in the interest rate are more meaningful to firms and households than changes in the level of reserves or the money supply. For example, if we hear that the interest rate just decreased by one percentage point, most people can readily assess what this means for their plans to buy a new house financed by a mortgage. In contrast, if we were to hear that the level of reserves in the banking system had just increased by $1 billion, it would not be clear to most people what this means, or that it would have any effect on the interest rate, or by how much. Even the Bank itself would be uncertain about the magnitude of these effects.

In summary, these are the advantages of conducting monetary policy by targeting the interest rate:

1. The Bank of Canada is able to control a particular interest rate.

2. Uncertainty about the slope and position of the M_D curve does not prevent the Bank of Canada from establishing its desired interest rate.

3. The Bank of Canada can easily communicate its interest-rate policy to the public.

The Bank of Canada and the Overnight Interest Rate

We have just explained why the Bank of Canada chooses to implement its monetary policy by targeting the interest rate rather than by targeting the money supply directly. But *how* does the Bank do this, and *which* interest rate among many does it target?

As we discussed in Chapter 27, there are many interest rates in the Canadian economy. Commercial banks pay different rates to depositors on different types of bank deposits. They also lend at different rates for different kinds of loans—home mortgages, small business loans, personal lines of credit, and car loans, to name just a few. In addition, government securities trade at different yields (interest rates) depending on the term to maturity. Economists refer to the overall pattern of interest rates corresponding to government securities of different maturities as the *term structure of interest rates*. Since inflation and other risks generally lead bondholders to require a higher rate of return in order to lend their funds for a longer period of time, yields on government securities generally increase as the term to maturity increases. At any given time, the yield on 90-day Treasury bills is usually less than that on 5-year government bonds, which in turn is less than the yield on 30-year government bonds. Furthermore, because these various assets are viewed as close substitutes by bondholders, the different interest rates tend to rise and fall together.

In Canada, the interest rate corresponding to the shortest period of borrowing or lending is called the **overnight interest rate**, which is the interest rate that commercial banks charge one another for overnight loans. Commercial banks that need cash because they have run short of reserves can borrow in the *overnight market* from banks that have excess reserves available. The overnight interest rate is a market-determined interest rate that fluctuates daily as the cash requirements of commercial banks change.

The Bank of Canada exercises enormous influence over the overnight interest rate. As this rate rises or falls, the other interest rates in the economy—from short-term lines of credit to longer-term home mortgages and government securities—tend to rise or fall as well.

> **By influencing the overnight interest rate, the Bank of Canada also influences the longer-term interest rates that are more relevant for determining aggregate consumption and investment expenditure.**

To see how the Bank of Canada influences the overnight interest rate, we need to make an important distinction between the Bank's target and the instrument that it uses to achieve that target. The Bank establishes a target for the overnight interest rate and announces this target eight times per year at pre-specified dates called *fixed announcement dates*, or FADs.

The Bank's instrument for achieving its target is its lending and borrowing activities with the commercial banking system. When the Bank announces its target for the overnight rate, it also announces the **bank rate**, an interest rate 0.25 percentage points above the target rate. The Bank promises to lend at the bank rate any amount that commercial banks want to borrow. At the same time, the Bank offers to borrow (accept deposits) in unlimited amounts from commercial banks and pay them an interest rate 0.25 percentage points below the target rate. With these promises by the Bank, the actual overnight interest rate stays within the 0.5-percentage-point range centred around the target rate, and is usually very close to the target rate itself.

overnight interest rate The interest rate that commercial banks charge one another for overnight loans.

bank rate The interest rate the Bank of Canada charges commercial banks for loans.

Consider an example that illustrates the Bank's control over the overnight interest rate. We begin by assuming that the Bank's announced target for the overnight interest rate is 2 percent. The Bank is then willing to lend to commercial banks at the bank rate, 2.25 percent. The Bank is also willing to pay 1.75 percent on any deposits it receives from commercial banks. In this case, what will be the *actual* overnight interest rate? Without knowing more details about commercial banks' demands and supplies for overnight funds, we cannot know exactly what the rate will be, but we can be sure that it will be within the Bank's target range—that is, *between* 1.75 percent and 2.25 percent. It will not be above 2.25 percent because any borrower would rather borrow from the Bank of Canada at 2.25 percent than at a higher rate from any commercial lender. Similarly, it will not be below 1.75 percent because any lender would rather lend to the Bank of Canada at 1.75 percent than accept a lower rate from any commercial borrower. Thus, the Bank can ensure that the actual overnight interest rate remains within its target range.[1]

The Bank of Canada establishes a target for the overnight interest rate; its instrument for achieving this target is its borrowing and lending activities with commercial banks. By raising or lowering its target rate, the Bank affects the actual overnight interest rate. Changes in the overnight interest rate then lead to changes in other, longer-term, interest rates.

Figure 28-2 shows the path of the actual overnight interest rate and the Bank's target rate since 2000. It is almost impossible to tell the difference between the two lines in the figure, which shows the considerable influence that the Bank of Canada's actions have on the actual overnight interest rate.

The Money Supply Is Endogenous

When the Bank of Canada changes its target for the overnight rate, the change in the actual overnight rate happens almost instantly. Changes in other market interest rates, from home mortgage rates and the prime interest rate to the yields on short- and long-term government securities, also happen very quickly, usually within a day or two. As these rates adjust, firms and households begin to adjust their borrowing behaviour, but these changes take considerably longer to occur. For example, if the Bank of Canada lowered its target for the overnight rate by 25 basis points (0.25 percentage points), commercial banks might follow immediately by reducing the rate on home mortgages. But individuals will not respond to this rate reduction by immediately increasing their demand for home mortgages. Usually such changes take a while to occur, as borrowers consider how interest-rate changes affect their own economic situations, the affordability of a possible house purchase, or, in the case of firms, the profitability of a potential investment.

As the demand for new loans gradually adjusts to changes in interest rates, commercial banks often find themselves in need of more cash reserves with which to make new loans. When this occurs, banks can sell some of their government securities to the

---

[1] The actual overnight rate is usually indistinguishable from the Bank's target rate, but it occasionally deviates by as much as 10 basis points (0.1 percentage point). When this occurs, typically only a few days per month, the Bank of Canada initiates further temporary lending and borrowing transactions with the commercial banks in order to push the overnight rate back toward the Bank's target rate.

FIGURE 28-2 The Overnight Interest Rate: Target and Actual

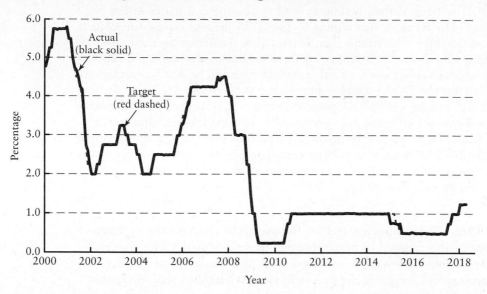

By setting a target for the overnight interest rate, the Bank of Canada exercises considerable influence over the actual overnight interest rate. By establishing an upper lending rate (the bank rate) and a lower borrowing rate, the Bank can ensure that the actual overnight interest rate remains within the Bank's target range. Since 2000, there have been only negligible differences between the actual overnight interest rate, the solid black line, and the Bank's target for the overnight rate, the red dashed line.

(*Source:* All data are monthly averages from the Bank of Canada: www.bankofcanada.ca. Overnight interest rate: Series V122514. Bank rate: Series V122530. The Bank's target rate is the bank rate minus 0.25 percentage points.)

open-market operation The purchase or sale of government securities on the open market by the central bank.

Bank of Canada in exchange for cash (or electronic reserves) and then use this cash to extend new loans. By buying government securities with cash in such an **open-market operation**, the Bank of Canada increases the amount of currency in circulation in the economy. This new currency arrives at the commercial banks as cash reserves, which can then be loaned out to firms or households. As we saw in Chapter 26, this process of making loans results in an expansion in deposit money and thus an expansion of the money supply.

> Through its open-market operations, the Bank of Canada changes the amount of currency in circulation. These operations, however, are generally not initiated by the Bank; it conducts them to accommodate the changing demand for cash reserves by the commercial banks.

Economists often say that the money supply is *endogenous*. Recall that the money supply is the sum of bank deposits and currency in circulation. The amount of bank deposits is not directly controlled by the Bank of Canada, but instead is determined by the economic decisions of households, firms, and commercial banks. And the Bank of Canada is *passive* in its decisions that change the amount of currency in circulation; it conducts its open-market operations to accommodate the changing demand for currency coming from the commercial banks. *Applying Economic Concepts 28-1* discusses in more detail how the Bank of Canada conducts open-market operations in response to this changing demand.

APPLYING ECONOMIC CONCEPTS 28-1

What Determines the Amount of Currency in Circulation?

The Bank of Canada uses its target for the overnight interest rate to influence the money market and implement its monetary policy. A reduction in the Bank's target for the overnight rate will reduce market interest rates and lead to a greater demand for borrowing and hence spending by firms and households. In contrast, an increase in the Bank's target for the overnight rate will tend to raise market interest rates and reduce the demand for borrowing and spending by firms and households.

In response to these changes in the demand for loans, commercial banks may find themselves either with too few cash reserves with which to make new loans or with too many cash reserves for the amount of loans they want to make. What happens in each case?

If Banks Need More Cash

Suppose that at the current market interest rates and level of economic activity, commercial banks are facing a growing demand for loans. If banks have excess reserves, these loans can be made easily. But once banks reach their target reserve ratio, they will be unable to extend new loans without increasing their cash reserves. Banks can increase their cash reserves by selling some of their government bonds to the Bank of Canada. In this case, the Bank of Canada is *purchasing* government bonds from the commercial banks. This transaction is called an *open-market purchase.*

Suppose a commercial bank wants to sell a $10 000 bond to the Bank of Canada. As the accompanying balance sheets show, this transaction does not change the total assets or liabilities for the commercial bank, although it changes the *form* of its assets. With more cash reserves (and fewer bonds), the commercial bank can now make more loans. For the Bank of Canada, however, there *is* a change in the level of assets and liabilities. Its holdings of bonds (assets) have increased and the amount of currency in circulation (liabilities) has also increased. Open-market purchases by the Bank of Canada are the means by which the amount of currency in the economy increases.

If Banks Have Excess Reserves

Now suppose that at the current market interest rates and level of economic activity the commercial banks cannot find enough suitable borrowers to whom they can lend their excess cash reserves. The commercial banks can reduce their excess cash reserves by using the cash to purchase government bonds from the Bank of Canada. In this case, the Bank of Canada is *selling* government bonds to the commercial banks. This transaction is called an *open-market sale.*

The changes would be the opposite of those shown in the accompanying balance sheets. The commercial bank would have less cash and more bonds, but its total assets and liabilities would be unchanged. The Bank of Canada would have fewer bonds and there would also be less currency in circulation in the economy.

Currency in a Growing Economy

If you look at the Bank of Canada's balance sheets (like the one we showed in Chapter 26) over several years, you will notice that the amount of currency in circulation rarely (if ever) falls. In an economy where national income is steadily growing, the demand for loans by firms and households is also usually growing, as is the demand for currency by commercial banks. In some years, the demand for currency is growing very quickly, in which case the Bank of Canada has many open-market purchases. In other years, the demand for currency grows only slowly, in which case the Bank has fewer (or smaller) open-market purchases. In a typical year, however, the amount of currency in circulation increases by about 4 percent, which in 2019 represented about $4 billion. Thus, in a typical week, the Bank of Canada purchases about $75 million of government bonds in the open market.

An Open-Market Purchase of Bonds from a Commercial Bank

Commercial Bank Balance Sheet

Assets		Liabilities
Bonds	− $10 000	No change
Cash Reserves	+ $10 000	

Bank of Canada Balance Sheet

Assets		Liabilities	
Bonds	+ $10 000	Currency in Circulation	+ $10 000

Expansionary and Contractionary Monetary Policies

We can now clarify the meaning of a *contractionary* or an *expansionary* monetary policy. Since what matters for the monetary transmission mechanism is the change in interest rates, economists label a monetary-policy action as being expansionary or contractionary depending on how the policy affects interest rates (rather than by the policy's impact on the money supply, which is harder to predict).

If the Bank of Canada wants to stimulate aggregate demand, it will reduce its target for the overnight interest rate, and the effect will soon be felt on longer-term market interest rates. Reducing the interest rate is an *expansionary* monetary policy because it leads to an expansion of aggregate demand. If the Bank instead wants to reduce aggregate demand, it will increase its target for the overnight interest rate, and longer-term market interest rates will soon rise as a result. Increasing the interest rate is a *contractionary* monetary policy because it leads to a contraction of aggregate demand.

As the longer-term market interest rates change, the various steps in the monetary transmission mechanism come into play. As we saw in Chapter 27, in an open economy like Canada's there are two separate channels in this transmission mechanism. First, desired investment and consumption expenditure will begin to change. At the same time, international capital flows in response to changes in interest rates will cause the exchange rate to change, which, in turn, causes net exports to change. Taken together, the total changes in aggregate expenditure lead to shifts in the *AD* curve, which then lead to changes in real GDP and the price level. The monetary transmission mechanism is reviewed in Figure 28-3.

FIGURE 28-3   The Monetary Transmission Mechanism

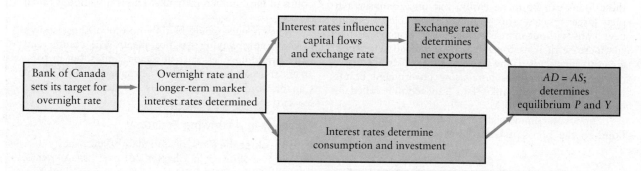

Monetary policy influences aggregate demand through the monetary transmission mechanism. The Bank of Canada sets a target for the overnight interest rate, which influences other market interest rates as well. The change in interest rates leads, via the monetary transmission mechanism, to changes in desired aggregate expenditure. Aggregate demand and aggregate supply then determine the price level and the level of real GDP.

▌ 28.2 Inflation Targeting

In the previous section we examined the technical details of how the Bank of Canada implements its monetary policy. In this section we examine the Bank's current policy objectives and how it conducts its monetary policy to achieve those objectives. Our emphasis is on the Bank's policy of *inflation targeting*.

Why Target Inflation?

Some people wonder why many central banks have established formal targets for the rate of inflation rather than for other important economic variables such as the rate of growth of real GDP or the unemployment rate. Central banks' focus on inflation comes from two fundamental observations regarding macroeconomic relationships: the costs associated with high inflation, and the ultimate cause of sustained inflation.

High Inflation Is Costly Economists have long accepted that high rates of inflation are damaging to the economy and are costly for firms and individuals. For those people whose incomes are stated in dollar terms, and are not indexed to adjust for changes in the price level, inflation can greatly reduce their purchasing power. For example, seniors whose pension incomes are not indexed to inflation suffer a reduction in their real incomes whenever inflation occurs. Similarly, those who have made loans or purchased bonds with interest rates that are fixed in nominal terms lose because inflation erodes the real purchasing power of their financial investments.

High inflation also undermines the ability of the price system to provide accurate signals of changes in relative scarcity through changes in relative prices. As a result, both producers and consumers may make mistakes regarding their own production and consumption decisions that they would not have made in the absence of high inflation.

Finally, the *uncertainty* generated by inflation is damaging to the economy in many ways. When inflation is high, it tends to be quite volatile, and this volatility makes it difficult to predict the future course of prices. As a result, periods of high inflation are often characterized as having much *unexpected* inflation. The risk of unexpected inflation makes it difficult for firms to make long-range plans, and such plans are crucial when firms undertake costly investment and R&D activities in order to expand their production facilities or to invent and innovate new products and new production processes. High and volatile inflation is thus harmful to economic growth.

> **High and uncertain inflation** reduces real incomes for many households and also hampers the ability of the price system both to allocate resources efficiently and to produce satisfactory rates of economic growth.

Monetary Policy Is the Cause of Sustained Inflation Until recent decades there was uncertainty about the causes of inflation. During the 1970s, many policymakers blamed inflation on the "cost push" exerted on wages by powerful unions and on prices by oligopolistic firms. In response, many governments adopted formal wage-and-price controls in an attempt to contain the inflations that they assumed were being generated from the supply side of the economy rather than from the demand side.

These attempts to control inflation proved to be costly failures as high inflation continued to plague many Western economies well into the 1980s. As a result of such failures, most economists soon came to adopt the argument that Milton Friedman had been making for many years, that inflation was mainly a monetary phenomenon.

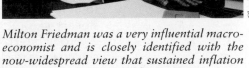

Milton Friedman was a very influential macro-economist and is closely identified with the now-widespread view that sustained inflation is ultimately a monetary phenomenon.

It was already recognized that shocks unrelated to monetary policy cause shifts in the *AD* and *AS* curves and thus cause temporary changes in the rate of inflation as the economy responds to these shocks. The change in view, however, was that *sustained* inflation was not caused by such shocks—instead, sustained inflation appeared to occur only in those situations in which monetary policy was allowing continual and rapid growth in the money supply. In other words, economists came to recognize that sustained inflation must ultimately be caused by central banks and their monetary policies.

With the acceptance of this view that sustained inflation is ultimately the result of monetary policy, central banks came to be seen as the main actors in the anti-inflation drama. If high and variable inflation rates were harmful to the economy and if central bank validation was a necessary condition for an inflation to be sustained, the central bank could prevent sustained inflation by adopting an appropriate monetary policy. In response to this belief, central banks around most of the developed world were given as their main responsibility the control of the price level and instructed to do this by adopting policies that targeted the rate of inflation.

> **Most economists and central bankers accept the idea that monetary policy is the most important determinant of a country's long-run rate of inflation.**

The Adoption of Inflation Targeting In 1990, New Zealand became the first country to adopt a formal system of *inflation targeting*. Canada was second, in 1991, followed soon by Israel, the United Kingdom, Australia, Finland, Spain, and Sweden. Since the mid-1990s, the list has grown to include Chile, Brazil, Colombia, Mexico, the Czech Republic, Poland, South Africa, Thailand, and the United States.

When the Bank of Canada first adopted its formal inflation targets in 1991 the annual rate of inflation was almost 6 percent. The targets were expressed as the midpoint of a 2-percentage-point band, in recognition of the fact that it is unrealistic to expect the Bank to keep the inflation rate at a single, precise value in the face of the many shocks that influence it in the short term. Beginning in 1992, the Bank of Canada's target range for inflation was 3 to 5 percent, with the range falling to 2 to 4 percent by 1993 and to 1 to 3 percent by the end of 1995. The Bank's formal inflation targets were renewed every five years between 1991 and 2016, with the current targets in place until 2021. (The Bank now emphasizes its 2 percent inflation target and places much less emphasis on the 1 to 3 percent range.) Figure 28-4 shows monthly data for two measures of Canadian inflation since 1992.

Inflation Targeting and the Output Gap

The Bank of Canada's currently stated policy objective is to keep inflation close to its formal 2 percent target. Achieving this objective requires the Bank to monitor the output gap and the associated pressures that may be pushing inflation above or below the target.

The Bank recognizes that because monetary policy has the potential to influence real GDP, it simultaneously has the potential to alter the size of the current output gap, from which comes the pressure for inflation to rise or fall. Faced with a persistent recessionary gap ($Y < Y^*$), which eventually tends to reduce inflation below the Bank's 2 percent target, the Bank can pursue an expansionary monetary policy. By doing so, it can attempt to close the output gap and bring real GDP back to Y^*, keeping the inflation rate close to 2 percent. Such a policy would be pursued until the output gap is eliminated and inflationary pressures threaten to move the inflation rate above the

2 percent target. Faced with a persistent inflationary gap ($Y > Y^*$), and the associated tendency for inflation to rise above the 2 percent target, the Bank can pursue a contractionary policy. By doing so, it can attempt to close the output gap and bring real GDP back toward Y^* and keep the inflation rate close to 2 percent.

> Persistent output gaps generally create pressure for the rate of inflation to change. To keep the rate of inflation close to the 2 percent target, the Bank of Canada closely monitors real GDP in the short run and designs its policy to keep real GDP close to potential output.

Inflation Targeting as a Stabilizing Policy

If the Bank of Canada is committed to keeping the rate of inflation near 2 percent, positive shocks that create an inflationary gap and threaten to increase the rate of inflation will be met by a contractionary monetary policy. The Bank will increase interest rates and shift the *AD* curve to the left. This policy will reduce the size of the output gap and push the rate of inflation back toward 2 percent. Similarly, if a negative shock creates a persistent recessionary gap, the Bank will respond with an expansionary monetary policy, reducing interest rates and shifting the *AD* curve to the right.

The short-run effects of the Bank's actions suggest that its policy of inflation targeting can be seen as an "automatic" stabilizer. But this is an exaggeration, as we can see by recalling our discussion in Chapter 24 of automatic fiscal stabilizers, which are caused by taxes and transfers that vary with the level of national income. Automatic fiscal stabilizers are truly "automatic" in the sense that no group of policymakers has to actively adjust policy—the stabilizers are built right into the tax-and-transfer system. With inflation targeting, however, there must be an active policy decision to keep inflation close to its target rate, and only then will the Bank's policy adjustments work to stabilize the economy in the face of shocks that create inflationary or recessionary output gaps.

> Inflation targets are not as "automatic" a stabilizer as the fiscal stabilizers built into the tax-and-transfer system. However, as long as the central bank is committed to achieving its inflation target, its policy adjustments will act to stabilize real GDP.

Complications in Inflation Targeting

So far, our discussion of inflation targeting makes the conduct of monetary policy seem relatively straightforward: Faced with a recessionary gap, the Bank of Canada implements an expansionary monetary policy; faced with an inflationary gap, the Bank of Canada implements a contractionary monetary policy. But there are several details that complicate the task considerably. In this section we discuss two complications for the conduct of monetary policy, and in the next section we address a more general difficulty.

Volatile Food and Energy Prices   Sometimes the rate of inflation increases for reasons unrelated to a change in the output gap. For example, many commodities whose prices are included in the Consumer Price Index (CPI) are internationally traded goods and their prices are determined in world markets. Oil is an obvious example, as are many raw materials and fruits and vegetables. When these prices rise suddenly, perhaps because of political instability in the Middle East (oil) or because of poor crop conditions in tropical countries (fruits and vegetables), the measured rate of inflation of the Canadian CPI also rises. Yet these price increases have little or nothing to do with the size of the output gap in Canada and thus have little implication for what policy action should be taken by the Bank of Canada. By focusing exclusively on the rate of inflation of the CPI, the Bank would be misled about the extent of inflationary pressures coming from excess demand in Canada.

For this reason, the Bank of Canada also monitors closely what is called the "core" rate of inflation. This is the rate of growth of a special price index, one that is constructed by extracting some food items, energy, and the effects of indirect taxes (such as the GST or excise taxes) from the Consumer Price Index. Figure 28-4 shows the paths of core and CPI inflation since 1992. As is clear from the figure, even though the two measures of inflation move broadly together, core inflation is much less volatile than is CPI inflation.

> Because the volatility of food and energy prices is often unrelated to the level of the output gap in Canada, the Bank of Canada closely monitors the rate of "core" inflation even though its formal target of 2 percent applies to the rate of CPI inflation. Changes in core inflation are a better indicator of short-run domestic inflationary pressures than are changes in CPI inflation.

FIGURE 28-4   Canadian CPI and Core Inflation, 1992–2018

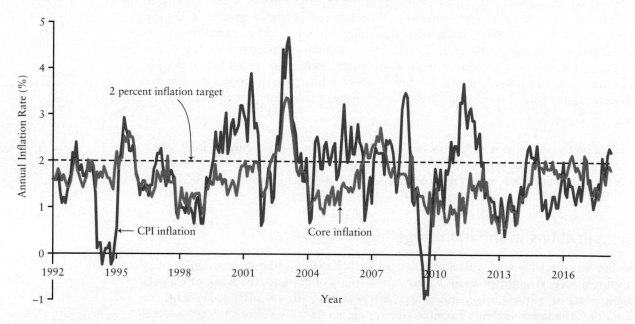

The CPI inflation rate is more volatile than the "core" inflation rate. The core rate of inflation in Canada is the rate of change of a special price index constructed by removing some food items, energy, and the effects of indirect taxes from the overall Consumer Price Index. For both series shown here, the inflation rate is computed monthly but is the rate of change in the price index from 12 months earlier.

(*Source:* Based on author's calculations using data from Statistics Canada, CANSIM database. CPI: Table 326-0020. Core: Table 176-0003.)

Note the sharp divergence between the two inflation rates in 1994. At that time, there were substantial decreases in the excise taxes on cigarettes. Since the resulting sharp decline in CPI inflation was caused by a reduction in taxes rather than by domestic excess supply, it would have been inappropriate for the Bank of Canada to respond to this decline in inflation by implementing an expansionary monetary policy. Instead, the Bank focused on the core inflation rate that excludes the effect of changes in indirect taxes. The core inflation rate in 1994 was relatively stable and close to the Bank's 2 percent target, indicating no need for a change in monetary policy.

Note also the volatility of the CPI inflation rate during 2008 and 2009. Energy and commodity prices had been rising for the previous few years, but they increased especially rapidly in the early part of 2008. This helped to push the CPI inflation rate well above 3 percent. But then the worst part of the global financial crisis occurred in the autumn of that year, energy and commodity prices plunged, and the CPI inflation rate fell quickly and was *negative* for a period of a few months in 2009. In contrast, the core rate of inflation was much less volatile during these events and remained much closer to 2 percent.

The Exchange Rate and Monetary Policy   Changes in the exchange rate—the Canadian dollar price of one unit of foreign currency—affect the relative prices of Canada's exports and imports. Since Canadian firms and households do a lot of trading with the rest of the world, a change in the exchange rate can have a major impact on aggregate demand, and hence on the output gap and the rate of inflation. For this reason, the Bank of Canada pays close attention to movements in the exchange rate. However, because changes in the exchange rate can have several different *causes*, care must be taken when drawing inferences about the desired change in monetary policy resulting from changes in the exchange rate. As we will see, there is no simple "rule of thumb" for how the Bank should react to a change in the exchange rate.

We consider two illustrative examples. In both cases, the Bank's actions are consistent with its objective of stabilizing real GDP and keeping the inflation rate near the Bank's 2 percent target.

For the first example, suppose that the economies of Canada's trading partners are booming and there is an increase in foreign demand for Canadian exports. This increase in demand for Canadian goods creates an increase in demand for the Canadian dollar in foreign-exchange markets. The Canadian dollar therefore appreciates. But the increase in demand for Canadian goods has added directly to Canadian aggregate demand and shifted the *AD* curve to the right. If this shock persists, it will eventually add to domestic inflationary pressures. In this case, if the Bank correctly determines the cause of the appreciation, it can take action to offset the positive demand shock by tightening monetary policy, which it does by raising its target for the overnight interest rate.

For the second example, suppose there is an increase in demand for Canadian *assets* rather than Canadian goods. This case has quite different implications. Suppose that investors, because of events happening elsewhere in the world, decide to liquidate some of their foreign assets and purchase more Canadian assets instead. The increase in demand for Canadian assets leads to an increase in demand for the Canadian dollar in foreign-exchange markets. The Canadian dollar therefore appreciates. In this case, however, as the dollar appreciates, Canadian exports become more expensive to foreigners. There will be a reduction in Canadian net exports and thus a reduction in Canadian aggregate demand. The *AD* curve shifts to the left. If this shock persists, it will create a recessionary gap. In this case, if the Bank correctly determines the cause of the appreciation, it can take action to offset the negative demand shock by loosening monetary policy, which it does by reducing its target for the overnight interest rate.

Notice in both examples that the Canadian dollar appreciated as a result of the external shock, but the causes of the appreciation were different. In the first case, there was a positive demand shock to net exports, which then caused the appreciation, which in turn dampened the initial increase in net exports. But the overall effect on the demand for Canadian goods was positive. In the second case, there was a positive shock to the *asset* market, which then caused the appreciation, which in turn reduced the demand for net exports. The overall effect on the demand for Canadian goods was negative. In the first case, the appropriate response for monetary policy was contractionary, whereas in the second case the appropriate response for monetary policy was expansionary.

Changes in the exchange rate can signal the need for changes in the stance of monetary policy. However, the Bank needs to determine the cause of the exchange-rate change before it can design a policy response appropriate for keeping real GDP close to potential and inflation close to the 2 percent target.

28.3 Long and Variable Lags

In Chapter 27 we encountered a debate that was prominent from the 1950s to the early 1980s. *Monetarists* argued that monetary policy was potentially very powerful in the sense that a given change in the money supply (or interest rates) would lead to a substantial change in aggregate demand, whereas *Keynesians* argued that monetary policy was much less powerful.

This debate had some of its roots in differing interpretations of the causes of the Great Depression. One interesting part of the debate is why Canada and the United Kingdom had collapses in economic activity similar in magnitude to that in the United States even though they did not suffer the widespread bank failures that featured in the U.S. experience. *Lessons from History 28-1* provides a brief summary of this interesting debate and applies some of the lessons about monetary policy we have learned in the past two chapters.

The debate between Monetarists and Keynesians was about more than just the *effectiveness* of monetary policy. The debate sometimes also focused on the question of whether active use of monetary policy in an attempt to stabilize output and the price level was likely to be successful or whether it would instead lead to *increased* economic instability. This debate is as important today as it was then, and at its centre is the role of *lags*.

What Are the Lags in Monetary Policy?

Experience has shown that lags in the operation of policy can sometimes cause stabilization policy to be destabilizing. In Chapter 24, we discussed how decision and implementation lags might limit the extent to which active use of fiscal policy can be relied upon to stabilize the economy. Although both of these sources of lags are less relevant for monetary policy, the full effects of monetary policy nevertheless occur only after quite long time lags. For two reasons, a change in monetary policy does not quickly affect the economy.

Changes in Expenditure Take Time   When the Bank of Canada changes its target for the overnight interest rate, the actual overnight rate changes almost instantly. Other, longer-term interest rates also change quickly, usually within a day or two. However, it takes more time before households and firms adjust their spending and borrowing plans in response to the change in interest rates. Consumers may respond relatively quickly and alter their plans for purchasing durable goods like cars and appliances. But it takes longer for firms to modify their investment plans and then put them into effect. It may take a year or more before the full increase in investment expenditure occurs in response to a fall in interest rates.

In an open economy such as Canada's, the change in the interest rate also leads to flows of financial capital and a change in the exchange rate. These changes occur very quickly. But the subsequent effect on net exports takes more time while purchasers of internationally traded goods and services switch to lower-cost suppliers.

The Multiplier Process Takes Time   Changes in consumption, investment, and net export expenditures brought about by a change in monetary policy set off the multiplier process that increases national income. This process, too, takes some time to work through. Furthermore, although the end result is fairly predictable, the speed with which the entire expansionary or contractionary process works itself through the economy can vary in ways that are hard to predict. Thus, though the overall effects of monetary policy might be reasonably straightforward to predict, the timing of those effects is difficult to predict.

> Monetary policy is capable of exerting expansionary and contractionary forces on the economy, but it operates with a time lag that is long and difficult to predict.

Economists at the Bank of Canada estimate that it normally takes between 9 and 12 months for a change in monetary policy action to have its main effect on real GDP, and a further 9 to 12 months for the policy action to have its main effect on the rate of inflation.

Destabilizing Policy?

The fact that monetary-policy actions taken today will not affect real GDP and inflation until one to two years in the future means that the Bank of Canada must design its policy for what *is expected* to occur in the future rather than what *has already been observed*. To see why a monetary policy guided only by past and current events may be destabilizing, consider the following simple example. Suppose that on January 1 the Bank observes that real GDP is less than potential output and concludes that an expansionary monetary policy is appropriate. It can reduce its target for the overnight rate at the next fixed announcement date (FAD), typically within a few weeks. By early February, the overnight interest rate will be reduced, as will the longer-term interest rates in the economy. The effects on aggregate demand, however, will not be felt in any significant way until late summer or early fall of that same year.

This policy action may turn out to be destabilizing, however. Some of the cyclical forces in the economy, unrelated to the Bank's actions, may have reversed since January, and by fall there may be an inflationary output gap. However, since the effects of the

LESSONS FROM HISTORY 28-1

Two Views on the Role of Money in the Great Depression

In most people's minds, the Great Depression began with the stock market crash of October 1929. In the United States, Canada, and Europe, the decline in economic activity over the next four years was massive. From 1929 to 1933, real output fell by roughly 25 percent, one-quarter of the labour force was unemployed by 1933, the price level fell by more than 25 percent, and businesses failed on a massive scale. In the many decades that have followed, no recession has equalled the Great Depression in terms of reduced economic activity, business failures, or unemployment.

The Great Depression has naturally attracted the attention of economists and, especially in the United States, these few years of experience have served as a kind of "retrospective laboratory" in which they have tested their theories.

The Basic Facts

The stock market crash of 1929, and other factors associated with a moderate downswing in business activity during the late 1920s, caused U.S. firms and households to want to hold more cash and fewer demand deposits in banks. The banking system, however, could not meet this increased demand for cash without help from the Federal Reserve System (the U.S. central bank). As we saw in Chapter 26, because of the fractional-reserve banking system, commercial banks are never able to satisfy from their own reserves a large and sudden demand for cash— their reserves are always only a small fraction of total deposits.

The Federal Reserve had been set up in 1913 to provide just such emergency assistance to commercial banks that were basically sound but were unable to meet sudden demands by depositors to withdraw cash. However, the Federal Reserve refused to extend the necessary help, and successive waves of bank failures followed as a direct result. During each wave, hundreds of banks failed, ruining many depositors, reducing the flow of credit, and worsening an already severe recession. In the second half of 1931, almost 2000 U.S. banks were forced to suspend operations. One consequence of these failures was a sharp drop in the money supply; by 1933, M2 was 33 percent lower than it had been in 1929.

Competing Explanations

For many years after the Great Depression was over, economists examined the data and constructed explanations for these dramatic events. To Monetarists, the basic facts seem decisive: To them, the fall in the money supply was clearly the major *cause* of the fall in output and employment that occurred during the Great Depression. Monetarists see the Great Depression as perhaps the single best piece of evidence of the strength of monetary forces and the single best lesson of the importance of monetary policy. In their view, the increased cash drain that led to the massive monetary contraction could have been prevented had the Federal Reserve quickly increased the level of cash reserves in the commercial banking system. In this case, the rise in cash reserves would have offset the increase in the cash drain, so that the money supply could be maintained.

monetary expansion that was initiated nine months earlier are just beginning to be felt, an expansionary monetary stimulus is adding to the current inflationary gap.

If the Bank now applies the monetary brakes by raising its target for the overnight interest rate, the output effects of this policy reversal will not be felt for another year or so. By that time, a contraction may have already set in because of the natural cyclical forces of the economy. Thus, the delayed effects of the monetary policy may turn what might otherwise have been a minor downturn into a major recession.

The long time lags in the effectiveness of monetary policy increase the difficulty of stabilizing the economy; monetary policy may have a destabilizing effect.

The Bank of Canada recognizes the possibility that if it responds to every shock that influences real GDP, the overall effect of its policy may be to destabilize the economy rather than stabilize it. As a result, it is careful to assess the causes of the shocks that buffet the Canadian economy. It tries to avoid situations in which it responds to

In contrast, Keynesians argued that the fundamental cause of the Great Depression was a reduction in autonomous expenditure. They cite a large decline in housing construction, a decline in automobile purchases, and a reduction in consumption driven largely by pessimism caused by the stock market crash. Although Keynesians accept the argument that the Federal Reserve's behaviour was perverse and exacerbated an already bad situation, they do not attribute a pivotal role to the Federal Reserve or to the money supply. Instead, they see the fall in the money supply as a *result* of the decline in economic activity, through a reduced demand for loans and thus reduced bank lending, rather than as its primary cause.

Lessons from Canada's Experience

Canada had broadly the same magnitude of economic collapse as did the United States during the Great Depression, but had *no* bank failures. Unfortunately, Canada's experience is not able to resolve the disagreement—both sides of the debate can offer explanations of the Canadian experience consistent with their central arguments.

Keynesians look to Canada's experience to support their view that money was not central to the cause of the economic collapse in the United States. They point out that since Canada did not escape the Great Depression but *did* escape the banking crisis and the associated collapse in the money supply, money was unlikely to have been the central cause of the U.S. economic collapse.

Monetarists accept the point that Canada did not have a massive reduction in the money supply, but they argue that the economic contraction in the United States (which *was* caused by the collapse in the money supply) spilled over into Canada, largely through a dramatic

reduction in demand for Canadian goods. This spillover implies a large decline in export expenditure for Canada, and thus a decline in Canadian national income. Thus, Monetarists essentially argue that money (and inappropriate monetary policy) in the United States was an important contributor to the economic decline in Canada.

During the Great Depression, bank failures were widespread in the United States but did not occur at all in Canada. This difference in experience can be used to test hypotheses regarding the causes of the Great Depression. But considerable disagreement still remains.

For a discussion of these two views, and some attempts to discriminate between them, see Peter Temin, *Did Monetary Forces Cause the Great Depression?* Norton, 1976.

---

shocks that are believed to be short-lived and then must reverse its policy in the near future when the shocks disappear. In general, the Bank responds only to those shocks that are significant in magnitude and are expected to persist for several months or more. For example, the global recession that began in 2008 was both large and long-lasting, and the Bank's expansionary policies had ample time to operate in the appropriate direction even after the expected lags in their effectiveness.

Communications Difficulties

Long lags in the workings of monetary policy also lead to some criticism of the central bank's policy actions.

Figure 28-5 shows a situation in which the current inflation rate is well below the 2 percent target but the expectation of future events suggests that inflation will soon rise and exceed the target. This situation is often faced by the Bank when the economy is in the late stages of an economic recovery, with real GDP still below Y^*, as was the case in mid-2017. At that time, monetary policy had been expansionary for over eight

FIGURE 28-5   Forward-Looking Monetary Policy

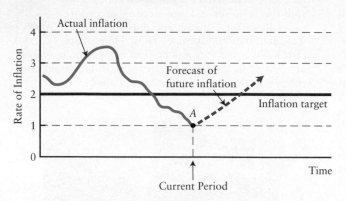

Since monetary policy works only with a considerable time lag, central-bank actions to keep inflation close to target must be taken in advance of expected future events. Suppose the economy is currently at point *A* with inflation well below the target. If events in the near future are expected to cause inflation to rise and exceed the target, then monetary policy must be tightened, even though *current* inflation is low.

years in an effort to stimulate the economy and offset the long-lasting effects of a global economic recession. But as real GDP began to grow and the existing recessionary gap began to narrow, the Bank needed to judge the appropriate time to begin tightening its policy in an attempt to keep inflation from rising above the 2 percent target.

What is the problem for the Bank's communications? Remember that because of the time lags involved, any policy change that occurs today has no effect on real GDP for roughly 9 months and the full effect on the rate of inflation does not occur for 18 to 24 months. If the economy is at point *A* in Figure 28-5, and inflation is expected to rise in the near future, then monetary policy must be changed *now* in order to counteract this future inflation. But this action could generate some criticism because the *current* inflation rate is low. In such situations, the Bank finds itself in the awkward position of advocating a tightening of monetary policy, in order to fight the expectation of future inflation, at a time when the *current* inflation rate suggests no need for tightening. But if the goal is to keep inflation close to the 2 percent target, such *pre-emptive* monetary policy is necessary because of the unavoidable time lags.

> Time lags in monetary policy require that decisions regarding a loosening or tightening of monetary policy be forward-looking. This often leads to criticism of monetary policy, especially by those who do not recognize the long time lags.

28.4 Four Decades of Canadian Monetary Policy

This section describes a few key episodes in recent Canadian monetary history. This is not done to teach history for its own sake, but because the lessons of past experience and past policy mistakes, interpreted through the filter of economic theory, provide our best hope for improving our policy performance in the future.

The OPEC oil-price shocks of 1973 and 1979–1980 led to reductions in GDP growth rates and increases in inflation in Canada—what came to be known as *stagflation*. At that time, the role of aggregate-supply shocks and their effect on macroeconomic equilibrium was not as well understood as it is today. The Bank of Canada's policy response involved considerable monetary expansion, and by 1980 the rate of inflation in Canada was more than 12 percent.

The Bank of Canada then embarked on policies designed to reduce the growth rate of the money supply and eventually reduce the inflation rate. Unfortunately, at the same time innovations in the financial sector led to unexpected increases in the demand for money. The result was a much sharper increase in interest rates (see Figure 28-6)

FIGURE 28-6   **Short-Term Interest Rates, Canada and the United States, 1975–2018**

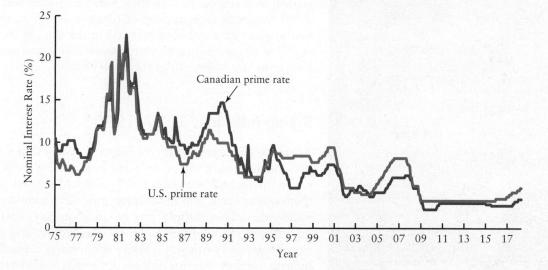

(*Source:* Based on Bank of Canada data, Tables 176-0043 and 176-0044. Both are monthly averages.)

than was intended by the Bank of Canada and the most serious recession since the 1930s. But the rate of inflation *did* fall, from more than 12 percent in 1980 to about 4 percent in 1984. This experience taught the Bank two important lessons:

1. Monetary policy can be *very* effective in reducing inflation.

2. Because of unexpected changes in money demand, monetary policy should focus more on interest rates than on the money supply.

As we saw earlier in this chapter, this second lesson is an important reason why the Bank now implements its policy by targeting the interest rate rather than by directly targeting the money supply.

Economic Recovery: 1983–1987

Following Canada's deep recession of 1981–1982, a sustained recovery began in 1983, and by mid-1987 real GDP had moved back toward potential. The main challenge for monetary policy in this period was to create sufficient liquidity to accommodate the recovery without triggering a return to the high inflation rates that prevailed at the start of the decade. In other words, the Bank of Canada had to increase the money supply to *accommodate* the recovery-induced increase in money demand *without* increasing the money supply so much that it refuelled inflationary pressures.

In spite of much debate and uncertainty, the Bank handled this "re-entry" problem quite well. The Bank allowed a short but rapid burst of growth in the nominal money supply, intended to accommodate the rise of money demand accompanying the

Tom Hanson/The CP Images

John Crow was the governor of the Bank of Canada from 1987 to 1994. In 1988 he announced that "price stability" would thenceforth be the Bank of Canada's objective.

recovery. It then reduced the growth rate of the money supply to a rate consistent with low inflation and the underlying growth in real income. The trick with this policy was that to avoid triggering expectations of renewed inflation, the Bank had to generate a one-shot increase in the *level* of the money supply without creating the impression that it was raising the long-term *rate of growth* of the money supply.

Rising Inflation: 1987–1990

By mid-1987, many observers began to worry that Canadian policymakers were too complacent in accepting the 4 percent range into which Canadian inflation had settled. Further, there was concern that inflationary pressures were starting to build—the money supply was growing quickly, real output growth was strong, unemployment was falling, and an inflationary gap was opening. Many economists argued that if monetary policy was not tightened, Canada would experience gradually increasing inflation until once again a severe monetary restriction would be required to reduce the rate of inflation.

In January 1988, Bank of Canada Governor John Crow announced that monetary policy would henceforth be guided by the goal of achieving long-term "price stability." Specifically, he said that "monetary policy should be conducted so as to achieve a pace of monetary expansion that promotes stability in the value of money. This means pursuing a policy aimed at achieving and maintaining stable prices."[2]

This explicit adoption of price stability as the Bank's only target set off a heated debate about the appropriate stance for monetary policy. The debate was fuelled by Crow's decision to give a high profile to his policy by repeatedly explaining it in speeches and public appearances. He believed that this was necessary because expectations of continuing inflation had become entrenched. In his view, until the public believed that the Bank was serious about controlling inflation, whatever the short-term consequences, inflation could not be reduced. Some critics said that price stability was unobtainable. Others said the costs of reaching it would be too large in terms of several years of recessionary gaps. Supporters said that the long-term gains from having low inflation would exceed the costs of getting there.

Despite the Bank's explicit policy of "price stability," the actual inflation rate increased slightly from about 4 percent in 1987 to just over 5 percent in 1990. The controversy reached new heights when in 1990 the country (and much of the world) entered a sustained recession. Maintaining a tight monetary policy with high interest rates (see Figure 28-6) seemed perverse to many when the economy was already suffering from too little aggregate demand to sustain potential output.

---

[2] John W. Crow, "The Work of Canadian Monetary Policy," speech given at the University of Alberta, January 18, 1988; reprinted in *Bank of Canada Review*, February 1988.

Furthermore, the high Canadian interest rates attracted foreign financial capital. Foreigners who wanted to buy Canadian bonds needed Canadian dollars, and their demands led to an appreciation of the Canadian dollar. This increased the price of Canadian exports while reducing the price of Canadian imports, putting Canadian export and import-competing industries at a competitive disadvantage and further increasing the unemployment that had been generated by the worldwide recession.

Inflation Targeting: 1991–2000

In spite of heavy political pressure to reduce interest rates, the Bank stood by its tight monetary policy. In 1991, it formally announced *inflation-control targets* for the next several years. Beginning in 1992, inflation was to lie within the 3 to 5 percent range, with the range falling to 2 to 4 percent by 1993 and to 1 to 3 percent by the end of 1995.

The inflation rate fell sharply, from about 5 percent in 1990 to less than 2 percent in 1992. For 1993 and 1994, inflation hovered around 2 percent. Furthermore, short-term nominal interest rates fell from a high of about 13 percent in 1990 to about 6 percent by the end of 1993. Recall that the nominal interest rate is equal to the real interest rate plus the rate of inflation. So this decline in nominal interest rates was the eventual result of the tight monetary policy that reduced inflation.

Gordon Thiessen became the governor of the Bank of Canada in 1994, after inflation had hovered around 2 percent for about two years.

The Bank had succeeded in coming close to its target of price stability. Controversy continued, however, on two issues. First, was the result worth the price of a deeper, possibly more prolonged recession than might have occurred if the Bank had been willing to accept slightly higher inflation? Second, would the low inflation rate be sustainable once the recovery took the economy back toward potential output?

The debate over the Bank's emphasis on maintaining low inflation became centred on Governor John Crow, especially during the federal election campaign of 1993. Some called for Crow's replacement with someone perceived to care more about the costs of fighting inflation. Others argued that the Bank's policy of "price stability" under Crow's stewardship was the right policy for the times and that the long-run benefits of maintaining low inflation would be worth the costs required to achieve it.

In 1994, at the end of Crow's seven-year term, the minister of finance appointed Gordon Thiessen, the former senior deputy governor of the Bank, to be the new governor. With some irony, the minister of finance, whose party had been severe critics of Crow's policy while they were in opposition, affirmed the previous monetary policy of the Bank and urged the new governor to maintain the hard-won low inflation rate. The new governor agreed and extended the formal inflation target of 2 percent until 2001.

For the next three years, the rate of inflation continued to hover between 1 and 2 percent. The main challenge for the Bank in the next few years was to keep inflation low while at the same time encouraging the economy to progress through what was viewed as a fragile recovery. Excessive stimulation of the economy would lead to the rise of inflation, which would sacrifice the hard-won gains achieved only a few years earlier. On the other hand, insufficient stimulation would itself be an obstacle to economic recovery.

Changes in stock-market values also created challenges for the Bank of Canada in the late 1990s. From 1994 through 1999, U.S. and Canadian stocks enjoyed unprecedented bull markets. The Dow Jones Industrial Average (an index of U.S. stock prices) increased from about 3500 in mid-1994 to about 11 000 in late 1999, an average annual increase of 26 percent. The Toronto Stock Exchange Index (now called the S&P/TSX) increased from roughly 4000 to 8000 over the same period, an average annual increase of 14 percent.

The concern for the Bank of Canada during this time was that the increase in wealth generated by these stock-market gains would stimulate consumption expenditures in what was already a steadily growing economy, thus increasing inflationary pressures. In December 1996, the chairman of the U.S. Federal Reserve, Alan Greenspan, warned market participants about their "irrational exuberance," a phrase that is now often quoted. Bank of Canada Governor Gordon Thiessen made similar remarks in Canada. Both central bankers were trying to dampen expectations in the stock market so that the stock-market gains, and thus the increases in wealth-induced spending, would not significantly contribute to inflationary pressures. But they had to be careful not to have their comments create a "crash" in the market that would have even more dramatic effects in the opposite direction.

As it turned out, the crash happened anyway. In both the United States and Canada, the stock markets had reached such levels that many commentators said it was only a matter of time before participants realized that stock prices no longer reflected the underlying values of the companies, at which point there would be massive selling and an inevitable crash. From the fall of 2000 to the spring of 2001, the major Canadian stock-market indexes fell by roughly 40 percent, driven to a large extent by huge reductions in the stock prices of high-tech firms. This stock-market decline is often referred to as the "dot-com" crash.

Inflation Targeting: 2001–2007

David Dodge became the new governor of the Bank of Canada in the spring of 2001. During his tenure as governor, the Bank faced several significant policy challenges.

When the terrorist attacks in New York and Washington occurred on September 11, 2001, the stock markets took another dramatic plunge. By late in 2003, stock markets were still far below their pre-crash levels. The main challenge for monetary policy was to provide enough liquidity to the banking systems to prevent the economy from entering a recession. In both Canada and the United States, the central banks dramatically lowered their key interest rates over a period of several months.

From 2002 to 2005, the Bank of Canada's target for the overnight interest rate was 3 percentage points below its level from the summer of 2000. During this period, two external forces on the Canadian economy became apparent and presented a further challenge for the Bank of Canada. First, strong world economic growth, especially in China and India, contributed to a substantial increase in the world prices of oil and other raw materials. Given Canada's position as a

David Dodge was the governor of the Bank of Canada from 2001 to early 2008. He needed to steer monetary policy during a time of a strong appreciation of the Canadian dollar, driven partly by rising world commodity prices.

Dick Loek/Toronto Star/Getty Images

major producer and exporter of these products, these price increases represented a significant positive external shock to aggregate demand. They also contributed to a substantial appreciation of the Canadian dollar, by more than 40 percent from 2002 to 2005. Taken by itself, this positive shock to Canadian aggregate demand created a justification for the Bank of Canada to tighten its monetary policy.

Working in the opposite direction was a second external shock, also contributing to an appreciation of the Canadian dollar. During the 2002–2005 period, partly in response to a large and growing U.S. current account deficit, the U.S. dollar was depreciating against the pound sterling and the euro. This "realignment" of the U.S. dollar also involved Canada and explained some part of the Canadian dollar's appreciation during that period. These exchange-rate changes, which were not themselves being caused by changes in the demand for Canadian goods and services, nonetheless tended to reduce Canadian net exports and aggregate demand, thus providing some justification for a loosening of Canadian monetary policy.

The problem for the Bank of Canada during this period was to determine the *relative* strength of these opposing forces and thus the appropriate *overall* direction for monetary policy. During the early part of this period, when Canadian real GDP was below potential, the Bank allowed the commodity–price-driven expansion to close the existing output gap. By the summer of 2005, however, when the output gap appeared to be all but closed yet commodity prices were still rising, the Bank began a series of increases in the target for the overnight interest rate. By the summer of 2006 it had increased its target rate by two percentage points.

Throughout 2006 and 2007, world commodity prices continued their steep ascent and the effect on the Canadian economy was dramatic. Employment grew rapidly, real GDP grew above the level of potential output, and serious concerns about inflation began to mount. During this period, the Bank of Canada continued to gradually raise its policy interest rate.

A related challenge for the Bank during this period involved regional and sectoral differences in economic performance within Canada. The strong growth in the prices of oil and raw materials naturally led to boom conditions in these sectors, which tend to be located in both Western and Atlantic Canada. However, these price increases harmed the profitability of many central Canadian manufacturing firms who used these products as important inputs. In addition, the appreciation of the Canadian dollar further challenged these firms, as foreign buyers reduced their demand for more expensive Canadian-made products.

Regional and sectoral differences highlight an inherent difficulty with monetary policy in a country as economically diverse as Canada. Because there must be a single monetary policy for the nation as a whole (as long as all parts of Canada continue to use the same currency), policy must be guided by the *average* level of economic activity in order to keep the *average* rate of inflation close to its target. But significant differences in economic activity across regions and/or sectors mean that many people will feel that monetary policy is being conducted inappropriately because economic activity in their specific region or sector is not the same as the national average.

Financial Crisis and Recession: 2007–2010

The next significant phase of Canadian monetary policy was determined largely by events in other countries. From 2002 to 2006, U.S. housing prices had been rising unusually rapidly, but they began to slow their ascent in the middle of 2006. In 2007,

Adrian Wyld/The CP Images

Mark Carney became the Bank of Canada's governor in early 2008, amid a global financial crisis and the beginning of a significant economic recession.

these prices reached their peak and then collapsed, falling by more than 30 percent in many parts of the country. On a large scale, U.S. homeowners began "walking away" from their houses, whose market values had fallen below the total amount owing on the associated mortgages. In these situations, the financial institution holding the mortgage no longer receives regular mortgage payments from the homeowner and instead takes ownership of the vacated house.

For the many financial institutions that held the mortgages—or the securities backed by the mortgages—the housing collapse led to a significant decline in the value of their assets. It soon became clear that millions of U.S. mortgages and mortgage-backed securities had been bought by financial institutions all over the world, and many large financial institutions in many countries were soon on the edge of insolvency and bankruptcy. What began as a collapse of U.S. housing prices soon became a global financial crisis.

Mark Carney became the new governor of the Bank of Canada in February 2008, just as the financial crisis was entering its most serious phase. With the collapse of major U.S. and U.K. financial institutions only a few months later, panic spread throughout the world's financial sector. It was unclear which institutions held large amounts of these "toxic" mortgage-backed securities and thus which institutions were in danger of going under. In this setting, the widespread fear in financial markets led to a virtual disappearance of short-term interbank lending. The flow of credit declined, and most lending that did take place was transacted at much higher interest rates. Given the importance of credit in a market economy, restoring the flow of credit was essential to maintaining the level of economic activity.

In Canada, it soon became clear that Canadian banks were far less exposed to these "toxic" mortgage-backed securities than were the banks in the United States and much of Europe. As a result, there was no significant danger of a Canadian bank becoming insolvent during this episode. However, because of the globalized nature of financial markets, short-term credit markets in Canada are highly integrated with those in other countries, with the result that Canada also experienced a decline in interbank lending and a rise in short-term interest rates. The Bank of Canada took two sets of actions during 2007–2008. First, it reduced its target for the overnight rate by more than 3.5 percentage points between the fall of 2007 and the end of 2008. Second, it eased the terms with which it was prepared to make short-term loans to financial institutions. Both sets of actions were designed to restore the flow of credit and reduce interest rates, thus helping to maintain the level of economic activity.

By late in 2008, however, it was clear that Canada would not be shielded from the global recession that was then beginning. The global financial crisis had a dramatic effect on the level of economic activity in the United States, the European Union, and many countries in Asia. With these economies experiencing recessions, there was a sharp decline in demand for Canada's exports. Canadian real GDP slowed sharply in late 2008 and began to fall in early 2009. The Bank of Canada's objective at this time was to provide as much monetary stimulus as was possible, complementing the large fiscal stimulus implemented by the Canadian government in its budget of 2009.

The Canadian economy experienced a significant recession through most of 2009 but returned to positive growth in real GDP in 2010. Despite the fact that the Bank was still holding its target for the overnight rate at historically very low levels, a significant recessionary gap persisted. Two external forces played an important role in dampening the growth of real GDP. First, the U.S. economy, though technically out of recession, was experiencing only a slow and gradual recovery; the low U.S. growth implied low demand for that economy's traditional imports of Canadian goods and services. Second, the global financial crisis of 2008 had eventually led to a "sovereign debt crisis" in Europe, in which government (sovereign) debt had increased dramatically in response to the recession and the provision of financial support to failing banks.

Slow Economic Recovery: 2011–Present

The next phase of Canadian monetary policy coincided with the long and gradual economic recovery that followed the global financial crisis. Historically, financial crises create a general lack of confidence in the future, and also lead banks, firms, and households to strive to reduce their debts and improve their balance sheets. The combination of lack of confidence and the desire to reduce debt contribute to weak growth in aggregate demand and thus to slow growth in GDP in the normal course of events. The aftermath of the global financial crisis of 2008–2009 was no different, but the recovery was more gradual, with the result that monetary policy remained very expansionary for a longer period than is normal following more "conventional" recessions. From 2011 to 2014, the Bank of Canada's target for the overnight interest rate remained at 1 percent. While inflation was slightly below the Bank's 2 percent target, real GDP remained significantly below Y^* and unemployment was elevated.

Two concerns affected the Bank's views on appropriate policy during this time. On the one hand, the existing recessionary gap pointed in the direction of further cuts to the Bank's policy interest rate to stimulate the economy (even though some argued that with interest rates already so low it was unlikely that further reductions would have much of an impact on aggregate demand). On the other hand, household debt and house prices were both rising to unprecedented levels during this time, generating concerns of a possible "crash" in house prices, which could then present even more problems. The Bank was concerned that further cuts to its policy interest rate would merely exacerbate these ongoing trends. Faced with a stubborn recessionary gap and also continuing increases in debt and house prices, the Bank chose to maintain an unchanged policy interest rate.

Stephen Poloz became the governor of the Bank of Canada in the summer of 2013. For the first 12 months of his term, the Bank's policy interest rate was held constant as the Canadian economy continued its gradual economic recovery. In mid-2014, however, the world price of oil began a rapid descent, from about U.S. $105 per barrel in June 2014 to below U.S. $40 per barrel by December 2015.

Stephen Poloz became the Governor of the Bank of Canada in 2013. The challenges associated with a slow economic recovery were worsened by a dramatic fall in the world price of oil during 2014 and 2015.

This decline represented a massive and sudden negative shock to Canada's aggregate demand, with especially negative effects in the oil-producing regions of Alberta, Saskatchewan, and Newfoundland and Labrador. In January 2015 Stephen Poloz surprised financial markets by reducing the Bank's target for the overnight interest rate by 0.25 percentage points, indicating the need for monetary policy to respond to the large reduction in aggregate demand. A further reduction, to a target rate of 0.5 percent, followed in July 2015.

For the next three years, the Canadian economic recovery proceeded gradually, aided by the combination of a gradually increasing world price of oil and growing export demand due to a faster recovery in the United States. The U.S. Federal Reserve raised its policy interest rate gradually during this period, as did the Bank of Canada.

One important complicating factor for Canadian monetary policy after 2016 was the election of U.S. President Donald Trump, who threatened to cancel the North American Free Trade Agreement (NAFTA) if Canada and Mexico did not agree to renegotiate the agreement with more favourable terms to the United States. The Canadian government actively engaged in these negotiations, working hard to save the considerable benefits to Canada that come with tariff-free trade with the United States. During the prolonged negotiation process, however, many businesses responded to the heightened economic uncertainty by cancelling or delaying their investment decisions. The result was continued slow growth in investment demand and thus, a reluctance by the Bank of Canada to raise its policy interest rate.

As this book went to press in the fall of 2018, the NAFTA negotiations were incomplete, the level of uncertainty regarding its future was considerable, and the Bank of Canada was being tentative with its policy actions.

SUMMARY

28.1 How the Bank of Canada Implements Monetary Policy   LO 1

- Monetary policy can be conducted either by targeting the money supply or by targeting the interest rate. But for a given negatively sloped M_D curve, both cannot be targeted independently.
- Because of its incomplete control over the money supply, as well as the uncertainty regarding both the slope and the position of the M_D curve, the Bank chooses to implement its policy by targeting the interest rate.
- The Bank establishes a target for the overnight interest rate. By offering to lend funds at a rate 25 basis points above this target (the bank rate) and to accept deposits

on which it pays interest at 25 basis points below the target, the Bank of Canada can control the actual overnight interest rate.
- Changes in the Bank's target for the overnight rate lead to changes in the actual overnight rate and also to changes in longer-term interest rates. The various steps in the monetary transmission mechanism then come into play.
- The Bank of Canada conducts an expansionary monetary policy by reducing its target for the overnight interest rate. It conducts a contractionary monetary policy by raising its target for the overnight interest rate.

28.2 Inflation Targeting   LO 2, 3

- It has long been understood that high inflation is damaging to economies and costly for individuals and firms.
- Experience with attempts to control inflation has led to the understanding that sustained inflation is ultimately determined by monetary policy.

- For these two reasons, many central banks now focus their attention on maintaining a low and stable rate of inflation.
- The Bank of Canada's formal inflation target is the rate of CPI inflation. It seeks to keep the annual inflation rate close to 2 percent.

- In the short run, the Bank closely monitors the output gap. By tightening its policy during an inflationary gap and loosening it during a recessionary gap, the Bank can keep the rate of inflation near 2 percent.
- The policy of inflation targeting helps to stabilize the economy. The Bank responds to positive shocks with a contractionary policy and responds to negative shocks with an expansionary policy.
- Two technical issues complicate the conduct of monetary policy:
  1. Volatile food and energy prices
  2. Changes in the exchange rate

28.3 Long and Variable Lags   LO 4

- Though the Bank of Canada can change interest rates very quickly, it takes time for firms and households to alter their expenditure in response to these changes. Even once those new plans are carried out, it takes time for the multiplier process to work its way through the economy, eventually affecting equilibrium national income.

- Long and variable lags in monetary policy lead many economists to argue that the Bank should not try to "fine-tune" the economy by responding to economic shocks. Instead, it should respond only to shocks that are significant in size and persistent in duration.

28.4 Four Decades of Canadian Monetary Policy   LO 5

- In the early 1980s, the Bank of Canada embarked on a policy of tight money to reduce inflation. This policy contributed to the severity of the recession.
- A sustained economic recovery occurred from 1983 to 1987. The main challenge for monetary policy during this time was to create sufficient liquidity to accommodate the recovery without triggering a return to the high inflation rates that prevailed at the start of the decade.
- In 1988, when inflation was between 4 and 5 percent, the Bank of Canada announced that monetary policy would henceforth be guided by the long-term goal of "price stability." By 1992, the Bank's tight money policy had reduced inflation to below 2 percent.
- Controversy concerned two issues. First, was the cost in terms of lost output and heavy unemployment worth the benefits of lower inflation? Second, could the low inflation rate be sustained?
- This controversy was partly responsible for the 1994 change in the Bank of Canada's governor, from John Crow to Gordon Thiessen. Despite this administrative change, the stated policy of price stability continued. By 2000, the rate of inflation had been around 2 percent for about seven years.
- Following the stock-market declines in 2000–2001 and the terrorist attacks in the United States in September 2001, the Bank of Canada and the U.S. Federal Reserve dramatically reduced their policy interest rates in an attempt to prevent a recession.
- In the 2002–2005 period, the main challenges for the Bank involved determining the relative strength of the two different forces leading to a substantial appreciation of the Canadian dollar. By summer of 2006, the Bank had increased its target for the overnight interest rate by two percentage points, to a level still below its previous peak in the summer of 2000.
- The onset of the global financial crisis in 2008 led the Bank of Canada to implement policies designed to restore the flow of credit and also to reduce interest rates.
- By 2018, eight years into a modest recovery, the Bank of Canada still had a historically low target for the overnight interest rate.

KEY CONCEPTS

Money supply vs. the interest rate	Endogenous money supply	The exchange rate and monetary policy
Overnight interest rate	Open-market operations	
The target overnight interest rate	Inflation targeting	Lags in the effect of monetary policy
The bank rate	CPI inflation vs. core inflation	

STUDY EXERCISES

MyLab Economics Make the grade with MyLab Economics™: All Study Exercises can be found on MyLab Economics™. You can practise them as often as you want, and many feature step-by-step guided instructions to help you find the right answer.

FILL-IN-THE-BLANK

1 Fill in the blanks to make the following statements correct.

a. In general, there are two approaches to implementing monetary policy. The central bank can attempt to influence _____ directly or to influence _____ directly.

b. The Bank of Canada chooses to implement its monetary policy by influencing the _____ directly. The Bank then uses _____ to accommodate the resulting change in money demand.

c. The Bank of Canada does not try to influence the money supply directly because (1) the Bank cannot control the process of _____ carried out by the commercial banks; (2) the Bank is unsure about the change in _____ that would result from a change in the money supply; and (3) the Bank is unsure of the position of the _____ curve at any given time.

2 Fill in the blanks to make the following statements correct.

a. The interest rate that commercial banks charge each other for overnight loans is called the _____.

b. The bank rate is _____ points above the target overnight interest rate. At this interest rate, the Bank stands ready to _____ to commercial banks. At a rate _____ points below the target, the Bank stands ready to _____ from commercial banks (and pay that rate as interest).

c. The Bank of Canada can change the amount of currency in circulation through _____. The Bank conducts these transactions to accommodate the changing demand for _____ by the commercial banks.

d. An expansionary monetary policy is one where the Bank of Canada _____ its target for the overnight interest rate. A contractionary monetary policy is one in which the Bank _____ its target for the overnight interest rate.

e. If the Bank of Canada wants to stimulate aggregate demand it can implement a(n) _____ monetary policy by _____ its target for the overnight interest rate. If the Bank wants to dampen aggregate demand it can implement a(n) _____ monetary policy by _____ its target for the overnight interest rate.

3 Fill in the blanks to make the following statements correct.

a. The long-run policy target for the Bank of Canada is the _____. The current target is to keep the inflation rate at _____ percent.

b. In the short run, the Bank of Canada closely monitors the _____.

c. The Bank of Canada conducts its monetary policy by announcing a change in the _____. It then conducts the necessary _____ in order to make this rate an equilibrium in the money market.

d. The conduct of monetary policy is made more difficult because of lags. Two reasons for these time lags are
   - _____
   - _____

e. Economists have estimated that a change in monetary policy has an effect on real GDP after a period of _____ months and an effect on the price level after a period of _____ months.

f. Because of the long time lags involved in the execution of monetary policy, it is very possible that the policy may in fact have a(n) _____ effect on the economy.

REVIEW

4 In the text we stated that the Bank of Canada's long-run policy target is the rate of inflation.

a. What observations have led many central banks to choose this long-run policy target?

b. The Bank of Canada closely monitors the level of real GDP and the output gap in the short run. How does it use this information in pursuit of its long-run policy of targeting the rate of inflation at 2 percent?

5 Milton Friedman was a professor of economics at the University of Chicago and was the most influential Monetarist of his generation. He was known for accusing the Federal Reserve (the U.S. central bank) of following "an unstable monetary policy," arguing that although the Federal Reserve "has given lip service to controlling the quantity of money . . . it has given its heart to controlling interest rates."

a. Explain why if the M_D function were approximately stable, targeting the growth rate in the money supply would produce a "stable" monetary policy. Show this in a diagram.

b. Explain why if the M_D function moves suddenly and in unpredictable ways, targeting the money supply produces an "unstable" monetary policy. Show this in a diagram.

c. The Bank of Canada conducts its policy by setting short-term interest rates. What is the implication for this policy of an "unstable" M_D function?

6 Suppose it is mid-2017 and the stock market has been growing rapidly for the past five years. Some economists argue that the stock market has become "overvalued" and thus a "crash" is imminent.

a. How does a rising stock market affect aggregate demand? Show this in an *AD/AS* diagram.

b. For a central bank that is trying to keep real GDP close to potential, explain what challenges are posed by a rapidly rising stock market.

c. Suppose the stock market "crashes," falling suddenly by 35 percent (as it did in 2008 after a similar "bull market" during 2003–2007). How does this affect aggregate demand? Show this in an *AD/AS* diagram.

7 Consider the relationship among exchange-rate changes, aggregate demand, and monetary policy. Assume we begin in a situation with real GDP equal to Y^*.

a. Suppose the world price for raw materials rises because of growing demand for these products. Given that Canada is a net exporter of raw materials, what is the likely effect on Canadian aggregate demand? Show this in an *AD/AS* diagram (assuming no change in the exchange rate).

b. Suppose instead that there is an increase in the demand by foreigners for Canadian financial assets such as government bonds. What is the direct effect on Canadian aggregate demand? Show this in an *AD/AS* diagram (assuming again no change in the exchange rate).

c. Both of the shocks described above are likely to cause an appreciation of the Canadian dollar on foreign-exchange markets. As the Canadian dollar appreciates, what are the effects on aggregate demand in part (a) and in part (b)? Show these "secondary" effects in your diagram and explain.

d. Given your answers to parts (a), (b), and (c), explain why the appropriate monetary policy response to a change in the exchange rate depends crucially on the *cause* of the exchange-rate change. What are the appropriate responses to each of the shocks (assuming they occur separately)?

8 In the last few years, the path of CPI inflation has deviated from the path of core inflation several times (see Figure 28-4).

a. Why is core inflation less volatile than CPI inflation?

b. Why might the Bank focus more on core inflation during some periods?

9 During the financial crisis of 2007–2008, the Bank of Canada took extraordinary actions to inject liquidity into the banking system. As a result, the amount of reserves in the banking system increased significantly.

a. Why might the Bank choose to increase reserves in the banking system in such an economic environment?

b. Despite the large increase in reserves, there was not a large increase in the Canadian money supply. Can you provide an explanation?

c. Given your answer to part (b), would you predict that the Bank's actions would lead to more inflation? Explain why or why not.

PROBLEMS

10 Read *Applying Economic Concepts 28-1*, which discusses the Bank of Canada's open-market operations and how these influence the amount of currency in circulation in the Canadian economy. Using simplified balance sheets like the ones shown below, suppose that a commercial bank uses $100 000 of excess cash reserves to purchase a government bond from the Bank of Canada.

a. What are the immediate effects on assets and liabilities for the commercial bank? Fill in the left-hand table.

b. What are the changes for the Bank of Canada? Fill in the right-hand table.

c. Explain what has happened to the amount of currency in circulation.

Commercial Bank		Bank of Canada	
Assets	Liabilities	Assets	Liabilities
Reserves	Deposits	Bonds	Commercial bank deposits
Bonds			Currency

11 The diagram below shows the demand for money and the supply of money.

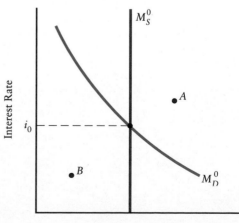

Quantity of Money

a. Given the position of the M_D curve, explain why it is not possible for the Bank of Canada to set the money supply and the interest rate at point A or at point B.

b. In the diagram, draw a new money demand curve, M_D^1, to the right of M_D^0. Suppose the M_D curve is shifting in unpredictable ways between M_D^0 and M_D^1. Why is a monetary policy that sets the interest rate more stable (and therefore preferable) to one that sets the money supply?

c. The Bank of Canada implements its monetary policy by setting the target for the overnight interest rate. Starting from money-market equilibrium and interest rate i_0, if the Bank reduces its target, explain what happens to the amount of money in the economy. What is the role of open-market operations in the Bank's policy?

29 Inflation and Disinflation

CHAPTER OUTLINE	LEARNING OBJECTIVES (LO)
	After studying this chapter you will be able to
29.1 ADDING INFLATION TO THE MODEL	**1** understand why wages tend to change in response to output gaps and inflation expectations.
	2 describe how a constant rate of inflation is incorporated into the basic macroeconomic model.
29.2 SHOCKS AND POLICY RESPONSES	**3** explain how *AD* and *AS* shocks affect inflation and real GDP.
	4 explain what happens when the Bank of Canada validates demand and supply shocks.
29.3 REDUCING INFLATION	**5** understand the three phases of a disinflation.
	6 explain how the cost of disinflation can be measured by the sacrifice ratio.

IN this chapter, we examine inflation, how it appears in our macro model, and why reducing a constant inflation is usually quite costly. In Chapter 30 we explore the costs and causes of high unemployment, and in Chapter 31 we discuss the problem of high government budget deficits. These three chapters offer a collection of some of the biggest macroeconomic challenges and policy debates of our time.

Unless you are older than the typical student taking a course in introductory economics, or you have come to Canada recently from a high-inflation country, inflation has not been a significant phenomenon in your life. It was not so long ago, however, that inflation was considered to be a serious problem in Canada and many other countries. Even though high inflation in Canada is no longer a "headline" issue, understanding the process of inflation, and how it can be reduced, is central to understanding why the Bank of Canada is so committed to keeping inflation low.

Recall that **inflation** is a rise in the average level of prices—that is, a rise in the price level. Figure 29-1 shows the rate of CPI inflation in Canada since 1965 and shows what is sometimes called the "twin peaks" of inflation. Rising from the mid-1960s, inflation peaked in 1974 at more than 12 percent, fell and then peaked again in 1981 at almost 13 percent, and then started its long but bumpy decline to its current level at around 2 percent, the Bank of Canada's current target rate of inflation.

FIGURE 29-1   Canadian CPI Inflation, 1965–2018

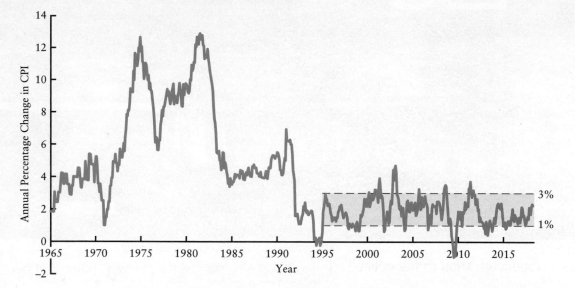

The rate of CPI inflation in Canada has been much lower and more stable since the adoption of inflation targeting in the early 1990s. The shaded band shows the Bank of Canada's target range for the annual rate of CPI inflation; it has been a range of 1–3 percent since 1995. It is evident that the average inflation rate has been much lower and also more stable since 1995 than it was during the previous three decades.

(*Source:* Based on author's calculations using data from the Bank of Canada, Table 326-0020, CPI all items. For each month, the inflation rate is computed as the percentage change from the CPI 12 months earlier.)

inflation A rise in the average level of all prices. Usually expressed as the annual percentage change in the Consumer Price Index.

This bumpy path for the rate of inflation nicely illustrates one of the reasons that inflation is a problem for the economy. As we mentioned in Chapter 19, economists make the distinction between *anticipated* and *unanticipated* inflation, and we showed why unanticipated inflation is the more serious problem. If firms and workers have difficulty predicting what inflation will be, they have problems determining how wages and prices should be set. The result will be unexpected changes in real wages and relative prices as inflation ends up being different from what was expected. These inflation-induced changes in real wages and relative prices cause redistributions of income and may lead to inefficient changes in employment, investment, or output. As you can imagine by looking at Figure 29-1, many of the changes in inflation between 1965 and 2018 were sudden and thus difficult to predict. To avoid this uncertainty in the economy, the Bank of Canada now strives to keep inflation both *low* and *stable*, near the official target of 2 percent. The result is an environment in which firms, workers, and households can more easily make plans for the future, secure in the knowledge that real wages, real interest rates, and relative prices will not be significantly affected by a volatile inflation rate.

What causes inflation? How can it be eliminated? And why have policies designed to reduce inflation been so controversial? These are the central topics of this chapter.

▌29.1   Adding Inflation to the Model

In the previous several chapters we examined the effects of shocks to aggregate demand and aggregate supply. In our macroeconomic model, *AD* and *AS* shocks influenced the values of both real GDP and the price level. Following these shocks, the economy's adjustment process tended to push the economy back toward potential GDP with a stable price level. In other words, any inflation that we have so far seen in our macroeconomic model was temporary—it existed only while the economy was adjusting toward its long-run equilibrium in which $Y = Y^*$.

In this chapter we modify our model to explain how *constant* inflation can exist. After all, even though Canadian inflation is very low by recent historical standards, over the past two decades it has been sustained and relatively stable at an average rate of 2 percent.

As we will soon see, one of the keys to understanding sustained inflation is to understand the role of *inflation expectations*. When combined with excess demand or excess supply, as reflected by the economy's output gap, such expectations give us a more complete explanation of why costs and prices change. Let's begin our analysis by examining in more detail why wages change.

Why Wages Change

Readers who have studied microeconomics will have examined why wages in *particular* firms and industries change relative to wages in other firms and industries. Movements in these *relative* wages are explained by many factors, including the power of industrial labour unions, firms' market power, the nature of work in specific industries, the skills of the workers, and much else. Here we ignore this microeconomic detail and focus instead on the *general* level of wages in the economy. Our emphasis is on the role played by broad macroeconomic forces.

In Chapter 24, when we examined the economy's adjustment process, we saw that increases in wages led to increases in firms' unit costs—because we maintained the assumption that technology was held constant. We continue with that assumption in this chapter. Thus, as wages and other factor prices rise, unit costs increase and the *AS* curve shifts up. Conversely, when wages and other factor prices fall, unit costs fall and the *AS* curve shifts down.

What are the macroeconomic forces that cause the overall level of nominal wages to change? The two main forces that we consider are the output gap and expectations of future inflation. Much of what we discuss in the case of the output gap was first seen in Chapter 24, but the points are important enough to bear repeating.

Wages and the Output Gap   In Chapter 24, we encountered three propositions about how changes in nominal (or money) wages were influenced by the output gap:

1. The excess demand for labour that is associated with an inflationary gap ($Y > Y^*$) puts upward pressure on nominal wages.

2. The excess supply of labour associated with a recessionary gap ($Y < Y^*$) puts downward pressure on nominal wages, though the adjustment may be quite slow.

3. The absence of either an inflationary or a recessionary gap ($Y = Y^*$) implies that demand forces are not exerting any pressure on nominal wages.

When real GDP is equal to Y^*, the unemployment rate is said to be equal to the NAIRU, which stands for the *non-accelerating inflation rate of unemployment* and is designated by U^*. The use of this particular name will be explained later in this chapter. Another name sometimes used in place of NAIRU is the *natural rate of unemployment*.

The NAIRU is not zero. Instead, even when $Y = Y^*$, there will be some amount of *frictional* and *structural* unemployment caused, for example, by the movement of people between jobs or between regions. When real GDP exceeds potential GDP $(Y > Y^*)$, the unemployment rate will be less than the NAIRU $(U < U^*)$. When real GDP is less than potential GDP $(Y < Y^*)$, the unemployment rate will exceed the NAIRU $(U > U^*)$.

We saw in Chapter 24 that nominal wages tend to react to various pressures of demand. These demand pressures can be stated either in terms of the relationship between actual and potential GDP or in terms of the relationship between the actual unemployment rate and the NAIRU. When $Y > Y^*$ (or $U < U^*$), there is an inflationary gap characterized by excess demand for labour, and wages tend to rise. Conversely, when $Y < Y^*$ (or $U > U^*$), there is a recessionary gap characterized by excess supply of labour, and wages tend to fall (although often slowly). This relationship between the excess demand or supply of labour and the rate of change of nominal wages is represented by the Phillips curve, which we also discussed in Chapter 24.

Wages and Expected Inflation   A second force that can influence nominal wages is *expectations* of future inflation. Suppose both employers and employees expect 2 percent inflation next year. Workers will tend to start negotiations from a base of a 2 percent increase in nominal wages, which would hold their *real wages* constant. Firms will also be inclined to begin bargaining from a base of a 2 percent increase in nominal wages because they expect that the prices at which they sell their products will rise by 2 percent. Starting from that base, workers may attempt to obtain some desired increase in their real wages while firms may attempt to reduce real wages. At this point, such factors as profits and bargaining power become important.

> The expectation of some specific inflation rate creates pressure for nominal wages to rise by that rate.

How do firms, workers, and consumers form their expectations about future inflation? There has been much debate about this over the years, but today most economists agree that expectations combine *backward-looking* and *forward-looking* elements. Many people will look backward, for example, and come to expect low inflation in the future largely as a result of experiencing many past years of low inflation. At the same time, most people are prepared to look forward and adjust their expectations in response to clear and credible announcements about future policy. For example, if the governor of the Bank of Canada announced today that the Bank's official inflation target would henceforth be 4 percent (rather than the current 2 percent), most people would adjust their expectations accordingly.

However people actually form their expectations, the key point for our current discussion is that nominal wages can be rising even if no inflationary gap is present. As long as people *expect* prices to rise, their behaviour will put upward pressure on nominal wages. Indeed, in every year since the Second World War, average nominal wages have increased in Canada, even though in some years there were notable recessionary gaps when nominal wages increased by less than prices. The reason is that in every year the price level was expected to increase (and did, in fact, increase). Clarifying the distinction between these two separate forces on nominal wages—excess demand and inflation expectations—is an important objective of this chapter.

Overall Effect on Wages   We can now think of changes in average nominal wages as resulting from two different macro forces:[1]

$$\text{Change in nominal wages} = \text{Output-gap effect} + \text{Expectational effect}$$

What happens to wages is the *net* effect of the two forces. Consider two examples. First, suppose both labour and management expect 2 percent inflation next year and are therefore willing to allow nominal wages to increase by 2 percent. Doing so would leave *real* wages unchanged. Suppose also there is a significant inflationary gap with an associated labour shortage and that the excess demand for labour causes wages to rise by an additional 1 percentage point. The final outcome is that nominal wages rise by 3 percent, the net effect of a 2 percent increase caused by expected inflation and a 1 percent increase caused by the excess demand for labour when $Y > Y^*$.

For the second example, assume again that expected inflation is 2 percent, but this time there is a large recessionary gap. The associated high unemployment represents an excess supply of labour that exerts downward pressure on wage bargains. Hence, the output-gap effect now works to dampen wage increases, say, to the extent of one percentage point. Nominal wages therefore rise only by 1 percent, the net effect of a 2 percent increase caused by expected inflation and a 1 percent *decrease* caused by the excess supply of labour when $Y < Y^*$.

From Wages to Prices

In Chapters 23 and 24 we saw that changes in wages and other factor prices lead to shifts of the *AS* curve. We have now determined that wage changes are themselves a response to output gaps and to expectations of future inflation.

> The net effect of the two macro forces acting on wages—output gaps and inflation expectations—determines what happens to the *AS* curve.

If the net effect of the output-gap effect and the expectational effect is to raise wages, then the *AS* curve will shift up. This shift will cause the price level to rise—that is, the forces pushing up wages will be *inflationary*. On the other hand, if the net effect of the output-gap effect and the expectational effect is to reduce wages, the *AS* curve will shift down—the forces reducing wages will be *deflationary*.[2]

---

[1] Average nominal wages may also be affected by things unrelated to output gaps and expected inflation, such as government guidelines and union activities. Such factors may be regarded as random shocks and analyzed separately from the two principal macro forces that we examine here.

[2] This is a good time to remind the reader that we are assuming constant productivity throughout this chapter. With ongoing productivity growth, the *AS* curve would shift upward when wages rise *faster than productivity* and shift downward when wages *rise slower than productivity*. But with constant productivity, any increase in nominal wages causes *AS* to shift up and any decrease in nominal wages causes *AS* to shift down.

Since anything that leads to higher nominal wages will shift the *AS* curve up and lead to higher prices, we can decompose inflation caused by wage increases into two component parts: *output-gap inflation* and *expected inflation*. But because the *AS* curve can also shift for reasons unrelated to changes in wages, we must add a third element. Specifically, we must consider the effect of non-wage supply shocks on the *AS* curve and thus on the price level. The best example of a non-wage supply shock is a change in the prices of materials used as inputs in production. We can then decompose actual inflation into its three components:

$$\text{Actual inflation} = \text{Output-gap inflation} + \text{Expected inflation} + \text{Supply-shock inflation}$$

As an example, consider an economy that begins with real GDP equal to Y^* and expectations of inflation equal to zero. In this case, the first two terms on the right-hand side are zero. But if an adverse supply shock then occurs, such as a significant increase in the price of oil or electricity, the *AS* curve shifts up and the price level rises. Actual inflation will be positive. As we will see later in the chapter, such supply shocks are not uncommon, and they generate challenges for the Bank of Canada in its attempt to maintain low inflation.

Having discussed these components of inflation, we are now in a position to see how a constant inflation can be included in our macroeconomic model.

Constant Inflation

Suppose the inflation rate is 2 percent per year and has been 2 percent for several years. This is what we mean by a *constant* inflation. In such a setting, people with backward-looking expectations about inflation will expect the actual rate to continue into the future. Furthermore, in the absence of any announcements that the central bank will be altering its monetary policy, people with forward-looking expectations will expect the actual inflation rate to continue. Thus, for the economy as a whole, the expected rate of inflation will equal the actual rate of inflation.

If inflation and monetary policy have been unchanged for several years, the expected rate of inflation will tend to equal the actual rate of inflation.

Suppose there are no supply shocks (we address these later in the chapter). Since actual inflation equals expected inflation, it follows from the equation above that there can be *no* output gap—real GDP must equal its potential level, Y^*.

In the absence of supply shocks, if expected inflation equals actual inflation, real GDP must be equal to potential GDP.[3]

---

[3] Another realistic possibility is that real GDP is below Y^* but there is only weak downward pressure on wages, and so relatively constant inflation. Recall our discussion from Chapter 24 that large and persistent recessionary gaps may be necessary to generate even small wage reductions. For simplicity, in this chapter we maintain the assumption that wages *do* fall when $Y < Y^*$, although we recognize that these forces may be both weak and slow.

Figure 29-2 shows a constant inflation in the *AD/AS* diagram. What is causing this inflation? As we will see, such a constant inflation requires both the *expectations* of inflation (which shift the *AS* curve) and the continuing monetary expansion by the central bank (which shifts the *AD* curve). Let's see how this works.

Suppose workers and employers expect 2 percent inflation over the coming years and employers are prepared to increase nominal wages by 2 percent per year. As wages rise by 2 percent, the *AS* curve shifts up by that amount. But in order for 2 percent to be the *actual* rate of inflation, the *intersection* of the *AS* and *AD* curves must be shifting up at the rate of 2 percent. This requires the *AD* curve to be shifting up at the same 2 percent rate—this *AD* shift is caused by the central bank's monetary expansion. So in this case there is no output-gap inflation ($Y = Y^*$), and actual and expected inflation are equal. When the central bank increases the money supply at such a rate that the expectations of inflation end up being correct, it is said to be *validating* those expectations.

> Constant inflation with $Y = Y^*$ occurs when the rate of monetary expansion, the rate of wage increase, and the expected rate of inflation are all consistent with the actual inflation rate.

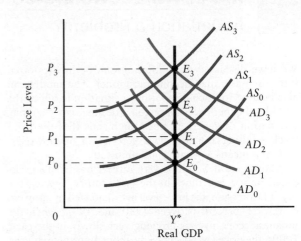

FIGURE 29-2   Constant Inflation

In the *AD/AS* model with no supply shocks, constant inflation occurs when $Y = Y^*$. Expectations of a constant rate of inflation cause wages and thus the *AS* curve to shift upward at a uniform rate from AS_0 to AS_1 to AS_2. Monetary expansion by the central bank is causing the *AD* curve to shift upward at the same time from AD_0 to AD_1 to AD_2. As a result, real GDP remains at Y^* as the economy moves from equilibrium E_0 to E_1 to E_2 and so on. The constant inflation rate takes the price level from P_0 to P_1 to P_2. Wage costs are rising because of expectations of inflation, and these expectations are being validated by the central bank's policy. (Note that if the inflation *rate* is constant, the successive increases in the price *level* become larger over time, as shown in the figure.)

The key point about constant inflation in our macro model is that there is no output-gap effect operating on wages. As a result, nominal wages rise exactly at the expected rate of inflation. The monetary expansion validates those expectations.

Note that in this constant-inflation equilibrium, interest rates are being kept stable by two equal but offsetting forces. The central bank is increasing the money supply, which tends to push interest rates down. But at the same time, rising prices are increasing the demand for money and pushing interest rates up. In equilibrium, the monetary policy is just expansionary enough to accommodate the growing money demand, thus leaving interest rates unchanged. As we will see later in this chapter, in order to *reduce* the rate of inflation, the central bank must implement a contractionary monetary policy—by reducing the growth rate of the money supply sufficiently to raise interest rates.

Figure 29-2 can be used to analyze any constant (and positive) rate of inflation. It could also be used to analyze the case of deflation, a situation in which the price level is falling so that the inflation rate is negative. In this case, the *AD* and *AS* curves would be shifting down at a constant rate, keeping $Y = Y^*$. *Applying Economic Concepts 29-1* discusses deflation, the reasons that some people seem to fear its effect on the economy, and why these fears may be misplaced.

APPLYING ECONOMIC CONCEPTS 29-1

Is Deflation a Problem?

We have discussed how inflation can be incorporated into our basic macroeconomic model. The model can also be used to discuss *deflation*, a situation in which the price level experiences an ongoing decline. For example, a deflation of 2 percent per year means that the price level is falling annually by 2 percent; in other words, deflation means a negative inflation rate.

Sustained deflation is very rare; it has been experienced only a few times in the last century. During the Great Depression, the price level in Canada fell by approximately 25 percent between 1930 and 1933; when the Japanese economy was growing very slowly in the early 2000s, the price level declined by about 1 percent per year.

In recent years, especially following the global recession of 2009, it was common to hear media discussion of the dangers of deflation and the need for central banks to take whatever actions were necessary to prevent it. The fear of deflation appears to stem from the belief that deflation causes a decline in economic activity, and this argument is usually based on the evidence drawn from the Great Depression, when real GDP fell by about 30 percent from 1929 to 1933.

How could deflation cause a decline in economic activity? A commonly heard argument is that when prices are falling, firms and consumers delay their spending because they know that prices will be lower in the future. The delay in spending leads to a leftward shift in the *AD* curve and, other things being equal, causes a decline in real GDP.

Economists who reject this line of argument usually make two observations, one about the historical evidence and the other about the proposed link from

deflation to recession. First, while it is certainly true that there was significant deflation during the Great Depression, it was probably a *result* rather than a *cause* of the economic events. In this view, a combination of the 1929 stock-market crash, widespread bank failures, inappropriate monetary and fiscal policies, and a significant rise in protectionist trade policies caused a major decline in aggregate demand. This decline in turn caused a leftward shift of the *AD* curve, resulting in *both* a decline in real GDP and a decline in the price level (deflation).

The second point relates to the possibility that buyers delay their purchases because of deflation, and that this delay can cause a recession. How important can this effect be? If the rate of deflation were 25 percent per year, it is easy to imagine that many firms and consumers would delay some purchases—after all, a saving of 25 percent provides a significant incentive to wait. But this effect is almost absent when deflation is only 1 or 2 percent per year, as it was in Japan during the early 2000s. And if this effect is absent, there is no fundamental danger associated with a small deflation.

Consider the opposite situation, that of prices rising by 1 or 2 percent annually. In this situation, do we expect firms and consumers to rush to purchase their products before prices rise, thereby pushing real GDP well above the economy's potential? The answer is no. When inflation is low and relatively stable, firms and consumers build it into their expectations, central banks build it into their policy decisions, and the economy can operate with real GDP equal to potential output, as we have shown in this chapter. The same would likely be true of a constant and anticipated deflation of 1 or 2 percent per year.

29.2 Shocks and Policy Responses

A constant rate of inflation is a special case in our macroeconomic model because the rising price level is not caused by an inflationary output gap. In many cases of inflation, however, the initial inflationary pressure is created by an aggregate demand or aggregate supply shock, and then, because of policy responses of the central bank, the inflation becomes entrenched. In this section we examine the effects of *AS* and *AD* shocks and the subsequent effects of the policy responses chosen by the central bank.

In this analysis, we make a central assumption in our macro model—that *AD* and *AS* shocks do not influence the level of potential output, Y^*. With this assumption in place, we know that a central prediction of our model is that the long-run effect of *AD* and *AS* shocks involves no change in real GDP because the economy's adjustment process brings real GDP back to (the unchanged) Y^*.

Demand Shocks

Any rightward shift in the *AD* curve that creates an inflationary output gap also creates what is called **demand inflation**. The shift in the *AD* curve could have been caused by a reduction in tax rates; by an increase in such autonomous expenditure items as investment, government, and net exports; or by an expansionary monetary policy. Demand inflation often occurs at the end of a strong upswing, as rising output causes excess demand to develop simultaneously in the markets for labour, intermediate goods, and final output. Demand inflation of this type occurred in Canada in 1989–1990 and to a lesser extent in 2003–2007.

demand inflation Inflation arising from an inflationary output gap caused, in turn, by a positive *AD* shock.

To begin our study of demand inflation, we make some simplifying assumptions. First, we continue to assume that Y^* is constant. Second, we assume that initially there is no ongoing inflation. These two assumptions imply that our starting point is a stable long-run equilibrium, with constant real GDP and price level, rather than the long-run equilibrium with constant inflation as shown in Figure 29-2. We then suppose that this long-run equilibrium is disturbed by a rightward shift in the *AD* curve. This shift causes the price level and output to rise. It is important next to distinguish between the case in which the Bank of Canada validates the demand shock and the case in which it does not.

No Monetary Validation Because the initial rise in *AD* takes real GDP above potential, an inflationary gap opens up. The pressure of excess demand soon causes nominal wages to rise, shifting the *AS* curve upward, as shown in Figure 29-3. As long as the Bank of Canada holds the money supply constant, the rise in the price level moves the economy upward and to the left along the new *AD* curve, reducing the inflationary gap. Eventually, the gap is eliminated, and equilibrium is established at a higher but stable price level, with output at Y^*. In this case, the initial period of inflation is followed by further inflation that lasts only until the new long-run equilibrium is reached.

Monetary Validation Suppose that after the demand shock creates an inflationary gap, the Bank of Canada attempts to sustain these "good economic times." It then validates the demand shock through an expansionary monetary policy. We illustrate this situation in Figure 29-4.

Two forces are now brought into play. Spurred by the inflationary gap, the increase in nominal wages causes the *AS* curve to shift upward. Fuelled by the expansionary monetary policy, however, the *AD* curve shifts further to the right. As a result of both of these shifts, the price level rises, but real GDP remains above Y^*. Indeed, if the shift in the *AD* curve *exactly* offsets the shift in the *AS* curve, real GDP and the inflationary gap will remain constant.

FIGURE 29-3 A Demand Shock with No Validation

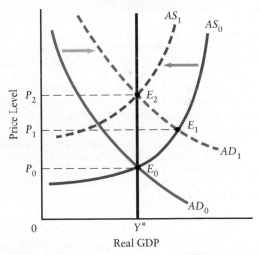

A demand shock that is not validated produces temporary inflation, but the economy's adjustment process eventually restores potential GDP and stable prices. The initial long-run equilibrium is at P_0 and Y^*. A positive demand shock shifts AD_0 to AD_1, generating an inflationary gap, but without monetary validation by the central bank there is no further shift of the *AD* curve. The excess demand puts upward pressure on wages, thus shifting AS_0 to AS_1. There is inflation as the economy moves from E_0 to E_1 to E_2, but at E_2 the price level is again stable.

FIGURE 29-4 A Demand Shock with Validation

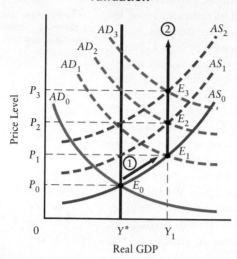

Monetary validation of a positive demand shock causes the *AD* curve to shift further to the right, offsetting the upward shift in the *AS* curve and thereby leaving an inflationary gap despite the ever-rising price level. An initial demand shock moves the economy along the path of arrow ①, taking output to Y_1 and the price level to P_1. The resulting inflationary gap then causes the *AS* curve to shift upward. This time, however, the Bank of Canada validates the demand shock with a monetary expansion that shifts the *AD* curve to the right. By the time the aggregate supply curve has reached AS_1, the aggregate demand curve has reached AD_2. The new equilibrium is at E_2. Output remains constant at Y_1, leaving the inflationary gap constant while the price level rises to P_2.

The persistent inflationary gap continues to push the *AS* curve upward, while the continued monetary validation continues to push the *AD* curve to the right. As long as this monetary validation continues, the economy moves along the vertical path of arrow ②.

supply inflation Inflation arising from a negative *AS* shock that is not the result of excess demand in the domestic markets for factors of production.

Continued validation of a demand shock turns what would have been transitory inflation into sustained inflation fuelled by monetary expansion.

In other words, the Bank of Canada could indeed choose to sustain the "good economic times" characterized by high output and low unemployment. But the result of this choice would be sustained inflation (and as we will soon see, the inflation rate would continually increase).

Supply Shocks

Any leftward shift in the *AS* curve that is *not* caused by excess demand in the markets for factors of production creates what is called **supply inflation**.

An example of a supply shock is a rise in the costs of raw materials, such as oil.[4] Another is a rise in domestic wages not due to excess demand in the labour market. The rise in wages might occur, as we saw earlier, because of generally held expectations of future inflation. These shocks cause the *AS* curve to shift upward.

The initial effects of any negative supply shock are that the price level rises while output falls, as shown in Figure 29-5. As with the case of a demand shock, what happens next depends on how the Bank of Canada reacts. If the Bank allows the money supply to increase, it validates the supply shock; if it holds the money supply constant, the shock is not validated.

No Monetary Validation The upward shift in the *AS* curve in Figure 29-5 causes the price level to rise and pushes output below Y^*, opening up a recessionary gap. Pressure mounts for nominal wages and other factor prices to fall. As wages and other factor prices fall, unit costs will fall. Consequently, the *AS* curve shifts down, increasing output while reducing the price level. The *AS* curve will continue to shift slowly downward, stopping only when real GDP is returned to Y^* and the price level is returned to its initial value of P_0. Thus, the period of inflation accompanying the original supply shock is eventually reversed until the initial long-run equilibrium is re-established.

A major concern in this case is the speed of wage adjustment. If wages do not fall rapidly in the face of excess supply in the labour market, the adjustment back to

---

[4] Recall our discussion in Chapter 23 of how some shocks affect *both* the *AD* and the *AS* curves. A rise in the world price of oil is one example. Since Canada both uses and produces oil, a rise in the world price of oil causes both the *AD* and *AS* curves to shift upward. In this discussion we confine ourselves to the effect of the *AS* shift.

potential output can take a long time. For example, suppose the original shock raised firms' costs by 6 percent. To reverse this shock and return real GDP to Y^*, firms' costs must fall by 6 percent. If nominal wages fell by only 1 percent per year, it would take several years to complete the adjustment.

> **Whenever wages and other factor prices fall only slowly in the face of excess supply, the recovery to potential output after a non-validated negative supply shock will take a long time.**

Concern that such a lengthy adjustment will occur is often the motivation for the Bank of Canada to validate negative supply shocks.

Monetary Validation What happens if the Bank of Canada responds to the negative supply shock with a monetary expansion, thus *validating* the shock? The monetary validation shifts the AD curve to the right and closes the output gap. As the recessionary gap is eliminated, the price level rises further, rather than falling back to its original value as it did when the supply shock was not validated. These effects are also illustrated in Figure 29-5.

> **Monetary validation of a negative supply shock causes the initial rise in the price level to be followed by a further rise, resulting in a higher price level but a much faster return to potential output than would occur if the recessionary gap were relied on to reduce wages and other factor prices.**

FIGURE 29-5 A Supply Shock With and Without Validation

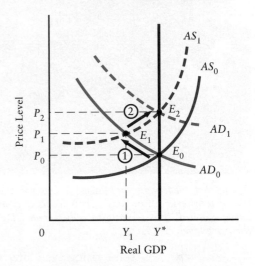

Adverse supply shocks initially raise prices while lowering output. An adverse supply shock causes the AS curve to shift upward from AS_0 to AS_1, as shown by arrow ①. Equilibrium is established at E_1. If there is no monetary validation, the reduction in wages and other factor prices makes the AS curve shift slowly back down to AS_0. If there is monetary validation, the AD curve shifts from AD_0 to AD_1, as shown by arrow ②. Equilibrium is re-established at E_2 with output equal to potential output but with a higher price level, P_2.

The most dramatic example of a supply-shock inflation came in the wake of the first OPEC oil-price shock. In 1974, the member countries of the Organization of the Petroleum Exporting Countries (OPEC) agreed to restrict output. Their action caused a threefold increase in the price of oil and dramatic increases in the prices of many petroleum-related products, such as fertilizer and chemicals. The resulting increase in industrial costs shifted AS curves upward in all industrial countries. At this time, the Bank of Canada validated the supply shock with large increases in the money supply, whereas the Federal Reserve (the U.S. central bank) did not. As the theory predicts, Canada experienced a large increase in its price level but almost no recession, while the United States experienced a much smaller increase in its price level but a deeper recession.

Is Monetary Validation of Supply Shocks Desirable? Suppose the Bank of Canada were to validate a large negative supply shock and thus prevent what could otherwise be a protracted recession. Expressed in this way, monetary validation sounds like a good

Ryan Remiorz/The CP Images

A contract settlement that raises wages for a large number of workers will increase firms' costs and shift the AS curve upward, thus tending to reduce real GDP and raise the price level.

policy. Unfortunately, however, the cost of monetary validation in this situation is the possibility of *extending* the period of inflation. If this inflation leads firms and workers to expect *further* inflation, then point E_2 in Figure 29-5 will not be the end of the story. As expectations for further inflation develop, and wages continue to rise, the AS curve will continue to shift upward. But if the Bank continues its policy of validation, then the AD curve will also continue to shift upward. It may not take long before the economy is in a *wage–price spiral*.

Once started, a wage–price spiral can be halted only if the Bank of Canada stops validating the expectational inflation initially caused by the supply shock. But the longer it waits to do so, the more firmly held will be the expectations that it will continue its policy of validating the shocks. These entrenched expectations may cause wages to continue rising even after validation has ceased. Because employers expect prices to rise, they go on granting wage increases. If expectations are entrenched firmly enough, the wage push can continue for quite some time, in spite of whatever downward pressure on wages is caused by the high unemployment associated with the recessionary gap.

Because of this possibility, some economists argue that the wage–price spiral should not be allowed to begin. One way to ensure that it does not begin is to refuse to validate any supply shock and accept whatever recessionary gap the shock creates, as the United States did after the OPEC oil-price shock in the early 1970s. The choice between a deeper recession with less expected inflation and a less severe recession with the possibility of higher entrenched inflation expectations involves an important value judgment and is not a matter that can be settled solely by economic analysis.

Accelerating Inflation

acceleration hypothesis The hypothesis that when real GDP is held above potential, the persistent inflationary gap will cause inflation to accelerate.

Consider a situation in which a demand or supply shock increases real GDP above Y^*. For example, a booming U.S. economy may lead to an increase in demand for Canadian goods, thus shifting Canada's AD curve to the right. Or a reduction in the world price of key raw materials may reduce firms' costs and shift the Canadian AS curve downward. In both cases, the effect in Canada would be to increase real GDP above Y^*— unemployment is low and businesses are booming. As we saw in Chapter 28, as real GDP rises above Y^*, the Bank of Canada would normally begin to tighten its monetary policy in order to prevent inflation from rising above its target. Some people, however, might argue that the Bank of Canada should not raise interest rates and "spoil the party," but instead should allow these boom conditions to continue. What would be the result if the Bank acted to maintain output above Y^*?

What would happen to the rate of inflation is predicted by the **acceleration hypothesis**, which says that when the central bank conducts its policy to hold the inflationary gap constant, the actual inflation rate will *accelerate*. The Bank of Canada may start by validating 2 percent inflation, but soon 2 percent will become expected, and given the demand pressure the inflation rate will rise to 3 percent and, if the Bank insists on validating 3 percent, the rate will become 4 percent, and so on, without limit. The process will end only when the Bank ends its policy of validation. Avoiding this possibility of steadily increasing inflation is one important reason that the Bank has adopted a formal (and unchanging) inflation target of 2 percent.

To see the argument in detail, recall our earlier discussion in this chapter about how actual inflation has three separate components: output gaps, inflation expectations, and non-wage supply shocks. It is restated here:

$$\frac{\text{Actual}}{\text{inflation}} = \frac{\text{Output-gap}}{\text{inflation}} + \frac{\text{Expected}}{\text{inflation}} + \frac{\text{Supply-shock}}{\text{inflation}}$$

To illustrate the importance of expectations in accelerating inflation, suppose the inflationary output gap creates sufficient excess demand to push up wages by 2 percent per year. As a result, the *AS* curve will also tend to be shifting upward at 2 percent per year.

When inflation has persisted for some time, however, people will likely come to expect that the inflation will continue. The expectation of 2 percent inflation will tend to push up wages by that amount *in addition to* the demand pressure. As the output-gap effect on wages is augmented by the expectational effect, the *AS* curve will begin to shift upward more rapidly (look back to Figure 29-4). When expectations are for a 2 percent inflation and demand pressure is also pushing wages up by 2 percent, the overall effect will be a 4 percent increase in wages. Sooner or later, however, 4 percent inflation will come to be expected, and the expectational effect will rise to 4 percent. This new expectational component of 4 percent, when added to the output-gap component, will create an inflation rate of 6 percent. And so this cycle will go on. As long as there is excess demand arising from an inflationary output gap, the inflation rate cannot stay constant because expectations will always be revised upward toward the actual inflation rate.

Now we see the reason for the name NAIRU. If real GDP is held above Y^* (and thus the unemployment rate is held below the NAIRU), the inflation rate tends to accelerate. The NAIRU is therefore the lowest level of sustained unemployment consistent with a *non-accelerating* rate of inflation.

According to the acceleration hypothesis, as long as an inflationary output gap persists, expectations of inflation will be rising, which will lead to increases in the actual rate of inflation.

The tendency for inflation to accelerate is discussed further in *Extensions in Theory 29-1*, which examines how expected inflation affects the position of the Phillips curve.

Inflation as a Monetary Phenomenon

For many years, a debate among economists concerned the extent to which inflation is a monetary phenomenon. Does it have purely monetary causes—changes in the demand or the supply of money? Does it have purely monetary consequences—only the price level is affected? One slogan that states an extreme position on this issue was popularized many years ago by the late Milton Friedman: "Inflation is *always* and everywhere a monetary phenomenon." To consider these issues, let us summarize what we have learned already. First, look at the various *causes* of inflation in our macro model:

- Anything that shifts the *AD* curve to the right will cause the price level to rise (demand inflation).

EXTENSIONS IN THEORY 29-1

The Phillips Curve and Inflation Expectations

As we first saw in Chapter 24, the Phillips curve describes the relationship between unemployment (or the output gap) and the rate of change of nominal wages. The Phillips curve was born in 1958 when Professor A.W. Phillips from the London School of Economics noted a relationship between unemployment and the rate of change of nominal wages over a period of 100 years in the United Kingdom.

Phillips was interested in studying the short-run behaviour of an economy subjected to cyclical fluctuations. In the years following Phillips's study, however, some economists treated the Phillips curve as establishing a long-term tradeoff between wage inflation and unemployment.

Suppose the government stabilizes output at Y_1 (and hence the unemployment rate at U_1), as shown by points

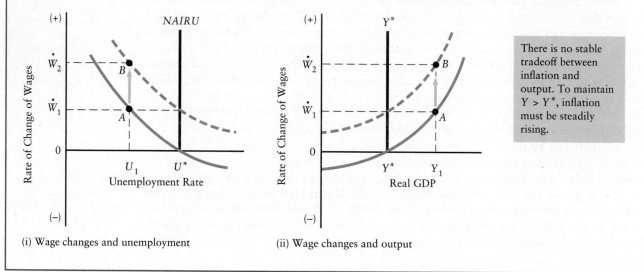

There is no stable tradeoff between inflation and output. To maintain $Y > Y^*$, inflation must be steadily rising.

(i) Wage changes and unemployment

(ii) Wage changes and output

- Anything that shifts the *AS* curve upward will cause the price level to rise (supply inflation).
- Increases in the price level caused by *AD* and *AS* shocks will eventually come to a halt unless they are continually validated by monetary policy.

The first two points tell us that a temporary burst of inflation need not be a monetary phenomenon. It need not have monetary causes, and it need not be accompanied by monetary expansion. The third point tells us that *sustained* inflation *must* be a monetary phenomenon. If a rise in prices is to continue indefinitely, it *must* be accompanied by a monetary policy that allows the money supply to continually increase. In our macro model, this is true regardless of the cause that set the inflation in motion.

Now, let us summarize the macroeconomic changes that accompany inflation, assuming that real GDP was initially at its potential level:

- In the short run, demand inflation tends to be accompanied by an *increase* in real GDP above its potential level.
- In the short run, supply inflation tends to be accompanied by a *decrease* in real GDP below its potential level.
- When all costs and prices are adjusted *fully* and real GDP has returned to its potential level, the only long-run effect of *AD* or *AS* shocks is a change in the price level.

A in the accompanying figures. To do this, it must validate the ensuing wage inflation, which is indicated by $\dot{W}_1$ in the figures. The government thus *appears* to be able to choose among particular combinations of (wage) inflation and unemployment, in which lower levels of unemployment are attained at the cost of higher rates of inflation.

In the 1960s, Phillips curves were fitted to the data for many countries, and governments made decisions about where they wanted to be on the tradeoff between inflation and unemployment. Then, in the late 1960s, in country after country, the rate of wage and price inflation associated with any given level of unemployment began to rise. Instead of being stable, the Phillips curves began to shift upward. The explanation lay primarily in the rise of inflation expectations.

It was gradually understood that the original Phillips curve concerned only the influence of the output gap and left out inflationary expectations. This was not unreasonable for Phillips's original curve, which was fitted mainly to nineteenth-century data where the price level was relatively constant and so expected inflation was negligible. But in the inflationary period following the Second World War, this omission proved important and unfortunate. An increase in expected inflation shows up as an upward shift in the original Phillips curve that was drawn in Chapter 24. The importance of expectations can be shown by drawing what is called an **expectations-augmented Phillips curve**, as shown by the dashed Phillips curves here. The height of the Phillips curves above the axis at Y^* and at U^* show the expected inflation rate. These distances represent the amount that wages will rise even when $Y = Y^*$ (or $U = U^*$) and there is neither excess demand nor supply in labour markets. The actual wage increase is shown by the augmented (dashed) curve, with the increase in wages exceeding expected inflation whenever $Y > Y^* (U < U^*)$ and falling short of expected inflation whenever $Y < Y^* (U > U^*)$.

Now we can see what was wrong with the idea of a stable inflation–unemployment tradeoff. Maintaining a particular output Y_1 or unemployment U_1 in the figures requires some inflation $\dot{W}_1$. And once this rate of inflation comes to be expected, people will demand that much just to maintain their real wages. The Phillips curve will then shift upward to the position shown in the figures and the economy will be at point B. Now there is inflation $\dot{W}_2$ because of the combined effects of expectations and excess demand. However, this higher rate is above the expected rate $\dot{W}_1$. Once this higher rate comes to be expected, the Phillips curve will shift upward once again.

As a result of the combination of output-gap inflation and expectational inflation, the inflation rate associated with any given positive output gap ($Y > Y^*$ or $U < U^*$) rises over time. This is the phenomenon of accelerating inflation that we discussed in the text.

The shifts in the Phillips curve are such that most economists agree that in the long run, when inflationary expectations have fully adjusted to actual inflation, there is no tradeoff between inflation and unemployment. In other words, the long-run Phillips curve is a vertical line above U^* (or Y^*).

The first two points tell us that inflation is not, in the short run, a purely monetary phenomenon because there are real consequences. The third point tells us that inflation is a monetary phenomenon from the point of view of long-run equilibrium. There is still plenty of room for debate, however, on how long the short run will last. Most economists believe that the short run can be long enough for inflation to have major real effects on important economic variables.

We have now reached three important conclusions:

- Without monetary validation, positive demand shocks cause inflationary output gaps and a temporary burst of inflation. The gaps are removed as rising factor prices push the *AS* curve upward, returning real GDP to its potential level but at a higher price level.
- Without monetary validation, negative supply shocks cause recessionary output gaps and a temporary burst of inflation. The gaps are eventually removed when factor prices fall sufficiently to restore real GDP to its potential and the price level to its initial level.
- Only with continuing monetary validation can inflation initiated by either supply or demand shocks continue indefinitely.

To put these conclusions differently, we can modify Friedman's statement slightly to represent the causes of inflation more accurately. While *AD* and *AS* shocks may lead

expectations-augmented Phillips curve The relationship between unemployment and the rate of increase of nominal wages that arises when the output-gap and expectations components of inflation are combined.

to temporary inflation even in the absence of any actions by the central bank, *sustained* inflation can occur only if there is continual monetary validation by the central bank.

Sustained inflation is always and everywhere caused by sustained monetary expansion.

▌29.3 Reducing Inflation

Suppose an economy has had high inflation for several years. What must the central bank do to reduce the rate of inflation? What are the costs involved in doing so?

The Process of Disinflation

disinflation A reduction in the rate of inflation.

Disinflation means a reduction in the rate of inflation. Canada has had two notable periods of disinflation—in 1981–1982, when inflation fell from more than 12 percent to 4 percent, and in 1990–1992, when inflation fell from 6 percent to less than 2 percent.

The process of reducing a high inflation can be divided into three phases. In the first phase, the monetary validation is stopped and any inflationary gap is eliminated. In the second phase, the economy still suffers from declining output and rising prices—*stagflation*. In the final phase, the economy experiences both increasing output and increasing prices, but the inflation then comes to an end. We now examine these three phases in detail.

The starting point for our analysis is an economy with an inflationary gap ($Y > Y^*$) and rising inflation.[5]

Phase 1: Removing Monetary Validation   The first phase consists of tightening monetary policy by raising interest rates and thus reducing the growth rate of the money supply. This policy action slows the rate at which the *AD* curve is shifting upward. An extreme case of monetary tightening in this setting is one where the Bank of Canada adopts a "cold-turkey approach": Interest rates are increased so much that the growth rate of the money supply is reduced to zero and the upward shift of the *AD* curve is halted abruptly. This extreme case is shown in part (i) of Figure 29-6.

The Bank's tight-money policy stops the *AD* curve from shifting. But under the combined influence of the present inflationary gap and expectations of continued inflation, wages continue to rise. Hence, firms' costs continue to increase and the *AS* curve continues to shift upward. Eventually, the inflationary gap will be removed, as real GDP falls back toward Y^*.

If the excess demand from the inflationary output gap were the only influence on nominal wages, the story would be ended. At $Y = Y^*$, there would be no upward demand pressure on wages and other factor prices. The *AS* curve would be stabilized, and real GDP would remain at Y^*. But it is usually not so simple.

---

[5] In the simpler case in which the economy begins with $Y = Y^*$ and constant inflation, only the second and third phases are relevant.

FIGURE 29-6 Eliminating a Sustained Inflation

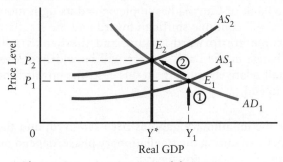

(i) Phase 1: Removing monetary validation

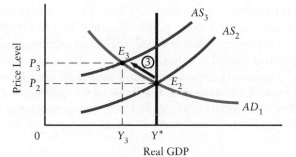

(ii) Phase 2: Stagflation

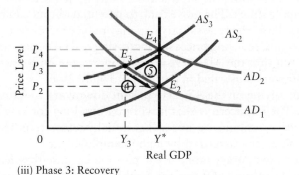

(iii) Phase 3: Recovery

(i) Phase 1: The elimination of a sustained inflation begins with a monetary tightening to remove the inflationary gap. The initial position is one where fully validated inflation is taking the economy along the path shown by arrow ①. When the curves reach AS_1 and AD_1, the central bank adopts a tight monetary policy, which halts the growth of the money supply, thus stabilizing aggregate demand at AD_1. Due to the output gap and inflation expectations, wages continue to rise, taking the AS curve leftward. The economy moves along arrow ②, with output falling and the price level rising. When aggregate supply reaches AS_2, the inflationary gap is removed, output is Y^*, and the price level is P_2.

(ii) Phase 2: Expectations and wage momentum lead to stagflation, with falling output and continuing inflation. The economy moves along the path shown by arrow ③. The driving force is now the AS curve, which continues to shift because inflation expectations cause wages to continue rising. The recessionary gap grows as output falls. Inflation continues, but at a diminishing rate. If wages stop rising when output has reached Y_3 and the price level has reached P_3, the stagflation phase is over, with short-run equilibrium at E_3.

(iii) Phase 3: After expectations are reversed, recovery takes output to Y^* and the price level is stabilized. There are two possible scenarios for recovery. In the first, the recessionary gap causes wages to fall (slowly), taking the AS curve back to AS_2 (slowly), as shown by arrow ④. The economy retraces the path originally followed in part (ii) back to E_2. In the second scenario, the central bank increases the money supply sufficiently to shift the AD curve to AD_2. The economy then moves along the path shown by arrow ⑤. This restores output to potential at the cost of further temporary inflation that takes the price level to P_4. Potential output and a stable price level are now achieved.

Phase 2: Stagflation As we explained earlier, wages depend not only on current excess demand but also on inflation expectations. Once inflation expectations have been established, it is not always easy to get people to revise them downward, even in the face of announced changes in monetary policies. Hence, the AS curve continues to shift upward, causing the price level to continue to rise and output to fall. A recessionary gap is created. The combination of rising prices and a reduction in output (or its growth rate) is called **stagflation**. This is phase 2, shown in part (ii) of Figure 29-6.

The ease with which the Bank of Canada can end such an inflation depends on how easy it is to change these expectations of continued inflation. This change is more

stagflation The simultaneous increase in inflation and reduction in output (or its growth rate) that is caused by an upward shift of the AS curve.

difficult to the extent that expectations are backward-looking and easier to the extent that expectations are forward-looking.

If most people are backward-looking when forming their expectations, inflation will remain high even well after the Bank of Canada has implemented its tight monetary policy. In this case, the *AS* curve will continue shifting upward and the stagflation will endure. However, if most people are forward-looking and the Bank's policy announcements are credible, the change in the Bank's policy will be widely acknowledged and expected inflation will fall relatively quickly. In this case, the upward shifts of the *AS* curve will soon come to an end.

> How long inflation persists after the inflationary gap has been removed, and the depth of the associated recessionary gap during the stagflationary phase, depend on how quickly inflation expectations are revised downward.

The importance of expectations explains why the Bank of Canada and other central banks emphasize their precise objectives in their many public speeches. In 1990–1991, the Bank's governor, John Crow, gave many speeches in an effort to convince the public that the Bank would stick to its newly adopted inflation target. This communications strategy was an attempt to reduce inflationary expectations and thus slow the upward shift of Canada's *AS* curve. Even now, the governor of the Bank of Canada regularly speaks publicly about the Bank's 2 percent inflation target and about the importance of achieving it. Such public communications help to "anchor" inflation expectations at the 2 percent target.

Phase 3: Recovery   The final phase is the return to potential output. When the economy comes to rest at the end of the stagflation, the situation is exactly the same as when the economy is hit by a negative supply shock. The move back to potential output can be accomplished in either of two ways. First, the recessionary gap may reduce factor prices, thereby shifting the *AS* curve downward, reducing prices but increasing real GDP. Second, an expansionary monetary policy can shift the *AD* curve upward, increasing both prices and real GDP. These two possibilities are illustrated in part (iii) of Figure 29-6.

Many economists worry about relying on the *AS* curve to shift downward to return the economy to potential output. Their concern is that it will take too long for wages to fall sufficiently to shift the *AS* curve—though output will eventually return to potential, the long adjustment period will be characterized by high unemployment.

Other economists worry about a temporary monetary expansion because they fear that expectations of inflation may be rekindled when the Bank's monetary expansion shifts the *AD* curve to the right. And if inflationary expectations *are* revived, the Bank will then be faced with a tough decision—either it must let another recession develop to break these new inflation expectations or it must validate the inflation to reduce unemployment. In the latter case, the Bank is back where it started, with validated inflation on its hands—and diminished credibility.

The Cost of Disinflation

As the forgoing discussion suggests, disinflation is a classic example of a policy that brings short-term pain for long-term gain. The long-term gain is the reduced costs to individuals and firms associated with the lower rate of inflation; the short-term pain is the temporary loss in economic activity and rise in unemployment that occurs during the process of disinflation.

The cost of disinflation is the loss of output that is generated in the process.

As we said earlier, the size and duration of the recession depends to a large extent on how quickly inflation expectations are revised downward as the disinflation continues. If expectations are mainly backward-looking and slow to adjust to the changes in policy, the recession will be deep and protracted. Conversely, if expectations are mainly forward-looking and quick to adjust to changes in policy, the recession may be mild and of short duration.

But *how costly* is the process of disinflation? Economists have derived a simple measure of the cost of disinflation based on the depth and length of the recession and on the amount of disinflation. This measure is called the **sacrifice ratio** and is defined as the cumulative loss of real GDP caused by a given disinflation (expressed as a percentage of potential GDP) divided by the number of percentage points by which inflation has fallen.

sacrifice ratio The cumulative loss in real GDP, expressed as a percentage of potential output, divided by the percentage-point reduction in the rate of inflation.

For example, the 1990–1992 disinflation in Canada reduced inflation by roughly 4 percentage points. Suppose the cumulative loss of real GDP caused by that disinflation was equal to $80 billion and that potential GDP at the time was equal to $800 billion. The cumulative loss of output would then have been 10 percent of potential output. The sacrifice ratio would therefore have been $10/4 = 2.5$. The interpretation of this number is that it "costs" 2.5 percent of real GDP for each percentage point of inflation that is reduced.

The numbers in the previous example are hypothetical, but typical estimates of the sacrifice ratio for many developed countries range between 2 and 4. Figure 29-7 illustrates the time paths of real GDP and inflation following a disinflation and shows how to compute the sacrifice ratio. Note an important assumption that is implicit whenever measuring the sacrifice ratio in this way: that all changes in the path of real GDP are *caused by* the disinflation.

FIGURE 29-7 The Cost of Disinflation: The Sacrifice Ratio

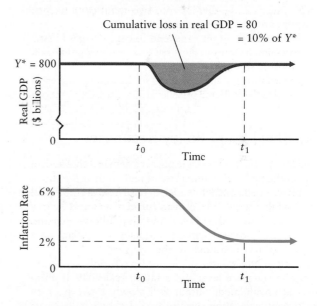

The sacrifice ratio is larger the deeper the recession and the longer it takes real GDP to return to potential. In this example, the economy begins with $Y = Y^*$ and inflation of 6 percent. At t_0, a tightening of monetary policy initiates a disinflation. A recessionary gap opens up and inflation falls only slowly. By t_1, real GDP has returned to Y^* and inflation has been reduced by four percentage points. In this figure, the cumulative loss of real GDP is 10 percent of Y^* and inflation has fallen by four percentage points. The sacrifice ratio is therefore $10/4 = 2.5$, indicating that it costs 2.5 percent of GDP to reduce inflation by one percentage point.

Conclusion

Throughout the history of economics, inflation has been recognized as a harmful phenomenon. The high inflation rates that Canada experienced in the 1970s and early 1980s (see Figure 29-1) were also experienced in many developed countries. In the past 50 years these countries have learned much about the causes of inflation, the policies required to reduce it, and the costs associated with doing so.

In particular, Canada and several other countries have adopted formal inflation-targeting regimes, which have been successful at keeping inflation low and stable. An important aspect of inflation targeting is to keep the *expectations* of inflation low. As we have seen in this chapter, keeping inflation expectations low is crucial to keeping actual inflation low.

In recent years, some commentators have argued that the dangers of inflation have been eliminated, that inflation is now "dead." Central to these arguments is the view that greater international competition through the process of globalization will keep inflationary pressures at bay. Yet, whatever forces globalization might bring, it remains true that *sustained* inflation is ultimately caused by monetary policy. Unless central banks remain committed to keeping inflation low and stable, damaging inflation could return as a potential threat to the economy.

SUMMARY

29.1 Adding Inflation to the Model

LO 1, 2

- Ongoing price inflation will be accompanied by closely related growth in wages and other factor prices such that the *AS* curve is shifting upward. Factors that influence wages can be divided into two main components: output gaps and expectations.
  1. Inflationary output gaps tend to cause wages to rise; recessionary output gaps tend to cause wages to fall, but only slowly.
  2. Expectations of inflation tend to cause wage increases equal to the expected price-level increases. Expectations can be backward-looking, forward-looking, or some combination of the two.
- With a constant rate of inflation and no supply shocks, expected inflation will eventually come to equal actual inflation. This implies that there is no output-gap effect on inflation.
- With real GDP equal to Y^*, a constant inflation can occur with the *AD* and *AS* curves shifting upward at the same rate.

29.2 Shocks and Policy Responses

LO 3, 4

- The initial effects of a single positive demand shock are a rise in the price level and a rise in real GDP. If the shock is unvalidated, output tends to return to its potential level while the price level rises further (as the *AS* curve shifts upward). Monetary validation allows demand inflation to proceed without reducing the inflationary gap (*AD* curve continues to shift upward).
- The initial effects of a single negative supply shock are a rise in the price level and a fall in real GDP. If inflation is unvalidated, output will slowly move back to its potential level as the price level slowly falls to its pre-shock level (*AS* curve slowly shifts down). Monetary validation allows supply inflation to continue in spite of a persistent recessionary gap (*AD* curve shifts up with monetary validation).
- If the Bank of Canada tries to keep real GDP constant at some level above Y^*, the actual inflation rate will eventually accelerate.
- Aggregate demand and supply shocks have temporary effects on inflation. But sustained inflation is caused by sustained monetary expansion.

29.3 Reducing Inflation

LO 5, 6

- The process of ending a sustained inflation can be divided into three phases.
  1. Phase 1 consists of ending monetary validation and allowing the upward shift in the *AS* curve to remove any inflationary gap that does exist.
  2. In Phase 2, a recessionary gap develops as expectations of further inflation cause the *AS* curve to continue to shift upward even after the inflationary gap is removed.
  3. In Phase 3, the economy returns to potential output, sometimes aided by a one-time monetary expansion that raises the *AD* curve to the level consistent with potential output.
- The cost of disinflation is the recession (output loss) that is created in the process. The sacrifice ratio is a measure of this cost and is calculated as the cumulative loss in real GDP (expressed as a percentage of Y^*) divided by the reduction in inflation.

KEY CONCEPTS

Temporary and sustained inflation
The NAIRU
Forward-looking and backward-looking expectations

Expectational, output-gap, and supply-shock pressures on inflation
Monetary validation of demand and supply shocks

Expectations-augmented Phillips curve
Accelerating inflation
Disinflation
Sacrifice ratio

STUDY EXERCISES

MyLab Economics Make the grade with MyLab Economics™: All Study Exercises can be found on MyLab Economics™. You can practise them as often as you want, and many feature step-by-step guided instructions to help you find the right answer.

FILL-IN-THE-BLANK

1 Fill in the blanks to make the following statements correct.

a. The term NAIRU stands for the _____.

b. Unemployment is said to be equal to the NAIRU when GDP is equal to _____.

c. Changes in nominal wages result from two effects: the _____ effect and the _____ effect. Both of these effects cause the _____ curve to shift.

d. The *AS* curve shifts up when nominal wages _____ and also shifts up with a negative _____ shock.

e. Actual inflation can come from any of its three component parts. They are _____, _____, and _____.

f. If the rate of inflation is constant at 6 percent and actual GDP equals potential GDP, then we can say that the central bank is _____ inflation expectations. That is, the central bank is permitting a(n) _____ in the money supply such that the expected and actual inflation rates are equal at _____ percent.

2 Fill in the blanks to make the following statements correct.

a. Suppose the economy is initially at potential GDP (Y^*) and then there is a sudden increase in the demand for Canadian exports. The *AD* curve shifts to the _____ and opens a(n) _____ gap.

b. With an inflationary gap, the economy is operating where GDP is above _____. In an effort to maintain the output gap, the Bank of Canada may choose to validate the inflation by _____ the interest rate and allowing the money supply to _____. The actual inflation rate will _____.

c. The alternative policy response to an inflationary gap is to not validate the inflation. The _____ curve stops shifting upward. The _____ curve shifts upward due to rising wages caused by _____. Real GDP eventually returns to _____ at a higher _____.

d. Sustained inflation can be said to be a(n) _____ phenomenon.

e. Reducing a sustained inflation requires that monetary _____ be stopped. Inflation will persist, however, until _____ of continued inflation are revised downward.

f. The cost of disinflation is the cost of the _____ that is generated in the process.

REVIEW

3 What sources of inflation are suggested by each of the following quotations?

a. A newspaper editorial in Manchester, England: "If American unions were as strong as those in Britain, America's inflationary experience would have been as disastrous as Britain's."

b. An article in *The Economist*: "Oil price collapse will reduce inflation."

c. A Canadian newspaper article in June 2015: "Tensions in Yemen fuel an oil-driven inflation."

d. A newspaper headline in October 2008: "Bank's fast growth of money will spur inflation."

e. A newspaper headline in July 2014: "Bumper crops across the West will dampen consumer inflation."

f. A newspaper headline in June 2018: "Wage growth suggests imminent interest-rate hikes."

4 Consider the following *AD/AS* diagram, beginning at AD_0 and AS_0. Suppose the economy experiences a positive aggregate demand shock—say, an increase in the demand for Canada's exports. Real GDP increases to Y_1.

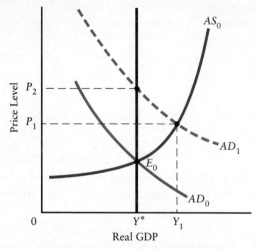

a. Explain what happens if the Bank of Canada does not react to the shock. Show this in the diagram.
b. Now suppose the Bank decides to maintain real GDP at Y_1—that is, it decides to validate the shock. Explain how this is possible, and show it in a diagram.
c. What is the effect on inflation from the policy in part (b)? Is inflation constant or is it rising? Explain.

5 Consider the following *AD/AS* diagram, beginning at AD_0 and AS_0. Suppose the economy experiences a negative aggregate supply shock—say, an increase in wages driven by a major union settlement. Real GDP falls to Y_1.

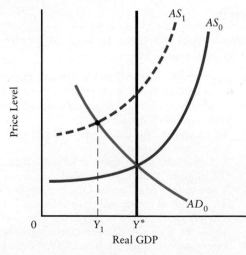

a. Explain what happens if the Bank of Canada does not react to the shock. Show this in the diagram.
b. Now suppose the Bank decides to offset the shock's effect on real GDP—that is, it validates the shock. Explain how this is possible, and show it in a diagram.
c. What danger do many economists see in validating such supply shocks? What is the alternative?

6 In the summer of 2018, a time when U.S. inflation was rising and output was close to potential, a story in *The Globe and Mail* reported that the release of strong employment-growth data for the United States led to a plunge in prices on the U.S. stock market.

a. Explain why high employment growth would lead people to expect the U.S. central bank to tighten its monetary policy.
b. Explain why higher U.S. interest rates would lead to lower prices of U.S. stocks.
c. How would you expect this announcement to affect Canada?

7 What is the relationship between the sacrifice ratio and the central bank's credibility?

a. Explain why a more credible policy of disinflation reduces the costs of disinflation.
b. Explain how you think the Bank of Canada might be able to make its disinflation policy more credible.
c. Can the Bank's policy responses to negative supply shocks influence the credibility it is likely to have when trying to end a sustained inflation? Explain.

PROBLEMS

8 The table below shows several macroeconomic situations, each with a given amount of excess demand (or supply) for labour and a level of inflation expectations. Both are expressed in percentage per year. For example, in Case A excess demand for labour is pushing wages up by 4 percent per year, and expected inflation is pushing wages up by 3 percent per year.

Case	Excess Demand	Inflation Expectations	Total Wage Change	AS Shift
A	+4	+3	——	——
B	+4	0	——	——
C	0	+3	——	——
D	−3	0	——	——
E	−3	+4	——	——

a. For each case, identify whether there is an inflationary or a recessionary output gap.
b. For each case, what is the total effect on nominal wages? Fill in the third column.
c. For each case, in which direction is the AS curve shifting (up or down)? Fill in the last column.

9 In the AD/AS diagram here, the economy is in long-run equilibrium with real GDP equal to Y^*; the price level is stable at P_0.

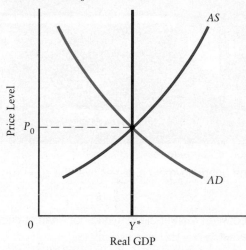

a. Suppose the central bank announces that it will implement an expansionary monetary policy that will shift the AD curve up by 5 percent. Show the likely effect of this announcement on the AS curve.
b. Does the shift of the AS curve in part (a) depend on whether workers and firms believe the central bank's announcement? Explain.
c. In a new AD/AS diagram, show how a sustained and constant inflation of 5 percent is represented (with $Y = Y^*$).
d. In the absence of any supply shocks, explain why a constant inflation is only possible when real GDP is equal to Y^*.

10 This exercise requires you to compute inflationary expectations based on a simple formula, and it will help you to understand why backward-looking expectations adjust slowly to changes in economic events. Suppose that the *actual* inflation rate in year t is denoted Π_t. *Expected* inflation for year $t + 1$ is denoted Π^e_{t+1}. Now, suppose that workers and firms form their expectations according to

$$\Pi^e_{t+1} = \theta\Pi^T + (1 - \theta)\Pi_t \quad (\text{with } 0 < \theta < 1)$$

where Π^T is the central bank's announced *inflation target*. This simple equation says that people's expectations for inflation at $t + 1$ are a weighted average of last year's actual inflation rate and the central bank's currently announced target. We will use this equation to see how the size of θ determines the extent to which expectations are backward-looking. Consider the table below, which shows the data for a reduction in actual inflation from 10 percent to 2 percent.

Year (t)	Π^T	Π_t	$\theta = 0.1$ Π^e_{t+1}	$\theta = 0.9$ Π^e_{t+1}
1	2	10	——	——
2	2	9	——	——
3	2	6	——	——
4	2	3	——	——
5	2	2	——	——
6	2	2	——	——
7	2	2	——	——
8	2	2	——	——

a. Assume that θ is equal to 0.1. Compute expected inflation for each year and fill in the table.
b. On a scale diagram, plot the time path of actual inflation, expected inflation, and the inflation target.
c. Now assume that θ equals 0.9. Repeat parts (a) and (b).
d. Which value of θ corresponds to more backward-looking expectations? Explain.
e. Given the different speed of adjustment of inflationary expectations, predict which disinflation is more costly in terms of lost output—the one with $\theta = 0.1$ or with $\theta = 0.9$. Explain.

11 The table that follows shows some data on various disinflations. In each case, assume that potential GDP is equal to $900 billion.

Case	Inflation Reduction (percentage points)	Cumulative GDP Loss ($ billion)	Sacrifice Ratio
A	5	100	——
B	2	30	——
C	6	60	——
D	8	80	——

a. In each case, compute the sacrifice ratio.
b. Explain why the sacrifice ratio can be expected to be smaller when expectations are more forward-looking.
c. Explain why the sacrifice ratio can be expected to be smaller when central-bank announcements are more credible.

30 Unemployment Fluctuations and the NAIRU

CHAPTER OUTLINE

LEARNING OBJECTIVES (LO)

After studying this chapter you will be able to

30.1 EMPLOYMENT AND UNEMPLOYMENT

1 compare employment and unemployment changes over the short run and long run.

30.2 UNEMPLOYMENT FLUCTUATIONS

2 describe the difference between market-clearing and non-market-clearing theories of the labour market.

30.3 WHAT DETERMINES THE NAIRU?

3 discuss the causes of frictional and structural unemployment.

4 explain the various forces that cause the NAIRU to change.

30.4 REDUCING UNEMPLOYMENT

5 discuss policies designed to reduce unemployment.

WHEN the level of economic activity changes, so do the levels of employment and unemployment. When real GDP increases in the short run, employment usually rises and unemployment usually falls. Conversely, when real GDP falls in the short run, employment falls and unemployment rises. Figure 30-1 shows the course of the unemployment rate in Canada over the past few decades. Recall from Chapter 19 that the unemployment rate is the percentage of the people in the labour force not working but actively searching for a job. It is clear that the unemployment rate has followed a cyclical path, rising during the recessions of 1981–1982, 1991–1992, and 2009, and falling during the expansions of the late 1980s, late 1990s, mid-2000s and the 2010–2018 period. In this chapter we examine theories designed to explain these short-run fluctuations.

In addition to examining short-run fluctuations in the unemployment rate, economists also study the concept of the NAIRU—the rate of unemployment that exists when real GDP is equal to potential output, Y^*. At points A, B, C, D, and E in Figure 30-1, real GDP was approximately equal to potential output, and thus the unemployment rates then were approximately equal to the NAIRU. We will see in this chapter several reasons why the NAIRU might change over time and thus offer some explanations for the gradual decline in the NAIRU apparent in the figure, from about 8 percent in 1977 (point A) to less than 6 percent in 2018 (point E).

We begin by examining some basic facts about employment and unemployment.

30.1 Employment and Unemployment

Look back at Figure 19-3, which shows the path of employment and the labour force in Canada since 1960. The most striking feature of part (i) of the figure is that both employment and the labour force have tripled over the past half-century, with only relatively minor fluctuations. Also notice in part (ii) of Figure 19-3, and again in Figure 30-1, that the unemployment rate displays considerable short-run fluctuations but no significant long-term trend. These two characteristics of the labour force—long-term growth in employment but short-term fluctuations in the unemployment rate—are common to most developed countries.

> Over the span of many years, increases in the labour force are more or less matched by increases in employment. Over the short term, however, the unemployment rate fluctuates considerably because changes in the labour force are not matched by changes in employment.

Changes in Employment

The amount of employment in Canada has increased dramatically over the past few decades. In 1976, there were approximately 9.7 million employed Canadians. By 2018, total employment was 18.5 million. The actual amount of employment, of course, is determined both by the demand for labour and by the supply of labour. How have the two "sides" of the Canadian labour market been changing?

FIGURE 30-1   Canadian Unemployment Rate, 1976–2018

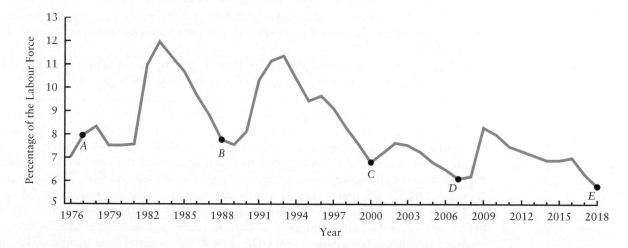

The unemployment rate displays considerable short-run fluctuations; the NAIRU shows a slight downward long-run trend. The points labelled *A* through *E* correspond to years when real GDP was equal to *Y** and so the unemployment rate was equal to the NAIRU.

(Source: Based on Statistics Canada, CANSIM database, Table 282-0087. Unemployment rate is for both sexes, 15 years and over, seasonally adjusted.)

On the supply side, the labour force has grown virtually every year since the end of the Second World War. There are three main causes of the increase in Canada's labour force: a rising population, which boosts entry into the labour force of people born 15 to 25 years previously; increased labour force participation by various groups, especially women; and net immigration of working-age persons.

On the demand side, many existing jobs are eliminated every year, and many new jobs are created. The technological improvements that drive economic growth often cause great disruptions in an economy. Some sectors of the economy decline while others expand. Jobs are lost in the sectors that are contracting and created in sectors that are expanding. Furthermore, even in relatively stable industries, many firms disappear and many new ones are set up. The net increase in employment is the difference between all the jobs that are created and all those that are lost.

In most years, enough new jobs are created both to offset the number of jobs that have been eliminated and also to provide jobs for the growing labour force. The result is a net increase in employment in most years.

In 2018, Canadian employment was 18.5 million workers. In a typical year employment increases by about 210 000 workers, an annual growth rate of just over 1 percent.

Changes in Unemployment

In the early 1980s, worldwide unemployment rose to high levels. The unemployment rate remained high in many advanced industrial countries and only began to fall, and even then very slowly, during the latter half of the decade. Canadian experience reflected these international developments rather closely. From a high of more than 12 percent in 1983, the Canadian unemployment rate fell to 7.5 percent in 1988, a point that many economists at the time thought was close to the Canadian NAIRU (see point *B* in Figure 30-1).

With the onset of another recession in the early 1990s, the unemployment rate then rose through 1990 and 1991, reaching 11.3 percent by 1992. During the next few years, the unemployment rate fell only slowly as the Canadian recovery was weak; by early 1994 the unemployment rate was still more than 10 percent. But the speed of the Canadian recovery quickened and unemployment began to drop. By early 2000, after five years of steady economic recovery, the unemployment rate was 6.8 percent.

With the onset of the 2008 global financial crisis, and the worldwide recession that immediately followed, unemployment again increased sharply. The Canadian economy fared much better than others, however, and unemployment increased only to 8.7 percent at the depth of the recession in mid-2009 (whereas it was considerably higher in the United States and most of Europe). After a decade of gradual economic recovery that brought Canadian real GDP close to its potential level by mid 2018, the unemployment rate was 5.8 percent.

During periods of rapid economic growth, the unemployment rate usually falls. During recessions or periods of slow growth, the unemployment rate usually rises.

Flows in the Labour Market

As we have just observed, many existing jobs are eliminated every year as existing firms adopt new technologies that require different types of workers, some industries shrink, and some firms disappear altogether. Similarly, new jobs are continually being created, as other industries expand and new firms are born. The public's and the media's focus on the labour market, however, tends to be on the overall level of employment and unemployment rather than on the amount of *job creation* and *job destruction*. This focus can often lead to the conclusion that few changes are occurring in the labour market when in fact the truth is quite the opposite.

For example, the Canadian unemployment rate was roughly constant at 7 percent from 2014 to 2016. Does this mean no jobs were created during the year? Or that the Canadian labour market was stagnant during this period? No. In fact, workers were finding jobs at the rate of between 500 000 and 600 000 *per month*. At the same time, however, other workers were leaving jobs or entering the labour force at roughly the same rate. These large flows *out of unemployment* were being approximately matched by the large flows *into unemployment*. The net result was that total unemployment changed only slightly.

> The amount of activity in the labour market is better reflected by the flows into and out of unemployment than by the overall unemployment rate.

By looking at the *gross flows* in the labour market, we are able to see economic activity that is hidden when we look just at changes in the overall amount of employment and unemployment (which is determined by *net* flows). Indeed, the gross flows are typically so large that they dwarf the net flows. See *Applying Economic Concepts 30-1* for more discussion of the gross flows in the Canadian labour market and how these gross-flows data can be used to compute the average length of unemployment spells.

Measurement Problems

The official labour-market data produced and reported by Statistics Canada understate the full effects of recessions on unemployment. The unemployment data refer to those individuals who are not currently working and who are actively searching for a job. As a recession continues, many workers who have been unable to find a job become discouraged and give up the search. Statistically, these *discouraged workers* are no longer included in the labour force; they are therefore not classified as unemployed, even though they would still accept a job if one were offered. In addition, this pool of discouraged workers generally becomes larger as the recession continues, which means that the official data become a larger understatement of the amount of "true" unemployment.

A second problem with the official measure of unemployment is that it fails to take account of situations where an individual is *underemployed*. Many workers who have lost their job and are still searching for a suitable replacement may temporarily take a part-time job or a low-paying job that does not require their qualifications. These workers prefer a part-time or low-paying job to the alternative of being totally unemployed, and they are appropriately represented in the data as being employed. Yet it is also true that they usually continue to search for a job better suited to their experience and qualifications.

APPLYING ECONOMIC CONCEPTS 30-1

Stocks and Flows in the Canadian Labour Market

In most reports about changes in unemployment, both in Canada and abroad, emphasis is typically on the changes in the *stock* of unemployment—that is, on the number of people who are unemployed at a particular point in time. But as we said in the text, the focus on the stock of unemployment can often hide much activity in the labour market, activity that is revealed by looking at *gross flows*.

What Are Labour-Market Flows?

The first figure in this box shows the difference between stocks and flows in the labour market. The blue circles represent the number of individuals at the end of each month (the *stocks*) in each possible "state"—employment (*E*), unemployment (*U*), and *not* in the labour force (*N*). The six red arrows represent the monthly *flows* of individuals among the various states. For example, arrow ① shows the monthly flow of individuals from *E* to *U*. These individuals begin the month in *E* (employed), leave their jobs sometime during the month, and end the month as unemployed individuals, in *U*. Arrow ③ shows the flow from *N* to *U*—these individuals are new entrants to the labour force during the month and begin their labour-force experience as unemployed individuals.

In the second figure, three series of data are shown for Canada from 1976 to 2003—a period that includes the major recessions of 1981 and 1991. (Unfortunately, Statistics Canada has stopped publishing these data, so more recent data are not available.) The top line is the stock of unemployment—the actual *number* of people unemployed at a specific point in time. During the severe recession of the early 1980s, unemployment peaked at approximately 1.7 million people and then fell during the recovery until 1989. With the onset of the next recession in 1990–1991, unemployment rose again, reaching nearly 1.8 million in 1992.

The two lower lines show *gross flows* in the labour market. (These data are not available for 1997 and 1998, which explains the break in the lines at that point.) The orange line shows the monthly flow into unemployment, corresponding to the sum of the flows in arrows ① and ③ in the first figure. This flow into unemployment represents

- workers losing jobs through layoffs or plant closure
- workers quitting jobs to search for different jobs
- new entrants to the labour force searching for jobs

In the figure, the monthly flow into unemployment varies between approximately 350 000 and 500 000 individuals *per month*.

The green line shows the monthly flow out of unemployment, corresponding to the sum of the flows in arrows ② and ④ in the first figure. This outflow represents

- unemployed individuals finding new jobs
- unemployed individuals becoming discouraged and leaving the labour force

During the period shown in the figure, the monthly flow out of unemployment is roughly the same size as the monthly inflow, 350 000 to 500 000 individuals per month. (Today, both monthly flows are in the range of 500 000 to 600 000 individuals.)

What is the connection between the flows and the stocks in the labour market? Whenever the flows into unemployment exceed the flows out of unemployment, the stock of unemployment rises. Conversely, whenever the flows out of unemployment exceed the flows into unemployment, the stock of unemployment falls.

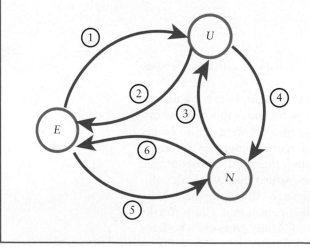

Using Flows Data

For two reasons data on flows can be very useful when studying the labour market. First, they show the tremendous amount of activity in the labour market even though the stock of unemployment may not be changing significantly. For example, between 1991 and 1992 the stock of unemployment in Canada varied between 1.4 million and 1.6 million persons. But during that two-year period, roughly 400 000 persons *per month* either became unemployed or ceased being unemployed. This number reflects the massive amount of regular turnover that exists in the Canadian labour market—turnover that is the essence of what economists call *frictional unemployment*.

The second reason flows data are useful is that the relationship between the flows and the stock can tell us about the amount of time the average unemployed person spends unemployed. If U_s is the stock of unemployment, and U_o is the monthly outflow from unemployment, then one simple estimate of the average length of an unemployment spell is

$$\text{Average duration of unemployment spell} = \frac{U_s}{U_o}$$

Consider the situation in 1999, at the peak of the business cycle (a low point for unemployment). At that time, the stock of unemployment was approximately 1 million people and the outflow from unemployment was approximately 400 000 persons per month. Thus, the average unemployed person in 1999 could expect to leave unemployment in about 2.5 months (1 000 000 people/ 400 000 people per month = 2.5 months). In contrast, in 1992, at the depth of the previous recession (and thus a high point for unemployment), the expected duration of an unemployment spell was 3.6 months (1 600 000/450 000 = 3.6).

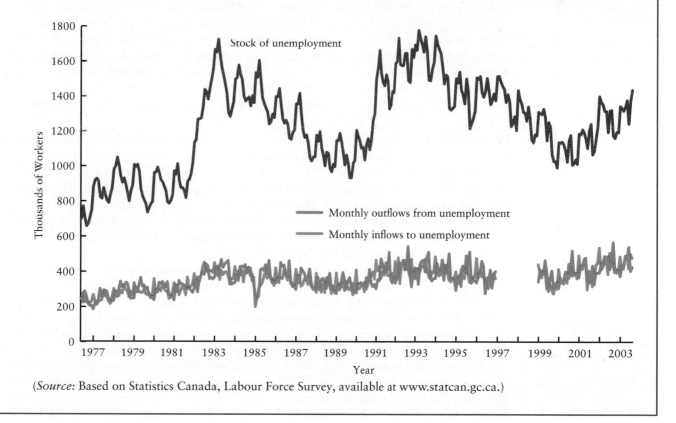

(*Source:* Based on Statistics Canada, Labour Force Survey, available at www.statcan.gc.ca.)

Care must therefore be taken when assessing the state of the labour market from the official unemployment data. A fall in the unemployment rate is sometimes caused by discouraged workers giving up the search and leaving the labour force. And just because individuals are recorded as being employed does not mean they are not still searching for jobs that better match their skills and experience.

Consequences of Unemployment

To most people, unemployment is seen as a "bad," just as output and income are seen as "good." But this does not mean *all* unemployment is bad, just as we know that not all output—such as noise or air pollution—is good. Indeed, we will see later in this chapter that some unemployment is socially desirable as it reflects the necessary time spent searching to make appropriate matches between firms who are seeking new employees and workers who are seeking new jobs.

We examine two costs of unemployment. The first is the associated loss in output and income. The second is the harm done to the individuals who are unemployed.

Lost Output   Every person counted as unemployed is willing and able to work and is seeking a job but has yet to find one. Hence, unemployed individuals are valuable resources who are currently not producing output. The output that is not produced, but potentially could be, is a loss of income for society. Once an unemployed person regains employment, however, output rises again and this loss no longer occurs. But nothing makes up for the *past* loss that existed while the person was unemployed. In other words, the loss of output and income that accompanies unemployment is lost forever. In a world of scarcity with many unsatisfied desires, this loss represents a serious waste of resources.

Personal Costs   For the typical Canadian worker, being unemployed for long periods of time is unusual. Most spells of unemployment are short. In 2008, *before* the onset of a major global recession, the OECD estimated that only 7.1 percent of Canadian unemployment spells lasted 12 months or longer; this number increased to 12 percent two years later, at the depth of the recession. In other words, the vast majority of unemployed workers find new jobs in just a few months. Moreover, many workers experiencing temporary unemployment have access to the employment-insurance program that provides some income during their spell of unemployment.

There are nevertheless problems associated with unemployment, especially for those relatively few workers who are unemployed for long periods of time. The effects of long-term unemployment, in terms of the disillusioned who have given up trying to make it within the system and who contribute to social unrest, is a serious social problem. The loss of self-esteem and the dislocation of families that often result from situations of prolonged unemployment are genuine personal and family tragedies.

In the United States, as in Canada, the amount of long-term unemployment has historically not been large. For example, in the depths of the recessions of 1982 and 1991, the fraction of total unemployed workers who were unemployed for six months or more was just under 25 percent. In the most recent recession of 2009–2010, however, long-term unemployment in the United States became a more serious problem. The amount of long-term unemployment reached 45 percent in 2010. Even by mid-2016, more than six years into a modest economic recovery, almost 30 percent of all unemployed U.S. workers had been out of work for over six months. As we will describe later in this chapter, extensive long-term unemployment can be an important force behind increases in the economy's NAIRU. The general case for concern about high unemployment has been eloquently put by Princeton economist Alan Blinder:

> A *high-pressure economy provides opportunities, facilitates structural change, encourages inventiveness and innovation, and opens doors for society's under-dogs . . . All these promote the social cohesion and economic progress that make democratic mixed capitalism such a wonderful system when it works well. A low-pressure economy slams the doors shut, breeds a bunker mentality that resists change, stifles productivity growth, and fosters both inequality and mean-spirited public policy. All this makes reducing high unemployment a political, economic, and moral challenge of the highest order.*[1]

30.2 Unemployment Fluctuations

It is clear from Figure 30-1 that the unemployment rate fluctuates considerably over relatively short periods of time. Over the years, economists have debated the sources of these fluctuations, and many different theories have been developed to try to explain them. These theories can be divided into two broad categories.

The first set of theories is based on the central assumption that real wages adjust instantly to clear the labour market after any *AD* or *AS* shock occurs. As a result, real GDP is always equal to *Y**. (As we saw in Chapter 24, if the economy's adjustment process works quickly, real GDP returns to *Y** very soon after any *AD* or *AS* shock.) In this perspective, the unemployment rate still fluctuates, but only due to changes in frictional or structural unemployment. In these "market-clearing" theories, the only unemployment is frictional and structural, and the unemployment rate is thus always equal to the NAIRU.

The second set of theories is based on a very different view of how the labour market functions. These theories emphasize the distinction between the unemployment that exists when real GDP is equal to *Y**, and unemployment that is due to deviations of real GDP from *Y**. The former refers to the NAIRU, and is made up of frictional and structural unemployment. The latter is often called **cyclical unemployment**, which falls (or rises) as real GDP rises above (or falls below) *Y**. As we will soon see, this second set of theories suggests that cyclical unemployment exists because real wages do not adjust quickly to clear labour markets in response to shocks of various kinds. We refer to these as "non-market-clearing" theories of the labour market, and they are consistent with the macro model that we have developed throughout this book.

cyclical unemployment Unemployment not due to frictional or structural factors; it is due to deviations of GDP from *Y**.

Market-Clearing Theories

Two major characteristics of modern market-clearing theories of the labour market are that firms and workers continuously optimize and markets continuously clear. In such models, there can be no *involuntary* unemployment. These theories then seek to explain unemployment as the outcome of voluntary decisions made by individuals who are choosing to do what they do, including spending some time out of employment.

Market-clearing theories explain fluctuations in employment and real wages as having one of two causes. First, as shown in part (i) of Figure 30-2, changes in technology that affect the *marginal product* of labour will lead to changes in the demand for labour. If

---

[1] Blinder, A.S., "The Challenge of High Unemployment," *American Economic Review*, 1988.

FIGURE 30-2   Employment and Wages When Labour Markets Clear

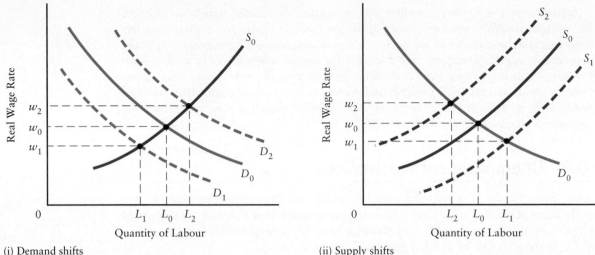

(i) Demand shifts   (ii) Supply shifts

In market-clearing theories of the labour market, real wages adjust quickly and so there is no involuntary unemployment. The figure shows a perfectly competitive market for one type of labour. In part (i), the demand curves D_1, D_0, and D_2 are the demands for this market corresponding to low, medium, and high values for the marginal product of labour. As demand rises from D_1 to D_0 to D_2, real wages rise from w_1 to w_0 to w_2, and employment rises from L_1 to L_0 to L_2. In part (ii), changes in workers' willingness to work causes the supply of labour to fluctuate from S_1 to S_0 to S_2, and wages to fluctuate from w_1 to w_0 to w_2. In both parts, real wages adjust quickly, the labour market always clears, and there is no involuntary unemployment.

these technological shocks are sometimes positive and sometimes negative, they will lead to fluctuations in the level of employment and real wages. Second, as shown in part (ii) of Figure 30-2, changes in the willingness of individuals to work will lead to changes in the supply of labour and thus to fluctuations in the level of employment and real wages. In both cases, however, note that the flexibility of real wages results in a *clearing* of the labour market. In this setting, whatever unemployment exists cannot be involuntary and must be caused by either frictional or structural causes, the two components of the NAIRU.

> **Market-clearing theories of the labour market assume that real wages quickly adjust to clear the labour market. People who are not working are assumed to have voluntarily withdrawn from the labour market for one reason or another. There is no involuntary unemployment.**

There are two major problems with these theories of labour markets. First, empirical observation is not consistent with the predicted fluctuations in real wages. In Canada and other developed economies, employment tends to be quite volatile over the business cycle, whereas real wages tend to be relatively stable—they do *not* show the cyclical variation depicted in Figure 30-2. The second problem is that the market-clearing theories predict no involuntary unemployment whatsoever, a prediction that many economists argue is unsupported by empirical observation. In Canada and other countries, a large fraction of unemployed workers are eligible for and collect employment insurance. In order to collect the insurance benefits, they are required to be actively searching for a job. For those who are truly engaged in an active job search, it is difficult to describe them as *voluntarily* unemployed. We will say more about the distinction between voluntary and involuntary unemployment later in the chapter.

Non-Market-Clearing Theories

The many economists who reject the market-clearing theories of unemployment fluctuations emphasize that labour markets do not operate in the extreme manner shown in Figure 30-2. Just as the prices of TVs, cars, blue jeans, sushi, and smartphones do not change daily, or even monthly, to equate current demand with current supply, so the wages paid to various types of labour, such as factory workers, schoolteachers, professors, architects, fast-food workers, train engineers, TV commentators, and product designers, do not change frequently to equate current demands with current supplies. These economists use non-market-clearing theories of the labour market in which "wage stickiness" plays a central role in explaining unemployment fluctuations. As we saw in Chapter 24, this wage stickiness is an important part of the macro model we have developed throughout this textbook.

When unemployed workers are looking for jobs during a recession, they do not knock on employers' doors and offer to work at lower wages than are being paid to current workers; instead, they answer help-wanted ads and hope to get the jobs offered but are often disappointed. Nor do employers, seeing an excess of applicants for the few jobs that are available, go to the current workers and reduce their wages until there is no one left looking for a job; instead, they pick and choose until they fill their needs and then hang a sign saying "No Help Wanted."

As a result of this wage stickiness, many people become involuntarily unemployed when the demand for labour falls during a recession. Their unemployment is involuntary in the sense that they would accept an offer of work in jobs for which they are trained, at the going wage rate, if such an offer were made. For example, such involuntary unemployment was evident during the recession that began in 2008 and extended into 2010 (and later in some countries). In the countries hardest hit by the recession, many workers had been unemployed for extended periods and their loss of income caused them to lose their homes and other possessions. In the European Union, where youth unemployment approached 50 percent in some countries, it was obvious that labour markets were not clearing to eliminate involuntary unemployment and that many unemployed workers would have gladly accepted work if it had been available. The cyclical behaviour of involuntary unemployment when wages are sticky is illustrated in Figure 30-3.

FIGURE 30-3 Unemployment and Sticky Wages When Labour Markets Do Not Clear

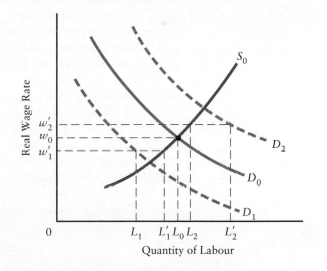

When the wage rate does not change enough to equate quantity demanded with quantity supplied, there will be unemployment in slumps and labour shortages in booms. When demand is at its normal level D_0, the market is cleared with wage rate w_0, employment is L_0, and there is no involuntary unemployment. In a recession, demand falls to D_1, but the wage falls only to w'_1. As a result, L_1 of labour is demanded and L'_1 is supplied. Employment is determined by the quantity demanded at L_1. The remainder of the supply for which there is no demand, $L_1L'_1$, is involuntarily unemployed. In a boom, demand rises to D_2, but the wage rate rises only to w'_2. As a result, the quantity demanded is L'_2, whereas only L_2 is supplied. Employment rises to L_2, which is the amount supplied. The rest of the demand cannot be satisfied, making excess demand for labour of $L_2L'_2$.

The main challenge for these non-market-clearing theories is to explain *why* wages do not quickly adjust to eliminate involuntary unemployment. This issue has been debated among economists for years, and several plausible reasons have been presented.

Long-Term Employment Relationships

The most obvious reason for wage stickiness over the business cycle is that many workers and their employers have long-term relationships in which the wages and conditions of work are determined for extended periods of time, often for one or more years. This situation applies to most groups of workers such as schoolteachers, professors, hospital technicians, office workers, supervisors, middle managers, and skilled construction workers.

To see why long-term employment relationships usually involve sticky wages, imagine a worker being faced with a choice between two employment arrangements:

1. A high average wage but one that fluctuates over the business cycle, and the chance of job loss during a recession.

2. A somewhat lower wage that is stable over the business cycle, and a reduced chance of job loss during a recession.

Most workers would prefer the second employment arrangement because they value the security that allows them to make long-term financial plans. For example, taking on a home mortgage or car loan is more manageable with a relatively secure job and income. The lower wage in the second employment arrangement can be seen as the price the worker pays for greater employment and income security.

Why do employers also prefer such long-term employment arrangements with sticky wages? Employers want to retain workers who have the knowledge required for a particular job—knowledge of the firm's organization, production techniques, operating procedures, and marketing plans. If all workers were identical, an employer would not mind laying off one individual from a particular job during a recession and then hiring a different worker for that job when demand recovers. But workers are not all the same, even in fairly routine jobs and even among workers having the same formal qualifications. What the worker learns through on-the-job experience is valuable to the firm and makes each individual a unique asset. If a firm laid off one worker and then later hired another worker for the same job, it would lose all the knowledge that the first worker had acquired on the job and would lose efficiency until the new worker acquired similar experience. In today's knowledge-intensive world, this loss can be substantial and typically applies for a wide range of workers.

For these and other similar reasons, wages tend to be insensitive to fluctuations in current economic conditions. Wages are often, in effect, regular payments to workers over an extended employment relationship rather than a device for fine-tuning the current supplies of and demands for labour. Employers tend to "smooth" the income of employees by paying a steady wage and letting profits and employment fluctuate to

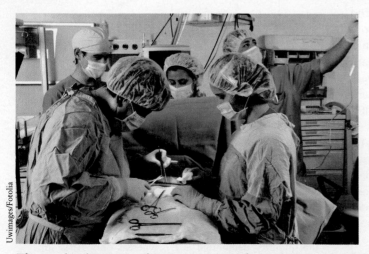

Uwimages/Fotolia

The quick adjustment of wages to excess demands and supplies is not a characteristic of labour markets in which employees and firms have long-term relationships, such as in the healthcare sector.

absorb the effects of temporary changes in demand. It is these fluctuations in employment over the business cycle that cause the fluctuations in involuntary unemployment.

Long-term relationships between firms and workers are important in most labour markets, and wages in such labour markets do not adjust frequently to eliminate involuntary unemployment.

Though long-term relationships between employers and workers have been the norm in most parts of the Canadian economy for many years, there is now an emerging trend toward workers being less connected to a single employer and more involved in short-term contract work—what is often referred to as the "gig economy." *Applying Economic Concepts 30-2* examines this phenomenon in more detail, and how its growth is likely to increase the economy's overall amount of wage flexibility.

Menu Costs   A second reason for wage (and price) stickiness relates to the costs associated with their changes. A typical large firm sells dozens of differentiated products and employs many different types of labour. Changing wages and prices in response to every fluctuation in demand is a costly and time-consuming activity. Many firms therefore find it optimal to keep their wage structures and price lists (*menus*) constant for significant periods of time. Since large firms are often operating in imperfectly competitive markets, they have discretion over the prices of their products. Hence, firms often react to short-term changes in demand by holding prices and wages constant and responding with changes in output and employment.

If firms did alter their prices dramatically over the business cycle, they would be more or less forced to alter wages correspondingly or else suffer losses that could threaten their existence during recessions. As it is, the presence of relatively sticky prices allows firms to keep wages relatively sticky over the cycle for all of the reasons we discussed when examining long-term employment relationships.

Efficiency Wages   A third reason for wage stickiness is that firms may find it profitable to pay workers a higher rather than a lower wage. Employers may find that they get more output per dollar of wages paid—that is, a more efficient workforce—when they pay labour somewhat more than the minimum amount that would induce people to work for them.

Suppose it is costly for employers to monitor workers' performance on the job so that some workers will be able to shirk duties with a low probability of being caught. Given prevailing labour-market institutions, it is generally impossible for employers to levy fines on employees for shirking on the job since the employees could just leave their jobs rather than pay the fines. So firms may instead choose to pay a wage premium—an *efficiency wage*—to the workers, in excess of the wage that the workers could get elsewhere in the labour market. With such a wage premium, workers will be reluctant to shirk because if they get caught and laid off, they will then lose this high wage.

Such high wages are rational responses of firms to the conditions they face and imply that firms will not alter wages in the face of temporary reductions in demand—that is, wages will be sticky.

Union Bargaining   A final important reason for wage stickiness comes from existing institutions in the labour market. In many employment situations, those already working ("insiders") have more say in wage bargaining than those currently not employed

APPLYING ECONOMIC CONCEPTS 30-2

Wage Flexibility and the Rise of the "Gig" Economy

For most of the twentieth century, "traditional" work involved individuals working for one employer at a time, sometimes for many years. An individual's career was spent mostly at one employer, perhaps working up through the ranks. This picture of the labour market is changing quickly, however, as we see increasing numbers of individuals working part-time at several jobs or working as self-employed contractors.

This development has been dubbed the "gig economy," in which rising numbers of individuals earn their income by working various "gigs" rather than maintaining a traditional long-term relationship with a single employer. Workers in this gig economy are characterized as (1) having their independence, (2) receiving payment for specific tasks, and (3) having short-term relationships with their clients.

A website designer, computer technician, or translator, for example, may sell their services on a contract basis, and their total income may come from these arrangements. Other individuals may work in the gig economy only to supplement their income from a traditional job. Uber drivers and people who advertise their various services on TaskRabbit are good examples.

Why is the gig economy growing, and what are the implications for wage flexibility?

What Do the Data Say?

A 2016 study by McKinsey & Company, an international consultancy, surveyed 8000 individuals in the United States and Europe and examined the nature of their work experience. The study found that between 20 and 30 percent of the working-age population was engaged in "independent work." As the table shows, such work in the gig economy, whether for primary or supplemental income, is the preferred choice of about 70 percent of the surveyed independent workers. In contrast, just over 30 percent of those involved in the gig economy claim to be doing so out of necessity, either because they cannot find a traditional job or because they need to earn extra money. (The fraction of Canadians involved in independent work is similar, and has been rising over time. Since 1997, the number of Canadians in temporary jobs has increased by 38 percent while the number in traditional jobs increased by only 17 percent.)

The McKinsey study also found that the individuals who have chosen to work in the gig economy report greater satisfaction with their working lives than those who do so out of necessity. This greater satisfaction is

The Characteristics of Workers in the Gig Economy
(162 million workers in the United States and Europe)

	Primary Income	Supplemental Income
Preferred Choice	Free Agents 30% (49 million people)	Casual Earners 40% (64 million people)
Out of Necessity	Reluctants 14% (23 million people)	Financially Strapped 16% (26 million people)

Source: Independent Work: Choice, Necessity, and the Gig Economy, McKinsey & Company, 2016.

("outsiders"). Employed workers are often represented by a union, which negotiates the wage rate with firms. The union will generally represent the interests of the insiders but will not necessarily reflect the interests of the outsiders. Insiders will naturally want to bid up wages even though to do so will harm the employment prospects of the outsiders. Hence, this theory generates an outcome to the bargaining process between firms and unions in which the wage is set higher than the market-clearing level, just as with efficiency wages.

There are several reasons why wages do not adjust quickly to clear excess demands or supplies in labour markets. Such wage stickiness is an important explanation for the existence of cyclical unemployment, which rises and falls as real GDP fluctuates.

true across countries, ages, income, and education levels. In short, while working in the gig economy appears to be an undesirable outcome for many, the clear majority prefers it to traditional work.

Why Is This Happening?

For many individuals, the gig economy offers independence and flexibility; the individual can choose which jobs to accept, for whom to work, and when to do the work. These are the "free agents" and the "casual earners" in the table. This independence naturally appeals to entrepreneurial types who prefer to be their own boss, even though it often comes with uncertainty regarding the source of the next paycheque. For these individuals, the rise of the gig economy signals an exciting opportunity, albeit one that demands hard work and perseverance.

For many other individuals, however, the gig economy is clearly a second choice, one unemployed workers may feel pushed into. These are the "reluctants" and the "financially strapped" in the table, and they would prefer to be a traditional employee in a traditional job. For these workers, the rise of the gig economy likely represents rising job insecurity and anxiety about the future.

From the perspective of firms, the rise of the gig economy reflects changes in technology and the nature of work. Profit-maximizing firms choose to hire workers in a traditional relationship when the benefits of doing so exceed the costs; and for many years it was simpler and cheaper to have workers "in house" rather than to be entering into repeated contractual arrangements with outside suppliers. But with the growing importance of service (rather than manufacturing) jobs and the rapid spread of low-cost digital technologies, it has become easier and cheaper for many firms to "outsource" jobs. The jobs may range from low-wage janitorial workers to high-wage engineers or IT technicians. No matter their income level, however, in most cases the workers receive a payment for services but do not earn the health, dental,

or pension benefits that were once standard with many traditional jobs.

Some current policies provide firms with an incentive to increase their outsourcing of workers. In many jurisdictions, firms are legally required to provide similar benefits to all of their workers, independent of their wages. Firms may respond to such requirements by choosing to outsource their lowest-wage workers, partly to avoid having to pay benefits. The firm then hires outside suppliers to replace those services, but the suppliers (or their workers) very often receive fewer benefits than they would have received with the initial employer. In such cases, the requirement to equalize benefits across workers has the unintended consequence of more outsourcing and an effective *decline* in benefits for low-wage workers.

What Are the Implications for Wage Flexibility?

In the text we argued that an important reason for sticky wages is that employers and workers are engaged in long-term relationships in which wages do not adjust frequently to changes in the economic environment. With the rise of the gig economy, what will happen to this wage stickiness?

As more individuals operate as independent contractors, their overall flexibility increases. They can take the jobs they like from the clients they like, and they can work the days and hours they prefer. They can also charge the fees they like, making adjustments for changes in the economic situation. Of course, the conditions of the contract need to be acceptable to their clients if their services are to be hired, so there are limits to this flexibility. But with the greater emphasis on the short-term nature of jobs, there is good reason to expect that the rise of the gig economy will increase the economy's degree of wage flexibility. If this turns out to be true, it will likely mean that the economy will adjust more quickly to *AD* and *AS* shocks, returning real GDP more quickly to potential output.

30.3 What Determines the NAIRU?

When the unemployment rate is equal to the NAIRU, there is only frictional and structural unemployment. Our interest here is in why the NAIRU changes over time and in the extent to which economic policy can affect it.

Frictional Unemployment

As we saw in Chapter 19, **frictional unemployment** results from the normal turnover of labour. One source of frictional unemployment is young people who enter the labour force and look for jobs. Another source is people who leave their jobs. Some may quit

frictional unemployment
Unemployment that results from the turnover in the labour market as workers move between jobs.

because they are dissatisfied with the type of work or their working conditions; others may be fired because of incompetence or laid off because their employers go out of business. Yet others may lose their jobs because the jobs themselves are eliminated by the introduction of new technologies. Whatever the reason, they must search for new jobs, which takes time. People who are unemployed while searching for jobs are said to be frictionally unemployed or in *search unemployment*.

> **The normal turnover of labour causes frictional unemployment to persist, even if the economy is at potential output.**

How "voluntary" is frictional unemployment? Some of it is clearly voluntary. For example, a worker may know of an available job but may not accept it so she can search for a better one, or one for which she is more appropriately trained. Some of it is also involuntary, such as when a worker gets laid off and cannot find *any* job offer for a period of weeks, even though he may be actively searching. However it is labelled, some amount of frictional (search) unemployemnt is desirable because it gives unemployed people time to find an available job that makes the best use of their skills.

Structural Unemployment

structural unemployment
Unemployment caused by a mismatch in skills, industry, or location between available jobs and unemployed workers.

Structural unemployment is defined as a mismatch between the current structure of the labour force—in terms of skills, occupations, industries, or geographical locations—and the current structure of firms' demand for labour. Since changes in the structure of the demand for labour are occurring continually in any modern economy, and since it takes time for workers to adjust, some amount of structural unemployment always exists.

The Pace of Economic Change   Changes that accompany economic growth shift the structure of the demand for labour. Demand might rise in such expanding areas as British Columbia's Lower Mainland or northern Alberta and might fall in parts of Ontario and Quebec. Demand rises for workers with certain skills, such as computer programming and electronics engineering, and falls for workers with other skills, such as paralegal services, assembly line work, and middle management. To meet changing demands, the structure of the labour force must change. Some existing workers can retrain and some new entrants can acquire fresh skills, but the transition is often difficult, especially for older workers whose skills become economically obsolete.

Increases in international competition can also cause structural unemployment. As the geographical distribution of world production changes, so does the composition of production and of labour demand in any one country. Labour adapts to such shifts by changing jobs, skills, and locations, but until the transition is complete, structural unemployment exists.

> **Structural unemployment will increase if there is either an increase in the pace at which the structure of the demand for labour is changing or a decrease in the pace at which labour is adapting to these changes.**

Following the Canada–U.S. Free Trade Agreement in 1989 and the North American Free Trade Agreement (NAFTA) in 1994, there were significant shifts of economic activity within Canada. For example, the textiles industry, much of which was located in Quebec, contracted; at the same time there was an expansion of the high-tech industry, much of which was located in the Ottawa Valley. The types of workers released from the textiles industry, however, were not exactly what were required in the expanding high-tech industry. This type of mismatch in skills and locations contributed to structural unemployment during the 1990s.

Structural unemployment also increased during the 2002–2008 period in response to the five-fold increase in the world price of oil. The demand for labour increased sharply in the petroleum-producing regions of Alberta, Saskatchewan, and Newfoundland. At the same time, many jobs were lost in the manufacturing heartland of Ontario and Quebec because the rising price of oil significantly increased firms' costs. Some of the displaced workers could find jobs relatively quickly in expanding firms in other regions or sectors, but for most workers this transition was slow. Structural unemployment was the result.

Increases in the world price of oil between 2002 and 2008 led to a reduction in manufacturing activity in Central Canada and economic expansions in oil-producing regions of the country, such as the Alberta oil sands shown here. Structural unemployment was created until workers could move from Eastern and Central Canada to Alberta. With the sharp decline in the world oil price in 2014–2015, these forces were reversed, causing structural unemployment.

With the massive decline in the world price of oil in 2014–2015, the structure of labour demand changed again, reversing the shifts from the earlier decade. Labour demand slowed in Alberta, Saskatchewan, and Newfoundland and sped up in the manufacturing sectors in Ontario and Quebec. Structural unemployment increased again.

Policies that Inhibit Change Government policies can influence the speed with which labour markets adapt to the kinds of changes just described. Some countries, including Canada, have adopted some policies that *discourage* movement among regions, industries, and occupations. These policies (which may be desirable for other reasons) tend to reduce the rate at which unemployed workers are matched with vacant jobs, and thus tend to raise the amount of structural unemployment.

For two related reasons, the employment-insurance (EI) program contributes to structural unemployment. First, the Canadian EI system ties workers' benefits to the *regional* unemployment rate in such a way that unemployed workers can collect EI benefits for more weeks in regions where unemployment is high than where it is low. The EI system therefore encourages unemployed workers to remain in high-unemployment regions rather than move to regions where employment prospects are more favourable. Second, workers are eligible for employment insurance only if they have worked for a given number of weeks in the previous year—this is known as the *entrance requirement*. In some cases, however, these entrance requirements are very low and thus seasonal workers may be encouraged to work for a few months and then collect employment insurance and wait for the next season, rather than finding other jobs during the off season.[2]

---

[2] That the EI system contributes to the amount of structural unemployment is not to deny the significant benefits from the system. First, EI encourages unemployed workers to search for jobs appropriate to their desires and skills. Second, EI provides a financial cushion that reduces the personal suffering which often accompanies periods of unemployment and low income.

Finally, labour-market policies that make it difficult or costly for firms to fire workers also make employers more reluctant to hire workers in the first place. Such policies, which are very common in the European Union, reduce the amount of turnover in the labour market and are believed to be an important contributor to the amount of long-term unemployment in those countries. In Germany, Italy, and Belgium, for example, the labour laws impose very high costs on firms whenever workers are laid off. In those countries, even when their economies are growing moderately, approximately 50 percent of all unemployment spells last for *longer* than 12 months.

The Frictional–Structural Distinction

As with many distinctions, the one between frictional and structural unemployment is not precise. In a sense, structural unemployment is really long-term frictional unemployment. Consider, for example, what would happen if there were an increase in world demand for Canadian-made car parts but at the same time a decline in world demand for Canadian-assembled cars. This change would require labour to move from one sector (the car-assembly sector) to another (the car-parts manufacturing sector). If the reallocation were to occur quickly, we would call the unemployment *frictional*; if the reallocation were to occur slowly, we would call the unemployment *structural*.

In practice, structural and frictional unemployment cannot be separated. But the two of them, taken together, *can* be separated from cyclical unemployment. Specifically, when real GDP is at its potential level, the *only* unemployment (by definition) is frictional and structural and thus the unemployment rate is equal to the NAIRU. For example, real GDP in Canada was approximately equal to potential GDP in 2007. (See Figure 30-1.) At that time, the unemployment rate was 6 percent, and thus the NAIRU was approximately 6 percent. In contrast, two years later in 2009, in the midst of the most recent recession, the unemployment rate was about 8.5 percent. If the underlying frictions and structural change in the economy were unaltered over those two years, we could conclude that in 2009, 2.5 percentage points of the actual unemployment rate was due to cyclical factors and the rest was due to frictional and structural factors.

Why Does the NAIRU Change?

The NAIRU can change for two broad reasons. First, anything that alters the *amount* of adjustment required between firms, occupations, sectors, or regions will cause a change in NAIRU. Second, anything that alters the *ability* of the labour force to make these adjustments will cause a change in NAIRU. We now examine four specific reasons for these kinds of changes.

Demographic Shifts Because young people usually try several jobs before settling into one for a longer period of time, young workers have more labour-market turnover and therefore higher unemployment rates than older, more experienced workers. The proportion of young workers in the labour force rose significantly as the baby-boom generation of the 1950s entered the labour force in the 1970s and

Young workers generally have higher unemployment rates than older workers. As the share of younger workers in the labour force changes, so will the economy's NAIRU.

Gideon Mendel/PhotoEdit, Inc.

1980s. This trend had the effect of increasing the NAIRU during the 1970s and 1980s. But as the baby-boom generation aged, and the fraction of young workers in the labour force declined in the late 1990s and early 2000s, the opposite effect was observed and tended to reduce the NAIRU.

A second demographic trend relates to the labour-force participation of women. During the 1960s and 1970s women tended to have higher unemployment rates than men. Since this was true at all points of the business cycle, the higher unemployment was higher frictional and structural unemployment. Thus, when female labour-force participation rates increased dramatically in the 1960s and 1970s, the NAIRU increased. In recent years, however, female unemployment rates have dropped below the rates for men, and so further increases in female participation will, if anything, tend to decrease the NAIRU.

Greater labour-force participation by groups with high unemployment rates increases the NAIRU.

See Figure 30-4 for Canadian unemployment rates for various demographic groups in 2018. Notice especially the significantly higher unemployment rates for youth of both sexes. These data form the basis for the often-heard view that while overall

FIGURE 30-4   Canadian Unemployment Rates by Demographic Groups, 2018

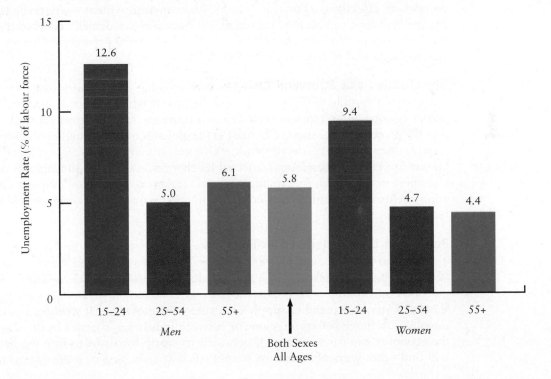

Unemployment is unevenly spread among different groups in the labour force. In 2018, when the overall unemployment rate was 5.8 percent, the unemployment rates for youths (of both sexes) were considerably higher.

(Source: Based on Statistics Canada CANSIM database, Table 282-0087.)

unemployment may be at acceptable levels, high youth unemployment may be a serious problem.

Hysteresis We saw in Chapter 27 that short-run changes in real GDP sometimes cause changes in the level of potential output, Y^*. One possible reason that we examined was due to the operation of labour markets, whereby the NAIRU can be influenced by the current rate of unemployment. Such models get their name from the Greek word *hysteresis*, meaning "lagged effect."

One mechanism that can lead to hysteresis arises from the importance of experience and on-the-job training. Suppose a recession causes a significant group of new entrants to the labour force to encounter unusual difficulty obtaining their first jobs. As a result, this unlucky group will be slow to acquire the important skills that workers generally learn in their first jobs. When demand increases again, this group of workers will be at a disadvantage relative to workers with normal histories of experience, and the unlucky group may take longer to find jobs and thus have unemployment rates that will be higher than average. Hence, the NAIRU will be higher than it would have been had there been no recession.

Another force that can cause hysteresis is emphasized by commentators in the European Union, which has a more heavily unionized labour force than Canada or the United States. In times of high unemployment, people who are currently employed ("insiders") may use their bargaining power to ensure that their own status is maintained and prevent new entrants to the labour force ("outsiders") from competing effectively. For this reason, high unemployment—whatever its initial cause—will tend to become "locked in." If outsiders are denied access to the labour market, their unemployment will fail to exert downward pressure on wages, and the NAIRU will tend to rise.

Globalization and Structural Change The ongoing process of globalization, especially since the mid-1970s, has increased the rate at which labour is being reallocated across regions and sectors in the Canadian economy.[3] While most economists argue that the growing integration of Canada in the global economy generates net benefits for Canada, they also recognize a downside. One unfortunate consequence is that Canadian labour markets are increasingly affected by changes in demand and supply conditions elsewhere in the world. As Canadian labour markets require more frequent and larger adjustments to economic events occurring in other parts of the world, the NAIRU will tend to increase.

Policy and Labour-Market Flexibility We mentioned earlier how policies such as employment insurance can increase structural unemployment and thereby increase the NAIRU. This is one example of a policy reducing the *flexibility* of the labour market.

Such inflexibility is an important cause of unemployment. If wages are inflexible, shocks to labour demand or supply can cause unemployment. If workers are unable or unwilling to move between regions or between industries, changes in the structure of the economy can cause unemployment. If it is costly for firms to hire workers, firms will find other ways of increasing output (such as switching to more capital-intensive

---

[3] Recall from Chapter 1 that we use the term *globalization* to refer to the significant declines in transportation and communication costs that have been taking place over the past two centuries (especially rapidly over the past 50 years) and which have led to an increased volume of world trade in goods, services, and assets.

methods of production). In general, since the economy is always being buffeted by shocks of one sort or another, the less flexible is the labour market, the higher structural unemployment will be.

Any government policy that reduces labour-market flexibility is likely to increase the NAIRU.

Another example of a policy that reduces labour-market flexibility is mandated job security for workers. In most Western European countries, firms cannot lay off workers without showing cause, which can lead to costly delays and even litigation. When firms do lay workers off, they are required either to give several months' notice before doing so or, in lieu of such notice, are required to make severance payments equal to several months' worth of pay. In Italy, for example, a worker who has been with the firm for 10 years is guaranteed either 20 months' notice before termination or a severance payment equal to 20 months' worth of pay.

Such job-security provisions greatly reduce the flexibility of firms. But this inflexibility on the part of the firms is passed on to workers. Any policy that forces the firm to incur large costs for laying off workers is likely to lead the same firm to be very hesitant about hiring workers in the first place. Given this reduction in labour-market flexibility, such policies are likely to increase the NAIRU.

Such mandated job security is relatively rare in Canada and the United States. Its rarity contributes to the general assessment by economists that North American labour markets are much more flexible than those in Europe. Many economists see this as the most important explanation for why unemployment rates in Canada and the United States are usually significantly below the unemployment rates in Europe.

30.4 Reducing Unemployment

In the remainder of this chapter we briefly examine what can be done to reduce unemployment. Other things being equal, all governments would like to reduce unemployment. The questions are "Can it be done?" and "If so, at what cost?"

Cyclical Unemployment

We do not need to say much more about cyclical unemployment because its control is the subject of stabilization policy, which we have studied in several earlier chapters. Monetary and fiscal policies implemented in response to negative *AD* or *AS* shocks will act to reduce cyclical unemployment.

There is room for debate, however, about *how much* the government can and should do in this respect. Advocates of stabilization policy call for expansionary fiscal and monetary policies to reduce cyclical unemployment (and increase output), especially when a recessionary gap is sustained for a long period of time. Advocates of a hands-off approach say that normal market adjustments can be relied on to remove recessionary gaps and that government policy, no matter how well intentioned, will only make things worse.

Despite this ongoing debate, policymakers have not yet agreed to abandon stabilization measures. In the recession that began in most countries in 2008, for example, governments were quite aggressive in their implementation of expansionary fiscal and monetary policies in an attempt to dampen the recession's effects on falling output and rising unemployment. Today, most economists look back to these decisions and agree that governments' aggressive policy actions helped to reduce what would have otherwise been a much deeper recession.

Frictional Unemployment

The turnover in the labour market that causes frictional unemployment is an inevitable part of the functioning of the economy. Some frictional unemployment is a natural part of the learning process for young workers. As we observed earlier, new entrants to the labour force have to try several jobs to see which is most suitable, and this leads to a high turnover rate among the young and hence high frictional unemployment.

Whatever the source of unemployment, employment insurance (EI) is one method of helping people cope with its costs. Although EI alleviates the suffering caused by unemployment, it also contributes to search unemployment, as we have already observed. As with any policy, a rational assessment of the value of EI requires an evaluation of its costs and benefits. Many Canadians believe that when this calculation is made, the benefits greatly exceed the costs, although many also recognize the scope for reform of certain aspects of the program.

Many provisions have been added to the EI program to focus it more on people in general need and to reduce its effect of raising the unemployment rate. For example, workers must be actively seeking employment in order to be eligible for EI. Also, workers who voluntarily quit their jobs (without cause) are not eligible to collect EI. In recent years, the benefits received by eligible unemployed workers have been reduced, thus decreasing the likelihood that job seekers will reject early job offers. These changes have contributed to a decline in the amount of frictional uncmployment.

Structural Unemployment

The reallocation of labour among occupations, industries, skill categories, and regions that gives rise to structural unemployment is an inevitable part of a market economy. Much of this required reallocation is driven by technological change, which occurs in different ways and at different paces in various parts of the economy. Ever since the beginning of the Industrial Revolution in the late eighteenth century, workers have resisted the introduction of new techniques that replace the older techniques at which they were skilled. Such resistance is understandable. New techniques often destroy the value of the knowledge and experience of workers skilled in the displaced techniques. Older workers may not even get a chance to start over with the new technique. Employers may perceive that younger workers are more adept at learning new skills and prefer to hire them rather than older workers.

Today, the rise of artificial intelligence, machine learning, and the related automation of jobs is leading to widespread concerns that structural unemployment will significantly increase in the near future. From society's point of view, new technologies are beneficial because they are a major source of productivity growth and rising average living standards. From the point of view of the workers they displace, however, new techniques can be an unmitigated disaster.

There are two basic approaches to reducing structural unemployment: try to resist the changes that the economy experiences or accept the changes and try to assist the necessary adjustments. Throughout history, both approaches have been tried.

Resisting Change   Over the long term, policies aimed at maintaining employment levels in declining industries run into increasing difficulties. Agreements to hire unneeded workers raise costs and can hasten the decline of an industry threatened by competitive products. An industry that is declining because of economic change becomes an increasingly large burden on the public purse as economic forces become less and less favourable to its success. Sooner or later, public support is withdrawn, and it is followed by a precipitous decline. Although policies such as these are not viable in the long run for the entire economy, they may be the best alternatives for the affected workers during their lifetimes.

There is often a conflict between the private interest of workers threatened by structural unemployment, whose interests lie in preserving existing jobs, and the social interest served by reallocating resources to where they are most valuable.

Assisting Adjustment   A second general approach to dealing with structural change is to accept the decline of specific industries and the loss of specific jobs that go with them and to try to reduce the cost of adjustment for the workers affected. A number of policies have been introduced in Canada to ease the adjustment to changing economic conditions.

One such policy is publicly subsidized education and retraining programs. The public involvement is motivated partly by positive externalities to education and partly by imperfections in capital markets that make it difficult for workers to borrow funds for education, training, or retraining. A major component of labour-market policies is a system of loans and subsidies for higher education.

Another policy is motivated by the difficulty in obtaining good information about current and future job prospects. Relative to what was possible 20 years ago, the development of the Internet greatly improved the flow of this type of information. The government of Canada created online services to speed up and improve the quality of matches between searching workers and firms. Today, however, the Internet is both more sophisticated and more widespread, and firms and workers are easily able to learn about labour-market opportunities through a large number of online search facilities. As a result, there is likely a reduced need for government to play an active role in providing labour-market information either to firms or workers.

Policies to increase retraining and to improve the flow of labour-market information will tend to reduce the amount of structural unemployment.

The federal government's 2018 budget responded to the need to improve the skills of Canadian workers in an economy increasingly subject to rapid change. New policies included providing better labour-market information to workers in seasonal industries, expanding funding so that young workers could access better summer jobs and acquire necessary skills, and funding partnerships between government and the private sector to develop experimental training programs for workers. In general, the government's policy approach was not one of resisting the economic changes that are occurring but rather accepting these changes, emphasizing the need for flexibility, and then developing policies that improve the labour force's ability to adapt.

Conclusion

Over the years, unemployment has been regarded in many different ways. Some see it as proof that the market system is badly flawed. Others regard it as a necessary evil of the market system and believe government policy can reduce its incidence and its harmful effects. More extreme observers believe its importance is overblown and that workers can obtain jobs if they really want to work.

Most government policy follows a middle route. Fiscal and monetary policies generally seek to reduce at least the most persistent of recessionary gaps, and a host of labour-market policies are designed to reduce frictional and structural unemployment. Social policies such as employment insurance seek to reduce the sting of unemployment for the many who suffer from it for reasons beyond their control.

As global economic competition becomes more intense and as new knowledge-driven methods of production spread, the ability to adjust to economic change will become increasingly important. Countries that succeed in the global marketplace, while also managing to maintain humane social welfare systems, will be those that best learn how to deal with changes in the economic landscape. This will mean avoiding economic policies that inhibit change while adopting social policies that reduce the human cost of adjusting to change. This is an enormous challenge for future Canadian economic and social policies.

SUMMARY

30.1 Employment and Unemployment

LO 1

- Canadian employment and the Canadian labour force increased along a strong upward trend throughout the twentieth century. The unemployment rate fluctuates significantly over the course of the business cycle.
- Looking only at the level of employment or unemployment misses a tremendous amount of activity in the labour market as individuals flow from unemployment to employment or from employment to unemployment. Such gross flows reflect the turnover that is a normal part of any labour market.
- It is useful to distinguish among several types of unemployment: cyclical unemployment, which is associated with output gaps; frictional unemployment, which is a result of normal labour-market turnover; and structural unemployment, which is caused by the need to reallocate resources among occupations, regions, and industries as the structure of demand and supply changes.
- Together, frictional unemployment and structural unemployment make up the NAIRU. The actual unemployment rate is equal to the NAIRU when real GDP is equal to Y^*.

30.2 Unemployment Fluctuations

LO 2

- Market-clearing theories assume labour markets clear continuously with perfectly flexible wages and prices. Such theories can explain cyclical variations in employment but predict no involuntary unemployment.
- Empirical evidence suggests that wages are relatively stable over the business cycle, in contrast to what is predicted by market-clearing theories of the labour market.
- Non-market-clearing theories of the labour market provide an explanation for involuntary unemployment based on wage stickiness; real wages do not adjust frequently in response to all shocks to labour demand and supply.
- To explain wage stickiness, non-market-clearing theories have focused on:
  1. the nature of long-term employment relationships
  2. the costs of changing wages and prices
  3. efficiency wages
  4. union bargaining

30.3 What Determines the NAIRU? LO 3, 4

- The NAIRU will always be positive because it takes time for labour to move between jobs both in normal turnover (frictional unemployment) and in response to changes in the structure of the demand for labour (structural unemployment).
- Because different workers have different sets of skills and because different firms require workers with different sets of skills, some unemployment—resulting from workers searching for appropriate job matches with employers—is socially desirable.

- Anything that increases the rate of turnover in the labour market, or the pace of structural change in the economy, will likely increase the NAIRU.
- Employment insurance also increases the NAIRU by encouraging workers to continue searching for an appropriate job. Policies that mandate job security increase the costs to firms of laying off workers. This makes them reluctant to hire workers in the first place and may increase the NAIRU.

30.4 Reducing Unemployment LO 5

- Cyclical unemployment can be reduced by using monetary or fiscal policies to close recessionary gaps.
- Frictional and structural unemployment can be reduced by making it easier to move between jobs and by raising the cost of staying unemployed (e.g., by reducing employment-insurance benefits).

- In a growing, changing economy populated by people who want to change jobs for many reasons, it is neither possible nor desirable to reduce unemployment to zero.
- Policies that assist workers in retraining and in moving between jobs, regions, or industries may be the most effective way to deal with the various shocks that buffet the economy.

KEY CONCEPTS

Gross flows in the labour market
Cyclical, frictional, and structural unemployment
Market-clearing theories of the labour market

Non-market-clearing theories of the labour market
Long-term employment relationships
Frictional and structural unemployment

Determinants of the NAIRU
Hysteresis
Policies to reduce the NAIRU
Labour-market flexibility

STUDY EXERCISES

MyLab Economics Make the grade with MyLab Economics™: All Study Exercises can be found on MyLab Economics™. You can practise them as often as you want, and many feature step-by-step guided instructions to help you find the right answer.

FILL-IN-THE-BLANK

❶ Fill in the blanks to make the following statements correct.

    a. The overall unemployment rate in Canada is not a good indicator of the level of *activity* in the labour market because it does not indicate _____.

    b. *Gross* flows in the labour market are much _____ than net flows in the labour market.

    c. In a typical month in Canada, _____ workers flow in each direction between unemployment and employment.

d. Cyclical unemployment exists when real GDP is _____ than potential GDP. When real GDP is equal to potential GDP, then all unemployment is either _____ or _____.

e. Market-clearing theories assume that the labour market always _____ with flexible _____ and that any unemployment that does exist is _____.

f. Non-market-clearing theories assume that wages do not instantly _____ to clear the market. A recessionary gap can persist and result in unemployment that is _____.

2 Fill in the blanks to make the following statements correct.

a. The NAIRU is composed of _____ unemployment and _____ unemployment. The NAIRU is always _____ than zero.

b. If there are 1000 loggers in British Columbia who are unemployed, and 1000 vacant positions for call-centre operators in New Brunswick, we say that this unemployment is _____.

c. Suppose the NAIRU in June 2018 was 6.0 percent. If the actual unemployment rate was 8.2 percent, we can conclude that _____ percentage points are due to _____ factors and the remaining _____ percentage points are due to _____ and _____ factors.

d. Suppose the government increased the number of weeks that an unemployed worker can collect EI benefits from 12 weeks to 16 weeks. The NAIRU is likely to _____ because of an increase in the amount of _____ unemployment.

e. Countries with greater labour-market flexibility are likely to have _____ unemployment rates than countries in which policies inhibit flexibility.

f. Cyclical unemployment can be reduced by closing a(n) _____ gap by using _____ and _____ policies.

REVIEW

3 Consider two hypothetical countries. In Country A, 20 percent of the labour force is unemployed for half the year and employed for the other half; the remaining 80 percent of the labour force is never unemployed. In Country B, 100 percent of the labour force is unemployed for 10 percent of the year and employed for the other 90 percent of the year. Note that both countries have an overall unemployment rate of 10 percent. Which of these countries seems to have the more serious unemployment problem, and why?

4 The diagram below shows a perfectly competitive labour market. The initial equilibrium is with wage w^* and employment L^*.

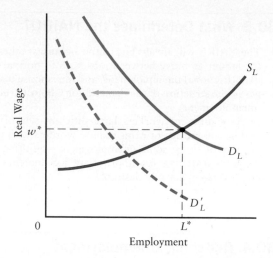

a. Suppose the demand for labour decreases to D_L'. If wages are perfectly flexible, what is the effect on wages and employment? Show this in the diagram.

b. Is there any involuntary unemployment in part (a) after the shock?

c. Now suppose wages can only adjust half as much as in part (a)—that is, wages are sticky. What is the effect on wages and employment in this case? Show this in the diagram.

d. Is there any involuntary unemployment in part (c) after the shock? How much?

5 Consider an economy that begins with real GDP equal to potential. There is then a sudden increase in the prices of raw materials, which shifts the *AS* curve upward.

a. Draw the initial long-run equilibrium in an *AD/AS* diagram.

b. Now show the immediate effect of the supply shock in your diagram.

c. Suppose wages and prices in this economy adjust instantly to shocks. Describe what happens to unemployment in this economy. Explain.

d. If wages and prices adjust only slowly to shocks, what happens to unemployment? Explain.

e. Based on evidence in the Canadian economy, which is the more realistic adjustment to the *AS* shock?

6 Interpret the following statements from newspapers in terms of types of unemployment.

a. "Recession hits local factory; 1800 workers laid off."

b. "Of course, I could take a job as a dishwasher, but I'm trying to find something that makes use of my degree in English literature," says a recent graduate in our survey of the unemployed.

c. "Retraining is the best reaction to the increased use of robots."

d. "Uneven growth: Alberta sputters while Ontario booms."

7 The diagram below shows a simple *AD/AS* diagram. The economy begins in long-run equilibrium at E_0 with real GDP equal to Y^*.

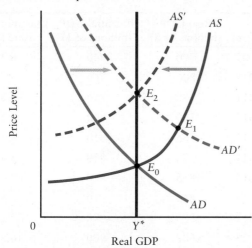

a. At E_0, the unemployment rate is 8 percent. What type of unemployment is this?
b. A positive aggregate demand shock now shifts the *AD* curve to *AD'*. At E_1 the unemployment rate is only 6.5 percent. Is there cyclical unemployment at E_1?
c. Describe the economy's adjustment process to E_2.
d. What is the unemployment rate at E_2? What kind of unemployment exists at E_2?

8 The diagram below shows a simple *AD/AS* diagram. The economy begins in long-run equilibrium at E_0 with real GDP equal to Y^*.

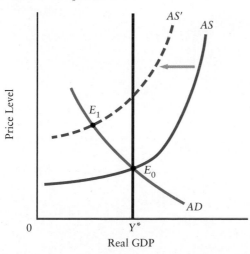

a. At E_0, the unemployment rate is 6 percent. What type of unemployment is this?
b. A negative aggregate supply shock now shifts the *AS* curve to *AS'*. At E_1 the unemployment rate is 7.5 percent. Is there cyclical unemployment at E_1? How much?

c. If monetary and fiscal policy do not react to the shock, describe the economy's adjustment process to its new long-run equilibrium.
d. What is the unemployment rate at the economy's new long-run equilibrium? What kind of unemployment exists there? Explain.

9 The Canadian government recently announced its plan to modify the employment-insurance (EI) program, generating a great deal of debate over the appropriate level of generosity for EI.

a. Explain what problem can be caused by having an EI system that is too generous.
b. Explain what problem can be caused by having an EI system that is not generous enough.
c. If EI generosity were reduced and the NAIRU declined as a result, is this necessarily a desirable outcome?

10 In its 2009 and 2010 budgets, the Canadian government significantly increased its planned spending on infrastructure projects in order to fight the existing recession and protect jobs.

a. Explain why such a policy may "create" jobs.
b. Is such a policy equally likely to create jobs during a recession as when the economy is already operating at potential output, as it was by mid-2018? Explain.

PROBLEMS

11 The table below provides employment and labour force data for a small economy over a 3-month period.

	Stock of Unemployment	Stock of Employment	Stock Outside the Labour Force	Total Population
Sept. 1	120 000	1 430 000	450 000	2 million
Oct. 1	120 000	1 380 000	500 000	2 million
Nov. 1	120 000	1 250 000	550 000	2 million

a. What is the unemployment rate on September 1, October 1, and November 1?
b. Explain why the unemployment rate changes even though the stock of unemployment remains stable.
c. Provide a likely explanation for the change in this economy's labour force. In this case, is the unemployment rate an accurate measure of the amount of slack (excess supply) in the labour market?

⑫ The table below shows the percentage of the labour force accounted for by youths (15 to 24 years old) and older workers (25 years and older) over several years. Suppose that because of their lower skills and greater turnover, youths have a higher unemployment rate than older workers (see Figure 30-4).

| Year | Percentage of Labour Force | |
	Youths	Older Workers
1	20	80
2	21	79
3	22	78
4	23	77
5	25	75
6	27	73
7	29	71
8	31	69

a. Suppose that in Year 1 real GDP is equal to potential GDP, and the unemployment rate among older workers is 6 percent but is 14 percent among youths. What is the economy's NAIRU?
b. Now suppose that for the next eight years real GDP remains equal to potential and that the unemployment rates for each group remain the same. Compute the value of the NAIRU for each year.
c. Explain why the NAIRU rises even though output is always equal to potential.

⑬ The following table shows the pattern of real GDP, potential GDP, and the unemployment rate for several years in Cycleland.

Year	Real GDP (billions of $)	Potential GDP (billions of $)	Unemployment Rate (%)
2009	790	740	6.3
2010	800	760	6.5
2011	780	780	6.8
2012	750	800	8.2
2013	765	810	8.4
2014	790	830	8.4
2015	815	850	8.0
2016	845	870	7.5
2017	875	890	7.2
2018	900	900	6.8
2019	930	920	6.7

a. On a scale diagram, draw the path of real GDP and potential GDP (with time on the horizontal axis).
b. On a separate diagram (below the first one) show the path of the unemployment rate.
c. For which years is it possible to determine the value of the NAIRU?
d. Does the NAIRU change over the 10-year period? Provide one reason that the NAIRU could increase.

31 Government Debt and Deficits

CHAPTER OUTLINE

31.1 FACTS AND DEFINITIONS

31.2 TWO ANALYTICAL ISSUES

31.3 THE EFFECTS OF GOVERNMENT DEBT AND DEFICITS

31.4 FORMAL FISCAL RULES

LEARNING OBJECTIVES (LO)

After studying this chapter you will be able to

1 explain how the government's annual budget deficit (or surplus) is related to its stock of debt.

2 describe the structural deficit and how it can be used to measure the stance of fiscal policy.

3 understand how budget deficits may crowd out investment and net exports.

4 describe why a high stock of government debt may hamper the conduct of monetary and fiscal policies.

5 explain why legislation requiring balanced budgets may be undesirable.

CANADA'S experience with government debt and budget deficits has been highly variable over the past half-century. From the mid-1970s through the early 1990s, most Canadian governments ran large budget deficits, and the county's stock of public debt grew significantly. By the mid-1990s, the debt was so large that many people viewed it as an economic time bomb, waiting to explode and cause serious harm to our living standards. By the early 2000s, after governments had taken drastic actions to reduce public spending, the federal and some provincial governments were achieving budget surpluses, and the debt had declined significantly in relation to GDP.

With the onset of the global financial crisis of 2008–2009, governments in many countries, including Canada, returned to running significant budget deficits. These deficits occurred partly because of a decline in revenues associated with a large economic recession and partly because of government efforts to stimulate the economy through an increase in public spending.

In the aftermath of the global financial crisis, several European countries, most notably Greece, suffered economic decline and near collapse due to their extreme levels of government debt. There was much debate about whether "fiscal austerity" was needed to reduce public debt or instead whether "fiscal stimulus" was needed to promote economic growth. There was a great deal of public tension as citizens, governments, and international organizations struggled to find the best path forward.

Any government's budget deficit and debt are important both economically and politically. As we saw in Chapters 22 and 24, the spending and taxation decisions that lead to deficits (or surpluses) can have potent effects on real GDP; as we will also see in this chapter, the accumulated level of government debt can have important impacts on the economy. As for politics, it is no exaggeration to say that governments' budget decisions are among their most important; in many political systems, governments win or lose elections largely on the basis of their economic policies.

We begin this chapter by considering the simple arithmetic of government budgets. This tells us how the deficit or surplus in any given year is related to the government's outstanding stock of debt. We then explore why deficits and debt matter for the performance of the economy.

▌31.1 **Facts and Definitions**

There is a simple relationship between the government's expenditures, its tax revenues, and its borrowing. This relationship is summarized in what economists call the government's *budget constraint*.

The Government's Budget Constraint

As is true for any individual's expenditures, government expenditures must be financed either by income or by borrowing. The difference between individuals and governments, however, is that governments typically do not earn income by selling products or labour services; instead, their income is generated by levying taxes. Thus, all government expenditure must be financed either by tax revenues or by borrowing. This point is illustrated by the following simple equation, which is called the government's budget constraint:

$$\text{Government expenditure} = \text{Tax revenue} + \text{Borrowing}$$

We divide government expenditure into two categories. The first is purchases of goods and services, G. The second is the interest payments on the outstanding stock of debt; this is referred to as **debt-service payments** and is denoted $i \times D$, where i is the interest rate and D is the stock of government debt (which has accumulated over time from the government's past borrowing). A third category of government spending is *transfers* to individuals and firms (such as employment-insurance benefits, public pensions, and industrial subsidies) but, as we did in earlier chapters, we include transfers as part of T, which is the government's *net tax revenue* (tax revenue minus transfers). The government's budget constraint can therefore be rewritten as

debt-service payments Payments that represent the interest owed on a current stock of debt.

$$G + i \times D = T + \text{Borrowing}$$

or, subtracting T from both sides,

$$(G + i \times D) - T = \text{Borrowing}$$

This equation simply says that any excess of total government spending over net tax revenues must be financed by government borrowing.

Debt and Deficits   The government's annual **budget deficit** is the excess of government expenditure over tax revenues in a given year. From the budget constraint just given, this annual deficit is exactly the same as the amount borrowed by the government during the year. Since the government borrows by issuing bonds and selling them to lenders, borrowing by the government increases the stock of **government debt**. Since D is the outstanding stock of government debt, ΔD is the *change* in the stock of debt during the course of the year. The budget deficit can therefore be written as

$$\text{Budget deficit} = \Delta D = (G + i \times D) - T$$

> **budget deficit** Any shortfall of current revenue below current expenditure.

> **government debt** The outstanding stock of financial liabilities for the government, equal to the accumulation of past budget deficits.

The government's annual budget deficit is the excess of expenditure over tax revenues in a given year. It is also equal to the change in the stock of government debt during the year.

Notice two points about budget deficits. First, a change in the size of the deficit requires a change in expenditures *relative* to tax revenues. For given tax revenues, a smaller deficit can come about only through a reduction in government expenditures; conversely, for given expenditures, a smaller deficit requires an increase in tax revenues. Second, since the budget deficit is equal to the amount of new government borrowing, the stock of government debt will rise whenever the budget deficit is positive. Even a drastic reduction in the size of the annual budget deficit is therefore not sufficient to reduce the outstanding stock of government debt; the stock of debt will fall only if the budget deficit becomes *negative*. In this case, there is said to be a **budget surplus**.

> **budget surplus** Any excess of current revenue over current expenditure.

A budget deficit increases the stock of government debt; a budget surplus reduces it.

The Primary Budget Deficit   One component of government expenditure is debt-service payments ($i \times D$). Since at any point in time the outstanding stock of government debt—determined by *past* government borrowing—cannot be influenced by current government policy, the debt-service component of total expenditures is beyond the immediate control of the government. In contrast, the other components of the government's budget (G and T) are determined by the current set of spending programs and tax policies, all of which can be adjusted if the government chooses to do so. To capture the part of the budget deficit that is attributable to current spending and tax policies, we can compute the **primary budget deficit**, defined to be the difference between government purchases and net tax revenues:

$$\text{Primary budget deficit} = G - T$$

> **primary budget deficit** The difference between the government's overall budget deficit and its debt-service payments.

The government's primary budget deficit shows the extent to which current tax revenues are sufficient to finance expenditure on current government programs.

Because of the need to make debt-service payments, there are often large differences between the government's overall budget deficit (or surplus) and its primary budget deficit (or surplus). In the 2005–2006 fiscal year, for example, the Canadian government had an *overall* surplus of $8 billion. So,

$$G + iD - T = -\$8 \text{ billion}$$

Since the debt-service payments during that year were $34 billion, we see that the government's *primary* surplus that year was $42 billion (or a primary deficit of −$42 billion).

$$G + \$34 \text{ billion} - T = -\$8 \text{ billion}$$

$$G - T = \text{primary deficit} = -\$42 \text{ billion}$$

In other words, total tax revenues in 2005–2006 were $42 billion more than *program* spending but only $8 billion more than *total* spending.

By the 2018–2019 fiscal year, the government's budget situation had changed considerably. The *overall* budget that year was projected to show a deficit of $18.1 billion, so

$$G + iD - T = \$18.1 \text{ billion}$$

But during that same year the government's projected debt-service payments were $26.3 billion:

$$G + \$26.3 \text{ billion} - T = \$18.1 \text{ billion}$$

$$\Rightarrow G - T = -\$8.2 \text{ billion}$$

so the government was projecting a *primary* budget surplus of $8.2 billion for that year. In other words, in 2018–2019 total tax revenues would not be enough to cover total government spending but would be more than sufficient to cover the government's program spending.

> The primary budget surplus or deficit shows the extent to which current tax revenues can cover the government's current program spending; it is equal to the overall budget deficit minus debt-service payments.

Deficits and Debt in Canada

In a growing economy, many macroeconomic variables, such as the levels of government expenditure and tax revenue, also tend to grow. As a result, rather than looking at the absolute size of the government deficit or debt, economists focus on government debt and deficits in relation to the overall size of the economy. Some budget deficits that would be unmanageable in a small country like New Zealand might be quite acceptable for a larger country like Canada, and trivial for a huge economy like the United States. Similarly, a government budget deficit that seemed crushing in Canada in 1919 might appear trivial in 2019 because the size of the Canadian economy is many times larger now than it was then.

Federal Government   The path of federal budget deficits since 1962 is shown in Figure 31-1. The top panel shows total federal spending and total federal tax revenues as percentages of GDP.[1] The bottom panel shows the total federal budget deficit as a percentage of GDP. Large and persistent budget deficits began in the mid-1970s. Throughout the 1980s and early 1990s, the average budget deficit was over 5 percent of GDP.

---

[1] In Figure 31-1 government expenditures include purchases, transfer payments, and debt-service payments. Tax revenues are not net of transfers.

In the mid-1990s, the federal government embarked on a successful policy of deficit reduction and by 1998 reported its first budget surplus in almost 30 years. The federal budget was then continually in surplus until the 2008–2009 fiscal year, at which point the budget returned to a deficit for several years, mostly as a result of a major recession. The budget deficit shrank as the economy recovered, but mildly expansionary policies then led it to increase again. By 2019 the budget deficit was below one percent of GDP.

As we saw in the previous section, a deficit implies that the stock of government debt is rising. Thus, the persistent budget deficits that began in the 1970s have their counterpart in a steadily rising stock of government debt. Figure 31-2 shows the path of Canadian federal government debt since 1940. At the beginning of the Second World War, the stock of federal debt was equal to about 45 percent of GDP. The enormous increase in the debt-to-GDP ratio over the next five years reflects wartime borrowing used to finance military expenditures. From 1946 to 1974, however, there was a continual decline in the debt-to-GDP ratio. The economy was growing quickly during this period, but equally important was that the federal government in the post-war years typically ran significant budget surpluses. These two factors explain the dramatic decline in the debt-to-GDP ratio between 1946 and 1974.

By 1974 the federal debt was only 14 percent of GDP. The large and persistent budget deficits beginning in the mid-1970s, however, along with a general slowdown in the rate of economic growth, led to a significant upward trend in the debt-to-GDP ratio. The ratio climbed steadily from 1979 to 1996, when it peaked at more than 69 percent of GDP. Then, with the significant reductions in the budget deficit beginning in 1996, the debt-to-GDP ratio began to fall. By 2008, the federal government's net debt was just above 30 percent of GDP, the lowest it had been since the early 1980s. The debt ratio then increased during the 2008–2009 recession, but by 2012 was again on a downward path and was forecast to be slightly below 30 percent by 2020.

FIGURE 31-1 **Federal Government Expenditures, Revenues, and Deficit, 1962–2017**

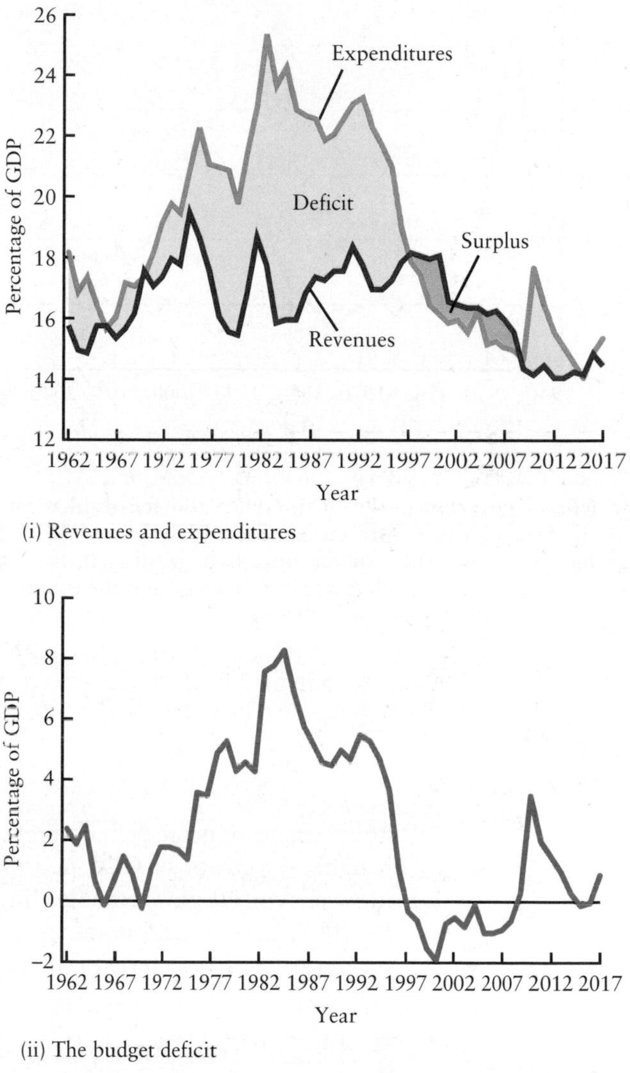

(i) Revenues and expenditures

(ii) The budget deficit

The federal budget was in deficit every year between 1971 and 1997. From 1998 to 2008 there were budget surpluses. The budget returned to deficit in 2009; it is now forecast to remain slightly below 1 percent of GDP for several years. Part (i) shows revenues and expenditures as a percentage of GDP. Part (ii) shows the budget deficit (or surplus) as a percentage of GDP.

(*Source:* Based on data from the Department of Finance, *Fiscal Reference Tables*, October 2017, Tables 4 and 8.)

FIGURE 31-2 Federal Government Net Debt as Percentage of GDP, 1940–2017

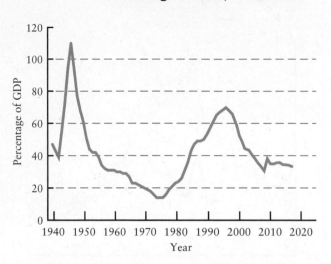

The federal government's debt-to-GDP ratio fell dramatically after the Second World War and continued falling until 1975. It then increased markedly for the next two decades. In the late 1990s when government deficits were reduced and the economy was in a healthy recovery, the debt-to-GDP ratio began to fall.

(*Source:* Based on author's calculations using data from Statistics Canada, CANSIM database. Nominal GDP; Table 380-0064. Net financial debt; Department of Finance's *Fiscal Reference Tables 2017.*)

Provincial Governments Canadian provincial governments are responsible for a significant fraction of total government revenues and expenditures. In many countries, sizable regional governments either do not exist, as in the United Kingdom and New Zealand, or are often legally required to run balanced budgets, as is the case for about two-thirds of the 50 states in the United States. In contrast, the size of Canadian provincial governments—measured by their spending and taxing powers relative to that of the federal government—means that an examination of government debt and deficits in Canada would not be complete without considering the provincial governments' fiscal positions.

> When examining the size and effects of budget deficits or surpluses, it is important to consider all levels of government—federal, provincial, territorial, and municipal.

During the 1970s, the provincial governments were running budget deficits and so the stock of provincial government debt was increasing. But the deficits were small enough for the debt not to be growing relative to GDP. During the 1980s and early 1990s, however, provincial deficits grew dramatically. Total provincial net debt grew from roughly 4 percent of GDP in 1980 to 29 percent in 1998. In the subsequent decade, most provincial governments eliminated their deficits and some had budget surpluses. By 2009, however, economic recession had driven them back into deficit. By 2018, the total provincial and territorial net debt was about 30 percent of GDP and rising.

▌ 31.2 Two Analytical Issues

Before we can discuss some of the macroeconomic effects of budget deficits and surpluses, we must examine two analytical issues: the stance of fiscal policy and changes in the debt-to-GDP ratio.

The Stance of Fiscal Policy

In Chapters 22 and 24 we examined *fiscal policy*, which is the use of government spending and tax policies. We noted there that changes in expenditure and taxation normally lead to changes in the government's budget deficit or surplus. Thus, it is tempting to view *any* change in the government's budget deficit as reflecting a change in its fiscal policy. For example, we could interpret an increase in the deficit as indicating an expansionary fiscal policy, since the rise in the deficit is associated with either an increase in government expenditures or a decrease in tax revenue (or both). Was the dramatic rise in the Canadian federal budget deficit between 2008 and 2010 *purely* the result of fiscal policy?

No. In general, only some changes in the budget deficit are due to changes in the government's fiscal policy. Other changes have nothing to do with explicit changes in policy, but instead are the result of changes in the level of economic activity, which nonetheless have an impact on the budget. If our goal is to determine how changes in fiscal policy affect the budget deficit, we need to distinguish the effects of a change in fiscal policy from the effects of changes in economic activity (GDP). To do this, we introduce the *budget deficit function*.

The Budget Deficit Function To see why the budget deficit can rise or fall even when there is no change in fiscal policy, recall the equation defining the government's overall budget deficit.

$$\text{Budget deficit} = (G + i \times D) - T$$

budget deficit function A relationship that plots, for a given fiscal policy, the government's budget deficit as a function of the level of real GDP.

As we first discussed in Chapter 22, the level of net tax revenues typically depends on the level of real GDP, even with unchanged policy. For example, as GDP rises the level of tax revenues also rises. In addition, as GDP rises there are typically fewer transfers (such as welfare or employment insurance) made to the private sector. Thus, net tax revenues, T, increase when GDP increases. In contrast, the level of government purchases and debt-service payments can be viewed as more or less independent of the level of GDP, at least over short periods of time. Thus, with no changes in the government's fiscal policies, the budget deficit will tend to increase in recessions and fall in booms. That is, there is a negative relationship between real GDP and the government's budget deficit.

> For a given set of expenditure and taxation policies, the budget deficit rises as real GDP falls, and falls as real GDP rises.

Figure 31-3 plots this basic relationship, which is called the **budget deficit function**. When the government determines its expenditure and taxation polices, it determines the *position* of the budget deficit function. A more expansionary fiscal policy, such as an increase in G, shifts the budget deficit function up. A more contractionary fiscal policy shifts the budget deficit function down. In contrast, a change in the level of real GDP in the absence of any policy change will represent a *movement along* the budget deficit

FIGURE 31-3   The Budget Deficit Function

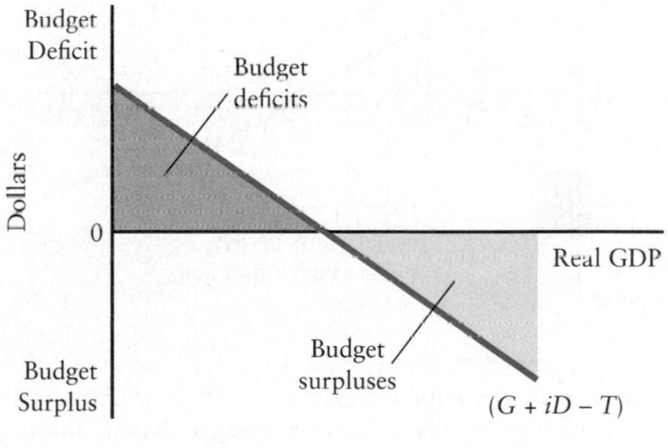

For given government purchases and debt-service payments, there is a negative relationship between real GDP and the government budget deficit. G and iD are assumed to be independent of the level of real GDP. In contrast, a rise in real GDP leads to higher tax revenues and lower transfers, and thus to higher net tax revenue, T. Thus, the budget deficit falls as real GDP increases. Therefore, even with unchanged fiscal policies, changes in real GDP will lead to changes in the budget deficit.

A more expansionary fiscal policy implies an increase in spending or a reduction in net taxes at *any level of real GDP* and thus an upward shift of the budget deficit function. A more contractionary fiscal policy shifts the budget deficit function down.

function. Thus, for a given set of fiscal policies, the budget deficit will decrease when GDP rises and increase when GDP falls.

> **Fiscal policy determines the position of the budget deficit function. Changes in real GDP lead to movements along a given budget deficit function.[2]**

Structural and Cyclical Budget Deficits At any given time, the actual budget deficit is the sum of two components—the *structural* and the *cyclical* deficits. The structural deficit reflects the amount of the deficit that is due to the underlying design of fiscal policy, independent of the current level of GDP. The cyclical deficit reflects the amount of the deficit that is due to actual GDP being either above or below the level of potential GDP, Y^*. By definition, the cyclical deficit is zero when real GDP equals Y^*; at the same time, the structural deficit may be positive, negative, or zero.

structural budget deficit An estimate of what the government budget deficit would be if real GDP were equal to Y^*; sometimes called a *cyclically adjusted deficit*.

FIGURE 31-4 The Structural Budget Deficit and Changes in Fiscal Policy

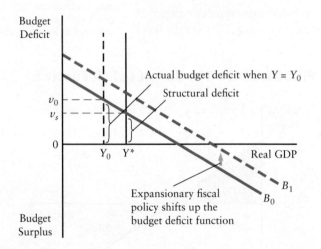

When real GDP equals Y^*, there is no cyclical component to the budget deficit. Whatever deficit then exists is the structural deficit.

The **structural budget deficit** is sometimes called the *cyclically adjusted deficit* because in order to measure it we estimate what the budget deficit would be with current policies in place but under the assumption that $Y = Y^*$. Figure 31-4 shows the budget deficit function and shows the structural deficit, v_s, measured when $Y = Y^*$. But if real GDP is actually equal to Y_0, which is less than Y^*, the budget deficit will be v_0, which exceeds v_s. In this case, the cyclical deficit is $v_0 - v_s$.

The change in the stance of fiscal policy is shown by the resulting change in the structural budget deficit. Initially, fiscal policy gives rise to the budget deficit function, B_0. The structural deficit (always measured at Y^*) is v_s. But the actual budget deficit depends on the actual level of real GDP. If real GDP is Y_0, the actual budget deficit is v_0. In this case, $v_0 - v_s$ shows the cyclical component of the deficit.

An expansionary change in fiscal policy shifts the budget deficit function up to B_1, increasing the structural deficit (and also increasing the actual deficit for any given level of real GDP).

> **During recessionary gaps ($Y < Y^*$), the actual budget deficit exceeds the structural budget deficit. During inflationary gaps ($Y > Y^*$), the actual budget deficit is less than the structural budget deficit.**

The Stance of Fiscal Policy We are now in a position to determine how a change in the stance of fiscal policy is best identified. We cannot merely examine the change in the budget deficit, because the deficit will change whenever Y changes even

---

[2] If we assume that net tax revenue, T, is given by $T = tY$, then a change in the net tax rate (t) leads to a change in the *slope* of the budget deficit function.

in the absence of a change in fiscal policy. Any change in the structural deficit, however, *does* reveal a change in underlying fiscal policy. As Figure 31-4 shows, an expansionary change in fiscal policy shifts the budget deficit function upward and increases the structural deficit. A contractionary change in fiscal policy shifts the budget deficit function downward and reduces the structural deficit.

Changes in the stance of fiscal policy are best identified by changes in the structural budget deficit.

Figure 31-5 shows the structural deficit in Canada and plots it together with the actual budget deficit. Both are expressed as percentages of GDP and represent the combined budget deficits of all levels of government. Unlike the actual budget deficit, which can be precisely measured, the structural deficit can only be estimated. The reason is that its value depends on the value of potential GDP, Y^*, which itself is not directly observable and hence must be estimated. Note from Figure 31-5 that the actual deficit is larger than the structural deficit during times of recessionary gaps, such as 1981–1985, 1991–1995, and 2009–2011. This relationship reflects the fact that during these periods actual GDP is less than potential GDP, and thus actual tax revenues are less than they would be if output were equal to potential. Conversely, the actual budget deficit is less than the structural deficit during periods of inflationary gaps, such as 1986–1990, 2000, and

FIGURE 31-5   Actual and Structural Budget Deficits, Combined Government, 1980–2016

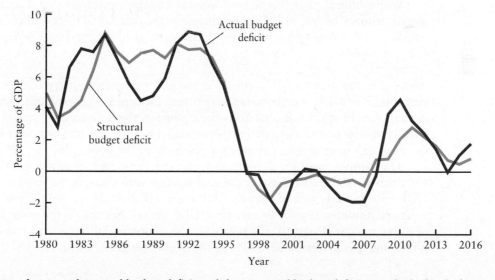

The difference between the actual budget deficit and the structural budget deficit reveals the level of output compared to potential. The changes in the structural deficit show changes in the stance of fiscal policy. The actual budget deficit is above the structural budget deficit when output is below potential; the actual deficit is less than the structural deficit when output is above potential. An increase in the structural deficit reveals a fiscal expansion; a decrease reveals a fiscal contraction.

(*Source:* Based on data from Statistics Canada, Government Finance Statistics, Table 385-0032.)

2004–2007, reflecting the fact that during these periods actual GDP is greater than potential and thus tax revenues are greater than they would be if output were equal to potential. In years where the actual deficit is approximately equal to the structural deficit, such as 1985, 1990, 1999, 2008, and 2013 real GDP is approximately equal to potential.

Changes in the expansionary or contractionary stance of fiscal policy are shown by the *changes* in the structural deficit. For example, the dramatic rise in Canada's structural deficit from 1982 to 1985 reveals a considerable fiscal expansion; the more gradual decline from 1985 to 1994 reveals a moderate fiscal contraction. From 1994 to 1999, the substantial fiscal contraction, at both federal and provincial levels, led to the sharp decline in the structural deficit, by over 7 percentage points of GDP. Between 2000 and 2007, the combined government sector had an actual and structural budget surplus of about 1 percent of GDP, and the stance of fiscal policy did not change markedly. Beginning in 2009, there was then a substantial increase in the actual budget deficit to just under 5 percent of GDP. Some of this rise in the deficit resulted from a decline in real GDP as the economy went into recession. But Canadian governments also increased their spending significantly and reduced some taxes so that the structural deficit also increased by over 3 percentage points of GDP.

Debt Dynamics

As we have already observed, in order to gauge the importance of government deficits and debt, they should be considered relative to the size of the economy. This is why economists often discuss the federal government's debt-to-GDP ratio rather than the absolute amount of government debt. Here we examine the link between the overall budget deficit, the primary budget deficit, and changes in the debt-to-GDP ratio.

With a little algebra, it is possible to write a simple expression that relates the government's primary budget deficit to the change in the debt-to-GDP ratio. Economists often use this relationship for analyzing the dynamics of government debt. The equation is

$$\Delta d = x + (r - g) \times d$$

where d is the debt-to-GDP ratio, x is the government's primary budget deficit as a percentage of GDP, r is the average real interest rate on government bonds, g is the growth rate of real GDP, and Δd is the *change* in the debt-to-GDP ratio. We will not spend the time necessary to derive this equation here, but readers who are interested in doing so can refer to the math notes at the back of the book. [36]

This simple equation shows two separate forces, each of which tends to increase the debt-to-GDP ratio. First, if the real interest rate exceeds the growth rate of real GDP (if r exceeds g), the debt-to-GDP ratio will rise for the simple reason that the debt accumulates at a faster rate than GDP grows. Second, if the government has a *primary* budget deficit (if x is positive), the debt-to-GDP ratio will rise because the government is incurring new debt to finance its program spending.

If the real interest rate on government debt is approximately equal to the growth rate of real GDP, reductions in the debt-to-GDP ratio require the government to run primary budget surpluses.

Recent Canadian data can be used to illustrate the use of this equation. We can do this for any year, but the last few years have seen few interesting swings in any components of this equation. In contrast, the 2008–2009 global financial crisis created a recession and a notable increase in Canada's federal debt-to-GDP ratio. For this reason, we apply the debt-dynamics equation to this more interesting time period.

The global financial crisis that began in 2008 was followed immediately by a worldwide recession and, like most of the G20 countries, Canada embarked on a major fiscal expansion to offset its effects. At the beginning of 2009, the federal debt-to-GDP ratio was 29 percent ($d = 0.29$). During that year, revenues fell sharply, expenditures increased, and the government ran a primary budget deficit of 1.7 percent of GDP ($x = 0.017$). The average real interest rate on government bonds in 2009 was 5.3 percent ($r = 0.053$) while real GDP *fell* in that year by 2.8 percent ($g = -0.028$).

Using all of these data, our equation for the change in the federal debt-to-GDP ratio over the course of 2009 becomes:

$$\Delta d = 0.017 + (0.053 \ - (-0.028)) \times (0.29)$$
$$= 0.017 + (0.081) \times (0.29)$$
$$= 0.017 + 0.023$$
$$= 0.04$$

which means that the government's debt-to-GDP ratio increased during 2009 by four percentage points, from 29 percent to 33 percent. Note that the *decline* in real GDP during 2009 ($g = -0.028$) substantially contributed to the increase in the debt ratio. In a typical year in which real GDP grows by 2 percent or more, a primary budget deficit of 1.7 percent of GDP would not generate such a large increase in the debt-to-GDP ratio.

After the worst of the recession was over in 2011, the federal government embarked on modest fiscal tightening, which helped to put the debt-to-GDP ratio back on a downward path. A smaller gap between r and g also helped, created by the increase in g that accompanied a gradual economic recovery. By mid-2018, after a few years of only mild changes in the government's fiscal stance, the debt-to-GDP ratio was 30.4 percent and was forecast to be just over 28 percent by 2023.

As a result of the 2008 global financial crisis and the recession that followed, many highly indebted European governments experienced significant further increases in their public debts. Some of this new debt was incurred as governments provided assistance to failing financial institutions; some was incurred through more conventional fiscal stabilization policies such as those we examined in Chapter 24. By 2011, the public debts in Greece, Portugal, Spain, and some other countries were so high that bondholders came to believe that these governments were effectively bankrupt and would be unable to repay or even service their existing debts. Fear of *debt defaults* by these governments led to massive increases in bond yields and created great uncertainty within the European Union. *Applying Economic Concepts 31-1* examines how our simple debt-dynamics equation can be used to understand Greece's extremely difficult fiscal situation in 2011—a situation that has still not been resolved.

APPLYING ECONOMIC CONCEPTS 31-1

The Continuing Greek Tragedy of Debt Dynamics

By 2011, the Greek economy had been in recession for three years, the unemployment rate was over 20 percent, and the government was implementing deep cuts in its spending programs in an effort to reduce its overall budget deficit of 9.2 percent of GDP. This toxic mixture of deep recession and large cutbacks in public services brought hundreds of thousands of Greek citizens into the streets—protesting the government's policies and demanding improvements in their country's economic situation.

Why was the Greek government cutting spending if the economy was in a deep recession? And how were these cuts related to the existing level of Greek government debt? We can use the debt-dynamics equation discussed in the text to shed light on these issues. Specifically, we can use the equation to determine how much fiscal adjustment would have been necessary to *stabilize* Greece's debt-to-GDP ratio at its 2011 level.*

Stabilizing the Debt-to-GDP Ratio

Consider the data for Greece as published by the International Monetary Fund (IMF). At the beginning of 2011, Greece's public debt was 143 percent of its GDP ($d = 1.43$). The average nominal interest rate on its government debt was 4.3 percent and inflation was 3.1 percent; the real interest rate, r, was therefore 1.2 percent ($r = 0.012$). The Greek economy was then

in its fourth continuous year of recession, and real GDP growth in 2011 was *negative* 6.9 percent ($g = -0.069$).

Using these data, we can compute the value of the primary budget balance that would have been necessary to stabilize the Greek debt-to-GDP ratio during 2011. Recall the equation that describes the change in the debt-to GDP ratio:

$$\Delta d = x + (r - g)d$$

If d is to be held constant ($\Delta d = 0$), the necessary value for x, which we call x^*, is

$$x^* = -(r - g)d$$

Using the data for Greece in 2011 we see that x^* is

$$x^* = -(0.012 - (-0.069)) \times (1.43)$$
$$= -(0.081) \times (1.43)$$
$$= -0.116$$

The interpretation of this number is that Greece would have needed a primary budget *surplus* of 11.6 percent of GDP in 2011 in order to stabilize its debt-to-GDP ratio that year. Its actual primary balance that year was a *deficit* of 2.3 percent. Thus, to stabilize d would have required a reduction in government expenditures and/or an increase in tax revenues of roughly 14 percent of GDP—an enormous

---

▌31.3 **The Effects of Government Debt and Deficits**

Let's now examine why we should care about the size of the government deficit and its debt. We begin with the important idea that deficits may *crowd out* private-sector activity and thereby harm future generations by reducing the economy's long-run growth rate. The opposite idea is equally important—that budget surpluses may *crowd in* private-sector activity and be beneficial to future generations by increasing the economy's long-run growth rate.

Before beginning our analysis, we must be clear about one of our assumptions in the macro model that we have developed in previous chapters. As we saw earlier in this chapter, when the government increases its budget deficit, it necessarily increases its borrowing. This increase in borrowing is a reduction in the government's saving. In our model, we make the assumption that any reduction in the government's saving has only small effects on the amount of saving by the private sector—with the result that *national* saving falls along with government saving. Thus, we assume in our model that an increase in the government's budget deficit leads to a reduction in national saving. We make this assumption because it is consistent with the bulk of empirical evidence on this issue.

fiscal adjustment for any government to make over several years, let alone in a single year.

An Impending Default?

By late in 2011 it was clear to most holders of Greek government bonds that any realistic fiscal adjustment by the Greek government would be insufficient to stabilize the debt-to-GDP ratio in the near future. Instead, the debt ratio would almost certainly continue to rise for several years. Bondholders then wondered how the Greek government would ever repay the existing bonds. Once these concerns became entrenched, the demand for Greek bonds plummeted and the bond yields increased sharply to reflect the risk of default by the Greek government. In 2011, the yields on Greek 10-year bonds were 34 percent—as compared to approximately 2 percent on 10-year bonds issued by the German government.

The increase in yields on Greek bonds exacerbated the fiscal situation of the Greek government and threatened the creation of a vicious cycle. The high bond yields made it more costly to finance its large overall budget deficit (9.2 percent of GDP in 2011) and also more costly to finance the "rollover" of existing bonds that occurs regularly in any modern economy. These greater financing costs increased the need for fiscal contraction as a means of reducing the existing budget deficit, but fiscal contraction would reduce aggregate demand and reduce real GDP growth even further. In addition, any further decline in real GDP growth would, as is clear from the debt-dynamics equation, cause an even larger increase in the debt-to-GDP ratio and thus cause further fears of default, thus driving up bond yields even further.

To break this vicious cycle, the Greek government turned to the IMF and other members of the European Union for substantial loans that would permit Greece to finance its budget deficit and bond rollovers at reasonable rates for a few years while Greece implemented its necessary fiscal adjustments and tried to restore its fiscal credibility in the eyes of global bondholders.

Resolution?

For the next five years, the Greek economy continued to shrink and the Greek government struggled to reduce the budget deficit. Though a contractionary fiscal policy caused the primary budget to fall sharply during this time, the shrinking economy contributed to further *increases* in the government's debt ratio. By 2016, even after a partial debt default, Greece's debt-to-GDP ratio was approximately 180 percent, and there was no resolution in sight to the overall fiscal situation. The Greek government could not agree on a set of fiscal policies that would satisfy Greek voters and at the same time satisfy the conditions set forth by the European countries that had become Greece's most important creditors.

---

*The economic situation in Greece was determined by a complex set of factors, including various problems encountered within a group of countries using a common currency. In this box, we focus only on the *fiscal* situation in Greece.

> In our macro model, we assume that an increase in the government's budget deficit leads to a decrease in national saving.

Do Deficits Crowd Out Private Activity?

It is useful to make the distinction between an economy that is *closed* to international trade in goods, services, and assets and one that is *open* to such trade. We consider the two cases separately.

Investment in Closed Economies   Recall from Chapter 25 the close long-run relationship between desired investment and desired national saving in a closed economy. In the long-run version of our macro model, with real GDP equal to Y^*, the real interest rate is determined by the equality of desired investment and desired national saving. What is the effect in this model of an increase in the government's budget deficit, caused either by an increase in government spending or a reduction in taxes? An increase in the budget deficit is assumed to cause a reduction in the supply of national saving. As we

FIGURE 31-6 A Fiscal Expansion Crowds Out Private Investment

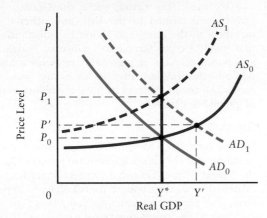

(i) Aggregate demand and supply

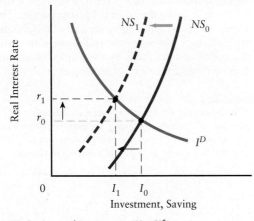

(ii) Saving and investment ($Y = Y^*$)

For a closed economy, the long-run effects of an increase in the budget deficit will be a higher real interest rate and a reduction in private investment. Consider a closed economy that is in long-run equilibrium at Y^* and P_0 in part (i). Suppose the government increases its spending or reduces its taxes, thus increasing the budget deficit. Either policy raises aggregate demand and shifts AD_0 to AD_1. The new short-run equilibrium is at Y' and P', but the adjustment process will then cause factor prices to rise, shifting the AS curve from AS_0 to AS_1. The new long-run equilibrium will be at Y^* and P_1.

The long-run effect of this change on saving and investment can be seen in part (ii), which shows the market for financial capital in the long run, with real GDP equal to Y^*. The increase in the government's budget deficit reduces national saving and shifts NS_0 to NS_1. The equilibrium real interest rate rises and the amount of investment falls from I_0 to I_1.

saw in Chapter 25, a reduction in the supply of national saving will shift the NS curve to the left, increase the equilibrium real interest rate, and reduce the amount of investment in the economy. This **crowding out** of investment by the expansionary fiscal policy is shown in Figure 31-6.

Note in the figure the different short-run and long-run effects of the fiscal expansion. In the short run, the fiscal expansion shifts the AD curve to the right and increases real GDP. In the long run, however, after wages and other factor prices have fully adjusted to the output gap, real GDP returns to Y^* at an increased equilibrium real interest rate. So the amount of investment in the new long-run equilibrium is less than it was prior to the increase in the budget deficit. The end result of the fiscal expansion is a "crowding out" of private investment.

> The long-run effect of a fiscal expansion is to drive up the real interest rate and crowd out private investment.

Net Exports in Open Economies There is a second effect in an open economy when financial capital is internationally mobile. Consider once again the possibility that the Canadian government increases its budget deficit either by increasing spending or by reducing taxes. What is the effect of the reduction in national saving in an open economy, like Canada's?

As real interest rates rise in Canada, foreigners are attracted to the higher-yield Canadian assets and thus foreign financial capital flows into Canada. But since Canadian dollars are required in order to buy Canadian interest-earning assets, this capital inflow increases the demand for Canadian dollars in the foreign-exchange market and leads to an appreciation of the Canadian dollar. If the currency appreciation is sustained over several months or longer, it will cause a reduction in Canada's exports and an increase in Canada's imports; Canadian net exports, NX, will fall.

In an open economy, the government budget deficit attracts foreign financial capital and appreciates the domestic currency. The long-run result is a crowding out of net exports.

How Much Crowding Out?   We have argued that the long-run effect of an increase in the government's budget deficit is to crowd out private investment and net exports. We have said nothing, however, about *how much* crowding out takes place. For example, does a $10 billion increase in the budget deficit reduce private expenditure by the full $10 billion, or by less, or by more?

To examine this issue, recall an equation of national income accounting from Chapter 20:

$$Y = C_a + I_a + G_a + NX_a$$

where the *a* subscripts denote actual (as opposed to desired) quantities. By definition, the sum of the four expenditure components is always exactly equal to real GDP. Now think about the change in these expenditure components as we follow the effects of a fiscal expansion in Figure 31-6. Suppose that we begin in a long-run equilibrium with $Y = Y^*$ and then the government increases its purchases of goods and services. In the short run in our macro model, this fiscal expansion leads to an increase in Y above Y^* and also causes an increase in consumption (which rises as Y rises). In the long run, however, after Y has returned to Y^*, the higher-than-initial value of government purchases implies that the sum of the three private expenditure components must be lower than it was at the initial long-run equilibrium. We cannot say precisely how the reduction in private spending is distributed across the three components, but in the long run in our model total private expenditure $(C_a + I_a + NX_a)$ has been crowded out by the full amount of the fiscal expansion.

Note, however, that full crowding out does *not* occur if the level of potential output, Y^*, increases as a result of the fiscal expansion. For example, suppose the government increases its spending on productivity-enhancing infrastructure projects or improvements in education or health-care programs. These kinds of expenditures are likely to increase the level of Y^*. If Y^* rises, then the long-run adjustment in Figure 31-6 brings the economy back to a *higher* level of Y^*, in which case the fiscal expansion crowds out less private expenditure. In other words, the extent of crowding out depends crucially on the change in Y^* which, in turn, depends on the nature of the increased government spending.

The larger is the increase in potential output caused by a fiscal expansion, the less private expenditure will be crowded out.

Do Deficits Harm Future Generations?

In a closed economy, a rise in the government's budget deficit pushes up interest rates and crowds out domestic investment. In an open economy, a rise in the deficit also appreciates the currency and crowds out net exports. In both cases, there may be a cost to future generations. Economists call this cost the *long-term burden of government debt*. Such a burden will be present if the private expenditure that is crowded out would have added more to the economy's productive capacity than what is added by the government's expenditure financed by the budget deficit.

crowding out The offsetting reduction in private expenditure caused by the rise in interest rates that follows an expansionary fiscal policy.

The previous paragraph suggests that whether government budget deficits harm future generations depends on the nature of the government goods and services being financed by the deficit (and also on the nature of the private expenditure that gets crowded out). At one extreme, the government borrowing may finance a project that generates a substantial return to future generations, and thus the future generations may be made better off by today's budget deficit. An example might be the government's financing of long-term medical research projects that generate a return in the distant future. Another example is the government's financing of a public transit network that reduces transport times for many years. At the other extreme, the government deficit may finance some government program that benefits mainly the current generation. An example might be the government's financing of temporary cultural or sporting events that benefit the current generation but produce little or no benefits for future generations.

> **Government budget deficits represent taxes that must be paid by future generations. Whether these future generations are harmed by the current budget deficit depends to a large extent on the nature of the government spending financed by the deficit.**

The concern that budget deficits may be inappropriately placing a burden on future generations has led some economists to advocate the idea of *capital budgeting* by the government. Under this scheme, the government would essentially classify each of its expenditure items as either consumption or investment; the former would be spending that mostly benefits the current generation while the latter would be spending that mostly benefits future generations.

With capital budgeting, undesirable redistributions of income between generations could be minimized, while still permitting some budget deficits. For example, the government might be committed to borrowing no more in any given year than the expenditures classified as investments. In this way, future generations would receive benefits from current government spending that are at least equal to the future taxes they will pay.

Does Government Debt Hamper Economic Policy?

The costs imposed on future generations by government debt are real, though they are often ignored because they occur in the very distant future. But other problems associated with the presence of government debt are more immediately apparent. In particular, high levels of government debt may make the conduct of monetary and fiscal policy more difficult.

Budget deficits used to finance investment projects may not harm future generations because the future generations will benefit from the investment.

James Wheeler/123RF

Monetary Policy To see how a large stock of government debt can hamper the conduct of monetary policy, consider a country that has a high debt-to-GDP ratio and that has a real interest rate above the growth rate of GDP. As we saw previously, the debt-to-GDP ratio will continue to grow in this situation unless the government starts running significant primary budget *surpluses*. But such primary surpluses require either increases in taxation or reductions in program spending, both of which tend to be politically unpopular. If such primary surpluses look unlikely to be achieved in the near future, both foreign and domestic bondholders may come to expect the government to put pressure on the central bank to purchase—or *monetize*—an increasing portion of its deficit. Such monetization means that the money supply is increasing and will eventually cause inflation. Any ensuing inflation would erode the real value of the bonds held by creditors.

Fears of future debt monetization will likely lead to expectations of future inflation and put upward pressure on longer-term nominal interest rates. Thus, even in the absence of any *current* actions by the central bank to increase the rate of growth of the money supply, a large government debt may lead to the *expectation* of future inflation, thus hampering the task of the central bank in keeping inflation and inflationary expectations low.

Fiscal Policy   In Chapter 22 we saw that fiscal policy can be used to stabilize aggregate demand and real GDP. For example, in a booming economy, the government might reduce spending or increase tax rates to reduce inflationary pressures. Or during a recession, the government might reduce tax rates and increase spending in an attempt to stimulate aggregate demand. Having fiscal expansions during recessions and fiscal contractions during booms is one way of implementing *counter-cyclical fiscal policy*.

How does the presence of government debt affect the government's ability to conduct such counter-cyclical fiscal policy? Perhaps the easiest way to answer this question is to recall the equation that describes the change in the debt-to-GDP ratio:

$$\Delta d = x + (r - g) \times d$$

This equation shows that the *change* in the debt-to-GDP ratio (Δd) depends on the current *level* of the debt-to-GDP ratio (d). For example, if the real interest rate exceeds the growth rate of real GDP, so that $r - g$ is positive, the increase in the debt-to-GDP ratio (Δd) will be higher if d is already high than if it is low (for any given value of x). We examine the case where $r - g$ is positive because this is the typical situation in a developed economy such as Canada's.

With this relationship in mind, consider the problem faced during a recession by a government considering an expansionary fiscal policy. Such a policy would increase the primary budget deficit and therefore increase x. On the one hand, there would be short-run benefits from the higher level of real GDP; on the other hand, the government may be wary of taking actions that lead to large increases in the debt-to-GDP ratio.

If d is relatively small, the government has a great deal of flexibility in conducting counter-cyclical fiscal policy. The small value of d implies that d will be rising only slowly in the absence of a primary deficit. Thus, the government may be able to increase the primary deficit—either by increasing program spending or by reducing tax rates—without generating a large increase in the debt-to-GDP ratio. But the government has significantly less flexibility if d is already very high. In this case, and with our assumption that r is greater than g, the high value of d means that even in the absence of a primary budget deficit, d will be increasing quickly. Thus, any increase in the primary deficit associated with the counter-cyclical fiscal policy runs the danger of generating increases in the debt-to-GDP ratio that may be viewed by creditors as unsustainable. Such perceptions of unsustainability may lead to an increase in the real interest rate on government debt, which exacerbates the problem by driving d up even faster.

The idea that a large and rising stock of government debt could "tie the hands" of the government in times when it would otherwise want to conduct counter-cyclical fiscal policy was brought to the fore of Canadian economic policy by the late Douglas

Purvis of Queen's University (and a co-author of this textbook for many years). Purvis argued in the mid-1980s that Canadian government deficits must be brought under control quickly so that the debt would not accumulate to the point where the government would have no room left for fiscal stabilization policy. These warnings were not heeded. By the onset of the next recession in 1991, the federal government had added roughly $200 billion to the stock of debt and the debt-to-GDP ratio was just less than 70 percent. Predictably, the government felt unable to use discretionary fiscal policy to reduce some of the effects of the recession.

By 2008, however, the federal debt-to-GDP ratio had fallen to less than 30 percent as a result of more than a decade of fiscal restraint and rapid economic growth. When the Canadian economy entered recession late in 2008, the Conservative government recognized that Canada's past fiscal prudence gave it the needed flexibility to design an aggressive counter-cyclical fiscal policy. The federal budgets of 2009 and 2010 announced large spending increases and tax reductions that were predicted to result in budget deficits that would increase the debt-to-GDP ratio by roughly 4 percentage points over the next two years. The government was careful, however, to indicate clearly its intentions of returning the debt-to-GDP ratio to less than 30 percent within a few years. The need for short-term fiscal stimulus was tempered by the recognition of the importance of long-term fiscal prudence.

31.4 Formal Fiscal Rules

Over the past 40 years in Canada, policymakers and economists have debated the appropriate sizes of budget deficits and surpluses. As part of these debates, the argument is often made that legislation should be passed to impose restrictions on the size of budget deficits. Would such legislation be desirable? We examine three different proposals.

Annually Balanced Budgets

It would be extremely difficult to balance the budget on an annual basis. The reason is that a significant portion of the government budget is beyond its short-term control, and a further large amount is hard to change quickly. For example, the entire debt-service component of government expenditures is determined by past borrowing and thus cannot be altered by the current government. Also, many spending programs such as public pensions and major transfers to provinces are set in current legislation and cannot be changed without the lengthy process of legislative reform. In addition, as we saw in our discussion of the structural budget deficit, changes in real GDP that are beyond the control of the government lead to significant changes in tax revenues (and transfer payments) and thus generate significant changes in the budget deficit or surplus.

Even if it were possible for the government to control its spending and revenues perfectly on a year-to-year basis, it would probably be *undesirable* to balance the budget every year. Recall that tax revenues naturally rise in booms and fall in recessions; and many expenditures on transfers fall in booms and rise in recessions. As we first saw in Chapter 22, this property of the tax-and-transfer system implies that fiscal policy contains an automatic stabilizer. In recessions, the increase in the budget deficit stimulates aggregate demand whereas in booms the budget surplus reduces aggregate demand.

Things would be very different with an annually balanced budget. With a balanced budget, government expenditures would be *forced* to adjust to the changing level of tax revenues. In a recession, when tax revenues naturally decline, a balanced budget would require either a *reduction* in government expenditures or an *increase* in tax rates, thus generating a major *destabilizing* force on real GDP. Similarly, as tax revenues naturally rise in an economic boom, a balanced budget would require either an increase in government expenditures or a reduction in taxes, thus stimulating aggregate demand when an inflationary gap may already exist.

An annually balanced budget would eliminate the automatic fiscal stabilizers and accentuate the swings in real GDP.

Cyclically Balanced Budgets

One alternative to the extreme policy of requiring an annually balanced budget is to require that the government budget be balanced over the course of a full economic cycle. Budget deficits would be permitted in recessions as long as they were matched by surpluses in booms. In this way, the automatic stabilizers could still perform their important role, but there would be no persistent build-up of government debt. In principle, this is a desirable treatment of the tradeoff between the short-run benefits of deficits and the long-run costs of debt.

Despite its appeal, the idea of cyclically balanced budgets has its problems as well. Perhaps the most important problem with a cyclically balanced budget is an operational one. In order to have a law that requires the budget to be balanced over the business cycle, it is necessary to be able to *define* the cycle precisely. But there will always be disagreement about what stage of the cycle the economy is currently in, and thus there will be disagreement as to whether the current government should be increasing or reducing its deficit. Compounding this problem is the fact that politicians will have a stake in the identification of the cycle. Those who favour increased deficits will argue that this year is an unusually bad year and thus an increase in the deficit is justified; deficit "hawks," in contrast, will always tend to find this year to be unusually good and thus a time to run budget surpluses.

A second problem is largely political. Suppose one government runs large deficits for a few years during a recession and then gets replaced in an election. Would the succeeding government then be bound to run budget surpluses after the recovery? What one government commits itself to in one year does not necessarily restrict what it (or its successor) does in the next year.

Balancing the budget over the course of the business cycle is in principle a desirable means of reconciling short-term stabilization with long-term fiscal prudence. The difficulty in precisely defining the business cycle, however, suggests that governments could best follow this as an approximate guide rather than as a formal rule.

Maintaining a Prudent Debt-to-GDP Ratio

A further problem with any policy that requires a balanced budget—whether over one year or over the business cycle—is that the emphasis is naturally on the overall budget deficit. But, as we saw earlier in this chapter, what determines the change in the debt-to-GDP ratio is the growth of the debt *relative* to the growth of the economy. With a growing economy, it is possible to have positive overall budget deficits—and thus a growing debt—and still have a falling debt-to-GDP ratio. Thus, to the extent that the debt-to-GDP ratio is the relevant gauge of a country's debt problem, focus should be placed on the debt-to-GDP ratio rather than on the budget deficit itself.

> **Most economists view a low and relatively stable debt-to-GDP ratio as the appropriate indicator of fiscal prudence. Their view permits a budget deficit such that the stock of debt grows no faster than GDP.**

This view recognizes that not all government debt represents a problem. As we argued earlier in this chapter, government expenditure on items that deliver benefits for many years can sensibly be financed by borrowing so that the future generations who benefit from the spending also bear some of the burden of repayment. However, admitting that some government debt may be appropriate is not to deny that genuine problems do exist when the government's debt-to-GDP ratio is very high. The challenge is then to permit government budget deficits necessary to finance worthwhile public investment while at the same time ensuring that the debt-to-GDP ratio does not become excessive. Such an approach to fiscal policy would be considered prudent by many economists.

By this standard, the Canadian federal budgets of the last several years have been prudent because they have led to a growth rate in the stock of debt smaller than the growth rate of real GDP, and thus a reduction in the debt-to-GDP ratio. For example, in 1996, the federal debt-to-GDP ratio reached its recent maximum of 70 percent. Significant fiscal contractions, combined with strong economic growth, led to a decline in the debt-to-GDP ratio to 50 percent by 2001, less than 40 percent by 2005, and less than 30 percent by 2008. The arrival of the 2008 global recession then led to substantial federal (and provincial) budget deficits, partly because of the recession-induced decline in net tax revenues and partly because of policy actions taken to stimulate the economy. The federal debt-to-GDP ratio increased to 38 percent by 2010. By 2018, however, after eight years of modest recovery, the budget deficit was less than one percent of GDP, the debt-to-GDP ratio was roughly 30 percent, and most forecasts showed the debt ratio to be approaching 28 percent by 2023.

SUMMARY

31.1 Facts and Definitions   LO 1

- The government's budget deficit is equal to total government expenditure minus total government revenue. Since the government must borrow to finance any shortfall in its revenues, the annual deficit is equal to the annual increase in the stock of government debt. Whenever the deficit is positive, the stock of government debt is growing.
- The primary budget deficit is equal to the excess of the government's program spending over total tax revenues.

- Large and persistent budget deficits beginning in the 1970s increased the stock of debt so that by 1996 the federal government net debt was equal to 70 percent of GDP. By 2008, after several years of fiscal contraction, the federal debt-to-GDP ratio was approximately 30 percent.
- The 2008–2009 recession increased the federal debt-to-GDP ratio to 38 percent, but it was projected to fall back down to 28 percent by 2023.

31.2 Two Analytical Issues

- Since tax revenues tend to rise when real GDP rises, the overall budget deficit tends to rise during recessions and fall during booms. This tendency makes the budget deficit a poor measure of the stance of fiscal policy.
- The structural budget deficit is the budget deficit that would exist with the current set of fiscal policies if real GDP were equal to potential GDP. Changes in the structural deficit reflect changes in the stance of fiscal policy.

- The change in the debt-to-GDP ratio from one year to the next is given by

$$\Delta d = x + (r - g) \times d$$

where d is the debt-to-GDP ratio, x is the primary deficit as a percentage of GDP, r is the real interest rate on government bonds, and g is the growth rate of real GDP.

31.3 The Effects of Government Debt and Deficits

- In a closed economy, the long-run effect of an increase in the budget deficit is to reduce national saving and increase real interest rates. This increase in interest rates reduces the amount of investment.
- In an open economy, the long-run effect of an increase in the budget deficit is to push up interest rates and attract foreign financial capital. This leads to a currency appreciation and a reduction in net exports.
- Unless government debt is incurred to finance worthwhile public investments, the long-term burden of the

debt is a redistribution of resources away from future generations and toward current generations.
- A large debt-to-GDP ratio may lead creditors to expect increases in inflation, as the government attempts to finance deficits through the creation of money. Such increases in inflationary expectations hamper the conduct of monetary policy.
- The higher is the debt-to-GDP ratio, the more constrained is the government in conducting countercyclical fiscal policy.

31.4 Formal Fiscal Rules

- Since tax revenues (net of transfers) naturally rise as real GDP increases, legislation requiring an annually balanced budget forces either expenditures to rise or tax rates to fall during booms. This produces destabilizing fiscal policy.
- Cyclically balanced budgets, in principle, permit the short-run benefits of deficits to be realized without incurring the long-run costs of debt accumulation. Implementation of this policy is difficult, however,

since the precise identification of the business cycle is controversial.
- Small budget deficits need not lead to increases in the debt-to-GDP ratio if the economy is growing.
- Prudent fiscal policy can permit budget deficits during recessions and allow the financing of worthwhile public investments, while ensuring that the debt-to-GDP ratio does not become excessive.

KEY CONCEPTS

Government's budget constraint	Debt-service payments	Crowding out of net exports
Primary budget deficit	Debt-to-GDP ratio	Long-term burden of the debt
The relationship between deficits and government debt	Structural and cyclical deficits	Annually balanced budget
	Crowding out of investment	Cyclically balanced budget

STUDY EXERCISES

MyLab Economics Make the grade with MyLab Economics™: All Study Exercises can be found on MyLab Economics™. You can practise them as often as you want, and many feature step-by-step guided instructions to help you find the right answer.

FILL-IN-THE-BLANK

❶ Fill in the blanks to make the following statements correct.

a. The government's budget constraint shows that total government expenditures must be equal to the sum of _____ and _____.

b. The government's annual budget deficit is the excess of total _____ over total _____ in a given year.

c. If we want to know how much of a government's budget deficit is attributable to *current* program spending and tax policies, we compute the _____ deficit. This measure tells us the difference between the government's overall budget deficit and its _____ payments.

d. If the government's total budget deficit is $20 billion and its debt-service payments are $18 billion, then its _____ is $2 billion. If the total budget deficit is $20 billion and its debt-service payments are $26 billion, then its _____ is $6 billion.

❷ Fill in the blanks to make the following statements correct.

a. When there is no change in the government's fiscal policy it is still possible for the budget deficit to fall because _____.

b. For a given set of fiscal policies, the budget deficit _____ as real GDP rises and _____ as real GDP falls.

c. The structural budget deficit is the deficit that would exist if real GDP equalled _____ and the government's _____ were at their current levels.

d. During a recession, when Y is less than Y^*, the actual budget deficit is _____ than the structural budget deficit. During an inflationary boom, when Y is greater than Y^*, the actual budget deficit is _____ than the structural budget deficit.

e. Suppose the real interest rate is 2 percent and the growth rate of real GDP is 1.5 percent. If the government wants to stabilize the debt-to-GDP ratio, then it is necessary to have a(n) _____.

❸ Fill in the blanks to make the following statements correct.

a. In a closed economy, when the government has a fiscal expansion, interest rates will _____ and some private investment will be _____.

b. In an open economy, when the government has a fiscal expansion, interest rates will _____, the Canadian dollar will _____, and net exports will _____.

c. Suppose a law was passed that required the government to balance its budget each year. Fiscal policy would then have a(n) _____ effect.

d. A cyclically balanced budget is difficult to implement because it is difficult to identify the _____.

REVIEW

❹ The figure below shows the budget deficit function for a country.

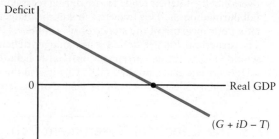

a. Explain why the budget deficit function is downward sloping.

b. If the government increases its level of purchases (G), what happens to the budget deficit at any level of real GDP? Show this in the diagram.

c. If the government increases the net tax rate, what happens to the deficit at any level of real GDP? Show this in the diagram.

d. Explain why a rise in the actual budget deficit does not necessarily reflect a change in fiscal policy.

e. How would a fiscal expansion appear in the diagram? A fiscal contraction?

❺ The Canadian federal budget moved from a surplus of $9.6 billion in the 2007–2008 fiscal year to a deficit of $5.8 billion the next year, and a large deficit of $55.6 billion in 2009–2010.

a. Suppose real GDP was at potential in each of the first two years. What can you conclude about the cause of the change in the budget deficit? Show this change in a diagram of the budget deficit function.

b. Suppose from 2008–2009 to 2009–2010, two things happened: real GDP fell and the government implemented an expansionary fiscal policy (both of which were true). Show these two separate events in a diagram of the budget deficit function.

❻ The diagram below shows an *AD/AS* diagram. The economy begins at E_0 with output equal to Y^*. Suppose the government in this closed economy increases G and finances it by running a deficit (borrowing). The *AD* curve shifts to the right.

a. How does the interest rate at E_1 compare with that at E_0? Explain.

b. Given your answer to part (a), how does investment at E_1 compare with investment at E_0?

c. Explain the economy's adjustment toward E_2. What happens to the interest rate and investment?

d. What is the likely long-run effect for the economy from the fiscal expansion? Explain.

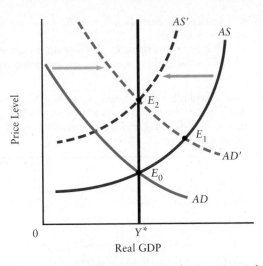

7 Refer to the diagram above in Study Exercise 6, but now suppose this is an open economy where financial capital is internationally mobile. Compared to the response to Study Exercise 6, describe the additional effect that takes place in an open economy.

8 The diagram below shows an *AD/AS* diagram. The economy begins at E_0 with output equal to Y^*. Suppose the government in this closed economy decreases its budget deficit by increasing T (and keeping G unchanged), thus causing the *AD* curve to shift to the left.

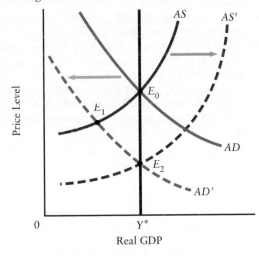

a. How does the interest rate at E_1 compare with that at E_0? Explain.
b. Given your answer to part (a), how does investment at E_1 compare with investment at E_0?
c. Explain the economy's adjustment toward E_2. What happens to the interest rate and investment?
d. What is the long-run effect of the government deficit on the growth rate of Y^*?

e. Comparing the short-run and the long-run effects of this policy, what dilemma does the government face in reducing its deficit?

9 Suppose a member of Parliament pronounces: "The prime minister's policies are working! Lower interest rates combined with tight fiscal policy have reduced the deficit significantly." What do interest rates have to do with government spending and taxes when it comes to deficit management?

10 The following headline appeared in *The Globe and Mail* in March 2018, when the Canadian and U.S. federal governments were planning increases in budget deficits: "As Canada, U.S. roll along deficit track, concerns emerge about ability to steer through next recession."

a. From online data sources, what were the Canadian and U.S federal debt-to-GDP ratios in early 2018?
b. Explain why any government with a high debt-to-GDP can find it difficult to "steer through the next recession."
c. Given your answers to parts (a) and (b), which of the two governments were in the more difficult situation? Explain.

PROBLEMS

11 The table below shows government spending data over eight years in Debtland. All figures are in billions of dollars. The symbols used are as defined in the text.

Year	G (1)	T (2)	iD (3)	Budget Deficit (4)	Primary Budget Deficit (5)	Stock of Debt (6)
2013	175	175	25	—	—	—
2014	180	180	26	—	—	—
2015	185	185	27	—	—	—
2016	188	190	26	—	—	—
2017	185	195	25	—	—	—
2018	185	200	24	—	—	—
2019	180	205	23	—	—	—
2020	175	210	22	—	—	—

a. Compute Debtland's budget deficit in each year and complete column 4 in the table. (Since we are computing the deficit, a negative number indicates a surplus.)
b. Compute Debtland's primary budget deficit in each year and complete column 5 in the table.
c. Suppose the initial stock of debt (in 2012) was $400 billion. Noting that the deficit in 2013 adds to the existing stock of debt, what is the stock of debt by the end of 2013?

d. Compute the stock of debt for each year and complete column 6 in the table.

e. Suppose you know that Debtland's debt-to-GDP ratio was the same in 2020 as in 2012. By what percentage did GDP grow between 2012 and 2020?

12 In the late 1990s, the U.S. government was slightly ahead of the Canadian government in reducing its budget deficit. The following table shows the actual budget deficit and the structural budget deficit (both as a percentage of GDP) for the United States from 1989 to 1997.

Year	Actual Deficit	Structural Deficit
1989	2.8	2.9
1990	3.9	3.2
1991	4.6	3.4
1992	4.7	3.7
1993	3.9	3.7
1994	3.0	2.8
1995	2.3	2.6
1996	1.4	1.6
1997	0.3	1.0

a. On a scale diagram (with the year on the horizontal axis), graph the actual deficit and the structural deficit.

b. From 1990 to 1994, the actual budget deficit is above the structural deficit. Explain why.

c. From 1995 to 1997, the actual budget deficit is below the structural deficit. Explain why.

d. Identify the periods when U.S. fiscal policy was expansionary.

e. Identify the periods when U.S. fiscal policy was contractionary.

f. Look back at Figure 31-5. How does the stance of U.S. fiscal policy over this period compare with Canada's?

13 The following table shows hypothetical data from 2013 to 2019 that can be used to compute the change in the debt-to-GDP ratio. The symbols used are as defined in the text.

Year	x (1)	r (2)	g (3)	d (4)	Δd (5)
2013	0.03	0.045	0.025	0.70	—
2014	0.02	0.04	0.025	—	—
2015	0.01	0.035	0.025	—	—
2016	0.00	0.035	0.025	—	—
2017	−0.01	0.03	0.025	—	—
2018	−0.02	0.03	0.025	—	—
2019	−0.03	0.025	0.025	—	—

a. Remember from the text that the change in the debt-to-GDP ratio (Δd) during a year is given by $\Delta d = x + (r - g)d$. Compute Δd for 2013.

b. Note that d at the beginning of 2014 is equal to d at the beginning of 2013 plus Δd during 2013. Compute d in 2014.

c. Using the same method, compute d and Δd for each year, and complete columns 4 and 5.

d. Plot d in a scale diagram with the year on the horizontal axis. What discretionary variable was most responsible for the observed decline in d?

e. Note that as the primary deficit (x) falls between 2013 and 2019, there is also a downward trend in the real interest rate. Can you offer an explanation for this?

32 The Gains from International Trade

CHAPTER OUTLINE	LEARNING OBJECTIVES (LO)
	After studying this chapter you will be able to
32.1 THE GAINS FROM TRADE	**1** explain why the gains from trade depend on the pattern of comparative advantage.
	2 understand how factor endowments influence a country's comparative advantage.
32.2 THE DETERMINATION OF TRADE PATTERNS	**3** describe the law of one price.
	4 explain why countries export some goods and import others.

TRADE between peoples and nations has been going on throughout human history, and humans have gone to great lengths and endured severe hardship in order to reap the benefits of trade. Centuries ago, for example, the inhabitants of remote islands in Southeast Polynesia travelled the open ocean in canoes for days at a time to trade oyster shells, volcanic glass, basalt, and food items with inhabitants of other, distant islands.

Today, the logistics for trade may be less demanding, but the transactions themselves are no less important. Canadian consumers buy cars from Germany, Germans take holidays in Italy, Italians buy spices from Africa, Africans import oil from Kuwait, Kuwaitis buy Japanese cameras, and the Japanese buy Canadian lumber. *International trade* refers to the exchange of goods and services that takes place across international boundaries.

The founders of modern economics thought deeply about the costs and benefits of foreign trade. The eighteenth-century British philosopher and economist David Hume (1711–1776), one of the first to work out the theory of the price system, developed his concepts mainly in terms of prices in foreign trade. Adam Smith (1723–1790), in *The Wealth of Nations*, attacked government restriction of international trade. David Ricardo (1772–1823) developed the basic theory of the gains from trade that we study in this chapter. The 1846 repeal of the Corn Laws—tariffs on the importation of corn and other grains into the United Kingdom—and the transformation of that country during the nineteenth century from a country of high tariffs to one of complete free trade were to some extent the result of arguments by economists whose theories of the gains from international trade led them to condemn tariffs.

FIGURE 32-1   The Growth in World Merchandise Trade, 1950–2017

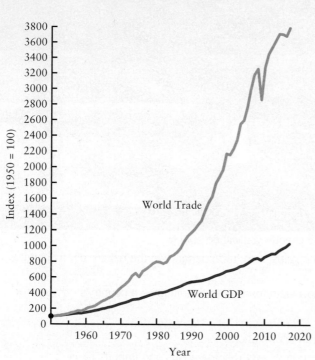

The volume of world trade has grown much faster than world GDP over the past six decades. The figure shows the growth of real GDP and the volume of trade since 1950. Both are expressed as index numbers, set equal to 100 in 1950. Real world GDP has increased more than ten times since 1950; world trade volume has increased by almost 38 times. The major global recession in 2009 is clearly evident with the sharp decline in the flow of trade in that year. Note that this figure shows only the trade in goods; if the trade in services were included, trade growth would be even larger.

(*Source:* Adapted from World Trade Organization, *International Trade Statistics*, Table A1. www.wto.org.)

Over the past 70 years, international trade has become increasingly important, not just for Canada but for the world as a whole. As Figure 32-1 shows, since 1950 the volume of world trade has grown much faster than world real GDP. The world's real GDP has increased by more than ten times, an average annual growth rate of 3.6 percent. Over the same period, however, the volume of world trade has increased by almost 38 times, an average annual growth rate of 5.6 percent.

Figure 32-2 shows some data for Canadian trade in 2017. The bar chart shows the value of Canadian exports and imports of goods in several broad industry groupings. There are three important points to note from the figure. First, international trade is important to Canada. In 2017, Canada exported $550 billion and imported $574 billion in goods—if we added trade in services, each of these values would be higher by about $100 billion; each flow (exports and imports) amounts to about 32 percent of GDP. Second, exports and imports are roughly the same size, so that the *volume* of trade is much larger than the *balance* of trade—the value of exports minus the value of imports. Third, in most of the industry groupings there are significant amounts of both imports and exports. Such *intra-industry trade* will be discussed later in the chapter. Canada does not just export resource products and import manufactured goods; it also imports many resource products and exports many manufactured goods.

In this chapter, we examine the increases in average living standards that result from international trade. We find that the source of the gains from trade lies in differing cost conditions among geographical regions. World income would be vastly lower if countries did not specialize in the products in which they have the lowest opportunity costs of production, and then trade these products to other countries in exchange for the products in which *they* specialize. The relevant opportunity costs are partly determined by natural endowments (geographical and climatic conditions), partly by public policy, and partly by historical accident.

open economy An economy that engages in international trade.

closed economy An economy that has no foreign trade—a situation referred to as *autarky*.

32.1 The Gains from Trade

An economy that engages in international trade is called an **open economy**; one that does not is called a **closed economy**. A situation in which a country does no foreign trade is called one of *autarky*.

FIGURE 32-2 **Selected Canadian Exports and Imports of Goods, 2017**

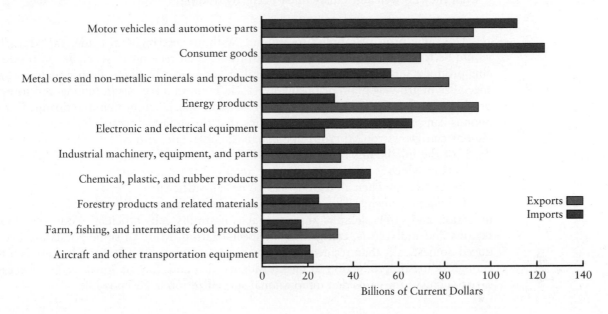

Canada exports and imports large volumes of goods in most industries. The data show the value of goods exported and imported by industry in 2017 (trade in services is not shown). The industries are ranked by the total volume of trade—exports plus imports. The total value of goods exported was $550 billion; the total value of goods imported was $574 billion.

(*Source:* These data are available on Statistics Canada's website: www.statcan.gc.ca.)

Although politicians often regard foreign trade differently from domestic trade, economists from Adam Smith on have argued that the causes and consequences of international trade are simply an extension of the principles governing trade between domestic firms and individuals. What are the benefits of trade among individuals, among groups, among regions, or among countries?

Interpersonal, Interregional, and International Trade

To begin, consider trade among individuals. Without trade, each person would have to be self-sufficient: Each would have to produce all the food, clothing, shelter, medical services, entertainment, and luxuries that he or she consumed. Because no individual could effectively produce such a large range of products, a world of individual self-sufficiency would be a world with extremely low living standards: individuals would work very hard but not be able to produce or consume very much.

Trade among individuals allows people to specialize in activities they can do well and to buy from others the goods and services they cannot easily produce. A good doctor who is a bad carpenter can provide medical services not only for her own family but also for a good carpenter without the training or the ability to practise medicine. Trade and specialization are intimately connected.

> Without trade, everyone must be self-sufficient; with trade, people can specialize in what they do well and satisfy other needs by trading.

The same principle applies to regions. Without interregional trade, each region would be forced to be self-sufficient. With trade, each region can specialize in producing products for which it has some natural or acquired advantage. Prairie regions can specialize in growing grain or raising livestock, mountain regions in mining and forest products, and regions with abundant power can specialize in manufacturing. Cool regions can produce wheat and other crops that thrive in temperate climates, and hot regions can grow tropical crops like bananas, sugarcane, and coffee. The living standards of the inhabitants of all regions will be higher when each region specializes in products in which it has some natural or acquired advantage and obtains other products by trade than when all regions seek to be self-sufficient.

This same principle also applies to countries. A national boundary is a political invention and rarely delimits an area that is naturally self-sufficient. Countries, like regions and individuals, can gain from specialization. More of some goods are produced domestically than residents want to consume, while for other goods there is not enough domestic production to meet residents' demand. International trade is necessary to achieve the gains that international specialization makes possible.

> With international trade, each country is able to concentrate on producing goods and services that it produces efficiently while trading to obtain goods and services that other countries produce more efficiently.

Specialization and trade go hand in hand because there is no incentive to achieve the gains from specialization without being able to trade the goods produced for goods desired. Economists use the term **gains from trade** to embrace the results of both.

gains from trade The increased output attributable to the specialization that is made possible by trade.

Illustrating the Gains from Trade

Our discussion so far has emphasized the differences that exist between individuals, regions, and countries, and how these differences lie behind the benefits derived from trade. In order to show these benefits more precisely, we will focus on trade between two countries. We make the important assumption that within each country the average cost of production of any good is independent of *how much* of that good is produced. That is, we are making the assumption of *constant costs*. (We relax this assumption later.) Our example involves two countries and two products, but the general principles apply to the case of many countries and many products.

absolute advantage When one country can produce some commodity at lower absolute cost than another country.

Absolute Advantage　One region is said to have an **absolute advantage** over another in the production of good *X* when an equal quantity of resources can produce more *X* in the first region than in the second. Or, to put it differently, if it takes fewer resources to produce one unit of good *X* there than in another country. Table 32-1 shows an example. The two "countries" are Canada and the European Union (EU), and the two goods are wheat and cloth. The table shows the *absolute cost* of producing one unit of wheat and one unit of cloth in each country. The absolute cost is the dollar cost of the labour, capital, and other resources required to produce the goods. Thus, the country that can produce a specific good with fewer resources can produce it at a lower absolute cost.

In Table 32-1, the absolute cost for both wheat and cloth is less in Canada than in the EU. Canada is therefore said to have an *absolute advantage* over the EU in the production of both wheat and cloth because it is a more efficient producer—it takes less labour and other resources to produce the goods in Canada than in the EU.

The situation in Table 32-1 is hypothetical, but it is encountered often in the real world. Some countries, because they have access to cheap natural resources or low-cost labour or more sophisticated capital equipment, are low-cost producers for a wide range of products. Does this mean that high-cost countries stand no chance of being successful producers in a globalized world of international trade? Will the low-cost countries produce everything, leaving nothing to be done by high-cost countries? The answer is no. As we will see immediately, the gains from international trade do *not* depend on the pattern of absolute advantage.

Comparative Advantage   The great English economist David Ricardo (1772–1823) was the first to provide an explanation of the pattern of international trade in a world in which countries had different costs. His theory of *comparative advantage* is still accepted by economists as a valid statement of one of the major sources of the gains from international trade. A country is said to have a **comparative advantage** in the production of good X if the cost of producing X *in terms of forgone output of other goods* is lower in that country than in another. Thus, the pattern of comparative advantage is based on *opportunity costs* rather than absolute costs. Table 32-2 illustrates the pattern of comparative advantage in the Canada–EU example. The opportunity cost in Canada for one kilogram of wheat is computed by determining how much cloth must be given up in Canada in order to produce an additional kilogram of wheat. From Table 32-1, the absolute costs of wheat and cloth were $1 per kilogram and $5 per metre, respectively. Thus, in order to produce one extra kilogram of wheat, Canada must use resources that could have produced one-fifth of a metre of cloth.

comparative advantage When a country can produce a good with less forgone output of other goods than can another country.

TABLE 32-1   Absolute Costs and Absolute Advantage

	Wheat (kilograms)	Cloth (metres)
Canada	$1 per kilogram	$5 per metre
EU	$3 per kilogram	$6 per metre

Absolute advantage reflects the differences in absolute costs of producing goods between countries. The numbers show the dollar cost of the total amount of resources necessary for producing wheat and cloth in Canada and the EU. Note that Canada is a lower-cost producer than the EU for both wheat and cloth. Canada is therefore said to have an absolute advantage in the production of both goods.

TABLE 32-2   Opportunity Costs and Comparative Advantage

Canada:	opportunity cost of 1 kg of wheat = 0.2 m cloth
EU:	opportunity cost of 1 kg of wheat = 0.5 m cloth
Canada:	opportunity cost of 1 m of cloth = 5 kg wheat
EU:	opportunity cost of 1 m of cloth = 2 kg wheat

Comparative advantages reflect opportunity costs that differ between countries. The opportunity costs are computed using the data provided in Table 32-1. For example, for Canada to produce one additional kilogram of wheat, it must use resources that could have been used to produce 0.2 metres of cloth; the opportunity cost of 1 kg of wheat in Canada is therefore 0.2 metres of cloth. The comparative advantages for each country are shown by the shaded rows. Canada has a comparative advantage in wheat production because it has a lower opportunity cost for wheat than does the EU. The EU has a comparative advantage in cloth because its opportunity cost for cloth is lower than that in Canada.

So the opportunity cost of one kilogram of wheat is 0.2 metres of cloth. By exactly the same reasoning, the opportunity cost of one metre of cloth in Canada is 5.0 kilograms of wheat. These opportunity costs are shown in Table 32-2.

Even though a country may have an absolute advantage in all goods (as Canada does in Table 32-1), it *cannot* have a comparative advantage in all goods. Similarly, even though a country may be inefficient in absolute terms and thus have an absolute disadvantage in all goods (as is the case for the EU in Table 32-1) it *cannot* have a comparative disadvantage in all goods. In Table 32-2, Canada has a comparative advantage in the production of wheat because Canada must give up less cloth to produce one kilogram of wheat than must be given up in the EU. Similarly, the EU has a comparative advantage in the production of cloth because the EU must give up less wheat in order to produce one metre of cloth than must be given up in Canada.

The gains from specialization and trade depend on the pattern of comparative, not absolute, advantage.

In our example, total world wheat production can be increased if Canada devotes more resources to the production of wheat and fewer resources to the production of cloth. Similarly, total world cloth production can be increased if the EU devotes more resources to the production of cloth and fewer to wheat. In the extreme case, Canada could *specialize* by producing *only* wheat and the EU could specialize by producing only cloth. Such reallocations of resources increase total world output because each country is producing more of the good in which it has the lowest opportunity cost. The gains from specialization along the lines of comparative advantage are shown in Table 32-3. In the table, we assume that Canada shifts its resources to produce slightly more wheat and slightly less cloth, while the EU does the opposite. Note that total world output of both goods increases.

TABLE 32-3 The Gains from Specialization

Changes from each country producing more units of the product in which it has the lower opportunity cost

	Wheat (kilograms)	Cloth (metres)
Canada	+5.0	−1.0
EU	−4.0	+2.0
Total	+1.0	+1.0

Whenever opportunity costs differ between countries, specialization can increase the world's production of both products. These calculations show that there are gains from specialization given the opportunity costs of Table 32-2. To produce five more kilograms of wheat, Canada must sacrifice 1.0 m of cloth. To produce two more metres of cloth, the EU must sacrifice 4.0 kg of wheat. This combination of changes increases world production of both wheat and cloth.

World output increases if countries specialize in the production of the goods in which they have a comparative advantage.

Not *every possible* pattern of specialization, however, is beneficial for the world. In our example, if Canada were to specialize in cloth and the EU in wheat, total world output would *fall*. To see this, note that in order to produce one extra metre of cloth in Canada, five kilograms of wheat must be sacrificed (see Table 32-2). Similarly, in order to produce four extra kilograms of wheat in the EU, two metres of cloth must be sacrificed. Thus, if each country produced these additional units of the "wrong" good, total world output of wheat would fall by one kilogram and total output of cloth would fall by one metre.

Specialization of production *against* the pattern of comparative advantage leads to a decline in total world output.

Production Possibilities Boundaries We have discussed comparative advantage in terms of opportunity costs. We can also illustrate it by considering the two countries' production possibilities boundaries. Recall from Chapter 1 the connection between a country's production possibilities boundary and the opportunity costs of production. The slope of the production possibilities boundary indicates the opportunity costs. The existence of different opportunity costs across countries implies comparative advantages that can lead to gains from trade. Figure 32-3 illustrates how two countries can both gain from trade when they have different opportunity costs, which are independent of the level of production. An alternative diagrammatic illustration of the gains from trade appears in *Extensions in Theory 32-1*, where the production possibilities boundary is concave (which means that the opportunity cost for each good is higher when more of that good is being produced).

FIGURE 32-3 The Gains from Trade with Constant Opportunity Costs

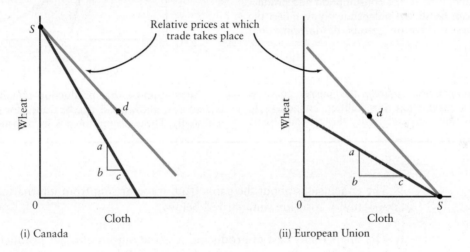

(i) Canada (ii) European Union

International trade leads to specialization in production and increased consumption possibilities. The bottom, purple lines in parts (i) and (ii) represent the production possibilities boundaries for Canada and the EU, respectively. In the absence of any international trade, these also represent each country's consumption possibilities.

The difference in the slopes of the production possibilities boundaries reflects differences in comparative advantage, as shown in Table 32-2. In each part the opportunity cost of increasing production of wheat by the same amount (measured by the distance *ba*) is the amount by which the production of cloth must be reduced (measured by the distance *bc*). The relatively steep production possibilities boundary for Canada thus indicates that the opportunity cost of producing wheat in Canada is less than that in the EU.

If trade is possible at some relative prices between the two countries' opportunity costs of production, each country will specialize in the production of the good in which it has a comparative advantage. In each part of the figure, the slope of the upper, green line shows the relative prices at which trade takes place. Production occurs in each country at point *S* (for specialization); Canada produces only wheat, and the EU produces only cloth.

Consumption possibilities for each country are now given by the upper, green line that passes through point *S*. Consumption possibilities are increased in both countries; consumption may occur at some point, such as *d*, that involves a combination of wheat and cloth that was not attainable in the absence of trade.

EXTENSIONS IN THEORY 32-1

The Gains from Trade More Generally

Examining the gains from trade is relatively easy in the case where each country's production possibilities boundary is a straight line. What happens in the more realistic case where the production possibilities boundary is concave? As this box shows, the same basic principles of the gains from trade apply to this more complex case.

International trade leads to an expansion of the set of goods that can be consumed in the economy in two ways:

1. By allowing the bundle of goods consumed to differ from the bundle produced

2. By permitting a profitable change in the pattern of production

Without international trade, the bundle of goods produced must be the same as the bundle consumed. With international trade, the consumption and production bundles can be altered independently to reflect the relative values placed on goods by international markets.

Fixed Production

In both accompanying figures, the purple curve is the economy's production possibilities boundary. In the absence of international trade, the economy must consume the same bundle of goods that it produces. Thus, the production possibilities boundary is also the consumption possibilities boundary. Suppose the economy produces and consumes at point a, with x_1 of good X and y_1 of good Y, as in the first figure.

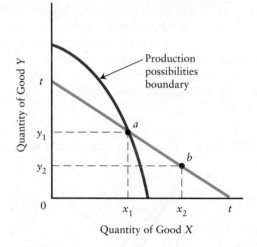

Next suppose that production remains at point a but we now allow good Y to be traded for good X internationally. The consumption possibilities are now shown

The conclusions about the gains from trade arising from international differences in opportunity costs are summarized below.

1. The opportunity cost of producing X is the output of other products that must be sacrificed in order to increase the output of X by one unit.

2. Country A has a comparative advantage over Country B in producing a product when its opportunity cost of production is lower. This implies, however, that Country A has a comparative *dis*advantage in some other product(s).

3. When opportunity costs for all products are the same in all countries, there is no comparative advantage and there is no possibility of gains from specialization and trade.

4. When opportunity costs differ in any two countries and both countries are producing both products, it is always possible to increase total production of both products by a suitable reallocation of resources within each country.

Though the concepts of comparative advantage and specialization are relatively straightforward, it is helpful to work through numerical examples to solidify your

by the line *tt* drawn through point *a*. The slope of *tt* indicates the quantity of *Y* that exchanges for a unit of *X* on the international market—that is, the relative price of *X* in terms of *Y*.

Although production is fixed at point *a*, consumption can now be anywhere on the line *tt*. For example, the consumption point could be at *b*. This could be achieved by exporting $y_2 y_1$ units of *Y* and importing $x_1 x_2$ units of *X*. Because point *b* (and all others on line *tt* to the right of *a*) lies outside the production possibilities boundary, there are potential gains from trade. Consumers are no longer limited by their own country's production possibilities. Let us suppose that they prefer point *b* to point *a*. They have achieved a gain from trade by being allowed to exchange some of their production of good *Y* for some quantity of good *X* and thus to consume more of good *X* than is produced at home.

Variable Production

In general, however, openness to trade with other countries will change the pattern of domestic production, and this will create *further* gains from trade. The country can now produce the bundle of goods that is most valuable in world markets. That is represented by the bundle *d* in the second figure. The consumption possibilities boundary is shifted to the line *t't'* by changing production from *a* to *d* and thereby increasing the country's degree of specialization in good *Y*. For every point on the original consumption possibilities boundary *tt*, there are points on the new boundary *t't'* that allow more consumption of both

goods—for example, compare points *b* and *f*. Notice also that, except at the zero-trade point *d*, the new consumption possibilities boundary lies *everywhere above the production possibilities boundary*.

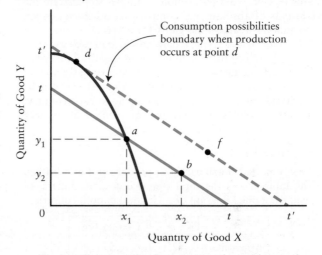

The benefits of moving from a no-trade position, such as point *a*, to a trading position, such as points *b* or *f*, are the *gains from trade* to the country. When the production of good *Y* is increased and the production of good *X* decreased, the country is able to move to a point, such as *f*, by producing more of good *Y*, in which the country has a comparative advantage, and trading the additional production for good *X*.

understanding. *Applying Economic Concepts 32-1* provides two examples and works through the computations of absolute and comparative advantage.

The Gains from Trade with Variable Costs

So far, we have assumed that opportunity costs are the same whatever the scale of output, and we have seen that there are gains from specialization and trade as long as there are differences in opportunity costs across countries. If costs vary with the level of output, or as experience is acquired via specialization, *additional* gains are possible.

Economies of Scale In many industries, production costs fall as the scale of output increases. The larger the scale of operations, the more efficiently large-scale machinery can be used and the more a detailed division of tasks among workers is possible. Small countries (such as Switzerland, Belgium, and Israel) whose domestic markets are not large enough to exploit economies of scale would find it prohibitively expensive to become self-sufficient by producing a little bit of everything at very high cost.

APPLYING ECONOMIC CONCEPTS 32-1

Two Examples of Absolute and Comparative Advantage

This box provides two simple examples to illustrate the concepts of absolute and comparative advantage. Each example also shows the gains from specialization. You will notice that the type of data provided in each example is different. The first example shows the absolute dollar cost of producing two goods in two countries; the second shows the amount of output of two goods that can be produced from the resources available in each country. In both examples, however, we can identify the pattern of absolute and comparative advantage.

Example #1

Argentina and Brazil can both produce fish and leather. The table shows the total resource cost, in dollars, of producing one kilogram of each good in both countries.

	Fish (kg)	Leather (kg)
Argentina	$2	$5
Brazil	$3	$4

Absolute Advantage Argentina is the more efficient producer of fish since its total resource cost ($2) is less than Brazil's ($3), and so it has the absolute advantage in producing fish. Brazil has the absolute advantage in producing leather.

Comparative Advantage To know the pattern of comparative advantage, we must compute the *opportunity costs of production*. In Argentina, producing one more kilogram of leather requires using $5 of resources—the amount that could have been used to produce 2.5 kg of fish. Thus, producing 1 kg of leather involves giving up 2.5 kg of fish. In Brazil, however, one extra kilogram of leather only requires a sacrifice of 1.33 kg of fish. Since Brazil has the lower opportunity cost for leather (it gives up the least fish), it has the comparative advantage in leather production.

The opportunity cost for fish production *must* be the inverse of that for leather. In Argentina, one extra kilogram of fish "costs" 0.4 kg of leather. In Brazil, one extra kilogram of fish "costs" 0.75 kg of leather. Since Argentina has the lower opportunity cost of fish, it has the comparative advantage in fish production.

Specialization If Argentina and Brazil were to trade with each other, total production would be increased if each country specialized in the production of the good in which it has the comparative advantage. Argentina should produce fish and buy its leather from Brazil; Brazil should produce leather and buy its fish from Argentina.

Example #2

Switzerland and Austria can both produce glass and chocolate. Each country has 1000 units of identical resources, which we will call "labour." The table shows the maximum amount of each good that each country could produce if it devoted all of its labour to the production of that good.

	Glass (tonnes)	Chocolate (kg)
Austria	5000	400 000
Switzerland	4000	200 000

Absolute Advantage Each unit of labour in Austria can produce 5 tonnes of glass or 400 kg of chocolate. The identical unit of labour in Switzerland can produce only 4 tonnes of glass or 200 kg of chocolate. Switzerland is less efficient than Austria in the production of both goods; Austria therefore has the absolute advantage in *both* goods.

Comparative Advantage Once again, we need to know the opportunity costs of production. In Austria, producing one extra tonne of glass requires giving up 80 kg (= 400 000/5000) of chocolate. In Switzerland, producing one extra tonne of glass "costs" 50 kg (= 200 000/4000) of chocolate. Switzerland has the lower opportunity cost for glass and thus has the comparative advantage in glass production. It follows that Austria *must* have the comparative advantage in the production of chocolate. Austria's opportunity cost of 1 kg of chocolate is 1/80 tonne of glass, whereas Switzerland's opportunity cost of 1 kg of chocolate is 1/50 tonne of glass.

Specialization If the two countries engaged in international trade, total output would be maximized if Austria specialized in the production of chocolate and Switzerland specialized in the production of glass.

One of the important lessons learned from patterns of world trade since the Second World War has concerned scale economies and product differentiation. Virtually all of today's manufactured consumer goods are produced in a vast array of differentiated product lines. In most industries, any one firm produces only one or a few of the different versions of the product. It does this because it is producing for a larger foreign market, and by focusing on only a few versions of the product, it can achieve the benefits of the associated scale economies. The result is that different countries specialize in different *versions* of similar products, and then trade with one another. Such trade is referred to as *intra-industry trade* and reflects the prevalence of scale economies and product differentiation in many industries.

This aspect of trade was first dramatically illustrated when the European Common Market (now known as the European Union) was established in the late 1950s. Economists had expected that specialization would occur according to the theory of comparative advantage, with one country specializing in cars, another in refrigerators, another in fashion and clothing, another in shoes, and so on. This is not the way it worked out. Instead, much of the vast growth of trade was in intra-industry trade—that is, trade of goods or services within the same broad industry. Today, one can buy French, English, Italian, and German fashion goods, cars, shoes, appliances, and a host of other products in Paris, London, Rome, and Berlin. Ships loaded with Swedish furniture bound for London pass ships loaded with English furniture bound for Stockholm, and so on. But the firms involved in this production are more likely to reap the benefits of the economies of scale than they could if they were producing only for their own domestic markets.

Wine is a good example of an industry in which there is much intra-industry trade. Canada, for example, imports wine from many countries but also exports Canadian-made wine to the same countries.

Jack Sullivan/Alamy Stock Photo

The same increase in intra-industry trade driven by scale economies happened with Canada–U.S. trade over successive rounds of tariff cuts that were negotiated after the Second World War, the most recent being those associated with the 1989 Canada–U.S. Free Trade Agreement, and its 1994 expansion into the North American Free Trade Agreement (NAFTA), which included Mexico. In several broad industrial groups, including automotive products, machinery, textiles, and forestry products, both imports and exports increased in each country. What free trade in Europe and North America did was to allow a proliferation of differentiated products, with different countries each specializing in different subproduct lines and reaping the benefits of the scale economies in production. Consumers have shown by their expenditures that they value this enormous increase in the range of choice among differentiated products, and producers have gained economies by being able to operate at a larger scale.

> In industries with significant scale economies, small countries that do not trade will have low levels of output and therefore high costs. With international trade, however, small countries can produce for the large global market and thus produce at lower costs. International trade therefore allows small countries to reap the benefits of scale economies.

Learning by Doing   The discussion so far has assumed that costs vary with the *level* of output. But they may also vary with the *accumulated experience* in producing a product over time.

FIGURE 32-4　Economies of Scale Versus Learning by Doing

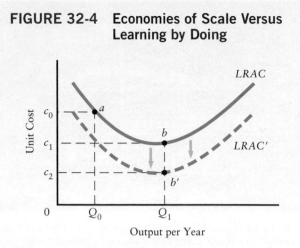

Output per Year

Early economists placed great importance on a concept that is now called **learning by doing**. They believed that as countries gained experience in particular tasks, workers and managers would become more efficient in performing them. As people acquire expertise, costs tend to fall. There is substantial evidence that such learning by doing does occur. It is particularly important in many of today's knowledge-intensive high-tech industries. The distinction between this phenomenon and economies of scale is illustrated in Figure 32-4. It is one more example of the difference between a movement along a curve and a shift of the curve.

The opportunity for learning by doing has an important implication: Policymakers need not accept current comparative advantages as given. Through such means as education and tax incentives, they can seek to develop new comparative advantages. Moreover, countries cannot complacently assume that their existing comparative advantages will persist. Misguided education policies, the wrong tax incentives, or policies that discourage risk taking can lead to the rapid erosion of a country's comparative advantage in particular products and industries.

Specialization may lead to gains from trade through scale economies, learning by doing, or both. Consider a country that wants to consume the quantity Q_0. Suppose it can produce that quantity at an average cost per unit of c_0. Suppose further that the country has a comparative advantage in producing this product and can export the quantity Q_0Q_1 if it produces Q_1. This may lead to cost savings in two ways.

First, the increased level of production of Q_1 compared with Q_0 permits it to move along its long-run average cost curve from a to b, thereby reducing costs per unit to c_1. This is an economy of scale.

Second, as workers and management become more experienced, they may be able to produce at lower costs. This is learning by doing and it shifts the cost curve from $LRAC$ to $LRAC'$. At output Q_1, costs per unit fall to c_2. The movement from a to b' incorporates both economies of scale and learning by doing.

Sources of Comparative Advantage

David Ricardo's analysis teaches us that the gains from trade arise from the pattern of comparative advantage. However, his analysis does not explain the *sources* of a country's comparative advantage. Why do comparative advantages exist? Since a country's comparative advantage depends on its opportunity costs, we could also ask: Why do different countries have different opportunity costs?

learning by doing The reduction in unit costs that often results as workers learn through repeatedly performing the same tasks. It causes a downward shift in the average cost curve.

Different Factor Endowments One answer to this question was offered early in the twentieth century by two Swedish economists, Eli Heckscher and Bertil Ohlin. According to their theory, the international cost differences that form the basis for comparative advantage arise because factor endowments differ across countries. This is often called the *factor endowment theory of comparative advantage.*

To see how this theory works, consider the prices for various types of goods in countries *in the absence of trade.* A country that is well endowed with fertile land but has a small population will find that land is cheap but labour is expensive. It will therefore produce land-intensive agricultural goods cheaply and labour-intensive goods, such as machine tools, only at high cost. The reverse will be true for a second country that is small in size but possesses abundant and efficient labour. As a result, the first country will have a comparative advantage in agricultural production and the second in goods that use much labour and little land.

According to the Heckscher-Ohlin theory, countries have comparative advantages in the production of goods that use intensively the factors of production with which they are abundantly endowed.

For example, Canada is abundantly endowed with forests relative to most other countries. According to the Heckscher-Ohlin theory, Canada has a comparative advantage in goods that use forest products intensively, such as paper, framing materials, raw lumber, and wooden furniture. In contrast, relative to most other countries, Canada is sparsely endowed with labour. Thus, Canada has a comparative disadvantage in goods that use labour intensively, such as cotton or many other textile products.

Different Climates   The factor endowment theory provides only part of the entire explanation for the sources of comparative advantage. Another important influence comes from all those natural factors that can be called *climate* in the broadest sense. If you combine land, labour, and capital in the same way in Costa Rica and in Iceland, you will not get the same output of most agricultural goods. Sunshine, rainfall, and average temperature also matter. You can, of course, artificially create any climate you want in a greenhouse, but it costs money to create what is freely provided elsewhere.

A country's comparative advantage is influenced by various aspects of its climate.

Of course, if we consider "warm weather" a factor of production, then we could simply say that countries like Costa Rica are better endowed with that factor than countries like Iceland. In this sense, explanations of comparative advantage based on different climates are really just a special case of explanations based on factor endowments.

Human Capital   Acquired skills, what economists call *human capital*, matter greatly in determining comparative advantage. Beginning in the late nineteenth century, Germany had an excellent set of trade schools that were attended by virtually every male who did not go on to higher academic education. As a result, Germany developed, and still maintains, a strong comparative advantage in many consumer goods that require significant engineering skills to produce, such as home appliances, power tools, and small machines. The people of Persia (now Iran) produced carpets of high quality over the centuries, and from childhood their workers developed skills in carpet making that few others could match. So they had a comparative advantage in high-quality carpets and some related commodities. Early on, Americans developed the skills necessary to mass-produce goods of reasonable quality made from standardized parts. So the United States developed a comparative advantage in many consumer goods made with mass-production techniques.

Canada is extremely well endowed with forests. It is no surprise, therefore, that it has a comparative advantage in a whole range of forestry products.

Acquired Comparative Advantage   The example of human capital makes it clear that many comparative advantages are *acquired*. Further, they can change. Thus, comparative advantage should be viewed as being *dynamic* rather than static. Many of today's industries depend more on human capital than on fixed physical capital or natural resources. The skills of a computer designer or a video game programmer are acquired by education and on-the-job training. Natural endowments of energy and raw materials cannot account for Silicon Valley's leadership in computer technology, for Canada's prominence in auto-parts manufacturing, for Taiwan's excellence in electronics, or for Switzerland's prominence in private banking.

If comparative advantage can be acquired, it can also be *lost*. If firms within one country fail to innovate and adopt the latest technologies available in their industry, but competing firms in other countries are aggressively innovating and reducing their production costs, the first country will eventually lose whatever comparative advantage it once had in that industry. In recent years, for example, pulp and paper mills in Canada have been closing, driven out of the industry by Scandinavian firms that more aggressively pursue improvements in productivity.

> **With today's growing international competition and rapidly changing technologies, no country's comparative advantages are secure unless its firms innovate and keep up with their foreign competitors and its education system produces workers, managers, and innovators with the requisite skills.**

Contrasting Views?   The view that a country's comparative advantages change over time and can be influenced by education, innovation, and government policy is a relatively modern one. It contrasts sharply with the traditional view that a country's natural endowments of land, labour, and natural resources are the prime determinants of its comparative advantage. The traditional view suggested that a government interested in maximizing its citizens' material standard of living should encourage specialization of production in goods for which it *currently* had a comparative advantage. If all countries followed this advice, each would have been specialized in a relatively narrow range of distinct products. Germans would have produced engineering products, Canadians would have produced resource-based primary products, Americans would have been farmers and factory workers, Central Americans would have been banana and coffee growers, the Chinese would have produced rice and cheap toys, and so on.

There are surely elements of truth in both views. It would be unwise to neglect the importance of resource endowments, climate, culture, social patterns, and institutional arrangements. But it would also be unwise to assume that all advantages are innate and immutable.

▌ 32.2 The Determination of Trade Patterns

Comparative advantage has been the central concept in our discussion about the gains from trade. If Canada has a comparative advantage in lumber and Italy has a comparative advantage in shoes, then the total output of lumber and shoes can be increased if Canada specializes in the production of lumber and Italy specializes in the production of shoes. With such patterns of specialization, Canada will naturally export lumber to Italy and Italy will export shoes to Canada.

It is one thing to discuss the *potential* gains from trade if countries specialized in the production of particular goods and exported these to other countries. But do *actual* trade patterns occur along the lines of comparative advantage? In this section of the chapter we use a simple demand-and-supply model to examine why Canada exports some products and imports others. We will see that comparative advantage, whether natural or acquired, plays a central role in determining actual trade patterns.

There are some products, such as coffee and mangoes, that Canada does not produce and will probably never produce. Any domestic consumption of these products must therefore be satisfied by imports from other countries. At the other extreme, there are some products, such as nickel and potash, for which Canada is one of the world's major suppliers, and demand in the rest of the world must be satisfied partly by exports from Canada. Finally, there are some products, such as concrete blocks and crushed stone, that are so expensive to transport that every country produces approximately what it consumes.

Our interest in this section is with the vast number of intermediate cases in which Canada is only one of many producers of an internationally traded product, as with beef, oil, copper, wheat, lumber, and newsprint. Will Canada be an exporter or an importer of such products? And what is the role played by comparative advantage?

The Law of One Price

Whether Canada imports or exports a product for which it is only one of many producers depends to a great extent on the product's price. This brings us to what economists call the *law of one price*.

> **The law of one price states that when a product is traded throughout the entire world, the prices in various countries (net of any specific taxes or tariffs) will differ by no more than the cost of transporting the product between countries. Aside from differences caused by these transport costs, there is a single world price.**

Many basic products—such as wheat, oil, lumber, paper, copper wire, steel pipe, iron ore, and computer RAM chips—fall within this category. The world price for each good is the price that equates the quantity demanded worldwide with the quantity supplied worldwide. The world price of an internationally traded product may be influenced greatly, or only slightly, by the demand and supply coming from any one country. The extent of one country's influence will depend on how important its quantities demanded and supplied are in relation to the worldwide totals.

The simplest case for us to study arises when the country, which we will take to be Canada, accounts for only a small part of the total worldwide demand and supply. In this case, Canada does not itself produce enough to influence the world price significantly. Similarly, Canadian purchases are too small a proportion of worldwide demand to affect the world price in any significant way. Producers and consumers in Canada thus face a world price that they cannot influence by their own actions.

In this case, the price that rules in the Canadian market must be the world price (adjusted for the exchange rate between the Canadian dollar and the foreign currency). The law of one price says this must be so. What would happen if the Canadian domestic price diverged from the world price? If the Canadian price were below the world price, no supplier would sell in the Canadian market because higher profits could be made by selling abroad. The absence of supply to the Canadian market would thus drive up the Canadian price. Conversely, if the Canadian domestic price were above the

FIGURE 32-5   An Exported Good

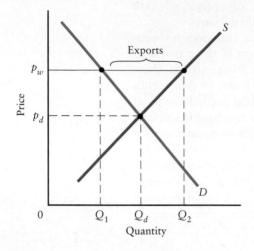

Exports occur whenever there is excess supply domestically at the world price. The domestic demand and supply curves are D and S, respectively. The domestic price in the absence of foreign trade is p_d, with Q_d produced and consumed domestically. The world price of p_w is higher than p_d. At p_w, Q_1 is demanded while Q_2 is supplied domestically. The excess of the domestic supply over the domestic demand is exported.

worldwide price, no buyer would buy from a Canadian seller because lower prices are available by buying abroad. The absence of demand on the Canadian market would thus drive down the Canadian price.

The Pattern of Foreign Trade

Let us now see what determines the pattern of international trade in such circumstances.

An Exported Product   To determine the pattern of Canadian trade, we first show the Canadian domestic demand and supply curves for some product, say, lumber. This is done in Figure 32-5. The intersection of these two curves tells us what the price and quantity would be in Canada *if there were no foreign trade*. In this situation, the price in Canada would be p_d and the quantity of lumber exchanged would be Q_d.

Now consider a situation in which international trade exists, and the world price of lumber is p_w.[1] If the world price is higher than the no-trade domestic price ($p_w > p_d$), there will be an excess of Canadian supply over Canadian demand. This excess domestic supply will be Canada's exports. In Figure 32-5, the amount of Canada's lumber exports at the world price is $Q_2 - Q_1$.

What is the role of comparative advantage in this analysis? We have said that Canada will export lumber if the world price exceeds Canada's no-trade domestic price. Note that in a competitive market the price of the product reflects the product's marginal cost, which in turn reflects the opportunity cost of producing the product. That Canada's no-trade price for lumber is lower than the world price reflects the fact that the opportunity cost of producing lumber in Canada is less than the opportunity cost of producing it in the rest of the world. Thus, by exporting goods that have a low no-trade price, Canada is exporting the goods for which it has a comparative advantage.

> Countries export the goods for which they are low-cost producers. That is, they export goods for which they have a comparative advantage.

An Imported Product   Now consider some other product—for example, computer RAM chips. Once again, look first at the domestic demand and supply curves, shown this time in Figure 32-6. The intersection of these curves determines the price that would exist in Canada if there were no foreign trade.

If we now consider a situation with international trade, we must compare the world price of RAM chips with the no-trade Canadian price. As shown in Figure 32-6,

---

[1] If the world price is stated in terms of some foreign currency (as it often is), the price must be converted into Canadian dollars by using the current exchange rate between the foreign currency and Canadian dollars.

the world price of RAM chips is below the Canadian no-trade price. At this low world price, domestic demand is larger and domestic supply is smaller than if the no-trade price had ruled. The excess of domestic demand over domestic supply is met by imports.

Again, this analysis can be restated in terms of comparative advantage. The high Canadian no-trade price of RAM chips reflects the fact that the production of RAM chips has a higher opportunity cost in Canada than elsewhere in the world. This high cost means that Canada has a comparative disadvantage in RAM chips. So Canada imports goods for which it has a comparative disadvantage.

Countries import the goods for which they are high-cost producers. That is, they import goods for which they have a comparative disadvantage.

Is Comparative Advantage Obsolete?

It is sometimes said that the theory of comparative advantage is nearly 200 years old, and things have changed so much since then that the theory must surely be obsolete.

Contrary to such assertions, comparative advantage remains an important and valid economic concept. At any one time—because comparative advantage is reflected in international relative prices, and these relative prices determine what goods a country will import and what it will export—the operation of the price system will result in trade that follows the current pattern of comparative advantage. For example, if Canadian costs of producing steel are particularly low relative to other Canadian costs, Canada will export steel at international prices (which it does). If Canada's costs of producing textiles are particularly high relative to other Canadian costs, Canada will import textiles at international prices (which it does). Thus, there is no reason to change the view that David Ricardo long ago expounded: *Current comparative advantage is a major determinant of trade under free-market conditions.*

The Role of Public Policy   What has changed, however, is economists' views about the *determinants* of comparative advantage. It is now clear that current comparative advantage is more open to change by private entrepreneurial activities and by government policy than was previously thought. Thus, what is obsolete is the belief that a country's current pattern of comparative advantage, and hence its current pattern of imports and exports, must be accepted as given and unchangeable.

The theory that comparative advantage is a major influence on trade flows is not obsolete, but the theory that comparative advantage is completely determined by forces beyond the reach of decisions made by private firms and by public policy has been discredited.

FIGURE 32-6   An Imported Good

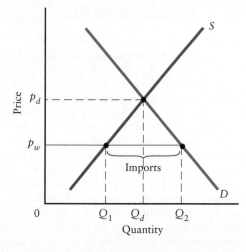

Imports occur whenever there is excess demand domestically at the world price. The domestic demand and supply curves are D and S, respectively. The domestic price in the absence of foreign trade is p_d, with Q_d produced and consumed domestically. The world price of p_w is less than p_d. At the world price Q_2 is demanded, whereas Q_1 is supplied domestically. The excess of domestic demand over domestic supply is satisfied through imports.

APPLYING ECONOMIC CONCEPTS 32-2

Comparative Advantage and Global Supply Chains

The discussion of comparative advantage developed in this chapter applies easily to many products with one or even a few components. One can sensibly speak of national comparative advantages for whole products, such as Costa Rica for bananas, Canada for sawn logs, Chile for copper, Korea for steel, and Saudi Arabia for oil.

For many manufactured products, however, and even for some resource-based products and service industries, production is carried out in complex and integrated "global supply chains," with a product's several different components being produced in different countries and often by different firms. In such a world, it is no longer clear where some products are "made," even though one could easily determine where each of the product's many components is produced and where they are all assembled into a final product.

This method of decentralized production has several causes. First, the existence of scale economies provides an incentive for individual firms to reduce their costs by concentrating the production of each individual component in a different specialized large factory. Second, differences in national wage rates for various types of labour

provide an incentive for these production facilities to be located in different countries. Third, the current very low costs of communication and transportation make it possible to coordinate supply chains globally and ship parts and final products anywhere at low cost. (If fuel becomes expensive enough to make transport costs a significant part of total costs, it will become economic to do much more production closer to final markets than it has been over the last several decades.)

Consider three examples. The iPhone sold by Apple clearly says "Made in China" on the box, but most of the value from its design occurs in the United States, many electronic components come from Korea and Japan, and only the iPhone's final assembly occurs in China. Apple chooses to locate assembly in China, using components manufactured elsewhere, because by doing so it can maximize its product quality and minimize costs.

Bombardier jet aircraft designed and assembled in Canada also involve global supply chains. Fuselage parts come from Japan, the wings are produced in Northern Ireland, engines are imported from the United States, and the avionics are engineered in the United States but

One caveat should be noted. It is one thing to observe that it is *possible* for governments to influence a country's pattern of comparative advantage. It is quite another to conclude that it is *advisable* for them to try. The case in support of a specific government intervention requires that (1) there is scope for governments to improve on the results achieved by the free market, (2) the costs of the intervention be less than the value of the improvement to be achieved, and (3) governments will actually be able to carry out the required interventionist policies (without, for example, being sidetracked by considerations of electoral advantage).

In many cases, governments have succeeded in creating important comparative advantages. For example, the Taiwanese government virtually created that nation's electronics industry and then passed it over to private hands in which it became a world leader. The government of Singapore created a computer-parts industry that became a major world supplier. However, there are also many examples in which governments failed in their attempts to create comparative advantage. The government of the United Kingdom tried to create a comparative advantage in computers and failed miserably, wasting much public money in the process. The government of Ireland tried to create a comparative advantage in automobile production and failed to create more than a modest, unprofitable industry that eventually disappeared. The world is strewn not only with spectacular successes, which show that it can be done, but also with abject failures, which show that the attempt to do so is fraught with many dangers.

The Importance of Modern Supply Chains One other comment needs to be made regarding the relevance of the concept of comparative advantage. For understanding international trade in copper wire, lumber, oil, bananas, coffee, textiles, and many other

sourced from Asian suppliers. Bombardier adopts this business model because costs can be reduced and quality maximized by using specialty suppliers at each link in the global supply chain.

Such global supply chains even exist for some products that appear to have few "components," such as fish. For example, a Canadian firm may hire a Chilean trawler to fish in the Indian Ocean, land its catch in Malaysia where it is frozen, and then send it to China for further processing before it is finally sold to Japanese wholesalers.

There are three implications for international trade in the presence of integrated global supply chains. First, we should not view countries as having comparative advantages in entire products but rather in the specific productive activities that take place along the global supply chain. China may not have a comparative advantage in "producing" consumer electronics but may have one in assembling them. Canada may not have a comparative advantage in "producing" jet aircraft but may have one in designing them.

Second, these comparative advantages may not be long-lasting because they are sensitive to changes in the economic environment and in technology. For example, significant changes in national corporate tax rates, exchange rates, and wages for factory workers will generally change the optimal location for the production of a product's various components. Also, newly developed

technologies for producing existing products and creating new ones can alter the patterns of comparative advantage significantly and quickly.

Third, traditional data on international trade does not capture the extent of integration in global supply chains. The iPhone assembled in China and exported to the United States appears simply as a Chinese export; but the significant value generated by the U.S.-based design team may appear in no trade statistics whatsoever. It follows that the measured flow of a country's exports of some products does not necessarily correspond closely with the level of local economic activity (production and employment) actually generated by those products. Even in Canada's resource sector, the domestic content of exports is not 100 percent, although it is typically more than 75 percent, meaning that up to one-quarter of the value of the final exported product comes from imported inputs. In most manufacturing industries, however, the domestic content of exports is 50 percent or lower, and in the automobile industry it is only 35 percent.

The presence of such highly integrated global supply chains indicates the importance of two-way trade in the Canadian economy: Access to low-price and high-quality imports is as crucial to the Canadian economy as is our access to world markets where we can sell our intermediate and final products.

relatively simple products, the concept of comparative advantage is very useful. In some manufacturing industries, however, where products have dozens or perhaps hundreds of components, the determinants of trade flows are more complex than the theory of comparative advantage suggests. For example, it is difficult to see why Canada might have a comparative advantage in the production of automobile transmissions but not in automobile brake systems or air-conditioning systems. Yet, the automobile sector is perhaps the best example of an industry in which a firm's "supply chain" includes products made by several other firms in several countries. *Applying Economic Concepts 32-2* discusses how economies of scale and the forces of globalization have led to the development of complex global supply chains and how these supply chains affect the way we think about comparative advantage and international trade.

The Terms of Trade

We have seen that world production can be increased when countries specialize in the production of the goods for which they have a comparative advantage and then trade with one another. We now ask: How will these gains from specialization and trade be shared among countries? The division of the gain depends on what is called the **terms of trade**, which relate to the quantity of imported goods that can be obtained per unit of goods exported. The terms of trade are measured by the ratio of the price of exports to the price of imports.

A rise in the price of imported goods, with the price of exports unchanged, indicates a *fall in the terms of trade*; it will now take more exports to buy the same quantity of imports. Similarly, a rise in the price of exported goods, with the price of imports

terms of trade The ratio of the average price of a country's exports to the average price of its imports.

FIGURE 32-7   An Improvement in the Terms of Trade

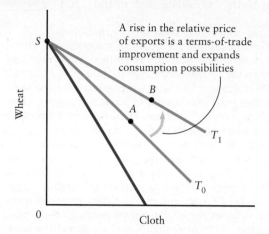

A rise in the relative price of exports is a terms-of-trade improvement and expands consumption possibilities

Changes in the terms of trade lead to changes in a country's consumption possibilities. The purple line shows the hypothetical production possibilities boundary for Canada. With international trade at relative prices T_0, Canada specializes in the production of wheat, producing at point S, but is able to consume at a point like A. It pays for its imports of cloth with its exports of wheat.

If the price of wheat rises relative to the price of cloth, production remains at S but the line T_1 shows Canada's new consumption possibilities. Consumption can now take place at a point like B where consumption of both wheat and cloth has increased. The increase in the terms of trade makes Canada better off because of the increase in consumption possibilities.

unchanged, indicates a *rise in the terms of trade*; it will now take fewer exports to buy the same quantity of imports. Thus, the ratio of these prices measures the amount of imports that can be obtained per unit of goods exported.

The terms of trade can be illustrated with a country's production possibilities boundary, as shown in Figure 32-7. The figure shows the hypothetical case in which Canada can produce only wheat and cloth. As we saw earlier, the slope of Canada's production possibilities boundary shows the relative opportunity costs of producing the two goods in Canada. A steep production possibilities boundary, as we see in Figure 32-7, indicates that only a small amount of cloth must be given up to get more wheat; thus cloth is relatively costly and wheat is relatively cheap. In contrast, a flatter production possibilities boundary indicates that a larger amount of cloth must be given up to get more wheat; thus cloth is relatively cheap and wheat is relatively expensive.

If, through international trade, Canada has access to different relative prices, Canada will be led to specialize in the production of one good or the other. In Figure 32-7, we show a case in which the world relative price of cloth is lower than the relative price Canada would have if it did not trade. (This lower *world* relative price of cloth reflects the fact that other countries can produce cloth more cheaply than Canada.) Faced with a lower relative price of cloth, Canada ends up specializing in the production of the relatively high-priced product (wheat), and importing the relatively low-priced product (cloth). This point of specialization is point S in Figure 32-7.

The upper two *green* lines in the figure show alternative values of the world relative prices—that is, alternative values for Canada's terms of trade. A rise in the terms of trade indicates a fall in the relative price of cloth (or a rise in the relative price of wheat). This increase in the terms of trade is shown as an upward rotation of the green line from T_0 to T_1. A reduction in the terms of trade is shown as a downward rotation in the green line, from T_1 to T_0.

It should be clear from Figure 32-7 why changes in the terms of trade are important. Suppose the international relative prices are initially given by T_0. Canada specializes in the production of wheat (point S) but consumes at some point like A, where it finances its imports of cloth with exports of wheat. Now suppose there is a shift in world demand toward wheat and away from cloth, and this leads to an increase in the relative price of wheat. The terms of trade increase to T_1 and, with unchanged production at point S, Canada can now afford to consume at a point like B where consumption of both wheat and cloth has increased.

A rise in a country's terms of trade is beneficial because it expands the country's consumption possibilities.

Conversely, a reduction in the price of a country's exports (relative to the price of its imports) is harmful for a country. In Figure 32-7, this is shown as a change of the terms of trade from T_1 to T_0. Even though production may remain unchanged, the range of goods available to be consumed falls, and this reduction in consumption possibilities leads to an overall loss of welfare.

How do we measure the terms of trade in real economies? Because international trade involves many countries and many products, we cannot use the simple ratio of the prices of two goods as in Figure 32-7. The basic principle, however, is the same. A country's terms of trade are computed as an index number:

$$\text{Terms of trade} = \frac{\text{Index of export prices}}{\text{Index of import prices}} \times 100$$

A rise in the index is referred to as a terms of trade *improvement*. A decrease in the index is called a terms of trade *deterioration*. For example, oil-exporting countries experienced significant terms-of-trade improvements when the world price of oil increased sharply in the mid-1990s and again in the mid-2000s. When world oil prices fell sharply in 2014–2015, the same countries experienced a large deterioration in their terms of trade. The opposite was true for oil-importing economies like the United States and the European Union.

Canada's terms of trade since 1961 are shown in Figure 32-8. As is clear, the terms of trade are quite variable, reflecting frequent changes in the relative prices of different

FIGURE 32-8   Canada's Terms of Trade, 1961–2017

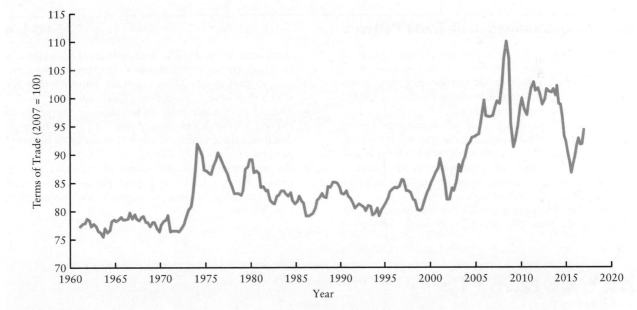

Canada's terms of trade have been quite variable over the past 60 years. The data shown are Canada's terms of trade—the ratio of an index of Canadian export prices to an index of Canadian import prices. As the relative prices of lumber, oil, wheat, electronic equipment, textiles, fruit, and other products change, the terms of trade naturally change.

(*Source:* Author's calculations using data from Statistics Canada, CANSIM database, Table 380-0066.)

products. Note the dramatic improvement in Canada's terms of trade in the early 1970s, reflecting the large increase in oil prices caused by OPEC's output restrictions. Since Canada is a net exporter of oil, its terms of trade improve when the price of oil increases. An even larger increase occurred in the 2002–2008 period, when the world prices of most commodities, especially energy-related commodities, increased sharply.

SUMMARY

32.1 The Gains from Trade

LO 1, 2

- Country A has an *absolute* advantage over Country B in the production of a specific product when the absolute cost of the product is less in Country A than in Country B.
- Country A has a *comparative* advantage over Country B in the production of a specific good if the forgone output of other goods is less in Country A than in Country B.
- Comparative advantage occurs whenever countries have different opportunity costs of producing particular goods. World production of all products can be increased if each country transfers resources into the production of the products for which it has a comparative advantage.
- International trade allows all countries to obtain the goods for which they do not have a comparative

advantage at a lower opportunity cost than if they were to produce all products for themselves; specialization and trade therefore allow all countries to have more of all products than if they tried to be self-sufficient.
- A nation that engages in trade and specialization may also realize the benefits of economies of large-scale production and of learning by doing.
- Traditional theories regarded comparative advantage as largely determined by natural resource endowments that are difficult to change. Economists now know that some comparative advantages can be acquired and consequently can be changed. Public policies may, in this view, influence a country's role in world production and trade.

32.2 The Determination of Trade Patterns

LO 3, 4

- The law of one price says that the national prices of tradable goods (net of taxes and tariffs) must differ by no more than the costs of transporting these goods between countries. After accounting for these transport costs, there is a single world price.
- Countries will export a good when the world price exceeds the price that would exist in the country if there were no trade. The low no-trade price reflects a low opportunity cost and thus a comparative advantage in that good. Thus, countries export goods for which they have a comparative advantage.
- Countries will import a good when the world price is less than the price that would exist in the country if

there were no trade. The high no-trade price reflects a high opportunity cost and thus a comparative disadvantage in that good. Thus, countries import goods for which they have a comparative disadvantage.
- The terms of trade refer to the ratio of the prices of exports to the prices of imports. The terms of trade determine the quantity of imports that can be obtained per unit of exports.
- An improvement in the terms of trade—a rise in export prices relative to import prices—is beneficial for a country because it expands its consumption possibilities.

KEY CONCEPTS

Interpersonal, interregional, and international specialization
Absolute advantage and comparative advantage
Opportunity cost and comparative advantage

The gains from trade: specialization, scale economies, and learning by doing
The sources of comparative advantage

Factor endowments
Acquired comparative advantage
The law of one price
The terms of trade

STUDY EXERCISES

MyLab Economics Make the grade with MyLab Economics™: All Study Exercises can be found on MyLab Economics™. You can practise them as often as you want, and many feature step-by-step guided instructions to help you find the right answer.

FILL-IN-THE-BLANK

1 Fill in the blanks to make the following statements correct.

    a. The "gains from trade" refers to the increased _____ attributable to specialization and trade.

    b. Suppose Argentina can produce one kilogram of beef for $2.50 and Brazil can produce one kilogram of beef for $2.90. Argentina is said to have a(n) _____ in beef production over Brazil. The gains from trade do *not* depend on _____.

    c. Comparative advantage is based on _____ rather than absolute costs.

    d. It is possible for a country to have a comparative advantage in some good and a(n) _____ in none.

    e. If all countries specialize in the production of goods for which they have a comparative advantage, then world output will _____.

    f. If opportunity costs are the same in all countries, there is no _____ and no possibility of _____.

2 Fill in the blanks to make the following statements correct.

    a. A product such as coffee beans is cheaply transported and is traded around the world. The law of _____ tells us that it will tend to have _____ worldwide price.

    b. If the no-trade domestic price of copper wire in Canada is $20 per unit and the world price is $24 per unit, then Canada will have an excess _____, which it will then _____. The opportunity cost of producing copper wire in Canada is _____ than the opportunity cost of producing it in the rest of the world.

    c. Canada will import goods for which it has an excess _____ at the world price. In the absence of trade, the _____ price of these goods would be less than the _____ price.

    d. A rise in Canada's terms of trade means that the average price of Canada's _____ has risen compared with the average price of Canada's _____. This change is referred to as a terms of trade _____.

    e. The terms of trade determine the quantity of _____ that can be obtained per unit of _____.

REVIEW

3 The following diagrams show the production possibilities boundaries for Canada and France, both of which are assumed to produce only two goods, wine and lumber.

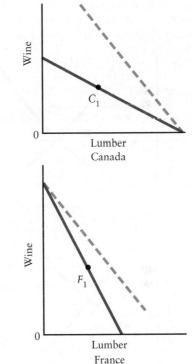

Canada

France

    a. Which country has the comparative advantage in lumber? Explain.

    b. Which country has the comparative advantage in wine? Explain.

    c. Suppose Canada and France are initially not trading with each other and are producing at points C_1 and F_1, respectively. Suppose when trade is introduced, the free-trade relative prices are shown by the slope of the dashed line. Show in the diagrams which combination of goods each country will now produce.

    d. In this case, what will be the pattern of trade for each country?

4 The following diagrams show the Canadian markets for newsprint and machinery, which we assume to be competitive.

a. Suppose there is no international trade. Show on the diagram the equilibrium price and quantity in the Canadian newsprint and machinery markets.

b. Now suppose Canada is open to trade with the rest of the world and the world price of newsprint is higher than the price of newsprint from part (a). Show in the diagram the quantities of domestic consumption and production and the quantity of newsprint that is either exported or imported.

c. Similarly, suppose the world price of machinery is lower than the price of machinery from part (a). Show in the diagram the quantity of domestic consumption and production and the quantity of machinery that is either exported or imported.

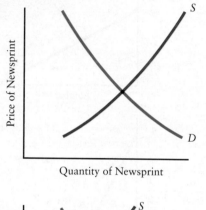

Quantity of Newsprint

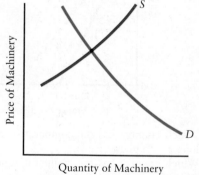

Quantity of Machinery

5 For each of the following events, explain the likely effect on Canada's terms of trade. Your existing knowledge of Canada's imports and exports should be adequate to answer this question.

a. A hurricane damages much of Brazil's coffee crop.

b. OPEC countries succeed in significantly restricting the world supply of oil.

c. Several new large copper mines come into production in Chile.

d. A major recession in Southeast Asia reduces the world demand for pork.

e. Russia, a large producer of wheat, experiences a massive drought that reduces its wheat crop by more than 30 percent.

f. Three major potash-producing firms form a cartel and restrict the world's output of potash.

6 Predict what each of the following events would do to the terms of trade of the importing country and the exporting country, other things being equal.

a. A blight destroys a large part of the coffee beans produced in the world.

b. Korean producers cut the price of the steel they sell to Canada.

c. General inflation of 4 percent occurs around the world.

d. Violation of OPEC output quotas leads to a sharp fall in the price of oil.

7 When the North American Free Trade Agreement (NAFTA) was being negotiated in the early 1990s, there was a great deal of debate. One critic argued that "it can't be in our interest to sign this deal; Mexico gains too much from it." What does the theory of the gains from trade have to say about that criticism?

8 In 2018, U.S. President Donald Trump argued that his country's trade agreements with other countries were bad for the United States and were unfairly benefiting America's trading partners. What does the theory of the gains from trade have to say about such arguments?

9 Adam Smith saw a close connection between a nation's wealth and its ability and willingness "freely to engage" in trade with other countries.

a. Based on what you have learned in this chapter, what is the connection?

b. Explain why trading with countries that are "most different" from our own is likely to generate the most benefits. Which differences are of central importance?

c. Under what circumstances are there *no* benefits from a country specializing and trading with other countries?

d. Illustrate the argument from part (c) in a simple diagram of a country's production possibilities boundary.

PROBLEMS

10 The following diagram shows the production possibilities boundary for Arcticland, a country that produces only two goods, ice and fish. Labour is the only factor of production. Recall that a linear production possibilities boundary reflects *constant* opportunity costs for both products.

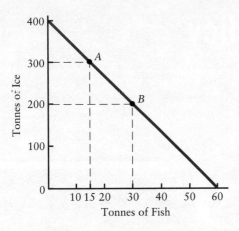

a. Beginning at any point on Arcticland's production possibilities boundary, what is the opportunity cost of producing 100 more tonnes of ice?
b. Beginning at any point on Arcticland's production possibilities boundary, what is the opportunity cost of producing 10 more tonnes of fish?

⑪ The following table shows the production of wheat and corn in Brazil and Mexico. Assume that both countries have one million acres of arable land and the same amount of other resources.

	Brazil	Mexico
Wheat	90 bushels per acre	50 bushels per acre
Corn	30 bushels per acre	25 bushels per acre

a. Which country has the absolute advantage in wheat? In corn? Explain.
b. What is the opportunity cost of producing an extra bushel of wheat in Brazil? In Mexico? Which country has the comparative advantage in wheat production? Explain.
c. Which country has the comparative advantage in corn production? Explain.
d. Explain why one country can have an absolute advantage in both goods but cannot have a comparative advantage in both goods.
e. On a single scale diagram with wheat on the horizontal axis and corn on the vertical axis, draw each country's production possibilities boundary.
f. What is shown by the slope of each country's production possibilities boundary? Be as precise as possible.

⑫ The following table shows how many tonnes of dairy products and beef products can be produced in New Zealand and Australia with one unit of equivalent resources.

	Dairy Products (tonnes)	Beef Products (tonnes)
New Zealand	12	4
Australia	12	16

a. Which country has an absolute advantage in dairy products? In beef products? Explain.
b. What is the opportunity cost of producing an extra tonne of dairy products in New Zealand? In Australia? What is the opportunity cost of producing an extra tonne of beef products in New Zealand? In Australia?
c. What is the pattern of comparative advantage between these two countries?
d. Assume that both countries have 100 units of equivalent resources. On scale diagrams with dairy products on the horizontal axis and beef products on the vertical axis, draw each country's production possibilities boundary.
e. What is the interpretation of the slope of the production possibilities boundary?

⑬ The table below shows indexes for the prices of imports and exports over several years for a hypothetical country.

Year	Import Prices	Export Prices	Terms of Trade
2014	90	110	——
2015	95	87	——
2016	98	83	——
2017	100	100	——
2018	102	105	——
2019	100	112	——
2020	103	118	——

a. Compute the terms of trade in each year for this country and fill in the table.
b. In which span of years do the terms of trade improve?
c. In which span of years do the terms of trade deteriorate?
d. Explain why a terms of trade "improvement" is good for the country.

33 Trade Policy

CHAPTER OUTLINE

LEARNING OBJECTIVES (LO)

After studying this chapter you will be able to

33.1 FREE TRADE OR PROTECTION?

1 describe the various situations in which a country may rationally choose to protect some industries.

2 discuss the most common invalid arguments in favour of protection.

33.2 METHODS OF PROTECTION

3 explain the effects of tariffs and quotas on the domestic economy.

4 understand why trade-remedy laws are sometimes just thinly disguised protection.

33.3 CURRENT TRADE POLICY

5 distinguish between trade creation and trade diversion.

6 discuss the main features of the North American Free Trade Agreement.

CONDUCTING business in a foreign country is not always easy. Differences in language, in local laws and customs, and in currency complicate transactions. Our concern in this chapter, however, is not with these complications but with government policy toward international trade, which is called *trade policy*. At one extreme is a policy of free trade—that is, an absence of any form of government interference with the free flow of international trade. Any departure from free trade designed to protect domestic industries from foreign competition is called *protectionism*.

In the decades following the end of the Second World War, most countries gradually moved away from protectionist policies and toward freer trade. This shift led to large increases in the flows of international trade and contributed to rising prosperity in those countries. In recent years, however, a backlash against freer trade has emerged in many countries, motivated in part by the economic disruptions that accompany freer international trade. In particular, U.S. President Donald Trump has argued that the United States no longer benefits from existing free-trade agreements and has sought to repeal or renegotiate several of them. This policy stance, from a country that for decades was a strong promoter of global free trade, has created concern among many of America's trading partners, including Canada. The tensions surrounding global trade and trade policy are likely to be of great importance for the next several years.

We begin this chapter by briefly restating the case for free trade and then go on to examine various valid and invalid arguments that are commonly advanced for some degree of protection. We then explore some of the methods commonly used to restrict trade, such as tariffs and quotas. Finally, we examine the many modern institutions designed to foster freer trade on either a global or a regional basis. In particular, we discuss the North American Free Trade Agreement (NAFTA) and the World Trade Organization (WTO).

33.1 Free Trade or Protection?

Today, most governments accept the proposition that a relatively free flow of international trade is desirable for the health of their individual economies. But heated debates still occur over trade policy. Should a country permit the *completely* free flow of international trade, or should it use policies to restrict the flow of trade and thereby protect its local producers from foreign competition? If some protection is desired, should it be achieved by tariffs or by non-tariff barriers? **Tariffs** are taxes designed to raise the domestic price of imported goods. **Non-tariff barriers (NTBs)** are policies other than tariffs designed to reduce the flow of imports; examples are import quotas and customs procedures that are deliberately more cumbersome than necessary.

tariff A tax applied on imports of goods or services.

non-tariff barriers (NTBs) Restrictions other than tariffs designed to reduce imports.

The Case for Free Trade

The gains from trade were presented in Chapter 32. Comparative advantages arise whenever countries have different opportunity costs. Free trade encourages all countries to specialize in producing products in which they have a comparative advantage. This pattern of specialization maximizes world production and hence maximizes average world living standards (as measured by the world's per capita GDP).

However, while freer trade generates real income gains for countries as a whole, it does not necessarily improve the income for *every individual* in the country. For example, reducing an existing tariff on the import of steel will be beneficial for the many consumers of steel who can now purchase the product at a lower price. At the same time, however, the lower tariff will reduce income for those domestic firms and workers involved in the production of steel. That the total gains to the first group are much larger than the losses to the second group in no way avoids the fact that some people get harmed by freer trade.

If we ask whether it is *possible* for free trade to improve everyone's living standards, the answer is yes because the larger total income that free trade generates could, at least in principle, be divided up in such a way that every individual is better off. If we ask whether free trade always does so in practice, however, the answer is, not necessarily.

> Free trade makes the country as a whole better off, even though it may not make every individual in the country better off.

In today's global economy, a country's products must stand up to international competition if they are to survive. Over even as short a period as a few years, firms that do not develop new products and new production methods fall seriously behind their foreign competitors. If one country protects its domestic firms by imposing a tariff, those firms are likely to become complacent about the need to adopt new technologies, and over time they will become less competitive in international markets. As the technology gap between domestic and foreign firms widens, the tariff wall will provide less and less protection. Eventually, the domestic firms will succumb to foreign competition. Meanwhile, domestic living standards will fall relative to foreign ones.

Given that any country can be better off by specializing in those goods in which it has a comparative advantage, one might wonder why most countries of the world continue in some way to restrict the flow of trade. Why do tariffs and other barriers to trade continue to exist two centuries after Adam Smith and David Ricardo argued the case for free trade? Is there a valid case for some protection?

The Case for Protection

protection Any government policy that interferes with free trade in order to protect domestic firms and workers from foreign competition.

A country engages in trade **protection** whenever it uses policies that restrict the flow of trade in a way that favours domestic firms over their foreign competitors. There are several valid arguments for protection, including

- promoting diversification
- protecting specific groups
- improving the terms of trade
- protecting infant industries
- earning economic profits in foreign markets

We will discuss each of these arguments briefly. Note that the first two arguments generally involve achieving some worthy objective at the cost of a *reduction* in national income. The last three arguments are reasons for protection as a means of *increasing* a country's national income.

Promoting Diversification   For a very small country, specializing in the production of only a few products—though dictated by comparative advantage—might involve risks that the country does not want to take. One such risk is that technological advances may render its basic product obsolete. Another risk, especially for countries specialized in producing a small range of agricultural products, is that swings in world prices lead to large swings in national income. By using protectionist policies, the government can encourage the creation of some domestic industries that may otherwise not exist. The cost is the loss of national income associated with devoting resources to production in industries in which there is no domestic comparative advantage. The benefit is that overall national income and employment become less volatile.

Countries whose economies are based on the production of only a few goods face risks from fluctuations in world prices. For this reason, protection to promote diversification may be viewed as desirable.

Tom Uhlman / Alamy Stock Photo

Protecting Specific Groups   Although specialization according to comparative advantage will maximize *average* per capita GDP, some specific groups may have higher incomes under protection than under free trade.

Of particular interest in Canada and the United States has been the effect that greater international trade has on the incomes of unskilled workers.

Consider the ratio of skilled workers to unskilled workers. There are plenty of both types throughout the world. Compared with much of the rest of the world, however, Canada has more skilled and fewer unskilled people. When trade is expanded because of a reduction in tariffs, Canada will tend to export goods made by its abundant skilled workers and import goods made by unskilled workers. (This is the basic prediction of the *factor endowment theory* of comparative advantage that we discussed in Chapter 32.) Because Canada is now exporting more goods made by skilled labour, the domestic demand for such labour rises. Because Canada is now importing more goods made by unskilled labour, the domestic demand for such labour falls. This specialization according to comparative advantage raises average Canadian living standards, but it will also tend to raise the wages and employment prospects of skilled Canadian workers relative to those of unskilled Canadian workers.

If increasing trade has these effects, then reducing trade by erecting protectionist trade barriers can have the opposite effects. Protectionist policies may raise the incomes of unskilled Canadian workers, giving them a larger share of a smaller total GDP. The conclusion is that trade restrictions can improve the earnings of one group whenever the restrictions increase the demand for that group's services. This benefit for one group is achieved, however, at the expense of a reduction in *overall* national income and hence the country's average living standards.

> Social and distributional concerns may lead to the rational adoption of protectionist policies. But the cost of such protection is a reduction in the country's *average* living standards.

Improving the Terms of Trade   Tariffs can be used to change the terms of trade in favour of a country that makes up a large fraction of the world demand for some product that it imports. By restricting its demand for that product through a tariff, it can force down the price that foreign exporters receive for that product. The price paid by domestic consumers will probably rise but as long as the increase is less than the tariff, foreign suppliers will receive less per unit. For example, the current 25 percent Chinese tariff on the import of U.S. automobiles might raise the price paid by Chinese consumers by 15 percent and lower the price received by American suppliers by 10 percent (the difference between the two prices being received by the Chinese government). This reduction in the price received by the U.S. suppliers is a terms-of-trade improvement for China (and a terms-of-trade deterioration for the United States).

Note that not all countries can improve their terms of trade by levying tariffs on imported goods. A *necessary* condition is that the importing country has *market power*—in other words, that its imports represent a large proportion of total world demand for the good in question, so that its restrictive trade policies lead to a decline in the world price of its imports. Large countries like China and the United States have market power in many products. Small countries, like Canada, do not. For small countries, therefore, tariffs cannot improve their terms of trade.

> Large countries can sometimes improve their terms of trade (and thus increase their national income) by levying tariffs on some imported goods; small countries cannot.

infant industry argument The argument that new domestic industries with potential for economies of scale or learning by doing need to be protected from competition from established, low-cost foreign producers so that they can grow large enough to achieve costs as low as those of foreign producers.

Protecting Infant Industries   The oldest valid arguments for protection as a means of raising living standards concern economies of scale or learning by doing. It is usually called the **infant industry argument**. An infant industry is nothing more than a new, small industry. If such an industry has large economies of scale or the scope for learning by doing, costs will be high when the industry is small but will fall as the industry grows. In such industries, the country that first enters the field has a tremendous advantage. A developing country may find that in the early stages of development, its industries are unable to compete with established foreign rivals. A trade restriction may protect these industries from foreign competition while they "grow up." When they are large enough, they will be able to produce as cheaply as their larger foreign rivals and thus be able to compete without protection.

Most of the now industrialized countries developed their industries initially under quite heavy tariff protection. (In Canada's case, the National Policy of 1876 established a high tariff wall behind which many Canadian industries developed and thrived for many years.) Once the industrial sector was well developed, these countries reduced their levels of protection, thus moving a long way toward free trade. Electronics in Taiwan, automobiles in Japan, commercial aircraft in Europe (specifically the consortium of European governments that created Airbus), and shipbuilding in South Korea are all examples in which protection of infant industries was successful. In each case, the national industry, protected by its home government, developed into a major player in the global marketplace.

The Chinese economy, although now the world's largest as measured by real GDP, is still much less developed than those of Canada, the United States, and Western Europe. China has tariffs that protect many of its industries and help them compete in global markets. With the ongoing rapid development of the Chinese economy, many economists wonder when this trade protection will be reduced, at which point Chinese firms will be forced to compete on a "level playing field" with firms from other countries.

One practical problem with the infant industry argument for protection is that some infants "never grow up." Once the young firm gets used to operating in a protected environment, it may resist having that protection disappear, even though all economies of scale may have been achieved. This problem is as much political as it is economic. Political leaders must therefore be careful before offering protection to infant industries because they must recognize the political difficulties involved in removing that protection in the future. The countries that were most successful in having their protected industries eventually grow up and succeed in fierce international competition were those, such as Taiwan and South Korea, that ruthlessly withdrew support from unsuccessful infants within a specified time period.

Earning Economic Profits in Foreign Markets   Another argument for protectionist policies is to help create an advantage in producing or marketing some product that is expected to generate economic profits through its sales to foreign consumers. If protection of the domestic market, which might include subsidizing domestic firms, can increase the chance that one of the domestic firms will become established and thus earn high profits, the protection may pay off. The economic profits earned in foreign markets may exceed the cost to domestic taxpayers of the protection. This is the general idea of *strategic trade policy*.

Opponents of strategic trade policy argue that it is nothing more than a modern version of age-old and faulty justifications for tariff protection. Once all countries try to be strategic, they will all waste vast sums trying to break into industries in which there is no room for most of them. Domestic consumers would benefit most, they say, if their governments let *other* countries engage in this game. Consumers could then buy the cheap, subsidized foreign products and export traditional non-subsidized products in return. The opponents of strategic trade policy also argue that democratic governments that enter the game of picking and backing winners are likely to make more bad choices than good ones. One bad choice, with all of its massive development costs written off, would require that many good choices also be made in order to make the equivalent in profits that would allow taxpayers to break even overall.

A long-simmering dispute between Canada and Brazil illustrates how strategic trade policy is often difficult to distinguish from pure protection. The world's two major producers of regional jets are Bombardier, based in Montreal, and Embraer SA, based in Brazil. For several years, each company has accused its competitor's government of using illegal subsidies to help the domestic company sell jets in world markets. Brazil's Pro-Ex program provides Embraer's customers with low-interest loans with which to purchase Embraer's jets. Export Development Canada (EDC) provides similar loans to Bombardier's customers.

For many years, Canada and Brazil have been in a trade dispute centred on each country's alleged support of aerospace manufacturers. Canada's Bombardier and Brazil's Embraer both receive considerable financial assistance from their respective governments.

There have been several complaints brought to the World Trade Organization (WTO) by both the Canadian and Brazilian governments. In various rulings the WTO determined that both governments were using illegal subsidy programs to support their aerospace firms. Both countries, however, naturally view their respective programs as necessary responses to the other country's subsidization. Many economists believe that an agreement to eliminate both programs would be fair to both parties, while saving Brazilian and Canadian taxpayers a considerable amount of money. As of 2018, however, governments in both countries continue to support their respective aerospace firms and both sets of taxpayers continue to foot the bill.

A country can potentially increase its national income by protecting infant industries and by subsidizing "strategic" firms. Unless carefully applied, however, such policies can end up being redistributions from consumers and taxpayers to domestic firms, without any benefit to overall living standards.

Invalid Arguments for Protection

We have seen that free trade is generally beneficial for a country overall even though it does not necessarily make every person better off. We have also seen that there are some situations in which there are valid arguments for restricting trade. Yet public discussion about free trade is laden with several invalid arguments, which often cloud the debate. Here we review a few arguments that are frequently heard in public debates concerning international trade.

Keep the Money at Home This argument says that if I buy a foreign good, I have the good and the foreigner has the money, whereas if I buy the same good locally, I have the good and our country has the money, too. This argument is based on a common misconception. It assumes that domestic money actually goes abroad physically when imports are purchased and that trade flows only in one direction. But when Canadian importers purchase Japanese goods, they do not send dollars abroad. They (or their financial agents) buy Japanese yen and use them to pay the Japanese manufacturers. They purchase the yen on the foreign-exchange market by giving up dollars to someone who wants to use them for expenditure in Canada. Even if the money did go abroad physically—that is, if a Japanese firm accepted a bunch of Canadian $100 bills—it would be because that firm (or someone to whom it could sell the dollars) wanted them to spend in the only country where they are legal tender—Canada.

Canadian currency ultimately does no one any good except as purchasing power in Canada. Actually, it would be miraculous if we could send nothing more than Canadian money to other countries in return for real goods. After all, the Bank of Canada has the power to create as much new Canadian money as it wants (at almost zero direct cost) and so this transaction would effectively mean Canada getting foreign products for free. But the reality is different: it is only because Canadian money can buy Canadian products and Canadian assets that others want it.

Protect Against Low-Wage Foreign Labour   This argument says that the products of low-wage countries will drive Canadian products from the market, and the high Canadian standard of living will be dragged down to that of its poorer trading partners. For example, if Canada imports cotton shirts from Bangladesh, higher-cost Canadian textile firms may go out of business and Canadian workers may be laid off. This argument suggests that Canada is worse off *overall* by trading with Bangladesh. Is this really true?

As a prelude to considering this argument, think what the argument would imply if taken out of the context of countries and applied instead to individuals, where the same principles govern the gains from trade. Is it impossible for a rich person to gain by trading with a poor person? Would Bill Gates and Elon Musk really be better off if they did all their own gardening, cooking and cleaning? No one believes that a rich person gains nothing by trading with those who are less rich.

Why, then, must a rich group of people lose when they trade with a poor group? "Well," some may say, "the poor group will price its goods too cheaply." Consumers in rich countries gain, however, when they can buy the same goods at a lower price. If Vietnamese, Mexican, or Indian workers earn low wages and the goods they produce are sold at low prices, all Canadian consumers will gain by obtaining imports at a low cost in terms of the goods that must be exported in return. The cheaper our imports are, the better off we are in terms of the goods and services available for domestic consumption.

As we said earlier in this chapter, *some* Canadians may be better off if Canada places high tariffs on the import of goods from Mexico or India or other developing nations. In particular, if the goods produced in these countries compete with goods made by unskilled Canadian workers, then those unskilled workers will be better off if a Canadian tariff protects their firms and thus their jobs. But Canadian income overall—that is, average per capita real income—will be higher when there is free trade.

Exports Are Good; Imports Are Bad   Exports create domestic income; imports create income for foreigners. Surely, then, it is desirable to encourage exports by subsidizing them and to discourage imports by taxing them. This is an appealing argument, but it is incorrect.

Exports raise GDP by adding to the value of domestic output and income, but they do not add to the value of domestic consumption. The standard of living in a country depends on the level of consumption, not on the level of income. In other words, income is not of much use except that it provides the means for consumption.

If exports really were "good" and imports really were "bad," then a fully employed economy that managed to increase exports without a corresponding increase in imports ought to be better off. Such a change, however, would result in a reduction in current standards of living because when more goods are sent abroad but no more are brought in from abroad, the total goods available for domestic consumption must fall.

The living standards of a country depend on the goods and services consumed in that country. If we could have imports for "free," meaning without having to provide exports in return, our consumption and living standards could be vastly increased. But no country will send us their products for free. In reality, the importance of exports is that they provide the resources required to purchase imports, either now or in the future.

Create Domestic Jobs   It is sometimes said that an economy with substantial unemployment, such as Canada during and immediately after the 2009 recession, provides an exception to the case for freer trade. Suppose tariffs or import quotas reduce the imports of Japanese cars, Indian textiles, Chinese electronics, and Polish sausages. Surely, the argument goes, these polices will create more employment in Canadian industries producing similar products. This may be true but it will also *reduce* employment in other industries.

The Japanese, Indians, Chinese, and Poles can buy products from Canada only if they earn Canadian dollars by selling their domestically produced goods and services to Canada (or by borrowing dollars from Canada).[1] The decline in their sales of cars, textiles, electronics, and sausages will decrease their purchases of Canadian lumber, software, banking services, and holidays. Jobs will be lost in Canadian export industries and gained in industries that formerly faced competition from imports. The major long-term effect is that the same amount of total employment in Canada will merely be redistributed among industries. In the process, average living standards will be reduced because employment expands in inefficient import-competing industries and contracts in efficient exporting industries.

The relationship between tariffs and employment was sharply illustrated in 2018 when U.S. President Trump imposed high tariffs on the import of foreign-produced steel and aluminum. Though firms and workers in these American industries favoured this policy, it was soon pointed out that far more jobs were at risk in the many U.S. industries that relied on low-priced steel and aluminum as vital inputs in the production of finished products. The tariffs would raise costs in these industries and place them at a competitive disadvantage with foreign firms who could purchase steel and aluminum more cheaply in other countries and then sell their finished products into the United States at low prices. After these concerns were raised, the U.S. president scaled back some of the new tariffs, applying them only to some countries.

A country that imposes tariffs in an attempt to create domestic jobs risks starting a "tariff war" with its trading partners. Such a trade war can easily leave every country worse off, as world output (and thus income) falls significantly. An income-reducing trade war followed the onset of the Great Depression in 1929 as many countries increased tariffs to protect their domestic industries in an attempt to stimulate domestic

---

[1] They can also get dollars by selling to other countries and then using their currencies to buy Canadian dollars. But this intermediate step only complicates the transaction; it does not change its fundamental nature. Other countries must have earned the dollars by selling goods to Canada or borrowing from Canada.

LESSONS FROM HISTORY 33-1

Donald Trump, Tariff Wars, and Stark Lessons from the Great Depression

In the first two years of Donald Trump's presidency, the United States—long an enthusiastic promoter of freer global trade—adopted an aggressively protectionist approach to trade policy. By imposing steep tariffs on a range of imported products, the United States appeared to be willing to engage in a "tariff war," ignoring important lessons from history. What are those lessons?

In 1929, at the start of the Great Depression, governments in many countries responded to internal political pressures to protect domestic jobs. In the United States, Congress passed the Smoot-Hawley Tariff Act in June 1930, legislation that raised tariffs on hundreds of different imported products. At the time, a petition against the legislation was signed by 1028 economists who argued that such tariffs would be costly for America and would initiate a "tariff war" between the United States and its trading partners, thereby worsening the economic situation.

In retrospect, the economists were clearly correct. Dozens of countries protested the increase in U.S. tariffs but then retaliated by increasing their own tariffs. Here in Canada, Liberal Prime Minister Mackenzie King raised tariffs on imported U.S. products and lowered them on imports from the rest of the British Empire. Confident that he would earn the public's support for his aggressive actions, he promptly called a federal election. But the Conservatives under R.B. Bennett argued that the Liberal actions were far too timid, and the voters apparently agreed. The Liberals were soundly defeated, Bennett became prime minister, and Canadian tariffs on U.S. products were raised even further.

Economists today agree that the widespread increase in tariffs in the 1930s contributed significantly to a reduction in global trade and made the economic situation worse. In January of 1929, before the onset of the Depression, the annual volume of world trade was $5.3 billion. Four years later, at the depth of the Depression, world trade had collapsed to $1.8 billion, a reduction of 66 percent. The net effect, instead of increasing employment in any country, was to shift jobs from efficient export-oriented industries to inefficient import-competing industries.

When the most recent worldwide recession began in the wake of the 2008 global financial crisis, world leaders were mindful of this important lesson from the Great Depression. When meeting in Washington, D.C., to coordinate their policy responses, the leaders of the world's largest developed and developing countries (the G20 group of countries) publicly committed to not raising any tariffs for at least one year.

Despite this commitment, however, protectionist measures soon emerged. In the United States, the fiscal stimulus package passed by Congress included a "buy American" clause prohibiting any funds from the package being spent on imported construction materials. Similar kinds of protection were built in to the fiscal stimulus packages in China and some European countries. Canada and other major trading nations were understandably concerned by these actions and soon began threatening their own retaliatory measures. The Canadian government went to great lengths to argue that U.S. trade protection would not only hurt Canada but would also hurt the United States by raising prices

production and employment. Most economists agree that this trade war made the Great Depression worse than it otherwise would have been. *Lessons From History 33-1* discusses how protectionist policies can lead to tariff wars and worsen overall income in all countries. This history should be kept in mind as we see the United States imposing new tariffs on imports from many countries.

▍33.2 Methods of Protection

We now go on to explore the effects of two specific protectionist policies. Both cause the price of the imported good to rise and the quantity demanded by domestic consumers to fall. They differ, however, in how they achieve these results.

for American consumers, thus making economic recovery more difficult.

Over the next few years, protectionist sentiment gradually declined and the merits of freer trade appeared to be more widely accepted. But things changed dramatically in the United States with the election of President Donald Trump in 2016.

Donald Trump's election campaign was full of both protectionist and nationalist rhetoric, and within his first term in office much of this rhetoric was reflected in U.S. trade policy. In 2017 President Trump threatened to repeal the North American Free Trade Agreement (NAFTA) and forced a major renegotiation of the Agreement with Canada and Mexico. In 2018, the United States imposed new tariffs on imported steel and aluminum, a policy seen by many to be primarily aimed at low-cost Chinese producers. This action led China to immediately impose tariffs on a range of imported U.S. products. In return, the United States imposed more tariffs on other Chinese imports. A tariff war had begun between the world's two largest economies.

Other countries, including Canada, watched these developments unfold with alarm, as the stark lessons from the Great Depression were recalled. Canada stands to gain much from an open global trading system; we stand to lose a great deal in a world with high protection and less trade. As this book went to press in the fall of 2018, there remained considerable uncertainty regarding the prospects for freer global trade.

Canadian Prime Ministers Bennett (left) and Mackenzie King (right) both learned in the 1930s that protectionist policies often make better politics than economics. U.S. President Trump in 2017–2018 appeared to think that protectionism was good politics and good economics; most economists and policymakers disagreed.

Tariffs

A tariff, also called an *import duty*, is a tax on imported goods. For example, consider a Canadian firm that wants to import cotton T-shirts from India at $5 per shirt. If the Canadian government levies a 20 percent tariff on imported cotton shirts, the Canadian firm pays $5 to the Indian exporter *plus* $1 (20 percent of $5) in import duties to the Canada Revenue Agency. The immediate effect of a tariff is therefore to increase the domestic firm's cost to $6 per T-shirt. This tariff has important implications for domestic consumers as well as domestic producers. The effect of a tariff in a competitive industry is shown in Figure 33-1.

The initial effect of the tariff is to raise the domestic price of the imported product above its world price by the amount of the tariff. Imports fall. The price received on

FIGURE 33-1 The Deadweight Loss of a Tariff

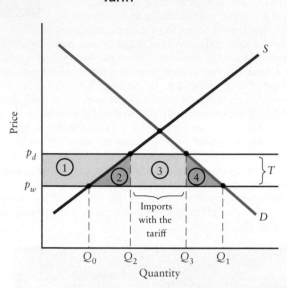

A tariff imposes a deadweight loss for the importing country. Before the tariff, the price in the domestic economy is the world price, p_w. Imports are Q_0Q_1. With a tariff of $\$T$ per unit, the domestic price rises to p_d. Domestic consumption falls to Q_3, and consumer surplus falls by areas ① + ② + ③ + ④. Domestic production rises to Q_2 and producer surplus increases by area ①. Imports fall to Q_2Q_3, and the government collects tariff revenue equal to area ③. The sum of areas ② and ④ represents the deadweight loss of the tariff.

domestically produced units rises, as does the quantity produced domestically. On both counts, domestic producers earn more. However, the cost of producing the extra production at home exceeds the price at which it could be purchased on the world market. Thus, the benefit to domestic producers comes at the expense of domestic consumers. Indeed, domestic consumers lose on two counts: First, they consume less of the product because its price rises, and second, they pay a higher price for the amount they do consume. This extra spending ends up in two places: The extra that is paid on all units produced at home goes to domestic producers, and the extra that is paid on units still imported goes to the government as tariff revenue.

The overall loss to the domestic economy from levying a tariff is best seen in terms of the changes in consumer and producer surplus. Before the tariff, consumer surplus was equal to the entire area below the demand curve and above the price line at p_w.

After the tariff, the price increase leads to less consumption and less consumer surplus. The loss of consumer surplus is the sum of the areas ①, ②, ③, and ④ in Figure 33-1. As domestic producers respond to the higher domestic price by increasing their production and sales, they earn more producer surplus, equal to area ①. Finally, the taxpayers gain the tariff revenue equal to area ③. This is simply a redistribution of surplus away from consumers toward taxpayers. In summary:

Loss of consumer surplus	= ① + ② + ③ + ④
Gain of producer surplus	= ①
Gain of tariff revenue	= ③
Net loss in surplus	= ② + ④

The overall effect of the tariff is therefore to create a deadweight loss to the domestic economy equal to areas ② plus ④. Domestic consumers are worse off, while domestic firms and taxpayers are better off. But the net effect is a loss of surplus for the economy as a whole. This is the overall cost of levying a tariff.

A tariff imposes costs on domestic consumers, generates benefits for domestic producers, and generates revenue for the government. But the overall net effect is negative; a tariff generates a deadweight loss for the economy.

Note that a domestic tariff also creates a loss for the countries from which we import. For example, since a Canadian tariff on imported machinery leads to a reduction in the volume of these imports, there is less Canadian demand for machinery from the exporting countries. This reduction in demand generates a loss in income for foreign producers and their workers. Tariffs therefore create losses for both importing and exporting countries.

Import Quotas

The second type of protectionist policy directly restricts the quantity of imports of a specific product. A common example is the **import quota**, by which the importing country sets a maximum quantity of some product that may be imported each year.

Figure 33-2 shows that a quantity restriction and a tariff have similar effects on domestic consumers and producers—they both raise domestic prices, increase domestic production, and reduce domestic consumption. But a direct quantity restriction is actually *worse* than a tariff for the importing country because the effect of the quantity restriction is to raise the price received by the foreign suppliers of the good. In contrast, a tariff leaves the foreign suppliers' price unchanged and instead generates tariff revenue for the government of the importing country.

> **Import quotas impose larger deadweight losses on the importing country than do tariffs that lead to the same level of imports.**

Tariffs Versus Quotas: An Application

The dispute that has raged for many years between Canada and the United States over the exports of Canadian softwood lumber (spruce, pine, fir, cedar) illustrates an important distinction between tariffs and quotas. Over the years, the United States has protected its softwood lumber industry in two different ways:

- by imposing tariffs on U.S. imports of Canadian softwood lumber
- by pressuring Canadian governments to place quotas on Canadian exports to the United States

Analysis of Figures 33-1 and 33-2 reveals that the choice between tariffs and quotas matters greatly for Canadian lumber producers.

In the case of a U.S. tariff on imported Canadian softwood lumber, Figure 33-1 illustrates the U.S. market. An import tariff raises the domestic price for U.S. lumber users and also increases the profits of U.S. lumber producers. Canadian lumber

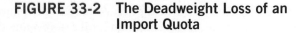

FIGURE 33-2   The Deadweight Loss of an Import Quota

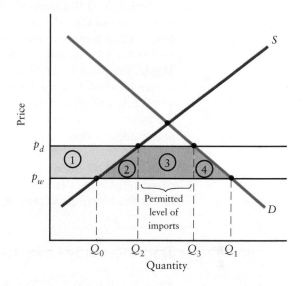

An import quota drives up the domestic price and imposes a deadweight loss on the importing country. With free trade, the domestic price is the world price, p_w. Imports are Q_0Q_1. If imports are restricted to only Q_2Q_3, the domestic price must rise to the point where the restricted level of imports just satisfies the domestic excess demand—this occurs only at P_d. The rise in price and reduction in consumption reduces consumer surplus by areas ① + ② + ③ + ④. Domestic producers increase their output as the domestic price rises, and producer surplus increases by area ①. Area ③ does not accrue to the domestic economy; instead this area represents extra producer surplus for the foreign firms that export their product to this country. The net effect of the quota is a deadweight loss for the importing country of areas ② + ③ + ④. Import quotas are therefore worse than tariffs for the importing country.

import quota A restriction on the quantity of a foreign product that may be imported in a given time period.

producers are harmed because there is less demand for their product at the unchanged world price. Area ③ in the figure represents U.S. tariff revenue collected on the imports of Canadian lumber—revenue that accrues to the United States government.

Figure 33-2 illustrates the U.S. market for softwood lumber when a quota is placed on the level of Canadian exports (U.S. imports). As with the tariff, the restricted supply of Canadian lumber to the U.S. market drives up the price to U.S. users and also raises profits for U.S. lumber producers. But with a quota there is an important difference: The higher price in the U.S. market is received by the Canadian lumber producers, as shown by area ③ in the figure.

While a tariff and quota may lead to the same reduced volume of trade in lumber, the tariff permits some surplus to be captured by the importing country, whereas the quota allows some surplus to be captured by the exporting country (area ③ in both cases). In the U.S.–Canadian softwood lumber dispute, both tariffs and quotas have been used. And while free trade in lumber would be better than any protection for both countries, Canada has an interest in imposing quotas on Canadian lumber exporters rather than having the same export reduction accomplished by a U.S. tariff.

Trade-Remedy Laws and Non-Tariff Barriers

As tariffs in many countries were lowered over the years since the Second World War, countries that wanted to protect domestic industries began using, and often abusing, a series of trade restrictions that came to be known as *non-tariff barriers* (NTBs). The original purpose of some of these barriers was to remedy certain legitimate problems that arise in international trade and, for this reason, they are often called *trade-remedy laws*. All too often, however, such laws are misused and over time become powerful means of simple protection.

Dumping   Selling a product in a foreign country at a lower price than in the domestic market is known as **dumping**. For example, if U.S.-made cars were sold for less in Canada than in the United States, the U.S. automobile firms would be said to be *dumping*. Dumping is a form of price discrimination studied in the theory of firms with price-setting power (see Chapter 10).

dumping The practice of selling a product at a lower price in the export market than in the domestic market for reasons unrelated to differences in costs of servicing the two markets.

> Dumping, if it lasts indefinitely, can be a gift to the receiving country. Its consumers get goods from abroad at lower prices than they otherwise would.

Despite the benefits to consumers from low-priced imports, most governments use anti-dumping duties designed to protect their own industries from what is viewed as unfair foreign pricing. Unfortunately, however, antidumping laws have been evolving over the past three decades in ways that allow antidumping duties to become barriers to trade and competition rather than to provide redress for genuinely unfair trading practices.

Several features of the antidumping system that is now in place in many countries make it highly protectionist. First, any price discrimination between national markets is classified as dumping and is subject to penalties. Thus, prices in the producer's domestic market become, in effect, minimum prices below which no sales can be made in foreign markets, whatever the nature of demand in the domestic and foreign markets. Second, many countries' laws calculate the "margin of dumping" as the difference between the price that is charged in that country's market and the foreign producer's average cost. Thus, when there is a global slump in some industry so that the profit-maximizing price for all producers is below average cost, foreign producers can be convicted of dumping. This gives domestic producers enormous protection whenever the market price falls temporarily below average cost. Third, law in the United States (but not in all other countries) places the onus of proof on the accused. Facing a charge of dumping, a foreign producer must prove that the charge is unfounded. Fourth, U.S. antidumping duties are imposed with no time limit, so they often persist long after foreign firms have altered the prices that gave rise to them.

Antidumping laws were first designed to permit countries to respond to predatory pricing by foreign firms. More recently, they have been used to protect domestic firms against any foreign competition.

Countervailing Duties A **countervailing duty** is a tariff imposed by one country designed to offset the effects of specific subsidies provided by foreign governments to their exporting firms. For example, if the German government provided subsidies to its firms that produce and export machine tools, the Canadian government might respond by imposing a countervailing duty—a tariff—on the imports of German machine tools designed to "level the playing field" between German and Canadian firms in that industry. Countervailing duties, which are commonly used by the U.S. government but much less so elsewhere, provide another case in which a trade-remedy law can become a covert method of protection.

countervailing duty A tariff imposed by one country designed to offset the effects of specific subsidies provided by foreign governments.

There is no doubt that countervailing duties have sometimes been used to counteract the effects of foreign subsidies. Many governments complain, however, that countervailing duties are often used as thinly disguised protection. At the early stages of the development of countervailing duties, only subsidies whose prime effect was to distort trade were possible objects of countervailing duties. Even then, however, the existence of equivalent domestic subsidies was not taken into account when decisions were made to put countervailing duties on subsidized imports. Thus, the United States levies some countervailing duties against foreign goods even though the foreign subsidy is less than the domestic (U.S.) subsidy in the same industry. This does not create a level playing field.

Over time, the type of subsidy that is subject to countervailing duties has evolved until almost any government program that affects industry now risks becoming the object of a countervailing duty. Because all governments, including most U.S. state governments, have programs that provide direct or indirect assistance to industry, the potential for the use of countervailing duties as thinly disguised trade barriers is enormous.

Countervailing duties can be used to offset the effects of foreign export subsidies, but often they are nothing more than thinly disguised protection.

Softwood lumber (spruce, pine, and fir) is used extensively in North America for the framing of houses and small buildings. For many years, the United States levied countervailing duties on Canadian softwood lumber exports, alleging that Canadian provinces unfairly subsidized production.

Discussions in Canada about countervailing duties are often related to the long-standing dispute regarding Canada's softwood lumber exports to the United States. The U.S. government's frequent claim is that Canadian provincial

Christina Richards/Shutterstock

governments provide a subsidy to domestic lumber producers by charging low *stumpage fees*—the fees paid by the companies to cut trees on Crown land. For many years the United States imposed a 27 percent tariff on imports of Canadian lumber; it was later replaced by export restrictions imposed by the Canadian government. But this issue shows no signs of being resolved. The United States continues to argue that Canadian provincial governments provide subsidies through low stumpage fees; Canadian governments continue to argue that low Canadian costs reflect our comparative advantage in softwood lumber.

33.3 Current Trade Policy

In the remainder of the chapter, we discuss trade policy in practice. We start with the many international agreements that govern current trade policies and then look in a little more detail at the NAFTA.

Before 1947, in the absence of any international agreement, any country was free to impose tariffs on its imports. However, when one country increased its tariffs, the action often triggered retaliatory actions by its trading partners. During the Great Depression in the 1930s, widespread increases in protection occurred as many countries sought to raise their employment and output by raising its tariffs. The end result was lowered efficiency, less trade, and a deeper economic decline. Since the end of the Second World War, much effort has been devoted to reducing tariff barriers, both on a multilateral and on a regional basis.

The GATT and the WTO

One of the most notable achievements of the post–Second World War era was the creation in 1947 of the General Agreement on Tariffs and Trade (GATT). The principle of the GATT was that each member country agreed not to make unilateral tariff increases. This prevented the outbreak of "tariff wars" in which countries raised tariffs to protect particular domestic industries and to retaliate against other countries' tariff increases. The GATT has since been replaced by the World Trade Organization (WTO), which continues the work of the GATT.

Through various "rounds" of negotiations under the auspices of the GATT and the WTO, the average level of tariffs has declined considerably since 1947. In addition to the tariff reductions, an important success of the WTO negotiations has been the creation of a formal dispute-settlement mechanism. This mechanism allows countries to take cases of alleged trade violations—such as illegal subsidies or tariffs—to the WTO for a formal ruling, and obliges member countries to follow the ruling. A notable failure of the WTO process has been the inability to significantly liberalize trade in agricultural products, an industry that still receives massive subsidies and other government support in many developed and developing countries.

There are currently 164 countries that are members of the WTO; 23 others are "observers" to the process.

Regional Trade Agreements

Regional agreements seek to liberalize trade over a much smaller group of countries than the entire WTO membership. Three standard forms of regional trade-liberalizing agreements are *free trade areas, customs unions*, and *common markets*.

A **free trade area (FTA)** is the least comprehensive of the three. It allows for tariff-free trade among the member countries, but it leaves each member free to establish its own trade policy with respect to other countries. As a result, members are required to maintain customs points at their common borders to make sure that imports into the free trade area do not all enter through the member that is levying the lowest tariff on each item. They must also agree on *rules of origin* to establish when a good is made in a member country and hence is able to pass tariff-free across their borders, and when it is imported from outside the FTA and hence is subject to tariffs when it crosses borders within the FTA. The three countries in North America formed a free-trade area when they created the NAFTA in 1994.

In recent years, Canada has signed bilateral free-trade agreements with Israel, Chile, Costa Rica, Peru, Colombia, and Jordan, among others. It is currently in negotiations with Japan and India for free-trade agreements, and it is in exploratory discussions with China. In 2017, the Comprehensive Economic and Trade Agreement (CETA) between Canada and the European Union took effect. In 2018, Canada along with 10 other Pacific-Rim countries signed the Comprehensive and Progressive Agreement for Trans-Pacific partnership.

A **customs union** is a free trade area in which the member countries agree to establish a common trade policy with the rest of the world. Because they have a common trade policy, the members need neither customs controls on products moving among themselves nor rules of origin. Once a product has entered any member country it has met the common rules and regulations and paid the common tariff and so it may henceforth be treated the same as one that is produced within the union. An example of a customs union is Mercosur, an agreement linking Argentina, Brazil, Paraguay, and Uruguay.

A **common market** is a customs union that also has free movement of labour and capital among its members. The European Union is by far the largest example of a common market.

In the fall of 2016, the people of the United Kingdom voted in a national referendum to leave the European Union. The U.K.'s decision to exit from the EU—now dubbed "Brexit" by many observers—created the need for a series of complex negotiations between the U.K. and the countries of the European Union. These negotiations mostly related to what extent the U.K. and EU will continue to share an open trading relationship once the formal ties of EU membership are severed. Since no country has ever before exited from the EU, much uncertainty was naturally created by the Brexit decision.

free trade area (FTA) An agreement among two or more countries to abolish tariffs on trade among themselves while each remains free to set its own tariffs against other countries.

customs union A group of countries that agree to have free trade among themselves and a common set of barriers against imports from the rest of the world.

common market A customs union with the added provision that labour and capital can move freely among the members.

Trade Creation and Trade Diversion

A major effect of regional trade liberalization is to alter the pattern of production and trade as countries reallocate their resources toward the production of goods in which they have a comparative advantage. Economists divide the effects on trade into two categories: *trade creation* and *trade diversion*.

Trade creation occurs when producers in one member country find that they can export products to another member country that previously were produced there because of tariff protection. For example, when the North American Free Trade Agreement (NAFTA) eliminated most cross-border tariffs among Mexico, Canada, and the United States, some U.S. firms found that they could undersell their Canadian competitors in some product lines, and some Canadian firms found that they could undersell

trade creation A consequence of reduced trade barriers among a set of countries whereby trade within the group is increased and trade with the rest of the world remains roughly constant.

their U.S. competitors in other product lines. As a result, specialization occurred, and new international trade developed among the three countries.

Trade creation represents efficient specialization according to comparative advantage.

trade diversion A consequence of reduced trade barriers among a set of countries whereby trade within the group replaces trade that used to take place with countries outside the group.

Trade diversion occurs when exporters in one member country *replace* more efficient foreign exporters as suppliers to another member country. For example, trade diversion occurs when U.S. firms find that they can undersell competitors from the rest of the world in the Canadian market, not because they are the cheapest source of supply, but because their tariff-free prices under NAFTA are lower than the tariff-burdened prices of imports from other countries. This effect is a gain to U.S. firms and Canadian consumers of the product. U.S. firms get new business and therefore they clearly gain. Canadian consumers buy the product at a lower, tariff-free price from the U.S. producer than they used to pay to the third-country producer (with a tariff), and so they are also better off. But Canada as a whole is worse off as a result of the trade diversion. Canada is now buying the product from a U.S. producer at a higher price with no tariff. Before the agreement, it was buying from a third-country producer at a lower price (and also collecting tariff revenue).

From the global perspective, trade diversion represents an inefficient use of resources.

The main argument *against* regional trade agreements is that the costs of trade diversion may outweigh the benefits of trade creation. While recognizing this possibility, many economists believe that regional agreements, especially among only a few countries, are much easier to negotiate than multilateral agreements through the WTO. In addition, regional agreements may represent effective *incremental* progress in what is a very lengthy process of achieving global free trade.

The North American Free Trade Agreement

The NAFTA dates from 1994 and is an extension of the 1989 Canada–U.S. Free Trade Agreement (FTA). It established a free trade area, as opposed to a customs union; each member country retains its own external trade policy, and rules of origin are needed to determine when a good is made within North America and thus allowed to move freely among the members.

National Treatment The fundamental principle that guides NAFTA is that of *national treatment*. The principle of national treatment is that individual countries are free to establish any laws they want, with the sole proviso that these laws must not discriminate on the basis of nationality. For example, Canada can choose to have stringent laws against releasing pollutants in waterways or against the emission of noxious gases into the atmosphere. The principle of national treatment requires that the Canadian government enforce these laws equally on all firms located in Canada, independent of their ownership or nationality. It is against NAFTA conditions to apply more stringent laws to foreign-owned firms than to domestic firms, or vice versa. Canada can also choose to impose strict product standards related to the chemical content of paint or the nutritional content of foods, but again the NAFTA condition requires that such laws be applied to products independent of where they are produced. For example, it would be against NAFTA rules to require a specific level of fuel efficiency on imported cars but not on those cars produced and sold in Canada.

The principle of national treatment allows each member country a maximum of policy independence while preventing national policies from being used as trade barriers. In the absence of national treatment, Canada could impose stringent environmental or product standards on the products of *foreign* firms only and thereby offer effective protection to its domestic firms who need only satisfy less stringent standards.

Dispute Settlement   A key provision of NAFTA is its dispute-settlement mechanism. Under it, the justifications required for levying antidumping and countervailing duties are subject to review by a panel of Canadians, Americans, and Mexicans. The international panel has the power to suspend any duties until it is satisfied that the domestic laws have been correctly and fairly applied.

The establishment of NAFTA's dispute-settlement mechanism was path breaking: for the first time in its history, the United States agreed to submit the administration of its domestic laws to *binding* scrutiny by an international panel that often contains a majority of foreigners.

Other Major Provisions   There are several other major provisions in NAFTA.

1. All tariffs on trade between Canada, the United States, and Mexico were eliminated as of 2010.

2. The principle of national treatment (described above) applies to foreign investment once it enters a country, but each country can screen foreign investment before it enters.

3. Some restrictions on trade and investment are not eliminated by the agreement. In Canada's case, the main examples are supply-managed agricultural products and cultural industries such as magazine and book publishing.

4. Trade in most non-agricultural service industries is liberalized and subject to the principle of national treatment.

5. A significant amount of government procurement is open to cross-border bidding, though a large part is still exempt from NAFTA.

Results   The Canada–U.S. FTA aroused a great debate in Canada. Indeed, the Canadian federal election of 1988 was fought almost entirely on the issue of free trade. Supporters looked for major increases in the security of existing trade from U.S. protectionist attacks and for a growth of new trade. Detractors predicted a flight of firms to the United States, the loss of many Canadian jobs, and even the demise of Canada's political independence.

Trade Creation.   By and large, however, both the Canada–U.S. FTA and the NAFTA agreements worked out just about as expected by their supporters. Industry restructured in the direction of greater export orientation in all three countries, and trade creation occurred. The flow of trade among the three countries increased markedly, but especially so between Canada and the United States. As the theory of trade predicts, specialization occurred in many areas, resulting in more U.S. imports of some product lines from Canada and more U.S. exports of other goods to Canada. In 1988, before the Canada–U.S. FTA took effect, Canada exported $85 billion in goods to the United States and imported $74 billion from the United States. By 2017, the value of Canada–U.S. trade had increased by five times—Canadian exports of goods to the United States had increased to $411 billion and imports from the United States had increased to $371 billion. (Note that these figures exclude trade in services; with services included, the increase in Canada–U.S. trade between 1988 and 2017 would be larger by about $200 billion in each direction.)[2]

Another aspect of the trade created by NAFTA relates to *global supply chains*, as we discussed in Chapter 32. As U.S., Mexican, and Canadian firms specialized in producing the goods in which they had a comparative advantage, the volume of *intra-industry trade* also increased. Nowhere was this more significant than in the auto and auto-parts sectors. Automobile assembly plants located in any of the three NAFTA countries now routinely receive parts from suppliers in the other two countries. In some cases, individual parts will cross the international border several times as they are combined with other parts to assemble large components (e.g., engines and transmissions) before the entire car is assembled in the final location.

Trade Diversion.   It is hard to say how much trade diversion there has been and will be in the future. The greatest potential for trade diversion is with Mexico, which competes in the Canadian and U.S. markets with a large number of products produced in other low-wage countries. Southeast Asian exporters to the United States and Canada have been worried that Mexico would capture some of their markets by virtue of having tariff-free access denied to their goods. Most estimates predict, however, that trade creation will dominate over trade diversion.

Transition and Surprises.   Most transitional difficulties were initially felt in each country's import-competing industries, just as theory predicts. Such an agreement as the NAFTA brings its advantages by encouraging a movement of resources out of protected but inefficient import-competing industries, which decline, and into efficient export-oriented industries, which expand because they have better access to the markets of other member countries. Southern Ontario and parts of Quebec had difficulties as some traditional exports fell and labour and capital were shifting to sectors where trade was expanding. By the late 1990s, however, Southern Ontario was booming again and its most profitable sectors were those that exported to the United States.

There were also some pleasant surprises resulting from free trade. Two Canadian industries that many economists expected to suffer from the FTA and the NAFTA were winemaking and textiles. Yet both of these industries prospered as Canadian firms improved quality, productivity, and benefited from increased access to the huge U.S. market. *Applying Economic Concepts 33-1* discusses the success of the Canadian wine industry after the tariffs on wine were eliminated.

---

[2] These data are in nominal dollars, which naturally grow over time along with real GDP and the price level. As a share of GDP, however, Canadian trade with the United States has also grown substantially. In 1988, exports and imports of goods (excluding services) with the United States were each roughly 13 percent of Canadian GDP; by 2017, they were each about 18 percent of Canadian GDP.

APPLYING ECONOMIC CONCEPTS 33-1

Canadian Wine: A Free-Trade Success Story

Before the Canada–U.S. FTA was signed in 1989, great fears were expressed over the fate of the Canadian wine industry, located mainly in Ontario and British Columbia. It was heavily tariff protected and, with a few notable exceptions, produced mainly cheap, low-quality products. Contrary to most people's expectations, rather than being decimated, the industry now produces a wide variety of high-quality products, some of which win international competitions.

The nature of the pre-FTA protection largely explains the dramatic turnaround of the Canadian wine industry once the FTA took effect. First, Canadian wine producers had been protected by high tariffs on imported wine but were at the same time required by law to produce wine by using only domestically grown grapes. The domestic grape growers, however, produced varieties of grapes not conducive to the production of high-quality wines, and with a captive domestic market, they had little incentive to change their behaviour. Thus, Canadian wine producers concentrated their efforts on "hiding" the attributes of poor-quality grapes rather than enhancing the attributes of high-quality grapes. The result was low-quality wine.

The second important aspect of the protection was that the high Canadian tariff was levied on a per unit rather than on an *ad valorem* basis. For example, the tariff was expressed as so many dollars per litre rather than as a specific percentage of the price. Charging a tariff by the litre gave most protection to the low-quality wines with low value per litre. The higher the per-litre value of the wine, the lower the percentage tariff protection. For example, a $5 per litre tariff would have the following

effects. A low-quality imported wine valued at $5 per litre would have its price raised to $10, a 100 percent increase in price, whereas a higher-quality imported wine valued at $25 per litre would have its price increased to $30, only a 20 percent increase in price.

Responding to these incentives, the Canadian industry concentrated on producing low-quality wines. The market for these wines was protected by the nearly prohibitive tariffs on competing low-quality imports and by the high prices charged for high-quality imports. In addition, protection was provided by many hidden charges that the various provincial governments' liquor monopolies levied in order to protect local producers.

When the tariff was removed under the FTA, the incentives were to move up-market, producing much more value per hectare of land. Fortunately, much of the Canadian wine-growing land in the Okanagan Valley in B.C. and the Niagara Peninsula in Ontario is well suited for growing the grapes required for good wines. Within a very few years, and with some government assistance to grape growers to make the transition from low-quality to high-quality grapes, Canadian wines were competing effectively with imported products in the medium-quality range. More recently, Canadian wineries have also started producing wines of higher quality.

The success of the wine industry is a good example of how tariffs can distort incentives and push an industry into a structure that makes it dependent on the tariff. Looking at the pre-FTA industry, very few people suspected that it would be able to survive, let alone become a world-class industry.

Dispute Settlement. Finally, the dispute-settlement mechanism seems to have worked well. A large number of disputes have arisen and have been referred to panels. Panel members have usually reacted as professionals rather than as nationals. Most cases have been decided on their merits; allegations that decisions were reached on national rather than professional grounds have been rare.

The Current Threat to NAFTA With the election in 2016 of U.S. President Donald Trump, it was only a matter of time before NAFTA became a target. Donald Trump's election campaign was full of nationalistic rhetoric extolling the costs to the United States from international trade, and from NAFTA in particular. In 2017, the United States forced a renegotiation of the Agreement with Canada and Mexico. Given the importance of trade with the United States, it is no surprise that this threat to NAFTA was taken very seriously by the governments of Canada and Mexico.

In Canada, the prime minister and provincial premiers displayed a united front on this issue. A coordinated effort was made to convince the U.S. administration, as well as members of Congress and state legislators, of the importance of Canada–U.S. trade and of the costs to both economies that would result from disruptions in these trade flows. The integrated nature of supply chains in several industries was also emphasized, and how any disruption in these supply chains would raise costs for firms and consumers in both countries. As of the fall of 2018, negotiations had finished on a new trade agreement—the United States, Mexico, and Canada Agreement (USMCA)—which is remarkably similar to NAFTA. This new agreement is planned to be ratified by the three countries' federal governments in 2019.

SUMMARY

33.1 Free Trade or Protection?   LO 1, 2

- The case for free trade is that world output of all products can be higher under free trade than when protectionism restricts regional specialization.
- Trade protection may be advocated to promote economic diversification or to provide protection for specific groups. The cost of such protection is lower average living standards.
- Protection can also be urged on the grounds that it may lead to higher living standards for the protectionist country than would a policy of free trade. Such a result might come

about by using market power to influence the terms of trade or by protecting infant industries until they become efficient enough to compete with foreign industries.
- Some invalid protectionist arguments are that (a) buying abroad sends our money abroad, while buying at home keeps our money at home; (b) our high-paid workers must be protected against the competition from low-paid foreign workers; (c) imports are to be discouraged because they reduce national income; and (d) trade protection increases domestic employment.

33.2 Methods of Protection   LO 3, 4

- A tariff raises the domestic price of the imported product and leads to a reduction in the level of imports. Domestic consumers lose and domestic producers gain. The overall effect of a tariff is a deadweight loss for the importing country.
- An import quota restricts the amount of imports and thus drives up the domestic price of the good. Domestic

consumers lose and domestic producers gain. The overall effect is a *larger* deadweight loss than with a tariff because, rather than the importing country collecting tariff revenue, foreign producers benefit from a higher price.
- Antidumping and countervailing duties, although providing legitimate restraints on unfair trading practices, are often used as serious barriers to trade.

33.3 Current Trade Policy   LO 5, 6

- The General Agreement on Tariffs and Trade (GATT), under which countries agreed to reduce trade barriers through multilateral negotiations and not to raise them unilaterally, has greatly reduced world tariffs since its inception in 1947.
- The World Trade Organization (WTO) was created in 1995 as the successor to GATT. It has 164 member countries and contains a formal dispute-settlement mechanism.
- Regional trade-liberalizing agreements, such as free trade areas and common markets, bring efficiency gains through trade creation and efficiency losses through trade diversion.

- The North American Free Trade Agreement (NAFTA) is the world's largest and most successful free trade area, and the European Union is the world's largest and most successful common market.
- NAFTA is based on the principle of "national treatment." This allows Canada, the United States, and Mexico to implement whatever social, economic, or environmental policies they choose providing that such policies treat foreign and domestic firms (and their products) equally.

KEY CONCEPTS

Free trade and protection
Tariffs and import quotas
Countervailing and antidumping
  duties
Word trade since 1945

The World Trade Organization (WTO)
Common markets, customs unions,
  and free-trade areas
Trade creation and trade diversion
Non-tariff barriers

The North American Free Trade
  Agreement (NAFTA)

STUDY EXERCISES

MyLab Economics Make the grade with MyLab Economics™: All Study Exercises can be found on MyLab
Economics™. You can practise them as often as you want, and many feature step-by-step
guided instructions to help you find the right answer.

FILL-IN-THE-BLANK

1 Fill in the blanks to make the following statements
correct.

  a. The case for free trade for an individual country is
     based on the gains from trade that are possible due
     to _____ advantage. Free trade allows each
     country to _____ in products for which they
     have a _____.

  b. Moving to freer trade can make the country as a
     whole better off, but some groups or individuals
     are likely to be made _____ off when trade
     protection is removed.

  c. A country may choose to protect certain industries
     from free trade, but the cost of such protection is
     usually _____ average living standards.

  d. The _____ argument provided the rationale
     for Canada's National Policy of 1876. A high tariff
     wall allowed many Canadian industries to develop
     where they may not have been able to compete
     otherwise.

  e. Advertisements that encourage us to "buy Can-
     adian" are promoting a(n) _____ argument for
     protection. Money spent on imported goods must
     ultimately be spent on _____ goods and servi-
     ces anyway.

  f. Invalid arguments for protection usually come
     from a misunderstanding of the gains from
     _____ or from the misbelief that protection
     can increase total _____.

2 Fill in the blanks to make the following statements
correct.

  a. A tariff imposed on the import of leather shoes
     will cause a(n) _____ in the domestic price.
     Total quantity of leather shoes sold in Canada will
     _____. Domestic (Canadian) production of
     leather shoes will _____ and the quantity of
     shoes imported will _____.

  b. The beneficiaries of the tariff described above are
     _____ because they receive a higher price for
     the same good and _____ because they receive
     tariff revenue. The parties that are clearly worse off
     are _____ because they now pay a higher price
     for the same good and _____ because they sell
     less in the Canadian market.

  c. The overall effect of a tariff on the importing coun-
     try is a(n) _____ in economic surplus. The
     tariff creates a(n) _____ loss for the economy.

  d. Suppose an import quota restricted the import of
     leather shoes into Canada to 20 000 pairs per year
     when the free trade imported amount was 40 000
     pairs. The domestic price will _____, total
     quantity sold in Canada will _____, and
     domestic production will _____.

  e. The beneficiaries of the quota described above are
     _____ and _____ because they both
     receive a higher price in the Canadian market. The
     party that is clearly worse off is _____ because
     they are now paying a higher price.

  f. The overall effect of an import quota on the
     importing country is a(n) _____ in economic
     surplus. The quota imposes a(n) _____ loss for
     the economy.

3 Fill in the blanks to make the following statements
correct.

  a. A regional trade agreement, such as NAFTA, or
     a common market, such as the European Union,
     allows for _____, whereby trade within the
     group of member countries is increased.

b. A regional trade agreement, such as NAFTA, or a common market, such as the European Union, also results in _____, whereby trade within the group of member countries replaces trade previously done with other _____.

c. The fundamental principle that guides the NAFTA is the principle of _____, which means that any member country can implement the policies of its choosing, as long as _____ and _____ firms are treated equally.

REVIEW

4 Canada produces steel domestically and also imports it from abroad. Assume that the world market for steel is competitive and that Canada is a small producer, unable to affect the world price. Since Canada imports steel, we know that in the absence of trade, the Canadian equilibrium price would exceed the world price.

a. Draw a diagram showing the Canadian market for steel, with imports at the world price.

b. Explain why the imposition of a tariff on imported steel will increase the price of steel in Canada.

c. Who benefits and who is harmed by such a tariff? Show these effects in your diagram.

5 The diagram below shows the Canadian market for leather shoes, which we assume to be competitive. The world price is p_w. If the Canadian government imposes a tariff of t dollars per unit, the domestic price then rises to $p_w + t$.

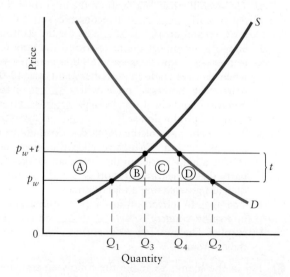

a. What quantity of leather shoes is imported before the tariff is imposed? After the tariff?

b. What is the effect of the tariff on the Canadian production of shoes? Which areas in the diagram show the increase in domestic producer surplus?

c. Which areas in the diagram show the reduction in domestic consumer surplus as a result of the higher Canadian price?

d. The Canadian government earns tariff revenue on the imported shoes. Which area in the diagram shows this tariff revenue?

e. What is the overall effect of this tariff on the economy? Which area in the diagram shows the deadweight loss?

6 Use the diagram from Study Exercise 5 to analyze the effects of imposing an import quota instead of a tariff to protect domestic shoe producers. Draw the diagram as in Study Exercise 5 and answer the following questions.

a. Explain why an import quota of Q_3Q_4 raises the domestic price to $p_w + t$.

b. With import quotas, the Canadian government earns no tariff revenue. Who gets this money now?

c. Is the import quota better or worse than the tariff for Canada as a whole? Explain.

7 Under pressure from the Canadian and U.S. governments in the early 1980s, Japanese automobile producers agreed to restrict their exports to the North American market. After the formal agreement ended, the Japanese producers decided unilaterally to continue restricting their exports. Carefully review Figure 33-2 and then answer the following questions.

a. Explain why the Japanese producers would voluntarily continue these restrictions.

b. Explain why an agreement to export only 100 000 cars to North America is better for the Japanese producers than a North American tariff that results in the same volume of Japanese exports.

c. Who is paying for these benefits to the Japanese producers?

8 Consider a mythical country called Forestland, which exports a large amount of lumber to a nearby country called Houseland. The lumber industry in Houseland has convinced its federal government that it is being harmed by the low prices being charged by the lumber producers in Forestland. You are an advisor to the government in Forestland. Explain which groups gain and which groups lose from each of the following policies.

a. Houseland imposes a tariff on lumber imports from Forestland.

b. Forestland imposes a tax on each unit of lumber exported to Houseland.

c. Forestland agrees to restrict its exports of lumber to Houseland.

d. Which policy is likely to garner the most political support in Houseland? In Forestland?

9 The United States recently threatened to impose duties on imported Canadian steel pipe. The allegation is that Canada is dumping its pipe into the U.S. market.

a. Who would benefit from such alleged dumping? Who would be harmed?

b. Who would benefit from the imposition of the antidumping duties? Who would be harmed?

c. Would the United States as a whole be made better off by the imposition of the duties? Explain.

10 In the past few years, trade between Canada and China has been growing quickly (though from a very low level). Many observers are concerned that Canadian firms are not able to compete with Chinese ones and that Canada may therefore be harmed by trading more with China. Comment on the following points in relation to the above worries:

a. "Chinese are the most expensive cheap labour I have ever encountered." Statement by the owner of a Canadian firm that is moving back to Canada from China.

b. The theory of the gains from trade says that a high-productivity, high-wage country can gain from trading with a low-wage, low-productivity country.

c. Technological change is rapidly reducing labour costs as a proportion of total costs in many products; in many industries that use high-tech production methods this proportion is already well below 20 percent.

❘ PROBLEMS

11 The diagram below shows the supply and demand curves for the Canadian domestic market for hockey sticks. Assume all hockey sticks are identical.

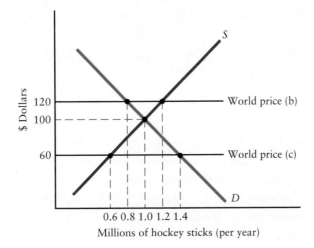

a. If Canada is a closed market and there is no international trade in hockey sticks, what is the price and quantity exchanged?

b. If Canada is an open market and the world price of hockey sticks is $120, describe the Canadian market. What is domestic production and consumption? Is Canada exporting or importing this product? How many per year?

c. If Canada is an open market and the world price of hockey sticks is $60, describe the Canadian market. What is domestic production and consumption? Is Canada exporting or importing this product? How many per year?

d. Suppose the world price is $60 and the Canadian government imposes a tariff of 50 percent on all imported hockey sticks. Describe the change in the Canadian market. What is the new price to Canadian consumers? What is domestic production and consumption? What is the new level of imports?

e. Describe which groups benefit and which groups lose due to the trade restriction described in part (d).

f. How much tariff revenue would the Canadian government collect with the 50 percent tariff in place?

12 The table below shows the prices *in Canada* of cotton towels produced in the United States, Canada, and Bangladesh. Assume that all cotton towels are identical.

Producing Country	Canadian Price ($) Without Tariff	Canadian Price ($) With 20% Tariff
Canada	4.75	4.75
United States	4.50	5.40
Bangladesh	4.00	4.80

a. Suppose Canada imposes a 20 percent tariff on imported towels from any country. Assuming that Canadians purchase only the lowest-price towels, from which country will Canada buy its towels?

b. Now suppose Canada eliminates tariffs on towels from all countries. Which towels will Canada now buy?

c. Canada and the United States now negotiate a free-trade agreement that eliminates all tariffs between the two countries, but Canada maintains the 20 percent tariff on other countries. Which towels now get imported into Canada?

d. Which of the situations described above is called trade creation and which is called trade diversion?

34

Exchange Rates and the Balance of Payments

CHAPTER OUTLINE

34.1 THE BALANCE OF PAYMENTS

34.2 THE FOREIGN-EXCHANGE MARKET

34.3 THE DETERMINATION OF EXCHANGE RATES

34.4 THREE POLICY ISSUES

LEARNING OBJECTIVES (LO)

After studying this chapter you will be able to

1 list the components of Canada's balance of payments and explain why the balance of payments must always balance.

2 describe the demand for and supply of foreign exchange.

3 discuss how exchange rates are determined.

4 describe the difference between fixed and flexible exchange rates.

5 discuss why a current account deficit is not necessarily undesirable.

6 understand the theory of purchasing power parity (PPP) and its limitations.

7 explain how flexible exchange rates can dampen the effects of external shocks.

CANADIANS import products from other countries and take vacations abroad. For both reasons, they care about the exchange rate between the Canadian dollar and foreign currencies. When the Canadian dollar depreciates, it costs more to purchase imported products, and foreign vacations become more expensive. On the other hand, Canadian firms that export their products to other countries usually benefit from a depreciation of the Canadian dollar because foreigners are induced to buy more Canadian products. In some way or another, most Canadians are affected by changes in the exchange rate.

In this chapter we examine what determines the exchange rate, why it changes, and the effects these changes have on the economy. The discussion will bring together material on three topics studied elsewhere in this book: the theory of supply and demand (Chapter 3), monetary policy and inflation (Chapters 28 and 29), and international trade (Chapter 32).

We begin by examining a country's balance of payments—the record of transactions in goods, services, and assets with the rest of the world. After introducing terms, we see why the balance of payments is defined in such a way that it *always* balances.

34.1 The Balance of Payments

Statistics Canada documents transactions between Canada and the rest of the world. The record of such transactions is made in the **balance of payments accounts**. Each transaction, such as the exports or imports of goods, or the international purchase or sales of assets, is classified according to whether the transaction generates a *payment* or a *receipt* for Canada.

balance of payments accounts A summary record of a country's transactions with the rest of the world, including the buying and selling of goods, services, and assets.

Table 34-1 shows the major items in the Canadian balance of payments accounts for 2017. Transactions that represent a receipt for Canada, such as the sale of a product

TABLE 34-1   Canadian Balance of Payments, 2017 (billions of dollars)

	Credit	Debit	Balance
CURRENT ACCOUNT			
Trade Account			
Merchandise exports	+549.5		
Service exports	+112.8		
Merchandise imports		−573.4	
Service imports		−137.8	
Trade balance			−48.9
Capital-Service Account			
Net investment income			−12.2
Net private and government transfers			−2.8
Current Account Balance			−63.9
CAPITAL ACCOUNT			
Net change in Canadian investments abroad (capital outflow from Canada)		−223.9	
Net change in foreign investment in Canada (capital inflow to Canada)	+280.4		
Official Financing Account			
Changes in official international reserves		−1.1	
Capital Account Balance			+55.4
Statistical Discrepancy			+8.5
Balance of Payments			0.0

The overall balance of payments always balances, but the individual components do not have to. In 2017, Canada had an overall trade deficit (including trade in goods and services) of $48.9 billion. There was also a deficit of $15 billion on the capital-service account. There was thus a $63.9 billion deficit on the current account. There was a surplus on the capital account of $55.4 billion because the trading of assets internationally resulted in a net inflow of capital. The statistical discrepancy entry of $8.5 billion compensates for the inability to measure some items accurately. The current account plus the capital account (plus the statistical discrepancy) is equal to the balance of payments—which is always zero.

(*Source:* Statistics Canada, CANSIM, Tables 376-0101 and 376-0102.)

or asset to foreigners, are recorded in the balance of payments accounts as a *credit* item. Transactions that represent a payment for Canada, such as the purchase of a product or asset from foreigners, are recorded as a *debit* item.

There are two main categories to the balance of payments: the *current account* and the *capital account*. We examine each account in turn.

The Current Account

current account The part of the balance of payments accounts that records payments and receipts arising from trade in goods and services and from interest and dividends that are earned on assets owned in one country and invested in another.

The **current account** records transactions arising from trade in goods and services. It also includes net investment income earned from foreign asset holdings. The current account is divided into two main sections.

The first section, called the **trade account**, records payments and receipts arising from the import and export of goods, such as computers and cars, and services, such as legal or architectural services. (Tourism constitutes a large part of the trade in services.) Canadian imports of goods and services require a payment to foreigners and thus are entered as debit items on the trade account; Canadian exports of goods and services generate a receipt to Canada and thus are recorded as credit items.

trade account In the balance of payments, this account records the value of exports and imports of goods and services.

The second section, called the **capital-service account**, records the payments and receipts that represent income earned from asset holdings. When a firm located in Canada, for example, pays dividends to foreign owners, the payments to foreigners are a debit item in Canada's balance of payments. In contrast, when Canadians earn income from their foreign-located investments, these receipts for Canada are recorded as credit items.

capital-service account In the balance of payments, this account records the payments and receipts that represent income earned on assets (such as interest and dividends).

As shown in Table 34-1, Canadian exports of goods and services in 2017 were $662 billion, while imports of goods and services were slightly larger at $711 billion. The trade account therefore had a deficit of $49 billion—meaning that Canada purchased $49 billion more in goods and services from the rest of the world than it sold to the world. The capital-service account that year was also in deficit—Canadians paid $15 billion more to foreigners as investment income (plus transfers) than they received from foreigners. The overall current account balance in 2017 (the sum of the trade and capital-service accounts) had a deficit of $63.9 billion.

The Capital Account[1]

capital account The part of the balance of payments accounts that records payments and receipts arising from the purchase and sale of assets.

The **capital account** records international transactions in assets, including bonds, shares of companies, real estate, and factories. When a Canadian purchases a foreign asset, the transaction is treated similarly to the purchase of foreign goods. Since purchasing a foreign asset requires a payment from Canadians to foreigners, it is entered as a debit item in the Canadian capital account. Note that when Canadians purchase foreign assets, financial capital is leaving Canada and going abroad, and so this is called a *capital outflow*. When a foreigner purchases a Canadian asset, the transaction is treated just like the sale of Canadian goods. It generates a receipt for Canada and thus is entered as a credit item in the Canadian capital account. When Canadians sell assets to foreigners, financial capital is entering Canada from abroad, and so this is called a *capital inflow*.

---

[1] Statistics Canada now calls this the "Capital and Financing Account," but its meaning is the same: It records international transactions in assets. For simplicity, we retain the shorter term.

As shown in Table 34-1, in 2017, Canadians increased their holdings of assets abroad by $224 billion, resulting in a capital outflow of that amount. At the same time, foreigners increased their holdings of assets in Canada by $280 billion, resulting in a capital inflow of that amount.[2]

One part of the capital account shows the government's transactions in its official foreign-exchange reserves. This *official financing account* is included as part of the capital account because official reserves are *assets* rather than goods or services. If the government increases its reserves, it does so by purchasing foreign-currency assets, and this is recorded as a debit item in the official financing account. (This transaction is a *debit* because a payment from Canada is made in Canadian dollars.) If the government instead reduces its reserves, it sells some foreign-currency assets, and this transaction would be recorded as a credit item in the official financing account. (This transaction is a *credit* because there is a receipt to Canada of Canadian dollars.) In 2017, the Government of Canada increased its official reserves by $1.1 billion.

In 2017, the overall capital account had a surplus of $55.4 billion, meaning that there was a net capital inflow of this amount to Canada from the rest of the world. In other words, foreign households, firms and governments increased their net holdings of Canadian assets by $55.4 billion in 2017.

The Balance of Payments Must Balance

The current account balance represents the difference between the payments and receipts from international transactions in goods and services. The capital account balance is the difference between payments and receipts from international transactions in assets. The balance of payments is the sum of current account and capital account balances. In any given period (usually a year) the *current account plus the capital account must equal zero*. In other words, the balance of payments is always equal to zero. In algebraic terms, we can write

$$\text{Balance of payments} = CA + KA = 0$$

where CA is the current account balance and KA is the capital account balance. Note that this is an *identity*—the accounting system used for the balance of payments defines transactions in such a way that $CA + KA = 0$. But there is an underlying logic to this accounting system. Let's consider an example that illustrates the logical connection between the current and capital accounts.

Consider a year in which Canadian households, firms, and governments, taken together, purchase $100 billion in goods and services from the rest of the world. During the same year, Canadians sell $150 billion of goods and services to the rest of the world. Exports are $150 billion and imports are $100 billion, so Canada has a current account surplus of $50 billion, $CA = 50$ billion. (Assume for simplicity that the capital-service account is zero.) The meaning of this $50 billion surplus is that Canadians now have claims on foreigners equal to $50 billion—that is, foreigners owe Canadians $50 billion. What does Canada do with these claims?

---

[2] Though not shown in the table, the capital account distinguishes between *direct investment* and *portfolio investment*. The former involves the purchase or sale of assets that alter the legal control of those assets, such as when a controlling interest of a company is purchased. The latter involves transactions in assets that do not alter the legal control of the assets, such as when a minority of a company's shares is purchased.

Consider two possibilities:

1. Canadians purchase $50 billion more of goods and services from the rest of the world. In this case, Canada's imports rise to $150 billion and the current account is now in balance ($CA = 0$). Since there have been no transactions in assets, the capital account is also in balance ($KA = 0$). It is clear now that $CA + KA = 0$.

2. Canadians purchase $50 billion more of assets from foreigners—a capital outflow from Canada. They could purchase land, bonds, corporate shares, or factories. But whatever they purchase, the capital account will now be in deficit by $50 billion ($KA = -50 billion). In this case, the current account surplus of $50 billion is exactly offset by the capital account deficit of $50 billion. Once again we have $CA + KA = 0$.

Of course, Canadians could do a combination of these two options—buy some more imports and some assets as well, with a total value of $50 billion. In this case, we would still have $CA + KA = 0$.

Some readers may wonder why Canadians couldn't simply leave their purchases of goods and services unchanged *and* decide not to purchase any additional assets. For example, couldn't we have the *CA* surplus of $50 billion but not make any transactions in the capital account (so that $KA = 0$)? With such a *CA* surplus, however, Canadians are holding an "IOU" from foreigners of $50 billion, and this IOU is itself an asset for Canada as a whole. That asset can be held in many forms (stocks, bonds, bank balances, etc.), any of which will appear in the balance of payments as a capital account deficit.

In other words, the accounting system for the balance of payments is *designed* so that any current account balance is matched by an increase of some assets in the capital account. The sum of the two accounts is always zero.

> **Any surplus on the current account must be matched by an equal deficit on the capital account. A current account surplus thus implies a capital outflow. The balance of payments is always zero.**

Notice that the opposite situation is also possible and that the balance of payments again sums to zero. Suppose Canadians purchase $75 billion more in goods and services from the rest of the world than they sell—so Canada has a current account deficit of $75 billion, $CA = -$75$ billion. (We continue to assume that the capital-service account is zero.) The rest of the world now has claims of this amount on Canadians, meaning that Canadians owe $75 billion to foreigners. Foreigners can either purchase more Canadian goods and services or more Canadian assets. If foreigners purchase $75 billion in additional Canadian goods and services, Canada's current account is balanced ($CA = 0$) and we again have $CA + KA = 0$. If foreigners choose instead to purchase $75 billion in Canadian assets, then Canada's capital account will be in surplus by $75 billion—a capital inflow. In this case, the current account will be in deficit ($CA = -$75$ billion) and the capital account will be in surplus ($KA = 75 billion), but again we see that the sum of the two accounts is zero.

> **Any deficit in the current account must be matched by an equal surplus in the capital account. A current-account deficit thus implies a capital inflow. The balance of payments is always zero.**

Let's go back and review the actual numbers from Table 34-1. In 2017, Canada had a current account deficit of $63.9 billion. In order to purchase these net imports of goods and services, Canadian firms and households had to sell the same value (aside from the statistical discrepancy) of assets to foreigners in that year, so there was a capital inflow, or capital account surplus. The balance of payments, as always, was in balance. That the balance of payments always sums to zero is important. This result is not based on assumptions about behaviour or any other theoretical reasoning—it is an *accounting identity*. Many people nonetheless find balance of payments accounting confusing. *Applying Economic Concepts 34-1* discusses an individual student's balance of payments with the rest of the world and illustrates why an individual's balance of payments must always balance.

There Can't Be a Balance of Payments Deficit!

Unless further qualified, the term "balance of payments deficit" does not make sense since the balance of payments must always balance. But such a term is nonetheless often used in the press and even by some economists. What does this mean? Most often the term is used carelessly—a balance of payments deficit is mentioned when what is actually meant is a current account deficit.

There are also occasions when people speak of a country as having a balance of payments deficit or surplus when they are actually referring to the balance of all accounts *excluding* the official financing account. In other words, they are referring to the combined balance on current and capital accounts, *excluding* the changes in the government's foreign-currency reserves. For example, consider a year in which the Government of Canada sells $5 billion of its foreign-currency reserves. This transaction is a credit item in the official financing account (part of Canada's capital account). It must be the case that *all other* items in the current and capital accounts *combined* sum to an overall deficit. In this case, some people might say that Canada's balance of payments "deficit" is being financed by the government's sale of foreign-currency reserves. But when we use the terms properly, we know that Canada's balance of payments, as always, is balanced.

Summary

This brings us to the end of our discussion of the balance of payments. Keep in mind that this is just an exercise in accounting. Though at times you may find it difficult to keep the various credits and debits in the various accounts straight in your mind, remember that the structure of the accounting system is quite simple. Here is a brief review:

1. The current account shows all transactions in goods and services between Canada and the rest of the world (including investment income and transfers). Think of this as the "income and expenditures" section.

2. The capital account shows all transactions in assets between Canada and the rest of the world. Part of the capital account shows the change in the government's holding of foreign-currency reserves. Think of this as the "change in assets" section.

APPLYING ECONOMIC CONCEPTS 34-1

A Student's Balance of Payments with the Rest of the World

Many students find a country's balance of payments confusing, especially the idea that the balance of payments *must always* balance. Why, they often ask, can't Canada export more goods and services to the world than it imports and at the same time have a net sale of assets to the rest of the world? The connection between the current-account transactions and the capital-account transactions is not always obvious.

Perhaps the easiest way to see this connection is to consider an individual's "balance of payments" with the rest of the world. Of course, most individuals would not normally compute their balance of payments, but by doing so we can recognize the everyday concepts involved and also see the necessary connection between any individual's "current account" and "capital account." The reason that Canada's balance of payments must always balance is exactly the same reason that an individual's balance of payments must always balance.

The table shows the balance of payments for Stefan, a university student. Stefan is fortunate in several respects. First, his parents are able to provide some of the funds needed to finance his education. Second, he has a summer job that pays well. Third, he was given some Canada Savings Bonds when he was born that provide him with some interest income every year.

Stefan's Balance of Payments

Current Account (Income and Expenditure)	
Labour income ("exports")	+$10 000
Purchase of goods and services ("imports")	−$17 000
Interest income	+$ 500
Transfers (from his parents)	+$10 000
Current Account Balance	+$3 500

Capital Account (Changes in Assets) (− denotes an increase in assets, or a "capital outflow")	
Purchase of mutual funds	−$1 500
Increase in savings account deposits	−$2 000
Capital Account Balance	−$3 500
BALANCE OF PAYMENTS	$0

The current account section of the table shows Stefan's income and expenditures for a single year. The capital account section shows the *change* in Stefan's assets over the same year. (Note that for Stefan as well as for any country, the capital account does not show the overall stock of assets—it only shows the *changes* in the stock of assets during the year.)

Let's begin with his current account. Stefan has a good summer job that earns him $10 000 after taxes. This $10 000 represents Stefan's "exports" to the rest of the world—he earns this income by selling his labour services to a tree-planting company. Over the year, however, he spends $17 000 on tuition, books, clothes, groceries, and other goods and services. These are Stefan's "imports" from the rest of the world. Stefan clearly has a "trade deficit" equal to $7000—he "imports" more than he "exports."

There are two other sources of income shown in Stefan's current account. First, he earns $500 in interest income. Second, his parents give him $10 000 to help pay for his education—a *transfer* in the terminology of balance of payments accounting. The interest income and transfer together make up Stefan's "capital-service account"—Stefan has a surplus of $10 500.

Stefan's overall current account shows a surplus of $3500. This means he receives $3500 more than he spends on goods and services. But where does this $3500 go?

This question brings us to Stefan's capital account, the bottom part of the table. The $3500 surplus on current account *must* end up as increases in Stefan's assets. He invests $1500 in a mutual fund and he also increases his savings-account deposits by $2000. In both cases he is purchasing assets—he buys units in a mutual fund and he also "buys" a bank deposit. Since Stefan must make a payment to purchase these assets, each appears as a debit item in his capital account. Stefan's capital account balance is a deficit of $3500; in other words, there is a "capital outflow" of $3500.

Finally, note that Stefan's current account and capital account *must* sum to zero. There is no way around this. Any surplus of income over expenditures (on current account) must show up as an increase in his assets (or a decrease in his debts) on his capital account. Conversely, any excess of expenditures over income must be financed by reducing his assets (or by increasing his debts). Stefan's balance of payments *must* balance.

What is true for Stefan is true for any individual and also true for any accounting unit you choose to consider. Saskatoon's balance of payments with the rest of the world must balance. Saskatchewan's balance of payments with the rest of the world must balance. Western Canada's balance of payments with the rest of the world must balance. And so must Canada's, and any other country's.

3. All transactions involving a payment from Canada appear as debit items. All transactions involving a receipt to Canada appear as credit items.

4. The balance of payments—the sum of the current account and the capital account—must always be zero.

We now go on to explore how exchange rates are determined in the foreign-exchange market. We will see that a knowledge of the various categories in the balance of payments will help in our understanding of why changes in exchange rates occur.

34.2 The Foreign-Exchange Market

Money is vital in any sophisticated economy that relies on specialization and trade. Yet money as we know it is a *national* matter. If you live in Argentina, you earn pesos and spend pesos; if you operate a business in Japan, you borrow yen and pay your workers in yen. The currency of a country is acceptable within the border of that country, but usually it will not be accepted by firms and households in another country. Just try buying your next pair of jeans in Canada with British pounds sterling or Japanese yen.

Trade between countries normally requires the exchange of the currency of one country for that of another.

The Exchange Rate

The exchange of one currency for another is called a *foreign-exchange transaction*. The **exchange rate** is the rate at which one currency exchanges for another. In Canada's case, the exchange rate is the Canadian-dollar price of one unit of foreign currency. For example, in June 2018, the price of one U.S. dollar was 1.27 Canadian dollars. Thus, the Canada–U.S. exchange rate was 1.27.

> **exchange rate** The number of units of domestic currency required to purchase one unit of foreign currency

Note that in the Canadian news media the exchange rate is usually expressed in the opposite way—as the number of U.S. dollars that it takes to buy one Canadian dollar. So instead of reporting that the Canadian–U.S. exchange rate in June 2018 was 1.27, the press would say that the Canadian dollar was "worth" 78.7 U.S. cents (1/1.27 = 0.787).

We can choose to define the Canada–U.S. exchange rate either way: as the Canadian-dollar price of one U.S. dollar (Cdn\$/U.S.\$) or as the U.S.-dollar price of one Canadian dollar (U.S.\$/Cdn\$). But we must choose one method and stick to it; otherwise, our discussions will quickly become very confusing. In this book we *always* define the exchange rate in the way Canadian economists usually do—as the Canadian-dollar price of one unit of foreign currency. This definition makes it clear that foreign currency, like any good or service, has a price expressed in Canadian dollars. In this case, the price has a special name—the exchange rate.

An **appreciation** of the Canadian dollar means that the Canadian dollar has become more valuable so that it takes fewer Canadian dollars to purchase one unit of foreign currency. For example, if the Canadian dollar appreciates against the U.S. dollar from 1.27 to 1.15, it takes 12 fewer Canadian cents to purchase one U.S. dollar. Thus, an appreciation of the Canadian dollar implies a *fall* in the exchange rate. Conversely, a

> **appreciation** A fall in the exchange rate—the domestic currency has become more valuable so that it takes fewer units of domestic currency to purchase one unit of foreign currency.

depreciation A rise in the exchange rate—the domestic currency has become less valuable so that it takes more units of domestic currency to purchase one unit of foreign currency.

depreciation of the Canadian dollar means that the Canadian dollar has become less valuable so that it takes more Canadian dollars to purchase one unit of foreign currency. Thus, a depreciation of the Canadian dollar means a *rise* in the exchange rate.

> **An appreciation of the Canadian dollar is a fall in the exchange rate; a depreciation of the Canadian dollar is a rise in the exchange rate.**

We now go on to build a simple theory of the foreign-exchange market. This will allow us to analyze the determinants of the exchange rate. To keep things simple, we use an example involving trade between Canada and Europe, and thus we examine the determination of the exchange rate between the two currencies: the Canadian dollar and the euro. In this example, think of Europe as a shorthand for "the rest of the world" and the euro as a shorthand for "all foreign currencies."

> **Because Canadian dollars are traded for euros in the foreign-exchange market, a demand for euros implies a supply of Canadian dollars, and a supply of euros implies a demand for Canadian dollars.**

For this reason, a theory of the exchange rate between dollars and euros can deal *either* with the demand and supply of dollars *or* with the demand and supply of euros; both need not be considered. We will concentrate on the demand, supply, and price of euros. Thus, the market we will be considering (in general terms) is the foreign-exchange market—the "product" is foreign exchange (euros in our case) and the "price" is the exchange rate (the Canadian-dollar price of euros).

We develop our example in terms of the demand and supply analysis first encountered in Chapter 3. To do so, we need only recall that in the market for foreign exchange, transactions that generate a receipt for Canada in its balance of payments represent a *supply* of foreign exchange. Foreign exchange is being supplied by the foreigners who need Canadian funds to purchase Canadian goods or assets. Conversely, transactions that are a payment from Canada in the balance of payments represent a *demand* for foreign exchange. Foreign exchange is being demanded by the Canadians who are purchasing foreign goods or assets. In what follows we make the (realistic) assumption that the Bank of Canada makes no transactions in the foreign-exchange market. Later we discuss the role of central-bank transactions.

Comstock/Stockbyte/Getty Images

Trade between countries that use different currencies requires that currencies also be exchanged; this takes place in foreign-exchange markets where exchange rates—the price of one currency in terms of another—are determined.

The Supply of Foreign Exchange

Whenever foreigners purchase Canadian goods, services, or assets, they supply foreign currency to the foreign-exchange market and demand, in return, Canadian dollars with which to pay for their purchases. Thus, the supply of foreign exchange (and the associated demand for Canadian dollars) arises from Canada's sales of goods, services, and assets to the rest of the world.

Canadian Exports   One important source of supply of foreign exchange is foreigners who wish to buy Canadian-made goods and services. A French importer of lumber is such a purchaser; an Austrian couple planning a vacation in Canada is another; the Hungarian government seeking to buy Canadian engineering services is a third. All are sources of supply of foreign exchange, arising out of international trade. Each potential buyer wants to sell its own currency in exchange for Canadian dollars that it can then use to purchase Canadian goods and services.

Asset Sales: Capital Inflows   A second source of supply of foreign exchange comes from foreigners who want to purchase Canadian assets, such as government or corporate bonds, real estate, or shares in a Canadian firm. To buy Canadian assets, holders of foreign currencies must first sell their foreign currency in return for Canadian dollars. As we saw earlier in the chapter, when Canadians sell assets to foreigners, we say there is a *capital inflow* to Canada.

Reserve Currency   Firms, banks, and governments often accumulate and hold foreign-exchange reserves, just as individuals maintain savings accounts. These reserves may be in several different currencies. For example, the government of Poland may decide to increase its reserve holdings of Canadian dollars and reduce its reserve holdings of euros; if it does so, it will be a supplier of euros (and a demander of Canadian dollars) in foreign-exchange markets.

The Total Supply of Foreign Exchange   The supply of foreign exchange (or the demand for Canadian dollars in the foreign-exchange market) is the sum of the supplies for all the purposes just discussed—for purchases of Canadian goods and services, Canadian assets, and for the purchase of Canadian dollars to add to currency reserves.

Furthermore, because people, firms, and governments in all countries purchase goods and assets from many other countries, the demand for any one currency will be the aggregate demand of individuals, firms, and governments in a number of different countries. Thus, the total supply of foreign exchange (or the demand for Canadian dollars) may include Germans who are offering euros, Japanese who are offering yen, Argentinians who are offering pesos, and so on. For simplicity, however, we go back to our two-country example and use only Canada and Europe.

The Supply Curve for Foreign Exchange   The supply of foreign exchange on the foreign-exchange market is represented by a positively sloped curve, such as the one shown in Figure 34-1. This figure plots the Canadian-dollar price of euros (the

FIGURE 34-1   The Foreign-Exchange Market

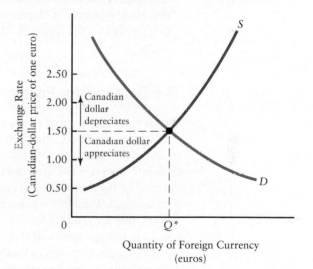

The demand for foreign exchange is negatively sloped, and the supply of foreign exchange is positively sloped, when plotted against the exchange rate, measured as the Canadian-dollar price of one unit of foreign currency. The demand for foreign exchange is given by the blue line D. It represents the sum of transactions on both current and capital accounts that require payments to foreigners. The supply of foreign exchange is given by the red line S. It represents the sum of transactions on both current and capital accounts that represent receipts from foreigners.

In this example, the equilibrium value of the exchange rate is 1.50—it takes 1.50 Canadian dollars to purchase one euro.

exchange rate) on the vertical axis and the quantity of euros on the horizontal axis. Moving up the vertical axis, more dollars are needed to purchase one euro—the Canadian dollar is depreciating. Moving down the vertical axis, fewer dollars are needed to purchase one euro—the dollar is appreciating.

Why is the supply curve for foreign exchange positively sloped? Let's consider what happens when Europeans are buying Canadian exports. If the Canadian dollar is depreciating (moving up the vertical axis), the euro prices of the Canadian exports are falling and so Europeans will want to buy more. To make these additional purchases, they increase their supply of euros to the foreign-exchange market in order to acquire the Canadian dollars they need to pay for the Canadian products. In the opposite case, when the dollar appreciates (moving down the vertical axis), the euro price of Canadian exports rises. European consumers will buy fewer Canadian goods and thus supply less foreign exchange.[3]

Similar considerations affect other sources of supply of foreign exchange. When the Canadian dollar depreciates (a higher exchange rate), Canadian securities and other assets become more attractive purchases, and the quantity purchased by foreigners will rise. With this rise, the amount of foreign exchange supplied to pay for the purchases will increase.

> The supply curve for foreign exchange is positively sloped when it is plotted against the exchange rate; a depreciation of the Canadian dollar (a rise in the exchange rate) increases the quantity of foreign exchange supplied.

The Demand for Foreign Exchange

The demand for foreign exchange arises from all international transactions that represent a payment for Canada in our balance of payments. What sorts of international transactions generate a demand for foreign exchange (and a supply of Canadian dollars)? They are the same sort of transactions we just discussed, but this time they are moving in the opposite direction—Canadians, rather than foreigners, are doing the purchasing. Canadians seeking to purchase foreign products will be supplying Canadian dollars and demanding foreign exchange for this purpose. Canadians may also seek to purchase foreign assets. If they do, they will supply Canadian dollars and demand foreign exchange. Similarly, a country with reserves of Canadian dollars may decide to sell them in order to hold some other currency instead.

The Demand Curve for Foreign Exchange When the Canadian dollar depreciates against the euro, the Canadian-dollar price of European goods rises. Because it takes more dollars to buy the same European good at an unchanged euro price, Canadians will buy fewer of the now more expensive European goods. The amount of foreign exchange being demanded by Canadians in order to pay for imported European goods

---

[3] We have assumed here that the foreign price elasticity of demand for Canadian exports is greater than 1, so that a price change leads to a proportionately larger change in quantity demanded. This is a common assumption in the analysis of international trade.

will fall.[4] In the opposite case, when the Canadian dollar appreciates, European goods become cheaper, and so Canadians demand more foreign exchange to pay for the greater volume of imports. This same argument applies in exactly the same way to the purchases of foreign assets. Figure 34-1 shows the demand curve for foreign exchange.

The demand curve for foreign exchange is negatively sloped when it is plotted against the exchange rate; an appreciation of the Canadian dollar (a fall in the exchange rate) increases the quantity of foreign exchange demanded.

▌ 34.3 The Determination of Exchange Rates

The demand and supply curves in Figure 34-1 do not include transactions in the foreign-exchange market made by the central bank in an attempt to alter the value of the exchange rate. Such transactions, if they occur at all, appear as a subset of the official financing account (look back to Table 34-1). To complete our analysis of the foreign-exchange market we need to consider three possibilities for central-bank behaviour:

1. When the central bank makes no transactions in the foreign-exchange market, there is said to be a purely *floating* or **flexible exchange rate**.

2. When the central bank intervenes in the foreign-exchange market to "fix" or "peg" the exchange rate at a particular value, there is said to be a **fixed exchange rate** or *pegged exchange rate*.

3. Between these two "pure" systems is a variety of possible intermediate cases, including the *adjustable peg* and the *managed float*. In the adjustable peg system, central banks fix specific values for their exchange rates, but they explicitly recognize that circumstances may arise in which they will change that value. In a managed float, the central bank seeks to have some stabilizing influence on the exchange rate but does not try to fix it at some publicly announced value.

flexible exchange rate An exchange rate that is left free to be determined by the forces of demand and supply on the free market, with no intervention by central banks.

fixed exchange rate An exchange rate that is maintained within a small range around its publicly stated par value by the intervention in the foreign-exchange market by a country's central bank.

Most industrialized countries today operate a mostly flexible exchange rate. It is mostly market determined but the central bank sometimes intervenes to offset significant short-run fluctuations. The countries of the European Union (EU) had a system of fixed exchange rates (relative to one another's currencies) between 1979 and 1999. In 1999 most of the countries of the EU adopted a common currency—the euro (an important exception being the United Kingdom). Within what is now called the *euro zone*, the countries have no exchange rates for national currencies but the single common currency has a flexible exchange rate relative to countries outside the euro zone. The United States, Japan, the United Kingdom, Australia, and most other major industrialized countries have flexible exchange rates with relatively small amounts of foreign-exchange intervention by their central banks.

---

[4] As long as the price elasticity of demand for imports is greater than 1, the fall in the volume of imports will exceed the rise in price, and hence fewer dollars will be spent on them. This condition (and the one in the previous footnote) is related to a famous long-standing issue in international economics, called the *Marshall-Lerner condition*. In what follows, we take the standard approach of assuming that both the price elasticity of demand for imports and the price elasticity of the demand for Canadian exports exceeds 1. This guarantees that the slopes of the curves are as shown in Figure 34-1.

Canada alternated between a system of fixed exchange rates and flexible exchange rates throughout most of the period between the Second World War and 1970. In contrast, most other countries pegged their currencies to the U.S. dollar under what was called the Bretton Woods system. Canada has had a flexible exchange rate since 1970. Later in the chapter we examine the issues involved in choosing between a flexible and fixed exchange-rate system. For now, let's explore the mechanics of how the various systems operate.

FIGURE 34-2 Fixed and Flexible Exchanges Rates

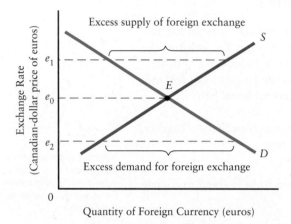

Quantity of Foreign Currency (euros)

In the absence of central-bank intervention, the exchange rate adjusts to clear the foreign-exchange market. The demand for and supply of foreign exchange are as in Figure 34-1. If there is no intervention by the central bank, there is a purely flexible exchange rate. It will adjust to equate the demand and supply of foreign exchange; this occurs at E with an exchange rate of e_0.

If the exchange rate is higher than that, say at e_1, the supply of foreign exchange will exceed the demand. The exchange rate will fall (the dollar will appreciate) until it reaches e_0, where equilibrium is achieved at E. If the exchange rate is below e_0, say at e_2, the demand for foreign exchange will exceed the supply. The exchange rate will rise (the dollar will depreciate) until it reaches e_0, where equilibrium is achieved at E.

In the case of a fixed exchange rate, the central bank intervenes to meet the excess demands or supplies that arise at the fixed value of the exchange rate. For example, if it chooses to fix the exchange rate at e_1, there will be an excess supply of foreign exchange. The central bank will purchase foreign exchange (and sell dollars) to meet the excess supply and keep the exchange rate constant. Alternatively, if the central bank chooses to fix the exchange rate at e_2, there will be an excess demand for foreign exchange. The central bank will sell foreign exchange (and buy dollars) to meet the excess demand and keep the exchange rate constant.

Flexible Exchange Rates

We begin with an exchange rate that is set in a freely competitive market, with no intervention by the central bank. Like any competitive price, the exchange rate fluctuates as the conditions of demand and supply change.

Suppose the current exchange rate is so high (say, e_1 in Figure 34-2) that the quantity of foreign exchange supplied exceeds the quantity demanded. There is thus an excess supply of foreign exchange. This excess supply of foreign exchange, just as in our analysis in Chapter 3, will cause the price of foreign exchange (the exchange rate) to fall. As the exchange rate falls (and the Canadian dollar appreciates) the euro price of Canadian goods rises, and this leads to a reduction in the quantity of foreign exchange supplied. Also, as the exchange rate falls, the Canadian-dollar price of European goods falls, and this fall leads to an increase in the quantity of foreign exchange demanded. The excess supply of foreign exchange leads to a fall in the exchange rate, which in turn reduces the amount of excess supply. Where the two curves intersect, quantity demanded equals quantity supplied, and the exchange rate is at its equilibrium or market-clearing value.

What happens when the exchange rate is below its equilibrium value, such as at e_2 in Figure 34-2? The quantity of foreign exchange demanded will exceed the quantity supplied. With foreign exchange in excess demand, its price will naturally rise, and as it does the amount of excess demand will be reduced until equilibrium is re-established.

A foreign-exchange market is like other competitive markets in that the forces of demand and supply lead to an equilibrium price at which quantity demanded equals quantity supplied.

Recall that we have been assuming that there is no intervention in the foreign-exchange market by the central bank. We now consider a system of fixed exchange rates in which such intervention plays a crucial role in the analysis.

Fixed Exchange Rates

If the central bank chooses to fix the exchange rate at a particular value, it must transact in the foreign-exchange market to accommodate any excess demand or supply of foreign exchange that arises at that exchange rate. These transactions are described in Figure 34-2.

The gold standard that operated for much of the nineteenth century and the early part of the twentieth century was a fixed exchange-rate system. The Bretton Woods system, established by international agreement in 1944 and operated until the early 1970s, was a fixed exchange-rate system that provided for circumstances under which exchange rates could be adjusted. It was thus an adjustable peg system; the International Monetary Fund (IMF) has its origins in the Bretton Woods system, and one of its principal tasks was approving and monitoring exchange-rate changes. The European Exchange Rate Mechanism (ERM), which existed from 1979 to 1999, was also a fixed exchange-rate system for the countries in the European Union; their exchange rates were fixed to one another but floated as a block against the U.S. dollar and other currencies. As mentioned earlier, this system of separate European currencies with fixed exchange rates was replaced in 1999 when most of the countries of the EU adopted a common currency—the euro.

Applying Economic Concepts 34-2 examines in more detail how a fixed exchange-rate system operates. It shows why a central bank that chooses to fix its exchange rate must give up some control of its foreign-exchange reserves, as occurred in Thailand in 1997 and is occurring in China today. We now go on to study the workings of a flexible exchange-rate system, the system used in Canada and most industrialized countries.

Changes in Flexible Exchange Rates

What causes exchange rates to vary? The simplest answer to this question is changes in demand or supply in the foreign-exchange market. Anything that shifts the demand curve for foreign exchange to the right or the supply curve for foreign exchange to the left leads to a rise in the exchange rate—a depreciation of the Canadian dollar. Conversely, anything that shifts the demand curve for foreign exchange to the left or the supply curve for foreign exchange to the right leads to a fall in the exchange rate—an appreciation of the Canadian dollar. These points are nothing more than a restatement of the laws of supply and demand, applied now to the market for foreign exchange; they are illustrated in Figure 34-3.

What causes the shifts in demand and supply that lead to changes in exchange rates? There are many causes, some transitory and some persistent. Let's look at several of the most important ones.

In 1999, 11 countries of the European Union adopted a common currency—the euro. By 2018, when 19 countries were in the euro zone, the price of one euro was 1.56 Canadian dollars.

A Rise in the World Price of Exports Suppose there is an increase in the world price of a major Canadian export, such as wheat, oil, copper, or nickel. For almost all of Canada's major exports, Canada's production is small relative to the world market and so no event in Canada is likely to cause a change in the world price. The higher world price means that the world's consumers are offering more foreign currency per unit of these Canadian exports.

APPLYING ECONOMIC CONCEPTS 34-2

Fixed Exchange Rates and Foreign-Exchange Reserves

This box provides some details on how a central bank operates a policy of fixed exchange rates, and how its actions relate to changes in its foreign-exchange reserves. We examine a hypothetical example for the Canadian–U.S. exchange rate as well as the actual situation for the Chinese–U.S. exchange rate.

A Hypothetical Canada–U.S. Example

Though Canada has a flexible exchange rate (with very rare foreign-exchange intervention by the Bank of Canada), we will imagine a situation in which the Bank of Canada pegs the Canadian–U.S. exchange rate. The figure

The Canada–U.S. Exchange Rate

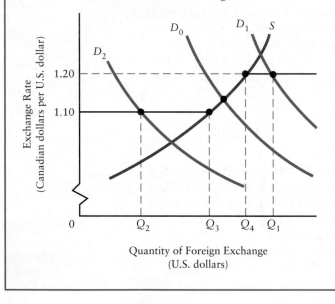

Quantity of Foreign Exchange
(U.S. dollars)

below shows the *monthly* demand for and supply of foreign exchange (U.S. dollars).

Suppose the Bank of Canada fixed the exchange rate between the narrow limits of, say, C$1.10 to C$1.20 to the U.S. dollar. The Bank then stabilizes the exchange rate in the face of seasonal, cyclical, and other fluctuations in demand and supply, transacting in the market to prevent the rate from going outside the permitted band. When the Bank buys U.S. dollars, its foreign-exchange reserves rise; when it sells U.S. dollars, its foreign-exchange reserves fall.

In the figure, we can see how the Bank's interventions have their effect. Consider three situations:

1. If the demand curve cuts the supply curve in the range 1.10 to 1.20, as D_0 does in the figure, the Bank need not intervene in the market.

2. If the demand curve shifts to D_1, there is an excess demand for U.S. dollars that the Bank must satisfy. The Bank sells U.S. dollars from its reserves to the extent of Q_4Q_1 per month in order to prevent the exchange rate from rising above 1.20.

3. If the demand curve shifts to D_2, there is an excess supply of U.S. dollars that the Bank must satisfy. The Bank buys U.S. dollars to the extent of Q_2Q_3 per month in order to prevent the exchange rate from falling below 1.10.

If, on average, the demand and supply curves intersect in the range 1.10 to 1.20, the Bank's foreign-exchange reserves will be relatively stable, with the Bank buying U.S. dollars when the demand is abnormally low and selling them when the demand is abnormally high. Over a long period, however, the average level of reserves will be fairly stable.

If conditions change, the Bank's foreign-exchange reserves will rise or fall more or less continuously. For

The increase in the supply of foreign exchange occurs even if the volume of Canadian exports is unchanged; if Canadian exports increase in response to the higher world price, the supply of foreign exchange increases further. The increase in the supply of foreign exchange shifts the supply curve to the right and causes a reduction in the exchange rate—an appreciation of the Canadian dollar.

A Rise in the Foreign Price of Imports   Suppose the euro price of European automobiles increases because of European supply disruptions. Suppose also that Canadian consumers have an elastic demand for European cars because they can easily switch to Canadian-made substitutes. Consequently, they spend fewer euros for European automobiles than they did before and hence demand less foreign exchange. The demand

example, suppose the average level of demand becomes D_1, with fluctuations on either side of this level. The average drain on the Bank's foreign-exchange reserves will then be Q_4Q_1 *per month*. But this situation cannot continue indefinitely because the Bank has only a limited amount of foreign-exchange reserves. In this situation, there are two alternatives: the Bank can change the fixed exchange rate so that the band of permissible prices straddles the new equilibrium price, or government policy can try to shift the curves so that the intersection is in the band 1.10 to 1.20. To accomplish this goal, the government must restrict demand for foreign exchange: it can impose import quotas and foreign-travel restrictions, or it can seek to increase the supply of U.S. dollars by encouraging Canadian exports.

The Actual Chinese–U.S. Exchange Rate

For most of the past 20 years, China has operated a form of fixed exchange rate for its currency, the yuan (sometimes called the renminbi). Between 1995 and 2005, the rate was rigidly fixed at 8.3 yuan per U.S. dollar. In the decade following 2005, the Chinese central bank adopted an adjustable peg system in which the yuan was permitted to gradually appreciate against the U.S. dollar; today the exchange rate is 6.3 yuan per U.S. dollar.

Our diagram shows two different regimes for China's exchange-rate policy. Up until 2014, the Chinese central bank was holding the exchange rate above its free-market equilibrium rate; in other words, the yuan was undervalued relative to what would have been observed with a flexible exchange rate. As a result, the Chinese central bank accommodated the excess supply of foreign exchange by selling yuan and increasing its holdings of foreign-exchange reserves. Between 2000 and 2014, the Chinese central bank accumulated just under $4 *trillion* in foreign-exchange reserves (valued in U.S. dollars).

After 2014, however, as global market conditions changed, the yuan-dollar exchange rate was below the free-market level, and so the yuan was then overvalued

relative to what would have been observed in a free market. Since 2014, the Chinese central bank has been intervening to accommodate the excess demand for foreign currency; it has lost approximately $1 trillion of its foreign-exchange reserves since that time.

This box and the Chinese example underline the importance of a key fact for any country operating a fixed or pegged exchange-rate system. Such systems require the central bank to intervene in the foreign-exchange market, using domestic currency to buy or sell foreign-exchange reserves. If the central bank is purchasing reserves with newly created domestic currency, there must be an associated monetary expansion. If the central bank is selling reserves for domestic currency, the domestic money supply must be falling. Such changes in the domestic money supply may conflict with the central bank's other objectives regarding the stabilization of output and inflation.

The Chinese–U.S. Exchange Rate

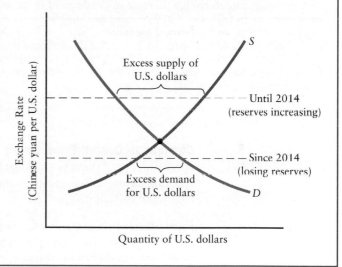

curve for foreign exchange shifts to the left, and the Canadian dollar appreciates. If instead the demand for foreign cars were inelastic, the rise in foreign prices would lead to an *increase* in the demand for foreign exchange (at least initially) and thus to a depreciation of the Canadian dollar. This is illustrated in part (i) of Figure 34-3.

Exchange rates often respond to changes in the prices of major exports and imports. A rise in the world price of Canadian exports causes the Canadian dollar to appreciate. A rise in foreign prices of Canadian imports can cause the Canadian dollar to appreciate or depreciate, depending on the elasticity of demand for those imports.

FIGURE 34-3 Changes in a Flexible Exchange Rate

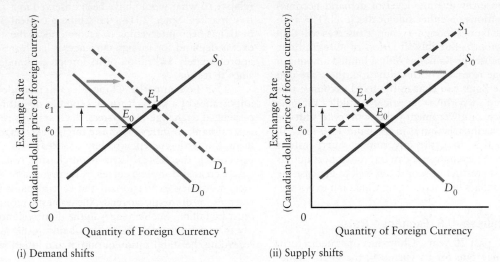

(i) Demand shifts   (ii) Supply shifts

An increase in the demand for foreign exchange or a decrease in the supply will cause the Canadian dollar to depreciate (the exchange rate to rise); a decrease in the demand or an increase in supply will cause the dollar to appreciate (the exchange rate to fall). The initial demand and supply curves are D_0 and S_0. Equilibrium is at E_0 with an exchange rate of e_0. An increase in the demand for foreign exchange from D_0 to D_1 in part (i), or a decrease in the supply of foreign exchange from S_0 to S_1 in part (ii), will cause the dollar to depreciate. In both parts, the new equilibrium is at E_1, and the dollar depreciation is shown by the rise in the exchange rate from e_0 to e_1. Conversely, a decrease in the demand for foreign exchange or an increase in the supply of foreign exchange will cause the dollar to appreciate and the equilibrium exchange rate to fall.

Changes in Overall Price Levels   Suppose that instead of a change in the price of a specific product there is a change in *all* prices because of general inflation. We consider separate cases, each corresponding to a different pattern of Canadian inflation relative to foreign inflation.

Equal Inflation in Both Countries.   Suppose inflation is running at 5 percent in both Canada and Europe. In this case, the euro prices of European goods and the dollar prices of Canadian goods are both rising by 5 percent per year. In this special case, the relative prices of imported goods and domestically produced goods will be unchanged and so demands will not be shifting between countries. As a result, the equilibrium exchange rate remains unchanged.

Inflation in Only One Country.   What will happen if there is inflation in Canada while the price level remains stable in Europe? The dollar price of Canadian goods will rise, and they will become more expensive in Europe. This increase in price will cause the quantity of Canadian exports, and therefore the amount of foreign exchange supplied by European importers, to decrease. The supply curve for foreign exchange shifts to the left.

At the same time, European goods in Canada will have an unchanged Canadian-dollar price, while the price of Canadian goods sold in Canada will increase because of the inflation. European goods have become relatively cheaper than Canadian goods, and thus more European goods will be bought in Canada. At any exchange rate, the amount of foreign exchange demanded to purchase imports will rise. The demand curve for foreign exchange shifts to the right.

If there is inflation in Canada, and no inflation in Europe, the supply curve for foreign exchange shifts to the left and the demand curve for foreign exchange shifts to the right. As a result, the equilibrium exchange rate *must* rise—there is a depreciation of the Canadian dollar relative to the euro.

Inflation at Unequal Rates. The two foregoing examples are, of course, just limiting cases of a more general situation in which the rate of inflation is different in the two countries. The arguments can readily be extended when we realize that it is the *relative* inflation in two countries that determines whether home goods or foreign goods look more or less attractive. If country A's inflation rate is higher than country B's, country A's exports are becoming relatively expensive in B's markets while imports from B are becoming relatively cheap in A's markets. This causes A's currency to depreciate relative to B's.

> Other things being equal, if Canada has higher inflation than other countries, the Canadian dollar will be depreciating relative to other currencies. If Canada has lower inflation than other countries, the Canadian dollar will be appreciating.

Capital Movements   Flows of financial capital can exert strong influences on exchange rates. For example, an increased desire by Canadians to purchase European assets (a capital outflow from Canada) will shift the demand curve for foreign exchange to the right, and the dollar will depreciate. In contrast, a desire by foreigners to increase their holdings of Canadian assets will shift the supply curve for foreign currency to the right and cause the Canadian dollar to appreciate.

Short-Term Capital Movements. An important motive for short-term capital flows is a change in interest rates. International traders hold transaction balances just as do domestic traders. These balances are often lent out on a short-term basis rather than being left idle. Naturally, the holders of these balances will tend to lend them, other things being equal, in markets in which interest rates are highest. This is often referred to as the *carry trade*. If one country's short-term interest rate rises above the rates in other countries (say, because that country undertakes a contractionary monetary policy), there will tend to be a large inflow of short-term capital into that country in an effort to take advantage of the high interest rate. This inflow of financial capital will increase the demand for the domestic currency and cause it to appreciate. Conversely, if a monetary expansion reduces short-term interest rates in one country, there will tend to be a shift of financial capital away from that country, and its currency will tend to depreciate. We saw this basic relationship between interest rates, capital flows, and the exchange rate in Chapter 27 when we discussed the monetary transmission mechanism in an open economy.

An increase in the world price of a major Canadian export, such as forestry products, generally leads to an appreciation of the Canadian dollar.

Changes in monetary policy lead to changes in interest rates and thus to international flows of financial capital. A contractionary monetary policy in Canada will lead to a rise in Canadian interest rates, a capital inflow, and an appreciation of the Canadian dollar. An expansionary monetary policy in Canada will lead to a reduction in Canadian interest rates, a capital outflow, and a depreciation of the Canadian dollar.

A second motive for short-term capital movements is speculation about the *future value* of a country's exchange rate. If foreigners expect the Canadian dollar to appreciate in the near future, they will be induced to buy Canadian stocks or bonds; if they expect the Canadian dollar to depreciate in the near future, they will be reluctant to buy such Canadian securities.

Long-Term Capital Movements.   Long-term capital movements are largely influenced by long-term expectations regarding the business environment in a country. For example, Canada will be an attractive destination for long-term investment if it is seen by foreigners as a country in which there are attractive profit opportunities, a stable and "business friendly" approach to public policy, an educated workforce, and good public infrastructure. Dramatic changes in tax and regulatory policy are often the causes of significant swings in long-term investment.

Structural Changes

An economy can undergo structural changes that alter the equilibrium exchange rate. *Structural change* is an all-purpose term for a change in cost structures, the invention of new products, changes in preferences between products, or anything else that affects the pattern of comparative advantage. Consider two examples.

Suppose firms in one country are slow to adopt technological innovations and, as a result, that country's products do not improve at the same speed as those in other countries. Consumers' demand will shift slowly away from the first country's products and toward those of its foreign competitors. This shift will cause a gradual depreciation in the first country's currency because fewer people want to buy that country's goods and thus fewer people want to buy that country's currency. As a general rule, a country with a slower pace of innovation than other countries tends to experience a depreciation of its currency.

A second example relates to the discovery of valuable mineral resources. Prominent examples are the development of natural gas in the Netherlands in the early 1960s, the development of North Sea oil in the United Kingdom in the 1970s, the more recent discovery of large diamond deposits in the Northwest Territories and the very recent development of shale oil deposits in the United States. If firms in one country make such a discovery and begin selling these resources to the rest of the world, the foreign purchasers must supply their foreign currency in order to purchase the currency of the exporting country. The result is an appreciation of the currency of the exporting country.

Anything that leads to changes in the pattern of trade, such as changes in costs or changes in demand, will generally lead to changes in exchange rates.

▌34.4 Three Policy Issues

This chapter has so far explained how the balance of payments accounts are constructed and how exchange rates are determined. It is now time to use this knowledge to explore some important policy issues. We examine three issues commonly discussed in the media. As we will see, these media discussions are not always as well informed as they could be. We pose the three policy issues as questions:

1. Is a current account deficit "bad" and a surplus "good"?

2. Is there a "correct" value for the Canadian dollar?

3. Should Canada have a fixed exchange rate?

Current Account Deficits and Surpluses

Figure 34-4 shows the path of Canada's current account balance (as a percentage of GDP) since 1961. In most years, Canada has a significant trade surplus since it exports more goods and services to the world than it imports. But because it makes more investment payments (both interest and dividends) to foreigners than it receives from

FIGURE 34-4   Canada's Current Account Balance, 1961–2017

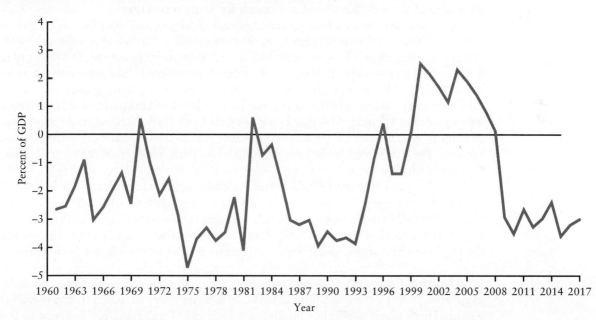

The changes in Canada's current account balance often reflect different economic performance in Canada and its trading partners. Canada typically has a current account deficit equal to a small percentage of GDP. Through the 2000s, however, rising world prices for petroleum products, which reflected a booming world economy, resulted in large Canadian exports and the appearance of a Canadian current account surplus. With the onset of the global recession starting in 2008, however, Canadian exports fell by more than Canadian imports, and the current account returned to deficit.

(*Source*: Statistics Canada, CANSIM database, Tables 376-0101 and 380-0064.)

foreigners, it has a deficit on the capital-service portion of the current account. During most of the 1960–1995 period, Canada had an overall current account deficit of between 2 and 4 percent of GDP. From 1999 to 2008, however, Canada's trade surplus increased by more than the capital-service deficit, and the result was a significant turn-around in the current account balance. The global recession in 2008, however, followed by a sluggish recovery in the world economy, caused Canada's exports to fall far more than its imports and the result was a return to current account deficits.

As we have learned, Canada's balance of payments accounts are defined in such a way that they must always balance, so during the 1960–1995 period the current account deficits were matched by capital account surpluses of the same size. During these years, Canada was selling more assets to the rest of the world—both bonds and equity—than it was buying from the rest of the world. Similarly, the current account surpluses from 1999 to 2008 were matched by capital account deficits, meaning that in those years Canada was buying more assets from foreigners than we were selling to foreigners.

It is common for news reporters to comment negatively on an increase in the current account deficit and positively on its decline. But are current account deficits really a problem? Should we be celebrating Canada's current account surpluses when they occur? We address this issue in three parts.

Mercantilism   Many people argue that a current account deficit is undesirable because it means that Canada is buying more goods and services from the world than it is selling to the world. Central to this view is the belief that exports are "good" and imports are "bad." We discussed this belief, and argued why it was incorrect, in Chapter 33 when we explored some of the invalid arguments for trade protection.

As a carryover from a long-discredited eighteenth-century doctrine called *mercantilism*, a current account surplus is sometimes called a "favourable balance," and a current account deficit is sometimes called an "unfavourable balance." Mercantilists, both ancient and modern, believe that a country's gains from trade arise only from having a "favourable" balance of trade—that is, by exporting more goods and services than it imports. But this belief misses the central point of comparative advantage that we explored in Chapter 32—that countries gain from trade because trade allows each country to specialize in the production of those products in which its opportunity costs are low. The gains from trade have *nothing* to do with whether there is a trade deficit or a trade surplus.

Lessons from History 34-1 discusses the doctrine of mercantilism. The lesson to be learned is that the gains from trade depend on the *volume* of trade (exports plus imports) rather than the *balance* of trade (exports minus imports). Since the 2016 election of U.S. President Donald Trump, there has been a rise in mercantilist rhetoric from the U.S. Administration, and it appears that this crucial lesson has not been learned.

International Borrowing   As we saw earlier, if Canada has a current account deficit, it must also have a capital account surplus. It is a net seller of assets to the rest of the world. These assets are either bonds, in which case Canadians are borrowing from foreigners, or they are shares in firms (equities), in which case Canadians are selling their capital stock to foreigners.

It follows that the question "Should Canada have a current account deficit?" is the same as the question "Should Canadians be net sellers of assets to foreigners?" It is not immediately clear that the answer to this question should be no. It is true that by selling bonds to foreigners, Canadians increase their indebtedness to foreigners and will eventually have to redeem the bonds and pay interest. And by selling income-earning

LESSONS FROM HISTORY 34-1

Donald Trump: Modern-Day Mercantilist

Media commentators, politicians, and much of the general public often appear to believe that a country should export more than it imports and thereby secure a current account surplus. U.S. President Trump shares this view when he points to any U.S. trade deficit—by product or by country—as bad for American economic interests. People who hold these views appear to believe that the benefits derived from international trade are measured by the size of the trade surplus rather than by the volume of two-way trade.

This view is related to the *exploitation doctrine* of international trade: one country's surplus is another country's deficit. Hence, one country's gain, judged by its surplus, must be another country's loss, judged by its deficit.

People who hold such views today are echoing an ancient economic doctrine called *mercantilism*. The mercantilists were a group of economists who preceded Adam Smith. They judged the success of trade by the size of the trade balance. In many cases, this doctrine made sense in terms of their objective, which was to use international trade as a means of building up the political and military power of the state, rather than as a means of raising the living standards of its citizens. A current account surplus allowed the country (then and now) to acquire assets. (In those days, the assets took the form of gold. Today, they are mostly claims on the currencies of other countries.) These assets could then be used to pay armies, to purchase weapons from abroad, and to finance colonial expansions.

If the government's policy objective is to promote the welfare and living standards of ordinary citizens, however, the mercantilist focus on the balance of trade makes no sense. The principle of comparative advantage shows that average living standards are maximized by having individuals, regions, and countries specialize in the things they produce comparatively well and then trading to obtain the things they produce comparatively poorly. With specialization, domestic consumers get access to products they want at the lowest possible prices, while domestic firms are able to sell their products at

Evan El-Amin/Shutterstock

higher prices than would otherwise be possible. The more specialization takes place, the more trade occurs and thus the more average living standards increase.

Note also that with greater specialization among countries there will be many situations in which any country will have a trade deficit for a specific product or with a specific country. For example, the United States may have a trade deficit with Canada for oil (as it does) whereas Canada may have a trade deficit with the United Stated for tourism (as it does). As we first saw in Chapter 32, these product–country deficits and surpluses often reveal the outcome of efficient specialization; it makes little sense to point to these imbalances, as President Trump frequently does, as evidence of unfair trading arrangements.

For the country as a whole, the gains from trade are to be judged by the *volume* of trade rather than by the *balance* of trade. A situation in which there is a large volume of trade even though each country has a zero balance of trade is thus entirely satisfactory. Furthermore, a change in policy that results in an equal increase in both exports and imports will generate gains because it allows for specialization according to comparative advantage, even though it causes no change in either country's trade balance.

equities to foreigners, Canadians give up a stream of income that they would otherwise have. But, in both cases, they get a lump sum of funds that can be used for any type of consumption or investment. Is it obviously "better" to have a lower debt or a higher future income stream than to have a lump sum of funds right now? If it were obviously better, no family would ever borrow money to buy a house or a car, and no firm would ever borrow money to build a factory.

A country that has a current account deficit is either borrowing from the rest of the world or selling some of its capital assets to the rest of the world. This is not necessarily undesirable.

To argue that it is undesirable for Canada to have a current account deficit is to argue that Canadians as a whole should not borrow from (or sell assets to) the rest of the world. But surely the wisdom of borrowing depends on *why* Canadians are borrowing. It is therefore important to know *why* there is a current account deficit.

Causes of Current Account Deficits There are several possible causes of a current account deficit. To analyze the possible causes, we will start with the following simple equation:

$$CA = S + (T - G) - I \tag{34-1}$$

where CA is the current account surplus (or deficit), S is private saving, I is private-sector investment, and $T - G$ is the budget surplus (or deficit) of the total government sector. This equation can be derived from the national income accounting identities we introduced in Chapter 20.[5]

This equation says that the current account balance in any year is exactly equal to the excess of national saving, $S + (T - G)$, over domestic investment I. If Canadians (and their governments) save more than is needed to finance the amount of domestic investment, where do the excess funds go? They are used to acquire foreign assets, and thus Canada has a current account surplus ($CA > 0$). In contrast, if Canadians do not save enough to finance the amount of domestic investment, the balance must be financed by foreign funds. Thus, Canada has a current account deficit ($CA < 0$).

Notice that this accounting identity showing the relationship between CA, S, I, and $(T - G)$ is known from our national accounting framework without any knowledge of exports or imports of particular products or of the exchange rate. Our accounting system ensures that these various values add up in such a way that Equation 34-1 is always true. This equation therefore provides a solid foundation for analyzing our questions about the desirability of current account deficits and surpluses.

We can re-arrange this equation very slightly to get

$$CA = (S - I) + (T - G) \tag{34-2}$$

which says that the current account balance is equal to the excess of private saving over investment plus the government budget surplus.

Equation 34-2 shows three separate reasons for any given increase in the current account deficit (a fall in CA). First, a reduction in private saving, other things being equal, will lead to a rise in the current account deficit. Second, a rise in domestic investment, other things being equal, will increase the current account deficit. Finally, other things being equal, a rise in the government's budget deficit (a smaller value of $T - G$)

---

[5] The derivation of Equation 34-1 is as follows. Recall from Chapter 20 that $GDP = C + I + G + NX$ (where all values are "actual" as opposed to "desired"). In an open economy, the total income accruing to domestic residents is equal to GDP *plus* net investment income from abroad, which we call R. This total income, $GDP + R$, can only be used in three ways: to finance consumption, to pay taxes, or to add to saving. Thus we have $C + I + G + NX + R = C + T + S$. It follows that $NX + R = S + (T - G) - I$. Finally, note that $NX + R$ is simply the sum of the trade balance and the capital-service balance, which equals the current account balance, CA.

will raise the current account deficit. This third case is often referred to as a situation of *twin deficits*. That is, a rise in the government's budget deficit will also have the effect (if S and I remain constant) of increasing the current account deficit.

> **An increase in the level of investment, a decrease in the level of private saving, and an increase in the government's budget deficit are all possible causes of an increase in a country's current account deficit.**

It makes little sense to discuss the desirability of a change in the current account deficit without first knowing the *cause* of the change. Knowing the cause is crucial to knowing whether the change in the current account deficit is undesirable. The following three examples illustrate this important point.

First, suppose business opportunities in Canada are very promising and, as a result, there is an increase in the level of private-sector investment. Most people would consider such an investment boom desirable because it would increase current output and employment and, by increasing the country's capital stock, it would also increase the level of potential output in the future. But as is clear from Equation 34-2, other things being equal, the effect of the rise in Canadian investment is an increase in the Canadian current account deficit. The current account deficit increases because, in the absence of increased domestic saving, the increase in domestic investment can only take place if it is financed by a capital inflow from other countries. This capital inflow represents a rise in Canada's current account deficit (or capital account surplus). In this case, however, it would be difficult to argue that the increase in Canada's current account deficit is undesirable as it simply reflects a boom in domestic business opportunities.

For a second example, suppose the domestic economy begins to slow and households and firms become pessimistic about the future. In such a situation, we expect households to increase their saving and firms to reduce their investment, thus increasing the value of $(S - I)$. As the economy slows we would also expect the government's net tax revenues to fall, thus decreasing the value of $(T - G)$. But it is possible that the first effect dominates the second effect, thus leading to an increase in the current account surplus. Is the increase in Canada's current account surplus desirable? Most people would probably agree that the onset of a recession as just described is surely undesirable, involving a loss of output and employment.

A third example relates to fiscal policy. Suppose S and I remain unchanged while the government increases its budget deficit. As $(T - G)$ falls, Canada's current account deficit increases (or its current account surplus falls). In this case, the rise in the current account deficit is clearly due to the rise in the government's budget deficit. But whether the larger budget deficit is itself undesirable depends on the many issues we examined in Chapter 31. As we saw there, some budget deficits are appropriate whereas others are probably undesirable; much depends on the details of the policy actions and the economic context.

An increase in domestic investment, other things being equal, will lead to an increase in the current account deficit. But there is little undesirable about this situation.

A country's current account deficit can change for a number of reasons. Whether any given change is desirable depends crucially on its underlying cause.

Is There a "Correct" Value for the Canadian Dollar?

In the late 1990s, the Canadian dollar depreciated by about 15 percent against the U.S. dollar. It was then common to hear financial commentators discuss how the Canadian dollar was "undervalued." Retailers selling imported products and firms using imported supplies complained that the weak Canadian dollar was undermining their business. Opposite statements were heard between 2002 and 2008 when, as a result of high world prices for raw materials, the Canadian dollar appreciated by about 50 percent. At the time, some financial commentators argued that the Canadian dollar was "overvalued." Canadian firms in the tourist-oriented hospitality industry and those exporting manufactured products complained that the strong Canadian dollar was damaging their business. In both cases, the observers appeared to believe that there was some "correct" value for the Canadian dollar. Is there?

As we saw in the previous section, a country that chooses to use a flexible exchange rate has its exchange rate determined by competitive forces in the foreign-exchange market. In Canada, and other countries as well, fluctuations in exchange rates have many causes. Some changes may be good for Canada, such as a worldwide shortage of wheat that drives up the world price of wheat, a major Canadian export. Others may be bad for Canada, such as the discovery of new copper deposits in Chile that drives down the price of copper, also a major Canadian export. But the various supply and demand forces are coming together in the foreign-exchange market to determine the equilibrium value of the exchange rate. Changes in this value may reflect positive or negative events for Canada, but it is difficult to think of this equilibrium value as being either "too high" or "too low."

With a flexible exchange rate, the market determines the value of the exchange rate. With respect to the forces of demand and supply, the equilibrium exchange rate is the "correct" exchange rate.

Saying that the current equilibrium exchange rate is the "correct" rate in no way suggests that this correct rate is constant. Indeed, foreign-exchange markets are so large, with so many participants in so many countries, each responding to a slightly different set of events and expectations, that the equilibrium exchange rate is constantly changing. In other words, as various forces lead to frequent changes in the demand for and supply of the Canadian dollar in foreign-exchange markets, the "correct" value of the Canadian exchange rate is always changing.

Some economists accept that the current exchange rate, as determined by the foreign-exchange market, is indeed the correct rate, but they also argue that there exists a "fundamental" value of the exchange rate that will hold in the long run. These economists argue that the exchange rate's long-run value is determined by *purchasing power parity*.

purchasing power parity (PPP) The theory that, over the long term, the exchange rate between two currencies adjusts to reflect relative price levels.

Purchasing Power Parity   The theory of **purchasing power parity** (PPP) holds that, over the long term, the value of the exchange rate between two currencies depends on the two currencies' relative purchasing power for goods and services. The theory holds that a currency will tend to have the same purchasing power when it is spent in its home country as it would have if it were converted to foreign exchange and spent in the foreign country. Another way to say the same thing is that the price of *identical baskets of goods* should be the same in the two countries when the price is expressed in the same currency. If we let P_C and P_E be the price levels in Canada and Europe, respectively, and let e be the Canadian-dollar price of euros (the exchange rate), then the theory of purchasing power parity predicts the following equality in the long run:

$$P_C = e \times P_E \qquad (34\text{-}3)$$

This equation simply says that if a basket of goods costs 1000 euros in Europe and the exchange rate is 1.5 (that is, 1.5 Canadian dollars per euro), then that same basket of goods should cost 1500 dollars in Canada ($1.5 \times 1000 = 1500$).

> According to the theory of purchasing power parity, the exchange rate between two countries' currencies is determined by the relative price levels in the two countries.

The idea behind PPP is a simple one. Suppose that Equation 34-3 did *not* hold—specifically, suppose that P_C was greater than $e \times P_E$, so that Canadian-dollar prices in Canada exceeded the Canadian-dollar prices of the same goods in Europe. In this case, people would eventually increase their purchases of the cheaper European goods and reduce their purchases of the expensive Canadian goods. These actions would have the effect of depreciating the Canadian dollar (a rise in e); this depreciation would continue until the equality was re-established.

The *PPP exchange rate* is the value of the exchange rate that makes Equation 34-3 hold. That is, the PPP exchange rate (between the Canadian dollar and the euro) is defined to be

$$e^{PPP} \equiv P_C/P_E \qquad (34\text{-}4)$$

Note that the PPP exchange rate is itself not constant. If inflation is higher in Canada than in Europe, for example, P_C will be rising faster than P_E and so the PPP exchange rate will be rising. Conversely, if inflation is lower in Canada than in Europe, P_C will be rising more slowly than P_E and the PPP exchange rate will be falling.

Theory Confronts Reality   Should we expect the *actual* exchange rate to equal the PPP exchange rate? The theory of purchasing power parity predicts that if the actual exchange rate (e) does not equal the PPP exchange rate (e^{PPP})—in which case the actual exchange rate is either "overvalued" or "undervalued"—then demands and supplies of Canadian and European goods will change until the equality holds. Thus, the theory of PPP predicts that the actual exchange rate will eventually equal the PPP exchange rate.

Figure 34-5 shows the path of the actual Canadian–U.S. exchange rate and the PPP exchange rate since 1981. It is clear from the figure that there are long periods over which the actual exchange rate deviates significantly from the PPP exchange rate. Why is this the case? Is there something wrong with the theory of purchasing power parity?

Recall from Equation 34-3 that P_C and P_E were defined as the prices of *identical baskets of goods* in Canada and Europe, respectively. Given that the goods are the same, the argument that the prices should (eventually) be equated across the two countries is sensible—if the prices are not equated across the two countries, there would be an incentive to purchase in the cheaper country rather than in the more expensive country, and this would lead to changes in the exchange rate until Equation 34-3 *did* hold.

FIGURE 34-5   Actual and PPP Exchange Rates, 1981–2017

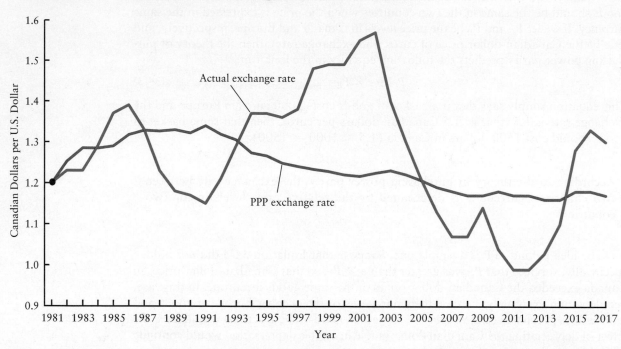

The actual exchange rate deviates from the PPP exchange rate for extended periods. The Canada–U.S. PPP exchange rate is the ratio of Canadian to U.S. price indexes. This PPP exchange rate increased during the 1980s when Canadian inflation was above that in the United States; it declined gradually over the next 20 years when Canadian inflation was slightly lower than in the United States. The actual Canada–U.S. exchange rate has fluctuated more dramatically and shows little tendency to track the PPP exchange rate. (The PPP exchange rate is a ratio of two price indexes; it has been constructed to be equal to the actual exchange rate in 1981, the first year of the sample period.)

(*Source:* Canadian CPI is from the Bank of Canada, annual average. U.S. CPI is from U.S. Bureau of Labor Statistics: www.bls.gov. Exchange rate is from Statistics Canada, CANSIM database, Table 176-0064, annual average.)

One problem, however, when we apply the theory of purchasing power parity to *national price indexes,* such as the Consumer Price Index or the implicit GDP deflator, is that the two baskets of goods are typically *not* the same—for two reasons.

Different Countries Produce Different Goods.   Suppose we apply the theory of PPP to the Canada–Europe exchange rate and we use the GDP deflators from the two countries as the measures of prices. Recall from Chapter 20 that the GDP deflator is an index of prices of goods *produced within the country*. But Canada and Europe clearly produce very different goods. The price of forest products will have a large weight in the Canadian GDP deflator but less weight in the European GDP deflator; in contrast, the price of wine will have a much larger weight in the European GDP deflator than in the Canadian GDP deflator.

The implication of these differences for the theory of PPP is important. As long as changes in the *relative* prices of goods occur, such as a change in the price of forest products relative to wine, then P_C (the Canadian GDP deflator) will change relative to P_E (the European GDP deflator) *even though the prices of individual goods might be equated across the two countries.* Thus, differences in the structure of the price indexes between two countries mean that using a PPP exchange rate computed on the basis of Equation 34-4 will be misleading. In other words, in the presence of changing relative prices, there is no reason to expect the actual exchange rate to equal the PPP exchange rate.

Non-Traded Goods Are Important.   The previous discussion emphasized that the *baskets* of goods across two countries might differ even though the products in the baskets were the same. But even if Canada and Europe produced exactly the same range of goods, so that the various weights in the GDP deflators were the same, there is another reason why the basket of goods in Canada differs from the basket of goods in Europe. Many products in any country are *not traded internationally*, such as haircuts, restaurant meals, dry cleaning, car-repair and landscaping services, and tickets to theatres or sporting events. But, since such products cannot be traded across international boundaries, there is nothing that will force their prices to be equal across the two countries. If haircuts are more expensive in Paris than in Toronto (as they are), we do not expect people to shift their consumption of haircuts away from Paris toward Toronto, and thus we should not expect the actual exchange rate to move to make Equation 34-3 hold.

The conclusion of this discussion is that we must be careful in selecting the price indexes we use when we apply the theory of purchasing power parity. We know that countries have different patterns of production and thus have different structures to their national price indexes. Thus, in the presence of changes in relative prices of various products, the national price indexes can change in ways that will not lead to changes in the exchange rate. Similarly, the presence of non-traded goods implies that some differences in prices across countries will not lead to changes in the location of demand and thus changes in the exchange rate.

Changes in relative prices and the presence of non-traded goods imply that the theory of purchasing power parity is generally a poor predictor of the actual exchange rate, even in the long run.

Should Canada Have a Fixed Exchange Rate?

In recent years, some economists have suggested that Canada peg the value of its currency to the U.S. dollar. Advocates of a fixed Canadian exchange rate see this policy as a means of avoiding the significant fluctuations in the Canadian–U.S. dollar exchange rate that would otherwise occur—fluctuations such as the 50 percent appreciation that occurred between 2002 and 2008 and the 25 percent depreciation that occurred between 2012 and 2015. They argue that exchange-rate fluctuations generate uncertainty for importers and exporters and thus increase the costs associated with international trade.

We examine this issue by comparing the main benefits of flexible and fixed exchange rates. Whereas flexible exchange rates dampen the effects on output and employment from external shocks to the economy, fixed exchange rates reduce the uncertainty faced by importers and exporters.

Flexible Exchange Rates as "Shock Absorbers"   For most of the years following the Second World War, Canada used a flexible exchange rate. Even when most other major countries chose to peg the value of their currencies to the U.S. dollar or to gold under the Bretton Woods system, Canada usually chose a flexible exchange rate. For all of its history Canada's economy has been heavily reliant on the export of resource-based products, the prices of which are determined in world markets and are often highly variable from year to year. Changes in these prices constitute changes in Canada's terms of trade and, as we saw earlier in this chapter, changes in a country's terms of trade are an important reason why exchange rates are so variable.

That the exchange rate adjusts in response to shocks is actually the main advantage of a flexible over a fixed exchange rate. A flexible exchange rate acts as a "shock absorber," dampening the effects on the country's output and employment from external shocks. To understand how this happens, consider a simple example.

Suppose a reduction in world demand leads to a reduction in the world prices of raw materials, which are major Canadian exports. When world demand for raw materials declines, there is a reduction in demand for Canadian exports and an accompanying reduction in demand for Canadian dollars (or a reduction in the supply of foreign exchange) in the foreign-exchange market. The effect on Canadian real GDP is shown in part (ii) of Figure 34-6 by the leftward shift of the AD curve. The effect in the foreign-exchange market is shown in part (i) by the leftward shift of the supply curve for foreign exchange. Consider the effect of this shock in two different situations. In the

FIGURE 34-6 Flexible Exchange Rates as a Shock Absorber

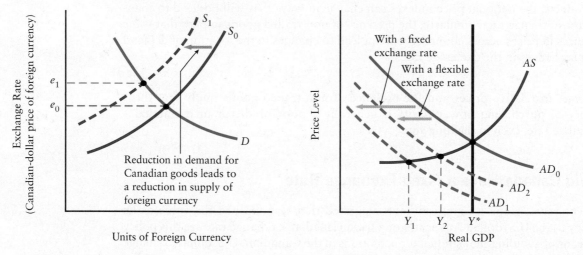

(i) Foreign-exchange market

(ii) AD and AS

Flexible exchange rates adjust to external shocks and thus dampen the effect on output and employment. The economy begins with the exchange rate equal to e_0 in part (i) and GDP equal to Y^* in part (ii). A reduction in the world price of Canadian exports causes a reduction in the supply of foreign exchange, shifting S_0 to S_1 in part (i).

With a fixed exchange rate, the Bank of Canada maintains the exchange rate at e_0, satisfying the excess demand for foreign exchange by selling its foreign-currency reserves. The reduction in the world price of Canada's exports is a negative aggregate demand shock. AD_0 shifts to the left to AD_1 in part (ii), causing GDP to fall to Y_1. The recessionary gap eventually pushes wages down, the AS curve shifts downward over time, and the economy moves along AD_1 to Y^*. The adjustment, however, may be very slow.

With a flexible exchange rate, the Bank of Canada allows the Canadian dollar to depreciate. The exchange rate rises to e_1 in part (i). The reduction in the price of Canadian exports still causes the AD curve to shift to the left in part (ii), but the shift is dampened by the depreciation of the dollar, which makes Canadian exports more attractive in world markets. The AD curve shifts only to AD_2 and so GDP falls only to Y_2. There is still a recession, but smaller than in the case with a fixed exchange rate.

first, the Bank of Canada maintains a fixed exchange rate; in the second, the Bank of Canada allows the exchange rate to be freely determined by demand and supply.

If the Bank of Canada fixes the exchange rate at e_0, the reduction in the supply of foreign exchange from S_0 to S_1 leads to an excess demand for foreign currency. To keep the exchange rate fixed at e_0, the Bank must sell sufficient foreign-exchange reserves to satisfy the excess demand. But the negative shock to aggregate demand still occurs and thus output and employment in Canada fall, as shown in part (ii) of Figure 34-6. If this shock is large and persistent enough, Canadian wages will eventually fall and the AS curve will eventually shift downward, returning real GDP to the level of potential output. But the closing of the recessionary gap may be slow and painful.

If Canada instead has a flexible exchange rate, the reduction in the world prices of raw materials will still lead to a reduction in the supply of foreign exchange but in this situation it will cause a depreciation of the Canadian dollar. The exchange rate will increase from e_0 to e_1. The AD curve will shift to the left, reducing Canada's GDP, just as in the fixed-exchange-rate case, *but it will not shift as far*. The sectors of the Canadian economy producing raw materials will still be in recession, for there has been a reduction in demand for these products. But the overall Canadian downturn will be dampened by the depreciation of the Canadian dollar. Other exporting sectors of the Canadian economy will actually *expand* as a result of the depreciation because their products are now less expensive in world markets. Thus, as shown in part (ii) of Figure 34-6, the leftward shift of the AD curve will not be as large as in the case of the fixed exchange rate. The overall result is that, with a flexible exchange rate, the decline in world demand for Canadian goods leads to a less severe Canadian recession than if Canada had a fixed exchange rate.

One of the advantages of flexible exchange rates is that, in response to shocks to the terms of trade, the exchange rate can act as a shock absorber, dampening the effects of the shock on output and employment.

The dramatic fall in the world price of oil in 2014–2015 illustrates the central point. As the price of oil fell from U.S.$105 per barrel in June 2014 to U.S.$40 per barrel in late 2015, the Canadian dollar also depreciated sharply—by almost 20 percent. Since Canada is a significant net exporter of oil, this shock represented a negative AD shock for the country as a whole, and the economic slowdown was concentrated in the oil-producing provinces of Alberta, Saskatchewan, and Newfoundland. The large depreciation of the Canadian dollar, however, stimulated production and employment in other sectors, notably Ontario's and Quebec's export-oriented manufacturing sectors. These changes dampened the effects of the overall AD shock. Had the Canadian dollar not been permitted to depreciate the overall impact of the oil-price decline would have been more severe.

Note that having a fixed exchange rate does not prevent a country from being subjected to shocks from the rest of the world. Some advocates of fixed exchange rates seem to think that by fixing the value of a country's currency, the country is shielding itself from undesirable fluctuations. But shocks to a country's terms of trade will always occur. As long as there are changes in the demand for and supply of various products around the world, there will also be changes in a country's terms of trade. What Figure 34-6 shows, however, is that by fixing the exchange rate and thus avoiding the fluctuations in the value of the currency, the effects of the shock merely show up as increased volatility in output and employment.

A country will always experience shocks in its terms of trade. A flexible exchange rate absorbs some of the shock, reducing the effect on output and employment. A fixed exchange rate simply redistributes the effect of the shock—the exchange rate is smoother but output and employment are more volatile.

Trade, Transaction Costs, and Uncertainty   Despite the benefits of international trade, there are costs involved in exporting and importing goods and services. The *transaction costs* of international trade involve the costs associated with converting one currency to another, as must be done either by the importer or by the exporter of the product that is traded. For example, if you have an import–export business in Canada and want to import some bicycles from Japan, you will probably have to purchase Japanese yen at a bank or foreign-exchange dealer and, with those yen, pay the Japanese seller for the bicycles. Even if the Japanese seller accepts Canadian dollars for the bicycles, and this often is the case, he will be required to convert those Canadian dollars into yen before he can use that money in Japan to pay his workers or pay for other costs of production.

The greater is the volume of trade between two countries, the higher are the aggregate transaction costs associated with international trade.

Such transaction costs exist even if trade takes place between two countries with fixed exchange rates. For example, if the Bank of Canada pegged the value of the Canadian dollar to the U.S. dollar, any trade between the two countries would still require the costly conversion of one currency to the other. Thus, the existence of transaction costs cannot be used as an argument in favour of fixed exchange rates and against flexible exchange rates. As long as there are two currencies, the transaction costs must be borne by one party or the other. These transaction costs could be avoided only if the two countries shared a common currency.

The volatility of flexible exchange rates generates another type of cost for importers and exporters. Specifically, the unpredictability of the exchange rate leads to *uncertainty* about the profitability of any specific international transaction. Such uncertainty, given risk-averse firms, can be expected to lead to a smaller volume of international trade and thus to fewer benefits from such trade.

For example, suppose a Canadian appliance manufacturer enters into a contract to purchase a specified amount of steel from a Japanese producer for a specified yen price in one year's time. In this case, the Japanese producer bears no *foreign-exchange risk* because the price is specified in yen. But the Canadian appliance manufacturer bears considerable risk. If the yen depreciates relative to the dollar over the coming year, fewer Canadian dollars will be required to pay for the steel. But if the yen appreciates relative to the dollar over the coming year, more Canadian dollars will be required to pay for the steel. The Canadian buyer therefore faces a risk in terms of the Canadian-dollar cost of the steel. If the firm is *risk averse*, meaning simply that it would be prepared to pay a cost to avoid the risk, the presence of the risk may lead to fewer international transactions of this type. Perhaps to avoid the foreign-exchange risk, the Canadian buyer will decide instead to buy Canadian-made steel, even though it may be slightly more expensive or not as appropriate for the task.

If the presence of foreign-exchange risk leads to less international trade, there will be a reduction in the gains from trade.

Many of the people who advocate Canada's move to a fixed exchange rate point to the avoidance of this foreign-exchange risk as the main benefit. They argue that if the Canadian dollar were pegged in value to the U.S. dollar, both importers and exporters would face less uncertainty on the most important part of their trade—that between Canada and the United States. With the greater certainty, they argue, would come greater trade flows and thus an increase in the overall gains from trade.

But many economists disagree. While accepting the basic argument regarding the risks created by flexible (and volatile) exchange rates, they note that importers and exporters already have the means to avoid this uncertainty. In particular, traders can participate in *forward markets* in which they can buy or sell foreign exchange *in the future* at prices specified today. For example, the Canadian appliance manufacturer could enter into a contract to purchase the required amount of yen in one year's time at a price specified today. In this case, no matter what happened to the yen–dollar exchange rate in the intervening year, the uncertainty regarding the Canadian-dollar price of the steel would be entirely eliminated.

Limitations for Monetary Policy   One final point should be noted about the choice between fixed and flexible exchange rates. If the Bank of Canada chooses to allow the exchange rate to fluctuate in response to shocks, it can focus its monetary policy on the control of inflation. In other words, it can adjust its monetary policy—sometimes tightening and other times loosening—to keep inflation close to the stated 2 percent target. But if the Bank chooses instead to fix the exchange rate, it is not *also* able to control inflation.

As we saw in Chapter 28, the Bank of Canada conducts its monetary policy by establishing a target for the overnight interest rate and maintaining that rate through its lending and borrowing activities with the commercial banks. If the Bank chooses to intervene in the foreign-exchange market to keep the exchange rate fixed—sometimes buying foreign exchange and other times selling it—these transactions will influence the Canadian money supply directly and thus influence Canadian interest rates. But these changes in interest rates may not be consistent with the Bank's policy objective of keeping inflation close to the 2 percent target.

Efforts by the Bank of Canada to maintain a fixed exchange rate are likely to be inconsistent with its efforts to keep inflation close to the 2 percent target.

Summing Up   So, should Canada give up its flexible exchange rate and instead peg the value of the Canadian dollar to the U.S. dollar? Advocates of this policy emphasize the foreign-exchange risk faced by importers, exporters, and investors, and the gains from increased trade that would result from a fixed exchange rate. Opponents to the policy emphasize the considerable shock-absorption benefits from a flexible exchange rate.

This debate will surely continue, partly because it is difficult to quantify the costs and benefits of a flexible exchange rate. Economists on both sides of the debate understand and accept the logic of the arguments from the other side. But researchers have so far been unable to determine how much of a shock is absorbed by a flexible exchange rate, and thus to estimate how much more volatile output and employment would be with a fixed exchange rate. Similarly, it is very difficult to estimate just how much more trade would take place if the foreign-exchange risk faced by traders were eliminated by means of a fixed exchange rate. Without convincing empirical evidence supporting the move to a fixed exchange rate, however, the status quo will probably remain. It is probably safe to assume that Canada will continue to have a flexible exchange rate, at least for the next several years.

SUMMARY

34.1 The Balance of Payments

LO 1

- Actual transactions among Canadian firms, households, and governments and those in the rest of the world are reported in the balance of payments accounts. In these accounts, any transaction that represents a receipt for Canada (Canadians sell goods or assets to foreigners) is recorded as a credit item. Any transaction that represents a payment from Canada (Canadians purchase goods or assets from foreigners) is recorded as a debit item.
- Categories in the balance of payments accounts are the trade account, the capital-service account, the current account (which is equal to the trade account plus the capital-service account), and the capital account (which includes the official financing account).
- If all transactions are recorded in the balance of payments, the sum of all credit items necessarily equals the sum of all debit items. The balance of payments must always balance.
- A country with a current account deficit must also have a capital inflow—a capital account surplus. A country with a current account surplus must also have a capital outflow—a capital account deficit.

34.2 The Foreign-Exchange Market

LO 2

- The exchange rate between the Canadian dollar and some foreign currency is defined as the number of Canadian dollars required to purchase one unit of the foreign currency. A rise in the exchange rate is a depreciation of the Canadian dollar; a fall in the exchange rate is an appreciation of the Canadian dollar.
- The supply of foreign exchange (or the demand for Canadian dollars) arises from Canadian exports of goods and services, capital flows into Canada, and the desire of foreign banks, firms, and governments to use Canadian dollars as part of their reserves.
- The demand for foreign exchange (or the supply of Canadian dollars to purchase foreign currencies) arises from Canadian imports of goods and services, capital flows from Canada, and the desire of holders of Canadian dollars to decrease the size of their holdings.
- A depreciation of the Canadian dollar lowers the foreign price of Canadian exports and increases the amount of foreign exchange supplied (to purchase Canadian exports). Thus, the supply curve for foreign exchange is positively sloped when plotted against the exchange rate.
- A depreciation of the Canadian dollar raises the dollar price of imports from abroad and hence lowers the amount of foreign exchange demanded to purchase foreign goods. Thus, the demand curve for foreign exchange is negatively sloped when plotted against the exchange rate.

34.3 The Determination of Exchange Rates

LO 3

- When the central bank does not intervene in the foreign exchange market, there is a purely flexible exchange rate. Under fixed exchange rates, the central bank intervenes in the foreign-exchange market to maintain the exchange rate at an announced value. To do this, the central bank must be prepared to buy or sell foreign currency, sometimes in large quantities.
- Under a flexible, or floating, exchange rate, the exchange rate is determined by supply of and demand for the currency.
- The Canadian dollar will appreciate in foreign-exchange markets if there is an increase in the supply of foreign exchange (an increase in the demand for Canadian dollars) or if there is a reduction in the demand for

foreign exchange (a reduction in the supply of Canadian dollars). The opposite changes will lead to a depreciation of the Canadian dollar.

- Changes in the exchange rate are caused by changes in such things as changes in world prices, the rate of inflation in different countries, capital flows, structural conditions, and expectations about the future exchange rate.

34.4 Three Policy Issues

LO 4, 5, 6

- The view that current account deficits are undesirable is usually based on the mercantilist notion that exports are "good" and imports are "bad." But the gains from trade have nothing to do with the balance of trade—they depend on the volume of trade.
- From national income accounting, the current account balance is given by

$$CA = (S - I) + (T - G)$$

- An increase in investment, a decrease in saving, and an increase in the government budget deficit can each be the cause of a rise in the current account deficit.
- With a flexible exchange rate, supply and demand in the foreign-exchange market determine the "correct" value of the exchange rate. But this value changes as market conditions vary.
- The theory of purchasing power parity (PPP) predicts that exchange rates will adjust so that the purchasing power of a given currency is the same in different countries. That is, the prices of identical baskets of goods will be equated in different countries (when expressed in the same currency).
- If price indexes from different countries are used as the basis for computing the PPP exchange rate, differences in the structure of price indexes across countries, together with the presence of non-traded goods, can be responsible for persistent deviations of the actual exchange rate from the PPP exchange rate.
- An important benefit of a flexible exchange rate is that it acts as a shock absorber, dampening the effects on output and employment from shocks to a country's terms of trade.
- An important benefit of fixed exchange rates is that they reduce transaction costs and foreign-exchange risk faced by importers and exporters.

KEY CONCEPTS

Balance of payments
Current and capital accounts
Changes in official reserves
Foreign exchange and exchange rates
Appreciation and depreciation

Sources of the demand for and supply of foreign exchange
Fixed and flexible exchange rates
Mercantilism
Purchasing power parity

PPP exchange rate
Flexible exchange rates as shock absorbers
Foreign-exchange risk

STUDY EXERCISES

MyLab Economics Make the grade with MyLab Economics™: All Study Exercises can be found on MyLab Economics™. You can practise them as often as you want, and many feature step-by-step guided instructions to help you find the right answer.

▌FILL-IN-THE-BLANK

❶ Fill in the blanks to make the following statements correct.

  a. If a wine shop in Alberta buys a case of wine from Chile, the transaction is recorded as a(n) _____ in the _____ account, which is a subsection of the _____ account.

  b. If a Canadian receives dividend payments from a firm in Britain, the transaction is recorded as a(n) _____ in the _____ account, which is a subsection of the _____ account.

c. If a German pension-fund manager purchases a B.C. Hydro bond, the transaction is recorded as a(n) _____ in the _____ account. If a Canadian sells her ownership stake in a newspaper chain to an American, the transaction is recorded as a(n) _____ in the _____ account.

d. The sum of the current account and the capital account is known as the _____ and must *always* equal _____.

2 Fill in the blanks to make the following statements correct.

a. The convention among Canadian economists is to express the Canada–U.S. exchange rate as the _____ -dollar price of one _____ dollar. This definition allows us to express the price of one unit of foreign currency in _____ dollars.

b. A depreciation of the Canadian dollar means that it takes _____ Canadian dollars to purchase one unit of foreign currency, and there has been a(n) _____ in the exchange rate. An appreciation of the Canadian dollar means that it takes _____ Canadian dollars to purchase one unit of foreign currency, and there has been a(n) _____ in the exchange rate.

c. Suppose a newscaster tells us that the Canadian dollar is valued at 89.6 U.S. cents. Using the definition from this chapter, we say the Canadian–U.S. exchange rate is _____, meaning that it takes _____ Canadian dollars to buy one U.S. dollar.

d. The exchange rate is determined at the intersection of the _____ curve for foreign exchange and the _____ curve for foreign exchange. An exchange rate above this level means an excess _____ foreign exchange, which is also an excess _____ Canadian dollars. The exchange rate will _____ and the Canadian dollar will _____.

e. If there is a rise in foreign GDP, and foreign demand for Canadian goods increases, there will be a(n) _____ in supply of foreign currency. The Canadian dollar will _____.

f. An increase in Canadian prices relative to foreign prices will cause a(n) _____ in the demand for foreign exchange, and a(n) _____ in the supply of foreign exchange. The exchange rate will _____ and the Canadian dollar will therefore _____.

3 Fill in the blanks to make the following statements correct.

a. If the exchange rate is determined by the equality of supply and demand for foreign exchange and the central bank makes no foreign-exchange transactions, we say there is a(n) _____ exchange rate.

b. If the central bank buys and sells foreign exchange in an effort to maintain the exchange rate at a specific value, we say we have a(n) _____ exchange rate.

c. If the central bank pegs the exchange rate above its free-market equilibrium level, there will be a(n) _____ foreign exchange and the central bank will _____ foreign currency.

d. If the central bank pegs the exchange rate below its free-market equilibrium level, there will be a(n) _____ foreign exchange and the central bank will _____ foreign currency.

REVIEW

4 The diagram below shows the demand for foreign currency and the supply of foreign currency. The equilibrium exchange rate is e^*. Assume that Canada has a purely flexible exchange rate.

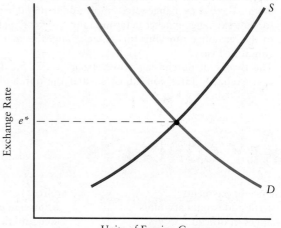

a. Show in the diagram the effect of a general inflation in Canada (when there is no inflation in the rest of the world). Explain.

b. Show what happens to the exchange rate if there is a large increase in foreign demand for Canadian telecommunications equipment. Explain.

c. Show the effect of an increase in Canadian investors' demand for Japanese government bonds. Explain.

5 What is the probable effect of each of the following on the exchange rate of a country, other things being equal?

a. The quantity of oil imports is greatly decreased, but the expenditure on imported oil is higher because of price increases.

b. The country's inflation rate falls much lower than that of its trading partners.

c. Rising labour costs of the country's manufacturers lead to a worsening ability to compete in world markets.

d. The government greatly expands its gifts of food and machinery to developing countries.

e. The central bank raises interest rates sharply.

f. More domestic oil is discovered and developed.

6 Many commentators are perplexed when they observe a depreciation of the Canadian dollar but not a reduction in the Canadian trade deficit. Explain why there is not a precise relationship between the value of the dollar and the trade balance. Give one example of an event that would give rise to each of the following:

a. Appreciation of the Canadian dollar and a fall in Canada's trade surplus

b. Depreciation of the Canadian dollar and a fall in Canada's trade surplus

7 The diagram below shows the demand for foreign currency and the supply of foreign currency. The equilibrium exchange rate is e^*.

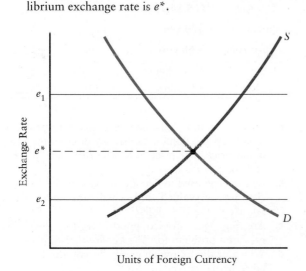

Units of Foreign Currency

a. Suppose the Bank of Canada decides to fix the exchange rate at e_1. What must the Bank do to accomplish its goal? How do the Bank's actions show up in the balance of payments accounts?

b. In part (a), explain why some people would call this a "a balance of payments surplus" even though the balance of payments is in balance.

c. Now suppose the Bank of Canada decides to fix the exchange rate at e_2. What must the Bank do to accomplish this goal? How do the Bank's actions show up in the balance of payments accounts?

d. With the exchange rate fixed at e_2, explain why some people would call this a "balance of payments deficit" even though the balance of payments is in balance.

8 Suppose Canadian real GDP is equal to potential output, the price level is stable, and the exchange rate is equal to e_0, its market-clearing value. There is then an upturn in the world demand for construction materials, especially lumber.

a. Draw a diagram of the foreign-exchange market. Assuming that Canada has a flexible exchange rate, show the likely effect on Canada's exchange rate of the increase in world demand for construction materials.

b. Explain the Bank of Canada's participation in the foreign-exchange market if Canada's exchange rate is fixed at e_0.

c. Now draw an *AD/AS* diagram for the Canadian economy. What is the likely effect of the shock on Canadian GDP under the conditions in part (a)?

d. On the same *AD/AS* diagram from part (c), show the effect of the shock on Canadian GDP under the conditions of part (b).

e. Explain how a flexible exchange rate acts as a shock absorber, insulating the economy from both positive and negative shocks.

9 A former Canadian prime minister once suggested that Canada should try to have balanced trade, industry by industry.

a. Do you think this makes sense? Explain.

b. How about the idea of balanced trade, country by country? Explain whether this makes sense.

10 A letter to a Canadian national newspaper argued that "the economy of this once wonderful country is in the sewer and the politicians keep on tinkering, not knowing how to fix it." The letter proposed a 20 percent depreciation of the Canadian dollar and argued that the immediate effects would be (among other things)

- a dramatic rise in exports
- a dramatic fall in imports
- a large net inflow of new foreign investment

a. What could the Bank of Canada do to generate a 20 percent depreciation of the Canadian dollar?

b. Would the action necessary in part (a) be consistent with the Bank's stated commitment to keeping inflation close to the 2 percent target? Explain.

c. However such a depreciation of the Canadian dollar might occur, is it possible to have the three effects claimed by the author of the letter? Explain.

| PROBLEMS

11 The table below shows Sophie's financial details for 2019. Answer the following questions about her "balance of payments." (Read *Applying Economic Concepts 34-1* to help answer these questions.)

Sophie's Financial Details, 2019	
Income from lifeguarding	$2500
Income from lawn mowing	3500
Gift from grandparents	1000
Interest from bank deposits	150
Expenditure on coffee and pastry	1000
Expenditure on tuition	3500
Purchase of mutual funds	1200
Bank balance at end of year	3500
Increase in bank balance during the year	1450

a. What is Sophie's "trade balance"? Explain.
b. What is Sophie's overall current account balance? Explain.
c. What is Sophie's capital account balance? Explain.
d. There is one (and only one) piece of information shown above that is not needed to compute Sophie's balance of payments. What is it? Explain why it is not needed.

⓬ Consider the balance-of-payments accounting information for FarawayLand as shown in the table below for the year 2018. All values are in billions of dollars.

Exports	126
Imports	−105
Net foreign-investment income	−31
Capital outflow from Canada (purchase of assets from foreigners)	−26
Capital inflow to Canada (sales of assets to foreigners)	36
Changes in official international reserves	0

a. What is the trade balance?
b. What is the current account balance?
c. What is the change in FarawayLand's net foreign assets?
d. What is capital account balance?
e. What is the balance of payments?
f. What exchange-rate regime does FarawayLand likely have? Explain your reasoning.

⓭ Every few months, *The Economist* publishes its "Big Mac Index." Using the current exchange rates, it compares the U.S.-dollar price of Big Macs in several countries. It then concludes that countries in which the Big Mac is cheaper (in U.S. dollars) than in the United States have "undervalued" currencies. Similarly, countries with Big Macs more expensive than in the United States have "overvalued" currencies. The table below shows data from January 2015. (Data from www.economist.com.) It shows the domestic-currency prices of Big Macs in various countries. It also shows the exchange rate, expressed as the number of units of domestic currency needed to purchase one U.S. dollar.

Country	Domestic Currency Price	Exchange Rate	U.S. Dollar Price
Canada	C$5.70	1.23	$__
U.S.A.	U.S.$4.79	1.00	$__
Japan	370 yen	117.77	$__
Euro zone	3.68 euros	0.86	$__
China	17.20 yuan	6.21	$__
Russia	89 rubles	65.23	$__

a. For each country, use the exchange rate provided to convert the domestic-currency price to the U.S.-dollar price. The price in terms of the currency for any country i is $P_i = e \times P_{U.S.}$.
b. By the logic used in *The Economist*, which currencies are overvalued and which are undervalued relative to the U.S. dollar?
c. Are Big Macs traded goods? If not, does this present a problem for *The Economist*? Explain.
d. Which of the following goods do you think would be a better candidate for this exercise? Explain your choice.
   (i) cement
   (ii) diamonds
   (iii) fresh fruit
   (iv) computer RAM chips

Mathematical Notes

1. Because one cannot divide by zero, the ratio $\Delta Y / \Delta X$ cannot be evaluated when $\Delta X = 0$. However, as ΔX *approaches* zero, the ratio $\Delta Y / \Delta X$ increases without limit:

$$\lim_{\Delta X \to 0} \frac{\Delta Y}{\Delta X} = \infty$$

Therefore, we say that the slope of a vertical line (when $\Delta X = 0$ for any ΔY) is equal to infinity.

2. Many variables affect the quantity demanded. Using functional notation, the argument of the next several pages of the text can be anticipated. Let Q^D represent the quantity of a product demanded and

$$T, \overline{Y}, N, \hat{Y}, p, p_j$$

represent, respectively, tastes, average household income, population, income distribution, the commodity's own price, and the price of the jth other product.

The demand function is

$$Q^D - D(T, \overline{Y}, N, \hat{Y}, p, p_j), \qquad j - 1, 2, \ldots, n$$

The demand schedule or curve is given by

$$Q^D = d(p) \Big|_{T, \overline{Y}, N, \hat{Y}, p_j}$$

where the notation means that the variables to the right of the vertical line are held constant.

This function is correctly described as the demand function with respect to price, all other variables being held constant. This function, often written concisely as $Q^D = d(p)$, shifts in response to changes in other variables. Consider average income: If, as is usually hypothesized, $\partial Q^D / \partial \overline{Y} > 0$, then increases in average income shift $Q^D = d(p)$ rightward and decreases in average income shift $Q^D = d(p)$ leftward. Changes in other variables likewise shift this function in the direction implied by the relationship of that variable to the quantity demanded.

3. Quantity demanded is a simple and straightforward but frequently misunderstood concept in everyday use, but it has a clear mathematical meaning. It refers to the dependent variable in the demand function from note 2:

$$Q^D = D(T, \overline{Y}, N, \hat{Y}, p, p_j)$$

It takes on a specific value whenever a specific value is assigned to each of the independent variables. The value of Q^D changes whenever the value of any independent variable is changed. Q^D could change, for example, as a result of a change in any one price, in average income, in the distribution of income, in tastes, or in population. It could also change as a result of the net effect of changes in all of the independent variables occurring at once.

Some textbooks reserve the term *change in quantity demanded* for a movement along a demand curve, that is, a change in Q^D as a result *only* of a change in p. They then use other words for a change in Q^D caused by a change in the other variables in the demand function. This usage is potentially confusing because it gives the single variable Q^D more than one name.

Our usage, which corresponds to that in more advanced treatments, avoids this confusion. We call Q^D *quantity demanded* and refer to any change in Q^D as a *change in quantity demanded*. In this usage it is correct to say that a movement along a demand curve is a change in quantity demanded, but it is incorrect to say that a change in quantity demanded can occur *only because of* a movement along a demand curve (because Q^D can change for other reasons, for example, a *ceteris paribus* change in average household income).

4. Similar to the way we treated quantity demanded in note 2, let Q^S represent the quantity of a commodity supplied and

$$C, X, p, w_i$$

represent, respectively, producers' goals, technology, the product's price, and the price of the ith input.

The supply function is

$$Q^S = S(C, X, p, w_i), \qquad i = 1, 2, \ldots, m$$

The supply schedule or curve is given by

$$Q^S = s(p)\Big|_{C, X, w_i}$$

This is the supply function with respect to price, all other variables being held constant. This function, often written concisely as $Q^S = s(p)$, shifts in response to changes in other variables.

5. Equilibrium occurs where $Q^D = Q^S$. For *specified values of all other variables*, this requires that

$$d(p) = s(p) \qquad [5.1]$$

Equation 5.1 defines an equilibrium value of p; although p is an *independent* or *exogenous* variable in each of the supply and demand functions, it is an *endogenous* variable in the economic model that imposes the equilibrium condition expressed in Equation 5.1. Price is endogenous because it is assumed to adjust to bring about equality between quantity demanded and quantity supplied. Equilibrium quantity, also an endogenous variable, is determined by substituting the equilibrium price into either $d(p)$ or $s(p)$.

Graphically, Equation 5.1 is satisfied only at the point where the demand and supply curves intersect. Thus, supply and demand curves are said to determine the equilibrium values of the endogenous variables, price and quantity. A shift in any of the independent variables held constant in the d and s functions will shift the demand or supply curves and lead to different equilibrium values for price and quantity.

6. The axis reversal arose in the following way. Alfred Marshall (1842–1924) theorized in terms of "demand price" and "supply price," which were the prices that would lead to a given quantity being demanded or supplied. Thus,

$$p^D = d(Q) \qquad [6.1]$$

$$p^S = s(Q) \qquad [6.2]$$

and the condition of equilibrium is

$$d(Q) = s(Q)$$

When graphing the behavioural relationships expressed in Equations 6.1 and 6.2, Marshall naturally put the independent variable, Q, on the horizontal axis.

Leon Walras (1834–1910), whose formulation of the working of a competitive market has become the accepted one, focused on quantity demanded and quantity supplied *at a given price*. Thus,

$$Q^D = d(p)$$

$$Q^S = s(p)$$

and the condition of equilibrium is

$$d(p) = s(p)$$

Walras did not use graphical representation. Had he done so, he would surely have placed p (his independent variable) on the horizontal axis.

Marshall's work influenced later generations of economists, in particular because he was the great popularizer of graphical analysis in economics. Today, we use his graphs, even for Walras's analysis. The axis reversal is thus one of those historical accidents that seem odd to people who did not live through the "perfectly natural" sequence of steps that produced it.

7. The definition in the text uses finite changes and is called *arc elasticity* because it is being computed across an *arc* of the demand curve. The parallel definition using derivatives is

$$\eta = \frac{dQ}{dp} \cdot \frac{p}{Q}$$

and is called *point elasticity*.

8. The propositions in the text are proved as follows. Letting *TE* stand for total expenditure, we can write

$$TE = p \cdot Q$$

It follows that the change in total expenditure is

$$dTE = Q \cdot dp + p \cdot dQ \qquad [8.1]$$

Multiplying and dividing both terms on the right-hand side of Equation 8.1 by $p \cdot Q$ yields

$$dTE = \left[\frac{dp}{p} + \frac{dQ}{Q}\right] \cdot (p \cdot Q)$$

Because dp and dQ are opposite in sign as we move along the demand curve, dTE will have the same sign as the term in brackets on the right-hand side that dominates—that is, on which percentage change is largest.

A second way of arranging Equation 8.1 is to divide both sides by dp to get

$$\frac{dTE}{dp} = Q + p \cdot \frac{dQ}{dp} \qquad [8.2]$$

From the definition of point elasticity in note 7, however,

$$Q \cdot \eta = p \cdot \frac{dQ}{dp} \qquad [8.3]$$

which we can substitute into Equation 8.2 to obtain

$$\frac{dTE}{dp} = Q + Q \cdot \eta = Q \cdot (1 + \eta) \qquad [8.4]$$

Because η is a negative number, the sign of the right-hand side of Equation 8.4 is negative if the absolute value of η exceeds unity (elastic demand) and positive if it is less than unity (inelastic demand).

Total expenditure is maximized when dTE/dp is equal to zero. As can be seen from Equation 8.4, this occurs when elasticity is equal to -1.

9. The distinction between an incremental change and a marginal change is the distinction for the function $Y = Y(X)$ between $\Delta Y/\Delta X$ and the derivative dY/dX. The latter is the limit of the former as ΔX approaches zero. We shall meet this distinction repeatedly—in this chapter in reference to marginal and incremental *utility* and in later chapters with respect to such concepts as marginal and incremental *product, cost,* and *revenue.* Where Y is a function of more than one variable—for example, $Y = f(X,Z)$—the marginal relationship between Y and X is the partial derivative $\partial Y/\partial X$ rather than the total derivative dY/dX.

10. The hypothesis of diminishing marginal utility requires that we can measure utility of consumption by a function

$$U = U(X_1, X_2, \ldots, X_n)$$

where $X_1, \ldots, X_n$ are quantities of the n products consumed. It really embodies two utility hypotheses: first,

$$\partial U/\partial X_i > 0$$

which says that the consumer can get more utility by increasing consumption of any specific product; second,

$$\partial^2 U/\partial X_i^2 < 0$$

which says that the utility of *additional* consumption of some product declines as the amount of that product consumed increases.

11. Because the slope of the indifference curve is negative, it is the absolute value of the slope that declines as one moves downward to the right along the curve. The algebraic value, of course, increases. The phrase *diminishing marginal rate of substitution* thus refers to the absolute, not the algebraic, value of the slope.

12. The relationship between the slope of the budget line and relative prices can be seen as follows. In the two-good example with prices held constant, a change in expenditure (ΔE) is given by the equation

$$\Delta E = p_C \cdot \Delta C + p_F \cdot \Delta F \qquad [12.1]$$

Expenditure is constant for all combinations of F and C that lie on the same budget line. Thus, along such a line we have $\Delta E = 0$. This implies

$$p_C \cdot \Delta C + p_F \cdot \Delta F = 0 \qquad [12.2]$$

and thus

$$\Delta C/\Delta F = -p_F/p_C. \qquad [12.3]$$

The ratio $\Delta C/\Delta F$ is the slope of the budget line. It is negative because, with a fixed budget, one must consume less C in order to consume more F. In other words, Equation 12.3 says that the negative of the slope of the budget line is the ratio of the absolute prices (i.e., the relative price). Although prices do not show directly in Figure 6A-3, they are implicit in the budget line: Its slope depends solely on the relative price, while its position, given a fixed money income, depends on the absolute prices of the two goods.

13. *Marginal product,* as defined in the text, is really *incremental* product. More advanced treatments distinguish between this notion and marginal product as the limit of the ratio as ΔL approaches zero.

Marginal product thus measures the rate at which total product is changing as one factor is varied and is the partial derivative of the total product with respect to the variable factor. In symbols,

$$MP = \frac{\partial TP}{\partial L}$$

14. We have referred specifically both to diminishing *marginal* product and to diminishing *average* product. In most cases, eventually diminishing marginal product implies eventually diminishing average product. This is not true in *all* cases, however, as the accompanying figure shows.

   In the figure below, marginal product diminishes after v units of the variable factor are employed. Because marginal product falls toward, but never quite reaches, a value of m, average product rises continually toward, but never quite reaches, the same value.

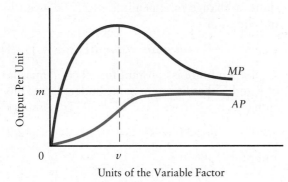

Units of the Variable Factor

15. Let Q be the quantity of output and L the quantity of the variable factor. In the short run,

$$TP = Q = f(L) \qquad [15.1]$$

We now define

$$AP = \frac{Q}{L} = \frac{f(L)}{L} \qquad [15.2]$$

$$MP = \frac{dQ}{dL} \qquad [15.3]$$

We are concerned with the relationship between AP and MP. Where average product is rising, at a maximum, or falling is determined by its derivative with respect to L:

$$\frac{d(Q/L)}{dL} = \frac{L \cdot (dQ/dL) - Q}{L^2} \qquad [15.4]$$

The right-hand side may be rewritten

$$\frac{1}{L} \cdot \left[\frac{dQ}{dL} - \frac{Q}{L} \right] = \frac{1}{L} \cdot (MP - AP) \qquad [15.5]$$

Clearly, when MP is greater than AP, the expression in Equation 15.5 is positive and thus AP is rising. When MP is less than AP, AP is falling. When they are equal, AP is neither rising nor falling.

16. The text defines *incremental cost*. Strictly, marginal cost is the rate of change of total cost with respect to output, Q. In other words, it is the derivative of total cost with respect to output,

$$MC = \frac{dTC}{dQ}$$

17. This point is easily seen if a little algebra is used:

$$AVC = \frac{TVC}{Q}$$

but note that $TVC = L \cdot w$ and $Q = AP \cdot L$, where L is the quantity of the variable factor used and w is its cost per unit. Therefore,

$$AVC = \frac{L \cdot w}{AP \cdot L} = \frac{w}{AP}$$

Because w is a constant, it follows that AVC and AP vary inversely with each other, and when AP is at its maximum value, AVC must be at its minimum value.

18. A little elementary calculus will prove the point:

$$MC = \frac{dTC}{dQ} = \frac{dTVC}{dQ} = \frac{d(L \cdot w)}{dQ}$$

If w does not vary with output,

$$MC = \frac{dL}{dQ} \cdot w$$

However, referring to note 15 (Equation 15.3), we see that

$$\frac{dL}{dQ} = \frac{1}{MP}$$

Thus,

$$MC = \frac{w}{MP}$$

Because w is fixed, MC varies negatively with MP. When MP is at a maximum, MC is at a minimum.

19. Strictly speaking, the marginal rate of substitution refers to the slope of the tangent to the isoquant at a particular point, whereas the calculations in Figure 8A-1 refer to the average rate of substitution between two distinct points on the isoquant. Assume a production function

$$Q = Q(K,L) \qquad [19.1]$$

Isoquants are given by the function

$$K = I(L, \overline{Q}) \qquad [19.2]$$

derived from Equation 19.1 by expressing K as an explicit function of L and Q. A single isoquant relates to a particular level of output, $\overline{Q}$. Define Q_K and Q_L as an alternative, more compact notation for $\partial Q/\partial K$ and $\partial Q/\partial L$, the marginal products of capital and labour. Also, let Q_{KK} and Q_{LL} stand for $\partial^2 Q/\partial K^2$ and $\partial^2 Q/\partial L^2$, respectively. To obtain the slope of the isoquant, totally differentiate Equation 19.1 to obtain

$$dQ = Q_K \cdot dK + Q_L \cdot dL$$

Then, because we are moving along a single isoquant, set $dQ = 0$ to obtain

$$\frac{dK}{dL} = -\frac{Q_L}{Q_K} = MRS$$

Diminishing marginal productivity implies $Q_{LL} < 0$ and $Q_{KK} < 0$, and hence, as we move down the isoquant of Figure 8A-1, Q_K is rising and Q_L is falling, so the absolute value of MRS is diminishing. This is called the *hypothesis of a diminishing marginal rate of substitution*.

20. Formally, the problem is to choose K and L in order to maximize

$$Q = Q(K, L)$$

subject to the constraint

$$p_K \cdot K + p_L \cdot L = C$$

To do this, form the Lagrangean,

$$\pounds = Q(K,L) - \lambda(p_K \cdot K + p_L \cdot L - C)$$

where λ is called the Lagrange multiplier.

The first-order conditions for this maximization problem are

$$Q_K = \lambda \cdot p_K \qquad [20.1]$$

$$Q_L = \lambda \cdot p_L \qquad [20.2]$$

$$p_K \cdot K + p_L \cdot L = C \qquad [20.3]$$

Dividing Equation 20.1 by Equation 20.2 yields

$$\frac{Q_K}{Q_L} = \frac{p_K}{p_L}$$

That is, the ratio of the marginal products, which is −1 times the MRS, is equal to the ratio of the factor prices, which is −1 times the slope of the isocost line.

21. Marginal revenue is mathematically the derivative of total revenue with respect to output, dTR/dQ. Incremental revenue is $\Delta TR/\Delta Q$. However, the term *marginal revenue* is used loosely to refer to both concepts.

22. For notes 22 through 24, it is helpful first to define some terms. Let

$$\pi_n = TR_n - TC_n$$

where π_n is the profit when Q_n units are sold.

If the firm is maximizing its profits by producing Q_n units, its profits must be at least as large as the profits at output zero. That is,

$$\pi_n \geq \pi_0 \qquad [22.1]$$

This condition says that profits from producing must be greater than profits from not producing. Condition 22.1 can be rewritten as

$$\begin{aligned} TR_n - TVC_n - TFC_n \\ \geq TR_0 - TVC_0 - TFC_0 \end{aligned} \qquad [22.2]$$

However, note that by definition

$$TR_0 - 0 \qquad [22.3]$$

$$TVC_0 = 0 \qquad [22.4]$$

$$TFC_n = TFC_0 = Z \qquad [22.5]$$

where Z is a constant. By substituting Equations 22.3, 22.4, and 22.5 into Condition 22.2, we get

$$TR_n - TVC_n \geq 0$$

from which we obtain

$$TR_n \geq TVC_n$$

This proves Rule 1.

On a per-unit basis, it becomes

$$\frac{TR_n}{Q_n} \geq \frac{TVC_n}{Q_n} \qquad [22.6]$$

where Q_n is the number of units produced.

Because $TR_n = Q_n \times p_n$, where p_n is the price when n units are sold, Condition 22.6 may be rewritten as

$$p_n \geq AVC_n$$

23. Using elementary calculus, we may prove Rule 2.

$$\pi_n = TR_n - TC_n$$

each of which is a function of output Q. To maximize π, it is necessary that

$$\frac{d\pi}{dQ} = 0 \qquad [23.1]$$

From the definitions,

$$\frac{d\pi}{dQ} = \frac{dTR}{dQ} - \frac{dTC}{dQ} = MR - MC \qquad [23.2]$$

From Equations 23.1 and 23.2, a necessary condition for attaining maximum π is $MR - MC = 0$, or $MR = MC$, as is required by Rule 2.

24. To prove that for a negatively sloped demand curve, marginal revenue is less than price, let $p = p(Q)$. Then

$$TR = p \cdot Q = p(Q) \cdot Q$$

$$MR = \frac{dTR}{dQ} = Q \cdot \frac{dp}{dQ} + p$$

For a negatively sloped demand curve, dp/dQ is negative, and thus MR is less than price for positive values of Q.

25. The equation for a downward-sloping straight-line demand curve with price on the vertical axis is

$$p = a - b \cdot Q$$

where a is the vertical intercept (when $Q = 0$) and $-b$ is the slope of the demand curve. Total revenue is price times quantity:

$$TR = p \cdot Q = a \cdot Q - b \cdot Q^2$$

Marginal revenue is

$$MR = \frac{dTR}{dQ} = a - 2 \cdot b \cdot Q$$

Thus, the MR curve and the demand curve are both straight lines, they have the same vertical intercept (a), and the (absolute value of the) slope of the MR curve ($2b$) is twice that of the demand curve (b).

26. The marginal revenue produced by the factor involves two elements: first, the additional output that an extra unit of the factor produces and, second, the change in price of the product that the extra output causes. Let Q be output, R revenue, and L the number of units of the variable factor hired. The contribution to revenue of additional labour is $\partial R / \partial L$. This, in turn, depends on the contribution of the extra labour to output $\partial Q / \partial L$ (the marginal product of the factor) and the contribution of the extra output to revenue $\partial R / \partial Q$ (the firm's marginal revenue). Thus,

$$\frac{\partial R}{\partial L} = \frac{\partial Q}{\partial L} \cdot \frac{\partial R}{\partial Q}$$

We define the left-hand side as marginal revenue product, MRP. Thus,

$$MRP = MP \cdot MR$$

27. The proposition that the marginal labour cost is above the average labour cost when the average is rising is essentially the same mathematical proposition proved in note 15. Nevertheless, let us do it again, using elementary calculus.

The quantity of labour supplied depends on the wage rate: $L^s = f(w)$. Total labour cost along the supply curve is $w \cdot L^s$. The average cost of labour is $(w \cdot L^s)/L^s = w$. The marginal cost of labour is

$$\frac{d(w \cdot L^s)}{dL^s} = w + L^s \cdot \frac{dw}{dL^s}$$

Rewrite this as

$$MC = AC + L^s \cdot \frac{dw}{dL^s}$$

As long as the supply curve slopes upward, $dw/dL^s > 0$; therefore, $MC > AC$.

28. In the text, we define MPC as an incremental ratio. For mathematical treatment, it is sometimes convenient to define all marginal concepts as derivatives: $MPC = dC/dY_D$, $MPS = dS/dY_D$, and so on.

29. The basic relationship is

$$Y_D = C + S$$

Dividing through by Y_D yields

$$\frac{Y_D}{Y_D} = \frac{C}{Y_D} + \frac{S}{Y_D}$$

and thus

$$1 = APC + APS$$

Next, take the first difference of the basic relationship to get

$$\Delta Y_D = \Delta C + \Delta S$$

Dividing through by ΔY_D gives

$$\frac{\Delta Y_D}{\Delta Y_D} = \frac{\Delta C}{\Delta Y_D} + \frac{\Delta S}{\Delta Y_D}$$

and thus

$$1 = MPC + MPS$$

30. The total expenditure over all rounds is the sum of an infinite series. If we let A stand for autonomous expenditure and z for the marginal propensity to spend, the change in autonomous expenditure is ΔA in the first round, $z \cdot \Delta A$ in the second, $z^2 \cdot \Delta A$ in the third, and so on. This can be written as

$$\Delta A \cdot (1 + z + z^2 + \ldots + z^n)$$

If z is less than 1, the series in parentheses converges to $1/(1 - z)$ as n approaches infinity. The total change in expenditure is thus $\Delta A/(1 - z)$. In the example in the box, $z = 0.80$; therefore, the change in total expenditure is

$$\frac{\Delta A}{1 - z} = \frac{\Delta A}{0.2} = 5 \cdot \Delta A$$

31. The "rule of 72" says that any sum growing at the rate of X percent per year will double in approximately $72/X$ years. For two sums growing at the rates of X percent and Y percent per year, the *difference* between the two sums will double in approximately $72/(X - Y)$ years. The rule of 72 is only an approximation, but at low annual rates of growth it is extremely accurate.

32. A simple example of a production function is $GDP = z(LK)^{1/2}$. This equation says that to find the amount of GDP produced, multiply the amount of labour by the amount of capital, take the square root, and multiply the result by the constant z, which is a technology parameter. This

production function has positive but diminishing marginal returns to either factor. This can be seen by evaluating the first and second partial derivatives and showing the first derivatives to be positive and the second derivatives to be negative.

For example,

$$\frac{\partial GDP}{\partial K} = \frac{z \cdot L^{1/2}}{2 \cdot K^{1/2}} > 0$$

and

$$\frac{\partial^2 GDP}{\partial K^2} = -\frac{z \cdot L^{1/2}}{4 \cdot K^{3/2}} < 0$$

33. The production function $GDP = z(LK)^{1/2}$ displays constant returns to scale. To see this, multiply both L and K by the same constant, θ, and see that this multiplies the whole value of GDP by θ:

$$z(\theta L \cdot \theta K)^{1/2} = z(\theta^2 \cdot LK)^{1/2} = \theta z(LK)^{1/2} - \theta \cdot GDP$$

34. This is easily proved. The banking system wants sufficient deposits (D) to establish the target ratio (v) of deposits to reserves (R). This gives $R/D = v$. Any change in D of size ΔD has to be accompanied by a change in R of ΔR of sufficient size to restore v. Thus, $\Delta R/\Delta D = v$, so $\Delta D = \Delta R/v$ and $\Delta D/\Delta R = 1/v$. This can be shown also in terms of the deposits created by the sequence in Table 26-7. Let v be the reserve ratio and $e - 1 - v$ be the excess reserves per dollar of new deposits. If X dollars are initially deposited in the system, the successive rounds of new deposits will be $X, eX, e^2 X, e^3 X, \ldots$ The series

$$X + eX + e^2 X + e^3 X + \ldots$$

$$= X \cdot [1 + e + e^2 + e^3 + \ldots]$$

has a limit of $X \cdot \dfrac{1}{1 - e}$

$$= X \cdot \frac{1}{1 - (1 - v)} = \frac{X}{v}$$

This is the total new deposits created by an injection of $\$X$ of new reserves into the banking system. For example, when $v = 0.20$, an injection of $\$100$ into the system will lead to an overall increase in deposits of $\$500$.

35. Suppose the public wants to hold a fraction, c, of deposits in cash, C. Now suppose that X

dollars are injected into the system. Ultimately, this money will be held either as reserves by the banking system or as cash by the public. Thus, we have

$$\Delta C + \Delta R = X$$

From the banking system's reserve behaviour, we have $\Delta R = v \cdot \Delta D$, and from the public's cash behaviour, we have $\Delta C = c \cdot \Delta D$. Substituting into the above equation, we get the result that

$$\Delta D = \frac{X}{v + c}$$

From this we can also relate the change in reserves and the change in cash holdings to the initial injection:

$$\Delta R = \frac{v}{v + c} \cdot X$$

$$\Delta C = \frac{c}{v + c} \cdot X$$

For example, when $v = 0.20$ and $c = 0.05$, an injection of $100 will lead to an increase in reserves of $80, an increase in cash in the hands of the public of $20, and an increase in deposits of $400.

36. Let d be the government's debt-to-GDP ratio and let Δd be the annual change in d. The percentage change in d over the year is therefore $\Delta d / d$, which for small percentage changes is very closely approximated by

$$\Delta d / d = \Delta D / D - \Delta \text{GDP} / \text{GDP}$$

where ΔD is the budget deficit and is equal to $G - T + iD$. The second term is the percentage change in *nominal* GDP, which is approximately equal to $g + \pi$, where g is the growth rate of real GDP and π is the rate of inflation. We therefore rewrite the expression as

$$\Delta d / d = (G - T + iD)/D - (g + \pi)$$

Now, multiply both sides by d to get:

$$\Delta d = (G - T + iD)/\text{GDP} - (g + \pi)d$$

We can now let x be the primary budget deficit $(G - T)$ as a share of GDP. The equation then becomes

$$\Delta d = x + (i - \pi - g)d$$

Finally, note that the real interest rate on government bonds is $r = i - \pi$, and so our final equation becomes

$$\Delta d = x + (r - g)d$$

Timeline of Great Economists

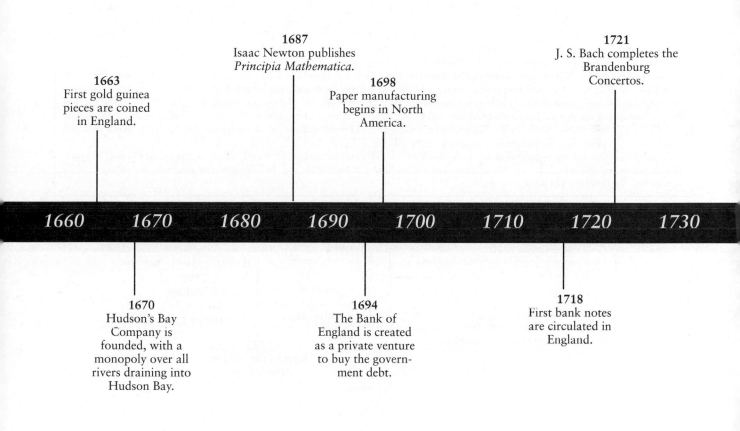

1663
First gold guinea
pieces are coined
in England.

1687
Isaac Newton publishes
Principia Mathematica.

1698
Paper manufacturing
begins in North
America.

1721
J. S. Bach completes the
Brandenburg
Concertos.

1660 1670 1680 1690 1700 1710 1720 1730

1670
Hudson's Bay
Company is
founded, with a
monopoly over all
rivers draining into
Hudson Bay.

1694
The Bank of
England is created
as a private venture
to buy the govern-
ment debt.

1718
First bank notes
are circulated in
England.

ADAM SMITH   (1723–1790)

Adam Smith was born in 1723 in the small Scottish town of Kirkcaldy. He is perhaps the single most influential figure in the development of modern economics, and even those who have never studied economics know of his most famous work, *The Wealth of Nations,* and are familiar with the terms *laissez-faire* and the *invisible hand,* both attributable to Smith. He described the workings of the capitalist market economy, the division of labour in production, the role of money, free trade, and the nature of economic growth. Even today, the breadth of his scholarship is considered astounding.

Smith was raised by his mother, as his father had died before his birth. His intellectual promise was discovered early, and at age 14 Smith was sent to study at Glasgow and then at Oxford. He returned to an appointment as professor of moral philosophy at University of Glasgow, where he became one of the leading philosophers of his day. He lectured on natural theology, ethics, jurisprudence, and political economy to students who travelled from as far away as Russia to hear his lectures.

In 1759, Smith published *The Theory of Moral Sentiments*, in which he attempted to identify the origins of moral judgment. In this early work, Smith writes of the motivation of self-interest and of the morality that keeps it in check. After its publication, Smith left his post at the University of Glasgow to embark on a European tour as the tutor to a young aristocrat, the Duke of Buccleuch, with whom he travelled for two years. In exchange for this assignment Smith was provided with a salary for the remainder of his life. He returned to the small town of his birth and spent the next 10 years alone, writing his most famous work.

An Inquiry into the Nature and Causes of the Wealth of Nations was published in 1776. His contributions in this book (generally known as *The Wealth of Nations*) were revolutionary, and the text became the foundation for much of modern economics. It continues to be reprinted today. Smith rejected the notion that a country's supply of gold and silver was the measure of its wealth—rather, it was the real incomes of the people that determined national wealth. Growth in the real incomes of the country's citizens—that is, economic growth—would result from specialization in production, the division of labour, and the use of money to facilitate trade. Smith provided a framework for analyzing the questions of income growth, value, and distribution.

Smith's work marked the beginning of what is called the Classical period in economic thought, which continued for the next 75 years. This school of thought was centred on the principles of natural liberty (laissez-faire) and the importance of economic growth as a means of bettering the conditions of human existence.

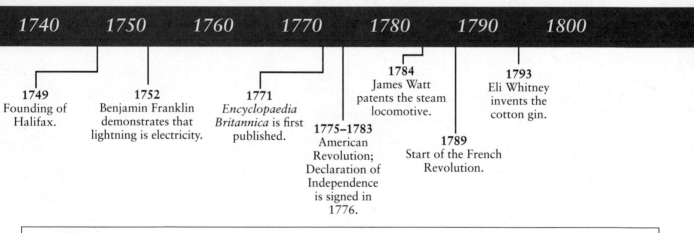

1740   1750   1760   1770   1780   1790   1800

1749
Founding of Halifax.

1752
Benjamin Franklin demonstrates that lightning is electricity.

1771
Encyclopaedia Britannica is first published.

1775–1783
American Revolution; Declaration of Independence is signed in 1776.

1784
James Watt patents the steam locomotive.

1789
Start of the French Revolution.

1793
Eli Whitney invents the cotton gin.

THOMAS MALTHUS   (1766–1834)

Thomas Malthus was born into a reasonably well-to-do English family. He was educated at Cambridge, and from 1805 until his death he held the first British professorship of political economy in the East India Company's college at Haileybury. In 1798 he published *An Essay on the Principle of Population as It Affects the Future Improvement of Society,* which was revised many times in subsequent years until finally he published *A Summary View of the Principle of Population* in 1830.

It is these essays on population for which Malthus is best known. His first proposition was that population, when unchecked, would increase in a geometric progression such that the population would double every 25 years. His second proposition was that the means of subsistence (i.e., the food supply) cannot possibly increase faster than in arithmetic progression (increasing by a given number of units every year). The result would be population growth eventually outstripping food production, and thus abject poverty and suffering for the majority of people in every society.

Malthus's population theory had tremendous intellectual influence at the time and became an integral part of the Classical theory of income distribution. However, it is no longer taken as a good description of current or past trends.

DAVID RICARDO   *(1772–1823)*

David Ricardo was born in London to parents who had emigrated from the Netherlands. Ricardo's father was very successful in money markets, and Ricardo himself was very wealthy before he was 30 by earning money on the stock exchange. He had little formal education, but after reading Adam Smith's *The Wealth of Nations* in 1799, he chose to divide his time between studying and writing about political economy and increasing his own personal wealth.

Ricardo's place in the history of economics was assured by his achievement in constructing an abstract model of how capitalism worked. He built an analytic "system" using deductive reasoning that characterizes economic theorizing to the present day. The three critical principles in Ricardo's system were (1) the theory of rent, (2) Thomas Malthus's population principle, and (3) the wages-fund doctrine. Ricardo published *The Principles of Political Economy and Taxation* in 1817, and the work dominated Classical economics for the following half-century.

Ricardo also contributed the concept of comparative advantage to the study of international trade. Ricardo's theories regarding the gains from trade had some influence on the repeal of the British Corn Laws in 1846—tariffs on the importation of grains into Great Britain—and the subsequent transformation of that country during the nineteenth century from a country of high tariffs to one of completely free trade.

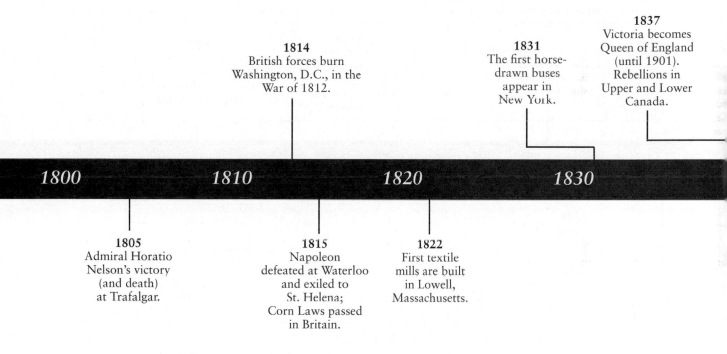

1814
British forces burn
Washington, D.C., in the
War of 1812.

1831
The first horse-
drawn buses
appear in
New York.

1837
Victoria becomes
Queen of England
(until 1901).
Rebellions in
Upper and Lower
Canada.

1800   *1810*   *1820*   *1830*

1805
Admiral Horatio
Nelson's victory
(and death)
at Trafalgar.

1815
Napoleon
defeated at Waterloo
and exiled to
St. Helena;
Corn Laws passed
in Britain.

1822
First textile
mills are built
in Lowell,
Massachusetts.

JOHN STUART MILL   *(1806–1873)*

John Stuart Mill, born in London, was the son of James Mill, a prominent British historian, economist, and philosopher. By age 12 he was acquainted with the major economics works of the day, and at 13 he was correcting the proofs of his father's book, *Elements of Political Economy.* J. S. Mill spent most of his life working at the East India Company—his extraordinarily prolific writing career was conducted entirely as an aside. In 1848 he published his *Principles of Political Economy,* which updated the principles found in Adam Smith's *The Wealth of Nations* and which remained the basic textbook for students of economics until the end of the nineteenth century. In *Principles,* Mill made an important contribution to the economics discipline by distinguishing between the economics of production and of distribution. He pointed out that economic laws had nothing to do with the distribution of wealth, which was a societal matter, but had everything to do with production.

Previous to Mill's *Principles* was his *System of Logic* (1843), which was the century's most influential text on logic and the theory of knowledge. His essays on ethics, contemporary culture, and freedom of speech, such as *Utilitarianism* and *On Liberty,* are still widely studied today.

KARL MARX (1818–1883)

Karl Marx was born in Trier, Germany (then part of Prussia), and studied law, history, and philosophy at the universities of Bonn, Berlin, and Jena. Marx travelled between Prussia, Paris, and Brussels, working at various jobs until finally settling in London in 1849, where he lived the remainder of his life. Most of his time was spent in the mainly unpaid pursuits of writing and studying economics in the library of the British Museum. Marx's contributions to economics are intricately bound to his views of history and society. *The Communist Manifesto* was published with Friedrich Engels in 1848, his *Critique of Political Economy* was published in 1859, and in 1867 the first volume of *Das Kapital* was completed. (The remaining volumes, edited by Engels, were published after Marx's death.)

For Marx, capitalism was a stage in an evolutionary process from a primitive agricultural economy toward an inevitable elimination of private property and the class structure. Marx's "labour theory of value," whereby the quantity of labour used in the manufacture of a product determined its value, held the central place in his economic thought. He believed that the worker provided "surplus value" to the capitalist. The capitalist would then use the profit arising from this surplus value to reinvest in plant and machinery. Through time, more would be spent for plant and machinery than for wages, which would lead to lower profits (since profits arose only from the surplus value from labour) and a resulting squeeze in the real income of workers. Marx believed that in the capitalists' effort to maintain profits in this unstable system, there would emerge a "reserve army of the unemployed." The resulting class conflict would become increasingly acute until revolution by the workers would overthrow capitalism.

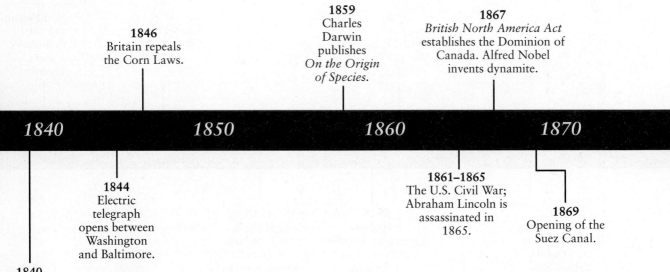

1846
Britain repeals
the Corn Laws.

1859
Charles
Darwin
publishes
*On the Origin
of Species.*

1867
British North America Act
establishes the Dominion of
Canada. Alfred Nobel
invents dynamite.

1840   **1850**   **1860**   **1870**

1844
Electric
telegraph
opens between
Washington
and Baltimore.

1861–1865
The U.S. Civil War;
Abraham Lincoln is
assassinated in
1865.

1869
Opening of the
Suez Canal.

1840
Act of Union
unites Upper
and Lower
Canada.

LEON WALRAS (1834–1910)

Leon Walras was born in France, the son of an economist. After being trained inauspiciously in engineering and performing poorly in mathematics, Walras spent some time pursuing other endeavours, such as novel writing and working for the railway. Eventually he promised his father he would study economics, and by 1870 he was given a professorship in economics in the Faculty of Law at the University of Lausanne in Switzerland. Once there, Walras began the feverish activity that eventually led to his important contributions to economic theory.

In the 1870s, Walras was one of three economists to put forward the marginal utility theory of value (simultaneously with William Stanley Jevons of England and Carl Menger of Austria). Further, he constructed a mathematical model of general equilibrium using a system of simultaneous equations that he used to argue that equilibrium prices and quantities are uniquely determined. Central to general equilibrium analysis is the notion that the prices and quantities of all commodities are determined simultaneously because the whole system is interdependent. Walras's most important work was *Elements of Pure Economics*, published in 1874. In addition to all of Walras's other accomplishments in economics (and despite his early poor performance in mathematics!), we today regard him as the founder of mathematical economics.

Leon Walras and Alfred Marshall are regarded by many economists as the two most important economic theorists who ever lived. Much of the framework of economic theory studied today is either Walrasian or Marshallian in character.

CARL MENGER   *(1840–1921)*

Carl Menger was born in Galicia (then part of Austria), and he came from a family of Austrian civil servants and army officers. After studying law in Prague and Vienna, he turned to economics and in 1871 published *Grundsatze der Volkswirtschaftslehre* (translated as *Principles of Economics*), for which he became famous. He held a professorship at the University of Vienna until 1903. Menger was the founder of a school of thought known as the "Austrian School," which effectively displaced the German historical method on the continent and which survives today as an alternative to mainstream Neoclassical economics.

Menger was one of three economists in the 1870s who independently put forward a theory of value based on marginal utility. Prior to what economists now call the "marginal revolution," value was thought to be derived solely from the inputs of labour and capital. Menger developed the marginal utility theory of value, in which the value of any good is determined by individuals' subjective evaluations of that good. According to Menger, a good has some value if it has the ability to satisfy some human want or desire, and *utility* is the capacity of the good to do so. Menger went on to develop the idea that the individual will maximize total utility at the point where the last unit of each good consumed provides equal utility—that is, where marginal utilities are equal.

Menger's emphasis on the marginal utility theory of value led him to focus on consumption rather than production as the determinant of price. Menger focused only on the demand for goods and largely ignored the supply. It would remain for Alfred Marshall and Leon Walras to combine demand and supply for a more complete picture of price determination.

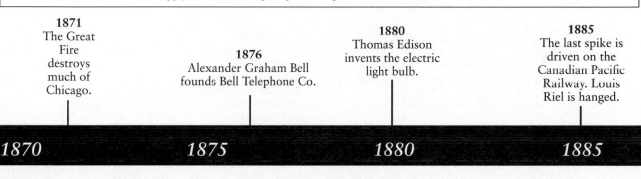

1871
The Great Fire destroys much of Chicago.

1876
Alexander Graham Bell founds Bell Telephone Co.

1880
Thomas Edison invents the electric light bulb.

1885
The last spike is driven on the Canadian Pacific Railway. Louis Riel is hanged.

1870   *1875*   *1880*   *1885*

ALFRED MARSHALL   *(1842–1924)*

Alfred Marshall was born in Clapham, England, the son of a bank cashier, and was descended from a long line of clerics. Marshall's father, despite intense effort, was unable to steer the young Marshall into the church. Instead, Marshall followed his passion for mathematics at Cambridge and chose economics as a field of study after reading J. S. Mill's *Principles of Political Economy*. His career was then spent mainly at Cambridge, where he taught economics to John Maynard Keynes, Arthur Pigou, Joan Robinson, and countless other British theorists in the "Cambridge tradition." His *Principles of Economics,* published in 1890, replaced Mill's *Principles* as the dominant economics textbook of English-speaking universities.

Marshall institutionalized modern marginal analysis, the basic concepts of supply and demand, and perhaps most importantly the notion of economic equilibrium resulting from the interaction of supply and demand. He also pioneered partial equilibrium analysis—examining the forces of supply and demand in a particular market provided that all other influences can be excluded, *ceteris paribus*.

Although many of the ideas had been put forward by earlier writers, Marshall was able to synthesize the previous analyses of utility and cost and present a thorough and complete statement of the laws of demand and supply. Marshall refined and developed microeconomic theory to such a degree that much of what he wrote would be familiar to students of this textbook today.

It is also interesting to note that although Alfred Marshall and Leon Walras were simultaneously expanding the frontiers of economic theory, there was almost no communication between the two men. Though Marshall chose partial equilibrium analysis as the appropriate method for dealing with selected markets in a complex world, he did acknowledge the correctness of Walras's general equilibrium system. Walras, on the other hand, was adamant (and sometimes rude) in his opposition to the methods that Marshall was putting forward. History has shown that both the partial and the general equilibrium approaches to economic analysis are required for understanding the functioning of the economy.

THORSTEIN VEBLEN (1857–1929)

Thorstein Veblen was born on a farm in Wisconsin to Norwegian parents. He received his Ph.D. in philosophy from Yale University, after which he returned to his father's farm because he was unable to secure an academic position. For seven years he remained there, reading voraciously on economics and other social sciences. Eventually, he took academic positions at the University of Chicago, Stanford University, the University of Missouri, and the New School for Social Research (in New York). Veblen was the founder of "institutional economics," the only uniquely North American school of economic thought.

In 1899, Veblen published *The Theory of the Leisure Class,* in which he sought to apply Charles Darwin's evolutionism to the study of modern economic life. He examined problems in the social institutions of the day, and savagely criticized Classical and Neoclassical economic analysis. Although Veblen failed to shift the path of mainstream economic analysis, he did contribute the idea of the importance of long-run institutional studies as a useful complement to short-run price theory analysis. He also reminded the profession that economics is a *social* science, and not merely a branch of mathematics.

Veblen remains most famous today for his idea of "conspicuous consumption." He observed that some commodities were consumed not for their intrinsic qualities but because they carried snob appeal. He suggested that the more expensive such a commodity became, the greater might be its ability to confer status on its purchaser.

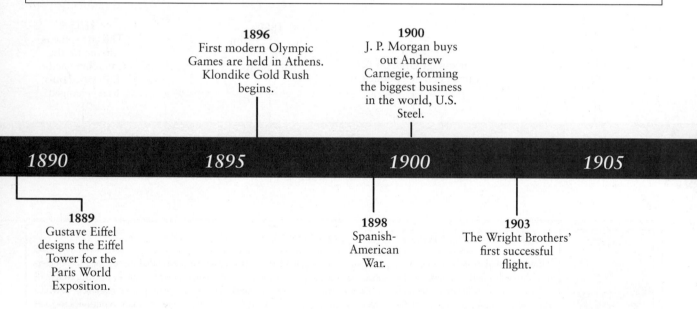

1896
First modern Olympic Games are held in Athens. Klondike Gold Rush begins.

1900
J. P. Morgan buys out Andrew Carnegie, forming the biggest business in the world, U.S. Steel.

1890   1895   1900   1905

1889
Gustave Eiffel designs the Eiffel Tower for the Paris World Exposition.

1898
Spanish-American War.

1903
The Wright Brothers' first successful flight.

VILFREDO PARETO (1848–1923)

Vilfredo Pareto was an Italian, born in Paris, and was trained to be an engineer. Though he actually practised as an engineer, he would later succeed Leon Walras to the Chair of Economics in the Faculty of Law at the University of Lausanne.

Pareto built on the system of general equilibrium that Walras had developed. In his *Cours d'économie politique* (1897) and his *Manuel d'économie politique* (1906), Pareto set forth the foundations of modern welfare economics. He showed that theories of consumer behaviour and exchange could be constructed on assumptions of ordinal utility, rather than cardinal utility, eliminating the need to compare one person's utility with another's. Using the indifference curve analysis developed by F. Y. Edgeworth, Pareto was able to demonstrate that total welfare could be increased by an exchange if one person could be made better off without anyone else becoming worse off. Pareto applied this analysis to consumption and exchange as well as to production. Pareto's contributions in this area are remembered in economists' references to *Pareto optimality* and *Pareto efficiency.*

JOSEPH SCHUMPETER   *(1883–1950)*

Joseph Schumpeter was born in Triesch, Moravia (now in the Czech Republic). He was a university professor and later a minister of finance in Austria. In 1932, he emigrated to the United States to avoid the rise to power of Adolf Hitler. He spent his remaining years at Harvard University.

Schumpeter, a pioneering theorist of innovation, emphasized the role of the entrepreneur in economic development. The existence of the entrepreneur meant continuous innovation and waves of adaptation to changing technology. He is best known for his theory of "creative destruction," where the prospect of monopoly profits provides owners the incentive to finance inventions and innovations. One monopoly can replace another with superior technology or a superior product, thereby circumventing the entry barriers of a monopolized industry. He criticized mainstream economists for emphasizing the static (allocative) efficiency of perfect competition—a market structure that would, if it could ever be achieved, retard technological change and economic growth.

Schumpeter's best known works are *The Theory of Economic Development* (1911), *Business Cycles* (1939), and *Capitalism, Socialism and Democracy* (1943).

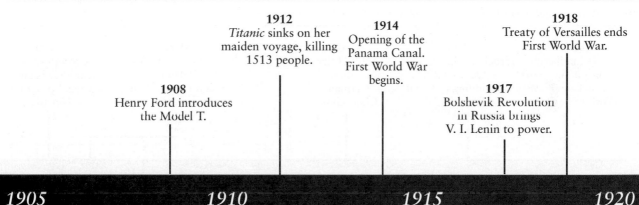

1912
Titanic sinks on her maiden voyage, killing 1513 people.

1914
Opening of the Panama Canal. First World War begins.

1918
Treaty of Versailles ends First World War.

1908
Henry Ford introduces the Model T.

1917
Bolshevik Revolution in Russia brings V. I. Lenin to power.

1905   *1910*   *1915*   *1920*

JOHN MAYNARD KEYNES   *(1883–1946)*

John Maynard Keynes was born in Cambridge, England. His parents were both intellectuals, and his father, John Neville Keynes, was a famous logician and writer on economic methodology. The young Keynes was educated at Eton and then at Kings College, Cambridge, where he was a student of Alfred Marshall and Arthur Pigou. His career included appointments to the Treasury in Britain during both world wars, a leading role in the establishment of the International Monetary Fund (through discussions at Bretton Woods, New Hampshire, in 1944), and editorship of the *Economic Journal* from 1911 to 1945, all in addition to his academic position at Kings College.

Keynes published extensively during his life, but his most influential work, *The General Theory of Employment, Interest, and Money*, appeared in 1936. This book was published in the midst of the Great Depression when the output of goods and services had fallen drastically, unemployment was intolerably high, and it had become clear to many that the market would not self-adjust to achieve potential output within an acceptable period of time. Fluctuations in economic activity were familiar at this point, but the failure of the economy to recover rapidly from this depression was unprecedented. Neoclassical economists held that during a downturn both wages and the interest rate would fall low enough to induce investment and employment and bring about a recovery. They believed that the persistent unemployment during the 1930s was caused by inflexible wages and they recommended that workers be convinced to accept wage cuts.

Keynes believed that this policy, though perhaps correct for a single industry, was not correct for the entire economy. Widespread wage cuts would reduce the consumption portion of aggregate demand, which would offset any increase in employment. Keynes argued that unemployment could be cured only by manipulating aggregate demand, whereby increased demand (through government expenditure) would increase the price level, reduce real wages, and thereby stimulate employment.

Keynes's views found acceptance after the publication of his *General Theory* and had a profound effect on government policy around the world, particularly in the 1940s, 1950s, and 1960s. As we know from this textbook, Keynes's name is associated with much of macroeconomics, from its basic theory to the Keynesian short-run aggregate supply curve and the Keynesian consumption function. His contributions to economics go well beyond what can be mentioned in a few paragraphs—in effect, he laid the foundations for modern macroeconomics.

EDWARD CHAMBERLIN   *(1899–1967)*

Edward Chamberlin was born in La Conner, Washington, and received his Ph.D. from Harvard University in 1927. He became a full professor at Harvard in 1937 and stayed there until his retirement in 1966. He published *The Theory of Monopolistic Competition* in 1933.

Before Chamberlin's book (which appeared more or less simultaneously with Joan Robinson's *The Economics of Imperfect Competition*), the models of perfect competition and monopoly had been fairly well worked out. Though economists were aware of a middle ground between these two market structures and some analysis of duopoly (two sellers) had been presented, it was Chamberlin and Robinson who closely examined this problem of imperfect markets.

Chamberlin's main contribution was explaining the importance of product differentiation for firms in market structures between perfect competition and monopoly. Chamberlin saw that though there may be a large number of firms in the market (the competitive element), each firm created for itself a unique product or advantage that gave it some control over price (the monopoly element). Specifically, he identified items such as copyrights, trademarks, brand names, and location as monopoly elements behind a product. Though Alfred Marshall regarded price as the only variable in question, Chamberlin saw both price and the product itself as variables under control of the firm in monopolistically competitive markets.

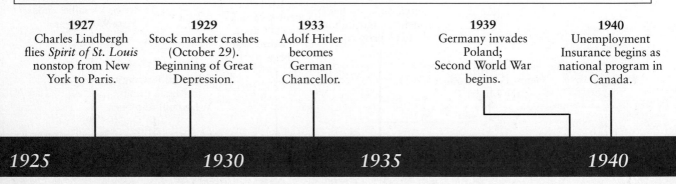

| **1927** | **1929** | **1933** | **1939** | **1940** |
| Charles Lindbergh flies *Spirit of St. Louis* nonstop from New York to Paris. | Stock market crashes (October 29). Beginning of Great Depression. | Adolf Hitler becomes German Chancellor. | Germany invades Poland; Second World War begins. | Unemployment Insurance begins as national program in Canada. |

1925   *1930*   *1935*   *1940*

1922
The Soviet Union is formed; Joseph Stalin named Secretary General of the Communist Party.

FRIEDRICH AUGUST VON HAYEK   *(1899–1992)*

Friedrich von Hayek was born in Vienna and studied at the University of Vienna, where he was trained in the Austrian tradition of economics (a school of thought originating with Carl Menger). He held academic positions at the London School of Economics and the University of Chicago. He returned to Europe in 1962 to the University of Freiburg in what was then West Germany and the University of Salzburg in Austria. He was awarded the Nobel Prize in Economics in 1974.

Hayek contributed new ideas and theories in many different areas of economics, but he is perhaps best known for his general conception of economics as a "coordination problem." His observation of market economies suggested that the relative prices determined in free markets provided the signals that allowed the actions of all decision makers to mesh—even though there was no formal planning taking place to coordinate these actions. He emphasized this "spontaneous order" at work in the economy as the subject matter for economics. The role of knowledge and information in the market process became central to Hayek, an idea that has grown in importance to the economics profession over the years.

Hayek's theory of business cycles provided an example of the breakdown of this coordination. A monetary disturbance (e.g., an increase in the money supply) would distort the signals (relative prices) by artificially raising the return to certain types of economic activity. When the disturbance disappeared, the boom caused by these distorted signals would be followed by a slump. Although Hayek's business-cycle theory was eclipsed by the Keynesian revolution, his emphasis on economics as a coordination problem has had a major influence on contemporary economic thought.

Hayek was also prominent in advocating the virtues of free markets as contributing to human freedom in the broad sense as well as to economic efficiency in the narrow sense. His *The Road to Serfdom* (1944) sounded an alarm about the political and economic implications of the then-growing belief in the virtues of central planning. His *Constitution of Liberty* (1960) is a much deeper philosophical analysis of the forces, economic and otherwise, that contribute to the liberty of the individual.

MILTON FRIEDMAN   *(1912–2006)*

Milton Friedman completed graduate studies in economics at the University of Chicago and at Columbia University, where he received his Ph.D. in 1946. Most of Friedman's academic career was spent as a professor at the University of Chicago, and after retiring in 1977 he was a senior research fellow at the Hoover Institution at Stanford University. Friedman is best known as one of the leading proponents of Monetarism and for his belief in the power of free markets. His work greatly influenced modern macroeconomics.

Friedman made his first significant mark on the profession with the publication of *The Theory of the Consumption Function* in 1957. There he developed the permanent income hypothesis and argued that consumption depends on long-run average income rather than current disposable income, as it does in Keynesian analysis. This was an early example of a macroeconomic theory that emphasized the importance of forward-looking consumers. In 1963, he co-authored with Anna Schwartz his most influential book, *A Monetary History of the United States, 1867–1960,* where they presented evidence in support of the Monetarist view that changes in the supply of money can cause dramatic fluctuations in the level of economic activity. Although this view was seriously challenged by subsequent research, Friedman helped the profession to understand the power of and the limitations of monetary policy.

Capitalism and Freedom (1962) and *Free to Choose* (1980), the latter co-written with his wife, Rose Friedman, are part of Friedman's attempts to communicate his ideas about economics and, in particular, the power of the free market, to a mass audience of non-economists. Both books became international bestsellers, and these books, in addition to his writing for newspapers and magazines, made Milton Friedman one of the most famous modern economists. He was awarded the Nobel Prize in Economics in 1976.

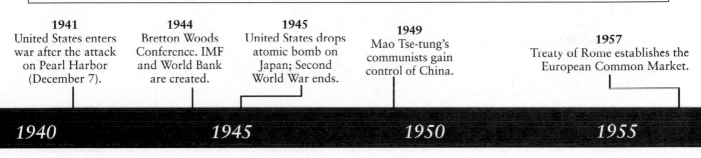

1941
United States enters war after the attack on Pearl Harbor (December 7).

1944
Bretton Woods Conference. IMF and World Bank are created.

1945
United States drops atomic bomb on Japan; Second World War ends.

1949
Mao Tse-tung's communists gain control of China.

1957
Treaty of Rome establishes the European Common Market.

1940   **1945**   **1950**   **1955**

JOHN KENNETH GALBRAITH   *(1908–2006)*

John Kenneth Galbraith was born on a farm in southeastern Ontario, to a family of Scottish-Canadian farmers. He began his undergraduate education at the Ontario Agricultural College in Guelph in 1926, where he studied agricultural economics and animal husbandry. He moved to California to study at the University of California at Berkeley and completed a Ph.D. in agricultural economics in 1934. Galbraith was hired by Harvard University in 1934 and, aside from his government and diplomatic postings, remained on staff there until his death.

Galbraith was heavily influenced by the ideas of John Maynard Keynes, Thorstein Veblen, and the "institutional" school of economics. He rejected the technical and mathematical approach of Neoclassical economics. Instead he emphasized the interplay of economics, politics, culture, and tradition, a combination that does not lend itself well to mathematical modelling. He was much more of a "political economist" in the style of the nineteenth century than a theoretical economist of the late twentieth century.

His most famous book was *The Affluent Society* (1958), where he argued that the United States had become obsessed with overproducing consumer goods and instead should be making large public investments in highways, education, and other public services. His expression "private opulence and public squalor" became well known, and many would agree is even more relevant today than it was when he wrote the words more than 50 years ago. In a later book, *The New Industrial State* (1967), Galbraith argued that very few U.S. industries fit economists' model of perfect competition, and that the economy was dominated by large, powerful firms. In general, Galbraith continued to write about topics that he believed the economics profession had neglected—topics such as advertising, the separation of corporate ownership and management, oligopoly, and government and military spending.

Because of Galbraith's desire to focus on the interplay of economics, politics, and society, he was often criticized (or ignored) by mainstream economists. But he was undeterred. And while many economists disagreed with his approach and some of his political views, he was widely recognized as a gifted and insightful writer and speaker.

KENNETH ARROW *(1921–2017)*

Kenneth Arrow was born and educated in New York City. He began graduate work at Columbia University and received an M.A. in mathematics in 1941. Over the following 10 years, after Arrow had completed his Ph.D. course work, he served in the U.S. Army Air Corps during World War II and held various research jobs while searching for a dissertation topic. His dissertation, which earned him his Ph.D. from Columbia in 1951, subsequently became a classic in economics, *Social Choice and Individual Values* (1951). Kenneth Arrow taught for most of his career at Harvard and Stanford Universities.

In his 1951 book, Arrow presented his "Impossibility Theorem," in which he shows that it is not possible to construct a set of voting rules for making public choices that is simultaneously democratic and efficient. This theorem led to decades of work by economists, philosophers, and political scientists in the field of social choice theory.

Arrow also made significant contributions in other areas of economics. In 1954 (with Gerard Debreu) he constructed a mathematical model of an economy with many individual, interrelated markets and proved the existence of a theoretical general market-clearing equilibrium. Arrow's work in the economics of uncertainty was also a major contribution. In *Essays in the Theory of Risk-Bearing* (1971), he introduced the concepts of moral hazard and adverse selection (among other ideas about risk), which we encounter in Chapter 16 of this book. Arrow was one of the first economists to develop the idea of "learning by doing," which has played an important role in modern theories of economic growth.

Arrow was awarded the Nobel Prize in 1972 (jointly with British economist John Hicks) and in 2004 was awarded the National Medal of Science, the United States' highest scientific honour.

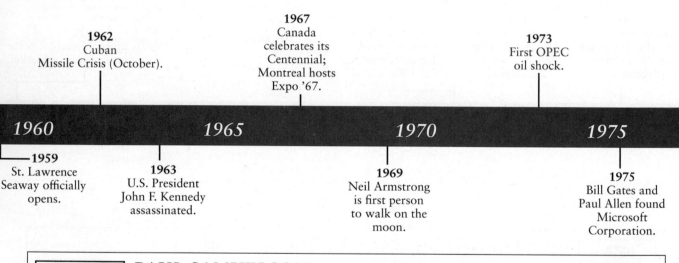

1962
Cuban
Missile Crisis (October).

1967
Canada
celebrates its
Centennial;
Montreal hosts
Expo '67.

1973
First OPEC
oil shock.

1960   **1965**   **1970**   **1975**

1959
St. Lawrence
Seaway officially
opens.

1963
U.S. President
John F. Kennedy
assassinated.

1969
Neil Armstrong
is first person
to walk on the
moon.

1975
Bill Gates and
Paul Allen found
Microsoft
Corporation.

PAUL SAMUELSON *(1915–2009)*

Paul Samuelson was born in Gary, Indiana, the son of a drugstore owner. He received his Ph.D. in economics in 1941 from Harvard University and spent his academic career at the Massachusetts Institute of Technology (MIT).

Samuelson is generally regarded as one of the greatest economic theorists of the twentieth century. While still a graduate student at Harvard, Samuelson wrote most of *Foundations of Economic Analysis* (1947), which was path-breaking at the time and used mathematical analysis and constrained optimization techniques to shed insight into economic behaviour. He systematized economic theory into a more rigorous mathematical discipline, which has had enormous effects on the way economics is studied today.

Though Samuelson made major contributions to many branches of economics, three are particularly notable. First, he showed how the central predictions of demand theory could be tested using the "revealed preferences" of consumers from observed market behaviour. Second, in international trade theory, he made important contributions in the analysis of the gains from trade and the effects of tariff protection on the distribution of income. Third, most familiar to readers of this book, he is credited with introducing the 45°-line model of short-run national income determination. This diagram, encountered throughout Chapters 21 and 22 of this book, has become the standard tool for teaching the Keynesian theory of national-income determination in the short run. Samuelson's work also provided valuable insights in other areas of economics, including government taxation and expenditure, capital theory, and theories of economic growth.

Samuelson was also well known for his famous introductory economics textbook, *Economics,* first published in 1948, which provided a systematic treatment of both micro- and macroeconomics in a way that had not been presented before. In general, he is credited with raising the level of scientific and mathematical analysis in economics. Samuelson was awarded the Nobel Prize in Economics in 1970, and was the first American scholar to receive this honour.

Index

A

absolute advantage, 806–807, 807*t*, 812
absolute changes, 34
absolute costs, 807*t*
absolute price, 68
accelerating inflation, 740–741, 742
acceleration hypothesis, 740–741
accounting identity, 855, 857
acquired comparative advantage, 815–816
adjustable peg, 863, 867
adjustment process (factor prices), 580, 582–585
  aggregate demand shocks, 581, 586–590, 588*f*, 589*f*
  aggregate supply shocks, 581, 590, 591*f*
  business cycle, (Not found in Current edition)
  downward wage stickiness, 584
  inflationary gap, 585
  long-run equilibrium, 591–592, 592*f*
  Phillips curve, 586, 586–587
  potential output, 582
  recessionary gap, 585
  when slow, 596
affluent societies, 4
aggregate demand
  aggregate demand *(AD)* curve. *See* aggregate demand *(AD)* curve
  aggregate demand shocks. *See* aggregate demand shocks
  changes in, and monetary transmission mechanism, 683, 683*f*
  decline in, 588
aggregate demand *(AD)* curve, 561
  AD/AS diagram, 592, 592*f*
  and aggregate expenditure curve, 683
  for any given price level, 561
  autonomous expenditure, increase in, 570
  derivation of, 562*f*
  increases in aggregate demand, 571*f*
  intersection with *AS* curve, 567
  not micro demand curve, 562–563
  and real GDP, 570–571
  shifts in, 563–564, 563*f*
  and simple multiplier, 563*f*, 564
  in simple short-run macro model, 561–564
  slope, 562–563, 685–686
aggregate demand shocks, 564, 569–572, 569*f*, 585–590
  aggregate demand, and real GDP, 570–572
  Asian crisis, 574

both demand and supply shocks, 573–574
  demand inflation, 737–738, 737*f*, 738*f*
  factor prices, 581, 586–590, 588*f*, 589*f*
  flexible wages, 588–589
  with monetary validation, 737–738, 738*f*
  multiplier when price level varies, 569–570
  negative shock, 568, 574, 588–590, 589*f*, 599
  with no monetary validation, 737, 737*f*
  positive shock, 569, 586–587, 588*f*
  potential output as "anchor", 585
  price level, change in, 569–570
  shape of *AS* curve, 570–571
  sticky wages, 589–590
aggregate expenditure (AE)
  function, 520–521, 521*f*, 542–544, 543*f*
  and *AD* curve, 683
  downward shifts, 526
  parallel shift of, 549
  shifts of, 514, 524–526, 525*f*, 548
  slope, 526
  upward shifts, 525–526
aggregate production function, 621, 622*f*
aggregate supply. *See* aggregate supply *(AS)* curve; aggregate supply shocks
aggregate supply *(AS)* curve, 565–566, 565*f*
  AD/AS diagram, 592, 592*f*
  Classical aggregate supply curve, 595
  flat range, 571
  increasing slope, 565–566
  input prices, changes in, 566
  intersection with *AD* curve, 568
  Keynesian range of the curve, 566, 571
  long-run aggregate supply curve, 591
  shape of, and aggregate demand shock, 569–570
  shifts in, 566–567, 567*f*
  slope, 565
  steep range, 571
  technological changes, 567
  vertical *AS* curve, 571
  vs. Phillips curve, 586
aggregate supply shocks, 566, 568, 572–573
  absence of, and constant inflation, 734–735, 735*f*
  Asian crisis, 574

both demand and supply shocks, 573–574
  factor prices, 581, 590–591, 591*f*
  with monetary validation, 739, 739*f*
  monetary validation, desirability of, 739–740
  negative shock, 568, 572, 572*f*, 591*f*
  with no monetary validation, 738–739, 739*f*
  oil prices, 572–573
  positive shock, 568, 572, 573, 574
  potential output as "anchor", 585
  price level and real GDP, 572
  supply inflation, 738–740, 739*f*
aggregates, 462
aggregation, 51*n*, 463
aging population, 2
agricultural subsidies, 61
allocation of resources. *See* resource allocation
American Economic Review, 28
American Revolution, 644
annually balanced budgets, 796–797
Antarctica, 634
anticipated inflation, 475, 730
antidumping duties, 840
appreciation, 477–478, 721, 859
Argentina, 643, 644, 812, 843
Asian economic crisis, 574
asset sales, 861
assumptions, 30–31
Australia, 708, 863
Austria, 812
autarky, 804
automatic stabilizers, 598–600, 709, 797
automatic teller machines (ATMs), 648
autonomous consumption, 512
autonomous expenditures, 509, 519–520, 520*f*, 564
average propensity to consume *(APC)*, 513
average propensity to save *(APS)*, 514
averages, 462

B

bachelor's degree, opportunity cost of, 6
balance of payments, 853–859
  accounting identity, 873, 874
  algebraic terms, 855
  balance, requirement of, 855–857
  balance of payments accounts, 853, 853*t*
  capital account, 854–855
  capital-service account, 855

credit item, 854
current account, 854, 871*f*
current account deficits and surpluses, 871–876
debit item, 854
direct investment *vs.* portfolio investment, 855*n*
"favourable balance", 872
mercantilism, 872
no balance of payments deficit, 857
official reserves, changes in, 855
student's balance of payments with the rest of the world, 858
trade account, 854
"unfavourable balance", 872
zero, 855
balance of payments accounts, 853, 853*t*
  see also balance of payments
balanced budget, 537, 784, 796–797
Bangladesh, 834
bank credit card, 654
bank deposits, 648–649, 654
bank notes, 646
Bank of Canada, 641, 650–653
  assets and liabilities, 652*f*, 653*n*
  balance sheet, 652*f*
  bank rate, 474, 702
  Canadian dollar, appreciation of, 477
  commercial banks, banker to, 651
  communications difficulties, 715–716
  economists at, 29
  federal government, banker to, 652
  financial markets, supporter of, 651–652
  fixed announcement dates, 702, 713
  functions of, 651–653
  inflation, control of, 707
  inflation targeting, 665, 693, 706–712, 719–720, 730
  see also inflation targeting
  interest rate, targeting, 701
  interest rates, influence on, 475
  lags, 712–713
  "lender of last resort", 651
  level of economic activity, influence on, 480
  monetary policy. *See* monetary policy
  money supply, measures of, 663
  money supply, non-targeting of, 700–701
  money supply, regulator of, 652–653
  oil-price shock, 739–740

Bank of Canada (*Cont.*)
open-market operations, 700, 704
open-market purchase, 705
open-market sale, 705
organization of, 650–651
overnight interest rate, 702–703, 704*f*
Bank of Canada Act, 651*n*
Bank of England, 650
bank panics, 647
bank rate, 474, 702
bank run, 656
banking system. *See* Canadian banking system
banks. *See* Bank of Canada; central banks; commercial banks
barter, 16, 642
base period, 35
base-period prices, 497
base year, 471
basket of goods, 36, 471, 877, 878, 879
Belgium, 768, 811
Bennett, R.B., 598, 836, 837*f*
Blinder, Alan, 759, 759*n*
Bolivia, 643, 644
Bombardier, 29, 820, 833–834
bond tables, 676
bond yield, 674, 676
bonds, 560*n*, 670
across countries, 684 (Found as 'across countries' in text)
bond tables, 676
bond yield, 673–674, 676
coupon payments, 671
default, 672*n*
and interest rates, 670–675, 673–675
market price, and present value, 672–673
and present value, 670–672
prices, 672–673,
promise of future payments, 671–672
riskiness of, 674
types of bonds, 672
understanding bonds, 670–675
booms, 466, 465, 583, 584
borrowing costs, 677
Brazil, 708, 708, 812, 833, 843
break-even level of income, 513
Bretton Woods system, 864, 865
Britain. *See* United Kingdom
Brown, E. Cary, 599
budget balance, 537
budget constraint, 780–782
budget deficit function, 785–786, 785*f*
budget deficits, 537, 599, 781
see also government debt and deficits
budget surplus, 537, 781
see also government debt and deficits
bull market, 513
business confidence, 519
business cycle, 464, 465, 480
business fixed investment, 490

C
Canada
and Asian crisis, 574
average house prices, 37*f*

banking system. *See* Canadian banking system
bilateral free-trade agreements, 843
Brazil, dispute with, 832–833
command principle, 19
credit market, 476
Crown corporations. *See* Crown corporations
deficits and debt, 782–784
economic growth, and top earners, 612
exchange rate, 477, 863, 879–884
exports, 478–479, 478*f*, 805*f*
federal debt-to-GDP ratio, 789
fiscal stimulus, 597
free trade agreements. *See* specific trade agreements
and global financial crisis. *See* global financial crisis
Great Depression, 714, 715, 736
high-inflation experience, 643
imports, 478–479, 478*f*
inflation targeting, 708
see also inflation targeting
key episodes in Canadian monetary history, 716–724
labour productivity, 470*f*
long-term unemployment, 758–759
market decisions, reliance on, 19
market economy, 20
oil-price shock, 739
productivity, 469
raw materials prices, 573
recession, 10
short-term interest rates, 1975-2018, 717*f*
softwood lumber, 842
subsidies, 61
terms of trade, 822, 822*f*
unemployment rate, 753*f*, 753, 754, 769*f*
U.S. trade, 846*n*
U.S. trade protection, effect of, 836
voluntary export restrictions (VER), (Not found in Current edition)
wine, and free trade, 84
Canada Deposit Insurance Corporation (CDIC), 656, 657
Canada Pension Plan (CPP), 492
Canada Revenue Agency (CRA), 837
Canada-U.S. exchange rate, 477, 477*f*, 877, 878*f*
Canada-U.S. Free Trade Agreement (FTA), 478–479, 766, 813, 843, 844, 845, 846
Canada-U.S. trade, 538
Canadian banking system, 650–657
Bank of Canada, 650–653
bank runs, 656
commercial banks, 650, 653–655
financial intermediaries, 650
fractional-reserve system, 656
money creation. *See* money creation
new deposit, 658–659, 660*f*
reserves, 655–657
Canadian Centre for Policy Alternatives, 29

Canadian dollar, 818*n*, 835*n*
see also exchange rate
appreciation, 477–478, 720, 859
"correct" value for, 876–879
depreciation, 477–478, 540, 860, 881
Canadian firms, 547
Canadian Index of Wellbeing, 503
Canadian Pacific Railway, 29
Canadian tariffs, 838–839
Canadian wage-adjustment process, 592–594
capital, 4
accumulation, 623–624
financial capital, 619, 683–684
human capital, 615, 623–624, 625, 815
movements, 869–870
physical capital, 615, 623–624
capital account, 854–855
Capital and Financing Account, 854*n*
capital budgeting, 794
capital inflows, 861
capital ratio, 657
capital-service account, 854
capital stock, 490
see also stocks
Capone, Al, 500
Carney, Mark, 722, 722*f*
carry trade, 869
cash drain, 861–862
causation, 30–31, 33–34
C.D. Howe Institute, 29
central banks, 647, 650, 651, 653*n*
see also Bank of Canada
central planning, 18, 19
see also command economy
centralized decision making, 18
Centre for the Study of Living Standards, 29
ceteris paribus, 50–51, 58, 67, 70
change
absolute changes, 34
in demand, 56
marginal change, 41
in quantity demanded, 56
in quantity supplied, 62
relative changes, 34
in supply, 62
change in demand, 56
change in quantity demanded, 56
change in quantity supplied, 62
change in supply, 62
chartered banks. *See* commercial banks
cheque, 648
Chile, 643, 646, 708, 843
China, 19, 67, 573, 612, 646*n*, 832, 837, 865, 867
Chinese-U.S. exchange rate, 867
choice
decision makers, 13–14
and opportunity cost, 5–6, 5*f*
and scarcity, 4–8
Chrysler, (Not found in Current edition)
circular flow of income and expenditure, 14*f*, 489*f*
Classical aggregate supply curve, 595
classical dichotomy, 686–687
Classical economics, 591*n*
clearing house, 654

climate change, 2, 815
"business as usual" approach, 635
and economic growth, 634–635
closed economy, 509, 562*n*, 792, 804
Club of Rome, 632
collective consumption goods. *See* public goods
Colombia, 708, 843
command economy, 18, 19
see also central planning
commercial banks, 650, 653–654
and amount of currency in circulation, 705
balance sheet, 658*f*, 659*f*
bank credit card, 654
Bank of Canada, as banker to, 651
clearing house, 654
consolidated balance sheet, 655*f*
credit, provision of, 653
excess reserves, 656, 661, 705
fractional-reserve system, 656
interbank activities, 654
new deposit, 658
pool loan, 654
as profit seekers, 654–655
reserve ratio, 656
reserves, 651, 655–657
target reserve ratio, 656, 660
commodities, 52*n*, 65*f*, 573, 709–710
common market, 843
comparative advantage, 15, 807–809, 807*t*, 810, 812
see also gains from trade; international trade
acquired comparative advantage, 815
and climate, 814–815
contrasting views, 816
dynamic nature of, 815
exported product, and trade patterns, 818*f*, 818
factor endowment theory of comparative advantage, 814, 831
and global supply chains, 820
governments, influence of, 820
Heckscher-Ohlin theory, 815
human capital, 815
imported product, and trade patterns, 818–819, 819*f*
obsolescence of, 819–821
sources of, 814–816
terms of trade, 821–824, 822*f*, 823*f*
trade patterns, 816–824
comparative statics, 65
competition, 62
complements
complements in consumption, 55
in production process, 61
complements in consumption, 55
Comprehensive Economic and Trade Agreement (CETA), 843
concave shape, 8
Conference Board of Canada, 29
constant costs, 806
constant dollar national income, 463
constant dollars, 497

constant inflation, 734–736, 735f
constant returns to scale, 622–623
Consumer Price Index (CPI), 36–37, 471, 498, 710f, 709, 878
consumers, 13, 54–56
consumption, 4
    see also consumption function
    autonomous consumption, 513
    changes in, and price level, 559–560
    complements in consumption, 55
    desired consumption. See desired consumption
    and disposable income, 510f
    distribution of consumption, 8
    of durable goods, 690n
    forgone consumption, 613
    induced consumption, 513
    marginal propensity to consume (MPC), 513, 542
    substitutes in consumption, 55
    and terms of trade, 822
    what is consumed and by whom, 8–9
consumption expenditure, 490
    see also desired consumption expenditure
    consumption function, 509–516, 512f
    average propensity to consume (APC), 513
    expectations, change, 516
    45° line, 513
    household wealth, change in, 514–515
    interest rates, change in, 515
    Keynesian consumption function, 511
    marginal propensity to consume (MPC), 513
    shifts of, 514–516, 515f
    slope of, 513
    theory of, 511
consumption goods, 7
consumption smoothing, 511
contractionary fiscal policy, 788
contractionary monetary policy, 706
Corn Laws, 803
corporation
    Crown corporations. See Crown corporations
    private corporations, 29
correlation, 33–34
Costa Rica, 843
costs
    absolute costs, 807t
    of borrowing, 515
    constant costs, 806
    of disinflation, 746–748, 747f
    of economic growth, 613–615
    of high inflation, 707
    marginal cost. See marginal cost (MC)
    market-development costs, 630–631
    menu costs, 763
    opportunity cost. See opportunity cost
    social costs, 613–614
    transaction costs of international trade, 882–833
    transportation costs, 16
    unemployment, personal costs of, 758–759

unit costs, 565
variable costs, 811–814
vs. market value, 491
counter-cyclical fiscal policy, 795
countervailing duty, 841–842
Coyne, James, 651n
Coyne Affair, 651n
CPI inflation, 710f, 730f
credit, 653
credit flows, 476
credit market, 476
cross-sectional data, 37, 37f
Crow, John, 718, 718f, 718n, 719, 746
crowding in, 790
crowding out, 790, 792–793, 792f
Crown corporations, 9, 494, 650
cryptocurrencies, 649
Cuba, 18
currency
    see also foreign-exchange market; money
    amount in circulation, 705
    as central bank liability, 653n
    debasement, 645
    exchange rate. See exchange rate
    in growing economy, 705
current account, 854, 871f
current account deficits and surpluses, 871–876
current-dollar national income, 463
current expenditure, 491n
curved line, slope of, 42
customers. See consumers
customs union, 843
cyclical budget deficits, 786
cyclical unemployment, 468, 559n, 759, 771–772
cyclically balanced budgets, 467
Czech Republic, 708

D
data series, comparison of, 34
deadweight loss
    import quota, 839f
    tariff, 838f
DeBeers, 63
debt defaults, 789
debt-service payments, 780
debt-to-GDP ratio, 783, 783f, 788–790, 794–795, 797–798
decentralized decision making, 19
decision lag, 601
decision making
    centralized decision making, 18–19
    decentralized decision making, 19
    described, 13
    how decisions are made, 13–14
    marginal decisions, 14
    maximizing decisions, 13
    and their choices, 12–14
decumulation, 490
deficits. See government debt and deficits
deflation, 739
demand, 53
    change in demand, 56
    demand-and-supply model, 63
    demand curve. See demand curve
    demand schedule, 52–53, 53f
    excess demand, 63, 64
    for foreign exchange, 860, 862

investment demand, 619f, 618–619
law of demand, 52
for money. See demand for money
quantity demanded. See quantity demanded
demand-and-supply model, 63
demand curve, 52–57, 54f
    foreign exchange, 862
    graphs, 65n
    investment demand curve, 617
    "micro" demand curve, 562
    movements along demand curve, 56–57, 57f
    and price, 65–67, 66f
    shifts in, 54–56, 55f, 57f, 65–67, 66f
demand deposits, 663
demand-determined output, 522, 527n, 549–550
demand for money, 675
    determinants of, 677–678
    and interest rate, 677, 677f
    liquidity preference, 678
    monetary equilibrium, 679–680, 679f
    precautionary demand for money, 675
    and price level, 678, 677f
    and real GDP, 677, 677f
    reasons for holding money, 675–677
    speculative demand for money, 675
    summary of, 678–679
    theory of money demand, 675–679
    transactions demand for money, 675
demand inflation, 737–738, 737f, 738f
demand schedule, 52–53, 53f
demand shocks. See aggregate demand shocks
demand side of the economy, 559–564
    aggregate demand (AD) curve, 561–564
    equilibrium GDP, 560–561
    price level, exogenous changes in, 559–560
demographic shifts, and NAIRU, 768–770, 769f
dependent variable, 65n
deposit money, 648–649, 658–661
deposits, 663
depreciation, 477–478, 491, 494, 540, 860, 881
depression, 565
desired aggregate expenditure (AE), 508, 542, 556
    aggregate expenditure (AE) function, 520–521, 521f
    autonomous expenditure, 509, 564
    consumption function, 509–516, 512f
    desired consumption expenditure, 509–516
    desired investment expenditure, 516–520
    induced expenditure, 509
    interest rates, fall in, 515

and price level, 561f
saving function, 513–514
desired consumption
    desired consumption expenditure, 509–516
    and monetary transmission mechanism, 682–683
    and national income, 542
desired consumption expenditure, 509–516
desired investment expenditure, 516–520
    autonomous expenditure, 519–520, 520f
    business confidence, 519
    real interest rate, 518–519
    sales, changes in, 519
Desjardins Inc., 676
destabilizing policy, 713–715
determination of price, 62–68
developed countries, 609
developing countries, 609
diamonds, 63
Diefenbaker, John, 651n
differentiated product, 63, 550, 812
diminishing marginal response, 41
diminishing marginal returns. See law of diminishing marginal returns
disagreements among economists, 20, 28–29
discouraged workers, 755
disequilibrium, 65
disequilibrium price, 65
disinflation, 744–747, 745f
disposable income, 509, 510f
distribution of income, 14
diversification, 830
dividends, 494
division of labour, 15
Dodge, David, 720, 720f
domestic price level, 686
double coincidence of wants, 16, 642
double counting, 486
double-entry bookkeeping, 488
downward wage stickiness, 584, 589–590, 589n
dumping, 840–841
durable goods, 515, 690n

E
Eastern Europe, 19
economic "bads", and GDP, 501
economic climate, (Not found in Current edition)
economic data, 34–38
    graphing, 37–38
    index numbers, 34–37, 35t, 36f
economic graphs, 44
economic growth, 466, 610
    balanced growth with constant technology, 624–625
    benefits of, 610–613
    case against economic growth, 614–615
    costs of, 613–614
    cross-country investment, and growth rates, 620f
    cumulative effect, 610t
    determinants of, 614–615
    and environmental degradation, 633–635
    and equilibrium price, 67

economic growth (*Cont.*)
  forgone consumption, 613
  and income inequality, 612–613
  in industrialized countries, 620
  limits to growth, 613, 632–636
  long-run economic growth, 579
  long-term economic growth, 463,
    479–480
  nature of, 581, 609–615
  and overall well-being, 614–615
  and poverty, 612–613
  production possibilities
    boundary, effect on, 9*f*
  real GDP, 609
  real GDP per employed worker,
    609–610
  real per capita GDP, 609
  and resource exhaustion,
    632–633
  social costs, 613–614
  sources of, 614–615
  sustainability of, 614, 636
  theories of. *See* economic growth
    theories
  three variables in, 609–610, 609*f*
  urgency for growth, 609
  vs. fluctuations, 479–481
economic growth theories
  advanced theories, 627–631
  basic relationships, 616–627
  endogenous technological change,
    627–629
  ideas-based theories, 631
  increasing marginal returns,
    630–631
  investment and saving, 617–620
  investment demand, 619*f*, 618
  knowledge-driven growth, 631
  long-run analysis, 616
  market-development costs,
    630–631
  national saving, 618, 619*f*
  Neoclassical growth theory,
    621–627
economic profit in foreign markets,
  832–833
economic recovery (1983-1987),
  717–718
economic recovery (2011-present),
  723–724
economic systems
  command economy, 18
  free-market economy, 18
  the great debate, 19–20
  mixed economies, 18–19, 20–21
  traditional economy, 17–18
  types of, 17–19
economic theories, 30–34
  abstraction from reality, 31
  assumptions, 30–31
  causation, 30–31, 33–34
  conditions of application, 31
  correlation, 33–34
  described, 30
  empirical observations, 32, 32*f*
  graphing economic theories, 38–44
  motives, 30
  predictions, 31
  statistical analysis, 32–33
  testing theories, 31–34
  variables, 30
economic values, 473
economic weather, (Not found in
  Current edition)

economics
  Classical economics, 591*n*
  definition, 4
  disagreements among economists,
    19–20, 28–29
  "dismal science", 631
  and government policy, 9–10
  key economic problems, 8–9
  macroeconomics, 9, 461, 462
  microeconomics, 9, 68
  Neoclassical economics, 591*n*
  normative statements, 27, 28*t*
  positive statements, 27, 28*t*
  resources, 4
  scarcity and choice, 4–8
  scientific approach, 32
  social science, 26
economies of scale, 811–813, 814*f*,
  832
economists
  disagreements among economists,
    19–20
  where economists work, 29
economy, 10
  closed economy, 509, 562*n*,
    791–792, 804
  decision makers and their
    choices, 13–14
  demand side of the economy,
    559–564
  factor inputs, 621
  market economies, 11–13
  open economy, 562*n*, 683–685,
    713, 792–793, 804
  supply side of the economy,
    564–567
efficiency
  and market economies, 12
  resource efficiency, 632
efficiency wages, 763
Elizabeth I, Queen of England, 645
embodied technical change, 625
Embraer SA, 833
empirical observations, 32, 32*f*
employment, 467, 468*f*
  see also unemployment
  changes in, 753–754
  full employment, 464*n*, 467
  long-term employment
    relationships, 762–763
  recent history, 468–469
  when labour markets clear, 760*f*
employment insurance, 767, 772
endogenous money supply,
  703–705
endogenous technological change,
  627–629
  knowledge transfer, 628–629
  learning by doing, 628
  market structure and innovation,
    629
endogenous variable, 30, 65, 541
energy prices, 709–711
entrance requirement, 767
Environment Canada, 29
environmental issues
  "business as usual" approach,
    635
  climate change. *See* climate change
  environmental degradation, and
    economic growth, 633–635
  global warming, 634–635
  pollution. *See* pollution
  and subsidies, 61

equilibrium, 64
  long-run equilibrium, 591–592,
    592*f*
  macroeconomic equilibrium,
    567–574
  market equilibrium. *See* market
    equilibrium
  market price of a bond, 673
  monetary equilibrium, 679–680,
    679*f*
equilibrium GDP, 560–561, 563
equilibrium interest rate, 617–618,
  681*f*
equilibrium national income,
  522–524, 522*t*, 524*f*, 544,
  549
  adding taxes to the consumption
    function, 542
  aggregate expenditure (AE)
    function, 524–526, 525*f*,
    542–544, 543*f*
  changes in, 524–531, 544–545
  equilibrium condition, 523
  fiscal policy, 547–549
  fluctuations as self-fulfilling
    prophecies, 529–531
  multiplier, 526–529, 527*f*, 529*f*,
    545–546
  net exports, 546–547
equilibrium price, 64, 64*ff*
equity, 21, 670
  see also fairness
euro, 541, 650, 860, 865*f*
euro zone, 863
Europe, 714
European Central Bank, 650
European Common Market, 813
  see also European Union
European Exchange Rate
  Mechanism (ERM), 865
European Union
  agricultural subsidies, 61
  common market, 843
  debt defaults, fear of, 789
  euro, 865*f*
  exchange rate, 864
  free trade agreements. *See* specific
    trade agreements
  government debt, 780
  hysteresis, 770
  labour-market policies, 768
  oil prices, 824
  voluntary export restrictions
    (VER), (Not found in
    Current edition)
excess demand, 63, 64
excess reserves, 656–657, 661, 705
excess supply, 63, 64
exchange rate, 476–477, 477*n*,
  477*f*, 859–860
  see also foreign-exchange market
  adjustable peg, 863, 867
  appreciation, 477–478, 721, 859
  Bretton Woods system, 864, 865
  Canada-U.S. exchange rate, 477,
    477*f*, 877, 878*f*
  depreciation, 477–478, 491, 494,
    540, 860, 881
  determination of, 863–870
  fixed exchange rate, 863, 865,
    864*f*, 866–867, 879–884
  flexible exchange rate, 863–864,
    864*f*, 865–870, 868*f*, 876
  floating exchange rate, 863

future value, 870
managed float, 863
and monetary policy, 711–712,
  883
news and the exchange rate, (Not
  found in Current edition)
pegged exchange rate, 863
PPP exchange rate, 876–879,
  878*f*
purchasing power parity (PPP),
  876–879, 878*f*
structural changes, 870
volatility of, (Not found in
  Current edition)
excise taxes, 494
execution lag, 600–601
exogenous forces, 568
exogenous variable, 30, 65, 541
expansionary fiscal policy, 788
expansionary monetary policy, 706
expectations, 516
expectations-augmented Phillips
  curve, 743
expected inflation, 582*n*, 587, 731,
  732–733, 734
expenditure
  autonomous expenditures, 509,
    519–520, 520*f*
  changes in, and lags, 712–713
  consumption expenditure, 490
  desired aggregate expenditure.
    See desired aggregate
    expenditure *(AE)*
  desired consumption expenditure,
    509–516
  desired investment expenditure,
    516–520
  flows of income and expenditure,
    14, 14*f*, 488, 489*f*
  GDP from the expenditure side,
    488, 490–493
  government expenditures,
    491–492
  induced expenditures, 509
  investment expenditure, 490–491
  public expenditure. *See*
    government spending
Export Development Canada, 29
exports, 478–479, 478*f*, 492
  Canadian exports, by industry,
    805*f*
  exported product, and trade
    patterns, 818, 818*f*
  foreign price elasticity of demand
    for Canadian exports, 862*n*
  net export function, 538,
    539–541, 539*f*, 540*f*
  net exports, 478, 478*f*, 492–493,
    538–539, 546–547, 560,
    792–793
  supply of foreign exchange, 860
  value of Canadian exports, 540*n*
  vs. imports, 834
  world price of, and flexible
    exchange rates, 865–866
externality, 21

F

factor endowment theory of
  comparative advantage,
  814–815, 831
factor incomes, 493–494
factor markets, 14
factor prices

adjustment process. *See* adjustment process (factor prices)
and aggregate demand shocks, 581, 586–590, 588f, 589f
and aggregate supply shocks, 581, 590–591, 589f
downward wage stickiness, 584
inflationary gap, 585
and output gap, 582–585
potential output, 583, 584
and real GDP, 583, 584
recessionary gap, 585
factors of production, 4
fairness, 10, 12
see also equity
federal government debt and deficit, 782–784, 784f, 785f
Federal Reserve, 650, 696, 714, 715, 720, 724, 725, 739
feudal system, 18
fiat money, 647–648
final goods, 486
Finance Canada, 29
financial capital, 618, 684, 685
financial crisis. *See* global financial crisis
financial intermediaries, 650, 653
financial markets, 651
financial stability, (Not found in Current edition)
fine tuning, 601–602
Finland, 708
firms
  price setters, 550, 551
  price taker, 565
fiscal austerity, 779
fiscal policy, 536
  "activist" fiscal policy, 594
  automatic fiscal stabilizers, 598–600
  bread-and-butter issues, 600
  and budget deficit function, 785–786, 785f
  and budget deficits and surpluses, 784–788, 786f
  contractionary fiscal policy, 785
  counter-cyclical fiscal policy, 795, 796
  decision lag, 601
  discretionary, 598, 600–602
  execution lag, 600–601
  expansionary fiscal policy, 788
  fine tuning, 600–601
  government debt, effect of, 794–796
  and government debt and deficits, 784–788
  government purchases, increase in, 602
  in Great Depression, 598–599
  gross tuning, 601–602
  and growth, 602–603
  limitations of, 600–602
  and paradox of thrift, 596–597
  stabilization policy. *See* fiscal stabilization policy
  structural budget deficits, 787, 787f
  taxes, reduction in, 602–603
  temporary *vs.* permanent tax changes, 601
fiscal stabilization policy, 594–603
  see also fiscal policy

automatic fiscal stabilizers, 598–600
basic theory of, 594–598
inflationary gap, closing, 595–596, 596f
limitations, 600–602
recessionary gap, closing, 594–595, 595f
fiscal stimulus, 10, 594, 597, 721, 780, 796, 836
fixed announcement dates, 702, 713
fixed exchange rate, 863–867, 871, 879–884
fixed factors, 507n
fixed investment, 490
fixed production, 810–811
Fleming, Donald, 651n
flexible exchange rates, 864, 864f
  capital movements, 869–870
  changes in, 865–870, 868f
  "correct" exchange rate, 876
  equal inflation in both countries, 868
  foreign price of imports, rise in, 866–868
  inflation at unequal rates, 869
  inflation in only one country, 868–869
  price levels, changes in, 868–869
  as "shock absorbers", 879–882, 880f
  uncertainty, 882
  world price of exports, rise in, 865–866
flexible wages, 588–589
floating exchange rate, 863
  see also flexible exchange rates
flows
  credit flows, 455
  gross flows in labour market, 755, 756
  of income and expenditure, 14, 14f, 488, 489f
  in labour market, 755, 756–757
  of purchases, 50
  vs. stocks, 50, 51
fluctuations
  real GDP, short-run fluctuations in, 592n
  as self-fulfilling prophecies, 529–531
  short-term fluctuations, 480–481
  in unemployment, 759–765
  vs. economic growth, 479–480
food prices, 709–711
forgone output, 807(Found as forgone output)
foreign exchange, 477, 860–862
foreign-exchange market, 477, 859–863, 861f
  demand curve for foreign exchange, 862–863
  demand for foreign exchange, 862–863
  exchange rate. *See* exchange rate
  supply curve for foreign exchange, 861–862
  supply of foreign exchange, 860–862
foreign-exchange risk, 882
foreign income, changes in, 539–540
foreign trade. *See* international trade

forgone consumption, 613
45° line, 513
forward-looking monetary policy, 716f
forward markets, 883
fractional-reserve system, 658
fractionally backed paper money, 646–647
France, 19
Fraser Institute, 29
free import, 835
free-market economy, 18
  see also market economy
free markets
  and efficiency, 12
  and fairness, 12
  market failures, 10
  vs. central planning, 19–20
free trade, 829–830
free trade area (FTA), 843
frictional unemployment, 467, 757, 765–766, 768, 772
Friedman, Milton, 511, 597, 692, 707, 726, 741, 743
FTA. *See* Canada-U.S. Free Trade Agreement (FTA); free trade area (FTA)
fuel consumption, 43f
full employment, 464n, 467
functional relation, 39
functions, 38–30
  graphing of functions, 39–43
  mathematical equation, 39
  with a minimum or a maximum, 42–43
  non-linear functions, 40–42, 41f
  slope of a straight line, 40
  table, 39
  words, 39
future generations, and deficits, 793–794

G
G20, 597, 789
gains from trade, 806
  see also international trade
  absolute advantage, 806–807, 807t, 811
  acquired comparative advantage, 815–816
  climate, 815
  comparative advantage, 807–809, 807t, 809, 812, 814–816
  economies of scale, 811–813, 814f
  factor endowment theory of comparative advantage, 814, 831
  fixed production, 810–811
  generally, 810–811
  human capital, 815
  illustration of, 806–811
  learning by doing, 813–814, 814f
  opportunity costs, 807, 809f, 810
  production possibilities boundary, 809–811
  specialization, 808t, 809, 812, 831
  variable costs, 811–814
  variable production, 811
  volume of trade, 872
GATT, 842
GDP deflator, 497–498, 878–879
GDP from the expenditure side, 488, 490–493, 493t

consumption expenditure, 490
government purchases, 491–492
investment expenditure, 490–491
net exports, 492
total expenditures, 493
GDP from the income side, 488, 493–496
  factor incomes, 493–494
  non-factor payments, 494–495
  total national income, 495–496
General Agreement on Tariffs and Trade (GATT), 842
General Motors (GM), (Not found in Current edition)
The General Theory of Employment, Interest and Money (Keynes), 591n
George V, King of England, 598
Germany, 643, 644, 768, 815
Gig economy, wage flexibility 764–765
global climate change. *See* climate change
global financial crisis, 21, 476, 564, 597, 654, 721–723, 754, 779, 789, 836–837
global financial stability, (Not found in current edition)
global recession, 10, 798
global supply chains, 846, 820
global warming, 634–635
  see also climate change
globalization, 16–17, 770n
  causes of, 16
  challenges of, 17
  and inflationary pressures, 748
  of markets, 629
  and structural change, 770
gold standard, 647
goods, 4
  basket of goods, 36, 471, 877, 879
  consumption goods, 7
  durable goods, 515, 690n
  final goods, 486
  identical basket of goods, 877
  inferior goods, 55
  intermediate goods, 486
  investment goods, 7, 490
  non-traded goods, 879
  nondurable goods, 515
  normal goods, 55
  production of different goods, 878–879
  public goods, 21, 631
  what is produced and how, 8
Goods and Services Tax (GST), 494
goods markets, 14
government
  Bank of Canada, as banker to federal government, 652
  budget balance, 537
  budget surplus, 537
  capital budgeting, 794
  comparative advantage, influence on, 820
  debt. *See* government debt and deficits
  as decision maker, 13
  deficits. *See* government debt and deficits
  in modern mixed economy, 20–21
  municipal governments, 537

government (*Cont.*)
  net tax revenues, 536–537
  provincial governments, 537
  purchases. *See* government
    purchases
  revenues, 783*f*
  in simple short-run macro model,
    536–538
  spending. *See* government
    spending
  taxes. *See* taxation
  transfers, 780
government debt, 781
  see also government debt and
    deficits
government debt and deficits, 537,
    781, 783*f*
  actual budget deficit, 787*f*
  analytical issues, 784–790
  annually balanced budgets,
    796–797
  balanced budget, 537, 784,
    796–797
  budget constraint, 780–782
  budget deficit, 537, 599,
    781–782
  budget deficit function, 785–786,
    785*f*
  budget surplus, 537, 779, 781
  in Canada, 782–784
  crowding in effects of surpluses,
    793
  crowding out effects of deficits,
    793, 791–793, 792*f*
  current account deficits, 871–876
  cyclical budget deficits, 786
  cyclically balanced budgets, 797
  debt defaults, 789
  debt dynamics, 788–789
  debt-service payments, 780
  debt-to-GDP ratio, 783, 784*f*,
    788–790, 795–796, 797–798
  economic policy, effects on,
    794–796
  effects of, 790–796
  facts and definitions, 780–784
  federal government, 782–783,
    783*f*, 784*f*
  fiscal policy, 784–788, 786*f*,
    796–797
  future generations, and deficits,
    793
  government debt, 781
  investment in closed economies,
    791–792
  long-term burden of government
    debt, 793
  net exports to open economies, 792
  primary budget deficit, 781–782
  provincial governments, 784
  structural budget deficits, 786,
    786*f*, 787*f*
  twin deficits, 875
government expenditures, 492, 780,
    783*f*, 784*f*
  see also government spending
government policy
  destabilizing policy, 713–715
  and economics, 9–10
  fiscal policy. *See* fiscal policy
  fiscal stabilization policy. *See*
    fiscal stabilization policy
  government debt, effect of,
    794–796

and idle resources, 9
  monetary policy. *See* monetary
    policy
  and NAIRU, 771
  stabilization policy, 547, 590,
    594–598
  and structural unemployment,
    767–768
  trade policy. *See* trade policy
government purchases, 491–492,
    536, 548, 602
government spending, 10
  deficit-financed increase in, 598
  government expenditures. *See*
    government expenditures
  government purchases. *See*
    government purchases
  productivity-enhancing
    infrastructure, (Not found in
    Current edition)
  program spending, 782
  transfer payments, 536
graphs
  cross-sectional data, 37–38, 37*f*
  demand curve, 65*n*
  economic data, 37–38
  economic theories, 38–44
  of functions, 39–43
  scatter diagram, 38, 38*f*
  slope. *See* slope
  supply curve, 65*n*
  time-series data, 37–38, 37*f*
Great Depression, 465, 480, 597,
    598–599, 692, 714–715,
    736, 835, 836–837
Greece, 644, 779, 790–791, 789
greenhouse-gas emissions, and
    economic growth, 634–635
Greenland, 634
Greenspan, Alan, 720
Gresham, Thomas, 645
Gresham's law, 645–646
gross domestic product (GDP),
    463, 488
  and economic "bads", 501
  and environmental damage, 501*f*
  equilibrium GDP, 560–561,
    563
  GDP deflator, 497–498, 878–879
  GDP from the expenditure side,
    488, 490–493, 493*t*
  GDP from the income side, 488,
    493–496
  and home production, 500
  and illegal activities, 500
  and living standards, 502–503
  nominal GDP, 496–499, 498*n*,
    499
  and non-market activities, 500
  omissions from GDP, 499–502
  potential GDP, 465, 466
  real GDP. *See* real GDP
  real per capita GDP. *See* real per
    capita GDP
  and underground economy, 500
gross flows in labour market, 755,
    756
gross investment, 491
gross tuning, 601
growth. *See* economic growth

H

Heckscher, Eli, 814
Heckscher-Ohlin theory, 815

home production, 500–501
homogeneous product, 52*n*
Hong Kong, (Not found in Current
    edition)
households
  expectations, 514
  wealth, 514–515, 559
housing market collapse, 564
human capital, 615, 623–624, 625,
    815
Hume, David, 803
Hungary, 644
Hydro Quebec, 63
hyperinflation, 471, 643, 644
hypotheses, 31
hysteresis, 687–688, 770

I

ideas-based theories, 631
identical basket of goods, 877
idle resources, 9
illegal activities, 500
IMF. *See* International Monetary
    Fund (IMF)
import duty, 837
  see also tariffs
import quota, 839, 839*f*
imports, 478–479, 478*f*, 492
  Canadian imports, by industry,
    805*f*
  foreign price of, and flexible
    exchange rate, 866–867
  imported product, and trade
    patterns, 818–819, 818*f*
  marginal propensity to import,
    538, 545
  price elasticity of demand for,
    863*n*
  vs. exports, 834–835
incentives, 12–13
income, 462–463
  break-even level of income, 513
  change in, and shifts in demand
    curve, 54–56
  consumers' income, and shifts in
    demand curve, 54–55
  disposable income, 509, 510*f*
  distribution of income, 14
  factor incomes, 493–494
  flows of income and expenditure,
    14, 14*f*, 488, 489*f*
  foreign income, changes in, 539
  GDP from the income side, 488,
    493–496
  national income. *See* national
    income
  net domestic income, 494
  permanent-income theory, 511
  real income, 502
income effect, 515*n*
income inequality, 3, 612
increasing marginal returns,
    630–631
independent variable, 65*n*
index numbers, 34–37, 35*t*, 36*f*
India, 67, 573
indirect taxes, 494
Indonesia, 573, 574
induced consumption, 513
induced expenditures, 509
inefficiency. *See* efficiency
infant industry argument, 832
inferior goods, 55
inflation, 471, 729

accelerating inflation, 740–741,
    743
anticipated inflation, 473, 730
Asian crisis and Canadian
    economy, 574
backward-looking expectations,
    732
and bonds, 560*n*
constant inflation, 734–735, 735*f*
core inflation, 710*f*, 710
costs of high inflation, 707
CPI inflation, 710*f*, 730*f*
debasing of coinage, 645
demand inflation, 737–738, 737*f*,
    738*f*
and demand shocks, 737–738,
    737*f*, 738*f*
disinflation, 744–746, 745*f*
and exchange rates, 869
expected inflation, 582*n*, 587,
    731, 732–733, 734
forward-looking expectations,
    732
and globalization, 748
high inflation, and money, 643
hyperinflation, 471, 643, 644
interest rate, 474–476
macroeconomic model, adding
    to, 731–736
as monetary phenomenon,
    741–744
monetary policy, and sustained
    inflation, 707–708
and money, 688, 689*f*
NAIRU (non-accelerating
    inflation rate of
    unemployment). *See* NAIRU
    (non-accelerating inflation
    rate of unemployment)
output-gap inflation, 734
and Phillips curve, 741, 742–743
prices, 733–734
recent history, 471–473
reducing inflation, 744–748, 745*f*
relative inflation, 869
rising inflation (1987-1990),
    718–719
sacrifice ratio, 747, 747*f*
significance of, 473–474
stagflation, 572, 590, 716,
    744–745
supply inflation, 738–740, 739*f*
and supply shocks, 738–740,
    739*f*
sustained inflation, 707–708,
    731, 742–743
temporary inflation, 731
twin peaks of inflation, 729
unanticipated inflation, 473, 730
and uncertainty, 707
unexpected inflation, 707
wages, changes in, 731–733
zero inflation, 734
inflation rate, 473*f*
inflation targeting, 665, 693,
    706–712, 719
  adoption of, 708
  complications, 709–712
  costs of high inflation, 707
  exchange rate and monetary
    policy, 707–708
  expectations of inflation, 747
  inflation-control targets, 719
  from 1991-2000, 719–720

and output gap, 708–709
reasons for, 707–708
as stabilizing policy, 709
from 2001-2007, 720–721
volatile food and energy prices, 709–711
inflationary gap, 465, 582, 583, 584, 585, 586–587, 588f, 746, 797
information technology, 16
innovations, 629, 631
Innovation, Science and Economic Development Canada, 29
inputs, 59–60, 566, 590
Inside the Black Box: Technology and Economics (Rosenberg), 628
Institute for Research on Public Policy, 29
interest, 494, 494n
interest rate. *See* interest rate
liquidity preference theory of interest, 680
interest rate, 474, 670n
bank rate, 474, 702
and bond prices, 670–672, 673–674
change in, 515, 690n
and credit flows, 476
and durable goods consumption, 690n
equilibrium interest rate, 618, 681f
expectation of increases in future rates, 675–676
inflation, 474–475
market interest rate, 673–674
and monetary transmission mechanism, 680–683, 681f
and money demand, 677, 677f
nominal interest rate, 474–475, 677n, 683n
overnight interest rate, 702–703, 704f
and present value, 670–672
prime interest rate, 474
real interest rate, 474–475, 518–519, 683n
short-term interest rates, 1975-2018, 717f
significance of, 475–476
targeting, in monetary policy, 701
term structure of interest rates, 676
vs. money supply, 699–701
intermediate goods, 486
intermediating, 476
international borrowing, 872–874
International Monetary Fund (IMF), 515, 790, 791, 865
international relative prices, 540–541, 540f
international trade, 803, 806
agreements. *See* international trade agreements
comparative advantage. *See* comparative advantage
exported product, and trade patterns, 818, 818f
gains from trade. *See* gains from trade
globalization. *See* globalization
growth in, 804f

importance of, 804
imported product, and trade patterns, 818–819, 819f
law of one price, 817–818
net export function, 539–541, 540f
net exports, 538–539
in simple short-run macro model, 538–541
terms of trade, 821–824, 822f, 823f, 831
trade creation, 843–844
trade diversion, 843–844
trade patterns, 816–824
trade policy. *See* trade policy
transaction costs, 882–883
international trade agreements
see also specific trade agreements
bilateral free-trade agreements, 843
common market, 843
customs union, 843
dispute-settlement mechanism, 843, 845
General Agreement on Tariffs and Trade (GATT), 842
regional trade agreements, 842–843, 844
trade creation, 843–844
trade diversion, 843–844
World Trade Organization (WTO), 842
Internet, 480
interpersonal trade, 805–806
interregional trade, 805–806
intra-industry trade, 804, 813
inventories, 490, 518
investment
actual total investment, 491
business fixed investment, 490
in closed economies, 791–792
cross country investment, and growth rates, 620f
crowding out of, 792–793
demand, 618, 619f
demand curve, 617
desired investment, and monetary transmission mechanism, 682–683, 682f
desired investment expenditure, 516–520
direct investment, 855n
and economic growth, 617–620
fixed investment, 490
gross investment, 491
in industrialized countries, 620
innovations, 630
investment goods, 7, 490
long-run connection between saving and investment, 617f
net investment, 491
portfolio investment, 855n
volatility of, 517f
investment expenditure, 490–491
see also desired investment expenditure
invisible hand, 12
involuntary unemployment, 759, 760, 761, 763
Iran, 815
Ireland, 688, 820
irrational exuberance, 720
Israel, 708, 811, 843
Italy, 492, 768

J
Japan, 628, 629, 835, 863
job creation, 755, 835–836
job destruction, 755
job-security provisions, 771
jobs for economists, 29
Jordan, 843

K
key economic problems, 8–9
Keynes, John Maynard, 511, 566, 566f, 591n, 597, 692
Keynesian consumption function, 511
Keynesian economists, 692–693, 715
Keynesian range of the *AS* curve, 566, 571
knowledge acquisition, 15
knowledge-driven growth, 631
knowledge transfer, 628–629

L
labour, 4
division of labour, 15
low-wage foreign labour, protection against, 834
marginal product, 621, 759
specialization of labour, 15
labour force, 467, 468f
and aging population, 2
growth in, 614, 623
Labour Force Survey, 467
labour market
economic climate *vs.* economic weather, (Not found in Current edition)
flexibility, 770–771
flows in, 755, 756–757
gross flows, 755, 756
market-clearing theories, 759–761, 760f
net flows, 755
non-market-clearing theories, 761–765, 761f
stocks, 756–757
labour productivity, 469, 470f, 610, 611
labour unions
"cost push" on wages, 707
wage stickiness and involuntary unemployment, 761
lags, and monetary policy, 712–713
laissez-faire capitalism, (Not found in Current edition)
land, 4
large countries, and terms of trade, 831
law of demand, 52
law of diminishing marginal returns, 621, 622f
law of diminishing returns, 565
law of one price, 817–818
learning by doing, 15, 628, 813–814, 814f, 832
legal tender, 648
leisure, 501
"lender of last resort", 651
"level playing field", 832
Lewis, William, 629
life-cycle theory, 511
The Limits to Growth (Club of Rome), 632
linearly-related variables, 39

liquidity preference, 678
liquidity preference theory of interest, 678
living standards, 2, 470, 502–503, 611–612, 610n, 636
long run
see also specific long-run terms
economic growth, analysis of, 616
macroeconomic state, 581
and paradox of thrift, 597
long-run aggregate supply curve, 591
long-run economic growth, 579, 609–610, 609f
see also economic growth
long-run equilibrium, 591–592, 592f
long-run macro model
see also macroeconomic model
assumptions, 581
equilibrium interest rate, 616, 617, 618
real GDP, 616
long-run money neutrality, 686–688, 687f
long-term burden of government debt, 793
long-term capital movements, 870
long-term economic growth, 463, 479–480
long-term employment relationships, 762–763

M
M1, 663
M2, 663, 664f
M2+, 663, 664f
M2++, 663
Mackenzie King, William Lyon, 836, 837f
macro model. *See* macroeconomic model
macroeconomic equilibrium, 567–574, 568f
aggregate demand shock, 569–572, 569f
aggregate supply shock, 572–573
assumptions, 580
changes in, 568–569
conditions for, 567
evolution into long-run equilibrium, 579
macroeconomic model
see also long-run macro model; short-run macro model
aggregate demand *(AD)* curve, 561–564
aggregate expenditure (AE) function, 520–522, 521f, 523, 525–526, 525f
aggregate supply *(AS)* curve, 565–566, 565f
algebraic exposition, 556–557
assumptions, 580, 581, 736–737
closed economy, 509
deflation, 736
demand-determined output, 549–550
demand side of the economy, 559–564
desired aggregate expenditure, 508–522
desired consumption expenditure, 509–516

macroeconomic model (*Cont.*)
  desired investment expenditure, 516–520
  equilibrium, 616
  equilibrium condition, 524, 544
  equilibrium GDP, changes in, 560–561
  equilibrium interest rate, 618, 619
  equilibrium national income, 522–524, 522*t*, 524*f*, 541–544, 548
  fluctuations as self-fulfilling prophecies, 529–531
  foreign trade, 538–541
  government, 536–538
  inflation, 731–736
  macroeconomic equilibrium, 567–574
  multiplier, 526–529, 527*f*, 529*f*
  price level, exogenous changes in, 559–560
  price level as endogenous variable, 558
  real GDP, 616
  results restated, 526
  simple multiplier, 527*f*, 528, 529*f*, 530, 545–546
  simplifying assumptions, 509
  supply side of the economy, 564–567
macroeconomic states
  factor prices, adjustment of, 580
  long run, 581
  short run, 580
  summary of, 581, 581*t*
macroeconomic variables
  appreciation, 477–478
  depreciation, 477–478
  employment, 467
  exchange rate, 476–478, 477*n*, 477*f*
  exchange rates and trade flows, 476–479
  exports, 476–477, 477*f*
  imports, 476–477, 478*f*
  income, 462–463
  inflation, 471–474
  interest rates, 474–476
  national income, 463, 466
  output, 462–466
  output gap, 582, 466*f*
  potential output, 464
  price level, 471–474
  productivity, 469–470
  unemployment, 467–469
macroeconomics, 9, 461, 462
Malaysia, 573, 574
Malthus, Thomas, 591*n*
managed float, 863
Manitoba Hydro, 29
margin of dumping, 840
marginal benefit, 14
marginal change, 41
marginal cost *(MC)*, 14
increasing marginal cost, 42, 42*f*
marginal decisions, 14
marginal product *(MP)*
  of labour, 621, 759
marginal propensity to consume *(MPC)*, 513, 542
marginal propensity to import, 538, 546
marginal propensity to save *(MPS)*, 514

marginal propensity to spend, 521, 528, 545
marginal propensity to spend on national income, 600
marginal response, 41–43
market, 62
  concept of, 62
  credit market, 476
  factor markets. *See* factor markets
  financial markets, 651
  foreign-exchange market. *See* foreign-exchange market
  forward markets, 883
  free markets. *See* free markets
  globalization of markets, 629
  goods markets, 14
  labour market. *See* labour market
  stock markets, 514–515
  use of term, 15
market-clearing theories of the labour market, 759–761, 760*f*
market demand curves, 51*n*
market-development costs, 630
market economy, 17
  alternative to, 17–21
  efficiency, 12
  globalization, effect of, 16–17
  incentives, 13
  nature of, 11–13
  self-interest, 12–13
  self-organizing, 11–12
  use of term, 16
market equilibrium, 63–65
  algebraic model, 67
  changes in, 65–67
market failure, 10, 20
market interest rate, 673–674
market power, 63, 831
market structure, and innovation, 629
market value, 491
Marshall, Alfred, 4, 52, 65*n*
Marshall-Lerner condition, 863*n*
Marx, Karl, 19
Mastercard, 654
material living standards, 610–611, 610*n*
maximizers, 13
maximum of a function, 42–43
medium of exchange, 642
menu costs, 763
mercantilism, 872
Mercosur, 843
metallic money, 643–645
Mexico, 479, 708, 813
  see also North American Free Trade Agreement (NAFTA)
"micro" demand curve, 562
microeconomics, 9
Mill, John Stuart, 591*n*
milling, 645
mineral resources, 870
minimum of a function, 42
mixed economies, 18–19, 20–21
models, 30
modern economies, complexity of, 10–17
modern money, 648–649
Modigliani, Franco, 511
Monetarist economists, 692, 692*n*, 714–715

monetary equilibrium, 679–680, 679*f*
monetary forces, strength of, 686–693
monetary policy, 480
  see also Bank of Canada
  "activist" monetary policy, 692*n*
  communications difficulties, 715–716
  contractionary monetary policy, 706
  Coyne Affair, 651*n*
  destabilizing policy, 713–715
  economic recovery (1983-1987), 717–718
  economic recovery (2011-present), 723–724
  effectiveness of, 690–692, 712
  endogenous money supply, 703–705
  and exchange rate, 711–712, 883
  expansionary monetary policy, 706
  financial crisis and recession (2007-2010), 721–723
  fine tuning, 601
  forward-looking monetary policy, 716*f*
  government debt, effect of, 794
  gross tuning, 601
  implementation of, 699–706, 699*f*
  inflation targeting, 706–712, 719–720
  interest rate, targeting of, 701
  key episodes in Canadian monetary policy, 716–724
  Keynesians *vs.* monetarists, 692–693, 692*n*
  lags, 712–713
  monetary transmission mechanism. *See* monetary transmission mechanism
  money supply, non-targeting of, 700–701
  money supply *vs.* interest rate, 699–701
  open-market operations, 700, 704
  overnight interest rate, 702–703, 704*f*
  rising inflation (1987-1990), 718–719
  and short-run changes in real GDP, 692
  and sustained inflation, 707–708
monetary reform, 688
monetary shocks, 690–693
monetary transmission mechanism, 680–683, 706*f*
  aggregate demand, changes in, 683, 683*f*
  desired consumption, changes in, 682–683
  desired investment, changes in, 682–683, 682*f*
  interest rate, changes in, 680–682, 681*f*
  open-economy modification, 683–685, 685*f*
  slope of *AD* curve, 685–686
  summary of, 684*f*
monetary validation

aggregate demand shocks, 737–738, 738*f*
aggregate supply shocks, 739, 739*f*
  removal of, 744
money
  bank notes, 646
  creation of. *See* money creation
  currency debasement, 645
  demand. *See* demand for money
  deposit money, 648–649, 658–661
  fiat money, 647–648
  fractionally backed paper money, 646–647
  gold standard, 647
  Great Depression, role in, 714–715
  and high inflation, 643
  hyperinflation and the value of money, 644
  hysteresis, 687–688
  and inflation, 643, 688, 689*f*
  legal tender, 648
  long-run money neutrality, 686, 687–689, 687*f*
  as medium of exchange, 642
  metallic money, 643–645
  modern money, 648–649
  monetary equilibrium, 679–680, 679*f*
  money supply. *See* money supply
  nature of, 642–649
  near money, 664
  neutrality of money, 686–688, 687*f*
  opportunity cost of holding money, 677, 677*n*
  origins of, 643–648
  paper money, 646–647, 646*n*
  purchasing power of money, 473
  real value of money, 473
  as store of value, 642–643
  strength of monetary forces, 686–690
  and trade, 15–16
  as unit of account, 643
money creation, 658–661
  cash drain, 661–662
  deposit money, 658–662
  excess reserves, 661
  multiple expansion of deposits, 659–660, 660*t*
  new deposit, 658–659, 660*t*
  realistic expansion of deposits, 662
  simplifying assumptions, 658
money demand. *See* demand for money
money market deposit accounts, 663
money market mutual funds, 663
money neutrality, 686, 686–688, 669*f*
money price, 68
money substitutes, 664
money supply, 658, 662
  and aggregate demand, 683*f*
  Bank of Canada, as regulator of, 652, 664–665
  change in, effect of, 691*f*
  definitions of, 663
  deposits, kinds of, 663
  endogenous, 703
  M1, 663

M2, 663, 664t
M2+, 663, 664t
M2++, 663
monetary equilibrium, 679–690, 679f
money substitutes, 664
near money, 664
non-targeting of, 700–701
vs. interest rate, 699–701
monopoly, and innovation, 629
mortgage-backed securities, 722
motives, 30
multiple expansion of deposits, 659–661, 660t
multiplier, 526–529
   and lags, 712–713
   price level, variations in, 569, 570f
   simple multiplier. See simple multiplier
   with taxes and imports, 545–546
municipal governments, 537

N

NAFTA. See North American Free Trade Agreement (NAFTA)
NAIRU (non-accelerating inflation rate of unemployment), 732, 752, 759, 768
   changes in, 768–771
   demographic shifts, 768
   determinants of, 765–771
   frictional-structural distinction, 768
   frictional unemployment, 765–766, 768
   globalization and structural change, 770
   hysteresis, 770, 769f
   labour-market flexibility, 770
   policies, effect of, 770–771
   structural unemployment, 766–768
national income, 463
   see also national income accounting
   actual national income, 522
   adding taxes to the consumption function, 542
   aggregation, 463
   constant dollar national income, 463
   current-dollar national income, 463
   equilibrium national income. See equilibrium national income
   importance of, 466
   marginal propensity to spend on national income, 600
   and national product, 489f
   nominal national income, 463
   real national income, 463
   recent history, 463–464
   short-run macro model. See short-run macro model
   total national income, 495
national income accounting
   see also national income
   arbitrary decisions, 494n, 496
   basics of, 488–496
   further issues, 496–503
   GDP and living standards, 502–503
   GDP deflator, 497–498

GDP from the expenditure side, 488, 490–493, 493t
GDP from the income side, 488, 493–496
   nominal GDP, 496–497
   omissions from GDP, 499–502
   real GDP, 496–497
National Income and Expenditure Accounts (NIEA), 488
national output, 486–488
National Policy of 1876, 832
national price indices, 878
   see also Consumer Price Index (CPI)
national product, 462, 489f
national saving, 617, 617n, 618, 619f
national treatment, 844–845
natural rate of unemployment, 732
natural resources, 621n
near money, 664
negatively-related variables, 39
Neoclassical economics, 591n
Neoclassical growth model, 621–627
   aggregate production function, 621, 622f
   balanced growth with constant technology, 624
   capital accumulation, 623–624
   constant returns to scale, 622–623
   diminishing marginal returns, 621, 622f
   economic growth in Neoclassical model, 623–625
   human capital accumulation, 623–624
   labour-force growth, 623
   physical capital accumulation, 623–624
   technological change, importance of, 625–626
   technological change, measurement of, 626–627
   vs. ideas-based theory, 631
net domestic income, 494
net export function, 538, 539–541, 539f, 540f
net exports, 478, 478f, 492, 538–539, 546–547, 560, 792
net flows in labour market, 755
net investment, 491
net tax rate, 536–537
net tax revenues, 536–537, 786n
the Netherlands, 870
neutrality of money, 686–688, 687f
new deposit, 658–659, 660f
new equipment, 490–491, 518
new plants, 490–491, 518
new residential housing, 491
New Zealand, 708, 782, 784
nominal GDP, 496–498, 499
nominal interest rate, 474–475, 677n, 683n
nominal national income, 463
nominal value, 473, 496
nominal wages, 584n, 586, 732, 733n
non-accelerating inflation rate of unemployment (NAIRU). See NAIRU (non-accelerating inflation rate of unemployment)

non-factor payments, 494–495
non-linear functions, 40–42, 41f
non-market activities, 500
non-market-clearing theories of the labour market, 761–765, 761f
non-tariff barriers (NTBs), 829, 840–842
non-traded goods, 879
nondurable goods, 515
normal goods, 55
normative statements, 27, 28t
North American Free Trade Agreement (NAFTA), 479, 724, 766, 813, 837, 843, 844–848
North Korea, 19
notice deposits, 663

O

official reserves, changes in, 855
Ohlin, Bertil, 814
oil prices, 572–573, 716, 739–740, 824
oligopoly prices, and inflation, 707
OPEC. See Organization of Petroleum Exporting Countries (OPEC)
open economy, 562n, 683–685, 685f, 713, 792, 804
open-economy monetary transmission mechanism, 683–685, 685f
open-market operations, 700, 704
open-market purchase, 705
open-market sale, 705
opportunity cost, 5–7, 5f
   and comparative advantage, 807, 807t
   gains from trade, 810, 809f
   of holding money, 675–677, 677n
   is a ratio, 5–7
   of university degree, 6
Organization of Petroleum Exporting Countries (OPEC), 31, 632, 716, 739, 824
Osberg, Lars, (Not found in current edition)
"other things being equal". See ceteris paribus
"other things given". See ceteris paribus
output, 462–463
   above potential, 583
   actual output, 464
   below potential, 584
   demand-determined output, 522, 527n, , 544, 549–550
   forgone output, 807
   national output, 486–488
   potential output, 464, 582, 746
   potential output as "anchor", 585
   profits as function of output, 43f
   supply of, and price level, 565
   total output, 488
   unemployment, and lost output, 758
output gap, 464–465, 466f, 582–585
   and factor prices, 585
   and inflation targeting, 708–709

potential output as "anchor", 585
   in short run, 583f
   unemployment, 585
   and wages, 731–732
output-gap inflation, 734
overnight interest rate, 702–703, 704f
overnight market, 702

P

paper money, 646–647, 646n
paradox of thrift, 596–597, 598
Paraguay, 843
part-time job, 755
peak, 465
pegged exchange rate, 863
   see also fixed exchange rate
percentage increase, 36
perfectly competitive markets, 62
permanent-income theory, 511
Persia, 815
Peru, 843
Philippines, 574
Phillips, A.W., 584, 586, 742
Phillips curve, 584–585, 586–587, 741, 742–743
physical capital, 615, 623–624
Poland, 708
policy. See government policy
policy imperialism, (: Not found in current edition)
pollution
   and economic growth, 634–635
   linear pollution reduction, 40f
   non-linear pollution reduction, 41f
Poloz, Stephen, 724, 723f
population
   aging population, 2
   and shifts in demand curve, 55
portfolio balance, 680
portfolio investment, 855n
Portugal, 789
positive statements, 27, 28t
positively-related variables, 39
potential GDP, 466, 466f
potential output, 464, 582, 746
potential output as "anchor", 585
poverty, 612
Powell, James, 648n
The Power of Productivity (Lewis), 629
PPP exchange rate, 877–879, 878f
precautionary demand for money, 675
predictions, 31
present value (PV), 670
   and interest rate, 670–672
   and market price of bonds, 672–674
   sequence of future payments, 671–672
   of single payment one year hence, 670–671
price
   absolute price, 68
   average house prices, 37f
   base-period prices, 497
   bonds, 672–674, 676
   commodities, 65f, 572
   determination of price, 62–69
   disequilibrium price, 65
   energy prices, 709–711

price (*Cont.*)
  equilibrium price, 64, 64f
  excess demand, 64
  excess supply, 64
  food prices, 709–711
  and inflation, 733–734
  input prices, 566, 590
  of inputs, and shifts in supply
    curves, 59–60
  international relative prices,
    changes in, 539–541, 540f
  and market equilibrium, 63–67
  money price, 68
  oil prices, 572–574, 716,
    739–740, 823
  of other goods, and shifts in
    demand curve, 55
  of other products, and shifts in
    supply curves, 61
  and quantity demanded, 51–52
  and quantity supplied, 58
  relative price, 68, 563, 590
  stability, 718
  volatile food and energy prices,
    709–711
  wage-price spiral, 740
price elasticity of demand, 862n,
  863n
price indexes, 36–37, 471–474
price level, 471
  and aggregate demand (AD)
    curve, 561
  and aggregate demand shock,
    569
  aggregate price level, 550
  and aggregate supply shocks, 572
  autonomous aggregate
    expenditure, changes in, 564
  constant price level, 509, 558
  and consumption, changes in,
    559–560
  and desired aggregate
    expenditure (AE), 561f
  effects of changes in price level,
    559–560
  as endogenous variable, 558
  and exchange rates, 867–868
  exogenous changes in, 559–560
  and inflation rate, 473f
  and money demand, 677–679,
    677f
  net exports, changes in, 560
  and price-setting firms, 565
  and price-taking firms, 565
  and real GDP, 567
  in simple short-run macro model,
    509, 558
  and supply of output, 565
  variations, and multiplier,
    569–570, 569f
price setters, 550, 565
price systems, 18
price taker, 565
primary budget deficit, 781–782
prime interest rate, 474
principal (loan), 518
Principles of Economics (Marshall),
  65n
private corporations, 29
producers, 13
product
  differentiated product, 63, 550,
    812
  national product, 462, 489f

product differentiation. *See*
  differentiated product
production, 4
  complexity of, 15
  division of labour, 15
  factors of production, 4
  fixed production, 810–811
  increasing marginal production
    costs, 42f
  specialization of labour, 15
  stages of, 486
  value added through stages of
    production, 487
  variable production, 811
production possibilities boundary,
  7–8, 7f, 9f, 809–811
productive capacity, 9
productivity, 469–470
  in Canada, 469
  importance of, 470
  labour productivity, 469, 470f,
    610, 611
  and per capita GDP, 502
  recent history, 469–670
productivity growth, 2, 611
  benefits of ongoing productivity
    growth, 615
  constant productivity, 733n
  and living standards, 462
  and per capita GDP, 609
profit maximization, 13, 30, 31
profits
  economic profit in foreign
    markets, 832–833
  as function of output, 43f
  maximization of. *See* profit
    maximization
  national income accounting, 494
protection, 828, 830
  see also trade policy
  case for, 830
  diversification, promotion of, 830
  domestic job creation, 835–836
  economic profits in foreign
    markets, 832–833
  exports *vs.* imports, 834–835
  infant industry argument, 832
  invalid arguments for, 833–836
  keeping the money at home,
    833–834
  low-wage foreign labour,
    protection against, 834
  methods of, 836–842
  and recession, 836
  specific groups, protection of,
    830–831
  terms of trade, improvement
    of, 831
protectionism. *See* protection
protectionist, 3
provincial governments, 537
provincial governments debt and
  deficits, 784
public goods, 21, 631
purchasing power, 502
purchasing power of money, 473
purchasing power parity (PPP),
  876–879, , 878f
Purvis, Douglas, 796

Q

quantity bought, 50
quantity demanded, 50–51, 56
  change in quantity demanded, 56

desired quantity, 50
and price, 51–52
vs. demand, 53
quantity exchanged, 50, 58
quantity sold, 58
quantity supplied, 57–58, 59, 61

R

Rasminsky, Louis, 651n
real GDP, 463, 465, 496–497, 499
  and aggregate demand shocks,
    570–571
  and aggregate supply shocks, 572
  and annually balanced budget,
    796–797
  and business cycle, (Not found in
    the current edition)
  and factor prices, 583, 584
  fluctuations, 463, 464f
  growth, 464f, 620
  in long run, 592
  and long-run economic growth,
    609
  and monetary policy, 691
  and money demand, 677, 677f
  per employed worker, 609–610
  per hour worked, 469
  and price level, 567
  short-run fluctuations, 592n
real income, 502
real interest rate, 474–475,
  475–476, 518–519, 683n
real national income, 463
real per capita GDP, 502, 609, 610
real value of money, 473
real wages, 470, 732
recession, 463, 466, 465, 752
  2007–2010, 721–723
  Asian crisis, 574,
  global recession, 10, 796
  and long-term unemployment,
    758–759
  and unemployment, 754
recessionary gap, 465, 582, 584,
  585, 586, 589, 594–595,
  596f, 734n
recovery, 465
  economic recovery (1983-1987),
    717–718
  economic recovery
    (2011-present), 723–724
  recovery phase, 746
regional trade agreements,
  842–843, 844
  see also specific trade agree-
    ments
relative changes, 34
relative inflation, 869
relative price, 68, 563, 590
relative wages, 731
reserve currency, 861
reserve ratio, 656
reserves, 651, 655–656
residential construction, 518
residential housing, 491
resource allocation, 8
resource efficiency, 632
resources, 4
  allocation of, 8
  exhaustion of, 632–633
  idle resources, 9
  mineral resources, 870
  natural resources, (Not found in
    the new edition)

retained earnings, 494
revenues
  federal government, 783f
  net tax revenues, 536–537, 780,
    786n
Ricardo, David, 591n, 803, 814,
  819, 830
risk, 674–675, 684, 882
risk averse, 882
Romania, 643
Roosevelt, Franklin, 598
Rosenberg, Nathan, 628
Royal Bank of Scotland, 676
rule of 72, 610
rules of origin, 843, 844
Russian Revolution, 844

S

sacrifice ratio, 747, 747f
salaries, 493
sales, changes in, 519
sales tax, 493
saving, 509
  average propensity to save (APS),
    514
  and economic growth, 616–620
  long-run connection between
    saving and investment,
    617f
  marginal propensity to save
    (MPS), 514
  national saving, 617, 617n, 618,
    619f
saving function, 513–514
savings deposits, 663
scarcity, 3–4
  and choice, 4–8
  opportunity cost, 5–7, 5f
  and production possibilities
    boundary, 7–8, 7f
  unattainable combinations, 7
scatter diagram, 38, 38f
Schumpeter, Joseph, 628
scientific approach, 32
search unemployment, 766
securities, 654
securitization, 653
self-fulfilling prophecies, 529–531
self-interest, 12–13
self-organizing economy, 11–12
September 11, 2001, 720
services, 3
shocks
  aggregate demand shocks. *See*
    aggregate demand shocks
  aggregate supply shocks. *See*
    aggregate supply shocks
  demand shocks. *See* aggregate
    demand shocks
  flexible exchange rates as "shock
    absorbers", 879–882, 880f
  and innovation, 629
  monetary shocks, 688–693
  oil-price shock, 739
  supply shocks. *See* aggregate
    supply shocks
short run, 507, 507n
  see also specific short-run terms
  macroeconomic state, 580
  monetary shocks, 690–693
  output gap, 583f
  paradox of thrift, 597
  short-run macro model. *See*
    short-run macro model

short-run macro model
  see also macroeconomic model
aggregate demand *(AD)* curve,
    561–564
aggregate expenditure (AE)
    function, 520–521, 521*f*,
    523, 524–526, 525*f*
aggregate supply *(AS)* curve,
    565–567, 565*f*
algebraic exposition, 556–557
assumptions, 580
closed economy, 509
demand-determined output,
    549–550
demand side of the economy,
    559–564
desired aggregate expenditure,
    508–521
desired consumption expenditure,
    509–516
desired investment expenditure,
    516–520
equilibrium, 597
equilibrium condition, 523, 544
equilibrium GDP, changes in,
    560–561
equilibrium national income,
    522–524, 522*t*, 524*f*,
    541–549
fluctuations as self-fulfilling
    prophecies, 529–531
foreign trade, 538–541
government, 536–538
macroeconomic equilibrium,
    567–574
multiplier, 526–529, 527*f*, 529*f*
price level, exogenous changes in,
    559–560
price level as endogenous
    variable, 550
real GDP, 597
results restated, 526
simple multiplier, 527*f*, 528–529,
    529*f*, 530, 545, 546
simplifying assumptions, 509
supply side of the economy,
    564–567
short-term capital movements, 870
short-term fluctuations, 480–481
simple multiplier, 527*f*, 528–529,
    530, 545–546
  see also multiplier
and aggregate demand *(AD)*
    curve, 563*f*, 564
algebra of, 530
numerical example, 528
realistic value for, 600
size of, 528–529, 529*f*, 546
simple short-run macro model. *See*
    short-run macro model
Singapore, 820
slope
aggregate demand *(AD)* curve,
    562–563, 685
aggregate expenditure (AE)
    function, 526
aggregate supply *(AS)* curve,
    565–566
consumption function, 513
of curved line, 42
demand curve for foreign
    exchange, 862–863
negative slope, 40–41
of net export function, 539

positive slope, 41
of a straight line, 40
slump, 465, 584
small countries, and terms of trade,
    831
Smith, Adam, 11, 15, 19, 591*n*,
    803, 805, 830
Smoot Hawley Tariff Act, 836
social costs, 613–614
social science, 26
Solow, Robert, 627
Solow residual, 627
South Africa, 708
South Korea, 573, 574
Southeast Asia, 573, 574
Soviet Union, 18
18S&P/TSX, 720
Spain, 708, 789
specialization, 806, 808, 808*t*,
    812, 830
specialization of labour, 15
specific groups, protection of,
    830–831
speculative demand for money, 675
stabilization policy, 547, 590, 709
  see also fiscal stabilization
    policy
stagflation, 572, 590, 716, 745–746
statistical analysis, 32–33
statistical discrepancy, 495
Statistics Canada, 29, 467, 468,
    471, 488, 502, 755, 854*n*
sticky wages, 584, 589–590, 589*n*,
    761*f*, 763
stock market crash, 598, 714, 720
stock markets, 514–515
stocks, 50, 51
  capital stock, 490
  labour market, 756–757
  vs. flows, 50, 51
store of value, 612–613
straight line, slope of, 40
strategic trade policy, 832–833
structural budget deficits, 786,
    786*f*, 787*f*
structural changes, 870
structural unemployment, 467,
    766–768, 772–773
stumpage fees, 842
subsidies, 60–61
  and countervailing duty, 841–842
  national income accounting, 495
substitutes
  in production process, 61
  substitutes in consumption, 55
substitutes in consumption, 55
substitution effect, 515*n*
suppliers, number of, 61
supply, 59
  change in supply, 61
  conditions of supply, 59
  demand-and-supply model, 63
  excess supply, 63, 64
  of foreign exchange, 860–862
  of money. *See* money supply
  of national saving, 618, 619*f*
  quantity supplied, 57–58, 59
  supply curve. *See* supply curve
  supply schedule, 58, 60*f*
supply chains, global, 820
supply curve, 58–61, 60*f*
  foreign exchange, 861–862
  graphs, 65*n*
  movements along supply curve, 61

for national saving, 617
and price, 65–67, 66*f*
shifts in, 59–61, 65–67, 66*f*
supply inflation, 738, 739*f*
supply schedule, 58, 59*f*
supply shocks. *See* aggregate supply
    shocks
supply side of the economy,
    564–567
  aggregate supply *(AS)* curve,
    565–566, 567*f*
  shifts in *AS* curve, 566–567, 568*f*
surplus
  budget surplus, 537, 779, 781, 782
  see also government debt and
    deficits
  current account surpluses,
    871–876
sustained inflation, 707–708, 731,
    742
Sweden, 708
Switzerland, 811, 812

T
Taiwan, 820
target reserve ratio, 656, 660
tariff war, 835, 836,742
tariffs, 829, 831, 835, 837–839,
    838*f*, 839–840
tastes, 55
tax-and-transfer system, 598–600
taxation
  excise taxes, 494
  Goods and Services Tax (GST),
    494
  indirect taxes, 494
  net tax rate, 536–537
  net tax revenues, 536–437, 780,
    786*n*
  reductions in taxes, 599
  sales tax, 494
  and shifts in supply curves, 60–61
  tax-and-transfer system, 598–600
  tax rates, changes in, 549, 598
  temporary *vs.* permanent tax
    changes, 601
technological change, 2, 60
  and aggregate supply *(AS)* curve,
    566–568
  balanced growth with constant
    technology, 624–625
  deterioration in technology, 567
  embodied technical change, 625
  endogenous technological change,
    627–629
  fear of, 626
  importance of, 625–626
  improvement in technology,
    562, 615
  knowledge intensity of, 626
  and limits to growth, 632
  measurement of, 626–627
  weakness of technological
    defence, 615
technology
  see also technological change
  deterioration in, 567
  improvement in, 567, 615
  information technology, 16
  and shifts in supply curves, 59–61
term deposit, 663
term premium, 676
term structure of interest rates,
    676, 702

terms of trade, 821–824, 822*f*,
    823*f*, 831
terms of trade deterioration, 824,
    831
terms of trade improvement, 824,
    831
terrorist attacks, 720
Thailand, 573, 574, 708, 865, 866
theories. *See* economic theories
Thiessen, Gordon, 719, 719*f*, 720
think tanks, 29
third-party effects. *See* externality
time-series data, 37–38, 37*f*
Toronto Stock Exchange Index,
    720
total factor productivity *(TFP)*,
    627
total output, 488
trade
  barter, 16
  carry trade, 869
  international trade. *See*
    international trade
  interpersonal trade, 805
  interregional trade, 805–806
  intra-industry trade, 804, 813,
    813
  and money, 15–6
  specialization, 806
trade account, 854
trade balance, 458
trade creation, 843–844
trade diversion, 843–844
trade patterns, 816–824
trade policy, 829
  countervailing duty, 841–842
  current trade policy, 842–848
  dumping, 840–841
  free trade, case for, 801
  import quota, 839, 839*f*
  international trade agreements.
    See international trade
    agreements
  non-tariff barriers (NTBs), 829,
    840–842
  protection, case for, 829–830
  protection, invalid arguments for,
    830–833
  protection, methods of, 837–842
  protectionism, 828
  strategic trade policy, 832
  tariffs, 829, 831, 839–839, 838*f*,
    839–841
  trade-remedy laws, 840–842
  voluntary export restrictions
    (VER), (Not found in the
    current edition)
trade protection. *See* protection
trade-remedy laws, 840–842
trade-weighted exchange rate, 477
traditional economy, 17
Trans-Pacific Partnership (TPP),
    843
transaction costs of international
    trade, 882–883
transactions demand for money,
    675
transfer payments, 492, 536
transition economies, 20
transportation costs, 16
Treasury bills, 670, 672
trough, 466
Trump, Donald, 872, 873
twin deficits, 875

U

unanticipated inflation, 473
uncertainty, 882
underemployed, 755
underground economy, 500
unemployment, 447–449, 448f
  see also unemployment rate
  changes in, 754
  consequences of, 758–759
  cyclical unemployment, 467,
    589n, 759, 771–772
  discouraged workers, 755
  fluctuations, 759–765
  frictional unemployment, 467,
    757, 765–766, 768, 772
  involuntary unemployment, 761,
    762, 763, 774
  long-term unemployment, 469,
    758–759, 768
  lost output, 758
  market-clearing theories of the
    labour market, 759–761,
    759f
  measurement problems, 754,
    758
  NAIRU (non-accelerating
    inflation rate of
    unemployment). *See* NAIRU
    (non-accelerating inflation
    rate of unemployment)
  natural rate of unemployment,
    732
  non-market-clearing theories of
    the labour market, 761–764,
    761f
  output gap, result of, 559
  personal costs, 758–759
  recent history, 468–469
  reducing unemployment,
    771–773
  search unemployment, 766, 772
  seasonal unemployment, 468
  short-term unemployment, 469
  significance of, 469
  structural unemployment,
    467–468, 766–768, 772–773
  underemployed, 755
  voluntary unemployment, 761

unemployment rate, 447
  see also unemployment
  in Canada, 753f, 753, 754, 769f
  changes in, 753
  NAIRU (non-accelerating
    inflation rate of
    unemployment). *See* NAIRU
    (non-accelerating inflation
    rate of unemployment)
unexpected inflation, 707
union bargaining, 763–764
unions. *See* labour unions
unit costs, 565–566
unit labour cost, 593
unit of account, 642
United Kingdom
  exchange rate, 864
  inflation targeting, 708
  monetary reform, 688
  no sizable regional governments,
    784
  North Sea oil, 870
United States
  agricultural subsidies, 61
  balanced budgets, 784
  computers, 820
  countervailing duty, 841
  credit market, 476
  current account deficit, 721
  exchange rate, 864
  Federal Reserve. *See* Federal
    Reserve
  fiscal stimulus, 836
  free trade agreements. *See* specific
    trade agreements
  and global financial crisis. *See*
    global financial crisis
  Great Depression, 714
  housing market collapse, 564
  inflation targeting, 708
  long-term unemployment,
    758–759
  market decisions, reliance on, 19
  market economy, 19
  oil prices, 739
  raw materials prices, 573
  September 11, 2001, 720
  shale oil deposits, 870

shocks and innovation, 629
short-term interest rates,
  1975-2018, 717f
Smoot-Hawley Tariff Act, 836
suppliers, 831
technological change, 626
voluntary export restrictions
  (VER), (Not found in the
  current edition)
university degree, opportunity cost
  of, 6
Uruguay, 843
U.S. Department of Defense, 480
utility, 13, 30

V

value added, 486–488
variable costs, 811–814
variable production, 811
variables, 28
  dependent variable, 65n
  in economics, 33
  endogenous variable, 30, 65, 541
  exogenous variable, 30, 64, 541
  independent variable, 65n
  key macroeconomic variables,
    462–466
  linearly related, 39
  negatively related, 39
  positively related, 39
Victor, Peter, 614n
Vietnam, 609
Viner, Jacob, (Not found in current
  edition)
Visa, 654
volatility
  exchange rate, (Not found in the
    current edition)
  food and energy prices, 709-711
voluntary export restrictions (VER),
  (Not found in the current
  edition)
voluntary unemployment, 761

W

wage-price spiral, 740
wage stickiness. *See* sticky wages

wages
  changes in, 731–733
  "cost push" on, 707
  deflationary forces, 733
  and demand shock, 587
  downward wage stickiness, 584,
    589–590, 589n
  economic climate *vs.* economic
    weather, (Not found in the
    current edition)
  efficiency wages, 763
  and expected inflation, 732–733
  flexible wages, 588–589
  forces of change, 733
  inflationary forces, 733
  national income accounting, 493
  nominal wages, 784n, 586, 732,
    733n
  and output gap, 731–732
  real wages, 474, 732
  relative wages, 731
  sticky wages, 584, 589–590,
    589n, 761f, 762, 765
  wage-price spiral, 740
  when labour markets clear, 760f
Watts, George, 651n
The Wealth of Nations (Smith),
  12, 803
weather, changes in, 55–56, 61
Weatherford, Jack, 646n
weighted average, 36
well-being, 610n, 614–615
Western Europe, 19, 573
World Bank, (Not found in current
  edition)
world trade. *See* international trade
World Trade Organization (WTO),
  29, 829, 833, 842
WTO. *See* World Trade
  Organization (WTO)

Y

yield curve, 676

Z

zero inflation, 734
Zimbabwe, 643, 644

Education and Employment Income, 2016

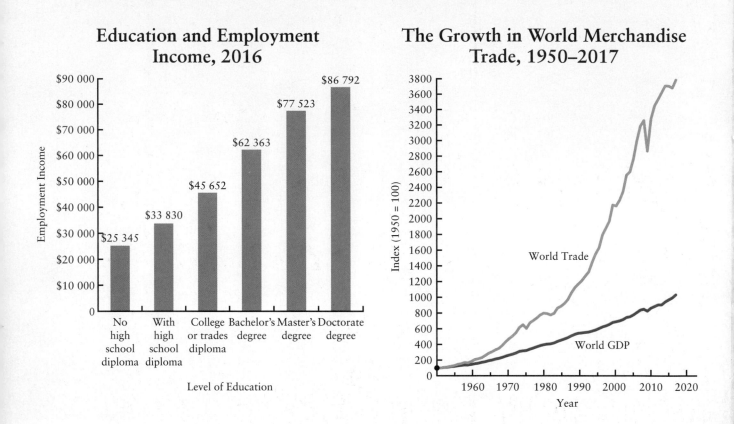

The Growth in World Merchandise Trade, 1950–2017

Inflation and Money Growth Across Many Countries, 1978–2017

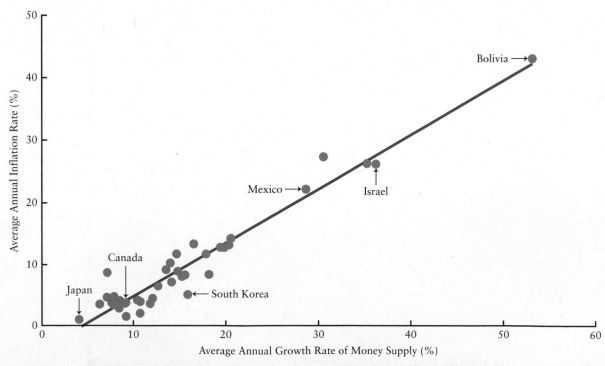